D1075040

BIBLE & MUSIC

Influences of
the Old Testament
on Western Music

ML
290
.S83
2011

BIBLE & MUSIC

Influences of the Old Testament on Western Music

MAX STERN

Nyack College - Bailey Library
One South Blvd.
Nyack, NY 10960

KTAV Publishing House, Inc.
Jersey City, New Jersey

Copyright © 2011 by Max Stern
Department of Israel's Heritage
Ariel University Center of Samaria

Library of Congress Cataloging-in-Publication Data

Stern, Max,1947 –
Bible & music: influences of the Old Testament on western music/ Max Stern
p. cm.
ISBN 978-1-60280-166-0
1. Bible. O.T. – Influence 2. Bible in music – History 3. Church music 4. Synagogue
music- History and criticism
I. Stern, Max. II. Title.
ML290.S83 2011
780/.dc22
2011026549

Layout: Marzel A.S–Jerusalem

Published by
KTAV Publishing House, Inc.,
888 Newark Avenue Suite 119
Jersey City, N.J. 07306
Email: orders@ktav.com • www.ktav.com
(201) 963-9524 • Fax (201) 9663-0102

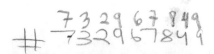

Table of Contents

French Romantic Opera
Wherewith thou mightest be bound (Judges 16: 6)
Biblical Opera

1 SAMUEL

Vocal-Instrumental Music
Place a king over us (1 Samuel 8:19)
A Prophetic Episode

Program Music
And took thence a stone and slung it (1 Samuel 17:49)
Tone Painting at the Keyboard

2 SAMUEL

Symphonic Psalm
And David danced before the Lord (2 Samuel 6:14)
Redemption as Popular Realism

I KINGS

Coronation Anthem
Long Live King Solomon (1 Kings 1:39)
Anthem and Motet

Romantic Oratorio
Art thou my lord Elijah? (1 Kings 18:7)
Biblical Music Drama

II KINGS

Italian Opera
And he carried away all Jerusalem (2 Kings 24:14)
Pathos as Eternal Truth

Preface

Whether in letter or spirit, the biblical word — interpreted and reinterpreted through the ages — includes a voice, a tone, and a resonance that awakens our deepest empathy, care, and attention. This study traces the influence of that voice on Western civilization's musical traditions — whether shallow or deep, sacred or secular. It is an approach to the Bible revealing a path of understanding illuminated more by imagination and intuition than critique or philology; a liturgy, through artistic means, no one needs to be initiated into. Thus, we cease to become judgmental observers who sit apart; rather, we become impassioned listeners who join together in an enchanted magic circle of intimates.

Each and every age reads and hears the Bible according to its own lights — perception, conception, rhythm, and style. This book has grown from an inquiry into the influence of the sacred on a panoramic variety of musical forms and idioms, historical and contemporary, pursued in lectures to my classes at the Ariel University Center in Israel; at Society of Biblical Literature meetings in Singapore, Edinburgh, Vienna, Tartu; and elsewhere in various public forums. Because music to the Psalms is vast, I anticipate dealing with the Psalter in a future volume, *Psalmody*.

I wish to express my gratitude to the Ariel University Center, Israel for the financial assistance, without which this book could not have been published. I also appreciate the interest, counsel and encouragement of many colleagues, teachers, friends and students. Among them are Professors Mayer Gruber and Howard Kreisel (Ben-Gurion University of the Negev), Moshe Yegar, Amnon Shiloach and Uri Epstein (Hebrew University), Uri Sharvit (Bar Ilan University), Allan Silver (Columbia University), Johanna Spector (Jewish Theological Seminary), William Kearns, Karl Kroeger, Jay Keiser and Joan Catoni Conlon (University of Colorado), Rivka Ulmer (Bucknell University), Zilla Sinuany-Stern, Amnon Shapira, Orzion Bartana and Uri Tzur (Ariel University Center), Mishael Caspi (Bates College), John Greene (Michigan State University) and Nick Strimple (University of Southern California). Also librarians Leah Katzenell (Ben Gurion University of the Negev), Thomas Bell (Kansas State University), and Stephanie Bonjack (University of

Southern California); proofreaders Shira Leibowitz-Schmidt (Netanya), Rabbi Dr. Jeremiah Unterman and Judith Seeligman (Jerusalem), Joan Avigur and Edith Hazan (Beer Sheba); graphics assistance by Yossi Shilon (Beer Sheba); and student research coordinator Dganit Shlomo (Ariel); Rabbis Shimon Kalazan (Jerusalem) and Meir Seroussi (Beer Sheba), Rev. Dr. Edgar Kellenberger (Switzerland), and Pastor Ulo Niinemagi (Tallinn). Last, but not least looms a beloved friend, violinist Kalmen Kinnory (d.2008, Jerusalem) and a sage, Rav Mordecai Neumann (d.1980, Mt. Zion).

Our translations from the Bible are taken from *The Soncino Books of the Bible*. Others are taken as the appear in the scores of the composers.

Introduction

The Ineffable Voice

The ineffable "Voice" within the biblical "Word" is the music of the Bible.[1] God desires that human beings listen to this voice. It is a request, an imperative beyond rationality and understanding: *Doth God delight in offerings and sacrifices as in listening to the voice of God (1 Sam. 15:22).* This seems to me to be the *modus vivendi* of the entire Bible. Human history began with the first disobedience, *I heard thy voice in the garden and I was afraid (Gen. 3:11).* In the same way humanity finds its redemption, *and in thy seed shall all the nations of the earth be blessed; because thou hast obeyed my voice (Gen. 22:18).* I would propose that it is not only the content of the word, but perhaps, the more intangible intention which the voice conveys in tone, tempo, enunciation, flow, rhythm, dynamic, and stress that constitutes its essential essence.

---

1. The Word is the crystallization of the abstract (cosmic) Will of God into vibration. Vibration has the power to physically create, simulate, and affect natural phenomena. A specific range of vibrations are in turn felt by the body, perceived by the ear, and intuited by the mind — i.e. heard, interpreted, and given meaning by man in sound, tone, and voice: *And God said, Let there be...and there was (Gen. 1:3).* The idea of "voice" here has moral intentions and implications. The Zohar describes the phrase *And God said* as an energy culled from the mystic limitless of thought *in silence without making a sound, but when it issued forth it became a voice which was heard* (Bereshith 16b, *The Zohar,* translated by Harry Sperling and Maurice Simon, Vol. 1 (London: Soncino Press [1934] 1978) 69, The opening of the Gospel of John alludes to this phenomenon, as well: *In the beginning was the Word, and the Word was with God, and the Word was God (John 1:1).* Do we understand the word in a cognitive way only (as an intellectual or academic exercise), or does it affect our behavior (in faith and actions)? Of interest in the link between the oral word of prophetic man and the written word of the Bible are the writings of Father (Professor) Walter J. Ong (1912–2003), especially *The Presence of the Word: Some Prolegomena for Cultural and Religious History* (New Haven, Connecticut: Yale University Press, 1967) and *Orality and Literacy: the Technologizing of the Word,* New Accents, ed. Terence Hawkes (New York: Methuen, 1988).

The austere monotheism of the Old Testament scorns indulgence in images (*Exod. 20:3–6*). From a strictly theological perspective, music and art, inevitably, disturb the orderly mathematical perfection of a divine universe of faith, reason, and ethical purpose, bringing to bear the imperfect and fallible human element of perception. On the other hand, books on music, more often than not, treat the biblical text transparently; accepting it as a given, they ignore its content, meaning, and message — preferring to discuss biographical and historical issues, and focus upon technical descriptions of style, form, and genre. This book attempts something different. Seeking a connection between biblical word and musical voice, it takes its stance on the narrow cultural bridge spanning the two worlds; it examines music from the perspective of the Bible, while trying to comment on and elucidate the Bible, through the prism of music.

Textually oriented interpretations reduce the spoken or sung word to the printed page, and search for cognitive understandings, extracting, as well, their denotative connotations. It is a literacy that traces the word on its varied permutations and peregrinations through Scripture. Its technique is revelation through analysis, from word to thought, but not, necessarily, from flesh to spirit. Often, this process evaporates mystery, excitement, and the sympathetic reader's emotive response to sacred writ: We gain in knowledge, what we lose in beauty; events and heroes of the Bible pale in a maze of logic and conundrum. Such biblical exegesis may be understood in four ways: literally, associatively, allegorically, or symbolically;[2] it is a rational, cognitive, and intellectual search for clarity and meaning. Textually oriented exegesis traditionally traces scriptural meaning through the derivation of word roots, grammatical construction, contextual syntax, or association of similar phrases found elsewhere in Scripture. In Hebrew, additional methodology is used, drawing connections based on the mathematical equivalents of letters in a word or phrase (*Gematria*) to release hidden meanings; or, through an acronymic play upon the letters in a word (*Notrikon*), in which each letter becomes a mnemonic aid in recalling substitute words. Biblical

---

2. This is akin to the basic medieval principles of Hebrew biblical exegesis (*PDRS*) representing *pashat* (plain meaning of the text), *drash* (interpretation or explanation of the text in others words), *remez* (symbolic meaning of the qualities or ideas implied by the text), and *sod* (the secret metaphysical or cosmological significance of the text).

exposition (i.e. application of the meaning of a text to a life situation), on the other hand, draws moral relevance from Scripture; seeking to influence human behavior for the better. All too often, these admirable interpretive tools must be supplemented by legend (*Aggadah*) in order to recapture the excitement and empathy aroused by the biblical tale. In all, through critique, we often gain in wisdom what we loose in pathos and beauty.

Tone, apart from this intellectual world of thought and abstraction is a sonorous, physical, resonating "voice" akin to Midrash, that awakens our care and concern.[3] Scripture, aware of the distinction between word and tone, at times even demands it, defining this distinction as *voice*. For, after idea and reason have exhausted their power, when only unconditional obedience regardless of insight, sense, or understanding is needed, Scripture bids us: *hearken unto the Voice of the words of God (1 Sam. 15:1).*[4]

A Historical Overview

Nyack college agrees with the

The history of biblical visual art and image is long — bas relief, statuary, illustrated manuscripts, stained glass windows, frescoes, and paintings — and gives testimony of the synagogue's and Church's sustained efforts to teach Bible stories to the ignorant and unlettered, while impressing the learned in non-verbal ways. Music has played a part in this drama, for it has always been integral to worship. As a functional tool in the service of religion, music has been taught, discussed, studied, analyzed, and performed for as long as there have been places of worship and people to worship in them. But, its role as a fine art — interpreting, elaborating and commenting upon a scriptural passage, lending expressive depth to a biblical episode, or fantasizing upon a theological concept, has rarely been explored. The reason for this is largely historical — fore, though music was highly regarded in its supportive role in liturgy, it did not develop a language pliable enough for artistic expression before the Late Middle Ages and Renaissance. Thus, throughout a millennium

---

3.   One of the earliest references confirming the reciprocal power of the human voice to awaken not only human care and concern, but, to effect divine sympathy, is found in the blessing of Moses to the tribe of Judah: *Hear, Lord, the voice of Judah (Deut. 33:7)* (See Judah Hahasid, *Sefer Hasidim*, paragraph 241).
4.   Samson Raphael Hirsch, *The Haftoroth*, translated and explained by Mendel Hirsch (Gateshead, England: Judaica Press, 1979) 538.

that witnessed the codification of fundamental religious doctrines and texts in the synagogue and Church, music's technical resources did not develop a sufficiently supple syntax, with the flexibility needed to realize its artistic potential.

Martin Luther was the German Reformer who recognized music's power to unite men in holy fervor. Later, Northern musicians, like Heinrich Schutz, went south to study their art with Italian masters. Their seriousness and intensity infused the light and airy play of Renaissance polyphony with a new kind of religious depth. In reaction to the in-roads that Luther's Reformation and chorales had made among the faithful, throughout Europe, the Church began to follow suit. If, previously, polyphonic music has been suspect, following the Council of Trent (1545–1563), the Roman Catholic Church, as a Counter-Reformation measure, revised its earlier position and sanctioned the performance of Palestrina's Masses and motets, opening up the way for sacred art music — a repertoire that was both serious in tone and inspired by Scripture. Since the 16th century composers and folk musicians have vastly enriched this artistic-philosophic perspective with a catalogue of compositions that have never quite found categorization — somewhere in-between in the worlds of liturgical, concert, popular, or folk music. It is this area, which is the focus of this study.

How This Book Is Organized

The sequence of this book follows that of the Bible;[5] it is the Bible's narrative, told through music. In presenting an aesthetic approach to the Holy Writ, it traces events from the Creation of the World until the Babylonian Exile — in works by composers of diverse times, places, and styles. The arrangement of works avoids musical-chronological

---

5. The Bible is not so much a book as a library; fathoming its depth seems endless. In seeking clarification of the term 'Bible,' we imply the 'Old Testament' or the original Hebrew Scriptures, and have excluded works inspired by the Gospels, Epistles, and other books of the New Testament, which are integral to the Protestant Bible, along with the Apocrypha and Pseudepigrapha, which appear in the Catholic Bible. Though, Christian interpretations and insights into the Old Testament and appropriate references from the above appear throughout. Part of our reason is practical, since treatment of the vast quantity of musical works based on the New Testament would have turned this book into a multi-volume encyclopedia, beyond our intentions. The subject of the New Testament and music awaits its own volume.

sequence — a departure from historical musicology's method of cataloging by epochs and periods (i.e. Greeks, Medieval, Renaissance, Baroque, Classical, Romantic, and Modern); and familiar rubrics: sacred, secular, liturgical, concert, art, and folk music. Rather, unity is sought in the relation of various kinds and styles of works to the biblical text. The Bible — and not aesthetic periods, genres, mediums, and styles — is our focal point. Meandering through music history, this book connects a panoply of works, circumstances, national styles, and historical periods — guided by the supra-historical prophetic 'yearning to give voice' to the biblical affirmation: *Credo in Unum Deum.*

Each chapter is a case study focusing on a biblical story, theme, or psalm text — understood from the standpoint of a specific musical work. It covers the biblical and literary sources of texts and subtexts; biographical and historical influences upon composers and/or librettists; and consideration of genre, medium, and style. Our ordering differs from the usual ways in which this material is arranged (historical period, alphabetical listing by composer, genre, or performing medium) in order to emphasize, what seems to us, a pivotal point, not to be overlooked or underestimated: The biblical voice is non-sequential. It enters and leaves history at will, appearing in one guise, then another; revealing itself to the learned, no less than to the ignorant and untutored, in forms that reflect elite art as well as vernacular culture. Examples have been selected from a variety of genres and styles; with preference given to works currently available in print, and, on recordings. Bibliographies and discographies are provided for further study.

Afterthought

My late teacher, Mordecai Neumann, who was as great a sage and saint as any I have ever met, once told me, alone, on Mount Zion, many years ago: "If, one reads the text of the Bible as literature, then, it is a book, like any other.[6] But, if one reads it, and believes that every word

---

6. For more than three thousand years the Bible has been taken as a document of faith. Studied by Jewish and Christian sages, edited and translated by the finest minds of their time, cited by saints, feared by sinners, it gave direction and meaning to the lives of a hundred generations. Empires (Rome), regimes (Communism), and nation states (USA), rose and fell, adapting or rejecting its principles. In the 19th century — subsequent to the Industrial Revolution, Enlightenment, and the emergence of Anti-Semitism (on the coat-tails of

is the Word of the Creator, then a new spirit enters and transforms you." Music is written from inspiration — however vague — and inspiration rooted in faith — however indefinable; no musical composition has ever been written based upon the findings of biblical criticism. Midrash reflects on the meaning of this statement in the verse: *and they believed in the Lord, and in His servant Moses. Then, sang Moses and the children of Israel this song unto the Lord (Exod. 14:31, 15:1)* — only he who believes can sing the song. To the artist, the only thing that matters, really, is the search for the burning inner light streaming through the oracles and prophecies of yore. Our interest, then, is in Eternal truths, beyond mere recitation of facts. Validation has been sought in ancient sources: Midrash, Mishnah, and Talmud, alongside the thoughts of the Early Church Fathers, Medieval Jewish commentators, the writings of historians, and the insights of literature.

---

an economic depression following the Franco-Prussian war) — the interpretation of the Bible took on a critical tone. Armed with a few Babylonian myths and a smattering of expertise in Hebrew, German scholars, dating from Julius Wellhausen (1844–1918) onwards, initiated a school of agnostic biblical criticism (directed primarily against the Old Testament). Inflated and exaggerated self-confidence elevated plausible conjecture into hypotheses, and mistook theory for positive proof, investing skepticism with the aura of intellectuality. This direction continues to be bolstered in academic circles, oblivious to the testimony of oral traditions, living witnesses to a voice once heard and passed through the generations, from father to son.

CHAPTER 1

This chapter focuses on Haydn's *Creation*, prototype for oratorios written in the language of Classical music. They are a genre of large concert works for soloists, chorus, and orchestra combining the sacred content of church music with the dramatic power of opera.

GENESIS

In the beginning God created the heaven and the earth. And the earth was without form, and void; and darkness was upon the face of the deep. And the spirit of God moved upon the face of the waters. And God said, Let there be light: and there was light   (Genesis 1:1–3).

That is all there is to the story of Creation as told in the Book of Genesis, and there is no other power or partner to assist or resist Him. The Word or Will of God is the sole and sovereign source of all reality. All the rest that we know about the Creation are products of prehistoric myth and epic woven into Midrash, Talmudic legends, apocryphal traditions, Zohar, medieval folklore, and modern commentaries.

Joseph Haydn: The Creation (Die Schopfung), Hob. XXI: 2
Libretto: Gottfried van Sweiten
Genre: Oratorio
Medium: Soprano, tenor, and bass soloists, chorus, and orchestra
Style: Classical
First performance: Palais Schwarzenberg, Vienna, 1798
Performance time: ca. 2 hours

The Creation by Joseph Haydn is a uniquely picturesque and richly textured work that tells the story of the first six days in the creation of the world as related in the first chapter of the Book of Genesis. Haydn was inspired by his visits to London in the late 1790s and his encounter with the English oratorio style of G. F. Handel. *The Creation* is the most important oratorio of the Classical period. Though written in an "Age of Reason," it bursts with religious awe.

Biographic Context

Franz Joseph Haydn (1732–1809) is a pivotal figure in the development of the language of music. Born near the Hungarian border in a provincial Austrian village, this boy from the artisan class (his father was a wheelwright and his mother a cook in the employ of a local count) became one of the most prominent men of his Era. His vocal talent was recognized early and by the age of eight young Franz Joseph was already a choirboy at St. Stephan's Cathedral in Vienna. There his education included: reading, writing, and perhaps, a little arithmetic — along with religious studies, singing, and playing instruments. For nine years the lad grew to maturity inside the confines of the Catholic Church — where religious services, liturgical chant, sermons, ecclesiastical holidays, and feast days were his daily fare.

General music history tends to minimize this early stage of Haydn's career, focusing more on his activities as a struggling young musician in Vienna, his thirty-year service as court musician to the Esterhazy family at Eisenstadt, and his friendship with the young genius, Mozart. Then, noting the dismissal of the musical establishment at Esterhazy, the successful London journeys, and final years in Vienna; for the most part, we encounter Haydn as a secular composer: father of the symphony and string quartet, progenitor and master of the piano sonata and sonata form, author of much chamber music and rarely performed operas. From whence does the religious spirit that wrote the *Creation* come? What were the internal workings of the soul which gave birth to this work? Surely, its origin was in childhood.

Haydn was a product of the Enlightenment, a period influenced by the empiricist philosophy of men like John Locke (i.e. *Essay Concerning Human Understanding, 1690*), and the scientific optimism of Isaac Newton (i.e. *Principia, 1687*). It was an aristocratic age — polite and polished, spacious and elegant — for men of quality, who would be ashamed to be cruel or gross or enthusiastic. Haydn flourished as a highly prized servant in this world of decorum and the harmonies of life. What was the place of religion in such an atmosphere? Was it out of place; probably not in Austria, but, elsewhere in Europe, maybe? Voltaire (1694–1778), the French philosopher, and the English historian,

Edward Gibbon (1734–1794) found religion perplexing, an atavism from an earlier age rather than a living force.[1] One wonders though, how accurately the testimony of a Voltaire and a Gibbon mirrors the climate and influence of religion on the vast majority of their Age. Certainly, for a person of Haydn's bent, the only entry into the Enlightenment was through the doors of the Church. How did this early education affect his mature outlook?

In the last ten years of his life, Haydn was befriended by Georg August Griesinger,[2] a representative of the music publishing firm Breitkopf & Hartel, who recorded all his conversations with Haydn and published them as a book just after Haydn died. He writes: *Haydn was very religiously inclined, and was loyally devoted to the faith in which he was raised. He was very strongly convinced in his heart that all human destinies are under God's guiding hand; that God rewards the good and the evil, that all talents come from above. All his larger scores begin: In nominee Domini (In the name of God) and end with Laus Deo (Praise God) or Soli Deo Gloria (Glory to God alone). 'If my composing is not proceeding so well,' I heard him say, 'I walk up and down my room with my rosary in my hand, say several Aves, and then ideas come to me again.' Haydn left every man to his own conviction and recognized all as brothers. In general, his devotion was not of the gloomy, always suffering sort, but rather cheerful and reconciled; and in this character, he wrote all his church music. His patriarchal, devout spirit is particularly expressed in Die Schopfung (Creation), and hence he was bound to be more successful than a hundred other masters. A natural consequence of Haydn's religios-*

---

1. The Encyclopaedists were a group of rebel spirits from the schools of the Jesuits. Hostile to religion, they were led by Diderot, who endeavored to place all knowledge in between the covers of many volumes produced over a very long time. This 18th-century desire to systemize all knowledge was felt on the musical scene, as well. Jean-Philippe Rameau established the first rational foundation for the principle of harmony, in his historic *Treatise on Harmony Reduced to Its Natural Principles* (1722). The subject matter of opera, at the time, was Greek mythology; the most popular work was Gluck's *Orpheus ed Euridice* (1762). Later, Mozart's works, particularly *The Marriage of Figaro* (1786), took man's social condition as a subject worthy of the operatic stage.
2. Georg August von Greisinger (1769 Stuttgart–1845 Vienna), lawyer and civil servant, he studied theology but did not go into the church. He was ennobled in 1819.

ity was his modesty, for his talent was not his own doing, rather a gracious gift from Heaven, to whom he believed he must show himself thankful.[3]

Text and Context

The principal textual sources for Haydn's *Creation* are the narrative of Creation, as related in Genesis 1:1–31, and Milton's *Paradise Lost* (1674 revised edition), with numerous fragmented citations from Psalms — particularly Psalm 19 and Psalm 145. Sections from the six days of creation alternate with paraphrased passages from *Paradise Lost* (mostly Book VII), which serve to comment upon and interpret the sacred word.

The Influence of Paradise Lost

The erudite English poet, Classical scholar, Hebraist, and Latin secretary to Cromwell in serving the Parliamentary cause, John Milton (1608–1674), was a virulent political activist and pamphleteer for 20 years. He was also a deeply religious man who did not affiliate with any particular Christian sect and "whose studies and meditations," according to English lexicographer Samuel Johnson (1709–1784), "were an habitual prayer."[4] After the Restoration, disillusioned and blind, Milton wrote *Paradise Lost*, among the supreme achievements of world literature:

> Of Man's First Disobedience, and the Fruit
> Of that Forbidden Tree, whose mortal taste
> Brought Death into the World, and all our woe.[5]

Paradise Lost details the revolt of the angels, led by Lucifer-Satan in heaven, before creation. Milton follows ancient tradition, which placed their creation long before that of our universe. It continues with the temptation and fall of Adam and Eve in the Garden of Eden. Milton

---

3. Georg August Greisinger, "Biographische Notizen uber Joseph Haydn." *Allegemeine Musikalische Zeitung* (July-September 1809). See H.P. Clive, *Beethoven and His World: A Biographical Dictionary* (London: Oxford University Press, 2001) 139.
4. As cited in Douglas Bush, "John Milton," *Encyclopedia Britannica*, Vol. 15 (London: William Benton, 1960) 572.
5. John Milton, *Paradise Lost*, Book 1, line 26, edited by Merrit Y. Hughes (New York: Odyssey Press, 1962) 6.

brings to the biblical text a humanist's perspective. His purpose is to "justify the ways of God to men."[6] This humanist attitude pervades both the libretto and the music to Haydn's *Creation*. The faithful archangels: Raphael, Uriel, and Gabriel[7] have major roles in *Paradise Lost*, in the biblical Midrashim of Creation, and in Haydn's oratorio.[8] Out of profound disappointment with the rebellious angels, God resolves to create another world, not one of angels, but of men, "which by man's work is to become the Kingdom of God."[9]

> Another World, out of one man a Race
> Of men innumerable, there to dwell,
> Not here, till by degrees of merit rais'd
> They open to themselves at length the way
> Up thither, under long obedience tri'd,
> And Earth be chang'd to Heav'n, and Heav'n to Earth,
> One Kingdom, Joy and Union without end.
>
> (*Paradise Lost*, Book VII)

God begins this new world out of chaos. It is the starting point of Haydn's *Creation*, too.[10]

> First there was Chaos,[11] the vast immeasurable abyss,

---

6. Ibid.
7. The biblical archangel Michael is not represented in Haydn's composition.
8. The fallen angels are those who deceived mankind and usurped God's worship, by masquerading as the gods of the pagan world. They "labored to affect a universal rebellion against the works of God...some in oracles, some as idols, such as Moloch; these are the very gods whom the Prophets denounced for seducing Israel." Introduction by Merritt Y. Hughes, i–xlix. For a more general overview of Milton's acquaintance with Jewish sources, see Harris F. Fletcher, *Milton's Rabbinical Readings* (Urbana: University of Illinois Press, 1930).
9. Martin Buber, *The Way of Man* (New York: Citadel Press, 1950) 34.
10. On all that went on before the Creation, the Bible is silent. Jewish legend, however, reveals that two thousand years before heaven and earth, seven things were created: Torah, the Throne of Glory, Paradise, Hell, the Celestial Sanctuary, the name of the Messiah, and Repentance. There is no mention of the battle of rebellious angels. According to Midrash, the angelic hosts — that are both the ministering angels and the angels of praise, were created on the second day; the reason being, lest men believe that the angels assisted God, in the creation of the heavens and the earth.
11. See Edith Hamilton, *Mythology* (New York: Little Brown/Mentor, 1957).

> Outrageous as a sea, dark, wasteful, wild.[12]

Milton reaches into Greek mythology to extend his theme.[13] In Part I, Haydn depicts this Greek vision of chaos in his instrumental prelude, shifting through an almost Wagnerian chromaticism. Suddenly, there is a transformation.

> From darkness and blind confusion,
> Love created Light with its companion, radiant Day.[14]

In Haydn's mind too, in between: *And God said* and *Let there be light* a new concept is inserted: Love. It is this profound message of love — God's love for His world, and, man's love for God, coupled with the angelic host's sense of wonder and appreciation for the beauty, majesty, and splendor of the Creation that is the animating force behind Haydn's oratorio.

Making of the Libretto

At the end of Haydn's second visit to London in 1794–95, the impresario Johann Peter Salomon (1745–1815), a German expatriate in London, gave the composer a copy of an anonymous libretto on the 'Creation of the World,' said to have been written, at least half a century earlier for Handel. It had never been set to music. Upon returning to Vienna, Haydn showed the libretto to his friend and patron, Baron Gottfried van Sweiten (1733–1803), an Austrian diplomat, who later served as prefect of the Imperial Library in Vienna. This aristocratic connoisseur endorsed the project with genial generosity, and set to work creating

---

12. Midrash informs us: "On the first day of creation God produced ten things: the heavens and the earth, formlessness and void, light and darkness, wind and water, the duration of the day and night." Louis Ginzberg, *Legends of the Bible* (Philadelphia: Jewish Publication Society, 1956) 1.

13. It is the tradition of battles between the Olympian gods and the Titans. He draws upon 8th-century B.C. Greek poet Hesiod's *Theogeny*: "Long before the gods appeared, in the dim past, uncounted ages ago, there was only the formless confusion of Chaos, brooded over by unbroken darkness. At last, but how, no one ever tried to explain, two children were born to this shapeless nothingness. Night was the child of Chaos, and so was Erebus, which is the unfathomable depth, where death dwells. In the whole universe there was nothing else; all was black, empty, silent, and endless." Hamilton, *Mythology*, 63–64.

14. Hamilton, ibid.

a German version of the text by adapting the English libretto to the contours of the German language.[15]

Music

The Creation is structured in three parts; each, a series of orchestral introductions and interludes, recitatives, arias, duets, ensembles, and choruses. The biblical words are set as recitatives. Arias and choruses paraphrase *Paradise Lost*, describing the phenomenon of nature in response to the divine word. Textual passages based on the Psalms are filled with astonishment and wonder at the biblical pronouncements, and echo the songful responses of the heavenly host. Each section concludes on a hymn of praise. *The first part (Nos. 1–14)* recounts the first four days of creation: 1. Heaven, earth, and light; 2. Division of the waters; 3. Land, plant and sea life; 4. Sun, moon and stars. *The second part (Nos. 15–26)* describes the fifth and sixth day: 5. Birds and fish; 6.

---

15. Haydn received generous financial support from van Sweiten as well, who organized the sponsors (*Gesellschaft der Associrten*), paid all the expenses of the performance, and presented the composer with the takings. Concerning the origin of the libretto, Baron van Sweiten wrote a revealing article for the *Allgemeine Musikalische Zeitung, 1799*, one of the first Viennese music periodicals:

     My part in the work, which was originally in English, is perhaps rather more than that of a mere translator: but not by any means so extensive that I could call the text my own…It was written by an unknown person (Griesinger, Haydn's first biographer, calls this person a Mr. Lidley or Lindley), who had compiled it largely from Milton's Paradise Lost, and had intended it for Handel. It is not known why this great composer never made any use of the work; but when Haydn was in London, the text was brought forth and it was suggested that he set it to music. At first glance, Haydn found the material of the text well chosen, but he did not accept the proposal immediately…and said he would give his answer when he returned to Vienna. He then showed it to me here and I agreed with his judgment of the piece. Moreover, I saw immediately that this work would provided Haydn with the ideal opportunity to display the full powers of his inexhaustible genius; and as I had longed hoped for this very possibility, I was encouraged to take the libretto and to give the English poem a German setting. While on the whole I followed the general outlines of the original piece, I changed details whenever it seemed prudent to do so for the sake of the musical line and expression. See H. C. Robbins Landon, liner notes to Haydn's *Creation*, Archiv Produktion 449–217-2 (1996) 6.

Animals and man. *The third part (Nos. 27–32)* evokes the praise of God and the mutual love of Adam and Eve.

The expressive and formal contrasts in the work shift between the timeless biblical Word of God (set in amorphous, harmonically static, recitatives), and the humanistic explanations and commentaries from *Paradise Lost*, conceived in clearly defined melody, animated rhythms, and varied textures. Motivic manipulation, familiar to us through the Classical symphonies of Haydn, is the essence of this style. Thematic nuggets take on manifold musical meaning by means of tonal inflection and modulation, cumulatively expanding, contracting, building, and generating large structural symmetries through contrast and comparison.

The most stunning effect in the entire work is the creation of light. It is Haydn's attempt to come to terms with the concept of the sublime.[16] The three archangels (soloists) and the heavenly host (chorus) sustain the biblical narrative. Raphael[17] — the angel of healing among the archangels, who defended God against the other angels in God's decision to create man[18] — opens the scene in a deep, majestic bass voice. Uriel, the leader of the angelic host and prince of light, is a portrayed as a clarion tenor; while Gabriel, the angel who rules Paradise, is a soprano.

RAPHAEL (bass)

In the beginning God created the heaven and the earth.
And the earth was without form and void;
And darkness was upon the face of the deep.

This opening recitative, *In the beginning*, is offset by dark string sonorities. Raphael sings unaccompanied in C minor. The harmony then shifts

---

16. The sublime refers to that which has incomparable greatness and power, whereas, beauty is simply that which is aesthetically pleasing. This dichotomy is as antithetical as light and darkness. These ideas were articulated in the treatise: *A Philosophical Inquiry into the Origin of Our Ideas of the Sublime and Beautiful* (1756), by the great British statesman, and political writer Edmund Burke (1729–1797), and had considerable vogue in English intellectual circles at the end of the 18ᵗʰ century. See John Morley, "Edmund Burke," *Encyclopedia Britannica*, Vol. 4, 413.

17. It is not quite clear if this angel is Raphael or Michael. See Louis Ginzberg, *The Legends of the Jews* (Baltimore: Johns Hopkins University Press, 1998 [1909–1937]) Vol. 5, notes 12 and 13, 12–14.

18. Talmud Yoma 37a.

Ex. 1. Haydn: *The Creation*, Part 1, No.1, excerpt from choral recitative "Let there be light," and Uriel's response "God saw the light that it was good."
Reprint of *Die Schopfung*, published by C.F. Peters, n.d., by Dover Publications (1990)

to an unusual E-flat minor tonality (mediant minor) to embrace the images of *void* and *darkness* that preceded creation. Next, the heavenly host (supported by throbbing strings) participates in a quasi arioso passage. It is the awakening *spirit of God*, as emphasized by a tonal modulation into E-flat major (parallel to E-flat minor and relative major to C-minor). The image of *the face of the deep* returns, in the key of C minor. Then, in stark unison, the chorus, very softly utters those ever so dramatic and fateful words: *And God said.*

CHORUS

> And the spirit of God moved upon the face of the waters.
> And God said, "Let there be light," and there was light.

Suddenly, the entire picture changes; through a simple tonal modulation, from C minor to C major, Haydn portrays the momentous shift from pitch darkness to brilliant light on the word "Light." The effect is sustained for a full four bars! We are awestruck by the immense dynamic range (from very soft *pianissimo* to very loud *fortissimo*), which affects us physically. In a flash, dull matter has been transmogrified into light energy, a hundred years before Einstein's theory: $E=mc^2$! This astonishing shift is further emphasized by an abrupt change of harmonic rhythm. The stroke of creative power at work is reinforced by instrumental registration and choral diction. Speech has become song!

URIEL (tenor)

> And God saw the light, that it was good;
> And God divided the light from the darkness.

The accompanied recitative and aria, and chorus that follow, enrich our knowledge with emotional depth, adding tonal visualization to understanding. It is an imaginative musical gloss on Scripture.

URIEL

> Now before the divine rays the gloomy shades of black darkness vanish.
> The first day begins. Chaos yields and order is established.
> The ghastly hosts of hell flee in terror down into the deep abyss to endless night.

The aria and chorus, *Now before the divine rays*, is laid out in 16 bar units, but phrased, in a prose-like, inner asymmetric structure — the musical equivalent of blank verse. It is within such varied tonal configurations, structures, and forms that Haydn actualizes the concepts of *chaos yielding to order*. This aria centers on A major-minor tonality.

Here, major symbolizes the sun beams which dispel darkness; while chromaticism, within minor mode modulations, symbolizes *gloom and darkness*. Furthermore, the metaphor — of light representing good, and dark representing evil — is sustained by a contrapuntal choral texture highlighting the *despairing, cursing, rage* of the damned.

CHORUS

> Despair, rage, and terror attend their fall.
> And a new world springs up at God's command.

The purity of the *new created world* is folk-like in structure; all is symmetrical and beaming in a major key. Motifs are no longer placed within asymmetric structures, but symmetrically repeat in square 8-bar periods and 16-bar phrases. The profound simplicity of this construction stands out in sharp relief to the previous phrase structures, which earlier had heralded in *the first day*. This plain, folk-like kind of music introduces a marvelous freshness into the picture, as if the earth were born anew under the footsteps of little children. In this instance, form and tonality function as symbols of human innocence, contrasting markedly with the subtle phrase construction that characterized the deep, creative cogitation of God. Summing up this selection, we hear the square formal balance and major tonality of this *newly created world*, played off against the fierce counterpoint and asymmetry of the rebelling angels.

Conclusion

Haydn teaches us how tonality — at the service of musical form and structure — may be used to embrace abstract ideas and concepts. It transforms religious content into a subject worthy of artistic treatment, far removed from the strictures of liturgical art. It is an exegesis that affects us in profound and subtle ways.[19]

---

19. There is a similarity in Haydn's thought process of contrast and comparison, to traditional principles of rabbinic exegesis: *Rabbi Ishmael says, the Torah may be expounded by these thirteen principles of logic: Inference from minor to major, or from major to minor; from similarity of phrases in texts; a comprehensive principle derived from one text or from two related texts.* See *Sifra* 1, as cited in Joseph Hertz, *Authorized Daily Prayer Book* (London: Soncino Press, 1946) 43.

If in the Age of Reason, the Bible and religion had taken on a rational basis — giving sanction to secular authority — the French Revolution and the Napoleonic wars shook the old aristocratic establishment of Europe from its comfortable moorings, and transformed the optimism of the 18th century into the ominous broodings of a burgeoning Romanticism. A preference for the excesses of the sublime, over the restrained balance of the beautiful, was to mark the transition from the Classical to the Romantic era. Men of the old order felt they had lost their footing. Perhaps, the mystery of religion was closer to new realities. Into this new order of things, Haydn stepped. In the *Creation*, this aged master managed to bridge the gap between the new and the old. He opens his discourse in the chromatic chaos of a world about to be born, colored in hues worthy of a Wagnerian twilight. Yet, his fundamentally aesthetic approach to religion and the worship of God is based on beauty, balance, and the common experience of nature. It is music for the concert hall, not the cathedral. Haydn's return to the Bible of his youth embodied a fresh image and outlook on the world. For him, and perhaps for others, it embraced the stable coordinate of simple faith that sustained a generation, during a period of emotional transition and turmoil.[20]

Related Directions

Musical compositions inspired by the Creation include various 18th-century settings of the "Morning Hymn" from *Paradise Lost*. These include: Klopstock's *Morgengesang am Schoepfungsfeste*, and a cantata by Carl Philipp Emanuel Bach (1784). Some later works on the creation theme are the Norwegian, J. Haarklou's *Skapelsen* (1891); *The Creation* (1924) by Louis Gruenberg; a ballet by Darius Milhaud, *La creation de monde* (1923), scored for 17 solo instruments in a jazz idiom and inspired by African creation myths; *In the beginning — the Seven Days of Creation* (1947) by Aaron Copland; and the oratorio *Genesis* (1958) by Franz Reizenstein. One of the most unusual works in this category is the composite composition, encompassing Chapters 1–11 of the Book of Genesis, entitled *Genesis Suite* (1945), with contributions by Arnold Schoenberg (*Prelude*), Nathaniel Shilkret (*Creation*), Alexandre

---

20. For further discussion of these ideas, and additional musical analysis, see Nicolas Temperley, *Haydn: The Creation* (Cambridge University Press, 1991).

Tansman (*Adam and Eve*), Darius Milhaud (*Cain and Abel*), Mario Castelnuovo-Tedesco (*The Flood*), Ernst Toch (*The Rainbow*), and Igor Stravinsky (*Babel*).

A contemporary work, *Bereshith* (1991), for soprano, flute, strings and percussion by Max Stern describes the mystery, wonder, and exhilaration of the Creation in the 'process of becoming.' It is structured as a fanciful theme with seven variations. The Seven Days of Creation are witnessed by an angel and a bird, both of whom were present at the dawn of time. The solo flutist flutters in birdsong throughout the orchestral texture, while the cherubic soprano, intones the words she heard from on High (Genesis, chapter 1). An Israeli pop song entitled *Bereshith* was written by Tzvika Pik to a text by Ehud Manor (1941–2005).

Works List

Badings, Henk (1907 Java–1987 Netherlands). *Genesis*, 4 percussions, electronic sound.

Barber, Samuel (1910 West Chester, Pa.–1981 New York). *In the beginning*, choir, organ.

Bialas, Guenter (1907–1995 Germany). *Im Anfang*, 3 echo voices / SSATTB, organ.

Copland, Aaron (1900 Brooklyn, NY–1990). *In the beginning*, mezzo soprano, a cappella choir.

Corigliano, John (b.1938 NYC). *Two Scenes from Genesis* (1972), narrator and orchestra.

Engel, A. Lehman (1910 Mississippi–1982 New York). *The Creation*, narrator, orchestra.

Fortner, Wolfgang (1907–1987 Leipzig). *The Creation*, baritone, chamber orchestra.

Gorecki, Henryk (b.1933 Poland). *Genesis III, monodrama* (1963), soprano, 13 metal percussion, 6 double bass.

Greenberg, Noah (1919–1966 New York). *Creation*, baritone, instruments.

Guttman, Oscar (1885–1942). *Breishit*, oratorio.

Harlap, Aharon (b.1941 Canada/1964 Israel). *For Dust You Are and to Dust You Shall Return* (1991), soprano, alto, baritone, narrator, chorus, orchestra.

Hunnicutt, Judy (20th C. Denver). *God, Creator* (Gen. 1:1–3), SATB, handbells.

Hurd, Michael (1928–2006 UK). Genesis (1965), bass, SATB.

Luening, Otto (1900 Milwaukee–1970 New York). *In the beginning*, electronic voice on tape.

Neuner, Carl Borromaeus (1778–1830 Munich). *Die Schoepfungstage*, 5 voices, choir, orchestra.

Norgard, Per (b.1932 Denmark). *Den fjerde dag* (1984).

Oertzen Rudolf (1888–1965 Zaghreb). *The Creation*, choir, jazz orchestra.

Pinkham, Daniel (1923–2006 USA). *In the Beginning of Creation* (1970) (Gen 1:1–3), SATB, electronic tape

Reizenstein, Franz Theodor (1911 Nuremberg–1968 London). *Genesis*, oratorio.

Sailer, Sebastian (1714–1777 Germany). *Die Schepfung des esrten Menschen, der Suendenfall und dessen Strafe*, soprano, tenor, bass, 2 violins, basso continuo.

Schidlowsky, Leon (b.1931 Chile/1969 Israel). *Genesis* (1986) for children's choir (SSA) a cappella.

Stern, Max (b.1947 USA/1976 Israel). *Bereshith*, soprano, flute, strings, percussion.

Ussachevsky, Vladimir (1911 Manchuria–1990 New York). *Creation*, 4 choirs and electronics.

Wagner-Regeny, Rudolf (b.1903 Hungary). *Genesis*, alto, choir, orchestra.

Wallace, William (1860 Scotland–1940 England). *The Creation*, symphonic poem.

Wigglesworth, Frank (1918 Boston–1996 New York). *Creation*, choir, orchestra.

Zur, Menachem (b.1942 Israel). *And There Arose a Mist* (1972) (Genesis, Giora Zur), Cantata for mixed choir, trumpet, 2 hns, trombone, percussion, tape.

Darius Milhaud's melodrama, *Cain and Abel*, applies an 18th-century musical-dramatic genre to a biblical subject. Interweaving spoken text and music, it affords opportunity to reflect on the contradictory nature of the 'Word' in performance. Is the sung word the same as the spoken word? Are there dimensions to narrative which cannot or ought not be sung?

CAIN and ABEL

And it came to pass, when they were in the field, that Cain rose up against Abel his brother and slew him. And the Lord said unto Cain: 'Where is Abel thy brother?' And he said: 'I know not; am I my brother's keeper?" And He said: 'What hast thou done? The voice of thy brother's blood crieth unto Me from the ground. And now cursed art thou from the ground, which hast opened her mouth to receive thy brother's blood from thy hand. When thou tillest the ground, it shall not henceforth yield unto thee her strength; a fugitive and a wanderer shalt thou be in the earth' (Genesis 4:8–12).

Sin came into the world with the disobedience of Eve, and, with the fratricide of Cain, the curse was born.[1] Murder is the fruit of jealousy, and all nature revolts at the deed. A Midrash relates that in consequence of Cain's crime, all the animals assembled to demand justice, while the ground refused to yield its fruitfulness. Christian theologians interpret the firstlings of Abel's flock and the fat as living works of charity (loving-kindness) and the heart, while explaining Cain's fruit of the ground as lifeless works of faith — cold, hard, and remorseless.

---

1.   In itself, the curse has neither dimension nor existence; it is the absence of the Holy in the life of man. The curse here only refers to Cain, not to any of the other descendents of Adam and Eve, else we would have no agriculture, whatsoever.

Darius Milhaud: Cain and Abel (1945)
Text: Genesis 4:1–16
Genre: Melodrama
Medium: Narration with orchestra
Style: Polytonal
Duration ca. 5 minutes

The monodrama *Cain and Abel* for narrator and orchestra is a dramatic monologue on the first fratricide in history. It forms the fourth movement of the *Genesis Suite*, a 7-movement work, by seven composers, depicting the earliest stories from the book of Genesis. The spoken text is interwoven with descriptive orchestral commentary.

Biographic Context

Darius Milhaud (1892–1974) was one of the most prolific composers of the 20th century and a leading exponent of polytonality, which he viewed as a "Latin" alternative to atonality. He was born into a cultured, middle-class Jewish family in Aix-en-Provence and studied at the Paris Conservatory, where he mastered academic compositional technique. On a stint in Brazil, he absorbed Latin-American rhythms. Negro jazz, another source, was the result of a visit to Harlem in New York City during the roaring '20s. These influences, along with French popular and folksong, and his own Jewish-Provencal heritage, Milhaud merged to create an intriguing, distinctively personal style. All of his works are marked by a musical language of unsentimental clarity and moderation. Few think of Milhaud as a Jewish émigré composer, yet, after the Nazi occupation of Paris, in 1940, Milhaud and his family fled to America, where he became associated with Mills College and the Aspen Festival and Music School. It was during this American sojourn that he turned more and more to biblical subjects and to his own Jewish roots for inspiration.

The Biblical Word: Logos or Pathos
Chanted, Spoken or Sung?

The historical precedent for biblical music is the cantillation of the

Pentateuch (*Torah* or "teaching").[2] According to tradition, Moses received its text and tone simultaneously: *And when the voice of the horn waxed louder and louder, Moses spoke and God answered him by a voice (Exod. 19:19).*[3] What was this voice (*neima*) — a tone, a recitative, a melos, or a melody? The public reading of the Law, established from the days of Moses as Tradition, condemns "He who reads [Scripture] without a tone, and he who studies [Scripture] without a tune, for he shows disregard for it and its laws."[4]

In the time of Ezra, we learn *and they read in the book, in the law of God distinctly and gave sense so that they understood the reading (Neh. 8:8).* This *sense* has been understood not only as reading the words, but, also, includes their accentuation and division into clauses, phrases, and sentences. This verse is further taken as a legal precedent sanctioning translation of the Bible into the vernacular because it allows for the translation of the original Hebrew text into a language *so that they understood the reading* (whether Aramaic, Greek, and Latin, the modern secular languages of Europe, or others around the globe). *Sense* as interpretation was to be communicated through vocal inflection[5] and emphasis, *distinctly* extended to include musical expression. We learn from the above citations, then, that there is a connection between sound and voice, tone and word. It denotes a unity between emotion and intellect, logos and pathos, word and feeling, head and heart; connotative meaning (associated overtones) and denotative understanding (explicit meaning). If the spoken word articulates denotative meaning, the sung word conjures up connotative depth. Tone is not merely a superficial additive to the Word — it is its essence, its inner being. Seen in this light, from whence comes

---

2. *And that you may teach the children of Israel all the statutes which the Lord hath spoken unto them by the hand of Moses (Lev. 10:11).*

3. R. Judah Hahassid (c.1150–1217), author of the classic medieval text *Sefer Hasidim*, writes, that not only the Torah, but also the Prophets and Writings each have their own tone, and that these are not to be interchanged. He further remarks that the relation between word and tone is a unity, and all are laws given to Moses on Mount Sinai. He comments on the word "voice" (Hebrew-*Kol*): "And with a tone (*neima* or pleasant sound) that he heard, with the same melos he [Moses] spoke to Israel." As cited in *Sefer Hasidim*, edited by Shimon Goodman (Jerusalem: Institute of Responsa Literature, 2006) 303, paragraph 302 (translation by Max Stern).

4. Mishnah Sukkoth iii.10 and Talmud Megillah 32a.

5. Talmud Nedarim 37b.

the "spoken word" of *Cain and Abel*? Why does Milhaud ignore the above precepts concerning word and tone, and narrate Holy Writ as if it were common speech? What are his precedents? Is it a narration with music or a biblical reading with orchestral accompaniment; a drama with musical accompaniment or a tone poem with narration? To what genre does *Cain and Abel* belong?

Melodrama

Milhaud's concept is based on the little known, almost extinct, 18th-century dramatic-musical form of melodrama.[6] The original melodrama was a genuine spoken drama with either a single actor (monodrama) or two actors (duo drama) and orchestra. Music contributed the hidden depth of the soul to their speech, beyond man's action's and words.[7] Milhaud has applied 20th-century musical idioms to this genre — sometimes notating the rhythm of the words (as they appear in the English Bible),[8] but never setting them to pitches.[9]

---

6. The glory of literary France, Swiss-born Jean Jacques Rousseau (1712–1778) was also a pioneer of melodrama, i.e. *Pygmalion*, 1762. Georg Benda, a Kapellmeister influenced by Rousseau, wrote two melodramas, *Ariade auf Naxos* (1775) and *Medea* (1778) — all on Greek mythology. After an early triumph, however, melodrama was rarely revived, but it did influence potions of larger works, such as the prison scene from Beethoven's *Fidelio*, Schoenberg's speech-song in *Pierrot Lunaire* (1912), the spoken narrations in Honegger's *King David* (1923), and others. There are sections in French opera comique, German singspiel, Viennese Operetta, and American Broadway musicals, which, in one way or another, also combine speaking and music.

7. Curt Sachs, *Our Musical Heritage* (Englewood Cliffs, NJ: Prentice Hall, 1955) 240.

8. Eighteenth-century musicians intensively studied the language arts of poetry, drama, and oratory, borrowing concepts from the art of rhetoric to designate various aspects of musical composition. They made distinctions between high, middle, and low style — "The high style encompasses all great, exalted, dreadful feelings and violent passions. The middle style includes softer and milder feelings, such as love, calmness, satisfaction, cheerfulness, and joy. The low style includes more trifling merriment, caricature and comedy." See Ernst Gerber in *Allegemeine musikalische Zeitung*, 1799, as cited in Leonard Ratner, *Classic Music: Expression, Form, and Style* (New York: MacMillan/Schirmer Books, 1980) 364.

9. In the Milkin Archive of American Jewish Music recording (Naxos 8.559442), three narrators dramatize the three voices of the story: the biblical narrator, the voice of the Lord, and the conscience of Cain.

Text and Music — Context and Exegesis

Analyses

Cain and Abel
Section 1 (4:1–5)

NARRATOR

And the man knew Eve his wife; and she conceived, and bore Cain, and said, 'I have gotten a man with the help of the Lord.' And again she bore his brother Abel. And Abel was a keeper of sheep, but Cain was a tiller of the ground. And in the process of time it came to pass, that Cain brought of the fruit of the ground an offering unto the Lord. And Abel, he also brought of the firstlings of his flock and of the fat thereof. And the Lord had respect unto Abel and to his offering: But unto Cain and his offering, He had not respect. And Cain was very wroth, and his countenance fell.

Musical gestures are freely interwoven with text and form a descriptive instrumental commentary. A sweeping upward-rocket theme indicates Cain's petulant nature. Its apogee climaxes in a harsh hammer-blow chord — symbolizing the violent stroke that slew Abel. A contrasting element is a pastoral theme, representing idyllic nature. It corresponds to Abel bringing the *firstlings of his flock* — an acceptable offering unto the Lord. These two themes are the building blocks of a through-composed musical structure, which traces and supports the archetypical narrative.

Section 2 (4:6)

LORD

And the Lord said unto Cain, 'Why art thou wroth? And why is thy countenance fallen? If thou doest well, shalt thou not be accepted? And if thou doest not well, sin coucheth at the door.' (The rest of the verse is omitted.)

Section 3 (4:8)

NARRATOR

And Cain spoke unto Abel his brother. And it came to pass, when they were in the field, that Cain rose up against Abel his brother, and slew him.

If the defining act of the episode is the fratricide of Abel, it poses an aesthetic dilemma: How does one set a crime such as murder to music? Let us, as Milhaud did, step outside the Bible and look to Greek sources for a clue. Murder is tragedy, and Greek tragedy was spoken and not sung. We learn of the high regard the spoken word held for the ancient pagan world through the treatise *Institutio oratoria* (Book XI, chapter 3), by the Roman writer Quintilian (35–100).[10] He detests Hebraic tonal melos and remarks, "the practice of chanting instead of speaking is the worst feature of our modern oratory." Quintilian cites the Roman statesman, philosopher, writer, and orator Cicero (106–43 B.C.) as his model, who, also, rejected the sing-song style of the East, informing us "that the rhetoricians of Lycia and Caria come near to singing their perorations."[11] To reinforce his argument, Quintilian adds, "Does anyone sing when his theme is murder, sacrilege, or patricide!"[12] This last citation clinches Milhaud's choice of speech, whether consciously or not, rather than song, for setting the biblical *Cain and Abel*. It also reflects an aesthetic derived from Classical models,[13] a hybridization between rationality and revelation. How different is this world from the biblical injunction: *Sing unto him, sing praises unto him; tell ye of all his marvelous works (1 Chron. 16:9).*

Section 4 (4:9–12)

LORD

> And the Lord said unto Cain: 'Where is thy brother?'

---

10. This work exerted its greatest influence during the Renaissance and Reformation. Undoubtedly, ideas derived from it influenced the creators of melodrama.
11. Lycia and Caria are regions in Asia Minor.
12. See Lacus Curtius Quintilian, *Institutio Oratoria*, Book XI, Chapter 3, translated by H.E. Butler, Vol. 4 (New York: Loeb Classical Library, 1920–22).
13. The spoken word is given greatest value in a society whose ideal is rationality — a social coordinate outside the circle of a community, held together by faith, family relationships, or historic revelation. Cicero remarks, *Nemo fere saltat sobrius* (No sober person dances). It illustrates the contempt of the rationalist, an intellect with no capacity for ecstasy. In contrast, *David danced before the Lord with all his might (2 Sam. 6:14)*. See also Curt Sachs, *World History of Dance* (New York: Norton, 1963) 245.

CAIN

'I know not; am I my brother's keeper?'

LORD

And He said: 'What hast thou done? The voice of thy brother's blood crieth unto Me from the ground. And now cursed art thou from the ground, which hath opened her mouth to receive thy brother's blood from thy hand. When thou tillest the ground, it shall not henceforth yield unto thee her strength; a fugitive and a wanderer shalt thou be in the earth.'

Section 5 (4:13–14)

CAIN

And Cain said unto the Lord: 'My punishment is greater than I can bear. Behold, Thou hast driven me out this day from the face of the land; and from Thy face I shall be hid; and I shall be a fugitive and a wanderer in the earth; and it will come to pass that whoever findeth me will slay me…'

Section 6 (4:15–16)

LORD

And the Lord said unto him, 'Therefore whosoever slayeth Cain, vengeance shall be taken upon him sevenfold.'

NARRATOR

And the Lord set a sign for Cain, lest any finding him should smite him. And Cain went out from the presence of the Lord.

Meter, Rhythm, and Meaning

The meter of Milhaud's monodrama is written in 4/4 or common time, the modern equivalent of *proportitio dupla* in the Middle Ages, or, *alla breve*[14] in the 18th century. Milhaud twists and pulls, distorts and syncopates this 'straight forward' duple meter, in order to transform something considered 'right and high'[15] into something 'base and

---

14. *Alle breve* signifies a melody comprised of whole and half notes.
15. The high style (*Alle breve*) was considered a descendent of plainsong, the musical counterpart of a liturgical text. See Ernst Gerber as cited in Ratner,

evil.' It is moral value expressed through meter and rhythm. Medieval music theory, too, conceived of meter and rhythm in terms of perfect[16] and imperfect[17] — a distinction analogous to the duality of human vs. Divine, mortal vs. immortal. It is represented as divisions of the number 2[18] vs. divisions by the number 3;[19] symmetry vs. asymmetry, reason vs. revelation. The whole medieval idea of musical proportions is based on such cosmological conceptions of rhythm, meter, and tempo. Milhaud applies this kind of thinking to his composition *Cain and Abel*. Throughout, we never encounter a three-fold division in the meter or in sub-divisions of the beats. Nowhere, either, is there a steady *tripla* pulse (as one finds, for instance, in the concluding sections of many Baroque settings).[20] What we do encounter, however, are spastic gesticulations,[21] all of which are rationalized by symmetric rhythmic

op. cit.

16. Perfect means Divine. Any combination or division of the *tactus* or beat into three is considered perfect. These relationships change as tempo changes (i.e. 3/4 is perfect in relation to meter, but imperfect in relation to beat; while 9/8 is perfect both in relation to meter and beat).

17. Imperfect means temporal and limited. Any combination or division of the beat into two is considered imperfect (i.e. 2/4, 4/4/, and all eighth, quarter, half, and whole notes).

18. The human body, the measure of man's physical being, with its exact symmetry of 2 arms, 2 legs, 2 eyes, and 2 ears is by nature imperfect.

19. See Gustave Reese, *Music in the Middle Ages*, for an extensive discussion of the rhythmic modes and proportionality in music.

20. The proportion of three or *tripla* is considered Divine, and, in Christian theology, a metaphor for the Trinity. Fourteenth-century French mathematician and philosopher Jean de Muris (1300–1351), in his treatise *Ars Novae Musicae*, writes: "All music is founded in perfection, combining in itself number and sound. The number which musicians consider perfect is the ternary number 3." Oliver Strunk, *Source Readings in Music History* (New York: Norton, 1950) 172–179. We add that numerology reaches back to remote antiquity, and was developed into a symbolic system by the Egyptians, Babylonians, Assyrians, Jews, and Greeks. The number 3 had typological significance, symbolizing completeness (i.e. beginning, middle, end; sun, moon, stars; father, mother, child). It stands for the three dimensions of time (past, present, future), as well as the three dimensions of space (length, width, height). The song of the angels praises the thrice holy Deity (*Kadosh, kadosh, kadosh*). The Sages of Ancient Israel grasped this as supernal wisdom, a crystallized ideation of the Divine.

21. The 20th-century composer Ralph Vaughan Williams employs similar "spastic" rhythms to symbolize Satan in his ballet *Job*.

divisions of whole notes and their sub-divisions in two's — as quarter notes, eighth notes, and sixteenth notes.

Conclusion

Mindful of the imperfection man's actions have thrust into the divine scheme of Creation, Milhaud struggles to affect a symbiosis between intellectual knowledge and spiritual presence in *Cain and Abel*. He solves the problem technically, revealing via musical metaphor, a deep sympathy for the problematic nature of the subject. This philosophical dichotomy of logos vs. pathos finds musical expression in two ways: one tonal and one rhythmic. The text as logos is spoken. The melodious presence of the Word's pathos, and its tonal link between heaven and earth, has been severed. It is a point of exegesis, as if to say, the man who cannot give wings to his spirit in song has no means through which to approach the Divine. Word as narration is rational; it is sense without soul.[22] The curse of Cain is the absence of a tonal connection by which to approach Holiness. In the life of this man, the voice of the orchestra underlines the emotional element in the story; its role awakens pathos and provides an ecstatic element to the work. However, here too, Milhaud is careful to frame his metric orchestral commentary in symmetric divisions of 2's and 4's, but never in asymmetric divisions of 3's. Again, he confirms and projects the symbolic absence of divinity through orchestral gesture, by means of metric prolation (or imperfect rhythmic sub-divisions of the beat), devoid of the redeeming 'perfection' of odd numbered threes. Thus, the curse of Cain, the man who *went out from the presence of the Lord (Gen. 4:16),* is made manifest.

Related Directions

Apart from some unimportant Italian oratorios of the early 17th century, the first significant musical treatment of the Cain and Abel story was an oratorio by Alessandro Scarlatti, *Cain, ovvero il primo omicido* (1706), the autograph score of which was rediscovered in 1966. *La Morte*

---

22. Milhaud's narrative mode, influenced by an ancient Greek and Roman aesthetic, derives from Renaissance models and ideals which 18th-century Europe adopted. In contemporary terms, it might be transposed as: form without content.

di Abele (1732), a libretto by Pietro Metastasio,[23] was set to music by Antonio Caldara, Leonardo Leo, and many others. The English translation was set by Thomas Arne as *The Death of Abel* (1744), the same work being later performed as *Abel* and *The Sacrifice*. J.H. Rolle's *Singspiel*, or ballad opera, *Der Tod Abels* (text by J.S. Patzke, 1769), was performed in many German towns until 1809. The reworking of the original text by the German poet Klopstock was set to music by Michael Haydn (1778), and Metastasio's text was used again by Franz Seydelman (1801). Two other 19th-century musical treatments were Conradin Kreutzer's *La mort d'Abel* (1810) and Max Zenger's minor opera *Cain* (1867), with a libretto based on Byron's poem. Some later works are E. d'Albert's opera *Kain* (1900), F. Weingartner's opera *Kain und Abel* (1914), and the ballet *Cain* (1930) by Marc Blitzstein.[24]

Works List

Aichinger, Gregor (c.1565–1628 Germany). *Where Is Now Abel? (Gen. 4:9–10)*, SAB.

D'Albert, Eugene (1864 Glasgow–1932 Riga). *Kain* (Heinrich Bulthaupt), opera.

Amadei, Filippo (1670–1729 Rome). *L'Abele*, oratorio.

Avondano, Pietro (18th C. Genoa). *La Morte d'Abel* (P. Metastasio), oratorio.

Benoit, Petrus (1834–1901 Antwerp). *Le Muerte d'Abel*, cantata.

Bigaglia, Diogemo (1676–1745 Venice). *L'Abele*, oratorio.

Blitzstein, Marc (1905 Philadelphia–1964 Martinique). *Cain*, ballet.

---

23. Pietro Metastasio (1698–1782) is considered the greatest Italian poet of the 18th century. His librettos were set to music by many composers, including Gluck, Handel, Mozart, Pergolesi, and Rossini. A child prodigy, his talent and charm endeared him to a series of powerful and influential patrons, who paved his way to becoming court poet at Vienna in 1729, where he created sacred *opera seria*. Those based on Old Testament oratorio texts include: *La morte d'Abel, Gioas re di Giuda, Giuseppe riconosciuto, Isacco, figura del Redentore*, and *La Betulia liberata*. Don Neville, "Opera or oratorio: Metastasio's sacred *opera seria*," Vol. 26, no. 4 (Oxford University Press: *Early Music*, November 1998) 596.

24. See Batia Bayer, "Cain and Abel," *Encyclopaedia Judaica* (Jerusalem: Keter Publishing House, 1972) Vol. 5, col. 24–25.

Borghi, Giovanni Battista (1738–1796 Italy). *La Morte d'Abele* (P. Metastasio).

Caldara, Antonio (1670 Venice–1736 Vienna). *La Morte d'Abele* (P. Metastasio).

Carissimi, Giacomo (1605–1674, Rome). *Historia di Cain*, oratorio.

Cazzati, Maurizio (1620–1677 Italy). *Caino Condannato* (M. Caccati), oratorio.

Crispi, Pietro Maria (1737–1797 Rome). *La Morte di Abele* (P. Metastasio), oratorio.

Czinzer, Giovanni (18th C. Florence). *Abele Ucciso da Caino* (P. Viviani), 4 voices.

Deden, Otto (1925 Holland). *Kain* (Roger van Aerde), baritone, chorus, and orchestra.

Fischietti, Domenico (1725 Naples–1810 Salzburg). *La Morte d'Abele* (P. Metastasio).

Foertsch, Johann (1652–1752 Germany). *Cain und Abel*, opera.

Frid, Geza (1904 Hungary/1926 Holland). *Abel et Cain* (Ch. Baudelaire) baritone, alto, orchestra.

Friebert, Johann (1742–1799 Germany). *Caino ed Abele* (Passau), oratorio.

Gallenberg, Wenzel (1783 Vienna–1839 Rome). *La Mort d'Abel*, oratorio.

Gatti, Luigi (1740 Italy–1817 Salzburg). *Abel's Tod* (P. Metastasio), oratorio.

Giordani, Giuseppe (1744 Naples–1798). *La Morte d'Abelle* (P. Metastasio), oratorio.

Graf, Friedrich (1727–1795 Germany). *Tod Abels*, oratorio.

Harlap, Aharon (b.1941 Canada/1964 Israel). *Cain and Abel* (1989), soprano, tenor, choir, and orchestra.

Harrer, Johann (1703–1755 Czech-German). *La Morte di Abele* (P. Metastasio), oratorio.

Henriques, Fini (1867–1940 Copenhagen). *Kain*, opera.

Kozeluch, Johann (1738–1814 Prague). *La Morte d'Abele* (P. Metastasio), oratorio.

Le Flem,Paul (1881–1984 France). *Cain*, cantata.

Leo, Leonardo (1694-1744 Italy). *La Morte di Abele* (P. Metastasio), oratorio.

Lorentzen, Bent (b.1935 Denmark). *Kain og Abel*, 2 sopranos, tenor, baritone, SATB, instruments.

Makoto, Moroi (b.1930 Tokyo). *Vision of Kain*, symphonic sketch for ballet.

Mazzei, Cesare (17th C. Italy). *Abele e Caino*, oratorio.

Melani, Alessandro (1639–1703 Italy). *Il Fratricidio di Caino* (B. Panfili), oratorio.

Melani, Atto (1626 Italy–1714 Paris). *Il Sacrificio d'Abel* (B. Panfili), oratorio.

Melani, Francesco (1628-c.1663 Italy). *Il Fratricidio di Caino* (B. Panfili), oratorio.

Melartin, Erkki (1875–1937 Finland). *Cain and Abel* (J. Linnankoski), cantata.

Meucci, Giovanni (18th C. Italy). *La Morte d'Abele* (P. Metastasio), oratorio.

Milhaud, Darius (1892 France–1974 Geneva). *Cain et Abel*, narrator, orchestra.

Morlacchi, Francesco (1784 Italy–1841 Austria). *La Morte di Abele* (P. Metastasio), oratorio.

Naumann, Johann (1741–1801 Dresden). *La Morte d'Abel* (P. Metastasio),oratorio.

Onslow, Andre-George (1784–1853 France). *La Mort d'Abel*, baritone, orchestra.

Pergolesi, Giovanni (1710–1736 Italy). *La Morte d'Abel*, oratorio.

Perotti, Giovanni-Agostino (1769–1855 Venice). *Abele* (P. Metastasio), oratorio.

Perry, George (1793–1862 London). *The Death of Abel*, oratorio.

Piccini, Nicola (1728–1800 Paris). *La Morte de Abele* (P. Metastasio), oratorio.

Queralt, Francisco (1740–1825 Barcelona). *La Muerte de Abel*, oratorio.

Reutter, Georg (1708–1772 Vienna). *Abel* (S. Padovano), oratorio.

Rolle, Johann (1716–1785 Germany). *Der Tod Abels* (Patzke), oratorio.

Scarlatti, Alessandro (1660–1725 Naples). *Cain Overo il Primo Omicido*, oratorio.

Searle, Humphrey (b.1915 Oxford–1982). *The Shadow of Cain* (E. Sitwell), speakers, mezzo soprano, chorus, orchestra.

Seydelmann, Franz (1748–1806 Dresden). *La Morte d'Abel* (P. Metastasio), oratorio.

Spilka, Frantisek (1877–1960 Prague). *Kain* (J. Karbulka), opera.

Spindler, Franz (1763 Bavaria–1819 Strasbourg). *Kain und Abel*, melodrama.

Stoelzel, Gottfried (1690–1749 Germany). *Caino Overo IL Primo Figlia Malvaggio*, oratorio.

Taverner, John (1944 England). *Cain and Abel*, cantata for soli, SATB, orchestra.

Tisne, Antoine (1932 France). *Abel et Cain*, choir.

Ullinger, Sebastien (18th C. Germany). *Kain und Abel*, Singspiel.

Umstatt, Josef (1711 Vienna–1762 Bamberg). *La Morte d'Abel*, oratorio.

Vannucci, Domenico (1718–1775 Italy). *L'Uccisione di Abele*, oratorio.

Weber, Jacob Gottfried (1779–1839 Germany). *Kain und Abel*, melodrama.

Weingartner, Felix (1863 Croatia–1942 Austria). *Kain und Abel*, opera.

Weinrauch, Ernestus (1730–1793 Germany). *Kain und Abel*, oratorio.

Wesley, Samuel (1766–1837 London). *The Death of Abel*, solo voices, chorus, orchestra.

Zador, Eugene (1894 Hungary–1977 Hollywood). *Cain* (Rupert Hughes), melodrama, baritone, orchestra.

Zenger, Max (1837–1911 Germany). *Kain* (Byron), oratorio.

G. Dore: The Dove Sent Forth from the Ark, *Bible Illustrations (1866)*

3

Benjamin Britten's children's opera *Noye's Fludde* portrays the bible story in an atmosphere of all-inclusive community music making. To realize this conception, he adapts texts from an English medieval mystery play and incorporates indigenous English hymns, setting them in a uniquely personal musical idiom.

NOAH

And the Lord saw that the wickedness of man was great in the earth, and that every imagination of the thoughts of his heart was only evil continually. And it repented the Lord that he had made man on the earth, and it grieved him at his heart. And the Lord said: 'I will blot out man whom I have created from the face of the earth; both man and beast, and creeping thing, and the fowl of the air; for it repenteth me that I have made them.' But Noah found grace in the eyes of the Lord   (Genesis 6:5–8).

Following expulsion from the Garden of Eden, men had sunken from the peaceful ideals of Creation and living in loving proximity to God. Humanity had evolved a civilization, which, for all its progress in arts, crafts, and inventions, proved godless; turning the good earth into a selfish, exploiting, grasping, and violent place. The deluge was a divine judgment upon an age in which might was right, and depravity degraded and enslaved humanity. Men of renown were unscrupulous and deified power. One alone was upright and blameless — Noah — who, believing in justice, practiced mercy. He preached to his generation to desist from iniquity and turn to righteousness, but failed. Noah built the ark at God's command, to save himself, his family, and all the animals and birds from the disaster that wiped out his generation.[1] *And*

---

1. Later ages criticized Noah, comparing him disparagingly to Abraham, whose proselytizing efforts spread Godliness in the world. In Jewish circles, the ark came to symbolize and justify the building of walls around sacred values, enabling a pious but insular society to survive. In its message of withdrawal,

God said unto Noah… Make thee an ark of gopher wood (6:14); and thou shalt come into the ark, thou, and thy sons, and thy wife and thy sons' wives with thee (6:18); And of every living thing of all flesh, two of every sort shalt thou bring into the ark (6:19).

Benjamin Britten: Noye's Fludde, op. 59 (1957)
Libretto: Chester Miracle Play
Genre: Community-Children's Opera
Medium: Professional soloists, choir, children's choir, church congregation, professional string quintet, school orchestra, recorder soloist & ensemble, seven percussionists, piano 4-hands, and organ
Style: Tonal
First performance: Aldeburgh Festival, Britain, 1958
Duration: ca. 50 minutes

Britten's *Noyes Fludde* is a children's opera styled in an accessible, tonal idiom that derives from the world of rural England and the Anglican Church. Written for professionals, amateurs, children, and congregation, it is a rare example of all-inclusive music making by a major 20th-century composer. Based on the Chester Mystery Play, *Noyes Fludde*, a fanciful retelling of the Bible story (*Gen. 6:9–9:18*). The work was first performed at the Aldeburgh Festival in 1958.

Biographic Context

Benjamin Britten (1913–1976) is among the most important British composers to emerge since the Second World War. His style synthesizes 18th and 19th-century idioms, techniques, and forms with English church and secular music; and 20th-century polytonality, atonality, and rhythmic innovations. Benjamin's earliest exposure to music came from his mother, an amateur singer. He started composing from the age of five, and by eleven began formal studies with Frank Bridge, continuing at the Royal College of Music with John Ireland. A life-long pacifist, Britten moved to America, in 1937, in an attempt to escape the war, returning home in 1943. In 1947, he founded the Aldeburgh Festival,

---

rather than engagement and confrontation with an evil and hostile world, the Ark came to be seen as a precursor to the Church — offering salvation to mankind.

with his friend, tenor Peter Pears, at the provincial seaside town of Aldeburgh (2,500 pop.).

Essentially a vocal composer, most of Britten's 17 operas touch on the theme of the individual and society, and the violation of innocence. Influenced by the landscape of the sea and the Anglican Church environment of Aldeburgh, Britten spent significant time performing in several churches near his home, and, until the end of his working life, focused his efforts primarily toward the Festival, composing music of all sorts, as well as performing and undertaking administrative duties. His two most successful operas, *Peter Grimes* (1945) and *Billy Budd* (1951), tell the stories of sailors and the sea. Britten's preoccupation with the sea and obsession with the conflict between a simple man and corrupt society found expression, also, in the biblical tale of Noah and the flood.

The Chester Mystery Plays

Mystery (or Miracle) plays developed throughout Europe from the 10th to 16th centuries. They are among the earliest forms of European drama.[2] The Chester Mystery Plays are a cycle of 24 plays, written in Middle English, which originated in 14th-century England. They focus on Bible stories, and were intended to be enacted in churches with accompanying song. Episodes from the Old Testament, which are seen to prefigure the life of Christ and emphasize his central place in history were specifically chosen. Noah's Flood, for example, is interpreted as anticipating the Last Judgment. At first, the monks at Chester Cathedral enacted these stories to help those who couldn't follow or understand the Scriptures in Latin. Eventually, this practice brought unruly crowds into the Cathedral and proved disruptive. The plays were moved outside, where the Church looked askance at clergy acting in public. Owing to their popularity, however, various guilds (i.e. grocers, bakers, millers, etc.) adopted and produced the plays, performing them on pageant wagons wheeled throughout city streets at various locations about town.

Under these conditions, the strictly religious nature of the plays became filled with satirical and everyday elements. For this reason, perhaps, the Chester Mystery Play cycles represent an intriguing

---

2. Strictly speaking, mystery plays focus on Bible stories or events from the life of Jesus; while, miracle plays, portray events in the lives of saints and martyrs.

balance between religious and secular. The nature of this balance is probably closer to the concept, often touched on in this study, of "religious but not necessarily liturgical." The very term "secularization" implies a growing irreverence and worldliness as the plays became more elaborate, as though they were no longer appropriate for association with church and clergy. On the contrary, the vernacular cycles were still the literary work of monks and cathedral canons. Comic characterization and incident, though often singled out by modern critics, were the peripheral fringes of a serious and reverent cosmic narrative.[3]

During the English Reformation under Queen Elizabeth I, the plays were banned as "Popery."[4] Ironically, in 1951, nearly 350 years later, they were revived for the festival of Britain, and continue to be popular to this day.

Text and Music, Music and Context

Noyes Fludde strives for the same unsophisticated style of presentation as the Chester Miracle Plays, which were performed by ordinary people (i.e. local craftsmen and tradesmen of the town and their families), with choristers from local churches and cathedrals taking the children's parts. It involves skilled professionals and unskilled amateurs, young and old alike. The score calls for characters who are accomplished professional singer-actors (i.e. Noye and his wife); a musical, though not necessarily professional actor with a rich speaking voice (i.e. God); trained young teenagers with lively personalities (for the parts of Sem, Ham, Jaffett and their wives); older girls (for the gossips); and numerous children (for the parts of the animals). The orchestra consists of a professional recorder soloist, professional string quintet, piano four-hands, organ and timpani, alongside amateurs and children playing violins, violas, cellos, basses, recorders, bugle, and hand bells. There are a slew of percussion instruments, as well: bass drum, tenor drum, side drum, tambourine, cymbals, triangle, whip, gong, Chinese

---

3. For a comprehensive overview see Ellen Catherine Dunn, "Drama, Medieval," *New Catholic Encyclopedia*, Vol. 4 (Farmington Hills, Minnesota: Gale, 2003) 897.
4. "Popery" is an anti-Catholic slur against those Christians loyal to the Roman Catholic Church and the Pope, in contrast to the Anglican Church of England.

blocks, a wind machine, sandpaper, and slung mugs — which imitate raindrops.[5]

Britten grafts onto the play three well-known Anglican Church hymns. These hymns form the structural cornerstones of Britten's musical design; they are a means of establishing a close relationship with his audience. At the outset of the opera the congregation joins in singing the anxious prayer, "Lord Jesus Think on Me." Later, when Noah's ark is adrift at sea, at the center of the action, the congregation participates in singing "Eternal Father," a prayer for deliverance. Finally, the entire cast and congregation unite for the solemn closing tableau, "The Spacious Firmament on High," invoking heaven's blessing of peace after the deluge. These hymn tunes serve as a musical quarry, from which the composer hews out new, original motifs. Weaving in and out of these tunes, Britten mixes and freely expands this hymnal adhesive into arioso-like recitatives and short arias. Thus, on many levels of expressive gesture and musical color, Britten realizes his central concept of community inclusiveness.

DETAIL 1

The Opening Congregational Hymn

1. Lord Jesus, Think on me
And purge away my sin;
From earth-born passions set me free
And make me pure within.

3. Lord Jesus, think on me
When floods the tempest high;
When on doth rush the enemy
O Savior be thou nigh.

4. Lord Jesus, think on me
That, when the flood is past,
I may eternal brightness see
And share thy joy at last.

While the people are singing the hymn, "Lord Jesus Think on Me," symbolizing the guilt of those for whom the flood is sent to cleanse the

---

5.   Britten, Benjamin, Noye's *Fludde* (London: Boosey & Hawkes, 1958).

earth of sin and impurity, Noye walks through the congregation onto the empty stage and kneels.[6] It is striking how Britten's fundamentally 'white note' palette, derived from the modality of the hymn, can, at the same time, evoke such originality. He achieves this effect by superimposing, upon simple modal melodies, a polytonal mix of triads, seventh and ninth chords, and quartal sonorities.

DETAIL 2a

The representation of the storm

The storm is announced by onomatopoeic sounds — thunder, lightning, and crashing waves. The wind howls through the rigging and the animals panic. Above the tumult, sung by Noye and the others as a prayer, rises the central hymn of the opera, "Eternal Father, Strong to save." The congregation participates in an effort to alleviate the fears of Noah's small family, trapped in a fragile vessel on a stormy sea.[7] A four-bar passacaglia theme, rising in whole tones (C-D-E-F-sharp), and constructed to synchronize with the hymn's four-bar phrasing, is repeated 18 times. This new structural frame, imposed by the passacaglia, serves as the basis for a series of free-flowing "storm" variations that precede and follow the hymn. Toward the climax of the flood the passacaglia theme also configures a bass counterpoint to the hymn tune.

---

6. The hymn "Lord Jesus Think on Me" is found as hymn #320 from the *Lutheran Hymnal* (St. Louis: Concordia Publishing House, 1941). It is based on Psalm 119: 133, *Order my steps in Thy Word; and let not any iniquity have dominion over me*, by Synesius of Cyrene (ca. 430) and translated from Greek to English by Allan W. Chatfield in *Songs and Hymns of Earliest Greek Christian Poets*, 1876. The music was composed by William Daman (1550 Liege, Flanders–c.1593, England), *Psalms of David in English Meter* (1579).

7. This hymn is found in most Protestant Hymnals. It was written by Rev. William Whiting (1825–1878), who resided on the English coast near the sea and penned it in 1860, after surviving a furious storm in the Mediterranean. Rev. John B. Dykes (1823–1876) adapted it in 1861, to music he had previously written to "Melita," an ancient name for the Mediterranean island of Malta. It is a benediction that has long held special appeal to seafaring men, particularly the Royal Navies of the British Commonwealth and the American Navy — where it has been adopted as the "Navy Hymn." (Text extracted from a publication of the Bureau of Naval Personnel, Department of the Navy, Naval Historical Center, Washington D.C.)

Ex. 2. Britten: *Noye's Fludde*, excerpt from hymn "Eternal Father"
© Copyright 1958 by Boosey & Hawkes. Used by permission.

DETAIL 2b

The Central Hymn

Eternal Father, strong to save,
Whose arm doth bind the restless wave,
Who bidd'st the mighty ocean deep
Its appointed limits keep:
O hear us when we cry to thee
For those in peril on the sea.

O Savior, whose almighty word
The winds and waves submissive heard,
Who walkest on the foaming deep,
And calm amidst its rage didst sleep:
O hear us when we cry to thee
For those in peril on the sea.

> O Sacred Spirit, who didst brood
> Upon the chaos dark and rude,
> Who bad'st its angry tumult cease,
> And gravest light and life and peace:
> O hear us when we cry to thee
> For those in peril on the sea.

The hymn, then, bursts out from the waves of the sea, so to speak. It is repeated three times as three stanzas are sung, each with greater emphasis and confidence. At its climax, the passacaglia emerges to accompany the diminishing flood waters — continuing for another seven repetitions. Slung mugs and staccato piano pitches, sounding above sustained chords, imitate the sparse sounds of raindrops. Britten employs cross relationships[8] derived from the middle phrase of "Eternal Father," to suggest dramatic uncertainty. At another juncture, he borrows and integrates a rising semi-tone pattern (E — F — F-sharp — G), taken from the closing phrase of the hymn, to evince images of rising flood waters.

DETAIL 3

Representation of the raven

As the storm slowly subsides and all the creatures in the Ark retire to sleep, Noye peers out the window of the Ark and reflects. He decides to send a raven to see if, yet, there is dry land, anywhere. The raven climbs out, flutters this way and that, then flies off and disappears into the distance. An asymmetric waltz for solo viola and strings accompanies the raven as it flutters about indecisively. Seamlessly, the waltz rhythm continues until a dove appears; her hovering here and there is

Ex. 3. Britten: *Noye's Fludde*, Representation of the raven
© Copyright 1958 by Boosey & Hawkes. Used by permission.

---

8. Cross relation refers to a sharpened and flatted version of the same tone, sounded simultaneously or successively (i.e. F and F-sharp).

symbolized by a recorder playing coo-coos, tremolos, and meandering scales. God's command to leave the Ark concludes this episode.

DETAIL 4

The animals exit the ark two by two. It is a parade of the entire cast and marked by the ecstatic *Jubilus*, sung successively to antiphonal Gregorian-like refrains of *Alleluia*, by pairs of children.

DETAIL 5

The Closing Congregational Hymn

The spacious firmament on high
With all the blue ethereal sky
And spangled heavens, a shining frame,
The great original proclaims.

Th'unwearied sun from day to day
Doth his Creator's power display,
And publishes to every land
The works of an almighty hand.

Soon as the evening shades prevail
The moon takes up the wondrous tale,
And nightly to the listening earth
Repeats the story of her birth:

Whist all the stars that round her burn,
And all the planets in their turn,
Confirm the tidings, as they roll,
And spread the truth from pole to pole.

What though in solemn silence all
Move round the dark terrestrial ball,
What though nor real voice nor sound
Amid their radiant orbs be found.

In reason's ear they all rejoice,
And utter forth a glorious voice;
For ever singing as they shine,
The hand that made us is Divine. Amen.

As a rainbow unfolds across the sky, the closing hymn, "The Spacious Firmament on High" is sung as a song of thanksgiving.[9] The sun appears, then, the moon and the stars. The Noyes' children slowly lead the animals off stage; while he remains alone in the empty ark, communing with God.

Conclusion

Through the metaphor of the Flood story, Benjamin Britten is trying to convey a message on the relationship between innocence and corruption; in spite of appearances, only the good, the pure, and the righteous are capable of regenerating the world. To do so requires the cooperation of all, all ages and all abilities. In keeping with this basic theme of all-inclusiveness, the composer uses basic musical materials in sophisticated ways. Simple diatonic melody is often offset with complex chromatic harmonic backgrounds. Amateurs and professionals join with children; and even the church congregation attending the performance is drafted to participate in its realization. What is the moral behind this all-encompassing approach of congregational-opera, which Britten has created? Perhaps, it is meant to project the idea that any society which is fractured into separate and selfish interest groups will perish. Mankind is a collective and cannot forever endure a world of quarrelsome, deceitful, vindictive, and hypocritical values — false to one another and false to themselves.

Related Directions

In music, there were two 19th-century oratorios on the theme of the Flood, one by Johann Christian Friedrich Schmerder (1823); and *Le Déluge* (1876; première at Boston, U.S., 1880) by Camille Saint-Saëns. *Two by Two*, a musical on the theme based on Clifford Odets' play with Danny Kaye in the star role, was staged on Broadway.

---

9. English essayist and poet Joseph Addison (1672–1719) paraphrased the words after Psalm 19:1, *The heavens declare the glory of God; the skies proclaim the work of His hands.* The music was adapted to the text from a canonic tune, composed by English composer Thomas Tallis (c.1505–1585), to a setting of Psalm 67 for the Archbishop of Canterbury. See Matthew Parker's *The Whole Psalter* translated into English Metre (1567).

Approaching the subject from an abstract, almost aleatory perspective, *Rainbow* (1985) by Max Stern is a descriptive account of Noah's Flood.

Rains — Winds — Gathering of the Waters — Scurrying of the Beasts — The Flood — Opening of the Windows of Heaven — Prevalence of the Waters — Sending Forth of the Raven and Doves — Rainbow

Scored for seven saxophones,[10] each instrument symbolizes one of the seven colors of the rainbow. To simulate naturalistic effects, performers are called upon to make extraneous noises and employ extended instrumental techniques, such as: blowing into instruments, clicking keys, and singing both pitched and non-pitched sounds while playing. Its structure follows the biblical narrative, building to a climax, then receding to behold the rainbow (*Gen. 7 and 8*).

A recent Israeli karaoke tune, *Yamim Shel Sheket* (Days of Serenity or Stillness) (2000), with casually flowing music by Avi Greinik and words by Yarden Bar Kochba, adapts Gen. 8:11 to reflect the quiet after the storm: *The days of stillness are coming, the two of us here on the mountain; the water already came down and there's a rainbow. It's possible to get up; the end of the world has passed.*

Works List

Anfossi, Pasquale (1727–1979 Rome). *Noe sacrificium* (Genesis 6–15) oratorio.

Arrieu, Claude (1903–1990 Paris). *Noe* (libretto, J. Limozin; based on play by A. Obey), opera.

Assmayer, Ignaz (1790 Salzburg–1862 Vienna). *Die suendflut*, oratorio.

Bochsa, Robert Nicolas (1789 France–1856 Sydney). *Le deluge universel*, oratorio.

Boyce, William (1710–1779 London). *Noah*, oratorio.

Britten, Benjamin (1913–1976 England). *Noyes Fludde* (Chester Miracle Play), canticle.

Burkhard, Willy (1900–1955 Zurich). *Die Sinflut*, choir.

Carissimi, Giacomo (1605–1674 Rome). *Diluvium universale*, oratorio.

---

10. The Saxophone Ensemble includes: B-flat Soprano, 2 E-flat Altos, 2 B-flat Tenors, E-flat Baritone, and B-flat Bass.

Castelnuovo-Tedesco, Mario (1895 Florence–1968 California). *The Flood* (from *Genesis Suite*), narrator, orchestra.

Cazzati, Maurizio (1620–1677 Italy). *Il diluvio*, oratorio.

Cowen, Frederik Hymen (1852 Jamaica–1935 London). *The Flood*, oratorio.

Donizetti, Gaetano (1797–1848 Bergamo, Italy). *Il diluvio universale* (D. Gilardoni), oratorio.

Drobisch, Karl Ludwig (1803 Leipzig–1834 Augsburg). *Die Suendflut*, oratorio.

Elwart, Antoine (1808–1877 Paris). *Noe ou le deluge universelle*, oratorio.

Graf, Friedrich Hartmann (1727–1795 Augsburg). *Due Suendflut*, oratorio.

Gregoir, Edouard (1822–1890 Antwerp). *Le deluge*, oratorio.

Halevy, Jacques Fromental (1799 Paris–1862 Nice). *Noe ou le deluge* (Saint-Georges), opera.

Jacquet de la Guerre, Elisabeth (1667–1729 Paris). *Le deluge* (A.H. de la Monte), cantata.

Kauer, Ferdinand (1751–1831 Vienna). *Die Suendflut oder Noahs Versoehngsopfer* (F.H. Dobenz), oratorio.

Koch, Friedrich (1862–1927 Berlin). *Die Suendflut*, oratorio.

Pasquali, Nicolo (1718–1757 Edinburgh). *Noah*, oratorio.

Perroni, Giovanni (1688 Italy–1748 Vienna). *Il sacrifizio die Noe*, oratorio.

Preyer, Gottfried (1807–1901 Vienna). *Noah*, oratorio.

Rieti, Vittorio (1898 Alexandria, Egypt–1994 New York). *L'arca de Noe*, ballet.

Saint-Saens, Charles-Camille (1835 Paris–1921 Algiers). *Le deluge* (L. Gallet), oratorio.

Schneider, Johann Christian Friedrich (1786–1853 Germany). *Die Suendflut* (E. Groote), oratorio.

Seyfried, Ignaz (1776–1841 Vienna). *Noah*, incidental music.

Sowash, Rick (b.1950) *Shenandoah's Ark* (Jacobus Revius), SATB.

Stampiglia, Silvio (1664–1725 Naples). *Il sacrificio di Noe* (G. Perroni), oratorio.

Stern, Max (b.1947 USA/1976 Israel). *Rainbow* (Genesis 7–8), seven saxophones.

Stravinsky, Igor (1882 Russia–1971 New York). *The Flood* (The York and Chester Miracle Plays) (Genesis 6–8).

Trento, Vittorio (1761–1833 Venice). *Il diluvio universale* (Buonavoglia), drama in 2 acts.

4

Stravinsky's *Abraham and Isaac* musters atonal serial technique and pointillist texture to interpret Scriptural text, in an archaic treatment that transforms Hebraic pathos into staid, almost Byzantine iconography.

ABRAHAM and ISAAC

And Abraham stretched forth his hand, and took the knife to slay his son. And the angel of the Lord called unto him out of heaven, and said: 'Abraham, Abraham.' And he said: 'Here I am.' And he said: 'Lay not thy hand upon the lad, neither do thou anything unto him; for now I know that thou art a God-fearing man. Seeing thou hast not withheld thy son, thine only son, from Me' (Genesis 22:10–12).

The *Akedah* (Sacrifice of Isaac) is the supreme example of self-abnegation and obedience to Divine Will in the Bible. At God's command, Abraham offers Isaac, the son of his old age, as a sacrifice. He takes Isaac to the place (Mount Moriah) and binds him to the altar. The angel of the Lord bids Abraham to stay his hand and a ram is offered in his stead. Among Christian writers, the sacrifice of Isaac is understood as foretelling the crucifixion; a parallel is drawn between Abraham sacrificing his son and God sacrificing His only begotten son.

Igor Stravinsky: Abraham and Isaac (1963)
Text: Genesis 22:1–19 (Hebrew)
Genre: Sacred Ballad
Medium: Baritone and chamber orchestra
Style: Atonal Serial
First Performance: Convention Center, Jerusalem, August 23, 1964

Abraham and Isaac: a sacred ballad for baritone and chamber orchestra, tells the story of the sacrifice of Isaac in an abstract, atonal musical language. Composed at Stravinsky's home in Beverly Hills, California (1962/3), following an invitation to visit Israel, its text cites Scripture directly (*Gen. 22:1–19*). One of the master's last works, we encounter here a composer, almost the age of the Patriarch, turning to an ancient language, acknowledging the suffering of an ancient people. Stravinsky dedicated this work to the people of the State of Israel, where it was premiered at the Israel Festival Jerusalem in 1964.

Biographic Context

Igor Stravinsky (1882–1971), one of the leading composers of the 20th century, is also one of its most cosmopolitan. Stravinsky traveled often, spending much of his life in transit, adjusting to new languages and cultures. Throughout his long career, he displayed an inexhaustible desire to learn and explore art and literature. A student of the Russian nationalist composer, Nikolai Rimsky-Korsakoff (1844–1908), his earliest successes were ballets written for the Ballets Russes.[1] Of these, the most notorious and savagely polytonal is *Rite of Spring* (1913), based on 'archaic' Russian folklore. Archaic is a word to remember in relation to Stravinsky; it became an aesthetic ideal he seemed to seek out and nurture; along with a philosophy, that music is incapable of expressing anything but itself.[2] Between the First and Second World Wars, Stravinsky established himself in Paris, and began composing upon Baroque and Classical models, frequently setting classical authors and Latin texts; and initiating new stylistic trends. Following the Second World War, he reestablished himself in America as an exponent of Serialism, creating a series of atonal religious works.[3]

What Is His Connection to the Bible?

As a boy in tsarist Russia, Igor attended church, read the Bible, and

---

1. The Ballets Russes was an itinerant dance company which performed under the directorship of Russian impresario Sergei Diaghilev between 1909 and 1929.
2. Igor Stravinsky, *Poetics of Music: In the Form of Six Lessons* (Cambridge, MA: Harvard University Press, 1947).
3. Serialism is a way of composing music using a series of notes arranged in a particular order. This ordering of musical elements may apply to other aspects (parameters) of music, such as rhythm and dynamics, as well.

observed the fasts and feasts of the Russian Orthodox Church. Like many, in adolescence, he rebelled. Then, years later, in his forties, following a religious experience, he reaffirmed the Russian Orthodox faith of his youth. Towards the end of his life, Stravinsky reflected, "I cannot evaluate the events that made me discover the necessity of religious belief."[4] During his American sojourn, Robert Craft, his interpreter, chronicler, assistant, and factotum, informs us: "Stravinsky prayed daily, prayed before and after composing, and prayed when having difficulty. He believed that God had created the world; he believed literally in all the events of the Bible."[5] In another interview, the sophisticated and cosmopolitan Stravinsky reveals, "I was born out of time, in the sense that by temperament and talent I would have been more suited to the life of a small Bach, living anonymously and composing regularly for the service of God."[6] It seems a paradoxical statement from an artist who established his reputation with a notorious ballet based on pagan folklore. Perhaps, after all, religion was the stable element in his world.[7]

Text and Context

Literary Sources

The sacrifice of Isaac is among the most frequently discussed profiles in Scripture. In medieval Jewish liturgy, it generated a genre of prayers for forgiveness *(Selichot),* known as *Akedah* poetry.[8] Their perspective is

---

4. Robert M. Copeland, "The Christian Message of Igor Stravinsky," *Musical Quarterly,* Vol. 68, no. 4 (London: Oxford University Press, October, 1982) 563–579.
5. Ibid.
6. Op. cit.
7. Robert Strasburg (1915–2003) was an American composer, musicologist, and music educator who studied under Igor Stravinsky, Walter Piston, and Paul Hindemith. As a student at Tanglewood in the 1940s, he saw it differently. He said to me, in a casual conversation at the Joseph Eisner Camp in Great Barrington, Massachusetts (Summer 1968), "Stravinsky was a cold, heartless, analytical brain; only his Christian faith made him human."
8. These writers include: Solomon ibn Gabirol (1021–1056), Ephraim ben Isaac (d.1175), Meir b. Isaac (c.1000), Sherira Gaon (920–1000) and Benjamin b. Zerach (c.1050), who contributed numerous paraliturgical poems to this genre. For *Akedah* poetry texts in Hebrew with English translation, see *Kinot,* translated and annotated by Abraham Rosenfeld (London: Judaica Press, 1965).

consistent with the oldest Midrash, which views sacrifice as a privilege: *Behold the fire and the wood. But, where then is the lamb for a burnt offering before the Lord. Abraham answered, 'The Lord hath chosen thee my son as a perfect burnt offering instead of the lamb.' And Isaac said to his father, 'I will do all that the Lord hath spoken with joy and cheerfulness of heart' (Genesis Rabbah 56).* It is an attitude that contradicts the moderns, who find only horror in the story, claiming it to be an example of misplaced piety, a relic of human sacrifice, an atavism. The ancients were aware of this ambiguity, but they conceived of lack of faith, as the work of the devil.[9] Yet, it is here, in comparison with *Akedah selichot,* that we detect, on the road to the sacred ballad *Abraham and Isaac,* an inverted parallel between Scripture and the neo-primitive *Rite of Spring;*[10] for, the *Rite of Spring* glorifies human sacrifice, itself, while the *Akedah* spiritualizes it.

A Complex and Untranslatable Ambiguity

Stravinsky's score is complex and convoluted. Few are capable of decoding its enigmatic script. Musical notation is itself a text. Stravinsky might have written it more accessibly, but chose to make it obtuse; why? Is there an idea glimmering behind this severe scholasticism;

---

9. *While Abraham and Isaac were proceeding along the road, Satan came in the figure of a very aged man, humble and contrite and said to Abraham, 'Art thou silly or foolish that thou doest this thing to thine only son? God gave thee a son in thine old age and wilt thou go and slaughter him and cause the soul of thine only son to perish from the earth? Doest thou not know and understand that this thing cannot be from the Lord? For the Lord would not do unto men such evil.' And Abraham chased him away!* Satan, not satisfied with the old man's response, then, sought to plant doubt into the younger man, Isaac. *And Satan returned and appeared as a young man, and said to Isaac: 'Doest thou not know that thy silly father bringeth thee to the slaughter this day for naught? Now, my son, do not listen to him, for he is a silly old man, and let not thy precious soul and beautiful figure be lost from the earth.' And Abraham said, 'Do not listen to his words for he is Satan endeavoring to lead us astray from the command of our God!'* Isaac followed Abraham's example. Thus, Scripture writes, *They walked together.* Louis Ginzburg, *Legends of the Bible* (1956) 130.

10. "I saw in my imagination," Stravinsky recalled, "a solemn pagan rite: sage elders, seated in a circle, watched a young girl dance herself to death. They were sacrificing her to propitiate the god of Spring" (Phillip Huscher, program notes to *The Rite of Spring: Scenes from Pagan Russia,* Chicago Symphony Orchestra, 2009).

how does it illuminate his concept and treatment of the biblical trial of the Patriarch? If Abraham's sacrifice is a postulate, not to be rationally grasped; how, then, can it be represented musically? Can musical notation itself give a clue towards clarification?

The biblical artist's challenge is always the same: to transform eternal truths into timely and relevant images; for, if clichés are stereotyped truisms, how, then, can such well-trodden and worn-out insights be given renewed vibrance? How does one project, artistically, a sense of the bitter trials that led to revelation, to those who have never experienced them? This qualitatively different way of understanding the Word, and grasping its profound truth, is exactly what Stravinsky is driving at with his contorted notation! He wants it to be difficult to read, to perform, and to understand. By implication, he is telling us — only one who struggles to fathom its complexity is worthy of the truth of its message;[11] it is the path of one who seeks the Voice behind the words.

The story of father and son going up the mountain together conceals a psychological complex of emotions under the simplest of exteriors — a journey. Stravinsky's ascetic aesthetic is the obverse of the Bible. His harsh atonality is, in fact, simpler than the original passage that serves as his text — because it avoids the profound inner emotional struggle of Abraham. In this sense, Stravinsky's portrayal is psychological simplicity, concealed under hyper-complexity, in contrast to Scripture, which conceals complexity underneath stark simplicity. Nonetheless, although there is little ambiguity in Stravinsky's treatment, still, the very complexity of its notation and language reveals a profound understanding and empathy with the more open interpretations suggested by the Bible. Perhaps, some insight into this multi-layered dilemma may be found in the unsuspecting Scriptural phrase, *saddled his ass*, fore the Hebrew original, *Vayakhavosh et khamoro* is rich in meanings.

*Vayashkeym Avraham baboker **vayakhavosh et khamoro***
And Abraham rose up in the morning and **saddled his ass**.

In Hebrew, the root *khavosh* is a triple homonym, meaning: to master, to overcome, and to saddle. The noun *khamor* means literally ass or donkey. But its root may be understood, in addition, as *homer*, which also denotes material and physical things or substances. On yet another

---

11. This is a viewpoint that Stravinsky shares with Schoenberg. See chapter 5, *Jacob's Ladder*.

level, *khamor,* meaning seriousness or graveness, may be understood spiritually. This short, seemingly superfluous phrase, then, constitutes a monumental declaration. Abraham has *saddled the ass* (that animal part within himself), which finds satisfaction in physical comfort, as well as all that spiritual part of himself that pertains to his personality. It implies abnegation of body and soul. In other words, Abraham has overcome the physical/material aspect of his being, and its spiritual essence, in order to pay undivided devotion to his maker.[12] It is with this understanding that the conflict of soul is revealed — which finds ultimate fulfillment in acts of loving-kindness, but forces itself, against its own will, harshly, to pick up the blade and slay a beloved son. Abraham has repressed all that he is, loves, and possesses in order to follow the Will of his Creator in complete faith![13]

Music and Musical Exegesis

Highly profiled atonal cantillation, supported by sparse, pointillist orchestration chisels the text into a cold, anti-melodic biblical intonation. Bridled is feeling. Quelled are music's sensual components. Only ascetic, disembodied spirituality, floating in space, remains. Stravinsky draws on serial technique, devoid of warm tonality, to simulate this archaic effect of ritual sacrifice.

Analyses

While the overall structure of *Abraham and Isaac* is a continuous through-composed narrative, its portrayal is subdivided into five sections, differentiated by short instrumental interludes:

- Section 1 — *And it came to pass* (v. 1–3)

---

12. In order to commit this abhorrent deed of slaughtering his own child, Abraham has 'saddled' the inclinations of his soul. Thus, he refrains or 'halters in' his natural feelings of love and compassion.

13. The Kabalists of 16th-century Safed inserted a meditation inspired by this interpretation into the prayer book. It reads, *Sovereign of the universe! Abraham mastered his compassion for his only son in order to perform Thy will with whole heart.* We witness, by means of this meditation, the awesome self-less-ness of the truly pious. See *Book of Prayers: According to the Custom of the Spanish and Portuguese Jews,* edited and translated by David De Sola Pool (New York: Union of Sephardic Congregations, 2001) 6.

- Section 2 — *Then on the third day* (v. 3–4)
- Section 3 — *And Abraham took the wood* (v. 6–12)
- Section 4 — *And Abraham lifted up his eyes* (v. 13–18)
- Section 5 — *So Abraham returned* (v. 18)

Ex. 4. Stravinsky: *Abraham and Isaac*
© Copyright 1965 by Boosey & Hawkes. Used by permission.

DETAIL 1
Section 1 (verses 1–3)

(Bars 11–25)
And it came to pass after these things, that God [Elohim] did tempt Abraham, and said unto him, Abraham, and he said, Behold, here I am. (Verse 1)

All motion is horizontal in this stark opening. Solo instruments shift colors every few notes, supporting an angular recitative articulated in wide, dissonant, and chromatic leaps. Suddenly, in response to the word *Elohim* (Lord), we encounter an odd sonority played *ponticello* and *tremolo* in the strings. This vertical element or sonority represents the omnipresent Eternal God — always a unity, always simultaneous, always timeless. It is incongruously out of context, but it signifies and reveals the cosmic reality that surrounds man's horizontal time-bound trajectory from birth to death.

Ex. 5. Stravinsky: *Abraham and Isaac*
© Copyright 1965 by Boosey & Hawkes. Used by permission.

(Bars 26–45)
And he said, Take now thy son, thine only son Isaac, whom thou lovest. And get thee into the land of Moriah; and offer him there for a burnt offering upon one of the mountains which I will tell thee of. (Verse 2)

God's utters his command, *Take now thy son, thine only son Isaac,* in the atonal equivalent of Hebraic cantillation. Instruments respond in sparse commentary. An extended melisma highlights *Yitzchak's* (Isaac's) name. However, why, then, is the name so curiously contorted; is it to show Abraham's love for Isaac? We hear a flute in the background. What does this symbolize? Perhaps it marks an angel, a holy spirit hovering in space above the men.

DETAIL 2

(Bars 52–72)
And Abraham rose up early in the morning and saddled his ass, and took

two of his young men with him, and Isaac his son, and clave the wood for the burnt offering, and rose up, and went unto the place of **which God has told him.** *(Verse 3)*

The deep bass instruments (bassoon and tuba) that initiate this phrase, metaphorically, trudge along with Abraham's little group toward Mount Moriah. Yet, the passage closes with high tremolo strings on the words *Asher amar lo ha Elohim* (which God has told him). It is a treble-bass dichotomy, bespeaking earth and heaven, expressing, through sonority and register, the enormous distance between human motivations and actions, when measured against the iridescent sheen of God's eternal Word.

Conclusion

Stravinsky did not speak Hebrew; for him, it was an archaic tongue. For this reason, his setting has none of the melody of spoken language. What were Stravinsky's reasons for setting a language he understood only in translation? The composer's remarks regarding earlier sacred works set to Latin liturgy are revealing. *I have always considered that a special language and not that of current converse was required for subjects touching on the sublime. The choice of Latin had the great advantage of giving me a medium not dead but turned to stone and so monumentalized as to have become immune from all risk of vulgarization. What a joy to compose music to a language of convention, almost of ritual, the very nature of which imposes a lofty dignity! One no longer feels dominated by the phrase, the literal meaning of the words cast in an immutable mold, which adequately expresses their value, they do not require any further commentary. The text thus becomes purely phonetic material for the composer. He can dissect it at will and concentrate all his attention on its purely constituent elements — that is to say, on the syllable.*[14] Remarkably, though, Stravinsky sets the inflections of each Hebrew syllable, with the skill of a linguist, and is thus, untranslatable as sung text. Perhaps, for this reason also, we feel that we are hearing an old tale told from very far away in *Abraham and Isaac*, as if all the leaves of a tree have defoliated and only its branches and trunk remain, starkly outlined against the sky. The strict discipline of serial technique, seen in this light, mirrors the Patriarch's severe mastery of his emotions. Tonal tendencies and

---

14. See Copeland, op. cit.

attractions play no part; atonality depicts human sensation, ossified. Spent are life's juices. The inner trial has passed.[15] It is the music of an old man confronting infinity. Like the *Akedah* itself, it is a musical statement, which breaches no compromise, nor attempt to engage the listener, per se. This single-minded cleaving (*devekut*) to the Almighty, in unquestioning devotion, is the unique heritage of the *Akedah*.[16] It strikes us as Stravinsky's Last Will and Testament, as well.

Related Directions

In European music there are at least 50 works on the sacrifice of Isaac, mostly oratorios. As in literature and art, the *Akedah* is often linked with the Crucifixion; Metastasio has stated this explicitly in the textbook title of his libretto *Isaaco, figura Del Redentore* (1740) which was performed in the court church during Passion Week. Many eminent 18th-century musicians composed settings for Metastasio's libretto which was originally written for the Viennese court. Popular German oratorios include J.H. Rolle's *Abraham auf Moria* (1776) and M. Blumner's *Abraham* (1859–60). In Poland, the biblical story inspired an opera by Chopin's teacher, Ksawery Joseph Elsner (1827), and an oratorio by W. Sowiński (1805–1880). In Abraham Goldfaden's Yiddish biblical operetta *Akedays Yitshok* (1897), the *Akedah* itself figures only near the end of the work. Hugo Adler wrote an *Akedah* (1938) based on the Buber-Rosenzweig German translation of the Bible and on selections from the Midrash and *Akedot piyutim*, which was modelled on the classical oratorio. Benjamin Britten introduces an ironic inversion of the story into his *War Requiem* (1962). It is a setting of Wilfred Owen's poem, "The Parable of the Old Men and the Young," in which Abraham does sacrifice his son: "But the old man would not so, but slew his son, and half the seed of Europe, one by one," underlining his bitterness towards those who send their

---

15. The main characteristics of this style consist in *what it is not*. Stravinsky's sparse textures avoid regular rhythmic pulsation, as his pitches avoid lyric melodic contour.

16. For the remainder of history, the *Sacrifice of Isaac* became an allegory for martyrdom. It is perhaps the only time in history, before or since, that a free-willed human being overcomes his physical limitations, needs, desires, and fears, to follow — in love and without question — the Will of his Creator (Rabbi Meir Seroussi in conversation with the author, September 1, 2007, Beer Sheba).

countries' children off to war. The music borrows themes from Britten's earlier *Abraham and Isaac* (1952).

Contemporary Israeli music identifies with the theme on many levels. *Akedah* (1977) by Aaron Charlap (1941 Canada/Israel) is a colorful narrative tableau for *a cappella* choir, set in quartal harmony. The post-modern *Akedah — It Wasn't Like That* (2005), for narrator and instrumental septet by kibbutz composer Yehuda Levi (b.1939), is a retelling of the story from the perspective of the father of a fallen Israel soldier. While the intimate song "Sacrifice of Isaac" (1968) by Naomi Shemer touches on the same theme in a popular form.

Works List

Adler, Hugo Chaim (1894 Germany–1955 USA). *Akedah* (Gen. 22), oratorio.

Adlgasser, Anton (1729–1777 Salzburg). *Abraham und Isaak*, oratorio.

Andreozzi, Gaetano (1763 Naples–1826 Paris). *Isaaco figura del redentore* (Metastasio), oratorio.

Antonelli, Abondio (16th C. Rome). *Abraham tolle filium tuum* (Gen. 22), 8 voices, basso continuo.

Avondano, Pietro (1714–1782 Lisbon). *Die Aufopferung Isaacs* (Metastasio), oratorio.

Bencini, Antonio (18th C. Rome). *Il sacrificio d'Abramo*, oratorio.

Bianchi, Franscesco (1752–1810 London) *Abraham sacrificium*, oratorio.

Blanghini, Felice (1781 Torino–1841 Paris). *Le sacrifice d'Abraham* (Colonel Saint-Mercel), oratorio.

Blummer, Martin (1827–1901 Germany). *Abraham*, oratorio.

Bonno, Giuseppe (1711 Italy–1788 Vienna). *Isaac figura del redentore* (Metastasio), oratorio.

Borghi, Giovanni (1738–1796 Italy). *Isacco* (Metastasio), oratorio.

Britten, Benjamin (1913–1976 England). *Abraham and Isaac* (Chester Miracle Play), canticle.

Brossard, Sebastian (1655–1730 France). *Abraham*, oratorio.

Cambini, Giuseppe (1746–1825 Italy). *Le sacrifice d'Isaac*, oratorio.

Capello, Giovanni (17th C. Venice). *Abraham*, dialogue (Motette e dialoghi, Venice 1618).

Carissimi, Giacomo (1605–1674 Rome). *Abraham et Isaac*, oratorio.

Carvalho, Joao de Sousa (1745–1798, Lisbon). *Isacco*, oratorio.

Charpentier, Marc-Antoine (1636–1704 Paris). *Sacrificium Abrahae*, oratorio.

Cimarosa, Domenico (1749–1801 Venice). *Il sacrificio d'Abramo*, oratorio.

Clerambault, Louis (1676–1749 Paris). *Abraham*, cantata, voice, instruments and basso continuo.

Crispi, Pietro (1737–1797 Rome). *Isaaco figura de redentore* (Metastasio), oratorio.

Danzi, Franz (1763–1826 Germany). *Abraham auf Moria*, oratorio.

Delanoy, Marcel (1898–1962 France). *Abraham et l'angel*, oratorio.

Dittersdorf, Karl Ditters von (1739–1799). *Issaco* (Metastasio), oratorio.

Ehrlich, Abel (1915 Germany–2003 Israel). *And Abraham Was One Hundred Years Old* (1964), soprano, clarinet.

Elsner, Ksawery (1769–1854 Warsaw). *Ofiara Abraham*, melodrama.

Felici, Bartolomeo (1695–1776 Florence). *Isacco figura del redentore* (Metastasio), oratorio.

Fiorillo, Ignazio (1715 Naples–1787 Germany). *Isacco* (Metastasio), oratorio.

Fortner, Wolfgang (1907–1987 Germany). *The Sacrifice of Isaac*, cantata.

Franck, Melchior (1579–1639 Germany). *Vater Abraham*, oratorio.

Furlanetto, Bonaventura (1738–1817 Italy). *Abraham et Isaac*, cantata.

Fuss, Johann (1777–1819). *Isaac* (J. Perinet after Metastasio), melodrama.

Gagnebin, Henri (1886–1977 Geneva). *Abraham sacrificani* (Th. de Beze), incidental music, a cappella choir.

Galuppi, Balassare (1706–1785 Venice). *Sacrificium Abraham* (P. Chiari), oratorio.

Gille, Jacob (1814–1880 Stockholm). *Abraham*, opera.

Goldfaden, Avraham (1840–1908). *Akedat Yitshak*, singspiel.

Harlap, Aharon (b.1941). *The Sacrifice of Isaac* (1979), mixed choir

Harrer, Johann (1703–1755 Karlsbad). *Isacco figura del redentore* (Metastasio), oratorio.

Haudebert, Lucien (b.1877). *Le sacrifice d'Abraham*, oratorio.

Himmel, Friedrich (1765–1814 Germany). *Isacco figura del redentore* (Metastasio), oratorio.

Holzbauer, Ignaz (1711 Austria–1783 Germany). *Isacco* (Metastasio), oratorio.

Jomelli, Niccolo (1714–1774 Italy). *Il sacrificio di Abramo* (Metastasio), oratorio.

Kunzen, Adolph (1720–1781 Germany). *Die Berufung Abrahams*, oratorio.

Lanciani, Flavio Carlo (1661–1706 Rome). *Lagioia seno d'Abramo*, oratorio.

Leopold I (1658–1705 Vienna). *Il sacrifizio d'Abramo*, oratorio.

Mangold, Carl (1813–1889 Germany). *Abraham* (Rieter-Biedermann), cantata.

Martinez, Marianne (1744–1812 Vienna). *Isacco, figura del redentore* (Metastasio), oratorio.

Martini (Padre) Giovanni (1706–1792 Bologna). *Il sacrificio d'Abramo* (G. Galuzzi), oratorio.

Masini, Antonio (1639–1678 Rome). *Il sacrificio d'Abramo*, oratorio.

Mayor, Charles (1876–1950). *Le sacrifice d'Abraham*, incidental music.

Mereaux, Jean (1745–1797). *Le sacrifice d'Abraham*, oratorio.

Messi, Franciscus de (c.1595–1665 Italy). *Isaach immolatus* (F. Clementi), oratorio.

Molique, Bernard (1802–1869 Germany). *Abraham*, oratorio.

Myslivecek, Josef (1737 Prague–1781 Rome). *Isacca figura del redentore* (Metastasio), oratorio.

Naumann, Johann (1741–1801 Germany). *Isacco figura del redentore* (Metastasio), oratorio.

Nicholi, Horace (1848–1922 USA). *Abraham*, oratorio.

Passarini, Francesco (1636–1694 Bologne). *Il sacrifizio d'Abramo* (G.B.F. Lutti), oratorio.

Pizetti, Ildebrando (1880 Parma–1968). *Rappresentatione di Abram e Isaac* (F. Belcari), 6 soloists, choir, orchestra.

Predieri, Luca (1688–1767 Bologne). *Il sacrificio d'Abramo* (F. Mensoni), oratorio.

Rabaud, Henri (1873–1949 Paris). *Le sacrifice d'Isaac*, cantata.

Reindl, Constantin (1738–1799 Luzern). *Abraham and Isaak*, oratorio.

Remick-Warren, Elinor (1900–1991 Los Angeles). *Abram in Egypt*, baritone, choir, orchestra.

Rolle, Johann Heinrich (1716–1785 Germany). *Abraham auf Moria* (Niemeyer), oratorio.

Scarlatti, Alessandro (1660–1725 Naples). *Il sacrifio di Abraham*, oratorio.

Schidlowsky, Leon (b.1931 Chile/1968 Israel). *The Sacrifice of Isaac* (1999), for narrator, tenor, baritone, chorus, orchestra.

Schiassi, Gaetano (1698 Bologna–1754 Lisbon). *Sacrificio d'Isaac* (P. Metastasio), oratorio.

Schuerer, Georg (1720 Bohemia–1786 Dresden). *Isacco figura del redentore* (P. Metastasio), oratorio.

Seyfried, Ignaz (1776–1841 Vienna). *Abraham*, oratorio.

Sirola, Bozidar (1889–1956 Zagreb). *Zrtva Abrahamova* (Abraham's sacrifice), oratorio.

Sowinski, Wojciech (1803 Poland–1880 Paris). *Poswiecenie Abrahama* (Abraham's sacrifice) (d'Anglemont), 4 voices, organ.

Stampiglia, Silvano (1664–1725 Naples). *La gioia nel seno di Abramo* (F. Lanciani), oratorio.

Sternberg, Erich Walter (1891–1974). *Opferung Issaks* (Sacrifice of Isaac) (1966), for soprano and orchestra.

Stravinsky, Igor (1882 Russia–1971 New York). *Abraham and Isaac* (Genesis 22:1–19), ballad for baritone and orchestra.

Tarchi, Angelo (1759 Naples–1814 Paris). *Isacco*, oratorio.

Torrance, George William (1835 Dublin–1907 Melbourne). *Abraham*, oratorio.

Umstatt, Josef (1711 Vienna–1762 Bamberg). *Isacco*, oratorio.

Viviani, Giovanni (17th C. Florence). *Abramo in Egitto*, oratorio.

Vuataz, Roger (1898–1988 Geneva). *Abraham* (libretto by composer), oratorio.

Zanata, Domenico (1665–1748 Verona). *Il sacrificio di Abram* (L. Nogarola), oratorio.

Zingarelli, Nicola Antonio (1752–1837 Naples). *Il sacrificio d' Abramo* (P. Metastasio), oratorio.

Other Directions

HAGAR and ISHMAEL

The story of Hagar — the daughter of Pharaoh, given to Sarah as a handmaid — is the subject of Genesis, chapter 16. It has been infrequently, set to music. Hagar was a woman of noble disposition, who followed Hebrew customs. She was offered to Abram by Sarai his wife, after they had dwelt ten years in the land of Canaan, without having children. Notwithstanding, as soon as Hagar conceived, she started to slander *her mistress [who] was despised in her eyes (Gen. 16:4)*. Sarai retaliated, forcing her do servile work, then, later, demanding that Hagar be sent away. The handmaid fled to the wilderness with her son, Ishmael, where, she, again resumed the idol worship of her father, Pharaoh. After the death of Sarah, Abraham married her: *Then Abraham took a wife and her name was Keturah (Gen. 25:1)*, and she returned to a life of virtue.[17]

Works List

Antil, John Henry (1904 Australia–1986). *Song of Hagar* (E.Anderson), oratorio.

Badia, Carlo-Agistino (1672 Venice–1738 Vienna). *Ismaele*, oratorio.

Beaulieu, Merie-Desire Martin (1791 Paris–1863). *Agar*, oratorio.

Bianchi, Francesco (1752 Cremona–1810 London). *Agar fugiens*, oratorio.

Cesarini, Carlo Francesco (1664–1730 Rome). *Ismaele soccorso dall'angelo*, oratorio.

Converse, Frederick (1871–1940 Massachusettes, USA). *Hagar in the Desert*, a dramatic narrative for low voice and orchestra.

Friebert, Johann Joseph (1742–1799 Passau). *Agar* (Passau), oratorio.

Fritellio, Jacobo (17ᵗʰ C.). *Ismael* (S. Mesquita), oratorio.

Scarlatti, Alessandro (1660–1725 Naples). *Agar e Ismaele Esiliati*, oratorio.

---

17. See Elimelech Epstein Halevy, "Hagar in the Aggadah," *Encyclopaedia Judaica*, Vol. 7, col. 1075–1076.

G. Dore: Jacob's Dream, *Bible Illustrations (1866)*

CHAPTER 5

Schoenberg's oratorio *Die Jakobsleiter* is a philosophical exegesis, in the language of twelve-tone expressionism, upon moral questions raised by this biblical episode.

JACOB'S DREAM

And he dreamed, and behold a ladder set up on the earth, and the top of it reached to heaven; and behold the angels of God ascending and descending on it. And, behold, the Lord stood above it, and said: 'I am the Lord, the God of Abraham thy father, and the God of Isaac. The land whereon thou liest, to thee will I give it and to thy seed... And behold, I am with thee, and will keep thee whithersoever thou goest, and I will bring thee back into this land; for I will not leave thee, until I have done that which I have spoken to thee of' (Genesis 28:12–13, 15).

In the passage, Jacob is a pilgrim about to take a wilderness journey, which, in the end, will transform him from Jacob into Israel — from the deceptive usurper who has acquired the birthright from his brother Esau through cunning, into a man of integrity — straightforward and righteous — who *strove with an angel and God and prevailed (Gen. 32:29)*.[1] Alone in the night, Jacob dreams of angels ascending and descending on a ladder extending from heaven to earth. But we have no idea who the angels of Jacob's Dream are; nor, why they are going up and coming down. Two things Jacob learns this night: the first is God's

---

1. As the consequence for his deception against his brother and father, Jacob must endure long years of toil and bondage in the house of a stranger (Laban). As he deceived his blind father with a goat skin, so his sons will deceive him, in the episode of Joseph's coat, with the blood of a goat.

determination to grant him the blessing of Abraham;[2] the second, that in spite of this special grace, he must suffer measure for measure.

Schoenberg envisions the angels as human souls striving for redemption. His oratorio is a magnified portrayal of humankind seen under the microscope of divine judgment; and struggling to overcome the endless cycles of pleasure and pain, illusion and disillusionment, which governed the emotional upheavals of their earthly existence — as they strive for a truth beyond pleasure and pain.

Arnold Schoenberg: Jacob's Ladder (Die Jakobsleiter) (1917–1922)
Libretto: Composer (published 1917)
Genre: Oratorio (fragment completed posthumously)
Medium: Soloists, chorus, and orchestra
Style: Twelve-Tone
First performance: Vienna, 1961
Duration: ca. 50 minutes

Jacob's Ladder is the first atonal oratorio ever written. It is a philosophical work, concerned with striving for self-knowledge and nearness to God. Unique is its concept of "music as idea." It was begun in 1917, in response to the intellectual and spiritual crisis brought on by the First World War;[3] though Schoenberg worked on the score sporadically throughout his life, it was still unfinished at his death. It was later completed by a former student[4] and first performed in 1961.

---

2. *And I will make thee a great nation, and I will bless thee, and make thy name great; and be though a blessing. And I will bless them that bless thee, and him that curseth thee will I curse; and in thee shall all the families of the earth be blessed (Gen. 12:2–3).*

3. The following quote may be applied to Schoenberg, as well as a number of other composers treated in this book, whose works were written in response to events surrounding World War I: "Everywhere there were unwonted privations; everywhere there was mourning. The tale of the dead and mutilated mounted to many millions. Men felt a crisis in the world's affairs. They were too weary and heartsick to consider complicated possibilities. They were not sure whether they were facing a disaster to civilization or the inauguration of a new phase of human association." See H.G. Wells, *Outline of History*, Vol. 1 (New York: Garden City Books, 1919 [1956]) 1.

4. Winfried Zillig (1905–1963), German composer, music theorist and conductor.

Biographic Context

Arnold Schoenberg (Vienna 1874–Los Angeles 1951) was one of the most influential composers and teachers of the 20th century. He introduced the concept of Expressionism[5] to music. Largely self-taught, Schoenberg learned his craft by imitating Baroque and Classical models, transcribing and arranging light music, marches, and operettas; and some private lessons from Alexander Zemlinsky. This process of independent discovery shaped his habits of mind and inner spiritual life.

Schoenberg's parents moved to the Jewish quarter of Vienna from Bratislava. The family was not well off. Arnold was brought up in the Orthodox faith, which he later abandoned. He left school and worked five years as a bank clerk, composing his earliest works by night. Gradually, with much effort and tribulation, he ascended to the post of Professor of Composition at the prestigious Prussian Academy of Arts in Berlin. In 1898, he converted to Christianity. But, unexpectedly, two decades later, something happened that radically changed his perceptions. While holidaying in the Austrian spa town of Mattsee in 1921, a summer resort known for being *Judenrei* or "Jew-free," Schoenberg experienced, firsthand, such anti-Semitic hostility that it forced his early departure and renewed his interest in the Jewish faith.[6] In 1933, follow-

---

5. Expressionism is characterized as a striving to give outer shape to inner, often subconscious, experience. Schoenberg's music gradually abandoned the principle of tonality, in pursuit of this goal, replacing it with extreme chromaticism, and later, the twelve-tone system.

6. It was a traumatic experience to which Schoenberg would frequently refer; a first mention appears in a letter addressed to Kandinsky (April 1923). "I have at last learnt the lesson that has been forced upon me this year, and I shall never forget it. It is that I am not a German, not a European, indeed perhaps scarcely even a human being (at least, the Europeans prefer the worst of their race to me), but that I am a Jew." Arnold Schoenberg, *Letters*, Erwin Stein, ed., translated by Eithe Wilkins and Ernst Kaiser (Berkeley: University of California Press, 1987). Schoenberg's statement echoes a remark made by composer-conductor Gustav Mahler (1860–1911), a convert to Catholicism, years earlier: "I am thrice homeless: as a Bohemian among Austrians, as an Austrian among the Germans, and as a Jew throughout the entire world. I am an intruder everywhere, welcome nowhere." See Alma Mahler, *Gustav Mahler: Erinnerungen und Briefe* (Amsterdam: Allert de Lange, 1940) as cited in Alfred Mathis-Rosenzweig, *Gustav Mahler: New Insights into His Life, Times and Work*, translated and annotated by Jeremy Barham (Surrey, UK: Ashgate Publishing, 2007).

ing the announcement of the German government's intention to remove Jewish elements from the Prussian Academy of Arts, he left Berlin and reconverted to Judaism, eventually making his way to America.[7]

Schoenberg was a seeker of truth, a true believer all his life. All great music was for him an expression of the longing of the soul for God. He saw life as change and religion as a quest. His faith bridged the rational and the intuitive. His orthodoxy expressed itself in processes rather than systems. For Schoenberg, religion was art and art was religion, and the composer was its prophet and priest. Three months before his death, he wrote to the Israel Academy of Music: *Those who issue from such an institution must be truly priests of art, approaching art in the same spirit of consecration as the priest approaches God's altar.*[8]

Text and Context

Mahler

Schoenberg metaphorically interprets Jacob's dream sequence[9] as a struggle through flesh to spirit, from feeling to idea. Music and humanity will be redeemed "through ideas and not through feeling."[10] His oratorio is peopled by saints and sinners on different rungs of the ladder of humanity. They must be purified through suffering, in order to inherit the blessing of Jacob. For his libretto, Schoenberg draws upon

---

7. One may deduce that both Mahler and Schoenberg were victims of the Austro-German outlook, which emerged with the German nation-state of the 1870s, and took on a "true" German nationalistic coloration. This ideology opposed the earlier liberal ideals of the Enlightenment and the French Revolution [i.e. liberty, equality, fraternity]. One German nationalist wrote before the outbreak of World War I, "the old terms have to be changed: instead of religion — language and artistic intuition; instead of humanity — race." Schoenberg's social consciousness was molded by this nationalist view, while, at the same time, his destiny as a composer was forged in confrontation with anti-Semitism. See Introduction by Abraham J. Peck in *The American Jewish Archives Journal*, Volume XL, number 2, Jacob Rader Marcus, editor (Cincinnati, November, 1988).

8. Schoenberg, *Letters*, op. cit.

9. *Genesis 28:10–22.*

10. This concept first appeared in print in the article "Where Is German Music Headed? — An Interview with Schoenberg in Paris," *Berliner Borsen Zeitung,* December 16, 1927, as cited in *Schoenberg and His World*, Walter Frisch, editor (Princeton, NJ: Princeton University Press, 1999) 270–272.

a number of diverse sources, all related in the basic concern of "man's duty towards God and the world."[11] His initial inspiration was Mahler's *Eighth Symphony*, a work which includes monumental choral movements.[12] In this work, Mahler sets texts from Faust and a well known Latin hymn. In the final scene from Goethe's *Faust, part 2*, disembodied souls in a kind of Purgatory purify themselves as they ascend towards God.

> Eternal burning brand,
> Glowing bond of Love,
> Seething pain of the breast,
> Foaming joy of God.
>
> (Goethe, *Faust*, part 2)

Schoenberg modeled the libretto to *Jacob's Ladder* to its content and truncated phrase structure. While the second text Mahler selected, *Veni, creator spiritus,mentes tuorum vista; Imple superna gratia, quae tu creasti,*[13] a Latin hymn of redemption and faith, voices a shared ideal of universal redemption.

Balzac — Strindberg — Swedenborg

Other sources, however, include the mystic novel by Honore De Balzac *Seraphita* (1835), subtitled "a tale of occult teaching for those lofty spirits who could discern Jacob's mystical stair." Of special interest is the last chapter, "Seraphita's Ascension." Another source is the fragment "Jacob Wrestles" (a retelling of the medieval "Faustian" tale of "Theophilus the Penitent") from the book *Legends* by August Strindberg, which Schoenberg had at a certain point considered setting to music. Both works are independently influenced by the writings

---

11. Tom Beck, "The Literary Sources of *Die Gluckiche Hand*," *Tempo* (New Series), No. 189 (Cambridge University Press, June 1994) 17–23.
12. Schoenberg originally conceived *Jacob's Ladder* as the last movement of a symphony he intended to write.
13. The Medieval text "Veni, Creator Spiritus" is attributed to Rabanus Maurus (776–856), and is one of the hymns most widely used in the Church (i.e. sung at Vespers, Pentecost, dedication of a Church, Confirmation and Holy Orders, and whenever the Holy Spirit is solemnly invoked). It reads: *Come, Creator Spirit. Visit the minds of your people. Fill with grace from on high the hearts which Thou didst create.*

of Emanuel Swedenborg (1688–1772),[14] 18th-century Swedish scientist, theologian, and religious mystic. For Swedenborg, the Bible must be interpreted according to a system of correspondences. He understands it as a description of a human being's transformation from a material to a spiritual entity. He felt there a series of finer worlds or heavens, populated by disembodied souls or angels, which exist "between the atoms" of our coarse reality. Swedenborg taught that every object in the material world corresponds to an object in the spiritual world.[15]

Libretto

In Schoenberg's libretto various personalities are striving for nearness to God.[16] We encounter malcontents, doubters, self-indulgent rejoicers,

---

14. Emanuel Swedenborg was a respected scientist, philosopher, and government official on the Swedish Board of Mines until 1745, when, at the age of 57, he had a number of strange visions and remarkable dreams, in which he was visited by a spirit, who told him that God needed a human to further reveal Him to mankind. From 1745 until his death, Swedenborg wrote a virtual library of theological books (*Arcana Coelestia* in 12 volumes, and *Apocalypse Explained* in 6 volumes).

15. *The whole world corresponds to the spiritual world — not just the natural world in general, but actually in details. So anything in the natural world that occurs from the spiritual world is called correspondent. It is vital to understand that the natural world emerges and endures from the spiritual world, just like an effect from the cause that produces it.* For a more detailed discussion of these points see John Covach, "Schoenberg and the Occult: Some Reflections on the "Musical Idea," *Theory and Practice: Journal of the Music Theory Society of New York State,* Vol. 17 (1992) 103–118.

16. The whole concept that humanity must raise itself step by step beyond the physical and earthly, obtains resonance in mystical interpretations of the *Zohar* (*Gen. 28:12–13*). Schoenberg is guided in the same direction by deeply personal insights and intuitions. He strives to embody these abstractions through artistic creativity. Midrash interprets these verses (*Gen. 28:12–13*) as symbolic rungs to a heavenly ladder. 1) *And behold a ladder* signifies humanity connecting with worlds beyond its own; 2) *Set up on the earth* indicates sense perception; 3) *And the top of it reached to heaven* represents the heavenly spheres; 4) *And behold the angels of God ascending and descending on it* is the transcendent world of Angels; 5) *And behold, the Lord stood above it* is the goal, leading to unity with God. These Kabalistic notions stress that the quest for truth must pass through four stages: conception, creation, doing, and shaping (i.e. a*siah, yetzirah, briah,* and *atzilut*), before achieving spiritualization. See Elie Munk, *The World of Prayer,* translated by Henry Biberfeld, Vol. 1 (Jerusalem: Feldheim Publishers, 1963) 11–12.

the indifferent, and the quietly resolved, the rebellious, as well as those who believe themselves "called" — all trying to overcome their conceit, preconceived notions, short sighted formulas, reliance on clichés, and deluded sense of self — in a word: hypocrisy. Only the one who is struggling, gains Schoenberg's sympathy, "to listen open mouthed, in wonderment, but not to contradict. But how can I avoid new sin?" he asks. The angel Gabriel replies, "Nibble at the word. Let each choose the small part he can preserve... In this, he resembles the Highest....Come closer, one who on a middle level is...as the distant overtone of the fundamental...while others, deeper, almost fundamentals themselves are farther removed from Him, as bright rock crystal is further from diamond than carbon."[17]

Music and Philosophy

Schoenberg seeks a kind of music able to penetrate, reveal, and express his innermost perceptions and experiences; and project his unrest, fear, horror, haunting loneliness, and tension into the world. This harsh attitude rejects external attractiveness as an aesthetic value. For Schoenberg — who conceives of his style as "idea" — philosophy, thought, and message count more than feeling, grace and beauty. In the search for the sublime, a musical language of complexity, compression and concentration has emerged — obliterating the distinction between dissonance and consonance. Chord clusters and patches of contrapuntal texture have replaced singable melody, literal repetition, and formal symmetry.[18] A soundscape of exaggerated gesticulations and poignant cries has been rationalized into a philosophy.

For many, dodecaphony is a mystical code. Others ask: How can a man-made series of twelve tones, termed a "row," replace the culturally ingrained, historically and scientifically sound principles of the

---

17. Gabriel is the angel sent to destroy Sodom (Gen. R. 50.2), as well as the angel with whom Jacob may have wrestled (Gen. R. 78.1). By choosing the archangel Gabriel as soloist of the oratorio, Schoenberg indicates acquaintance with this Midrash, perhaps.

18. The 'New Music of idea' is an intense, free chromaticism that is rationalized by means of dodecaphony: The principle that all twelve tones of the chromatic scale are to be sounded before any are repeated. Simple traditional chords and major-minor scales have been replaced by complex sonorities, tone clusters, and textures — which swiftly follow one another.

"natural" acoustic and diatonic scale that is at the heart of tonality? All pitch material in *Jacob's Ladder* originates in, and derives from, a single six-note hexachord: C-sharp — D — E — F — G — A-flat. Through extreme rhythmic articulation, and the permutation and transposition of pitches — a wealth of musical shapes emerges, which, for all their topsy-turvy variety, may be perceived as a coherent whole.[19] Schoenberg's system imposes numerical order upon a chaotic universe and opens up a new concept of musical composition. His exegesis is neither the plain meaning of the text (*peshat*), nor its explanation or interpretation (*drash*). It dwells in mathematics and the numerology (*gematria*) of mysticism, the shadowy world of allusions, and the secret meanings of acrostics (*notrikon*).[20]

Musical Exegesis

Jacob's Ladder (*Die Jakobsleiter*) is one continuous movement structured in three sections. It is scored for shifting groupings of singers (ranging from solo voices to conglomerates of voices) within a 12-part mixed chorus.

Soprano I / Soprano I / Mezzo-Soprano I / Mezzo-Soprano II / Alto I / Alto I / Tenor I / Tenor II / Baritone I / Baritone I / Bass I / Bass II

These singers both sing and speak-sing.[21] They represent angels. Gabriel's speech-song alternates with their choral textures. Five groups are represented, each with its own neurotic traits: Malcontents are never satisfied. Doubters are never sure. The Rejoicers are hedonistic

---

19. This sounding can be melodic or harmonic. It may also be transposed, played backwards, and heard in mirror images of itself. Basically, the row is a fixed succession of tones from which the composer selects. There is in the system, it seems to me, a correspondence with the endless possibilities of artificial intelligence: building complex chains of DNA from a few basic chemical elements.

20. I have drawn an analogy between a musical technique and Hebrew biblical hermeneutics, symbolized by the notrikon *PRDS,* an acrostic for *Peshat* ('plain' meaning), *Drash* (interpretation and commentary), *Remez* (application of a text to a context different from the one it was originally intended by means of analogy, allegory, and metaphor), and *Sod* (a secret, hidden, mystical, metaphysical, or eschatological meaning).

21. *Sprechgesang* (spoken-song) and *Sprechstimme* (spoken-voice) refer to expressionist vocal techniques, which fall between singing and speaking.

pleasure-seekers. The Indifferent could care less. While the Quietly Resigned are completely passive.

DETAIL

Jacob's Ladder, section 1

Excerpted from the libretto

Section 1 is a solo — response form.
Section 1 (Gabriel, the angels and the various groups)

GABRIEL

> Whether to right or left, forward or back, uphill or down,
> One must go on, without asking what lies ahead or behind.

Ex. 6. Arnold Schoenberg: *Die Jakobsleiter*

© Copyright 1980 by Belmont Music Publishers. Reproduced by permission of Universal Edition AG.

The archangel Gabriel hardly ever sings. His pronouncements are delivered in "Sprechstimme" (speech-song). Schoenberg is fond of this inflected recitative, which has a musical quality, yet avoids the necessity for lyricism.

CHORUS (in several groups)

The intolerable pressure! The heavy burden! What fearful pains! Burning longing! Hot desires! Illusion of fulfillment! Inconsolable loneliness! Duress of formulae! Annihilation of the will! Lies for the sake of happiness! Murder, robbery, blood, wounds! Possession, beauty, enjoyment! Pleasure in futility, self-esteem! Intimate hours, sweet delights! Bounding energy and successful action!

GAB\RIEL

No matter! Onward!

CHORUS (in several groups)

Onward…Whither? How Long?

The Malcontents sing together in block harmonies, indicating their collective comfort wallowing in discontent. Their speech-song always takes identical melodic direction, falling from high to low, thus implying that no matter what they possess they are always dissatisfied with their lot and find reason to complain.

MALCONTENTS

No beginning and no end!

The melodic line of the Doubters zigzags up and down in singsong, indicating that perhaps they should have done this, or possibly that — a combination of maybe yes, and maybe no.

DOUBTERS

Deceptive illusion: Endless doubt!

The Doubters frequently sing *fortepiano*, demonstrating, that no sooner do they voice a thought then they change their mind and regret it. Maybe it wasn't what we thought? Maybe it wasn't what we meant?

REJOICERS

O glorious sunlight! Endless pleasure!

The rejoicers are the hedonists of the world. They sing shapely, arched melodic curves, accompanied by harp and celesta with lush harmonies. Immune to spiritual values, they enjoy the good life.

CHORUS

> Onward? Is it really to go on forever like this?

The Indifferent dream, while the world goes on. They believe in nothing at all. They sing in unisons, offset by instrumental counterpoint. Their textures are the thinnest of all, proving that not much of either intellectual or emotional import occupies their attention.

INDIFFERENT

> And so we take things as they come

The Quietly Resigned seems to fade away. The structure of their phrases is square, dull and plodding — reflections of the boredom which is their lot.

QUIETLY RESIGNED

> O, yet how well one can live in the mire.

Rather than exert themselves in willful melody, the Quietly Resigned (expressed through extended harmonies as well) indulge in their own unfulfilled feelings and desires.

GABRIEL

> No matter! Onward! Come here,
> Those of you who believe you have been brought here by your deeds.

Section 2

Section 2 is a series of dialogues between the archangel and the soloists. Five protagonists present their respective positions in the development section of the oratorio. Each in turn is challenged by Gabriel. As the texts are aphoristic and philosophical, so is the music. Their cryptic statements are imitated, transformed, and commented upon by the orchestra.

Section 2 (Soloists)

ONE WHO IS CALLED

> I sought beauty. To it I sacrificed everything.

The One Who Is Called is selfish and self-centered but gifted beyond the norm, someone who considers himself an "artist." He never looks beyond himself to meaningful relationships with others.

GABRIEL

> You are self-satisfied. Self-sufficiency keeps you warm.

The nature of the One who is Rebellious is arrogant and short sighted. Unbridled will is his god. He is a scoffer, blind to the feelings of others, and a stranger to social responsibility.

ONE WHO IS REBELLIOUS

> How the god of impulses mocks him of commandments!
> For he lets the wolves prosper.

GABRIEL

> This Either and this Or, like short-sightedness and arrogance

Only the One who is Struggling has Schoenberg's wholehearted approval.

ONE WHO IS STRUGGLING

> I sought happiness. When it was denied, I strove for painlessness —
> Which also failed. I felt it does not matter what one is unhappy about.

GABRIEL

> You are wrong. The more sensitive you be, the nearer you are.

ONE WHO IS STRUGGLING

> But how can I avoid new sin?

GABRIEL

> Come closer, so they can see you!

The One who is Chosen is the misunderstood prophet. Perhaps he is created in Schoenberg's own self-image. The Monk voices the wisdom of convention. While, to He Who Is Dying, the world and its images fade away.

ONE WHO IS CHOSEN

> I must go among them although my word will still not be understood.

GABRIEL

> So long as he is unclean, he must create himself from himself!

MONK

> Lord, forgive my presumption; it gratified my vanity to be
> a good servant.

GABRIEL

> But how you falter, how uncertain you are! Go spread the word.

HE WHO IS DYING

> A thousand lives! To one who knows, they are no longer to be feared.
> What is appalling is one life, one suffering.

Section 3

Section 3 combines a wordless vocalise for solo soprano with Gabriel's soothing singing (for the first time).

Section 3 (disembodied souls)

The soloists are supported by slow, sustained chords sung by a female choir of disembodied souls, with occasional speech-song commentary by the larger chorus.

GABRIEL

> You approach the light; your ego will be eradicated.

THE SOUL (vocalizing)

HIGH FEMALE VOICES

> Sins fade away, the senses, the intellect melt away!

SPEAKING VOICES

> Transparent lightness. State of nearness.

HIGH FEMALE VOICES and THE SOUL (vocalizing)

Ex. 7. Arnold Schoenberg: *Die Jakobsleiter*

© Copyright 1980 by Belmont Music Publishers. Reproduced by permission of Universal Edition AG.

Conclusion

The biblical import of Jacob's dream is a message of hope — in all ages, in all places, under all conditions. It is that the Almighty is not far off in his heavenly abode, neither heedless of what men do nor oblivious to their plight; every spot on earth may be the gateway to heaven. The world of *Jacob's Ladder* is a world peopled by sinners positioned on different rungs of the ladder of life. Each must undergo suffering in order to transform and inherit the blessing of God. Their redemption is dependent upon their willingness to undergo pain and torment in order to achieve completeness, and reap fulfillment and salvation. Schoenberg's music strives to articulate the contorted turmoil involved in this heroic inner process.

Related Directions

Works on other aspects of Jacob's life include J.H. Rolle's oratorio *Jakobs Ankunft in Aegypten* (1746); *Jacobs Heyrath* and *Jakobs Tod und Begraebnis,* nos. 3 and 6 of Johann Kuhnau's *Biblische Sonaten* for keyboard instrument (1700); and the setting of Jacob's blessing of Judah (*Gen. 49:10–12*) in Heinrich Schuetz's *Geistliche Chormusik* (1648). In Jewish folksongs, Jacob appears symbolically in the many settings of *Al Tira Avdi Ya'akov* (Fear Not My Servant Jacob), often with textual additions in Yiddish, such as *Amar Adonai le-Ya'akov — yo foterl yo* (see A. Z. Idelsohn, *Melodien* (1932), no. 485). Mordechai Ze'ira was the composer of the well-known Israeli *hora* tune, *Al Tira Avdi Ya'akov,* to a poem by Emanuel Harussi. There are a number of works on Jacob's Dream, Jacob and Rachel, Jacob and the Angel, and Jacob and Joseph.[22]

Jacob's Dream

Some 16th-century motets set the text of the vision, such as *Vidit Jacob scalam* by Crecquillon (publ. 1556) or *O quam metuendus est locus iste* by Gallus (publ. 1603). A "dialogo" (quasi-oratorio), *Il Vecchio Isaac* by G. Fr. Anerio (publ. 1619), treats the story of Jacob, Esau, and the birthright. One notable curiosity was the oratorio *La Vision de Jacob* (1900) which Marcel Dupré wrote at the age of 14. For the Moscow performances of Richard Beer-Hofmann's *Jaakob's Traum* by the Habimah

---

22. See Batia Bayer, "Jacob," *Encyclopedia Judaica,* Vol. 9, col. 1204–1205.

Theater, music was written by M. Milner; the play was later turned into an opera by the Israeli composer Bernard Bergel. An orchestral work, *Jacob's Dream*, was written by Karol Rathaus (1941); and in 1949, Darius Milhaud composed a dance suite for five instruments, *Les Rêves de Jacob* (op. 294), for the Jacob's Pillow dance festival held in the Massachusetts village of that name. The song *Sulam Ya'akov* (Jacob's Ladder)(1972) by Nurit Hirsh to words by Yoram Tahar Lev is often used for popular circle dancing.

Jacob and Rachel

The story of Jacob and Rachel is treated in a motet, *Da Jakob Labans Tochter nahm*, by Joachim à Burck (1599); a "Singspiel" (comic opera), *Von Jakobs doppelter Heyrath*, by Johann Philipp Krieger (1649–1725); and a duo-drama, *Jakob und Rachel*, by J.E. Fuss (1800). It is also found, somewhat unexpectedly, in two Spanish polyphonic songs of the 17th century (*Siete años de pastor* and *Romances y letras a tres vozes*), edited by M. Querol Gavaldá, 1956. For the Ohel Theatre production of *Jacob and Rachel*, music was written by Solomon Rosowsky, later to be reworked into an orchestral suite by Julius Chajes.

Jacob Struggling with the Angel

Jacob's word to the angel in the struggle at the Jabbok is the title text of Bach's Cantata no. 157, *Ich lasse dich nicht, du segnest Mich denn* (but with "*Mein Jesu*" added). A motet for double choir on the same text was written by Johann Christophe Bach (1642–1703), published in English as *I Wrestle and Pray*.

Max Stern's *Jacob and the Angel* is an instrumental treatment spanning night into day. There are two versions: *Jacob Struggling with the Angel (1991)*, a toccata for piano and orchestra, and *Jacob and the Angel (1998)* for harp and piano (with both players also singing, humming, stomping feet, and blowing kazoos). It is a knock-down drag out battle between Jacob's angry tone clusters and the angel's lustrous chords. The protagonists oppose one another with Stone Age brutality, while, at the same time, passionately embracing in a dance of eternal love.[23] In the

---

23. This image is depicted in the stone statue "Jacob and the Angel" (1941) by sculptor Sir Jacob Epstein (1880–1959), at the Tate Gallery, London.

end, the morning light breaks through the darkness. The angel ascends to heaven and the victorious Patriarch limps away, exhausted.

Jacob's Lament over Joseph

Jacob's mourning over Joseph was set as a motet by many composers of the 16th century. The works begin with *Vixens Jacob vestment Joseph* (German: *Da Jakob nun est Kleid ansah*) or *Lamentabatur Jacob*, and the list of composers includes Clemens non Papa, Cristobal Morales, Jacob Regnart, and Cosmas Alder (for "Joseph's play" performed at Basle). The message to Jacob that Joseph is alive appears in Orlando di Lasso's *Dixit Joseph indecim fratribus.*

Works List

Abaelard, Petrus (1079–1142 France). *Planctus Jacob super Joseph* (Gen. 37:33), lament.

Acciarello, Franciscus (18th C.). *Jacob fidelis servitus*, oratorio.

Alder, Cosinas (1497 Baden–1561 Bern). *Da Jakob nun das Kleid ansah* (Gen. 37:33), 5 voices.

Alexander, Haim (1915 Berlin/1936 Jerusalem). *Mah tovu ohalekha Ya'akov* (Num. 24:5), soprano, choir, pianoforte.

Alman, Shmuel (1887–1947 London). *Mah Tovu Ohalekha Ya'akov* (Num. 24:5), choir.

Borlasca, Bernadino (c.1560–1631 Italy). *Scala Jacob* (Genesis 8), 8 voices, 8 instruments.

Bottario, Dominico Philioop (18th C.). *Jacob et Rachelis* (P. Gini), oratorio.

Burnell, I (19th–20th C. UK). *Surely the Lord Is in This Place (1921)* (Gen. 28:16–17), Anthem, SATB (organ. ad. lib.).

Burroughs, Bob (c.1930 Tazewell, Virginia). *Surely the Lord is in This Place* (Gen. 28:16–17), SAB.

Casali, Giovanni Battista (1715–1792 Rome). *La benedizione di Giacobbe*, oratorio.

Casini, Giovanni Maria (1652–1719 Florence). *Giacobbe in Mesopotamia*, oratorio.

Clemens Non Papa, Jacobus (c.1510–c.1556 Antwerpen).*Videns Jacob vestimenta Joseph* (Gen. 37:33), motet.

Donceanu, Felicia (b.1931 Romania). *Scara lui Iacob* (Bakonsky), voice, guitar.

Dupré, Marcel (1886 Rouen–1971 Paris). *La vision de Jacob,* oratorio.

Franck, Melchior (1579–1639 Germany). *Und da Jacob vollendet hatte,* cantata.

Furlanetto, Bonaventura (1738–1817 Venice). *Nuptie in domo Labani,* cantata.

Fuss, Johann Evangelist (1777–1819 Hungary). *Jacob and Rachel,* melodrama.

Hallgimsson, Haflidi (b.1941 Iceland). *Jacob's Ladder* (1984), guitar.

Hiles, Henry (1826–1904 England). *The Patriarchs* (Hiles), oratorio.

Hurford, Peter (b.1930 UK) *Truly the Lord Is in This Place* (Gen. 28:16–17), SATB, organ.

Jacquet de la Guerre, Elisabeth (1667–1729 Paris). *Jacob et Rachel* (A.H. de la Monte), cantata, voice, basso continuo.

Koechlin, Charles (1867–1950 Paris). *Jacob chez Laban* (Ch. Koechlin), 2 soloists, choir, orchestra, biblical pastorale.

Kuhnau, Johann (1660–1722 Leipzig). *Jakob's Tod und Begraebnis,* Biblical Sonatas, keyboard.

Kunzen, Adolph Carl (1720–1781 Germany). *Jakobs Vermaehlung mit Lea,* oratorio.

Lederer, Joseph (1733–1796 Germany). *Die Liebe Rachel und Jakobs,* musical comedy.

Lorenz, Ellen Jane (1907–1996 Dayton, Ohio). *The Gate of Heaven* (Gen. 28:16–17), SATB, organ/hand bells.

Mayr, Johannes (1763–1845 Germany). *Jacob a Labano fugiens,* oratorio.

McEwen, John Blackwood (1868–1948 London). *The Vision of Jacob,* soloist, choir, organ.

Milhaud, Darius (1892 France–1974 Geneva). *Les reves de Jacob* (Gen. 28), dance suite, oboe, strings.

Milner, Moshe Michael (1886–1952 Kiev). *Jakob's Traum* (R. Beer-Hoffmann), incidental music.

Morales, Christobal de (1512 Seville–1553 Malaga). *Lamentabatur Jacob,* motet, 5 voices.

Nicholl, Horace (1848 England–1922 New York). *Jacob,* oratorio.

Powell, Robert J. (b.1932 USA). *Surely the Lord Is in This House* (Gen. 28: 16–17), SATB.

Raimondi, Pietro (1786–1853 Rome). *Putifar, Guiseppe e Giacobbe* (G. Sapio), opera.

Rathaus, Karol (1895 Tarnopol–1954 New York). *Jacob's Dream* (R. Beer-Hofmann), suite.

Rolle, Johann Heinrich (1716–1785 Germany). *Jakobs Ankunft in Aegypten* (Roetger), oratorio.

Rosowsky, Solomon (1878 Riga–1962 New York). *Jacob and Rachel*, suite, 2 pianoforte, flute, drum, triangle and tambourine.

Routley, Erik (1917–1982 UK). *Come O Thou Traveler Unknown* (Wesley) (Gen. 32: 24, 26–27, 29b–30), SATB, organ.

Sabatino, Giovanni (1667–1742 Napoli). *L'aurora foriera della pace fra Giacobbe es Esau*, oratorio.

Samburski, Daniel (1909 Koenigsberg–1970 Tel-Aviv). *Yaakov*, baritone, orchestra.

Sances, Giovanni Felice (1600 Rome–1679 Vienna). *Jacob*, oratorio.

Schein, Johann Hermann (1586–1630 Leipzig). *Da Jakob vollendet hatte* (Gen. 49:33; 50:1), madrigal, 5 voices, basso continuo.

Schoenberg, Arnold (1874 Vienna–1951 Los Angeles). *Die Jakobsleiter*, oratorio.

Schorr, Baruch (1823–1904 Lviv, Ukraine). *Mah tovu ohalekha* (Num. 24:5), baritone, choir, organ.

Schuetz, Heinrich (1585–1672 Dresden). *Er wird sein Kleid in Wein waschen* (Gen. 49:1), choir.

Senfl, Ludwig (1486 Basel–1555 Munich). *Da Jakob nun das Kleid ansah*, choir.

Smart, Henry (1813–1879 London). *Jacob*, sacred cantata.

Wagner-Regeny, Rudolf (1903 Romania–1969 Germany). *Esau und Jakob*, 4 singers, narrator, strings, orchestra.

Williamson, Malcolm (1931 Sydney–2003 Cambridge, England). *Wrestling Jacob*, soprano, choir, organ.

G. Dore: Joseph Makes Himself Known to his Brothers, *Bible Illustrations* *(1866)*

Andrew Lloyd Webber's rock musical *Joseph and the Amazing Technicolor Dreamcoat,* affords us opportunity to examine the Bible as a source penetrating the world of contemporary musical theater and popular culture.

JOSEPH and HIS BROTHERS

Now Israel loved Joseph more than all his children, because he was the son of his old age; and he made him a coat of many colors. And when his brethren saw that their father loved him more than all his brethren, they hated him, and could not speak peaceably unto him. And Joseph dreamed a dream, and he told it to his brethren; and they hated him yet all the more. And he said unto them: 'Hear, I pray you, this dream which I have dreamed for, behold, we were binding sheaves in the field, and lo, my sheaf arose, and also stood upright; and, behold, your sheaves came round about, and bowed down to my sheaf.' And his brethren said to him: 'Shalt thou indeed reign over us? Or shalt thou indeed have dominion over us?' And they hated him yet the more for his dreams, and for his words   (Genesis 37:3–8).

The story of Joseph and his Brothers, the longest episode in the Book of Genesis (37–50), is the saga of how a family becomes a nation. Filled with jealousy and rage at Joseph's preferred status,[1] prim ways and

---

1.   In Joseph, the eldest offspring of Jacob's late wife, Rachel, we encounter the brilliant, but pampered son of an aged father. Joseph is Jacob's link to the love of his life, Rachel, and Jacob's preference for Joseph, inadvisable as it is, in this context is understandable. *And Jacob served seven years for Rachel; and they seemed unto him but a few days, for the love he had to her (Gen. 29:20).* It was only for love of Rachel that Jacob consented to marry her sister Leah and their handmaids Bilhah and Zilpah, who became, except for Benjamin, the mothers of all of his other sons.

dreams, his older half-brothers plotted to rid themselves of him, they *thought to slay him...cast him into a pit...and sat down to eat bread (Genesis 37:24–25)*. But, while quarreling over tactics, Joseph, unexpectedly, is rescued by a caravan of traveling merchants and taken to Egypt. Whether by the vicissitudes of design or destiny, mishap, chance, or folly, a fantastic tale of rags to riches opens up before us, and we are privy to a glimpse into the mechanisms by which the Almighty acts in the world to fulfill a near forgotten promise and blessing, made many years before, to a desperate youthful Jacob, fleeing his brother Esau's rage.[2] We witness too, the power of education, seen not so much as formal schooling, but as human anxiety and feelings of fear and remorse, transforming the thoughtless behavior of Joseph's asinine brothers into men of noble character and worth. *God meant it unto good...and will surely...bring you... unto the land which he swore to Abraham, Isaac and to Jacob (Genesis 50:20, 24)*.

Andrew Lloyd Webber:
Joseph and the Amazing Technicolor Dreamcoat (1968–1976)
Libretto: Tim Rice
Genre: Musical Theater
Medium: Soloists, chorus, children's chorus, dancers, and rock orchestra
Style: Pop-Rock
First performance: Colet Court School, London March 1, 1968
Duration: ca. 1 hour and 30 minutes

Joseph and the Amazing Technicolor Dreamcoat projects the biblical saga of Joseph into the late 20th century via musical idioms ranging from classical to pop, jazz, hip-hop and electro-acoustic rock. Originally written for an English prep school concert (1968), the show was later expanded into a full length London West End musical. It began as an informal commission from Alan Doggett, head of music at the Colet Court prep school in West London, who had known Andrew for some time. Doggett was looking for something original, but also religious, for his end term concert. As the fate would have it, Webber and his collaborator Tim Rice flipped opened the Bible and found there the

---

2. *The land whereon thou liest, to thee will I give it, and to thy seed; and thy seed shall be as the dust of the earth...and in thy seed shall all the families of the earth be blessed (Gen. 23:13–14)*.

story of Jacob and his son Joseph. After two months, they'd written a fifteen-minute rock n' roll musical. Rice's irreverent libretto follows the sequence of the Bible. Except for the story outline, though, there is little else to suggest its biblical origin; it could as well have been an up-dated fantasy in ancient Egyptian décor.

Biographic Context

Composer

Andrew Lloyd Webber (b.1948, London) is arguably the most successful composer of popular musicals in the late twentieth century. He revitalized musical theatre and brought pop rock to the stage. From an early age Andrew played instruments at home and soon afterwards began composing. Lloyd Webber's father, William, was a professor of theory and composition at the Royal College of Music, and organist at the Westminster School. It was natural, then, that his son was educated at this prestigious institution, where school days began with Latin prayers or service in the Abby.[3] Following graduation, Andrew was admitted to Oxford as a Queens Scholar (1963), but left college after a year to compose pop songs and musicals.

Librettist

Tim (Miles Bindon) Rice (b.1944, Buckinghamshire) attended private prep schools, performed as a teenage singer with a pop-rock group, did a stint at the Sorbonne in Paris (1961–63), attended law school (1963–66), and served as a management trainee at EMI Records (until 1968), before hooking up with Andrew Lloyd Webber. Their initial meeting came by

---

3. Westminster is a prestigious prep-school. Its origins can be traced to 1179, when the Benedictine monks of Westminster Abby were required by Pope Alexander III to set up a small, charity school for the poor. It continued under Henry VIII and received royal patronage under Elizabeth I in 1560. Music holds a central place in its curriculum (former graduates include Henry Purcell, Adrian Boult, and Roger Norrington). A wide variety of music is studied, from chamber music to jazz. The choir leads the school's services in Westminster Abby. At Westminster, there is a tradition of teaching composition and featuring works composed by pupils in concerts and recitals. When pupils leave Westminster, they emerge informed, articulate, and well able to hold their own intellectually (from the bulletin of the Westminster School).

way of an auto-introductory letter.[4] Both were well-bred British youths who shared artistic identity in the world of popular music. We can understand the sophisticated "tongue in cheek" of their productions as high-brows slumming as low-brows; it is a privilege reserved exclusively for the elite and socially pampered.

Text and Context — Music and Musical Exegesis

Joseph and the Amazing Technicolor Dreamcoat is a crass, glossy by-product of the Beatles generation. The hot sauce of percussion covers everything with a pulsating beat. Prosaic melodic materials are given variety through simple counterpoints. Its uniqueness, though, lies in the transformation of a teen-boppers musical palette into entertainment for adults. Impressively revamping, updating, and aping a panoply of commercial styles; not innovation, but skilled pantomime, mimic, and stand-up comic stylizations mark its originality.

Analyses

ACT I

Prologue

The musical is set as a play within a play, a story told to children through sung narrative and songs, encouraging them to dream.

Any Dream Will Do

This song is the story of Joseph, a dreamer. It is a straightforward tune, offset with responses from a children's chorus, supported by a funky rhythmic background.

---

4. *Dear Andrew — I've been told you're looking for a "with it" writer of lyrics for your songs, and as I've been writing pop songs for a while and particularly enjoy writing the lyrics, I wonder if you consider it worth your while meeting me. Tim Rice* (Cited in Sa Larsdottier, Andrew Lloyd Webber, 1997). Internet resource: http://hem.passagen.se/musicals/bio_and.html

Jacob and Sons

This song introduces Jacob and his twelve sons. It is a syncopated tune, parsed between the narrator and the sons, over a heavy 4/4 beat.

Coat of Many Colors and Joseph's Coat

Joseph's brothers are jealous of his multi-colored coat, a symbol of their father's preference for him. It is a two-phrase tune built upon a blues progression.

Joseph's Dreams

But, it becomes evident to the brothers that Joseph, because of his dreamcoat and dreams, is destined to rule over them. It alternates a slow Irish jig, colored in Baroque instrumentation, with a sassy "king of the road" type beat supplied by a men's chorus.

Poor, Poor Joseph

In order to eliminate Joseph as a competitor and ensure that his dreams do not materialize, the brothers sell him as a slave to passing Ishmaelites, who transfer him to Egypt. The song alternates a mix of African influenced punk with English anthem and hymn styles.

One More Angel in Heaven

Back home, the brothers, accompanied by their wives, break the news of Joseph's alleged demise to Jacob, by displaying his tattered coat smeared with the blood of a goat, to his distraught father. It is styled as a cross between a Country and Western ballad, and the St. Louis blues.

Potiphar

In Egypt, Joseph is slave to Egyptian millionaire, Potiphar. Joseph's gifts become evident, and he rises through the ranks of slaves and servants until he is running Potiphar's house. The master's wife attempts to seduce him, but, just as Joseph is spurning her advances, Potiphar barges in, sees the two together and jumps to conclusions, jailing his young attractive slave. Potiphar's wife's music is the Charleston, the flapper style of the Roaring '20s. Lloyd Webber characterizes her musically — not as a sensual, breathy femme fatale, but as a risqué, sociably amenable woman from the world of the well to do and idle rich. Potiphar's wife is a brazen beauty who has it all and flaunts it.

Close Every Door and Go, Go, Go Joseph

Depressed, Joseph's sings a slow waltz. His spirits rise when he interprets the dreams of his cellmates, two prisoners, who were formerly servants of Pharaoh. Joseph foretells the baker's execution, but predicts the butler will return to serve the king, in an upbeat choral number.

ACT II

Pharaoh's Story and Poor, Poor Pharaoh

The narrator sings of impending changes in Joseph's fortunes. Pharaoh is having dreams which no one can interpret. The reinstated butler informs Pharaoh of Joseph's skill in interpreting dreams. Pharaoh, seen as a rock n' roll superstar, enters as greasy haired "Elvis." It is a grotesque that brings archaeology up-to-date. Webber and Rice compare the adoration of Pharaoh to the idolatry cults of today's pop-music industry, and thus, they highlight, in their own way, the down-side of power as something coarse, crude, and self-indulgent.

Song of the King (Seven Fat Cows)

Pharaoh orders Joseph to be brought forth and discloses his two dreams of seven fat cows, seven skinny cows; seven healthy ears of corn, and seven dead ears of corn. It is a classic 1950's "rock n' roll around the clock" type of setting.

Pharaoh's Dream Explained and Stone the Crows

Joseph interprets the dream as seven plentiful years followed by seven years of famine. It is the upbeat, hit tune of the show. An astonished Pharaoh puts Joseph in charge of implementing the preparations needed to endure the impending famine. Joseph, second only to Pharaoh, now becomes the most powerful man in Egypt. This is a wordy song that, in addition, brings in a children's chorus on a kindergarten tune.

Those Canaan Days

Back home, in the land of Canaan, famine has overtaken Joseph's brothers, who express regret at selling him and deceiving their father. It is set to a nostalgic sentimental waltz-like tune, with a violin obbligato straight out of the Yiddish theater.

The Brothers Come to Egypt

They hear that in Egypt there is food, and resolve to go there, not realizing with whom they will be dealing. Pharaoh, king of Egypt, surrounded by celebrity groupies, again enters in a parody of Elvis, king of rock n' roll. It is set as a Latin American cha-cha.

Grovel, Grovel

Joseph's questioning alternates with his brothers' moans of "trouble, trouble," set as a jazz waltz. He supplies his brothers with food and sends them on their way; but not before he plants a golden cup into the sack of his brother, Benjamin.

Who's the Thief? A Benjamin Calypso

In the process of returning to Canaan, Joseph halts his brothers exit, inquiring about the "stolen cup." Each brother empties his sack, uncovering the cup in the possession of Benjamin, at which point Joseph accuses Benjamin of robbery. The older brothers beg for mercy, to the accompaniment of a Latin-American calypso beat. They implore Joseph to imprison them as his slaves, but to set Benjamin free. The calypso style and its Latin American rhythm is a vehicle for vigorous stage movement, which contains, however, an innuendo of violence. It recollects, perhaps unintentionally, a Midrash concerning Judah's determination to use three means, if necessary, to liberate Benjamin: *He was prepared to convince Joseph by argument or move him by entreaties or resort to force in order to accomplish his end.*[5]

---

5. Midrash Tanachuma, Genesis chapter 44, 18–34, as cited in Ginzberg, *The Legends of the Jews*, Vol. 2, note 267, 103.

Joseph All the Time and Jacob in Egypt

A nostalgic, French ballad-styled torch song is the vehicle used to symbolize the brother's regret at the sale of Joseph. Apprehending their penitence, Joseph reveals himself and sends for his father. A parody of Country & Western music is used here to underline the breaking news of Joseph's existence to Jacob.

Finale

The two are happily reunited in a square dance. Is this hoedown meant to convey familial normalcy, or, is it a mockery on domestic tranquility? It is never quite clear.

Conclusion

Andrew Lloyd Webber and Tim Rice, by extracting the story of Joseph from its original context in the Book of Genesis and reinventing it as a 21st-century fantasy for matured "lollipoppers," have managed to personalize the tale for a whole new generation of listeners, often with intriguing insights and irreverent correspondences. By their hand, something of the eternal message within the story is confirmed and brought about, ironically with the same unexpected twisting and turning of fortune and destiny, fate and history. It is a transmutation of sacred values into vernacular genres, that, nonetheless, ingests plot and substance from the timeless resilience of the original.[6] Catapulting ancient Egypt into the realm of hip-hop, biblical consciousness has entered the well-springs of popular culture and deepened it.

Each musical style and form — whether dramatic or comic, high or low, sophisticated or naïve — seeks its own level and targets its own audience. *Joseph and the Amazing Technicolor Dreamcoat* is as much a spoof on conventional thinking and acceptable values for the Beatles' generation, as Gilbert and Sullivan were for Victorian England. In a way, sacrilege and parody are forms of appreciation. The medieval Chester Mystery Plays seemed, perhaps, as irreverent to some living

---

6. It is quite a different approach than the epic novel by Thomas Mann. See Thomas Mann, *Joseph and His Brothers*, translated by John E. Woods (New York: Everyman's Library, 2005).

in the Middle Ages as Weber and Rice are today.[7] What the present shares with the past is its concern for, and determination to, recreate 'relevance.' Lloyd Webber seeks inspiration in his own neighborhood, so to speak, deriving stylistic materials and models from contemporary culture, commercial trends, fads, and popular music. These he recycles into pop-rock, Latin-American, and disco styled parodies accompanying the biblical scenario. It is a unique solution to the ageless striving — by means of metaphor and allegory, numerology and typology — to make the Bible relevant to its time and place.

Related Directions

The theme of Joseph and his Brothers is also found among the earliest oratorio subjects at the beginning of the 17th century. The greatest numbers of settings are those of Pietro Metastasio's *Guiseppe riconscuito* (Vienna, 1733).[8] Its composers include J.A. Hasse (1741), Luigi Boccherini (1756), and Carl Friedrich Fasch (1774). Other librettos of the period were J.B. Neri's *Guiseppe che interpreta I sogni*, set by Antonio Caldara (1726), who had already set a libretto by A. Zeno in his opera *Guiseppe* (Vienna, 1722); and Handel's oratorio *Joseph and His Brethren*, to a text by James Miller (first performed at Covent Garden Theatre, London, 1744).

The 19th century opens with Méhul's opera *Joseph* (1807; text by Duval), for male voices only, which has remained a classic; the century ends with two parodies: Victor Roger's *Joséphine vendue par ses soeurs* (Paris, Bouffes Parisiennes, 1886) and Edmond Diel's operetta *Madame Potiphar* (Paris, 1897). In the 20th century Richard Strauss's ballet *Die Josephlegende* (1914) had a libretto by Hugo von Hofmannsthal and H. Kessler. Another ballet, Werner Josten's *Joseph and His Brethren* (première in New York, 1936), was also arranged as a symphonic suite (1939). The Israeli composer Erich Walter Sternberg wrote a suite for

---

7. A parallel can be found in some of modern translations, which call themselves the *Holy Bible*. There is nothing holy about these popular versions, which are nothing more than veiled commentaries and "dumbed-down" rewriting of biblical texts for public consumption, interjected with personal biases. The Sacred Sandwich (2008). Internet resource: http://sacredsandwich.com/bible_versions.htm

8. Pietro Metastasio (1698–1782) is considered the greatest Italian poet and librettist of the 18th century.

string orchestra entitled *The Story of Joseph* (1942). Two settings are based on Thomas Mann's novel cycle: David Diamond's *Young Joseph* for three-part women's chorus and string orchestra (1944), and Hilding Rosenberg's cycle of four opera-oratorios, *Josef och hans bröder* (composed between 1945 and 1948). Israeli composer Dov Zeltser set Yiddish poet Yitzhak Manger's poem *Yosef HaTzadik* based on *Gen. 39:6*.

Works List

Abaelard (Abelard), *Petrus* (1079 Le Pallet/Nantes–1142 St. Marcel, France). *Planctus Jacob super Joseph*, a liturgical drama.

Accorimboni, Agostino (1739–1818 Rome). *Giuseppe riconosciuto*, oratorio.

Anfossi, Pasquale (1727–1797 Rome). *Giuseppe riconosciuto (Gen. 37–56)*, oratorio.

Bertoni, Ferdinando-Gasparo (1725 Salo/Brescia–1813 Italy). *Il Giuseppe riconosciuto* (P. Metastasio), oratorio.

Bijvanck, Henk (1909–1969 Java–Haarlem). *Joseph en zijn broers*, opera.

Bitgood, Roberta (1908–2007 Connecticut). *Joseph*, choir, cantata.

Blanchino, Ioan (17th C.). *Oratorium de Josepho Vendito a fratribus*.

Boccherini, Luigi (1743 Lucca–1805 Madrid). *Il Giuseppe riconosciuto* (P. Metastasio), oratorio.

Bonno, Giuseppe (1711–1788 Vienna). *Il Giuseppe riconosciuto* (P. Metastasio), oratorio.

Buti, Francesco (d.1682 Narni). *Giuseppe figlio di Giacobbe*, oratorio.

Byvanck, Henk (1909–1961 Holland). *Joseph and His Brothers* (Byvanck), opera.

Caldara, Antonio (1670 Venice–1736 Vienna). *Giuseppe figliolo di Giacob e di Rachele* (J.B. Neri), oratorio.

_____. *Gioseffo che interpreta i sogni* (J.B. Neri), oratorio.

Castelnuovo-Tedesco, Mario (1895 Florence–1968 California). *The Stories of Joseph*, Suite for pianoforte.

Conti, Francesco Bertholomeo (1682 Florence–1732 Vienna). *Giuseppe de interpreta i Sogni* (Neri), oratorio.

Cosmas Alder (1497–1550 Switzerland). *Joseph Play*, liturgical drama.

De Leone, Francesco (1887 Italy–1948 Ohio). *The Triumph of Joseph*, oratorio.

Duni, Egidio Romoaldo (1709–1775 Paris). *Giuseppe riconosciuto* (P. Metastasio), oratorio.

Fasch, Karl Christian (1736–1800 Berlin). *Giuseppe riconosciuto* (P. Metastasio), oratorio.

Ferradini, Antonio (1718 Naples–1779 Prague). *Giuseppe riconosciuto* (A. Zeno), oratorio.

Fesch, Willem de (1687 Holland–1757 London). *Josef,* oratorio.

Freibert, Johann Joseph (1742–1799 Passau). *Il Giuseppe riconosciuto* (P. Metastasio), oratorio.

Furlanetto, Bonaventura (1738–1817 Venice). *Joseph pro Rex Aegypti,* oratorio.

Gibelli, Lorenzo (1719–1812 Bologna). *Il Giuseppe riconosciuto,* oratorio.

Handel, George Frederick (1685 Halle–1759 London). *Joseph and His Brethren* (J.Miller) (Gen. 37–44), oratorio.

Hasse, Johann-Adolf (1699 Bergedorf–1783 Venice). *Giuseppe riconosciuto* (P. Metastasio), oratorio.

Horsley, William (1774–1858 London). *Joseph,* oratorio.

Jacquet, de La Guerre), Elisabeth (1667–1729 Paris). *Joseph* (A.H de la Motte), cantata for voice, basso continuo.

Josten, Werner (1885 Elberfeld–1963 New-York). *Joseph and His Brethren,* ballet.

Kay, Ulysses (1917 Arizona–1995 NJ). *As Joseph Was a Walking* (Gen. 36), choir.

Konvalinka, Milos (1919 Moravia–2000). *Josef a jeho bratri* (Hickmet), incidental music/concert suite.

Kosa, Gyorgy (1897–1984 Budapest). *Josef,* chamber oratorio.

Kunzen, Adolf Carl (1720–1781 Germany). *Joseph und seine Brueder* (J. D. Overbeck), oratorio.

Lasso, Orlando di (1532 Mons–1594 Munich). *Joseph verkauffet ist,* choir.

MacFarren, George Alexander (1813–1887 London). *Joseph,* oratorio.

Martelli, Simone (16ᵗʰ C.). *Joseph figliaolo di Jacob,* sacra representazione.

Mattheson, Johann (1681–1764 Hamburg). *Der gegen seine Brueder barmherzige Joseph,* oratorio.

McEwen, John Blackwood (1868–1948 London). *Joseph,* oratorio.

Mehul, Etienne Nicolas (1763–1817 Paris). Joseph (A. Duval), opera.

Myslivecek, Josef (1737 Praha–1781 Rome). *Giuseppe riconosciuto* (P. Metastasio), oratorio.

Naumann, Johann Gottlieb (1741 Blasewitz–1801 Dresden). *Giuseppe riconosciuto* (P. Metastasio), oratorio.

Porsile, Giuseppe (1672 Naples–1750 Vienna). *Giuseppe riconosciuto* (P. Metastasio), oratorio.

Pratti, Alessio (1750–1788 Ferrara). *Giuseppe riconosciuto* (P. Metastasio), oratorio.

Raimondi, Pietro (1786–1853 Rome). *Potiphar, Giuseppe e Giacobbe* (G. Sapio), opera.

Rosenberg, Hilding Constantin (1892 Boisjokloster–1985). *Josef och hans broder* (*Joseph and His Brothers*) (Thomas Mann), opera.

Rossi, Luigi (1598–1653 Rome). *Giuseppe, figlio di Giacobbe* (F. Butti), oratorio.

Sales, Pietro Pompeo (1729 Brescia–1797 Hanau). *Giuseppe ricognosciuto* (A. Zeno), oratorio.

Schiassi, Gaetano M. (1698 Bologna–1754 Lisbon). *Giuseppe riconosciuto* (P. Metastasio), oratorio.

Silvani, Giuseppe Antonio (1672–1727 Bologna). *La Verita in sogno spiegata da Giosefo hebreo*, oratorio.

Starer, Robert (1924 Vienna/1935 Israel/1941 Kingston, NY–2001). *Joseph and His Brothers*, oratorio.

Sternberg, Erich-Walter (1898 Berlin/1931 Israel–1974 Tel Aviv). *The Story of Joseph*, suite for strings.

Strauss, Richard (1864–1949 Germany). *Joseph slegende* (H. Hofmannsthal & H. Kessler), ballet.

Terradellas, Doming (1713 Barcelona–1751 Rome). *Giuseppe riconosciuto*, oratorio.

Vieru, Anatol (1926 Iasi–1998). *Josif si frati sai* (*Joseph and His Brethren*) (Thomas Mann) ensemble, instruments, magnetophone.

Vinaccesi, Benedetto (c.1670 Brescia–1719 Venice). *Gioseffo che interpreta i sogni*, oratorio.

Vogt, Gustave (1781 Strassburg–1870 Paris). *Variations on a theme of 'Joseph'* (Mehul), orchestra, opera.

Vorotnikov, Pavel (1804–1876). *Blagoobrazny Yosif* (*Joseph the Handsome*), choir.

Werner, Gregor Joseph (c.1695 Austria–1766 Eisenstadt). *Der keusche Joseph*, oratorio.

CHAPTER 7

George Frederick Handel's English oratorio *Israel in Egypt* tells the story of the Exodus with Baroque pomp and worldly grandeur: in a series of recitatives, solo arias and ensembles, and choral movements. Part one depicts the plagues of Egypt, while Part two sings the song of deliverance at the Red Sea — without sets, staging, or costumes.

EXODUS

And he said unto Abram: 'Know of a surety that thy seed shall be a stranger in a land that is not theirs, and shall serve them four hundred years; and also that nation, whom they shall serve, will I judge; and afterward shall they come out with great substance   (Genesis 15:13–14).

The Exodus of the children of Israel from Egypt is the central event of Jewish history, an archetype for the struggle of all oppressed peoples longing for freedom.[1] The deliverance from slavery through ten plagues, the crossing of the Red Sea, and the revelation of the Law at Sinai echo through world history as miraculous incidents of divine intervention in the lives of men and nations. The story highlights the impotence of man's most resolute determination to frustrate divine purpose.[2]

George Frederick Handel: Israel in Egypt (1739)
Libretto: Charles Jennens
Genre: English Oratorio

---

1. As is true of every Scriptural narrative, its purpose is not so much to give an exhaustive chronicle of events, as it is to demonstrate the moral and religious truth that all destiny is under the guiding hand of the Eternal. No proof text interprets this message better than the phrase, *I am the Lord your God, which brought you out of the land of Egypt, to be your God (Numbers 15:41).*
2. S.R. Driver, *Introduction to the Literature of the Old Testament* as cited in *The Pentateuch,* edited by J. H. Hertz (London: Soncino Press, 1976) 400.

Medium: Soloists (2 sopranos, alto, tenor and 2 basses), chorus, and orchestra
Style: Late Baroque
First performance: King's Theatre, Haymarket, London, 1739

Israel in Egypt is a seminal work. Its forthright treatment of biblical subject matter and its impressive choral conceptions influenced and inspired generations of composers as diverse as Haydn, Berlioz, Mendelssohn, Gounod, Elgar, Dvorak, Walton, Tippett, and others, into the twentieth century.

Biographic Context

George Frederick Handel (1785 Halle–1759 London), the creator of the English oratorio, was born in Germany. Handel's father, a court surgeon, did not encourage young George's musical inclinations, and sent his son to study at a grammar school, where ironically, as fate would have it, he met F.W. Zachow, the organist at the Liebfrauenkirche and a sympathetic man and teacher who laid Handel's lifelong foundations in organ playing and polyphonic composition. On his father's death, the 17-year-old Handel abandoned his legal studies and served a few months as organist at the Calvinist Cathedral in Halle, before seeking his fortune in Hamburg. There, he entered the opera house orchestra as a second violin player. During his tenure, the ambitious youth acquired both the essentials of vocal style,[3] and the kind of worldly adroitness needed to get ahead. Before he left Hamburg, Handel managed to get his first opera successfully produced. Not yet 22, seeking to master operatic art, Handel departed for Italy. He arrived there a gifted but crude composer and left a polished master.

Against a background of music-loving princes and cardinals, George Frederick spent three years in and about Rome, Florence, and Venice — charming patrons with his virtuoso harpsichord playing, and getting his operas, oratorios, and cantatas played under their patronage. Handel's characteristically rich, free, varied, and long-breathed melodic style dates from this period. At 25, he returned to Germany

---

3. J. Mattheson, *Georg Friedrich Handel's Liebensbeschreibung* (Hamburg 1761/R1976), as cited in Winton Dean, "Georg Frederic Handel," *The New Grove Dictionary of Music,* Vol. 8 (London: Macmillan, 1980) 84.

as Kapellmeister to the Elector of Hanover, shortly to become, King George of England. At his former employer's invitation, Handel came to London.[4] Versatile and comfortable in both monarchial and theatrical worlds, Handel composed ceremonial pieces and anthems for the nobility at court; while, at the same time, he produced operas, bullied divas and castrati, and wrestled with managers and audiences at the theatre. Over the years, however, British tastes changed, and, while struggling to keep his Italian opera company afloat, the indefatigable Handel suffered a stroke in 1737 at 52. His operatic career was over; oratorio proved his salvation.

The Birth of English Oratorio

Old Testament subject matter had a strong appeal for Handel's British audiences. Not only were they generally familiar with the stories, but they perceived a parallel between themselves and the ancient Israelites: both were intensely nationalistic and led by heroic figures, and both regarded themselves as being under the special protection of God — who was to be worshipped with pomp and splendor.[5] In 1732, a version of the oratorio *Esther* (originally written in 1720) had been "staged" informally with boys of the Chapel Royal.[6] Later that year, encouraged by its reception, Handel intended to mount a theatrical production at the King's Theatre in Haymarket. This ambition was foiled by the Dean of the Chapel

---

4. Under this royal patronage the composer-impresario began writing operas specifically for London, where he settled permanently in 1712. When the Royal Academy of Music was established in 1719, with the stated goal of promoting Italian opera, Handel became its principal conductor and music director. It was in this capacity, and with the support of the English aristocrats who founded the academy, that he brought Italian opera to London. For nearly thirty years, through thick and thin, these stiff lipped British aristocrats proved a loyal support group for the immigrant German composer.
5. We find similar correspondences, between the British nation and the ancient Hebrews, in the hymns of English theologian Isaac Watts (1674–1748), a contemporary of Handel.
6. Its ambiance was, perhaps, not unlike the Medieval Jewish *Purim spiel* (Purim Play). On the other hand, this event shares similarities with the genesis of the musical *Joseph's Amazing Technicolor Dreamcoat*, created for a prep school in London. Again and again, we encounter composers, at defining moments in their careers, turning to the Bible, and finding therein, something for their lives.

Royal (and Bishop of London), who considered the opera house an immoral place for boys and forbade the representation of biblical characters on stage. Forced to compromise, Handel accepted the continental manner of performing oratorio without costumes, sets, or action of any kind.[7] Soloists sang operatic arias, while Greek chorus-like choruses were given prominence. The success of *Esther* encouraged Handel to compose further works in this genre. The English oratorio was born.

Text and Context

PART I

The Plagues of Egypt

He sent Moses His servant; and Aaron whom He had chosen.
They shewed his signs among them, and wonders in the land of Ham

(Psalm 105:26–27)

Overture

1. RECITATIVE (tenor) Now there arose a new king
2. ALTO and CHORUS And the children of Israel sighed
3. RECITATIVE (tenor) Then sent he Moses, His servant
4. CHORUS They loathed to drink of the river
5. AIR Their land brought forth frogs
6. CHORUS He spake the word, and there came flies and lice
7. CHORUS He gave them hailstone
8. CHORUS He sent a thick darkness
9. CHORUS He smote all the first-born of Egypt
10. CHORUS But as for His people, He led them forth like sheep
11. CHORUS Egypt was glad when they departed
12. CHORUS He rebuked the Red Sea
13. CHORUS He led them through the deep
14. CHORUS But the waters overwhelmed their enemies
15. CHORUS And Israel saw that great work that the Lord did

---

7. Though, it was familiar to him through performances in Rome, he had experienced many years before, on his Italian sojourn.

PART II
The Song at the Red Sea

He rebuked the Red sea also, and it was dried up; so
He led them through the depths as through the wilderness.
(Psalm 106:9)

1. CHORUS Moses and the children of Israel
2. DUET (soprano I, II) The Lord is my strength and my song
3. CHORUS He is my God
4. DUET (bass I, II) The Lord is a man of war
5. CHORUS The depths have covered them
6. CHORUS Thy right hand, O Lord is become glorious in power
7. CHORUS Thou sentest forth thy wrath
8. CHORUS And with the blast of thy nostrils
9. AIR (tenor)The enemy said, I will pursue, I will overtake
10. AIR (soprano)Thou didst blow with the wind, the sea covered them
11. CHORUS Who is like unto Thee, O Lord
12. DUET (alto and tenor) Thou in thy mercy hast led forth Thy people
13. CHORUS The people shall hear and be afraid
14. AIR Thou shalt bring them in, and plant them
15. CHORUS The Lord shall reign for ever and ever
16. RECITATIVE (tenor) For the horse of Pharaoh went in with his chariots
17. DOUBLE CHORUS The Lord shall reign for ever and ever
18. RECITATIVE And Miriam the prophetess
19. SOPRANO and CHORUS Sing ye to the Lord

The story *Israel in Egypt* and the splitting of the Red Sea is spread over fifteen chapters in the Book of Exodus (Exod. 1–15). Ingeniously, the libretto for Part 1 was not compiled from Exodus, but was pieced together by Handel's friend, Charles Jennens,[8] from three didactic psalms that graphically recount the ten plagues of Egypt (Ps. 105:23–38; Ps. 78:12–13, 43–54; and Ps. 106:9–12). Part 2, on the other hand, is based entirely on the "Song at the Red Sea" (Exod. 15:1–18).

---

8. Charles Jennens (1700–1773) was an English landowner and patron of the arts. He was educated at Balliol College, Oxford, and put together librettos for five of Handel's oratorios: *Messiah, Saul, Belshazzar, Israel in Egypt* and *L'Allegro il Penseroso ed il Moderato*. See Clifford Bartlett, Introduction to *Messiah*, Oxford Choral Works (Oxford University Press, 1998).

Israel in Egypt is first and foremost a theatrical work, replete with color, atmosphere, and oppositions of all kinds — high and low, loud and soft, massive and thin. All of these dichotomies — diversity vs. unity, and complexity vs. simplicity — serve to enhance the biblical message of the work, a contest between polytheism and monotheism, the many gods of Egypt and the One God of Israel. Separate movements are clearly defined, both in subject matter and form: chorus and orchestra, recitatives and arias, solo ensembles and massed choruses alternate.[9] Each is conceived as a single mood or *affect*, carried through with sweeping momentum and full rounded forms; there is nothing episodic in Handel's approach. Contrast is sought, also within each movement: fugal polyphony and homophonic chordal blocks, for instance, are frequently juxtaposed.

Music and Musical Exegesis

Analyses

Excerpts from Part 1

Musical Imagery

The following examples demonstrate Handel's method of tone painting the ten plagues of Egypt. In the Air for alto solo, *Their land brought forth frogs, yea, even in their king's chambers (Psalm 105:30)* (Part 1, No. 5), we almost hear frogs leaping, portrayed in wide-spaced dotted-note orchestral figures.[10] In the Chorus, *He spake the word* (Part 1, No. 6),[11] we can almost picture flies and lice buzzing through the air, as the strings race frantically up and down the fingerboard. In *He smote all the first born of Egypt, the chief of all their strength (Psalm 105:36, 37)* (Part 1, Chorus No. 9), hammer blow chords in the orchestra depict the smiting

---

9. Handel expanded upon these techniques, borrowed from Venetian polychoral style, in his English Oratorios.

10. Handel's cosmopolitan style combines the aristocratic dotted-note flare of the French march with the graceful and flexible long vocal line of Italian opera. It blends the seriousness of the Lutheran chorale with the involved counterpoint of the German Baroque. It grounds them all in the solid structural designs of the English anthem.

11. *He spake the word, and there came all manner of flies and lice in all quarters. He spake; and the locusts came without number, and devoured the fruits of the ground (Psalm 105:31, 34, 35).*

of the first born. The character of each motif is shaped with clarity and precision, concise thematic elements projecting meaning though musical imagery. It is an extension of the madrigal technique of textual tone painting that Handel undoubtedly absorbed on his Italian sojourn.

Fugue

Chorus No. 11, *Egypt was glad when they departed* is a fugue in two parts. Set in Phrygian mode (e f g a b c d e), it marches along in moderate tempo, characterized by dactyl (long-short-short) and pyrrhic (short-short) rhythms. This theme, repeated 22 times, interprets the first half of the verse. It modulates briefly to the subdominant (A minor) and then back again.[12] A secondary subject, on the latter half of the sentence *for the fear of them fell upon them*, is a diminution of the theme (twice as fast) and set to anapest-like (short-short-long) rhythms. Its fixed rhythm counterpoints the main subject, while its melodic shape twists and turns, adapting itself to the context, like one in *fear*.

Declamation

Ex. 8. Handel: *Israel in Egypt*, Part 1, No.12
Reprinted from original Novello, Ewer and Co.'s Octavo Edition, n.d.

---

12. Fundamentally, it is a diatonic style, in which no attempt is made to exhaust tonal space, so familiar in the works of Bach. Modulations, to closely related keys, do not enter into realms of 'mystical intensity' or chromatic brooding.

A study in contrasts, No. 12, *He rebuked the Red Sea (Ps. 106:9a)* is a double-chorus (SATB/SATB) declamation. Set in high tessitura, the first half verse, *He rebuked the Red Sea* is proclaimed in majestic major mode choral blocks with full orchestral support: a tonal realization of the divine command. The second half of the verse, *and it was dried up (Ps. 106:9b)* is scored for *a cappella* voices in a low register. Its minor mode character is darker and more somber, and underscores the image of the sea humbly obeying its Creator's word.

Tone Painting

Ex. 9. Handel: *Israel in Egypt*, Part 1, No. 13
Reprinted from original Novello, Ewer and Co.'s Octavo Edition, n.d.

Chorus No. 13, *He led them through the deep as through a wilderness (Ps. 106:9)* is a polyphonic movement. The theme marches stepwise, upwards, painting the text, *He led them through the deep.* It then descends by the leap of a seventh, downwards, conveying the *deep* graphically. This duality, between the waters of the sea, *led them through the deep* and the dry expansive desert, *as through a wilderness*, is mirrored in the tonality: an alternation between tonic and dominant (E-flat and B-flat). A meandering sixteenth note figure emerges from the orchestral texture in counterpoint to the theme. Suddenly, this contrasting motif, given choral voice, takes on the character of a second theme, wandering about *as through a wilderness.* All these elements combine in apotheosis.

Texture

Chorus No. 14 contrasts chorus and orchestra. *But the waters overwhelmed their enemies, there was not one of them left (Ps. 106:11)* is declaimed in choral block harmonies, with the orchestra racing around in triplets, graphically symbolizing the *waters overwhelming the enemies.*

Contrasts

The verse, *And Israel saw that great work that the Lord did unto the Egyptians; and the people feared the Lord, and believed the Lord and His servant Moses (Exod. 14:31)* is divided into two separate movements. The first, *And Israel saw that great work* is set massively for double chorus and orchestra (Chorus No. 15). The second (Chorus No. 16), *the people feared the Lord, and believed the Lord and His servant Moses* is a calm and confident fugue.

Excerpts from Part 2

The three sections of Part 2 Nos. 15–17 constitute a rounded three-part unit (ABA): declamation, solo recitative, and chorale-like euphony. It culminates in a climaxing cadence that sums up the entire musical argument in a few chords. This technique, in which various elements are succinctly drawn together and concluded in unity, is akin to a moralizing maxim at the conclusion of a sermon.

Tonality

Ex. 10. Handel: *Israel in Egypt*, Part 2, No. 15
Reprinted from original Novello, Ewer and Co.'s Octavo Edition, n.d.

The Lord shall reign for ever and ever (Ex. 15:18), colored in brilliant C-major, lends this subject a hymn-like voice. The choral declamation is coupled to a rapidly chugging bass line, enriched by high skipping strings.

Recitative

Ex. 11. Handel: *Israel in Egypt*, Part 2, No. 16
Reprinted from original Novello, Ewer and Co.'s Octavo Edition, n.d.

The narrative recitative for solo tenor succinctly summarizes the *Song at the Red Sea: For the horse of Pharaoh went in with his chariots and with his horsemen into the sea, and the Lord brought again the waters of the sea upon them; but the children of Israel went on dry land in the midst of the sea (Exod. 15:19)*.

Double Chorus

This massive concluding affirmation rounds out the form by repeating the verse, *The Lord shall reign for ever and ever (Exod. 15:18)*. Its climaxing cadence is a majestic tonal symbol of the Bible, as seen through British eyes.[13]

---

13. All that is unique to the aesthetic of English oratorio — i.e. its expansiveness, grandeur and pomp — might be embodied in the phrase *Rule Britannica*,

Nyack College Library

Conclusion

The relation between Part 1 and Part 2 of the oratorio contrasts different approaches to narrative and poetic text. Handel's graphic descriptions of the *Ten Plagues*, in Part 1, draw from narrative prose episodes, but present them in concise rounded forms. The poetic *Song at the Sea* treats singular verses with the same expansive attention. The plagues of Egypt took place over the period of a year; yet, the *Song at the Sea* occurs almost at once.[14] This approach offers us opportunity to discuss the treatment of artistic 'time' from different perspectives. How does Handel convey the significance of time passing *vis a vis* human experience? At the sea, action comes to a standstill, as the emotion of a single moment is savored in all its cosmic resonance. Here, Handel's devotes fully as much attention to the momentary exaltation of the redeemed at the sea, as the prolonged suffering of the enslaved in Egypt. Particularly striking is Handel's economical use of text,[15] which functions as scaffolding for original and highly musical exegesis. In depicting the ten plagues, for example, a single motive (*affect*) and a few words, suffice for an entire movement. In the verse by verse settings of *Song at the Red Sea*, each short verbal statement provides enough material to inspire in Handel an intense musical probing into the depths of exaltation, overflowing in a well of joy and salvation.[16]

The Bible is essentially more concerned with historiography and the

---

a microcosm of 18th-century Britain's self-image. This phrase first appeared, after Handel died, in a popular song. *When Britain first, at Heaven's command, / Arose from out the azure main; This was the charter of the land,/ And guardian angels sang this strain: "Rule, Britannia! rule the waves: "Britons never will be slaves."* See The *Works of James Thomson* by James Thomson, published 1763, Vol II, 191.

14. Undoubtedly, its text was repeatedly culled by the redeemed Israelites on endless nights in the desert, as they mulled over the miraculous circumstances that led to their deliverance.

15. The great Italian master Monteverdi, wrote in the early 17th century: "Speech should be master of music, not its servant." Curt Sachs, *Our Musical Heritage* (Englewood Cliffs, NJ: Prentice-Hall, 1955) 172. Handel does not follow speech, in the manner of the early Baroque, but rather, imposes his will upon the text.

16. The conception of praise as something deep and broad is characteristic of the great composers, beyond a merely superficial release of energy (i.e. let's be happy).

import of the moral act than it is with a recitation of historical facts. Handel contrives to reorient chronological time in relation to emotional and spiritual significance, just as episodes are presented in the Bible; many years vanish in an instant, while a poignant moment may endure for eternity. His approach to text and time reflects, in music, one of the great mysteries of art and life: Is it rationality or revelation, pathos or logos, feeling or logic, wisdom or beauty — the eschatological puzzle of the Bible.

Other Directions

Gioachino Rossini: Moses in Egypt (1818)
Text: Leon Tottola
Genre: Italian Opera Seria
Libretto: Andrea Leone Tottola
Medium: Soloists, chorus and orchestra
Style: Bel Canto
First Performance: Naples, 1818

Characters:
Moses
Pharaoh
Amenophis, Pharaoh's son, loves Anai, a Hebrew slave at court
Eliezer (Aaron), Moses' brother
Osiride, High Priest of Isis
Sinaide, Pharaoh's wife
Anai, Miriam's daughter, loves Amenophis, son of Pharaoh
Marie (Miriam), Moses' sister

This three-act Italian opera by Gioachino Rossini (1792–1868), chronicles the story of Moses liberating the Israelites and guiding them out of Egypt. The plot is interwoven with a dramatic love story, not found in the Bible. The affair between Pharaoh's son, Amenophis, and Moses' niece, Anai, is based on an eighteenth-century drama in which Miriam's daughter had to choose between her love for Amenophis and her loyalty to God and her people. Gioachino Rossini's opera *Mosé in Egitto* was later revised in a French version, entitled *Moïse*. Included in the work is the "Prayer of Moses," a favorite subject (throughout the 19th century) for fantasias, variations, and arrangements. A French adaptation, entitled *Moise et Pharaon (ou Le Passage de la Mer Rouge)* (Moses and Pharaoh or Passage through the Red Sea) was premiered at the Paris Opera on March 26, 1827, with a libretto by Luigi Balocchi and Etienne de Jouy. This is Grand Opera at its best — with virtuoso arias, vast choral scenes, spectacular tableaux and ballet.[17]

Folk Song

From the Renaissance era, the story of Moses and the Israelites inspired many musical compositions, as well as Jewish and other folk songs. Better know than many operas and oratorios is the Afro-American Spiritual, *Go Down Moses*. Originating as a plea to free the slaves, before the American Civil War (1860–1865), the phrase, "Let my people go" has been associated with the American Civil Rights Movement of the 1960s, as well as with the Free World's support of Soviet Jewry's resistance to the Communist regime in the 1970s and 1980s.

> When Israel was in Egypt's land; let my people go.
> Oppressed so hard they could not stand; let my people go.
> Go down Moses, way down in Egypt's land,
> Tell ole Pharaoh to let my people go.

> "Thus spoke the Lord," bold Moses said; let my people go.
> If not I'll smite your first born dead; let my people go.
> Go down Moses, way down in Egypt's land,
> Tell ole Pharaoh to let my people go.

Related Works

Some historical settings of texts and episodes from the Book of Exodus include: Jachet van Berchem, *Locutus est Dominus ad Moysen; Stetit Moyses coram Pharaone* (motets, printed 1538–59); Claudio Monteverdi, *Audi coelum* (motets, added to the *Vesperae* of 1610); Giovanni Paolo Colonna, *Mosé legato di Dio e liberatore del popolo ebreo* (oratorio, 1686); Giovanni Battista Bassani, *Mosé risorto dalle acque* (oratorio, 1694); Antonio Vivaldi, *Moyses Deus Pharaonis* (oratorio, 1714; libretto

---

17. The success of the opera coincided with interest in things Egyptian, as a result of Napoleon's Egyptian campaign, which brought Egyptian antiquities to France, among them, the Rosetta stone in 1822, and led to the decipherment of hieroglyphs.

only preserved); Johann Adolf Hasse (1699–1783), *Serpentes in deserto* (oratorio); Nicolo Porpora (1686–1768), *Israel ab Aegyptiis liberatus* (oratorio); Carl Philipp Emanuel Bach, *Die Israeliten in der Wueste* (oratorio, text by Schiebler, 1775, and first performed in Breslau, 1798); François Giroust, *Le Mont-Sinai ou Le Decalogue* (oratorio, Latin text, 1785); Johann Christophe Friedrich Bach, *Mosis Mutter und ihre Tochter* (duo drama, 1788); Giovanni Paisello (1740–1816), *Mosé in Egitto* (cantata for three voices); Konradin Kreutzer, *Die Sendung Mosis* (oratorio, 1814).

Works List

Moses

Admon, Jedidiah (1894 Russia–1974 Israel). *U-Moshe hikah al sela*, 2 voices and choir.

Alcedo, Jose Bernardo (1788–1878 Lima). *Cantemus Domino* (Exod. 15), 6 voices and organ.

Alman, Shmuel (1887 Ukraine–1947 London). *Mi kamokha baelim Adonay* (Exod. 15:11–12), choir and organ.

Antonelli, Abondio (16th C. Rome). *Cantemus Domino* (Exod. 15:1–3), 4 voices and basso-continuo.

Bach, Johann Christoph Friedrich (1642–1703 Germany). *Mosis Mutter und ihre Tochter*, duodrama.

Barberio, Francesco (18th C. Italy). *Moyses e Nilo servatus*, oratorio.

Bassani, Giovanni Battista (1657–1716 Italy). *Mosé risorto dale acque*, oratorio.

Bazzani, Francesco Maria (17th C. Italy). *Mosé in Egitto*, oratorio.

Beaumesnil, Henriette Adelaide Villard de (1758–1813 Paris). *Les Israelites poursuivis par Pharaon*, oratorio.

Bencini, Antonio (18th C. Rome). *Angelo e Mosé*, 2 voices and violoncello.

Berlijn, Anton Aron (1817–1870 Amsterdam). *Moses auf Nebo* (L. Philippson), oratorio.

Boisdeffre, Rene Le Mouton de (c.1834–1906 France). *Moise sauve des eaux* (P. Colin), oratorio.

Bonfichi, Paolo (1769–1840 Italy). *Mose ossia di passaggio del Mare Rosso*, oratorio.

Borghi, Gionvanni Battista (1738–1796 Italy). *La spozalizio di Moze*, cantata.

Bruch, Max (1838 Koln–1920 Berlin). *Moses* (L. Spitta), oratorio.

Casali, Giovanni Battista (1715–1792 Rome). *Il roveto di Mose*, oratorio.

Castrisanu, Constantin (1888 Bucharest–1923). *Moise* (De Vigny), voice and pianoforte.

Colonna, Giovanni Paolo (1637–1695 Bologne). *Il Mose* (G.B. Giardini), oratorio.

Columbani, Quirino (fl.1690 Italy). *Acta Moysis in deserta* (A. Checchio), oratorio.

Conti, Francesco Bartholomeo (1682 Florence–1732 Vienna). *Mosé preservato*, oratorio.

Czernohorsky, Bohuslav M. (1684–1742 Europe). *Praecatus est Moises*, choir.

Dallapiccola, Luigi (1904–1975 Florence). *Canti di liberatione* (Exod. 15:3–5), choir and orchestra.

David, Felicien-Cesar (1810–1876 France). *Moise au Sinai*, oratorio.

De Grandis, Vincenzo (1631–1708 Italy). *L'esodo de Mose dall'Egitto* (G. Giardini), oratorio.

Dett, R. Nathaniel (1872 Quebec–1943 Ohio). *The Ordering of Moses*, soloists, choir and orchestra.

Drobisch, Karl Ludwig (1803 Leipzig–1854 Augsburg). *Moses auf Sinai*, oratorio.

Duquesnoy, Charles (1759–1822 Brussels). *Song of Moses*, cantata.

Engel, Joel (1868 Russia–1927 Tel Aviv). *Be-Erets Goshen* (Halperin), voice & pianoforte.

Ettinger, Max (1874 Lviv–1951 Basel). *Az yashir Mosheh* (Exod. 15), soloist, choir and orchestra.

Franck, Cesar (1822–1890 Paris). *Cantique de Moise* (Exodus 14), cantata.

Fromm, Herbert (1905 Germany–1995 Boston). *Mi kamokha ba-elim Adonay* (Exodus 15), tenor, choir and organ.

_____. *Shirat Miryam* (Exodus 15), choir and organ.

Furlanetto, Bonaventura (1738–1817 Venice). *Moyses in Nilo*, oratorio.

Galuppi, Baldassare (1706–1785 Venice). *Exitus Israelis de Aegypto* (P. Chiari), oratorio.

_____. *Moyses de Synai revertens* (P. Chiari), oratorio.

Gasparini, Francesco (1668–1727 Rome). *Moise liberato dal Nill*, oratorio.

Gaul, Alfred (1837–1913 England). *Israel in the wilderness*, oratorio.

Grandis, Renato de (b.1927 Venice). *L'esorto de Mose dall'Egitto*, oratorio.

Hajdu, Andre (1932 Budapest/1966 Israel). *The Song of the Sea* (Exod. 15), choir.

Handel, George Frederick (1685–1759 London). *Israel in Egypt*, oratorio.

Hassler, Leo (1564–1612 Germany). *Die zehn Gebote Gottes* (Exodus 20), choir.

Hast, Marcus (1871 Warsaw–1911 London). *The Death of Moses*, oratorio.

Haudebert, Lucien (1877–1963 France). *Moise*, oratorio.

Hemsi, Alberto (1898 Rhodes–1964 Paris). *Adonay, Adonay, El rahum* (Exod. 34:6), choir.

Jacquet de la Guerre, Elisabeth (1667–1729 Paris). *Le passage de la Mer Rouge* (A.H. de la Monte), cantata, voice, instruments, and basso-continuo.

James, Philip (1890–1975 New Jersey). *Shirat ha-yam* (Exodus 15), choir and organ.

Jumentier, Bernard (1749–1829 France). *La passage de la Mer Rouge*, oratorio.

Konigsloew, Johann (1745 Hamburg–1833). *Die Rettung des Kindes Mose*, oratorio.

Kozeluch, Leopold Anton (1784 Prague–1818 Vienna). *Mose in Egitto*, sacred act.

Kreutzer, Konradin (1780 Germany–1949 Riga, Latvia). *Moses Sendung*, oratorio.

Kunzen, Adolph Carl (1720–1781 Germany). *Israel's Abgoettery in der Wuesten*, oratorio.

Lachner, Franz Paul (1803–1890 Munich). *Moses* (E. Bauernfeld), oratorio.

Lang-Zaimont, Judith (b.1945 Queens, New York). *Moses supposes*, 3 part canon, voices, and percussion.

Lange, Samuel (1840 Rotterdam–1911 Stuttgart). *Moses*, oratorio.

Laurenti, Bartolomeo-Girolamo (1644–1726 Bologna). *Mosé infante liberato dal fiumme*, oratorio.

Leopold I (1658–1705 Vienna). *Die Erloesung des menschliden Geschlechts in der Figur des aus Aegypten gefuehren Volks Israel* (J.A. Rudolf), oratorio.

Lockwood, Normand (1906 New York–2002 Denver). *The Birth of Moses* (Exod. 2), women's voices, flute, and pianoforte.

Ludkewicz, Stanislaw (1879–1980 Lvov). *Moysey* (J. Franko), symphonic tableau.

Lugojan, Trifon (1874–1948 Romania). *La muntele Sinaiului*, religious concert.

Mangold, Carl Amand (1813 Darmstadt–1889). *Israel in der Wueste*, cantata.

Marx, Adolf Bernhard (1795–1866 Berlin). *Moses*, oratorio.

Massenet, Jules (1842–1912 Paris). *La Terre Promise*, oratorio.

Mendelssohn, Felix (1809 Hamburg–1847 Leipzig). *Da Israel aus Aegypten zog* (Ps. 114), 8 voices and choir.

Milhaud, Darius (1892 France–1974 Geneva). *The Man of Midian Opus Americanum No. 2)*, suite for orchestra.

Mondonville, Jean Josephe (1711–1772 France). *Les Israelites a la montagne d'Horeb*, oratorio.

Naylor, John (1838–1897 England). *The Brazen Serpent*, cantata.

_____. *Meribah*, cantata.

_____. *Manna*, cantata.

Orefice, Giacomo (1865–1922 Milano). *Mosé* (H. Orvieto), opera.

Paganini, Nicolo (1782 Genoa–1840). *Dal tuo stellato soglio da Mose di Rossini*, violin and pianoforte.

Paisible, Louis Henri (1745 Paris–1782 St. Petersburg). *Les Israelites sur la montagne d'Horebe*, oratorio.

Paisiello, Giovanni (1740–1816 Naples). *Mosé in Egitto*, cantata, 3 soloists, choir and orchestra.

Pasquini, Bernardo (1637–1710 Rome). *I fatti di Mosé in deserto* (G.B. Giardini), oratorio.

Perosi, Lorenzo (1872–1956 Rome). *Il Mose*, oratorio.

Persius, Luis-Luc (1769–1862 London). *Le passage de la Mer Rouge*, oratorio.

Perti, Giacomo Antonio (1661–1756 Bologne). *Mose* (G.B. Giardini), oratorio.

Piosello, Ioannes Baptisa (18th C. Italy). *Moses infantulus Nilo expositus*, oratorio.

Porpora, Nicola (1686–1768 Naples). *Israel ab Aegyptus liberatus*, oratorio.

Porsile, Giuseppe (1672 Naples–1750 Vienna). *Mosé liberato dal Nilo*, sacred act.

Predieri, Giacomo Cesare (1671–1753 Bologne). *Mosé bambino esposto al Nilo*, oratorio.

Pulkingham, Betty Carr (b.1928 North Carolina). *The Song of Moses* (Exod. 15:1–6, 15), 2 mixed voices, piano or guitar.

Rigel, Heinrich Joseph (1741–1799 Paris). *La sortie d'Egypte*, oratorio.

Rogers, Bernard (1893–1968 New York). *The Exodus*, cantata.

Rolle, Johann Heinrich (1716–1785 Germany). *Die Befreiung Israels*, oratorio.

Rollin, Jean Louis (1906 Paris–1977). *Moise* (A. de Vigny), oratorio.

Rosowsky, Boruch-Leib (1841 Vilnius–1919 Riga). *El erekh apayim* (Num. 34), tenor, choir, and organ.

Rosowsky, Solomon (1878 Riga–1962 New York). *Shirat Mosheh* (Exod. 15), tenor, choir, and pianoforte.

Rossini, Gioacchino Antonio (1792–1868 Paris). *Mose in Egitto* (A.L. Tottola), oratorio.

_____. *Moise et Pharaon* (L. Balocchi), opera.

Rubinstein, Anton (1829–1894 St. Petersburg). *Moses* (S. Mosenthal), oratorio.

Rudnicki, Antin (1902 Ukraine–1975 USA). *Moysey* (I. Franko), tenor and symphony orchestra.

Russel, William (1777–1813 London). *The Deliverance of Israel*, oratorio.

Sabra, Wadia (1876–1952 Lebanon). *Le chant de Moise*, oratorio.

Saint-Saens, Charles-Camille (1835 Paris–1921 Algier). *Moise sauve des eaux* (V. Hugo), oratorio.

Schneider, Johann Christian Friedrich (1786–1853 Germany). *Pharao* (A. Brueg-gemann), oratorio.

Schmitt, Aloys (1788–1866 Frankfurt). *Moses*, oratorio.

Schoenberg, Arnold (1874 Vienna–1951 Los Angeles). *Moses and Aaron* (A. Schoenberg), opera.

Schorr, Baruch (1823–1904 Ukraine). *Adonay, Adonay, El rahum ve-hanun* (Exodus 34:6), tenor and choir.

Schuster, Joseph (1748–1812 Dresden). *Mose riconosciuto* (G.A. Migliavacca), oratorio.

Schutz, Heinrich (1585–1672 Dresden). *Der Herr ist meine Staerke* (Exod. 15:1–11), choir.

Seter, Mordechai (1916 Russia–1994 Tel Aviv). *Va-yehi va-yamim ha-rabim ha-hem* (Exod. 2:23–25), motet, a cappella choir.

Sharet, Jehuda (1901 Russia–1979 Neveh Yam, Israel). *Seder shel Pesah*, narrator, choir and folk instruments.

Suessmayr, Franz Xaver (1766–1803 Vienna). *Moses, oder der Auszug aus Aegypten*, opera.

Tal, Joseph (1910 Germany/1936 Israel–2008). *Exodus*, choreographic poem.

_____. *Mot Moshe* (Y. Ya'ari), choir, soloist, orchestra and electronic music.

_____. *Exodus I* (1946) for baritone & orchestra.

Telemann, Georg Philipp (1681–1767 Hamburg). *Das befreite Israel* (Exod. 15), oratorio.

Toch, Ernst (1887 Vienna–1964 Santa Monica, California). *Cantata of Bitter Herbs*, voices and instruments.

Tuczek, Johann (1755 Prague–1820 Budapest). *Moses in Aegypten* (Gleich), oratorio.

Uber, Christian Benjamin (1746–1812 Wroclaw). *Moses* (Klingermann), incidental music.

Ulbrich, Ignaz (1706–1796 Vienna). *Die Israeliten in der Wueste*, oratorio.

Veracini, Francesco-Maria (1690–1768 Florence). *La liberazione del popolo ebreo dal naufragio di Faraone*, oratorio.

Vincenzo de Grandis de (1631–1708 Italy). *Il nascimento di Mose* (G. Giardini), oratorio.

_____. *Ritrata di Mose dall'Egitto e suoi sponsali con Sefora* (Exodus 2), oratorio.

Vivaldi, Antonio (1675 Venice–1741 Vienna). *Moyses Deus Pharaonis* (G. Casetti), oratorio.

Vogt, Gustave (1781 Strassburg–1879 Paris). *Trio on a theme from Moise* (Rossini), oboe, violin, viola, pianoforte.

Vuataz, Roger (1898–1988 Geneva). *Moise* (R. Vuataz), oratorio.

Wagenseil, Georg Christoph (1715–1777 Vienna). *Il roveto di Mosé* (G. Pizzi), oratorio.

Wambach, Emiel-Xaver (1854–1924 Antwerp). *Mozes op de Nijl* (E. Van Herendael), oratorio.

Weil, Kurt (1900 Germany–1950 New York). *Passover Haggadah* (M. Brod, J. Langer).

Weinberg, Jacob (1879 Odessa–1956 New York). *Moses*, soloist, choir, orchestra and organ, oratorio.

Wolfurt, Kurt (1880 Latvia–1957 Munich). *Siegeslied des Moses*, choir, tenor, orchestra, and organ.

Wolpe, Stephan (1902 Germany–1972 New York). *Exodus*, choreographic, symphonic poem.

Zacharia, Freidrich-Wilhelm (1663 Leipzig–1712). *Das befreite Israel* (Exod. 15), soloists, soprano, alto, tenor, 1 bass, 2 basses, orchestra.

Israel/Exodus

Adler, Samuel (b.1928 Germany/1939 USA). *A Song of Exaltation* (Exod. 15:1–6, 11, 18), SATB, organ.

Alman, Shmuel (1887 Ukraine–1947 UK). *Adonay el rachum* (Exod. 34–6), tenor & chorus.

Bach, Carl Philipp Emanuel (1714–1788). *Die Israeliten in der Wueste*, oratorio.

Baristow, Edward (1874–1946 UK). *Sing Ye to the Lord* (Exod. 15: 4, 21), SATB, organ.

Berger, Jean (1909 Germany–2002 USA). *Who Is Like Unto Thee* (Exod. 15:11), SATB.

Bloch, Ernest (1880 Geneva–1959 Portland, Oregon). *Mi kamokha ba-elim* (Exod. 15:11), baritone, choir, orchestra.

Dessau, Paul (1894 Cesje Budejovice/Hamburg/1939 USA–1979 Berlin). *Haggadah* (M. Brod and J. Langer after the Passover Haggadah), oratorio.

Feliciano, Richard (b.1930 USA). *I Will Sing to the Lord* (from *Songs for Darkness and Light*) (Exod. 15:1–2), 3 equal voices.

Gilboa, Jacob (1920 Slovakia/1938 Israel–2007). *Twelve Chagall Windows* (12 Israeli tribes) Deut., soprano, vocal ensemble and orchestra.

Gottlieb, Jack (b.1930 NYC). *Mi Chamocha* (Exod. 15:11), SATB, cantor, organ, percussion.

Grandis, Renato de (b.1927 Venice). *L'Esorto de Mose dall 'Egitto* Exodus, oratorio.

Hassler, Leo (1564 Nuemberg–1612). *Cantemus Domino* (Exod. 15:1–2), chorus.

Hopson, Hal (b.1933 Texas). *The Lord Is My Strength and My Song* (Exod. 15:2), unison, keyboard, bells and percussion.

Lasso, Orlando di (1532 Mons–1594 Muenchen). *Das vokck von Israel verfolgt Pharao*, from In exitu Israel (Ps. 113) 6 vs.

Levy, Ernst (1895–1981 Basel). *Symphonia* (Shema Israel), chorus and orchestra.

Nowakowski, David (1848 Kiev–1921 Odessa). *V'shomru vney Israel* (Exod. 31:16–18), choir and organ.

_____. *Mi chamocha* (Exod., 15), chorus.

Pethel, Stan (b.1950 Georgia). *I Will Sing Unto the Lord* (Exod. 15:1–2), SATB, 2 trumpets, horn, 2 trombones.

Reynolds, William J. (b.1920 Texas). *I Will Sing Unto the Lord* (Exod. 15: 1–2, 11), unison w. descant, keyboard.

Saint-Saens, Charles-Camile (1835 Paris–1921 Algier). *La Terre promise*, oratorio.

Scarlatti, Francesco (1660–1725 Palermo). *Israel per Foeminam triumphans* (Ph. Capistrellius), oratorio.

Sternberg, Erich-Walter (1898 Berlin/1931 Israel–1974 Tel Aviv). *Twelve Tribes of Israel*), orchestra.

Viviani, Giovanni Bonaventura (17ᵗʰ C. Florence). *Faraone* (Exodus), oratorio.

Weisgall, Hugo (1912 Moravia–1997 USA). *Who Is Like Unto Thee* (Exod. 15: 11, 18), baritone, SATB, keyboard.

Miriam

Fromm, Herbert (1905 Germany–1995 USA). *Song of Miriam* (Exod. 15: 20–21), SSA, baritone or soprano, piano, percussion.

Dett, Nathaniel (1882–1943 USA). *The Song of Miriam* (Exod. 15:20–22), SSA, soprano, keyboard.

The Ten Commandments

Giroust, Francois (1750 Paris–1799). *Le Mont-Sinai ou la Decalogue*, cantata.

Haydn, Joseph (1732–1809). *The Holy Ten Commandments* (Exod. 20: 2–17), canon 3–5 voices.

Lee, T. Charles (1915–1994 USA). *The Face of Moses Shone* (Exod. 19:1, 16–17), SATB, organ.

Schalit, Henrich (1886 Austria–1951 USA). *The Sacred Covenant* (Exod. 19:5–6), SATB, organ.

G. Dore: The Giving of the Law Upon Mount Sinai, *Bible Illustrations (1866)*

8

Ernest Bloch's *Sacred Service (Avodath Hakodesh)*, based on Reform Jewish liturgy, is a 20th-century concert work whose character and spiritual ethos derive from forms of worship and prayer traceable to rituals in the Book of Leviticus.

LEVITICUS

And Aaron lifted up his hands toward the people and blessed them; and he came down from offering the sin-offering, and the burnt offering, and the peace offerings. And Moses and Aaron went into the tent of meeting, and came out and blessed the people; and the glory of the Lord appeared unto all the people. And there came forth fire from before the Lord, and consumed upon the altar the burnt offering and the fat; and when all the people saw it, they shouted, and fell on their faces (Leviticus 9:22–24).

The central feature of the Sanctuary cult was the sacrifice. The Book of Leviticus describes the functions of the Priesthood, the details of animal sacrifice, and the duty of Holiness: *Ye shall be holy; for I the Lord your God am holy (Lev. 19:2).* Various individual and communal sacrifices are enumerated in the first ten chapters of Leviticus, while additional Daily public sacrifices and Festival Offerings appear in the Book of Numbers (chapters 28 and 29).

Ultimately, all Western liturgies can be traced back to the daily sacrifices offered by Moses, through the high priest Aaron and his sons, at the Tabernacle in the desert.[1] The procedure of the service was as

---

1. The well-known Talmudic prescription, 'a teaching of Moses from Sinai' *(Halacha le-Moshe mi-Sinai),* refers to laws, prayers, and ritual practices which have no Scriptural origin. It is an authentic description of a cultural heritage, buried beneath the sands of time. These "laws given to Moses at Sinai" are ancient "received traditions" neither stated nor derived from

follows: The priests would offer sacrifices; then, the High Priest would raise his hands and bless the people. While sacrifices were being burnt on the altar, Levites, accompanied by instruments, would sing psalms.[2] Around these rituals, Jewish liturgy evolved. Christian rite and its chant, which are rooted in Jewish liturgy, borrowed and stylized many ritualistic elements from the Temple and the synagogue.[3] The Office Hours of the Church are modeled after the prayer hours of the Jews; while the Mass, a mystic repetition of the Last Supper, derives from the Jewish Passover Seder that Jesus celebrated with his disciples.[4]

Ernest Bloch: Sacred Service (Avodath Hakodesh) (1930–1933)[5]

Text: Sabbath Morning Service
Genre: Liturgical
Medium: Cantor, choir, and orchestra (or organ)
Style: Modal
First Performance: Radio Turin, Italy, 1934
Duration: ca. 1 hour

Ernest Bloch wrote from the Swiss village, where he settled to compose *Avodath Hakodesh* (1930–1933), "I have now memorized entirely the whole service. Though intensely Jewish in its roots; this message seems to me above all a gift of Israel to the whole of humanity."[6] Bloch's *Sacred Service* is the first work ever written on a Jewish liturgical text, which is, at the same time, also frequently performed as a universal expression of religious devotion in churches and concert halls. Bloch conducted its premiere at Turin in 1934.

Scripture, but possessing biblical authority.

2.   A.Z. Idelsohn, "Forms of Worship and Prayer during the First Temple," in *Jewish Liturgy and Its Development* (NY: Shocken, 1972) 10–16.

3.   The traditional Passover Seder is found in the *Haggadah*. For further information on the interconnection between Early Christian and Jewish rituals, see Eric Werner, "The Liturgical and Musical Traits of the Earliest Christian Community," *The Sacred Bridge* (NY: Columbia University Press, 1963) 17–26.

4.   Willi Apel, "The Pre-Christian Roots," *Gregorian Chant* (Bloomington: Indiana University Press, 1958) 34–35.

5.   *Avodath Hakodesh* was commissioned with guidance from Cantor Reuben Rinder (1887–1966) by Gerald Warburg for Temple Emanuel Reform Synagogue in San Francisco (1929).

6.   Strassburg, Robert, *Ernest Bloch: Voice in the Wilderness* (Los Angeles: California State University, 1977).

Biographic Context

Ernest Bloch (1880 Geneva–1959 Portland, Oregon) is the foremost creator of Jewish music in the 20th century and the first composer of world stature to think in terms of Jewish consciousness. He studied violin, eurhythmics, and composition in Geneva, Brussels, Munich, and Paris. In 1916, he came to the United States with Maud Allan's ballet company,[7] as conductor of her American tour and remained in the United States, later to assume directorship of the Cleveland Institute of Music (1920–1925) and San Francisco Conservatory (1925–1930). He left for Switzerland in 1930, but returned to the U.S. before World War II. He served as professor of music at the University of California in Berkeley, until his retirement in 1952.

The following essay seeks to bridge the conceptual gap between the liturgy set to music by Bloch and its biblical origin.[8]

From Sacrifice to Liturgy

Longer than recorded history, so long as men have worshiped "sacred spirit," they have done so through the sacrificial cult, with altar and sanctuary. Primitive people would offer prayers at regular, fixed times: at sunrise and sunset, at the changes of the moon and seasons of the year, and on occasions of sowing and reaping. In the Bible, the building of altars and the offering of sacrifices formed an essential part of public ritual. Prayers and blessings without

---

7. Maud Allan (1873 Toronto–1956 Los Angeles) trained in Europe, danced to critical acclaim in London, and from 1910–1918 toured the world. Her style of interpretive dancing helped expand the horizons of modern dance. Although she is now almost forgotten, at the height of her success, Maude Allen was as well known as Isadora Duncan.

8. The traditional Sabbath service is divided into six sections: 1. Daily Morning Blessings (*Birchat Hashachar*) 2. Verses of Song (*Pesuke D'Zimra*) 3. *Shema* and its blessings 4. Standing Prayer (*Amidah*) 5. Torah reading 6. Closing psalms, readings, adoration, and closing hymn. Bloch sets *Avodath Hakodesh* in 5 movements, telescoping sections 1, 2 and 3 into Part 1; Extracting the Sanctification from the *Amidah* for Part 2; Dividing the Torah service in half, turning the removal and return of the scroll into Parts 3 and 4. Part 5 sets the final adoration and closing hymn, while the closing priestly benediction or dismissal (also in the Catholic Mass), derives from the ancient priestly rite in the Tabernacle.

sacrifices, however, reach back as far as the patriarchs.[9] The Bible records prayers made by Abraham, Isaac, and Jacob. Moses, whose prayers are often cited, is never recorded as having prayed during sacrifices. Thus, while public and private prayer appears to have coexisted with sacrifice in the Bible, sacrifice, without prayer and confession is devoid of spiritual significance. *The sacrifice of the wicked is an abomination to the Lord; but the prayer of the upright is his delight (Proverbs 15:8).*

Symbolism and Character of the Sacrificial Rites

The essence of worship, in all liturgies is Praise and Petition. Praise, adoration, or thanksgiving finds expression in the burnt offering, meal offering, and peace offering. Petition, as supplication or confession, finds expression in the sin offering and guilt offering. The sublimation of the physical act of sacrifice, by means of verbalization, is the catalyst that created liturgical texts we utter to this day: *Take with you words, and turn to the Lord: say unto him, Take away iniquity, and receive us graciously; so will we offer [the words of] our lips [instead of] calves (Hosea 14:2).* It was Moses who organized and arranged the sacrificial cult and established the classical patterns of public worship, which later evolved into Jewish liturgy.[10] It would seem that the singing of psalms and chanting of prayers during services dates back to the very beginnings of Israel.[11] These traditions continued in the Tabernacle, and at a later date, all authorities concur that the laudations and prayers of David became the foundation for the Temple Service. Frequently cited is 1 Chronicles, chapters 15 and 16. Mishneh *Tamid* describes the sacrificial rituals as they were practiced during the Second Temple period.

The Daily Public Sacrificial Ritual

The following passage is the basis for the daily public sacrificial ritual: *And the Lord spake unto Moses saying, Command the children of Israel, and say unto them, My oblation, my food for my offerings made by fire, of a sweet savor unto me, shall ye observe*

9. A.Z. Idelsohn, op. cit. 5.
10. Sacrificial procedures (Leviticus 7–10) and their appropriate prayers, confessions, and psalmody date from the period of Israel's wandering in the Sinai desert. By the time of King David these rituals were established traditions.
11. R. Kittel, *Die Psalmen* (Leipzig, 1914) xxxvii, as cited in Idelsohn, note 6, chapter one, op. cit. 353.

to offer unto me in its due season. And thou shalt say unto them, This is the offering made by fire which ye shall offer unto the Lord: he-lambs of the first year without blemish, two, day by day, for a daily burnt offering. The one lamb shalt thou offer in the morning, and the other lamb shalt thou offer at even; and the tenth part of an ephah of fine flour for a meal offering, mingled with the fourth part of a hin of beaten oil. It is a continual burnt offering, which was ordained on Mount Sinai for a sweet savor, an offering made by fire unto the Lord. And the drink offering thereof shall be the fourth part of a hin for the one lamb: in the holy place shalt thou pour out a drink offering of strong drink unto the Lord. And the other lamb shalt thou offer at even; as the meal offering of the morning, and as the drink offering thereof, thou shalt offer it, an offering made by fire, of a sweet savor unto the Lord (Numbers 28:1–8).

The times of the daily sacrifices, eventually developed into the hours of liturgical Jewish prayer, as well as the Office Hours of the Church. The following selection presents, in graphic detail, the procedures of ritual sacrifice in the Second Temple: *This is the rite of the daily burnt-offering in the Service of the House of our God.*

The Sacrifices

1. The **burnt offering** was a male animal of the herd or flock, and was entirely burnt on the altar. It symbolized closeness to God, submission to the will of God, and the desire to place one's life in the service of God.
2. The **meal offering** consisted of a mixture of flour and oil. These are products of the soil, which are produced and processed by human toil. They symbolize dedicating and consecrating man's works to the service and "glory of God."
3. The **peace offering** is a joyous sacrifice, a festive celebration in solidarity with others. Only a small part was burnt on the altar. Most of it was eaten in a solemn feast of thanksgiving and gratitude to God, in fulfillment of a vow, or as expression of a blessing received.
4. The **sin offering** is just the opposite. It was offered either by the individual or the community as an admission of error, in expiation for an unfulfilled vow, or for an act committed in a state of ritual impurity. The blood was poured and sprinkled, the fat and inwards were burnt on the altar, while the animal was burnt outside the camp (but not on an altar).
5. The **guilt offering** was in some ways a heroic sacrifice, for it involved public admission of an offence not punishable by law.

It offered new hope to a man burdened by a guilty conscience, restoring him to purity before society and God. It involved: unintentional appropriation of sacred and public property, false oaths, inappropriate use of a deposit or pledge, oppression of others, or some form of embezzlement. It required both a ram, and, the payment of a fine (twenty percent above the trespass committed).[12]

Procedures of Ritual Sacrifice
(Mishneh Tamid 7.3)

1. At the Cockcrow those who would perform the morning sacrifice rise, immerse themselves, sanctify their hands and feet, and choose their respective tasks by lot. They clean the ashes from the evening sacrifice, bring logs for the fire, take coals for the incense, prepare the candlestick, prepare the cakes for the meal offering; and select, slaughter, and quarter the animal.
2. When all is ready, a group of nine priests standing in a row, hold: 1) head, 2) two fore legs, 3) haunch and hind leg, 4) breast and neck, 5) two flanks, 6) innards in a dish, 7) fine flour for a meal offering, 8) cakes, 9) wine for the libation.
3. This group then recites (for themselves) a series of benedictions and passages from Scripture. These selections have become a part of the prayer book liturgy to this day. These are: 1) With abounding love[13] 2) Ten Commandments (Exod. 20:1–17) 3) Shema (Deut. 6:4–9) 4) And it shall come to pass (Deut. 11:13–21).
4. Then, they pronounce three blessings, with the people, in the forecourt. These are: 1) True and firm[14] 2) *Avodah* which became

---

12. These are not empty ceremonial acts, devoid of content or devotion. One must enter hidden recesses of mental anguish and exaltation, in order to fathom their meaning, though. Considerable numbers of people take medication, receive shock therapy, and spend endless sums on psychological treatments — sometimes even undergoing hospitalization — to alleviate the mental burden of guilt, remorse, and depression these ancient rites addressed, and purportedly remedied.
13. *With abounding love hast thou loved us, O Lord our God, and great and overflowing tenderness hast thou shown us... (from Daily Morning prayer).*
14. *True and firm, established and enduring, fair and faithful, beloved and cherished, delightful and pleasant, awesome and powerful, correct and accepted, good and beautiful is this affirmation to us forever and ever... (Daily Morning prayer).*

the original sixteenth blessing of the *Amidah* Prayer[15] 3) Priestly Blessing (Num. 14:37–41).

5. When this row of priests arrived near to the altar, one of them made a loud noise, hurling a tympanum (probably an ancient drum-like instrument, perhaps a *magrepha*), as a signal to the chief priest and the Levite musicians, to take their places, fore the sacrifice ritual was about to begin.

6. They, then, burn the incense and light the candlestick. Then, the priests recite the priestly blessing and utter the Name of the Eternal (Tetragrammaton-YHWH).

7. The Chief Priest, standing on the ramp to the altar, is presented with the various parts of the sacrifice. He lays hands on them, while uttering confessions, prayers, or benedictions, then places them on the altar. When he pours the final wine libation, the Levites begin their service.

8. Two silver trumpets sound blasts, the cymbal is struck, and the Levites break into "words of song" (a kind of chanting). They sing the Psalm of the day, pausing at the end of each line (or paragraph), at which time, the trumpets are sounded, and the people prostrate themselves.

Ever since the erection of the Tabernacle in the desert (c.1440 B.C.), the daily continual sacrifice, offered twice daily throughout the year, constituted a model for structured public worship. This paradigm, which continued during Temple times, was spiritualized after its destruction. With the cessation of ritual sacrifice the blessings, prayers, and confessions of the priests, supplemented by Scriptural readings, formed the conceptual framework for synagogue liturgy. Divine Service as prayer, fulfilled the complex human needs for praise, petition, and historic recollection. The qualities and attitudes of these prayers became a sublimated sacrificial act, addressing Indwelling Essence, which sacred music aspires to arouse and give voice to.[16]

Text and Context

The Book of Leviticus (chapters 1–6) details sacrificial offerings, which,

---

15. *Accept O Eternal, our God your people...and may the service of your people Israel always be favorable to You... (Amidah prayer).*

16. The prophet Hosea coined the classic phrase, which gives legal sanction to the procedure of substituting prayer for animal sacrifice: *We will render the offering of our lips in place of bullocks (Hosea 14:3).*

in their essence, are attuned to basic emotional attitudes, responses, and conceptions about the nature of the human soul and its relationship to God. The character and symbolism of sacrifice, thus, found expression in the music of the synagogue and church. Bloch sets the "Sabbath Morning Service" from the Reform Jewish ritual according to the *Union Prayerbook* (1918), an abridgement of traditional liturgy, which, itself is based on ancient sources reaching back to Temple rituals.[17] *Avodath Hakodesh* strives to evoke a spirit, whose essence is the Word.

Music and Musical Exegesis

Bloch's motifs are derived from word rhythms and word inflections. Notably absent are repetitive pulsations and rhythmic energies of dance. Harmonic style is modal, fundamentally triadic, but enriched with exotic, augmented seconds and fourths. Sonorities are often colored by shifting planes of parallel perfect fourths and fifths, recalling primitive organum, and lending a ritualistic tinge to the work.

Analyses

PART III
Torah Service

This section of the Sabbath Morning liturgy involves opening the Ark of the Law, removing the Torah scroll, and carrying it to the reader's desk. Bloch invests the whole procedure, which takes less than a minute to perform in the synagogue, with an archaic grandeur that derives from the ceremony of ritual sacrifice. Selections from the Torah Service (Part III) are linked by solo instrumental and orchestra interludes, which function as congregational meditations.

---

17. Reform Jewish liturgy revised traditional religious concepts, such as: Jews as a Chosen people, a personal Messiah, Resurrection, and the expectation of a return to the Land of Israel. References to the role of the priesthood and sacrificial offerings were also removed, notably, the excision of the *Musaf* service on Sabbath and Holidays.

Ex. 12. Ernest Bloch: *Avodath Hakodesh (Sacred Service)*

© Copyright 1934 Summy-Birchard, renewed 1962 by Broude Brothers. Used by permission.

SILENT DEVOTION

The Silent devotion is a spare instrumental dialogue, designed to awaken sacred atmosphere. It is a prelude to worship, and may be understood as the preparation of the priests for the service.

CHOIR (Meditation before the Ark)

O Lord, may the words of my mouth and the meditations of my heart be acceptable before Thee, Adonoy, my Rock and Redeemer. Amen.

(Psalm 19:15)

The meditation which precedes the sacrificial act is a Psalm verse.[18] Midrash Tehillim comments on David's intention in writing it: *May my songs be composed for the benefit of future generations, and may they be preserved for them. Let them not be read like ordinary poetry, but let them be studied with the same rewarding reflection as religious law.*[19] In this setting, Bloch sets the pliable flow of spoken prose, frequently using syncopations, cross-accents, and changes of meter to circumvent regular pulsations and symmetrical rhythms. He studiously avoids just those characteristics which make for the "catchy" quality of secular vocal music.

CANTOR AND CHOIR (Opening the Ark)

Lift up your heads, O ye portals! Lift, ye everlasting doors!
That the King of Glory may enter.

(Psalm 24:9–10)

These verses are recited by the celebrant, as he approaches the ark of the Law. The directness of these cantorial recitatives, mainly because of syllabic setting of text, is Western in character.[20] Again, a sense of the Holy pervades — alluding to the ancient priestly approach to the altar. Its inclusion, at this point in the service, has significance as a recol-

---

18. In Christian worship, a verse, such as this, which was chanted before or after a psalm, canticle or prayer, took on the name: antiphon.

19. See *The Psalms*, Samson Raphael Hirsch, editor (Jerusalem: Feldheim Publishers, 1978), commentary to Psalm 149.

20. At other times — reiterated notes, passionate outbursts, and melismatic figurations of Eastern Oriental character are shared stylistic elements which Bloch employs in his earlier works of the "Jewish Cycle": *Shelomo, Voice in the Wilderness, Baal Shem,* and *Israel Symphony.*

lection of the historical dedication of the first Temple by Solomon (II Chronicles 5–6). According to Midrash, after Solomon built the Temple and was on the threshold of bringing the ark into the Holy of Holies, the doors locked and were impossible to open. Although Solomon had already uttered 24 psalms (I Kings 8:23–53), his prayers were to no avail until he exclaimed: *Lift up your heads ... (Psalm 24:9–10)*, recalling the good deeds of David, whereupon the gates opened of themselves.[21]

CHOIR

Who is this King of Glory?

This phrase from Psalm 24: 8 has many liturgical overtones. It derives from the Sabbath morning *Musaph* prayer: *Where is the place of his glory?* This in turn is linked to Moses' revelation: *Show me, I pray Thee, Thy glory (Exod. 33:18)*. This brief imitative passage exhibits, also, the influence of Renaissance polyphony on the work's rich choral modality.

CANTOR

Adonoy of Sabaoth, He is the King of Glory!

This heraldic phrase, with its emphasis on octaves and fifths, recalls (in its motivic structure) the ritual blowing of the *shofar* on the Jewish New Year.

CHOIR

Selah!

Selah is a difficult concept to translate. It is used either as an exclamation or to punctuate psalm verses, indicating a pause or instrumental interlude. Hirsch reflects that it tells the reader to "meditate once more upon that which has just been said."[22] Bloch seems to have intuited all these meanings, for his threefold repetition of the word in shifting dynamics — now soft, now loud — transitions a text message into an instrumental interlude.

---

21. Midrash attributes the phrase *Lift up thy gates* to the angelic host, who, in this instance, question Solomon, crying: *Who is the king of Glory?* The following is Solomon's reply, *The Lord, strong and mighty*. Then, he repeats, *Lift up your heads (Psalm 24:7)* ... at which point the gates open. See Talmud Sabbath 30a.
22. *The Psalms*, Hirsch, 17.

INTERLUDE (Removing the Scroll from the Ark)

A six-note motif (G-A-C-B-A-G) heard at the outset of *Avodath Hakodesh*, functions as a *cantus firmus*.[23] In this interlude, as elsewhere, this motif permeates the entire work, cementing the contrasting moods and characters of the *Sacred Service* into an organic unity.

CANTOR AND CHOIR

> The Torah, which God gave through Moses,
>> is the law of the house of Jacob.
>>> (Deuteronomy 33:4)

In citing this verse, recalling the blessing of Moses to the children of Israel before his death, liturgy refers back to the ark of the Tabernacle in the desert — bringing historic continuity to bear upon the ceremonial act — tracing a line between the congregants in the synagogue and their ancient forebears in the desert. It signifies the continuing acceptance and ratification of the Torah and its teachings by all succeeding generations.[24]

> O house of Jacob, come ye, walk in the light of the Lord.
>> (Isaiah 2:5)

All of these settings for cantor and choir follow traditional patterns of responsorial-antiphonal psalmody. Here, the choir echoes the soloist in short exchanges. At other times, the choir trades off whole phrases with the soloist. In still other places, the choir amplifies cantorial intonations. This verse, extracted from Isaiah's prophecy, describes the glories of the Messianic age — the dissemination of true religion and the spontane-

---

23. *Cantus firmus* or 'fixed song' is a compositional technique used extensively in the Middle Ages, especially in musical settings of the Mass, where each section was composed around the same pre-existing melody. This form reached a pinnacle in the 15th and 16th centuries in the 'cantus firmus masses' of Dufay, Ockeghem, and Obrecht.

24. The medieval Spanish biblical exegete Nachmanides (1194–1270), comments that the word *kehillot*, here translated as *house*, is in fact, more correctly translated as *congregation*. It indicates that numerous Gentiles would join the fold of Israel and share in the heritage of Torah, thus, confirming Bloch's universalist conception. Nachmanides, *The Sonchino Chumash*, note 4 (London: Soncino Press, 1975 [1947]) 1176–77.

ous submission of the nations to the authority of God. It places the ceremonial act within a universal context.

CANTOR AND CHOIR (Affirmation of the Faith)

> O hear Israel *(Shema Yisrael)*, our God, our Creator, our God is One!
> (Deuteronomy 6:4)

As the *Shema* is the watchword of the faith, its declaration by cantor and choir is the highpoint of the service,[25] emphasized by the Torah being raised into the air. Bloch has set this dramatic celebratory act with symbolic flames ablaze in the orchestra. The connotative power of the act derives from associations lodged deep in the recesses of consciousness, particularly the image of lifting the sacrificial animal in air, above the sacred fire of the altar. In stirring and expansive musical gesture, Bloch highlights the word *One*, by setting it to an unusual augmented fourth interval or tritone (A to D-sharp). Characterized as Hebraic Orientalism, these colorful strains pick up on, and find appropriate expression for, each nuance of text. It is music that transforms coolly objective liturgical rite into fiery prophetic utterance.[26]

CHOIR (Processional to the Readers Desk)

> And thine, Adonoy is the greatness, and all dominion, and Thine
> the pow'r. For all things in heaven and on earth are Thine; Thine the
> Kingdom, O Lord our God, and be Thou exalted, O Lord, over all!
> (1 Chronicles 29:11)

On the day when King David presented his plan for the building of the Temple to the leaders of Israel, this verse constituted his final blessing and thanksgiving prayer. Thus, it functions to conclude the Torah service, as well.[27] Bloch's tutti-fortissimo setting is glorious.

---

25. *Shema Yisrael, Adonoy Elohenu, Adonoy Echad (Deut. 6:4)!*
26. Bloch may well have drawn his musical imagery from the pagan "fire music" leitmotif from Wagner's mythical music drama, "Ring Cycle."
27. Verses from 1 Chronicles 29:10–13 are included in the Morning service of traditional Jewish liturgy.

Conclusion

The Path from Liturgy to Music

From its very inception the ritual of sacrifice was closely identified with music, and music, thus, became an indispensable part of worship. Singing was considered integral to sacrifice, and lack of singing, even invalidated the sacrificial action.[28] The earliest synagogue rituals in Babylon and Palestine were undoubtedly seen as substitutes for the Temple service, and their prayers strove to conceptualize meanings implied or inherent in the sacrificial rituals of the central Temple cult. In the course of time, however, the original spiritual intentions of Scripture were forgotten. The idea of sacrifice, itself, appeared as an atavism from an archaic past.[29] Even the recital of texts memorializing sacrifice became burdensome, and lost to the hearts of some of the worshippers. Reform Judaism, striving for relevance within 19th-century European society, omitted all references to the sacrificial cult.

One of the early architects of Reform Judaism in America, Rabbi David Philipson, wrote: "The chief and underlying principle of the reform movement is the universalistic interpretation of Judaism, as over against the nationalistic."[30] Bloch thoroughly identified with this universalistic interpretation of Judaism. In giving it voice, however, his artistic soul reaches back beyond Reform to intuitive inner resources. Bloch taps into these sources and reshapes their intent. His musical language echoes pathos, born not of abstract reason and logical argument, but inspired from hidden springs of revelation and faith.[31] These

---

28. The Talmud discusses this issue extensively, citing Rav Yehuda in the name of Samuel, who derives the obligation of song from the Bible: *He should serve in the Name of his God (Deut. 18:7)*. What is "service in the Name of God?" he asks, "Singing in the Temple." Rabbi Meir and other Sages continue arguing about the degree to which the sacrifice is dependent upon song *(shira)*. See Talmud Arakhin 11a.

29. The laws of sacrifice, though studied continually as intellectual exercises, had lost a living emotional grip "in their hearts," and became a blunted and dulled habit.

30. David Philipson (1862–1949), Reform Rabbi, orator, author, and one of the architects of the American Reform Movement, *The Reform Movement in Judaism* (1907) 222 and 357–359, as cited in Idelsohn, *Jewish Liturgy*, 278.

31. Bloch expresses his feelings in this oft cited quote: *It is the Jewish soul that interests me, the complex, glowing, agitated soul that I feel vibrating throughout the Bible; the freshness and naïveté of the Patriarchs; the violence of the*

elemental passions created liturgy at its inception and continue to endow it with strength. For similar reasons, throughout the ages, the ideal of sacrifice and Levitical song has never ceased to inspire musical creativity.

Related Synagogue Collections and Services

The following classic 19th-century synagogue collections include choral compositions for cantor and choir. Most are reprints of original editions issued by Sacred Music Press of the Hebrew Union School of Sacred Music and the American Conference of Certified Cantors.

Baer, Abraham (1834–1894 Prussia). *Baal Tefillah.* Cantor, soli, choir (SATB).

Birnbaum, Abraham (1865–1922 Poland-Russia). *Art of Hazzanut,* Volumes 1 (Sabbath) & 2 (High Holidays). Cantor, choir (SATB).

Dunajewsky, A. (1843–1911 Odessa). *Thirty Israelite Temple Compositions for the Sabbath.* Cantor, choir (SATB).

Gerovitsch, Elieser (1844–1914 Kiev). *Shirei Tefillah,* Volumes 1 & 2. choir (SATB).

_____. *Shirej Simroh* (synagogue recitatives and choruses). Volumes 1 & 2. Cantor and choir (SATB).

Lewandowski, Louis (1821–1894 Berlin). *Kol Rinnah U'Tefillah.* Cantor.

_____. *Todah W'Simrah.* Vol. 1 (Sabbath), Vol. 2 (Festivals), Vol. 3 (High Holidays/Festivals).

Naumbourg, Samuel (1815 Bavaria–1880 Paris). *Zemirot Yisrael.* Vol. 1 (liturgical Sabbath chants), Vol. 2 (Festival chants), Vol. 3 (religious chants). Cantor, soli, choir (SATB) (piano/organ).

Nowakowsky, David (1848–1921 Odessa). *Sabbath Eve.* Cantor, choir (SATB).

_____. *Schlussgebet fur Jom Kippur,* Vol. 2 (*Neilah*).

Prophetic Books; the savage Jewish love of justice; the despair of Ecclesiastes; the sorrow and the immense greatness of the Book of Job; the sensuality of the Song of Songs. All this is in us, all this is in me, and it is the better part of me. It is all this that I endeavor to hear in myself and to transcribe in my music: the venerable emotion of the race that slumbers way down in our souls. See Peter Gradenwitz, The Music of Israel — From the Biblical Era to Modern Times (Portland, Oregon: Amadeus Press, 1966) 287.

Rossi, Salamone (c.1570-c.1630 Mantua, Italy). *Shir Hashirim.* Volumes 1 & 2. Cantor, choir (SATB) (piano/organ).

Sulzer, Salomon (1804–1890 Vienna). *Schir Zion.* Volumes 1, 2, 3. Cantor, choir (SATB), organ.

Weintraub, Hirsch (1817–1881 Konigsberg). *Schire Beth Adonai,* Volumes 1, 2, 3. Cantor, choir (SATB).

The following are functional and artistic 20th-century liturgical settings of Weekday Evening, Sabbath Eve, or Sabbath Morning Services.

Aloni, Aminadav (1928 Palestine–1999 USA). *Shir Chadash (A New Song): Sabbat Evening Service,* mixed choir, children's choir, solo voices, keyboard.

Ben-Haim, Paul (1897 Germany/1933 Israel–1984). *Kabbalat Shabbat.* Cantor and choir.

_____. *Friday Evening Service* (1966), for soprano, cantor, mixed choir, children's choir and orchestra.

_____. Liturgical Cantata (1950) (Psalms, Morning Prayer), baritone, mixed choir, orchestra.

Berlinski, Herman (1910 Germany/1939 USA–2001). *Avodat Shabbat,* cantor, choir, and orchestra.

Braun, Yehezkel (b.1922 Germany/1924 Palestine). *Evening Service for the Sabbath* (1964), cantor (baritone), mixed choir, orchestra.

Castelnuovo-Tedesco, Mario (1895 Italy–1968 USA). *Sacred Service for the Sabbath Eve, Op. 122.*

Drosin, Garth (20th C.). *Sacred Service.* Solo, SATB, brass quintet, and organ.

Fromm, Herbert (1905 Germany/1937 USA–1995). *Maariv.* Solo, SATB, narrator, and winds.

Gottlieb, Jack (b.1930 USA). *Love Songs for Sabbath: Friday Evening Service* (1967), SATB, cantor, female reader, dancers, percussion and organ.

Glantz, Yehuda Leib (1898 Ukraine–1964 Israel). *Friday Evening Service,* tenor, choir, organ.

_____. *Sabbath Morning Service,* tenor, choir, organ.

_____. *Hallel and Three Festivals,* tenor, choir, organ.

_____. *High Holidays,* tenor, choir, organ.

Helfman, Max (1901 Poland/1909 USA–1963). *The Holy Ark (Aron HaKodesh)* (Torah Service), solo, SATB, orchestra.

Janowski, Max (1912 Germany/1937 USA–1991). *Sabbat Service for Friday Evening.* Cantor, congregation, SATB, solo, organ.

Janowski, Max. *Sabbat Service for Saturday Morning,* cantor, congregation, soli, SATB, solo, organ.

Lavry, Marc (1903 Riga/1935 Israel–1968). *Sabbath Eve Sacred Service,* cantor, choir, and orchestra.

Milhaud, Darius (1892 France–1974). *Service Sacre* for cantor, choir, and orchestra.

Natra, Segiu (b.1924 Romania/1961 Israel). *Sacred Service* (1976), baritone, mixed choir, organ.

Rossi, Salomone (c.1570-c.1630). *Sacred Service for Sabbath Eve* (arranged by Isadore Freed), solo, SATB, string quartet.

Seter, Mordecai (1916–1994). *Sabbath Cantata* (1940) (Song of Songs, Psalms, Shlomo Halevy Al-Kabbetz, Sabbath Prayers, Genesis, and Kaddish), soprano, alto, tenor, bass, mixed choir, strings (or organ).

Shalt, Heinrich (1886 Austria–1951 USA). *Sabbath Eve Liturgy,* cantor, SATB, congregation, organ.

Starer, Robert (1924 Vienna–2001 USA). *Sabbath Evening Service* (1967), 4 soloists, choir and brass quartet.

Steinberg, Ben (b.1930 Canada). *Crown of Torah,* solo, choir, children's choir, flute, oboe, violoncello, harp, organ.

Weiner, Lazar (1897 Russia–1982 USA). *Shir L'Shabbatot,* solo, SATB, flute, oboe, clarinet, bassoon, strings.

Wyner, Yehudi (b.1929 USA). *Friday Evening Service* (1963), cantor, choir, organ.

Zaimont, Judith Lang (b.1945 USA). *Sacred Service for the Sabbath Eve,* baritone solo, choir, and orchestra.

G. Dore: The Angel Appearing to Balaam, *Bible Illustrations (1866)*

This chapter focuses on Max Stern's *Balaam and the Ass*, an instrumental retelling of the biblical tale as avant-garde program music.

NUMBERS

And the angel of the Lord went further, and stood in a narrow place, where there was no place to turn either to the right hand or to the left. And the ass saw the angel of the Lord, and she lay down under Balaam; and Balaam's anger was kindled, and he smote the ass with his staff and the Lord opened the mouth of the ass, and she said unto Balaam: "What have I done unto thee, that thou hast smitten me these three times   (Numbers 22: 26–28)?"

The Book of Numbers is a chronicle of outstanding events which took place during the forty years journey of the children of Israel in the wilderness. It includes: the census, appointment of the seventy elders, mission of the spies, rebellion of Korach, the sin of Moses, the deaths of Miriam and Aaron, and numerous civil and ritual laws. In the last stage of the journey (chapters 22–24), we find a holy people about to enter the Promised Land. Overcome with dread at this prospect, Balak, king of Moab (c.1200 B.C.) summons the heathen prophet Balaam: *Come now and curse this people… for they are too mighty for me… that I may drive them out of the land, for I know that whom thou blessest is blessed, and whom thou cursest is cursed (22:6).*

The story of Balaam and the ass takes place on the journey Balaam traveled on his path to meet Balak. It is one of the few humorous tales in Scripture. Beaten, because she strays from the way, on beholding an angel, the dumb animal miraculously speaks back to her heathen master. Considered a supernatural phenomenon,[1] for over a thousand years commentators have been divided and perplexed in their understanding and interpretation of this biblical episode: Is it a real incident or a dream?

Max Stern: Balaam and the Ass (1990)
Subtext: Numbers 22: 21–35
Genre: Chamber music
Medium: Duo for trombone and percussion
Style: Aleatory[2]
First performance: Lieberson Prize Competition, Beit Ariela, Tel Aviv, December 16, 1990
Duration: 15 minutes

Balaam and the Ass is programmatic chamber music for trombone and percussion. It was written for a prize competition of Israeli composers, anonymously judged in a public concert, and won the coveted Lieberson Prize. Eliciting overwhelming response, the work was subsequently chosen for inclusion in the music curriculum of Israel's public schools. Studied and enjoyed by a generation of young listeners, more than a humorous animal tale, *Balaam and the Ass* is a commentary on what it means to be human.

---

1. The Mishnah relates that *the mouth of the ass was one of ten things created on the eve of Sabbath in the twilight of Creation (Avot 5.9).* Hertz, *Prayer Book,* 687.

2. Aleatory music means many things to many people. Sometimes coined 'chance music' or 'indeterminate music', it signifies a technical procedure by which one or more elements of a musical composition are not fully notated, but left to the discretion of the performer. These elements vary from composition to composition, and include: pitch, rhythm, dynamic, tempo, or form. Indeterminacy and improvisation know many levels. In *Balaam and the Ass,* all pitches, dynamics, tempi, and note sequences are fixed. The freedom given the performers is in the parameter of rhythm — which is determined to the accuracy of a second. This allows for a greater degree of spontaneous interaction than might be possible with conventional notation. See Max Stern, "Organizing Procedures Involving Indeterminacy and Improvisation," *Interface,* edited by Marc Leman, Herman Saabe, Jos Kunst, and Frits Weiland, Vol. 17, no. 2 (The Netherlands: Swets & Zeitlinger, 1988) 103–114.

Biographic Context

Max Stern (b.1947 Long Island, New York/1976 Israel) has created a series of compositions which synthesize biblical themes with ancient sounds and modern techniques. Already, a mature professional musician in New York City before coming to Israel in 1976, Stern followed an inner calling to the land of his fathers, and there embarked on a spiritual odyssey "in the footsteps of the Prophets"[3] that led from Jerusalem to the Negev. Uri Mayer, conductor of the Israel Sinfonietta, wrote of his compositions, "Israel's most soulful composer, his works are beautifully crafted and expressive." A pioneer music educator in Israel, Max Stern has devoted much time to bringing music into the lives of ordinary people, for which he was acknowledged by the Histadrut-Israel Federation of Labor (2003). A recipient of MacDowell Colony Fellowships (1974, 1975) and international awards in Japan (1991) and Italy (2004), Stern has represented Israel at numerous international festivals and conferences. Thirteen CDs of his compositions have been released in cooperation with the Israel Broadcasting Authority and the National Council for Culture and Art. He is founding professor of music at the Ariel University Center (2001), and music critic for *The Jerusalem Post* since 1988.[4]

---

3.   From the article "Inspiration in the Desert of Israel" by Alex Svamberk, culture editor of the newspaper "Mlada Fronta DNES," Prague, September 8, 1995.

4.   The composer writes: *I began my musical life in the public schools of Valley Stream, and performed extensively on the contrabass, before studying composition with Bernard Rogers (a student of Ernest Bloch) and Samuel Adler (a student of Aaron Copeland and Paul Hindemith) at the Eastman School of Music, and privately in New York City with Hall Overton. Later, at Yale University, I worked with British composer, Alexander Goehr. Following participation in the First International Kodaly Seminar in Hungary (1970), and a subsequent Ford Foundation grant to study pedagogy and conducting with Peter Erdei, at the Kodaly Musical Training Institute, Wellesley, Massachusetts, I became intrigued by the relationship between art and a people's culture and destiny, and subsequently enrolled at the Jewish Theological Seminary in New York City, studying ethnomusicology with Johanna Spector. After many years of professional involvement as a performing musician, conductor, and teacher, I received a doctorate from the University of Colorado, Boulder, where my advisors included the noted American musicologists William Kearns and Karl Kroeger, and Pulitzer Prize winning composer Richard Toensing.*

Text and Subtext, Music and Musical Exegesis

Balaam and the Ass is a mini drama.[5] The form of the work follows the biblical narrative in a steady crescendo of continuity. Instruments are used to convey the story and portray its three characters literally: Balaam, Ass, and Angel.[6] The heathen prophet beats and curses; the Ass brays, bawls and speaks; the angel of God draws its sword of judgment under wings of mercy. Unique is the carefully graded balance between tonality, atonality, and non-tonality — employed allegorically, to depict various levels of consciousness and awareness distinguishing man from beast.

This duo for trombone and percussion explores a broad spectrum of sonorities and timbres within a flexible rhythmic time-frame.[7] At first, the animal snores and growls in undefined pitches. Later, as the work develops, the Ass is transformed. In consequence of her encounter with the Angel, she begins to speak, sing, and eventually pray her braying song to God. This metamorphosis involves exchanging for non-pitched sound effects, definite pitches, in ever clearer tonality; gradually, almost imperceptibly, consolidating isolated notes into conglomerates that coalesce into warm, resonant sonorities. From brutish cacophony to euphonious song, through grunts and groans and spoken words, the process of human evolution, growth, and development is translated into sound.

---

5. *And Balaam rose up in the morning, and saddled his ass, and went. And the angel of the Lord placed herself in the way as an adversary. And the ass saw the angel of the Lord, and turned aside out of the way. And Balaam smote the ass, and she spoke: 'What have I done unto thee, that thou hast smitten me these three times' (Num. 22).*

6. **Balaam** is represented by non-pitched percussion instruments (bass drum and side drum, bongos, tom-toms, timpani, and wood blocks). The **Angel** is characterized by both pitched metallic instruments (vibraphone, xylophone, and glockenspiel), and non-pitched gongs, cymbals and triangle. The **Ass** (trombone) plays both non-pitched sounds and pitched notes in various relationships. Extended instrumental techniques (the insertion and removal of tuning of slides, the use of half valves, flutter tonguing, speaking and singing into the trombone) create onomatopoeic effects and illustrate the action.

7. Aleatory describes a wide range of unpredictability. In *Balaam and the Ass* non-pitched sounds and rhythm are only partially determined by notation.

Ex. 13. Max Stern: *Balaam and the Ass*

Analyses

1. Introduction

And Balaam rose up in the morning, and saddled his ass (22:21).

The trombone yawns in indistinct glissandos. The bass drum and wood block try to awaken him.

2. Andante

Now, he was riding upon his ass (22:22).

Traveling together, percussion and trombone partake in an asymmetric rhythmic repartee.

3. Tranquillo

And the angel of the Lord, stood in the way (22: 23).

Sustained sonorities of vibraphone and bells merge into a harmony of ethereal calm.

4. Agitato

The ass turned aside out of the way…
And Balaam smote the ass (22: 23).

The trombone frantically signals her master, trying to warn him of danger ahead. It is an *angel of the Lord, standing in the way, and his sword drawn in his hand* is about to slay Balaam. But, the poor beast, rather than being rewarded for her efforts, is beaten soundly by the drums (representing Balaam).

5. Tranquillo

But the angel of the Lord stood in a path of the vineyards...
And when the ass saw the angel of the Lord (22: 24).

The calm of eternity returns. This time, the trombone seeks a relationship with the shimmering harmonies of the vibraphone and glockenspiel (Angel).

6. Agitato

She crushed Balaam's foot...and he smote her again (22: 25).

Even more mercilessly than before, drums and assorted percussion beat the trombone down, again and again.

7. Senza Misura

And the ass said...What have I done unto thee (22:28)?

Prostrate and exhausted, the trombone miraculously speaks back through her mouth-piece. It is a turning point in the work.

8. Cantabile

And the ass said...am I not thine ass,
Upon which thou has ridden...unto this day (22: 30).

The trombone attempts to grasp the heavenly vision and relate to the angel. She begins by singing in a gawky, tentative way.

9. Maestoso

Was I ever wont to do so unto thee (22: 30)?

Privy to divine revelation, the trombone undergoes a miraculous transformation. Metamorphosed, she is changed into something more than a dumb animal; she has attained awareness and begins to pray.[8]

10. Andante

And Balaam said...I have sinned (22:34).

Having completed her braying song, the trombone returns back to her previous state,[9] for, after all, she is only a beast. Then, both Balaam and the ass continue on their way, in a rhythmic interplay, akin to section 2.

Conclusion

Some say that what happened to Balaam on the way is an allegory and took place in a prophetic vision.[10] Others are convinced that it truly occurred. *The ass, through her speaking, was to instruct the man that the mouth and the tongue are in God's hand. The ass died the moment she had spoken what she had to say, for God feared that heathens might worship this ass, were she to stay alive. It is out of consideration to mankind that God has closed the mouth of animals; for were they to speak, man could not use them for his service — since the ass, the most stupid of animals, when she spoke, confounded Balaam, the wisest of the wise.*[11] Max Stern's *Balaam and the Ass* interprets the story as an allegory for awakening spiritual growth, from ignorance to enlightenment. It depicts the momentous process of maturity as revelation, a "chance" encounter, from infancy to old age, with divine grace.

---

8. The nature of revelation itself is not rational. It is its unique prerogative to effect instantaneous transformation of spirit and soul, through insight. This new, changed consciousness, however, then, requires time and effort to actualize.
9. Even though Balaam's ass has been graced to behold the angel of the Divine, she is still fated to remain an animal.
10. Medieval Jewish philosopher Moses Maimonides (1135–1204) and others consider the episode as a dream, or vision of the night, depicting the mental and moral conflict in Balaam's soul. See Maimonides, *Guide for the Perplexed*, translated by M. Friedlander (New York: Dover, 1956 [1904]) 237.
11. Ginzberg, *Legends of the Bible*, 467–68.

Other Directions

Few musical works have been written on the specific theme of Balaam and the ass.[12] More frequently, however, are settings devoted to Balaam's blessing the children of Israel: *How lovely are your tents, O Jacob; your dwelling places, O Israel (24:5)!* Many independent compositions based on texts from the Book of Numbers focus on the Priestly Blessing: *The Lord bless you, and keep you. The Lord cause his face shine to upon you, and be gracious unto you. The Lord lift up his countenance unto you, and give you peace (6: 24–26).*

Works List

Adler, Hugo (1894 Belgium–1955 USA). *Balak and Bil'am* (Num. 21–24) (translation Martin Buber), cantata.

Lutkin, Peter (1858 Wisconsin–1931 Illinois). *The Lord Bless You and Keep You* (1959) (Num. 6:24–26), SATB.

Mueller, Carl F. (1892–1982 USA). *The Lord Bless You* (1934) (Num. 6:24–26), SATB.

Nystedt, Knut (b.1915 Norway). *The Benediction* (1966) (Num. 6:24–26), SATB.

Orgad, Ben-Zion (1926–2006 Israel). *The Story of the Spies* (1952) (Num., Deut., Jer.), cantata for narrator, choir, orchestra.

Shaw, Kirby (20th C. USA). *Benediction* (1971) (Num. 6:24–26), SATB.

Smith, Gregg (b.1930s USA). *The Lord Bless Thee and Keep Thee* (1969) (Num. 6:24–26), S/SSA.

Willan, Healey (1880 UK–1968 Canada). *The Aaronic Benediction* (1958) (Num. 6:24–26), SATB.

Gottlieb, Jack (b.1930 NY). *Mah Tovu* (1971) (Num. 24:5), Cantor, SATB, organ.

Ouseley, F. A. Gore (1825–1889 England). *How Goodly are Thy Tents* (Num. 24: 5), SATB, organ.

---

12. A number of 16th and 17th-century Dutch paintings by Rembrandt (1606–1669), Bartholomeus Breenbergh (1598–1657), Hans Bols (1534–1593), Peter Lastman (1583–1633) and others have been inspired by the subject of *Balaam and the Ass.*

Max Stern's instrumental cantata *Ha'azinu*, for solo contrabass and orchestra, draws upon Jewish traditional and ethnic musical sources to illuminate epic biblical poetry and trace the dramatic trajectory of the *Song of Moses.*

DEUTERONOMY

Assemble unto me all the elders of your tribes, and your officers, that I may speak these words in their ears, and call heaven and earth to witness against them. For I know that after my death ye will in any wise deal corruptly, and turn aside from the way which I have commanded you; and evil will befall you in the end of days; because ye will do that which is evil in the sight of the Lord, to provoke him through the work of your hands. And Moses spoke in the ears of all the assembly of Israel the words of this song, until they were finished   (Deuteronomy 31:28–30).

Deuteronomy is the last of the Five Books of Moses and consists in the final addresses, teachings, and testimonies of Moses to the children of Israel,[1] shortly before his death. The absence of God, who neither speaks nor reveals himself, as He did in the other four books of the Pentateuch, is a striking feature of Deuteronomy. The importance of these discourses cannot be overestimated. They became prototypes for the biblical understanding of law, history, sanctity, and the prophetic concepts of blessing and curse, reward and punishment. In a series of three orations: the Lawgiver reviews Israel's journeys through the wilderness (1:6–4:40); summarizes the divine teachings by which men may live in harmonious community (4:44–26:19); and entreats the people to remain faithful to the ethical ideal of righteousness — whereby they

---

1.   The authors of the Gospels and Acts of the Apostles have reinterpreted the concept of the 'Children of Israel' to mean the Church. They find in Deut. 18:18–19 (as cited in Acts 3: 22–23), a prediction of the Savior of Christianity.

may inherit the promise of the Covenant in perpetuity (chapters 27–30). He crystallizes this message in a visionary epilogue *Ha'azinu* (Song of Moses), a poetic addition to the prose orations of the Book, reviewing the people's history and destiny and giving lyricism full reign: *Give Ear O Ye Heavens, and I will speak; And let the earth hear the words of my mouth (32:1).*

Max Stern: Ha'azinu (1989)
Subtext: Deuteronomy 32: 1–43
Genre: Instrumental Cantata
Medium: Contrabass and orchestra
Style: Tonal
First performance: Jerusalem Theatre, March 24, 1993
Duration: ca. 32 minutes

Ha'azinu, a cantata for contrabass and orchestra, is an instrumental characterization of Moses' farewell song to the children of Israel. It foretells the history and prophetic mission of the Jewish people, and contrasts God's promise of loving kindness and faithfulness — with Israel's ingratitude and faithlessness. It was premiered by contrabassist, Gary Karr and the Jerusalem Symphony Orchestra, under conductor, Arthur Fagan (1993).[2]

Text and Subtext, Music and Musical Exegesis

In *Ha'azinu*, the contrabass — slow of speech and heavy of tongue, as Moses is purported to be in the Bible — takes on the part of the Law-giver: exhorting, reproving, justifying the ways of God to man. The eternal witnesses of heaven and earth are portrayed by the orchestra. This unique musical conception rests upon a number of traditional sources, evoking powerful overtones in relation to the Jewish experience: the spirit of European cantorial song, a liturgical hymn *Yigdal*[3] as

---

2. In 1996 Stern revised the work for contrabass, harp, and organ, and performed it himself as soloist in a series of ten concerts throughout Germany, in collaboration with Das Duo — harpist Brigitte Langnickel-Kohler and organist Reinhard Langnickel.

3. The *Yigdal* is a liturgical poem based on the 13 principles of faith as articulated by Maimonides: 1) God's existence, 2) God's unity 3) God's in

sung in the Yemenite tradition,[4] and a Hasidic wedding *nigun* played at the bridal canopy.[5] Personifying the sacred union between bride and groom, a metaphor for the covenant between the children of Israel and their God. The deep string voice and its declamation of text purport to render, faithfully, a truth that shakes the universe. Motifs are not so much quotations as stylizations of traditional prayer modes and cantorial idioms, drawn from the world of synagogue song. Harmonic sonorities and textures vary from spare unisons and open intervals to chords and polychords of many colors and complexities. The cantata is structured in eight scenes, which flow together in episodic fashion.[6]

The following is extracted from the composer's notes to the concert program of the Jerusalem Symphony Orchestra at Henry Crown Hall, Jerusalem Theatre on March 24, 1993.

My first trip to Israel in 1971 was by way of Rome, where I visited, among other places, the Vatican, and was particularly impressed by the magnificent sculptures and frescos that depict the prophets of Israel and the events of the Bible. I thought, at the time, if this is Rome, what glory must Jerusalem, the place where it all happened, hold. But, when I got to Jerusalem, nothing. What a disappointment. It has taken many years to understand the profoundly internal nature of Jewish culture.

'Ha'azinu' is a rare composition, in that it is an artistic conception which comes from the heart of Jewish tradition. It strives for a musical expression of fundamental bedrock in the experience of the Jewish people

---

corporality, 4) God's eternity, 5) God is worthy of worship, 6) Prophecy, 7) Moses unsurpassed prophet, 8) Torah given by Moses, 9) Divine Law is complete and unchangeable, 10) God knows the actions of men, 11) Reward and Punishment, 12) Coming of the Messiah, 13) Resurrection of the dead.

4. I cannot forget when and where I first heard this tune, nor the impression it made upon me. It was on a Sabbath evening in a Yemenite synagogue in the Katamonim neighborhood of Jerusalem in 1976. It was sung collectively, at the top of their lungs, by old white bearded Jews from Yemen (dressed in long flowing tunics), alongside young men and children with sidelocks (*peyot*). Everything was white, all was aglow with purity and devotion, the very walls of the building seemed to vibrate in sympathy with their chant. I felt I was no longer on earth, I was witness to the angels of heaven.

5. This Hasidic tune is often heard at weddings (played by *klezemer* musicians in Jerusalem), while accompanying the bridal procession to the canopy (*chuppah*).

6. The instrumental cantata (without words) originated in the early Baroque period as a transitional genre in between vocal and instrumental music.

— chosenness, a vision of the Promised Land, reward and punishment, and ultimate salvation. It is based on the spirit of synagogue chant, a Yemenite tune to the 'Yigdal' prayer, and a Hasidic nigun sung at the bridal canopy. These elements, however, are fused into a new unity, and there is little of the hodgepodge of Jewish music or the Galut [Diaspora] per se. It is neither a modern work nor a conservative one; it is a sacred work — but not liturgical. The voice of the contrabass is low, rough, indistinct, and hardly flexible when compared to a violin or piano, yet this is the voice of Moses, a truth of heaven and earth, and around this sound, the entire orchestra reverberates. Each grunt, or squeak of that bass shakes the universe, and all the splendor of the orchestra is needed to frame that 'heavy speech and slow tongue' (Exod. 4:10). It was conceived for the concert hall, but it is not profane. It is a product of here and now, a living expression that is possible only in Israel.

Analyses

Part 1

Scene 1, section 1: *Invocation to Heaven and Earth*

Give ear, ye heavens, and I will speak;
And let the earth hear the words of my mouth (32:1).

The contrabass represents Moses invoking the eternal witnesses of heaven and earth, depicted by the orchestra. Although his intent is clear, his words are unintelligible. Perhaps, this indistinct rumble is the way the children of Israel actually heard Moses speaking to them in the plains of Moab.

section 2:

Remember the days of old,
Consider the years of many generations (32:7).

Cantorial idioms are exchanged between the contrabass soloist and solo instruments in the orchestra. The orchestra follows no specific text, but, rather, responds with sonorous imagery to the implied text and articulated 'speech' of the soloist.

Scene 2, section 1: *A Desert Encounter*

He found him in a desert land,
And in the waste, a howling wilderness;

Swirling orchestral textures and sonorities seem to emerge from nowhere. Chords and whole tone scales alternate with contrabass recitatives — evoking echoes of heaven, earth, desert, anger, and divine love.

section 2:

He compassed him about, He cared for him,
He kept him as the apple of His eye (32:10).

The music to this section *(compassed him about... cared for him)* symbolizes the adoration of angels and heavenly host. It is adapted from a Yemenite tune to the hymn *Yigdal* — a liturgical poem about the revelation of the Divine as seen through sacred ideals and principles of faith.

Scene 3: *Admonition*

But Jeshurun waxed fat, and kicked — Thou didst wax fat,
Thou didst grow thick, thou didst become gross —
And he forsook God, who made him,
And contemned the Rock of his salvation (32:15).

This admonition is depicted in truncated solo contrabass declamations and thunderous bass drum responses.

Scene 4: *Divine Anger*

They roused Him to jealousy with strange gods,
With abominations did they provoke Him (32:16).

Divine indignation, characterized by impassioned cantillation, is rendered in agitated orchestral interludes and oft-repeated notes in the strings.

Scene 5: *Divine Disappointment*

And the Lord saw and spurned,
And He said: 'I will hide my face from them,
I will see what their end shall be (32:19–20).

Sect. 1: part 5

Ex. 14. Max Stern: *Haʾazinu*, scene 5

Contrabass and orchestra swoon in lament. It draws on and elaborates upon musical materials first presented in the second scene of Part 1, *Remember the days of old.*

Scene 6: *Divine Love*

O that you were wise that I might love you
With an everlasting love.
(Deut. 32:29, Ps. 81:14–17 paraphrase)

A Hasidic wedding *nigun* is introduced by solo contrabass, symbolizing the covenant between God and His people. It gradually transforms from sobs to song, and then is taken up by the entire orchestra.

Scene 7: *Divine Justice*

Vengeance is Mine, and recompense,
Against the time when their foot shall slip (32:35).

Admonitions hurled by the contrabass are adopted and echoed in the winds, while, simultaneously, reproachful repeated notes are sounded in the strings. The thematic material for scene 7, parallels similar subject matter, formerly associated with the text *Jeshurun waxed fat, and kicked,* from scene 3.

Scene 8: *Divine Salvation*

Sing aloud, O ye nations, of His people;
For He doth make expiation for the land of His people (32:43).

Shining a beacon onto the future, a rhythmically animated finale concludes the song hopefully, in hymn-like affirmation. *'Happy art thou, O Israel: Who is like unto thee, a people saved by the Lord, the shield of thy help, and that is the sword of thy excellency (32:29)!'*[7] It foretells of Salvation awaiting the people at the ends of days.

---

7. "With these words, he at the same time answered a question that Israel had put to him, saying, *O tell us, our teacher Moses, what is the blessing that God will bestow upon us in the future world?* He replied: *'I cannot describe it to you, but all I can say is, happy ye that such is decreed for ye!'* See Midrash *Petirat Mosheh* 126 and 2 *Petirat Mosheh* 381, as cited in Louis Ginzberg, *The Legends of the Jews,* Vol. 3, 463.

Conclusion

Standing on the brink of the grave, Moses gives his parting benediction to the tribes whose religious and political welfare had been the devoted labor of his life. He turns, ascends the heights to the sepulcher which no man knows, and is seen no more: *And Moses went up from the plains of Moab unto the Mountain of Nebo. And there hath not arisen a prophet since in Israel like unto Moses (34:1).*[8] The moral of this work is its message of faith.

Other Directions

Moses und Aaron is a twelve-tone opera in two-acts by Arnold Schoenberg, a major atonal statement in the 20th century. Its libretto focuses on the contrasting characters of Moses and Aaron, and, the abstract nature of the biblical 'Word'.

Arnold Schoenberg: Moses and Aaron (1932)
Text: Arnold Schoenberg (after Exodus)
Genre: Opera
Medium: Speaker (Moses), tenor (Aaron), various soloists, 6 voices, chorus, and orchestra
Style: Twelve-tone
First Staged Performance: Zurich, 1957
Duration: 1 hour 40 minutes

Moses und Aaron has its roots in Schoenberg's earlier *Der Biblische Weg* (The Biblical Way, 1926–27), which evolved from a play into an oratorio (1928), and then, into an opera composed between 1930 and 1932. Composition was resumed in 1951, but it remained unfinished at the composer's death, as the third act was sketched out, but never finished. *Moses and Aaron* was first heard in concert form, as a radio broadcast from Hamburg (1954), and first staged in Zurich (1957). Despite its unfinished status *Moses and Aaron* is widely regarded as Schoenberg's masterpiece.

---

8. See Hertz, *Pentateuch*, 735.

Text and Context, Music and Musical Exegesis

Synopsis

Act I

Scene 1: The Call of Moses
Scene 2: Moses meets Aaron in the Wasteland
Scenes 3 & 4: Moses and Aaron bring God's Message to the People

Act II

Scenes 1 & 2: Aaron and the Seventy Elders before the Mountain of Revelation
Scenes 3 & 4: The Golden Calf and the Altar
Scene 5: Moses and Aaron

Act III (uncompleted)

Moses enters. Aaron a prisoner in chains follows, dragged by two soldiers who hold him fast. Behind come the Seventy Elders.

In this highly philosophical work, Schoenberg reveals his deeply conflicted artistic identity — expressed as an aesthetic dichotomy between idea and form. It was a topic that obsessed Schoenberg his entire life, both in music and in his personal interactions with society. His thesis addresses the tension between prophet and priest, or, composer and performer. The Lawgiver, as visionary creator, is incapable of communicating his vision to the people; while, the more adept Aaron, portrayed as a slick salesman and politician, is incapable of grasping the essence of the vision or idea. The unique voice of God is represented by 6 voices (three women and three men): singing and speaking simultaneously from within the orchestra. The abstract, strictly 12-tone score he produced is similar in quality to that which he composed for *Jacob's Ladder*, but only more thoroughly worked out in technical, textural, and structural detail.

DETAIL

Act 3 *(excerpt)*

The following extract from the unfinished third act of the libretto is one of the most profound comments on the nature of Monotheism ever expressed through an artistic medium. Schoenberg sums up the argument of the opera in a deeply disinterested and uncompromising tone, both difficult to grasp and hard to digest.

Aaron:

> I was to speak in images while you spoke in ideas;
> I was to speak to the heart, you to the mind.

Moses:

> To serve the divine idea is the purpose of the freedom for which this folk has been chosen….The almighty one is not obliged to do anything, is bound by nothing. He is bound neither by the transgressor's deeds, nor by the prayers of the good, nor by the offerings of the penitent…Your gifts had led you to the highest summit, then, as a result of that misuse, you were ever hurled back into the wasteland.

Schoenberg's attempt to confront absolute truth and unveil the *face* of Eternity is disturbing. It exposes a side to reality, which the Almighty Himself refused to reveal to His prophet Moses: *And he said, Thou canst not see my face: for no man can see me and live (Exodus 33:20)*. The divine attributes which man is vouchsafed to know are the Eternal's back: *Thou shalt see my back parts: but my face shall not be seen (33:23)*. Not absolute truth, but compassion, mercy, forgiveness, and love are the subjects of art: *The Lord, the Lord, merciful and gracious, longsuffering, and abundant in goodness and truth (34:6)*. In tackling this subject, Schoenberg seems to be knocking on doors opened by Grace alone. He has stepped unto holy ground, where angels fear to tread.

Other Directions

The following works deal with events in the life of Moses. Some relate specifically to the "Song of Moses," others to the events of the Exodus. Additional works on the life of Moses are found in bibliographies of chapter 7 (Exodus).

Among the earliest musical notations made by Obadiah the Norman Proselyte (11th–12th centuries) there is a setting of a *piyut* in honor of Moses, *Mi al Har Horev ha-Amidi*. Artistic treatments include: Franz Schubert, *Miriam's Siegesgesang* (for soprano solo, mixed choir, and piano, opus 136; text by Franz Grillparzer, 1828); Karl Loewe, *Die eherne Schlange* (cantata for men's choir a cappella, 1834); Adolf Bernhard Marx, *Moses* (oratorio, 1841); Felicien David, *Moïse au Sinai* ("ode symphonique," i.e. oratorio, 1846); Camille Saint-Saëns, *Moise sauve des eaux* (cantata, text by Victor Hugo, c. 1851); Anton Berlijn, *Moses auf Nebo* (oratorio); Anton Rubinstein *Moses* (oratorio, 1892); Marcus Hast, *The Death of Moses* (oratorio, 1892); Jules Massenet, *La Terre Promise* (oratorio, 1900); Bernard Rogers, *The Exodus* (cantata, 1932). Other works includes Darius Milhaud, *Opus Americanum 2*, op. 219 (orchestral suite, 1940); Wadi'a Sabra (1876–1952), Lebanese Maronite composer, *Le chant de Moïse* (oratorio); Roger Vuataz, *Moïse* (oratorio for five reciters, soprano, choir, and orchestra, 1947); Jacob Weinberg, *The Life of Moses* (oratorio, 1955); Josef Tal, *Exodus*, first version for piano and drums, as a "choreographic poem"; second version ("Exodus I"), for baritone and orchestra (1945/46); third version ("Exodus II"), electronic composition, including processed human voices (1958/59).

Jewish folk song tradition contains a large number of songs about Moses, such as *Yismah Moshe*, found in almost all communities; the religious Ladino songs, e.g. *Cantar vos queiro un mahase* (on the birth of Moses) and *A catorce era del mes* (on the Exodus); and the epic Aramaic songs of the Jews of Kurdistan about Moses and Pharaoh's daughter; the battle between Israel and Amalek; and the death of Moses. Many of these songs are sung on *Shavuot* or *Simhat Torah*. Among modern Israel folk songs are Yedidyah Admon's *U-Moshe Hikka al Zur*, and two children songs: *Benei Yisrael Po Kullanu* (Joel Engel, after a Yemenite melody) and *Dumam Shatah Tevah Ketannah* (K.Y. Silman, after an Ashkenazi melody). Yehuda Sharett's setting of the *Haggadah* ("*Nisan Yagur*") was composed as a "liturgy" for kibbutz use. (3) Other folk song traditions include American Negro Spirituals, as well as a few songs about Moses and the Exodus which exist in older Christian music. The Palestinian Arab tradition of mass pilgrimage to the legendary tomb of Moses on the festival of Nebi Musa has given rise to its own repertory of mass chants. One these, *Ya halili ya habibi, ya hawaja Musa*, has become an Israel *Hora-song*.

Works List *(see additional references in chapter 7)*

Amram, David (b.1930 Philadelphia). *Thou Shalt Love the Lord Thy God* (Deut. 6:5–9), SATB.

Brahms, Johannes (1833 Hamburg–1897 Vienna). *Where Is Such a Nation*, op. 109, no. 3 (Deut. 4:7, 9), SATB/SATB.

Bruch, Max (1838 Koln–1920 Berlin). *Moses* (L. Spitta), oratorio.

Castrisanu, Constantin (1888 Bucharest–1923). *Moise* (De Vigny), voice and pianoforte.

Colonna, Giovanni Paolo (1637–1695 Bologne). *Il Mose* (G.B. Giardini), oratorio.

Duquesnoy, Charles (1759–1822 Brussels). *Song of Moses*, cantata.

Feliciano, Richard (b.1930 USA). *Give Ear O Heavens* (Deut. 32:1–4) (from Songs for Darkness and Light), 3-part choir.

Geisler, Johann (18th C. Colonial America). *The Lord Keepeth Thee* (Deut. 28:9–10), SATB, piano.

Hast, Marcus (1871 Warsaw–1911 London). *The Death of Moses*, oratorio.

Haudebert, Lucien (1877–1963 France). *Moise*, oratorio.

Holman, Derek (b.1931 UK). *Blessed Be the Lord for His Land* (Deut. 33:13–16), SATB, organ.

Lachner, Franz Paul (1803–1890 Munich). *Moses* (E. Bauernfeld), oratorio.

Lange, Samuel (1840 Rotterdam–1911 Stuttgart). *Moses*, oratorio.

Ludkewicz, Stanislav (1879–1980 Lvov). *Moysey* (J. Franko), symphonic tableau.

Marx, Adolf Bernhard (1795–1866 Berlin). *Moses*, oratorio.

Mechem, Kirke (b.1925 Kansas City). *The Song Moses* (Deut. 37:7–43) (from Songs of Wisdom) SATB.

Milhaud, Darius (1892 France–1974 Geneva). *The Man of Midian* (Opus Americanum No. 2), suite for orchestra.

Nelson, Ronald (b.1929 Illinois). *Hear O People* (Deut. 6:4–5), unison, keyboard.

Orefice, Giacomo (1865–1922 Milano). *Mosé* (H. Orvieto), opera.

Perosi, Lorenzo (1872–1956 Rome). *Il Mose*, oratorio.

Perti, Giacomo Antonio (1661–1756 Bologne). *Mose* (G.B. Giardini), oratorio.

Powell, Robert J. (b.1932 USA). *Give Ear, O Ye Heavens* (Deut. 32: 1–4), SATB, keyboard.

Rubinstein, Anton (1829–1894 St. Petersburg). *Moses* (S. Mosenthal), oratorio.

Rudnicki, Antin (1902 Ukraine–1975 USA). *Moysey* (I. Franko), tenor, orchestra.

Sabra, Wadia (1876–1952 Lebanon). *Le chant de Moise*, oratorio.

Schmitt, Aloys (1788–1866 Frankfurt). *Moses*, oratorio.

Schoenberg, Arnold (1874 Vienna–1951 Los Angeles). *Moses and Aaron*, opera.

Shenderovas, Anatoly (b.1945 Lithuania). *Shema Yisrael* (Deut., Traditional sources, Vilna Gaon) (1997), cantor, men's choir, boy's choir, orchestra.

Shifrin, Seymour (1926 Brooklyn, NY–1929 Boston). *Give Ear, O Ye Heavens* (Deut. 32:1–4), SATB, organ.

Sternberg, Erich-Walter (1898 Berlin/1931 Israel–1974 Tel Aviv). *Sh'ma Israel*, poeme symphonique.

Sulzer, Salomon (1804–1890 Wien). *Sh'ma Israel* (Deut. 6:4–5), chorus.

Vinaver, Chemjo (1900 Warszawa/1939 Israel–1973 Jerusalem). *Sh'ma Israel* (Deut. 6:4–9), tenor, choir a cappella.

Vuataz, Roger (1898–1988 Switzerland). *Moise* (R. Vuataz), oratorio.

Ward-Steinman, David (b.1936 USA). *The Song of Moses* (1964) (libretto by composer after Deuteronomy), oratorio, SATB, s tenor tenor bass, orchestra.

Weinberg, Jacob (1879 Odessa–1956 New York). *Moses* oratorio, soloist, choir, orchestra and organ.

West, John E. (1863–1929 UK). *The Lord Came from Sinai* (Deut. 33:2–3).

_____. *The Eternal God Is Thy Refuge* (Deut. 33:27–29), SATB, organ.

Winslow, Richard Kenelm (b.1918 Middletown, Connecticut). *I Call Heaven and Earth* (Deut. 30:19), SATB.

Wood, Dale (1934–2003 USA). *Give Ear, O Ye Heavens* (Deut. 32:1–4), SATB, organ.

G. Dore: Ezekiel Prophesying, *Bible Illustrations (1866)*

Introduction to the Books
of the Prophets

Inspired poets, preachers, statesmen, social critics, political activists, and moralists, the Prophets of Israel were men in whom the divine light of Eternity was refracted through the voice of man (*Hear O' Israel, Dt.6:4*). The formula, *Thus spake the Lord*, more than a bibliographic citation, is a seal of infinite worth. Overwhelmed by the idea of a holy people, the Prophets sought to bring the Israelite nation to God.

Joshua, Samuel, Isaiah, Jeremiah, Ezekiel and the Twelve Minor Prophets neither preached nor wrote in a vacuum. They spoke to the body politic of their time, and addressed the principal conflict between prophet and king — not whether to let faith in God prevail as a guide in personal life, but whether to let righteousness be the guide in public life, as well. The kings of Israel and Judah were intelligent, capable leaders, and astute politicians. Their responses to influxes of Assyrian customs, foreign religious practices, and increasing luxury were rational. They dealt with realities of the moment. The Prophets, in contrast, saw the present through the eyes of Eternity. But, what were they trying to say? Why did neither the kings nor the people understand? *The significance of the Hebrew prophets lies in the fact that at a time when political turmoil and dissolving views threatened not only the political independence of the Hebrew state, but the spiritual life of the body politic, the prophets strove to strengthen values, seeing in ethical behavior and moral conduct the salvation of the future.*[1]

The Prophets tried to impress a spiritual truth upon their generation: The ultimate value is the altruistic act of faith, done without seeking reward. Through this conduit, the infinite blessing which God yearns to bestow upon mankind enters into the world. Beyond a personal ethic, however, they strove to make it a social principle. It

---

1. Calmann Levy, "The Prophets of Israel," *The New York Times* (1892). Internet resource: http://query.nytimes.com/gst/abstract.html?res= 9805E2DB1E39E033A2575BC2A96E9C94639ED7CF

is a revolutionary idea, which has yet to be tried: *O that my people would hearken unto me that Israel would walk in my ways. I would soon subdue their enemies, and turn my hand against their adversaries (Ps. 81: 14–15).* Ridiculed, pursued, imprisoned — sometimes even executed, the Prophet's willingness to sacrifice all, to bring this message into the world, is the power that stood by this people Israel, through the long, dark ages of exile: *So I let them go in the stubbornness of their heart that they might walk in their own counsels (Ps. 81:13).*

Prophetic teaching centers around three principles: 1) God judges all things according to justice and righteousness, rewarding and punishing according to the principle of "measure for measure." 2) All things — physical and natural, inanimate and living are instruments in the realization of the Divine Will, but, only humanity has the possibility of free will, necessary to affect blessing or catastrophe. 3) The purpose of history is that people shall *walk in the light of the Lord (Isa. 1:20, 2:5),* and nations *neither shall they learn war any more (Isa. 2:4).* If, these prophetic words are truth, why are they so inoperative?

Theologians and philosophers teach that idolatry and corruption blind the eye, interpreting the idea of 'false gods' as living by principles which profane truth, pervert good, and prevent "Blessing" from entering into the world.[2] The biblical condemnations of Assyria, Egypt, and Babylon are understood as metaphors, symbolically representing various degrees of rationality. Assyria, thus, stands for reasoning from intelligence and information; Egypt represents knowledge and power; Babylon signifies the lust for domination. Each stands in contradistinction to biblical revelation. The earlier prophets railed against the sin of idolatry. The latter prophets denounced ethical and moral impropriety. There is no real conflict; both heard the same voice, saw the same light. The difference is one of emphasis.[3]

What were self-evident truths to earlier generations, needed elaboration and explanation, in order to be understood by succeeding ones.

---

2. Emanuel Swedenborg (1688–1772), *Arcana Coelestia,* as cited in William C. Dick, 'The Prophets," *The Bible: Its Letter and Spirit* (London: J.M. Dent and Sons, 1943) 185–195.

3. Idolatry includes, and, is inseparable from, ethical and moral conduct. The deception of human will and intelligence is the categorization of reality between thought, word, and deed. In the divine scheme, everything is interdependent. It is this holistic approach that got lost.

What appeared to earlier generations as a single beam of white light, appeared to later generations, as light diffracted through a prism. This process of diffusion continued until it was no longer possible to distinguish the pure colors of good from evil, nor the ethical distinctions between right and wrong. Everywhere, nothing was straightforward and clear — thought, word, behavior, and deed all appeared in multiple shades of grey. When this became the norm, the 'Voice' ceased to speak. Prophets ceased to hear. The message was spent. Malachi, the last of the prophets writes: *Behold, I will send you Elijah the prophet before the coming of the great and terrible day of the Lord (Mal. 3:23).* 'The creative period of prophecy is past, and the way of salvation lies in conformity to the wisdom of the past.'[4] It was time for teachers and sages, historians and chroniclers, to untangle the literary remains of revelation through interpretation, exegesis, and exposition.

4. I.G. Matthews (Christian Hebraist) from *An American Commentary on the Old Testament*, as cited in Malachi, Eli Cashdan, ed., *The Twelve Prophets* (London: Soncino Books of the Bible, 1974) 336.

G. Dore: Walls of Jericho Falling, *Bible Illustrations (1866)*

11

Focusing upon the Afro-American Spiritual *Joshua Fit de Battle of Jericho*, this chapter discusses the heritage of the Bible in relation to the experience of Negro slaves in Colonial America and the United States in the early 19th century.

JOSHUA

And the seven priests bearing the seven ram's horns before the ark of the Lord went on continually, and blew with the horns; and the armed men went before them; and the rearward came after the ark of the Lord, the priests blowing continually. And the second day they compassed the city once, and returned into the camp; so they did six days. And it came to pass on the seventh day, that they rose early at the dawning of the day, and compassed the city after the same manner seven times; only on that day they compassed the city seven times. And it came to pass at the seventh time, when the priests blew the horns, that Joshua said to the people: 'Shout; for the Lord hath given you the city.' So the people shouted, and the priests blew the horns (6:13–16)...and it came to pass, when the people heard the sound of the horn, and the people shouted with a great shout, that the wall fell down flat, so that the people went into the city...and they took the city (Joshua 6:20).

Although Joshua accompanied Moses forty years in the desert, and fought the wars of resettlement another twenty years, no battle looms as large as the defeat of the city of Jericho, on which his enduring fame rests. The Bible describes in detail the circling of the walls by the priests and the blowing of seven shofars, which caused the walls of Jericho to collapse. It stresses, thereby, the spiritual and religious basis for the conquest of the land — a gift of God conditional on faithfulness to the covenant: *Every place that the sole of your foot shall tread upon, to you I have given it, as I spoke unto Moses* (1:3). According to tradition, Joshua wrote the book that bears his name.[1]

Anonymous: Joshua Fit de Battle of Jericho
Text and Music: Folksong
Genre: Negro Spiritual (19th C. America)
Medium: Improvised vocal music
Performance time: ca. 1':30

Biblical Folksong and the Spiritual

Biblical subjects, which were disseminated largely through oral transference by way of sermons, prayers learnt by rote, and stories are found in the folksongs of many nations, which introduced the contents, ideas, and idioms of the Bible into their own national histories and literatures. One of the richest and most varied repertories of songs dealing with biblical events and personalities are Spirituals, the religious folksongs of the American Negro. *Joshua Fit de Battle of Jericho* retells the story with lively syncopation and colloquial black dialect; and represents the essence of biblical folksong: short, simple, and direct, which reduces a complex of events from the Bible into a few concise and pithy phrases. Many learned oratorios have been written about Joshua, but none has immortalized his achievements more than this single folksong, created in antebellum America by unnamed and illiterate slaves. What is it about the story of the siege and capture of Jericho that impressed black men in 18th and 19th-century America, enough, to make a song of it?

The origin of the Spiritual is veiled in mystery. Such texts express the black man's understanding of the white man's religion and his longing to be free. They reflect an understanding of the Bible that his ear caught from evangelist's preaching, sermons in churches, and singing at Camp meetings. His imagination transformed these recollections into words, rhythm, and tone. The anonymous black folk who wrote *Joshua Fit de Battle of Jericho* were not biblical scholars; they were taken by force from Africa

---

1. Talmud Baba Bathra 15a. The Book of Joshua is the first of the historical books of the Bible and the former Prophets, which includes also the books of Judges, Samuel, and Kings. It is divided into three parts: the conquest of the land (chapters 1–12), apportionment of the land among the tribes (chapters 13–22), and the last words of Joshua (chapters 23–24).

by Spanish, Portuguese, and British slave traders to fill manpower shortages at home, as early as 1619. The British colonies, between 1680 and 1786, imported over two million slaves. With the inven-tion of the cotton gin (1793) and the development of plantations, the need for cheap and abundant labor encouraged the slave trade. This labor force would remain in bondage until the end of the Civil War.[2]

Those Negroes who were kidnapped and brought screaming to America, had their own religions — witchcraft, voodoo, ancestor worship, animism, and various other pagan cults. They neither spoke, nor read, nor wrote, nor heard of the Bible. But, in cap-tivity, systematic attempts were made to de-Africanize the blacks — forbidding them to speak their native language, play drums, or practice their animist faiths.[3] Slave owners used Christianity to teach these enslaved beings to be longsuffering, forgiving, and obedient.[4]

Slaves were ordered to desist from the pagan practice of spiri-tual possession and urged to identify as Christians. Their owners insisted upon having them attend religious services, go to church, listen to sermons, and sing hymns. Special galleries were set apart in colonial churches for this purpose. But, rows of benches, in places of worship, discouraged captive congregants from spontane-ously jumping to their feet and dancing, while musical instruments were forbidden.

The message of Christianity, however, proved more mean-ingful and effective than its abusive prohibitions. The Christian gospel that those who suffer on earth hold a special place with God in heaven spoke to them and gave them hope. They related to this message deeply. The black slave learned from the suffering of Jesus, and genuinely embraced Christianity, saying, "Lord I want to be a Christian; I want to be like Jesus."[5] For those incarcer-ated and chained Africans who crossed the Atlantic and for their

---

2. See W.E. Burghardt Dubois, *The World and Africa* (New York: Viking Press, 1947) 54.
3. Animism is the belief that objects and natural phenomena possess souls.
4. *Servants, obey in all things your masters according to the flesh; not with eye service, as men pleasers; but in singleness of heart, fearing God (Colossians 3:22). Servants, be subject to your masters with all fear, not only to the good and gentle, but also to the forward (1 Peter 2:18).*
5. William Dawson, "Interpretation of the Religious Folk Song of the American Negro," *Etude Magazine* (Philadelphia: Theodore Presser, 1955), as cited in the booklet jacket notes to the CD, *Spirituals*, MCA Records (1992).

descendents, the Christian Bible became that instrument and guide which carved out new visions and revelations in the New World. In Virginia, for instance, it meant more than just a history of the ancient Hebrews; it was a book of liberation, as well as redemption, that protected and defended the poor and powerless slave.[6] The story of Moses and the Exodus resonated profoundly with these men and women in bondage, who saw the plantation owner as Pharaoh; and identified themselves with the enslaved children of Israel. They longed for a redeemer, like Moses. In the words and music of the Spiritual, the slave was able to vent his dissatisfaction with his station in life, voice his longing to live as a free man, humbly seeking peace and salvation from God.

Because blacks were unable to express themselves meaningfully in the white man's church, they often slipped away into the night to secret religious services, hidden "bush meetings" in invisible churches, where they were able to engage in African rituals, such as: spiritual possession, speaking in tongues, and shuffling to communal shouts and chants — sung with intricate multi-part harmonies. There, they synthesized the Bible stories they'd heard from white preachers, improvised upon psalms, spiritual songs, and hymns, and made up their own songs of suffering, struggle, overcoming, faith, and forbearance. They applied biblical metaphors to communicate ways of escape, secret codes known only to the initiate. These include such songs as: *Swing Low Sweet Chariot*, *Gospel Train*, and *Wade in the Water*. For most peoples the folksong is a product of secular life; with the Negro slave, who was kept in continuous bondage for nearly 300 years and deprived of every medium for mental and emotional expression, the folksong was his only means of getting relief from pain and frustration. Into song he put his miseries and hopes, desires and faith. He put into them, also, his longing for deliverance, sometimes expressed in secret codes. Over 100 Negro spirituals have been identified, which use texts taken from the Bible. The spiritual *Deep River*, for example, which includes the words, *My home is over Jordan*, substitutes the Jordan for the Ohio River — the boundary, beyond which runaway slaves could feel they were safe from recapture[7]

Often, these songs catalyzed around a "fixed line" which caught their imagination. It might be a Scriptural verse, such as: *Joshua fit*

---

6. Rudolph Lewis, "Nathaniel of Southampton or Balaam's Ass: God's Revelations in the Virginia Wilderness," *Chicken Bones: A Journal*. Internet resource (2007).

7. See Dawson, op. cit.; and Lewis, op. cit.

de battle of Jericho, and de walls come a' tumblin down, or *Ezekiel saw de wheel, way up in de middle of the air*, or something someone said to them at work that day in the fields. But, whatever its initial source, that key line — repeated over and over again — served as a refrain for a song. Freely invented texts — often improvised by the singers — were later added, to elaborate and fanticize upon it. When asked how such a song was born, a black informant in the 19th century gave the following description: *I'll tell you; it's dis way: My master, call me up an' order me a short peck of corn and a hundred lash. My friends see it, and is sorry for me. When dey come to de praise meeting dat night dey sing about it. Some's very good singers and know how; and dey work it in, work it in, ya know, till dey get it right; and dat's de way.*[8]

Text and Context

The form these religious folksongs took was generally verse/refrain — a synthesis of improvised native African call and response,[9] and Protestant Church hymns sung in New World churches. Texts were recombined and sung in an infinite variety of ways. "Call and response" performance was always improvised on the spur of the moment.

Analyses

The main event in the story of the battle of Jericho is ingeniously worked into a single sentence.[10] The refrain is a masterpiece of compression, reducing the complex narrative of the Bible to its essence. Reference to "the walls come-a tumblin' down" is a descriptive metaphor connected to time and place, and voicing the slaves' desire for the bonds of slavery removed and their longing to be free.

---

8. Quoted from William Francis Allen, Charles P. Ware and Lucy Mckim Garrison (eds.), *Slave Songs of the United States* (New York: A Simpson and Company, 1867), as reprinted by Peter Smith, New York (1929), and cited in Chase, *America's Music* (1955) 242.
9. Call and response is a style of singing in which a melody sung by one singer is echoed by others — either soloists or groups.
10. *And it came to pass, when the people heard the sound of the horn, that the people shouted with a great shout, and the wall fell down flat, so that the people went up into the city, every man straight before him, and they took the city (Joshua 6:20).*

Refrain

> Joshua fit de battle ob Jericho, Jericho, Jericho
> Joshua fit de battle ob Jericho
> An' de walls come tumblin' down.

The following verses have nothing to do with the Book of Joshua. They are an exchange between fellow travelers on the freedom trail, "O tell me where you travelin' to," who speak a secret code of escape, "to be that I am found."

Verse-call

> Good morning brother pilgrim
> Pray tell me where you's bound;
> O tell me where you travelin' to
> On the disenchanted ground.

Verse-response

> My aim it is poor pilgrim
> To be that I am found,
> A travelin' through this wilderness
> On the disenchanted ground; Dat mornin'.

The above interjection, *Dat mornin'* — is an invitation for all to join in the refrain. But, it may also indicate a prearranged time of escape.

Refrain

> Joshua fit de battle ob Jericho, Jericho, Jericho
> Joshua fit de battle ob Jericho
> An' de walls come tumblin' down.

The following verses reveal the awesome stature of Joshua, not only in the eyes of the slaves, but also in the eyes of the Bible. Gideon as judge and Saul as king were heroic figures. Yet, neither commanded the unquestioned authority of Joshua, who was appointed by Moses, the man of God.[11] These slaves sensed this nuance and put it into words.

---

11. When the Book of Joshua was included in early Hebrew manuscripts of the Five Books of Moses, it was referred to as the Hexateuch.

Verse

> You may talk about yo' king ob Gideon,
> You may talk about yo' man ob Saul,
> Dere's none like good ole Joshua
> At de battle ob Jericho.

> Up to de walls ob Jericho
> He marched with spear in han',
> "Go blow dem rams horns," Joshua cried,
> "Cause de battle am in my han.'"

Remarkably, black slaves were also familiar with an obscure Jewish ritual instrument blown by the priests at Jericho, the *shofar* (frequently translated as ram's horn). Their understanding bespeaks knowledge of what a *shofar* is, and, where it comes from. Yet, all this is stated simply as "den lam' ram sheep."[12]

> Den de lam' ram sheep begin to blow,
> Trumpets begin to soun'
> Joshua commanded de children to shout
> An' de walls come tumblin' down; Dat mornin'.

Refrain

> Joshua fit de battle ob Jericho, Jericho, Jericho
> Joshua fit de battle ob Jericho
> An' de walls come tumblin' down.

Music and Musical Exegesis

To the white man's psalmody and hymnody, the black man added his African tribal twists and traditions.[13] Negro slaves spent nights singing

---

12. Only the male (ram) has horns which were used as *shofars*. Sheep are females and have no horns. But, it is not so obvious that *shofars* of this sort were blown by the priests (*Den de lam' ram sheep* is a young ram). The horns of other animals may have been used, as well (see Mishneh Rosh Hashanah).

13. *The poor Negro slaves, here, never heard of Jesus or his religion till they arrived at the land of their slavery in America ... The number of these who attend on my ministry is ... about 300. And never have I been so much struck ... with so many black countenances, eagerly attentive to every word they heard, and some of them covered with tears ... They express the sensations of their hearts*

psalms and hymns and produced a veritable torrent of sacred song. He softened the clear and distinct gutturals of English pronunciation, making them closer to African dialectics (t and th became d; the phrase "that is" was contracted into "dat's"). He brought the Western diatonic scale closer to native African tribal intonations.[14] He endowed the rigidity of metrical psalmody with a new rhythmic freedom.[15] This newborn Christian enthusiastically introduced improvisation, vocal sliding, hand clapping, and body slapping into worship — sounds he 'd recollected from trance and possession rituals left behind in Africa.[16] The English musician, Henry Russell, who was in the United States from 1833 to 1841, writes of his visit to a Negro service: *When the minister gave out his own version of the Psalm, the choir commenced singing so rapidly, that the original tune absolutely ceased to exist — in fact, the fine old psalm tune became thoroughly transformed into a kind of negro melody, by accelerating the time; and so sudden was the transformation, that, for a moment, I fancied that not only the choir, but the little congregation, intended to get up and dance as part of the service.*[17]

Analyses

The tune to "Joshua Fit de Battle of Jericho," though set in the so-called

---

so much in the language of simple nature, and with such genuine indications of artless sincerity... They are exceedingly delighted with [Dr. Isaac] Watt's [Hymns and Spiritual] Songs... They have an ecstatic delight in psalmody; nor are there any books they so soon learn, or take so much pleasure in, as those used in that heavenly part of divine worship. See the letter of Rev. John Davies of Virginia to John Wesley in England, extracted from the *Journal of John Wesley*, Vol. 2, 303, as cited in Gilbert Chase, *America's Music* (New York: McGraw-Hill, 1955) 79 and 81.

14. Musical theory since the Middle Ages has noted the significance of the half-steps between the third note and the fourth note (mi-fa), and the seventh note and the octave (ti-do), as the tones which determine the mode (d r m^f s l t^d'). African intonations, however, neutralized the diatonic scale (with its distinct third and high leading tone) by lowering the third and seventh tones that came to be known as "blue notes."

15. Protestant metrical psalmody was notated and not improvised.

16. See Dawson, *Spirituals*, op. cit.

17. Henry Russell, *Cheer! Boys, Cheer! Memories of Men and Music* (London: John Macqueen, Hastings House, 1895) 84–85, as cited in Chase, *America's Music*, 235–36.

Ex. 15. Spiritual: *Joshua Fit de Battle O' Jericho*
Transcribed by the author

'sad' minor mode, is lively in tempo and marked by joyous syncopation.[18] Its structure is a balance of motivic contrasts and cadence patterns. Embedded within, but, concealed because of rhythmic activation, are recitation tones.[19] This suggests a Gregorian connection. Particularly, in the bi-partition of the tune, which exhibits the same parallelism and structural construction as Psalmody. The parallel construction between biblical verses, plainsong, the 'antiphonal' call and response' of the Spiritual, and the presence of recitation tones, generally never linked, are usually considered entirely separate, unrelated categories. This may not be so.[20] Much of the culture of Ancient Israel was formed in Egypt. Egypt is a part of Africa. Midrash relates that Moses spent 40 years as king of Cush (Ethiopia) before returning to Egypt to lead the Hebrew slaves out of bondage. Some of the kings of Egypt were black and of Ethiopian origin. There is reason to speculate that parallelism in the poetic portions of the Five Books of Moses and the Psalms may

18. This joyous-minor character is found in many religious folk songs (*piyutim*) and table songs (*zemiroth*) adopted by Jewish communities in Europe and the Middle East.
19. The Psalms reflect the high culture of the ancient world, while the Spiritual is relatively recent folk music. I would speculate that the distinction is probably more closely related, than meets the eye, and actually reflects a common origin in pre-historic Africa.
20. See Dubois, op. cit.

derive from pre-historic African models (no less than Babylonian and Mesopotamian roots). These ancient models constitute a common heritage, from which the primordial subconsciousness of the Negro slave in America, drew.

The structure of the tune is marked by two repeated periods (8 bar phrases). The refrain (opening period) contains five tones — outlining a minor pentachord (D E F G A). This may be subdivided into two 4-bar phrases. The whole of **A A** consists of three short motifs: (a) a dotted-note rhythm, outlining a rising pentachord (D E F G); (b) a syncopated third (A F A) that repeats as a lower neighboring seesaw tone-like figure (G E G), before returning (A F A); and (c) a falling pentachord dotted-note rhythm (A G F E D). It is question and answer construction, marked by a half cadence on the fifth (A), and answered by a full cadence on the tonic (D).

The verse (second period) **B B** contrasts two short motifs: (d) an upbeat figure (D C D), followed by the descending leap of a fourth (D A), and landing on a recitation tone (A A A A A A). This patterning — with its free flowing initial hovering on the fifth (A), before closing on a cadential formula (F G A G F E D) and rounding out the tune on the tonic (D) — strikes us as the country cousin of an ecclesiastic mode. These features, pretty much, also echo the proportions and structure of plainsong *(initial-tenor-medio-tenor-finalis)*.

Formal design

Part One	Part Two
8 bar period	8 bar period
4 bars 4 bars	4 bars 4 bars
A = (a b b b) + A = (a b b c)	B = (d d d c) + B = (d d d c)

Conclusion

Spirituals, a product of plantation life, ceased to be created after emancipation. It was after its generative period that the Spiritual first came to the attention of the broader public through performances by the Fisk Jubilee Singers in 1871. The group was given its name by George White, Fisk University treasurer and music professor, who created a nine-member choral ensemble of students, and took them on tour, to earn money for the university, as a gesture of encouragement to the students, who had been former slaves. White named them "The Jubilee Singers," a biblical reference to the year of the Jubilee: *Proclaim liberty throughout the land unto all the inhabitants thereof; it shall be a jubilee unto you... (Lev. 25:10).* However, their unique appeal evolved in a wide range of artistic treatments and popular arrangements,[21] continuing into the 20th century as Gospel — a popular form of urban black Christian religious music.[22]

If, in the 19th century "Joshua Fit de Battle of Jericho" drew its model from the serious cantional style of white hymns, by the 1950s, even commercial music produced by white-American rock-and-roll artists, such as Elvis Presley, recycled Spirituals in their own image as rhythm and blues, country and western, and boogie woogie. Today, rap music performers transmogrify the Spiritual, yet again, by improvising new words, and generating innovative beat and break patterns, while adding complex harmonies and electronic effects to its original verse-refrain structure.

Perhaps the influence of African pre-history and the continuing interest in the Bible, evidenced in contemporary 'Soul' music of all kinds, may be more than skin deep. After many years, Joshua's decisive battle succeeded in fulfilling its promise of claiming the land as a possession for the children of Israel.[23] The black man is now free; but his fascination with the Bible continues. The connection, we have observed, between the American-Negro Spiritual folksong and the psalmody of the ancient children of Israel, who absorbed something of black Africa on their Egyptian sojourn, clings to primordial roots and supplies deep

---

21. These songs were published under the title, *Jubilee Songs as Sung by the Jubilee Singers of Fisk University* in 1872. Later, recordings of the group were made in the early 1900s. See Fisk Jubilee Singers-Our History (2007). Internet resource: http://www.fiskjubileesingers.org/our_history.html

22. *Joshua Fit de Battle O' Jericho* has been adapted and sung as "hard metal," a form of Black-American Gospel music.

23. Its inheritance rests on two principles: 1) the voluntary acceptance of the law must be wholehearted; 2) its application involves collective responsibility: *And Israel served the Lord all the days of Joshua, and all the days of the elders that outlived Joshua, and had known all the work of the Lord, that He had wrought for Israel (24:31).*

structural clues explaining the universal appeal of the Bible within Black Culture.[24]

Other Directions

Joshua has inspired a comparatively large number of compositions. The sudden appearance of several oratorios on the subject — mainly about the fall of Jericho — beginning with G.M. Bononcini's *Il Giosuè* (1688), is no doubt directly linked with political events of the time, particularly the victories of Charles of Lorraine over the Turks at Mohacs, and of Prince Eugene of Savoy.[25] Some early 18th-century works of note are Marc Antoine Charpentier's *Josuè* (c. 1700); the oratorio-pasticcio *I trionfi di Giosuè* (1703), jointly written in Florence by more than ten composers (including Veracini and Bononcini); and other oratorios by Veracini (c. 1715), Logroscino (1743), Hasse (1743) and Handel's oratorio *Joshua*. The only noteworthy example in France is of slightly later date, *La Prise de Jèricho*, an opera put together from various sources (chiefly Mozart) by Ludwig Wenzl Lachnith (1746–1820) and Friedrich Kalkbrenner (1755–1806) in 1805.

Of the few works on the subject written during the 19th century, only Mussorgsky's retain significance. His *Jesus Navin* ("Joshua, the Son of Nun"), for baritone, alto, mixed choir, and piano, is based on melodies which he heard from Jewish neighbours in St. Petersburg about 1864. Later works about Joshua include C. Frankenstein's opera *Rahab* (première in Hamburg, 1911); Franz Waxman's oratorio *Joshua* (première in Dallas, 1959), and Ben-Zion Orgad's *The Story of the Spies* for chorus and orchestra (1953).[26] New additions include a popular Israeli children's song, *Yehoshua Hakatan* by Meir Vizltir (b.1941).

---

24. These observations, proposed as hypotheses, are confirmed in the biblical account of the origin of the races of mankind and the brotherhood of man from the sons of Noah: Shem (the Semite of the Middle East), Jafet (the Caucasian of Europe), and Ham (the Negro of Africa).

25. The Battle of Mohács (1687) was fought between Ottoman troops and the forces of the Holy Roman Empire, commanded by Charles of Lorraine. The result was a defeat for the Ottomans. Prince Eugène of Savoy (1663–1736), who made an important contribution to this victory, secured fame with his crushing victory against the Ottomans at the Battle of Zenta in 1697, which laid the foundation of Hapsburg power in central Europe.

26. Batia Bayer, "Joshua in Music," *Encyclopaedia Judaica*, Vol. 10, col. 269–270.

Works List

Bazzani, Francesco Maria (17ᵗʰ C. Parma). *La caduta di Gerico* (Josh 2–6), oratorio.

Blanchino, Ioan (17ᵗʰ C. Italy). *Impii per luestum in Josue Jericho demoliente* (Ph. Capistrellius), oratorio.

Bononcini, Giovanni (1670 Modena–1747 Vienna). *Giosue* (T. Stanzani), oratorio.

Caldara, Antonio (1670–1736 Vienna). *La caduta di Gerico* (A. Garieria), oratorio.

Charpentier, Marc-Antoine (1636–1704 Paris). *Josue*, oratorio.

Crispi, Pietro Maria (1737–1797 Rome). *La caduta di Gerico* (G. Pasquini), oratorio.

Davesne, Pierre-Just (1745–1786 Paris). *La conquete de Jericho*, oratorio.

Fatioli, Mercurio (18ᵗʰ C. Italy). *Casus Jericho sub Josue* (J. Magnani), oratorio.

Furlanetto, Bonaventura (1738–1817 Venice). *Jericho*, cantata.

Handel, George Frederic (1685–1759 London). *Joshua* (T. Morell), oratorio.

Hasse, Johann-Adolf (1699–1783 Venice). *La caduta di Gerico* (G. Pasquini), oratorio.

Jacobi, Frederick (1891 San Francisco–1952 New York). *Hagiographa: Joshua*, string quartet and piano.

Kalkbrenner, Christian (1755 Munich–1806 Paris). *La Prise de Jericho*, oratorio.

Lachnith, Ludwig Venceslav (1746 Prague–1820 Paris). *La prise de Jericho*, oratorio.

Lanciani, Flavio Carlo (18ᵗʰ C. Italy). *Gesta Josue* (Josh. 6–9), oratorio.

Mussorgsky, Modest (1839–1881 Russia). *Joshua* (Byron), choir and orchestra.

Orgad, Ben-Zion (1926 Germany–2006 Tel-Aviv). *Sipur ha-meraglim* (Story of the Spies), choir, orchestra, cantata.

Persius, Luis-Luc (1769–1819 Paris). *La conquete de Jericho*, oratorio.

Richter, Ferdinand Tobias (1649 Wurzburg–1711 Vienna). *La caduta di Gerico, oratorio.*

Rigel, Henri Jean (1772 Paris–1852). *Destruction de Jericho*, oratorio.

Saint-Amans, Louis-Joseph (1740 Marseille–1820 Paris). *La destruction de Jericho*, oratorio.

Tarp, Svend Eric (1908–1994 Denmark). *The Battle of Jericho*, orchestra.

Tuczek, Johann (1755 Prague–1820 Budapest). *Joshua am Jordan,* oratorio.

Veracini, Francesco di Nicolo (1638–1720 Florence). *Il trionfo del Giosue* (C.P. Berzini), oratorio.

Veracini, Francesco-Maria (1690–1768 Florence). *L'empieta distrutta nella cadutta di Gerico,* oratorio.

Waxmann, Franz (1906 Poland–1967 Los Angeles). *Joshua* (Forsyth), oratorio.

CHAPTER 12

Representing biblical episodes without sets, staging, or costumes, the Latin oratorio *Jephte* by Giacomo Carissimi, became a reference point for all subsequent attempts at placing Scriptural text in a sacred-dramatic context.

JUDGES

And Jephthah vowed a vow unto the Lord and said: 'If thou wilt indeed deliver the children of Ammon into my hand, then it shall be, that whatsoever cometh forth of the doors of my house to meet me...it shall be the Lord's and I will offer it up for a burnt offering'... And Jephthah came to Mizpah unto his house, and, behold, his daughter came out to meet him with timbrels and with dances; and she was his only child...And it came to pass, when he saw her, that he rent his clothes, and said: 'Alas, my daughter thou hast brought me very low, and thou art my troubler; for I have opened my mouth unto the Lord, and I cannot go back' (Judges 30–31, 34–35).

The Book of Judges deals with the period from the death of Joshua to the birth of Samuel. The transition from the austere morality of the desert to the life of agricultural settlers lasted for more than three centuries, and was wrought with difficulties and unforeseen consequences. In times of tranquility, the Israelites, forgetting their divine calling, absorbed heathen customs of their neighbors; in times of crises, leaders of outstanding military ability, political acumen, or moral authority arose to unite and defend the people, terrified of fearsome raids by surrounding peoples, or depressed by the oppression of their resentful neighbors, who sought to expand their own territories at the newcomers expense.[1] Tradition attributes its authorship to the prophet Samuel.

---

1. The Judges were regional rulers who did not transfer their positions through heredity. Scripture lists 14 such figures: Othniel, Ehud, Shamgar, Deborah

Jephthah was not only a brave fighter, he was also a skilled politician. His negotiations with the king of the Ammonites (11:12–28) are among the earliest examples of diplomatic letters of exchange in history. Yet, for all his courage and piety, Jephthah could not overcome the fatal flaw of pride.[2] The story of Jephthah's daughter, tells of a rugged warrior, whose victory over the enemy was overshadowed by terrible sorrow and personal tragedy. So anxious was Jephthah to lead Israel to victory and prove his might, that he made a vow to God: *Whatever cometh forth out of my house first to meet me when I return, I will offer up unto Thee for a burnt-offering* (11:31). After the battle, his daughter, happy to see her father honored at last, hurried to be the first to greet him.[3]

Giacomo Carissimi: Jephte (ca. 1649)

Libretto: Unknown author (composer?)
Genre: Latin Oratorio
Medium: Six solo voices (SSSATB) and organ continuo
Style: Early Baroque
First performance: Oratory of the Most Holy Crucifix, Rome, ca.1650
Duration: ca. 30 minutes

Jephte, one of the landmark works of music history, is among the earliest oratorios to have retained a place in the repertory to this day. It was first written and performed at the *Oratorium,* a chapel for religious study and discussion in Rome, which, from the middle of the 17th century, gave its name to an entire genre of musical composition. *Jephte* is scored for six solo voices and continuo (organ and bass instrument)

and Barak, Gideon, Abimelech, Tola, Jair, Jephtah, Ibzan, Elon, Abdon, and Samson. While in victory, security, and prosperity, many relinquished their spiritual heritage, lapsed into indifference, and embraced foreign customs; there were untold others who remained faithful to the God of Israel and the Laws of Moses; throughout this period, daily sacrifices in the Tabernacle continued, uninterrupted.

2. Jephthah's strange vow would have been impossible under settled conditions. The Rabbis blame Jephtah for not having his vow annulled. Phinehas, the High Priest at the time, could have done so, but for the rivalry between them (Midrash Leviticus Rabbah 37.4).

3. According to early Christian commentators, Jephthah's daughter was typologized as the forerunner of consecrated virginity, and, later, considered a paradigm of Christian virtue and martyrdom. See David Gunn, *Commentary on Judges* (Malden, MA: Blackwell, 2007) 138.

and consists in a series of short recitatives, arioso arias, duets, trios, and choruses.

Biographic Context

Master of the Latin oratorio, Giacomo Carissimi (1605–1674 Rome) was among the most influential composers and teachers of the 17th century. He adapted the new operatic style of secular monody (*stile nuovo*) to sacred composition with the idea of renewing and deepening religious feeling in an increasingly secular age. His style is characterized by alternatively expressive and energetic ariosos and choruses, and fluent accompanied recitative (*stile rappresentativo*).

The youngest son of a barrel maker, Giacomo sang in the choir at Tivoli Cathedral as a boy, remaining there as organist, until 1628. The next year, he served as choir master at the nearby city of Assisi, before accepting an offer to become maestro di cappella at the Jesuit *Collegio Germanico* in Rome, one of the most influential centers of the Counter Reformation in Europe. There, Carissimi was responsible for the education of choirboys, teaching of seminary students, and the organization of music at the Church of St. Apollinaire.[4] He was ordained in 1637 and remained at the college until his death. Contemporaries described him as "tall and thin and prone to melancholy, very gracious in his relations with friends and others."[5]

Origins of Oratorio

The precedents of oratorio, if this means the combination of biblical story with music, are many. They begin with the interspersing of hymns within liturgical forms (such as the Mass), and extend

---

4. The German College, established in 1552, trained Jesuit priests to serve as missionaries in German-speaking Protestant lands. It developed a following for its music, and, by the 17th century, during Carissimi's tenure, this reputation reached its peak. The Jesuit order was dissolved in 1773, and the College's records and manuscripts were destroyed thirty years later, when Napoleon's troops sacked Rome. We know of Carissimi's compositions only through copies made by his pupils.

5. A. Cametti, 'Primo contributo per una biografia di Giacomo Carissimi' RMI, xxiv (1917) 383. As cited in Gunther Massenkeil, "Giacomo Carissimi," *The New Grove Dictionary of Music*, Vol. 3, 785.

into incidental music and songs for medieval liturgical drama. Another important source is the collective plainchant recitation of the Passion story from the Gospels during Holy Week. Here, the narrative was taken by a solo tenor, while the words Jesus spoke (*ipissima verba*) were given to other soloists, with the utterances of the disciples and the responses of the crowds (*responsa turbae*) taken by the assembled.

In Italy and especially in Florence, a tradition developed in which bible stories (*rappresentazione* or *storia*) were recited, interspersed with hymns of praise and devotion in the vernacular (*Laudi spirituali*). One particular type of religious poem — the *dialogue laude* (dialogues between God and the Soul, and Heaven and Hell) — was sung with 3 or 4 different voice parts. At Saint Philip Neri's Congregation of the Oratorio in Rome, begun in the 1550's, *Laudi* were sung as entertainment, to attract the public to their discussions on serious spiritual matters. In time, the musical component became more sophisticated. Carissimi was the most accomplished of those who managed to weave the diverse elements of narrative recitative, sung dialogue, and contemplative choral response into a coherent artistic unity.

Text and Context

The innovative genre of Latin oratorio is a kind of devotional music, in which biblical narrative takes artistic form. Deeply connected to the life of the church, Carissimi collaborated extensively with the Congregation of the Oratory.[6] His settings of the biblical story are geared for an informed and committed congregation, rather than a more casual secular audience. His compositional style reflects this choice. Veering away from popular and folk idioms, it applies operatic conventions to sacred ends, ignoring costumes or staging.[7] At first acquaintance, the

---

6. The room (*oratorium*), where this work was (most likely) first performed, gave its name to the musical genre conceived there — Oratorio. The community — who met at the *oratorium*, organized a century before by Philip Neri, to educate and convert the common people, through sermons and vernacular dramatizations of Bible stories — consisted of lay worshippers and priests. Musical performances took place during Lent, the season beginning forty days before Easter.

7. Other subjects treated by Carissimi in this way, include the oratorios: *Abraham and Isaac, Belshazzar, Hezekiah, Job, Jonah,* and *Judgment of Salomon.*

monodic speech-song style of the Early Baroque,[8] strikes the ear as dull and simplistic — consisting mostly in dry recitations, stepwise melodic lines, and broken triadic gestures. On closer acquaintance, Carissimi's exquisite sensitivity to clarity of diction and linear direction, transforms what might seem like prosaic declamation into vivid pictorial imagery.

Probing depths of emotion and character with a unique feeling for the asymmetric phrase, and, with an unexpected ingenuity of rhythmic pacing, he endows rudimentary chords with fresh, original, and refined harmonic movement. The first, more dramatic part of *Jephte* depicts scenes of battle and triumph. The second, more inward part focuses on her lament and intimate feelings between father and daughter. Its Latin text, by an unknown writer (probably the composer), is a free paraphrase of the biblical episode, with additions and invented passages drawn from other scriptural sources. The entire story of Jephthah covers the Book of Judges, chapter 11 and chapter 12:1–7; the libretto follows chapter 11, verses 28–38,

Music and Musical Exegesis

Analyses

Part I

1. *Historicus* (narrator recitative) (11:28–30)

Cum vocasset in proelium filios Israel rex filiorum Ammon et verbis Jephte acquiescere noluisset, factus est super Jephte Spiritus Domimi et progressus ad filios Ammon votum vovit Domini discens:

Now the King of the Ammonites,
Gathered in Gilead, fought with the children of Israel;
And would not hear nor heed the messengers sent by Jephthah.
Then the Spirit of the Lord God came upon Jephthah,
And he challenged the children of Ammon,
Then he vowed a vow to God, saying:

---

8. Monodic style arose about 1600, as an attempt to emulate the ethos of ancient Greek music. It placed emphasis on proper articulation, as well as expressive interpretation of texts; and was achieved by abandoning the elaborate imitative counterpoint of the Renaissance, and replacing it with simple accompanied recitative.

The opening scene of the oratorio is structured as a complete formal unit. It contains three affects: a pronouncement by the narrator, an action by Jephte, and a response by the spectators. The *Historicus* delivers the narrative against sustained chords in the continuo with considerable variety — sometimes in fast speech rhythm (*parlando*), sometimes in triadic declamation of text. If, at first, this speech-derived music seems nothing more than innocuous filler, as the work progresses, little by little, in retrospect, these simple phrases gain in thematic stature and meaning.

2. *Jephte* (solo recitative) (11:30–31)

Si tradiderit Dominus filios Ammon in manus meas, quicumque primus de domo mea occurrerit mihi, offeram illum Domini in holocaustum.

Ex. 16. Carissimi: *Jephte,* "*Si tradiderit*"

© Copyright 1977 by Casa Ricordi. Used by permission.

> If the Lord indeed render up the children of Ammon into my hands,
> Whoever first comes through the doors of my house to meet me,
> I give to God as sacrifice, a burnt offering.

For example, *Jephte* communicates his battle prayer as a trumpet call, set against a static F major triad in the continuo. His second phrase (*whoever first comes…*) is accompanied by chromaticism in the bass. The dreadful vow is approached subtly, from below, by a single semitone (F — F-sharp). It is the first time that chromaticism appears in the work. This connotation he gives to chromaticism is no accident, for it is reconfirmed four bars later. As *Jephte's* prayer approaches a final cadence, the semitonal C to C-sharp in the bass, supports the phrase, *a burnt offering*. This chromatic touch in the harmony becomes profoundly significant in Part 2, when it is metamorphosed melodically and employed to give expression to the daughter's grief-filled "Lament." In this one interval, then, we see both the vow and its consequence realized in tone.

3. *Historicus* (chorus — narrative) (11:32)

Transivit ergo Jephte ad filios Ammon,
Ut in spiritu forti et virtute Domini pugnaret contra eos.

Ex. 17. Carissimi: *Jephte, "Transvit"*
© Copyright 1977 by Casa Ricordi. Used by permission.

> Then did Jephthah fight with the children of Ammon;
> In the strength of the spirit and the power of God on high he fought
> against them.

Throughout, choruses of six solo voices function as structural pillars, summing up aspects of the story and defining the work's formal design. In the above example, all six voices are transformed into "ideal spectators" to the drama, and assume the role of *Historicus*. Sentence structure and content are emphasized by heightened speech accents.[9] These two phrases are stylized in contrasting musical textures: the first, in vigorous metrical chords (*stile concitato*), and the second, with all six solo voices echoing one another. Insistently "hammering" the point across, they draw the opening section of the oratorio to a close: *He fought against them, fought against them, fought against them!*

Part II

Filia (aria — solo) (free invention)

Oh, ye meadows mourn me. Oh, ye mountains guard me, and to my heart's and soul's affliction join your lamentations (Echo — 2 sopranos).

Part 2

Now I must die a virgin, and alone in my hour of death, I have no children to give me comfort. Sob and sigh for me, forests, fountains and rivulets. For a virgin's sacrifice spare no weeping (Echo).

Part 3

Woe for my sorrows. In the joy of the multitude, in the victory of Israel, and glory that is my father's, I in my virginity childless, I an only begotten daughter, am sworn to death and not living. Shake and shudder ye valleys, quake and cower, ye summits, caverns and volcanoes reecho to the fearful sound loud as thunder (Echo)!

---

9. Though the people are ancient Israelites, they take on the role of a Greek chorus, commenting and responding to the action. In such a context as sacred oratorio, their presence reveals Christianity's deep and contradictory symbiosis of Classical and Hebraic values — participating in the Renaissance revival of pagan antiquity, while functioning within the Hebraic ethos of the Bible.

Part 4

Lament me children of Israel, for Jephthah's only begotten child,
in many songs of sorrow, shed your tears for her.

Jephthah's daughter's lament is voiced in sobs, characterized as semitonal appoggiatura (a melodic chromaticism, which we encountered in
Jephthah's first recitative as bass harmony). In this moving monologue,
we experience both the soul's longing for life and its deep resignation,
as the daughter takes upon herself to fulfill the rash vow of her father.
Carissimi endows the most fleeting emotional traces of heart and mind
with tonal presence. A victim of destiny, the innocent child has accepted
the vow of Jephthah, as if it were her filial duty. The magnitude of her
self-sacrifice, caused later generations to view the daughter of Jephthah
as a paradigm of Christian virtue and martyrdom. Her aria is an incomparable example of profound psychological insight and subtle depth.

Conclusion

The exact fate of Jephthah's daughter is uncertain. Some say, Jephthah
built her a house, in which she lived a solitary life.[10] Midrash reveals
that Jephthah, however, died a lingering death six years later. He lost
his limbs, one by one, in the course of his movement through the land.[11]
The commentator, Gershonides,[12] adds that at his request, his arms and
legs were buried in the different cities, where he had achieved victory
over the Ammonites, as a memorial, seeing he had no children to per-
petuate his memory. Carissimi's *Jephte* reveals the lyric side of biblical
epic, creating a profoundly human portraiture of an era: *In those days
there was no king in Israel; every man did that which was right in his own
eyes (Judges 21:25).*

Related Works[13]

The story of Jephthah's Daughter has attracted the attention of many

---

10. Medieval biblical commentator David Kimchi (1160–1235), as cited in *Soncino
Books of the Bible*, Judges (1950) 259.
11. Midrash Genesis Rabbah 60.3.
12. Rabbi Levi Ben Gershom (1288–1344).
13. See Batia Bayer, "Jephthah," *Encyclopaedia Judaica*, Vol. 9, col. 1344–1345.

oratorio composers since Giacomo Carissimi wrote his *Jephte*. The works which followed include G.B. Vitali's *Il Gefte overo Il zelo impudente* (1672; libretto only extant); A. Draghi's *Jefte* (1690); A. Lotti's *Il voto crudele (Jefta)* (1712); and *Il Sacrifizio de Jeptha* by L. Vinci (1690–1730; date of composition unknown). Michel de Monteclair's *tragédie lyrique, Jephté*, to a libretto by the abbé, S.J. Pellegrin, was the first opera on a biblical subject licensed for stage performance in France. It had its première at the Academie Royale de Musique in 1732 and was restaged in 1733 and 1734, but was immediately afterward forbidden by Cardinal de Noailles. The subject, with a text by Thomas Morell was destined to inspire Handel's last work, *Jephte*. The first performance took place in the Covent Garden Theatre, London, on Feb. 26, 1752.

During the 19ᵗʰ century, the operatic potential of the story could be realized, since religious restrictions were no longer a deterrent, and the gruesome ending with a human sacrifice attracted, rather than repelled, the Romantics. Giacomo Meyerbeer's oratorio *Jephtas Geluebde*, written in 1812 at the age of 21, has remained in manuscript. Two operas were written and performed in Spain: *Jephté* (1845) by Luis Cepeda and *La Hija de Jefté* (1876) by Ruperto Chapi. Two Jephthah cantatas figure in the list of works which won their composer the Prix de Rome of the Paris Conservatory: one by Samuel David (1858) and another by Alexandre-Samuel Rousseau (1878). Byron's *Jephthah's Daughter* was the first set to music by Isaac Nathan and subsequently among others, by Karl Loewe (1826, in a German translation) and Robert Schumann (in his *Drei Gesange*, opus 95, 1849).

Among 20ᵗʰ-century works are Lucien Haudebert's *La fille de Jephté* (1929; for orchestra); Lazare Saminsky's *The Daughter of Jephthah*, "a cantata pantomime" for solo, choir, orchestra, and dancers (1937); and Ernst Toch's "rhapsodic poem" for orchestra, *Jephta* (1963). A.Z. Idelsohn's *Yiftah*, written in Jerusalem and published in 1922, was the first opera composed in Palestine. Idelsohn wrote the (Hebrew) text himself; the music is a singular combination of various Jewish traditions — both Western and Eastern — which he had by then collected for his ethno musicological studies. Modern Israeli works on the subject include Mordechai Seter's orchestral work *Jephthah's Daughter* (1965) and several settings in the form of a pageant, created for the kibbutzim. Two dances by Amittai Ne'eman, one slow and one debkah-like and fast, both called *Bat Yiftah*, are in the Israel folk dance repertory.

Works List

Abaelard, Petrus (1079–1142 France). *Planctus virginem Israel super Filia Jephte* (Judg. 11:40), lament.

Agthe, Carl Christian (1762–1979 Germany). *Mehala die Tochter Jephta* (Judg. 11–12), musical drama, 4 voices, choir and orchestra.

Assmayer, Ignaz (1790 Salzburg–1862 Vienna). *Das Geluebde* (J. Haslauer), oratorio.

Avondano, Pedro Antonio (1714–1782 Lisbon). *Il voto di Jefte* (G. Tonioli), oratorio.

Avondano, Pietro Giorgio (18th C. Genoa). *Il voto di Jefte* (G. Tonioli), oratorio.

Balde, Jacobus (1604–1668 Germany). *Jephtias*, incidental music.

Barthelemon, Francois Hyppolite (1741 Bordeaux–1808 London). *Jefte* (Abbe Semplici), oratorio.

Berger, Jean (1909 Germany–2002 USA). *Jiphtach and His Daughter* (1972) (Judg. 11:34–49), choir, soloist and instruments.

Berton, Henry Montan (1767–1844 Paris). *Jephte*, oratorio.

Bittoni, Bernado (1756–1826 Italy). *Jephte*, oratorio.

Bloch, Augustyn Hipolit (1929 Poland–2006). *Ajelet corka Jeftego*, mystery opera.

Busoni, Ferrucio (1866 Toscana–1924 Berlin). *I saw thee weep* (Byron), voice and pianoforte.

Carissimi, Giacomo (1605–1674 Rome). *Jephte*, oratorio.

Cimarosa, Domenico (1749–1801 Venice). *Jephte*, oratorio.

Cipolla, Francesco (18th C. Naples). *La figlia di Jephte*, oratorio.

Clasing, Johann Heinrich (1779–1829 Hamburg). *Die Tochter Jephtas*, soloist, 3 choirs and orchestra.

David, Samuel (1836–1895 Paris). *Jephte*, cantata.

Deshayes, Prosper-Didier (c.1750–1820 Paris). *Le sacrifice de Jephte*, oratorio.

Draghi, Antonio (1635 Rimini, Italy–1700 Vienna). *Jefte* (G. Apolloni), oratorio.

Federici, Francesco (17th C. Rome). *Sacrificium Jephte* (S. Mesquita), oratorio.

Franchi, Giovanio Pietro (c.1650–1731 Italy). *Jephte*, oratorio.

Furlanetto, Bonaventura (1738–1817 Venice). *Il trionfo di Jefte*, oratorio.

Galuppi, Baldassare (1706–1785 Venice). *L'Jephta osia il tionfo della religione* (Vannucchi), oratorio.

Green, Maurice (1695–1755 London). *Jephta*, oratorio.

Guglielmi, Pietro (1728–1763 Naples). *Il sacrificio de Jefte*, sacred drama.

Handel, George Frederic (1685–1759 London). *Jephta* (T. Morell) (Judg. 11–12), oratorio.

Haudebert, Lucien (1877–1963 France). *La fille de Jephte*, oratorio.

Hemmerling, Carlo (1903–1968 Switzerland). *La fille de Jephte*, incidental music, soprano, tenor, baritone, choir and orchestra.

Idelsohn, Abraham Zvi (1882 Lithuania–1938 USA). *Yiftah* (Idelsohn) (1908–12) a musical drama for soprano, alto, 3 tenors, baritone, mixed choir & piano.

Jacquet de la Guerre, Elisabeth (1667–1729 Paris). *Jephte* (A.H. de la Monte), cantata, 2 voices and basso continuo.

Jensen, Adolf (1837 Konigsberg–1879 Baden-Baden). *Jephtas Tochter* (Byron), soloist, choir and orchestra.

Klein, Bernhard (1793–1832 Koln). *Jephta*, oratorio.

Konigsloew, Johann (1745 Hamburg–1833). *Jephte*, oratorio.

Lefevre, Charles Edouard (1843 Paris–1917). *La fille de Jephte* (A. De Vigny), soloist, women's choir and orchestra.

Loewe, Karl (1796–1869 Germany). *Jephtas Tochter*, song.

Lotti, Antonio (1667–1740 Venice). *Il voto crudele* (P. Pariati), oratorio.

Manfredini, Francesco (c.1688–1748 Italy). *Il sacrificio di Jefte*, oratorio.

Masini, Antonio (1639–1678 Rome). *Jefte*, oratorio.

Maurice, Pierre (1868–1936 Geneva). *La fille de Jephte*, oratorio.

Mayr, Johannes (1763–1845 Germany). *Il ritorno di Jefte*, oratorio.

Meyerbeer, Giacomo (1791 Berlin–1864 Paris). *Jephta's Geluebde*, one-act opera.

Monteclair, Michel (1666–1737 Paris). *Jephte*, opera.

Moreau, Jean Baptiste (1656–1733 Paris). *Jephte* (J. Boyer), incidental music.

Paisiello, Giovanni (1740–1816 Naples). *Jefte sacrificium*, oratorio.

Peranda, Marco Giuseppe (1625 Rome–1675 Dresden). *Il sacrificio di Jefte, oratorio.*

Piroye, Charles (1665–1728 Paris). *Jephte*, musical tragedy.

Pistocchi, Francesco-Antonio (1659 Palermo–1726 Bologna). *Il sacrificio di Gefte*, oratorio.

Pollarolo, Carlo Francesco (1653–1722 Venice). *Jefte*, oratorio.

Porsile, Giuseppe (1672 Naples–1750 Vienna). *Il sacrificio di Gefte*, sacred act.

Predieri, Giacomo Cesare (1671–1753 Bologna). *Il Gefte*, oratorio.

Radoux, Jean-Theodore (1835–1911 Liege, Belgium). *La fille de Jephte*, cantata.

Raitio, Vaino (1891 Russia–1945 Helsinki). *Jeftan tytar* (J. Linnankowski & S. Ranta), opera.

Reinthaler, Karl Martin (1822–1896 Germany). *Jephta und seine Tochter*, oratorio.

Rigel, Heinrich Joseph (1741–1799 Paris). *Jephte*, oratorio.

Righetti, Gertrude (1793–1862 Bologne). *La figlia di Jefte* (G. Pistelli), oratorio.

Rolle, Johann Heinrich (1716–1785 Germany). *Mehalia, doe Tochter Jephta's* (Niemeyer), oratorio.

Rousseau, Alexandre-Samuel (1853–1904 Paris). *La fille de Jephte* (E. Guinard), cantata.

Ruloffs, Bartholomeus (1741–1801 Amsterdam). *Jephta* (F. Meritus), cantata.

Sacchini, Antonio Maria (1730 Florence–1786 Paris). *Jephtes sacrificium* (Ascenzione), oratorio.

Sales, Pietro Pompeo (1729 Brescia, Italy–1797 Hanau, Germany). *Giefte* (M. Verazi), oratorio.

Schletterer, Hans Michael (1824–1893 Augsburg). *Die Tochter Jephta's*, soprano, alto, women's choir and pianoforte, cantata.

Schmidt, Johann Michael (1720–1792 Mainz). *Gefte* (M. Veracini), oratorio.

Schumann, Robert (1810–1856 Germany). *Die Tochter Jephtas* (Byron), voice and pianoforte.

Seter, Mordechai (1916 Russia–1994 Tel-Aviv). *Bat Yiftah*, dance symphony for orchestra.

Stanley, John (1713–1786 London). *Jephta* (F. Frere), oratorio.

Toch, Ernst (1887 Vienna–1964 St. Monica, California). *Jephta*, rhapsodic poem.

Vinchioni, Cinthyo (18th C.). *Jephte* (A. Magnani), oratorio.

Vinci, Leonardo (1690–1730 Naples). *Il sacrificio di Jephta*, oratorio.

Vitali, Giovanni Battista (1632 Bologne–1692). *Il Gefte overo il zelo impudente* (Monti), oratorio.

Zagwijn, Henri (1878–1957 Netherlands). *Jephta* (I. Vondel), narrator and choir.

Zannetti, Francesco (1737–1788 Italy). *Il sacrificio di Giefte*, oratorio.

Other Directions[14]

GIDEON

The story of Gideon consists in a divine calling, a battle, and a victory celebration (Judges 6–8). One of the major works on the subject is *Il Gedone* by Nicola Porpora[15] (Text: A Perucci), an elaborate 18th-century Italian oratorio lasting nearly two hours. It was composed and performed at the Habsburg Imperial Court Chapel in Vienna (1737). I attended a revival of this historic work, at the Hofbrung Chapel in Vienna (2006). Styled in-between the Baroque and the Classical, its impressive recitatives are reminiscent of the Latin oratorio, while its arias and choruses look ahead to the mature works of Haydn and Mozart.

An early musical interpretation on a Gideon theme occurs in the allegorical minnesang "Gideon's Wollen Fleece" (*Daz Gedeones wollenvlius*) by Rumelant (c.1270), which combines biblical prototypes of knightly ideal with the mystical concept of divine love. Later compositions include the keyboard sonata *Gideon-Der Heyland Israel's* from J. Kuhnau's *Biblische Sonaten*. Johann Mattheson's oratorio *De siegende Gideon* was written for the celebration of Prince Eugene of Savoy's victory over the Turks (1717). Other compositions include Camille Saint-Saens: *Les soldats de Gedeon* (1868), a choral work for men's voices.

Works List

Benicini, Giuseppe (18th C. Florence). *Il Trionfo di Gedeone*, oratorio.
Cola, Gregorius (17th–18th C.). *Gedeon in Harad*, oratorio.
Furlanetto, Bonaventur (1738–1817 Venice). *Gedeone*, oratorio.
Gatti, Luigi (1740 Italy–1817 Salzburg). *Trionfo di Gedeone*, oratorio.
Horsley, William (1774–1858 London). *Gideon*, oratorio.

---

14. See "Gideon in the Arts," *Encyclopaedia Judaica*, Vol. 7, col. 559–560 and "Deborah in the Arts," *Encyclopaedia Judaica*, Vol. 5, col. 1433.
15. Nicola Porpora (1686 Naples–1768 Vienna) was a famed voice teacher in Vienna, and, in a sense, mentor to the young Joseph Haydn, who served as accompanist for his voice classes, and whose countrapuntal exercises he corrected.

Kuhnau, Johann (1660–1722 Leipzig). *Der Heyland Israelis/Gideon*, Biblical Sonatas, keyboard.

Lavry, Marc (1903 Riga/1936 Israel–1968). *Gideon* (H. Hefer), oratorio.

Mattheson, Johann (1671–1764 Hamburg). *Der siegende Gideon* (Glaucke), oratorio.

Meinardus, Ludwig (1827–1896 Germany). *Gideon*, oratorio.

Porpora, Nicola (1686–1768 Naples). *Gedeone* (Perruci), oratorio.

Rigel, Heri (1772 Paris–1852). *Gedeon*, concert spiritual.

Rumsland, von Sachsen (13th C.). *Daz Gedeones wollenvlius (Gideon's Wollend Fleece)*, song.

Saint-Saens, Camille (1835 Paris–1921 Algiers). *Les Soldats de Gedeon*, double men's chorus.

Schneider, Johann Friedrich (1786–1853 Germany). *Gideon* (A. Brueggemann), oratorio.

Smith (Schmidt), John Christopher (1712 Ansbach–1795 London). *Gideon* (T. Morelli), oratorio.

Speer, Charlton (1859–1921 England). *Gideon*, opera.

Stainer, John (1840 London–1901 Italy). *Gideon*, oratorio.

Tozzi, Antonio (1736–1812 Bologna). *Il Trionfo di Gedeone* (G.F. Fattiboni), oratorio.

DEBORAH and JAEL

Deborah and Jael were popular subjects for composers. About a dozen 17th and 18th century works on these themes are known, including some of historical interest, such as: G. Fr. Rubini's dialogo, *Debora* (1656), and Porsile's *Sisara* (1719). Handel's oratorio *Deborah*, with text by Samuel Humphreys (1739) is among his earliest oratorios. Baldassare Galuppi's oratorio *Jahel* (1747, Venice), features an unusual aria, accompanied by two mandolins. 18th-century compositions were often performed in honor of women rulers, such as the empress Maria Theresa. Two successful later works were: Josef Foerster's opera *Deborah* (1893), and Ildebrando Pizzetti's opera *Debora e Jaele* (1915–1921), first performed in Milan, 1922. Settings of the verse "Thus May Thine Enemies Perish" (Judg. 5:31) by Uri Givon and Sara Levi-Tannai ("Thine Enemies, O Israel") and others, have been made into Israeli folk dances. In similar vein is the rhythmic *Hevron Sheli* (Judg. 1:20) by American Hasidic singer-composer Avraham Fried (b.1959).

Works List

Deborah

Admon, Yedidya (1894–1982). *Song of Deborah* (1955), narrator, mezzo soprano, mixed choir and orchestra, oratorio.

Algazi, Isaac (1892 Turkey–1964 Montevideo). *The Song of Deborah* (Judg. 5), soprano and choir.

Eberlin, Johann (1702–1762 Salzburg). *Debora,* oratorio.

Galuppi, Baldassare (1706–1785 Venice). *Debora Prophetissa* (P. Chiari), oratorio.

Gibbs, Cecil (1889–1960 England). *Deborah and Barak* (A. Noyes), oratorio.

Green, Maurice (1695–1755 London). *Song of Deborah and Barak* (Judg. 5), oratorio.

Guglielmi, Pietro (1728–1763 Naples). *Debora e Sisera* (C. Sernicola), azione sacra (sacred scene).

Handel, G.F. (1685 Halle–1759 London). *Deborah* (S.Humphreys) (Judg. 4–5), oratorio.

Kozeluch, Leopold (1784 Prague–1818 Vienna). *Debora e Sisera* (C. Sernicola), opera.

Kozlovski, Jozef (1757 Warsaw–1831 St. Petersburg). *Debora* (Szachowski), incidental music.

Le Fem, Paul (1881–1984 France). *Debora,* oratorio.

Le Seur, Jean-Francois (1760–1837 Paris). *Deborah,* oratorio.

Levi-Tanai, Sara (1911–2005 Jerusalem). *Debora's Song,* music for dance-theater.

Manna, Christoforo (b.1704 Naples). *Debora,* oratorio.

Moreau, Jean Baptiste (1656–1733 Paris). *Debora* (J.F. Duche), incidental music.

Natra, Sergiu (1924 Bucharest–1961 Israel). *Song of Deborah,* mezzo soprano and chamber orchestra.

Pizzetti, Ildebrando (1880–1968 Italy). *Debora e Jaele* (I. Pizzetti), opera.

Porsile, Giuseppe (1672 Naples–1750 Vienna). *Sisara,* oratorio.

Rubini, Giovanni (17th C.). *Debora* (A. Spagna), dialogue.

Valls, Josep (b.1904–1999 Barcelona). *The Song of Deborah*, symphony for orchestra.

Werner, Gregor (c. 1695–1766 Austria). *Debora*, oratorio.

Jael

Bigaglia, Diogemo (1676–1745 Venice). *Giaele* (D. Giupponi), oratorio.

Borri,Baptista (17th–18th C. France). *Jahel Sisare Debellatrix* (F. Laurentinus), drama sacrum.

Coquard, Arthur (1846 Paris–1910). *Jahel* (S.Arnaut and L.Gallet), opera.

Costanzi, Giovanni Batista (1704–1778 Rome). *Giaele*, oratorio.

Daniels, Mabel Wheeler (1878 Massachusettes, USA–1971). *Song of Jael* (Judg. 4), soprano, choir, and strings, cantata.

Galuppi, Baldassare (1706–1785 Venice). *Jahel* (Mendicanti), oratorio.

Grua, Caralo Pietro (1700 Milan–1773 Mannheim). *Jaele*, oratorio.

Pizzetti, Ildebrando (1880–1968 Italy). *Debora e Jaele* (I. Pizzetti), opera.

Sandoni, Pietro Giuseppe (1680 Bologna–1748). *Il Trionfo de Jaele*, oratorio.

G. Dore: Samson and Delilah, *Bible Illustrations (1866)*

13

Camille Saint-Saens' opera *Samson and Delilah* approaches the characters and plots of the Bible from a secular perspective, as human beings with desires and longings and struggles for supremacy.

SAMSON and DELILAH

And it came to pass, when she pressed him daily with her words, and urged him, so that his soul was vexed unto death; that he told her all his heart, and said unto her: There hath not come a razor upon my head; for I have been a Nazarite unto God from my mother's womb. If I be shaven, then my strength will go from me, and I shall become weak, and be like any other man (Judges 16:16–17).

A folk hero of the Jewish people, endowed with superhuman size and strength, Samson was the last of the judges and ruled Israel for 20 years. Righteous, unselfish, and devoted to his people, he would never couple the name of God with an untruth. Yet, in contrast to other biblical judges, who were generally upright and God-fearing examples for others, Samson was mischievous, vehement, and full of impetuous devil-may-care bravado. By succumbing to the temptations of Philistine hedonism, Samson dooms himself and endangers the national struggle of his people.[1]

Camille Saint-Saens: Samson and Delilah (1877)
Libretto: Ferdinand Lemaire
Genre: Biblical Opera
Medium: Soloists, chorus, orchestra, and ballet
Style: French Romantic

---

1.   Adin Steinsaltz, "Samson," *Biblical Images*, translated by Yehuda Hanegbi and Yehudit Keshet (Landham, MD: Jason Aronson, 1994).

First Performance: December 2, 1877, Hoftheater, Weimar

A melodramatic story of love, hate, and desire — *Samson and Delilah* is considered one of the outstanding French operas of the 19th century. Its highlight is the love scene in Delilah's tent, in which Samson's physical and spiritual conflicts and inner trials, along with the theme of disintegration of personality, are forcefully projected. It was an unusual choice as an operatic subject, since most historic libretti of its day were based either on Greek mythology, Roman history, or national subjects. Composed in the early 1870s, the work was premiered in Germany (1877).

Biographic Context

Camille Saint-Saens (1835 Paris–1921) represents the quintessential French-Romantic style — a model of proportion and balance, distinctively melodic, refined, and elegant. A child prodigy, young Camille entered the Paris Conservatoire at the age of 13, studying piano, organ, and composition with Jacques Halevy (1799–1862). His intellectual interests were many and varied: Latin Classics, astronomy, archaeology, and philosophy — the Bible was not among them. Saint-Saens' vision was clear, stoic, and uncluttered by sentiment. In his philosophical book *Problemes and Mysteres* (Paris, 1894), he writes, "As science advances God recedes...Christian virtues are not social values...Nature is without aim, she is an endless circle." While in the preface to a book by a Dr. Regnault, entitled *Hypnotism and Religion* (1897), he wrote, "Artistic faith must be an eclectic one; not appealing to any supernatural revelation, and not venturing to assert the affirmation of absolute verities."[2] Saint-Saens' interest in the story of Samson was its human dimension and the tragedy of lust in action.

Text and Context

Originally, he intended to write an oratorio on the subject; but it was Ferdinand Lemaire, a young Creole from Martinique and husband to one of Saint-Saens' cousins, who suggested that an operatic treatment

---

2. Internet resources: www.oldandoldsold.com/articles18/music-19.shtml and http://www.jstor.org/pss/737853

might be preferable. Saint-Saens agreed and invited Lemaire to draft verses, the composer remaining firmly in charge of the actual scenario.

From beginning to end, the tension between moral responsibility and carnal desire, heightened by Samson's sincere sense of duty to God and his nation, is the thread binding the entire work together. At the very heart of the opera is the great seduction scene (Act 2, Scene 3), testing whether Samson will prove faithful his calling or, forsake his duty as a righteous Judge in Israel, and plunge headlong into a sea of dark, unbridled lust. While the entire Samson saga is found in the Book of Judges, chapters 14–16, the libretto to the opera is based on events from chapter 16.

Music and Musical Exegesis

A cast of soloists, chorus, and orchestra recreate the story in fully-developed recitatives, arias, duets, and choruses, with lavish sets, spectacular stage effects, elaborate costumes, large-scale group scenes, and ballet. Saint-Saens molds natural inflections of the French language into a flexible sung recitative, underlined by descriptive orchestral accompaniment. Declamation, arioso, and aria are blended into a continuous musical tissue, which transforms biblical pronouncement into a living operatic experience. Tonal and textural duality color the temperament of the musical idiom: diatonic harmonies and clear textures symbolize virtues of faith, confidence, and repose; turbid waves of sound and dense chromaticism are metaphors for passion and carnal lust raging in Samson's soul.

DETAIL

Act 2, Scene Three (excerpt)
English translation: Walter Duculox

In the encounter with Delilah, Samson is caught in a web of his own making, held by the deepest forces of his nature. In his final surrender to physical passion, we encounter a biblical hero reduced to flesh-and-blood, and brought to ruin through his obsession for a woman. The opera *Samson and Delilah* not only recounts biblical narrative, it fills-in the turbulent human passions imbedded between the stone-like pronouncements of Scripture. The scene races along as a single impulse, in six sections.

Section 1

Enter Samson gripped by a passionate curse. He seems to be disturbed, troubled, and uncertain. He glances about. It grows darker and darker. Distant flashes of lightning.

Ex. 18. Saint-Saens: *Samson and Delilah*
© Copyright 1964 by G. Schirmer, Inc. Reproduced by permission.

Samson

Once again, to my shame, I have come here today. In vain I fought alas, this cursed sway! Yes, I still am in love, though my conscience has told me: Away, away from here, where hellish demons hold me!

Samson's passion and guilt are mirrored in rhythmically agitated syncopations of shifting sonorities and stepwise sequences of chromatic scales racing up and down, reflections of Samson's unstable mentality. The intensely emotional world of Nature calls forth in flashes of lightning from the wind instruments, and thunder from heaven via percussive bellows in short, hammer-stroke chords from the orchestra. Ominous tremolos in the strings portray storm clouds hovering above.

Section 2 — *Samson's last farewell*

Played out in musical repartee, this next section brings to the fore the dramatic clash of the opera. Mountains of theological and philosophical writings have rarely touched the crux of the conflict between Samson's monotheistic faith and Delilah's pagan polytheism, as deeply as Saint-Saens has, in this dialogue of human hearts. Delilah's confidence is spun out in suave, long-lined cantilena, supported by sensual tonalities. It is rapturous music, luxuriating in harmonic refinement. Pulsating chords, supported by harp arpeggios, evoke images of wafting scented breezes. Samson's farewell to Delilah starts as an admission of love, evolving into a tortuous contest between Samson's loyalties to God and Delilah's cynical hedonism.

Ex. 19. Saint-Saens: *Samson and Delilah*
© Copyright 1964 by G. Schirmer, Inc. Reproduced by permission.

Delilah (glides swiftly up to Samson)

It's you! You've come, you whom I love! Yes, I love you and fear you. You've

come, and all my suffering ends when I am near you! My friend, my love,
my lord and master!

Samson

Delilah, speak no more of this love, of my shame, of all I deplore!

Delilah

Samson, you whom I admire! Why scorn me and spurn my yearning?
Wherefore should you flee my desire? Why fight the burning flame that sets
your heart on fire?

Samson

Torn and tormented I still adore you. In vain I fought my heedless passion.
Once more, in sorrow, I stand before you. Once again I stumbled and fell!

Delilah

Ah, come near me, hold me close! Let me ease your needless worry! Could
you have doubts that my heart be yours, you my master, my leader, my
lord? My love, how could it lose its magic spell?

Samson

My God has chosen me as servant. I shall follow where He will lead me.
Therefore I must leave you forever, break the tender bond that held me,
and offer you at last farewell!
Israel will rise and be victorious. The Almighty hath set the day of our
triumph, sublime and glorious!
Out of heaven I heard his voice: "You shall go on and lead your people!
Have faith in them, trust in God, and rejoice! I say unto you that their night
will be ended!"

Section 3 — *Delilah's response*

Delilah

What comfort is there in my heart in Israel's glory and splendor, when now
they will tear us apart, while to your duty you surrender? For love I did
give you my life, though reason told me to refuse you. And now at last you
plunge the knife into the heart that soon will lose you!

Samson

> Delilah, do not wrong me so! I must answer the call of duty. I love you more
> than you can know, Delilah, Delilah, I love you!

Interplay of motives, in antiphony, underline the deep sexual hunger burning in the veins of the protagonists. Fleeting human feelings, ossified in between lines of scriptural narrative, have been juiced into life. Hebraic ethos and loyalty to God are depicted in primary chords, heroic wind sonorities, and sweeping surges in the strings. Clear diatonic harmonies and noble textures give expression to Samson's unflinching loyalty to God and commitment to his people. In contrast, sensual melody and chromatic harmony mirror Delilah's seductive wiles.

Section 4 — *Delilah's seduction of Samson*

The themes of both characters interact, expand, and develop throughout this section. After prolonged inner struggle, Samson succumbs to passion, uttering, "Delilah, Delilah, I love you!"[3] His unabashed admission marks the climax of the entire opera, and commences the unraveling of his personality.

Delilah

> A god more sublime than your own, through me did lay his claim upon
> you. It's the only god I know, the mighty god of love has won you!
> Remember the days of delight, remember the words you have spoken,
> promises made in a starlit night, vows that were, alas, to be broken!

Samson

> This is madness! Reproach me no more! I give in to you, I surrender. Yes,
> may the Lord strike me at once, his lightning destroy the offender:
> My heart shall beat for you alone, no God, no duty stand above you!
> See, I challenge my fate unknown: Delilah, Delilah, I love you!

---

3. But, to what does he succumb? If we examine his actions, from the perspective of the Bible, we realize that Samson succumbs, not to Delilah, but, to desires and illusions, he, himself, has created and fostered (i.e. "evil inclination"). Delilah is only a vehicle; if it were not her, it would have been someone or something else. Biblical commentators also understand the scene from a national perspective, enabling Samson to enter the Temple of the Philistines and destroy them.

Delilah (Introduction and Aria)

Wondrous and beautiful fall, like dewdrops on roses, on my heart your words so tender. Yet, I who love you so, in whom my heart reposes, to my tears I must surrender! Oh, tell me once again that you'll always be mine! Dispel the doubt and sorrow that are clouding my soul, by a lone, loving sign!
Ah, return to my caresses, feel my love that balms and blesses!
Come back to my caresses, to all that love possesses!

Seduction, symbolized in Delilah's luxuriant lulling music, is followed by a reprise of the passionate strains that opened this scene. Its very attractiveness underlines a deceit, designed to extract from Samson the secret of his strength.

Samson

Delilah, Delilah, I love you!

Delilah

Wooed by the summer breeze, all blossoms will tremble in her kisses freely granted. So, when you speak to me, deep in my heart assemble tender thoughts and dreams enchanted. No dart can fly so fast to the foe whom it harms, as I, if you still want me, will submit to your charms and fly into your arms!

DUET:

Delilah — Return to my caresses, feel my love that balms and blesses!
Samson — Let me ease the fears that cause your sighing, kiss from your eyes all the tears you are crying!

Section 5 — *Delilah rejects Samson*

In this highly charged exchange, leading to Samson's revelation of his secret, the orchestra functions as both active participant and passive spectator. The orchestra floods the action in a sensuous blanket of sound; remembers past events (by repeating previously sung phrases); and reveals undercurrents of motivation and emotion. In this way, fashioned and developed out of the scene's themes and motifs, orchestral textures undergo continuous variation, making a running commentary to the vocal repartee. Metaphorically, orchestral evocations of the forces of nature (i.e. storm, thunder, and lightning), externalize, through tonal imagery, the turbulent inner world of the characters.

Delilah (Recitative)

Yet, no … No more of this! Delilah in her heart knows that you will deceive her. You have done it before, when ardent love you swore,
and still you sought to leave her.

Samson

Yet, for you I'm flouting all, my people, my God and his call! My Lord, in whose glory is founded, what marks my life, my strength unbounded!

Delilah

Well then, you shall know my concern: God, whom you praise as your Creator, this God, by whose will you were born, this God has made you a traitor to me, whose devotion you scorn: What mysterious vow did you offer? To be so strong, what have you sworn?
Answer the fears from which I suffer!

Samson

What you ask I can never do. Why make me suspicious of you?

Delilah

If still it is true that I charm you, if Samson is still in your sway, why can you not prove it today? Your trust in me, how could it harm you?

Samson

But why, Delilah, should you care, what resolve will bind me forever,
one I swore I never would share?

Delilah

Share it with me to comfort my despair!

Samson

Useless and vain is your endeavor! *(Lightning without thunder)*

Delilah

Yes, I ask you in vain, for vain is your affection! All I meet is disdain, scorn and spiteful rejection! When my heart wants to know what may mean our perdition, instead of love you show nothing but wild suspicion.

Samson

What a heart rending choice, an ordeal past endurance!
To God I raise my voice, asking him for assurance.

Delilah

He took my youth from me, all my charms he tasted,
and now I am to be shamed, abandoned and wasted!

Samson

Almighty God, reply unto my plea!

Delilah

I cannot bid you stay. My voice is weak from crying.
Flee from here! Go away! Leave Delilah dying!

Samson

No, not that!

Delilah

Will you tell?

Samson

Do not ask!

Delilah

If you want me to live, you must reveal your secret!

(Lightning without thunder)

Samson

The Lord in righteous wrath is sending us a warning.
If I stray from my path, we'll never see the morning.

Delilah

His command I defy. Come!

Samson

No! God on high will rend us asunder.

Delilah

And I laugh at his thunder.

Samson

It's the voice of my God!

Delilah

Liar! You and your God! Now I despise you! Away!

(Thunder and lightning. Delilah runs towards her dwelling. The storm breaks in all its fury. Samson raising his hands to heaven seems to call upon God. Then he springs in pursuit of Delilah, hesitates, and finally enters the dwelling.)

Section 6 — Philistine soldiers capture Samson

The brutal capture of Samson, by the Philistines, rounds out the act, pulling together, into a single knot, all the strands of Samson's lust and Delilah's vengeance. With respect to the structure of the overall scene, this section functions as the musical equivalent of an orchestral coda.

(Philistine soldiers enter and softly approach Delilah's dwelling. Tremendous crash of thunder. Delilah appears on the terrace.)

Delilah

To me, Philistines!

Samson

Ah, betrayed!

(The soldiers rush into the house. The curtain falls.)

Conclusion

In *Samson and Delilah*, the "medium is the message." Saint-Saens rejected the static form of oratorio in favor of the dramatic pathos of opera, because his perspective on the biblical story is human desire and will, not divine concern. He views biblical heroes as "earthly" creatures of flesh and blood, neither as prophets nor saints. The concern of the Bible, however, is not, ultimately, the exploration of the free will of man, nor its entanglement in a web of passion. Rather, it is the fate of the Blessing of God: Where is it? With whom is it? Who is worthy of bearing it? Who is responsible for it? Who forfeits it — the people, the nation, or a single individual? The Bible is not quite literature, and the people of the Bible are not, exclusively, literary studies in character types.

Scripture grants Samson free will, but tests and judges his way of life from a moral standpoint. The ethical blindness of his decisions, clearly suggested by Samson's physical blindness at the end of the opera, is his responsibility, alone. The complex emotive excesses that led to Samson's demise are a consequence of that free will, bestowed upon him. Yet, in a larger sense, the chosen are never totally abandoned; through penitence and suffering, they may again attain forgiveness and reconciliation. In the end, Samson is granted the power he forfeited, so as to wreak vengeance upon his oppressors.

Opera is a forum for pathos, not a platform for ideas; unlike the Bible, it has no ethical agenda. Conceived as music-drama, it affords opportunity for artistic imagination to express the human dimension within the biblical imperative, in this case, the void between what man desires and cosmic duty obliges. It is so easy to listen to the voices of sensuous idols, and so hard to receive the Voice of the One God. Samson succumbed to the first, but remained faithful to the second. For better or for worse, it is the privilege and prerogative of musical art to step back and view the mystery of revelation as a totality; to enter into this space of free-will and give it substance.[4]

---

4. Books of the Bible are interconnected. Events in the Book of Ruth, for example, took place during the period of the Judges; and there is a connection between the story of Samson and the Book of Ruth. Midrash reveals *Boaz made for his sons and daughters 120 wedding feasts. To none of them did he invite Manoach, the father of Samson.* And since Manoach, before the birth of Samson, had no children, whose wedding feasts he could invite him to, Boaz retorted: *Whereby will the barren mule repay me?* In consequence of this callousness, all of Boaz's 30 sons and 30 daughters died in his lifetime (Judges 12:8); while Manoach's only child became a judge in Israel (Talmud Baba Bathra 91a). In a tragic twist of fate, the son of Manoach, Samson, was tested through the same quality of arrogant thoughtlessness that had

Other Directions

Biblical Opera[5]

Though operas on biblical characters and subjects have existed since the 17th century, the term *Biblical opera*, as a genre, seems to have originated with the Russian pianist and composer Anton Rubinstein (1824–1894), whose concept of *Sacred opera* (*Geistliche Oper*) has been understood as an offshoot of Wagner's "Ring Cycle," and conceived as a monotheistic counterbalance to this profoundly and consciously pagan music drama, based on Nordic mythology.

If Baroque opera originated as musical dramatizations of Greek fables and tragedy, and Roman History; their sacred counterparts consisted in the Mystery and Miracle Plays of the Middle Ages, that portrayed Bible stories with music and song. Greek tragedy, with its heroic conflicts, tragic loves, and pride-filled fates — spurned Classical drama. While Hebrew ethos, and its poetic dialogue with the invisible, omnipresent, and omnipotent (in praise and prayer, prophetic denunciation, promise, and calls to repentance) — evolved into liturgy. Nonetheless, these two strands came together in the 17th century, in an attempt to give dramatic and musical realization to the characters and events of the Bible.

There is a connection between those who grew up, so to speak, in the embrace of the church, and those who did not. German composer Johann Theile (1646–1724), one of the last pupils of the Protestant composer of the Bible, Heinrich Schutz, wrote one of the first biblical operas — *Adam und Eva* (1678). In England, Edward Eccleston

---

mocked his father — to see if the offspring of the injured, when placed in a superior position, would have acted differently than the mocker of his father. It was a challenge that revealed a fatal flaw in Samson's make-up. Moral: The poor man will decry the injury of the privileged, but, when conditions are reversed, would he behave any better? This is the deep measure of truth, lurking behind the imperatives and judgments of God — measure for measure. The resolution of these subtle dissonances, shifting in every combination and permutation from generation to generation, leads humanity, in increments, towards climax, resolution, and the perfection, which constitutes the content of history.

5. See American music critic Henry Edward Krehbiel (1854–1923), *A Second Book of Operas — Their Histories, Their Plots, and Their Music*, chapters 1–3 (UK: Orth Press, 2007) [1917]) 1–48. Internet resource: www.gutenberg.org/etext/3770

produced an opera called *Noah's Flood* or the *Destruction of the World* (1679). Johann Philipp Förtsch (1652–1732), a statesman and a physician was another German composer of the period, who, in addition to operas on Classical mythology, produced also *Kain and Abel* (1689). German opera composer Reinhard Keiser (1674–1739) — an early influence on Handel, during his years of apprenticeship in Hamburg — wrote over a hundred operas; one of these on Nebuchadnezzar: *Der gestürzte und wieder erhöhte Nebukadnezar, König zu Babylon* (1704). Keiser was not only the son of an organist, but, from the age of 11, had been educated at the Thomas School in Leipzig, where his teachers included Johann Kuhnau, a direct predecessor of Bach.

A landmark work was the opera *Joseph* (1807) (inspired by the play *Omasis, ou Joseph en Égypte*) by French composer Etienne Henri Méhul (1763–1817), one of the earliest French Romantic composers, and highly regarded by Berlioz. He studied in childhood with the blind organist of a convent, and later took organ lessons with Wilhelm Hauser, a German musician at the monastery of Lavaldieu. Curiously, this background in ecclesiastical music emerges in the religious sentiments expressed in the drama, with "simplicity, grandeur, and lofty sentiment." Numerous operas were also written on the Jephtah story (Rolle: *Mehala, die Tochter Jephrtas*, 1784; Meyerbeer: *Jephtha's Tochter*, 1784; Generali: *Il voto di Jefte*, 1827; Sanpieri: *La Figlia di Jefte*, 1872).

Works by Verdi: *Nabucco* (1840) and Saint-Saens: *Samson and Delilah* (1877) supplement this list. Anton Rubinstein presents another perspective. He was born of a Jewish father and mother, who converted to Russian Orthodoxy because of anti-Semitism. For him, his commitment to sacred opera takes on the dimension of a quest for personal identity. An oft quoted line from his notebooks, reads: 'To the Christians I am a Jew, to the Jewish I am a Christian, to the Russians I am a German, to the Germans I am a Russian.' (Sentiments similar to Guastav Mahler, *see note 6, chapter 5*). He not only wrote the one act, *Der Thurm zu Babel* (1870); the biblical representation, *Sulamith* (1883); *Das verlorene Paradies* (after Milton), published around 1860; the sacred operas *Moses* (Riga, 1894); and *Christus* (Bremen 1895); but, also sought, unsuccessfully, to find a place, like Wagner's Bayreuth, which would be a sympathetic home for the performance of these works.

Related Works on the Samson Theme[6]

In the second half of the 17th century, there were stock Italian oratorios, including *La caduta de'Filistei* by Veracini (1665; libretto only survived) and *Samson vindicatus* by Alessandro Scarlatti (1696; music lost). Voltaire's *Samson* was set by Rameau (1732) but not performed; another setting was made at the beginning of the 19th century by Stanislas Champein and a third in 1790 by Wekerlin. Milton's *Samson Agonistes* was the basis for the libretto to Handel's oratorio, *Samson* (1744). Works on the subject composed at the end of the 18th and beginning of the 19th century are notable in transferring the subject to the stage. Rubin Goldmark wrote a symphonic poem, *Samson* (1913); Nicholas Nabokov wrote incidental music to Milton's *Samson Agonistes* (1938); and Bernard Rogers devoted a one-act opera, *The Warrior*, to the Samson and Delilah story (1947). At the beginning of the Israel War of Independence, Marc Lavry wrote *Ze'ad Shimson* (text by Avigdor Hameiri)("March, Samson, towards Philistia...march, thou regiment of a desperate nation ...") for tenor solo, three-part men's choir, and orchestra as a topical choral piece. Recent songs include Delilah's regretful love song by Russian-American, Regina Spector: *Samson* (2006) and Samson's rhythmic prayer (16:28) to topple the pillars on the Philistines by Israeli Dov Shurin: *Zochreni Na* (2002).

Works List

Abaelard, Petrus (1079–1142 France). *Planctus fili Israel super Samson* (P. Abaelard), lament.

Basili, Francesco (1767–1850 Rome). *Sansone in tamnata* (A.L. Tottola), tragico-sacred act.

Brossard, Sebastian de (1655–1730 France). *Samson et Dalila*, cantata.

Cambini, Giuseppe Maria (1746 Italy-ca.1825). *Samson* (F. Voltaire), oratorio.

Cesarini, Carlo Francesco (1664–1730 Rome). *Samson vindicatus*, oratorio.

---

6. A musical dialogue between Samson and Delilah, *Samson dux fortissime*, is something of a historical enigma (G. Reese, *Music in the Middle Ages* (1940) 244). See Batia Bayer, "Samson in Music," *Encyclopaedia Judaica*, Vol. 14, col. 776–777.

Colonna, Giovanni Paolo (1637–1695 Bologne). *Sansone*, oratorio.

Ferrari, Benedetto (1597–1681 Italy). *Sansone* (F. Cavalotti), oratorio.

Foerster, Joseph Bohuslav (1859–1931 Prague). *Samson* (J. Vrchlicky), incidental music.

Frontini, Francesco Paolo (1860–1939 Sicily). *Sansone e Dalila* (P. Mobilia), biblical act.

Gallenberg, Wenzel Robert (1783 Vienna–1839 Rome). *Samson oder die Niederlage der Philister*, ballet.

Gazzaniga, Giuseppe (1743–1818 Italy). *Samsone*, oratorio.

Goldmark, Rubin (1872–1936 New York). *Samson*, orchestra.

Graupner, Christoph (1683–1760 Darmstadt). *Der Fall des grossen Richters in Israel* (Simson Feind), oratorio.

Grechaninoff, Alexander (1864 Moscow–1956 New York). *Samson*, oratorio.

Handel, Georg Frederic (1685–1759 London). *Samson* (N. Hamilton after Milton), oratorio.

Jacquet de la Guerre, Elisabeth (1667–1729 Paris). *Samson* (A.H. de la Motte), cantata, voice, instruments and basso-continuo.

Laurenti, Bartolomeo-Girolamo (1644–1726 Bologne). *Il ginochini di Sansone*, oratorio.

Maconchy, Elisabeth (1907 Ireland–1994 England). *How Samson bore away the gates of Gaza* (N.V. Lindsay), voice, pianoforte.

Mereaux, Jean Nicolas (1745–1797 France). *Samson*, oratorio.

Nabokov, Nikolai (1903 Belarus–1978 New York). *Samson Agonistes* (J. Milton), incidental music.

Pasterwitz, George (1730–1803 Austria). *Samson*, religious play with music.

Pessard, Emile (1843–1917 Paris). *Dalila*, oratorio.

Rameau, Jean-Philippe (1683–1764 Paris). *Samson* (F. Voltaire), tragic-lyrical opera.

Rogers, Bernard (1893–1968 New York). *The Warrior*, opera.

Rolle, Johann Heinrich (1716–1785 Germany). *Simson* (Patzke), oratorio.

Saint-Saens, Charles-Camille (1835 Paris–1921 Algier). *Samson et Dalila* (F. Lamaire), opera.

Scarlatti, Alessandro (1660 Valencia–1656 Vienna). *Samson vindicatus* (B. Pamphily), oratorio.

Stephanescu, George (1843–1925 Bucharest). *Dalila*, soloist, choir, orchestra, cantata.

Szokolay, Sandor (b.1931 Hungary). *Samson* (S. Szokolay after L. Nemeth), opera.

Tuczek, Johann (1755 Prague–1820 Budapest). *Samson, Richter in Israel* (Schuster), oratorio.

Veracini, Francesco di Nicolo (1638–1720 Florence). *La caduta de Filistei nella morte di Sansone* (C.P. Berzini), oratorio.

Weckerlin, Jean Baptiste (1821–1910 France). *Samson* (F. Voltaire), soloist, choir, orchestra.

Zamrzla, Rudolf (1869–1930 Prague). *Simson* (Zavrel), opera.

G. Dore: Samuel Blessing Saul, *Bible Illustrations (1866)*

14

Prophetic oracle is given voice and political slant via speaking, singing, shouting, hooting, and whistling in Max Stern's contemporary vocal-instrumental episode, *Prophet or King*.

SAMUEL 1

Then all the elders of Israel gathered themselves together, and came to Samuel unto Ramah, and they said to him, "Behold, you are grown old, and your sons have not followed your ways. Therefore appoint a king for us, to judge [govern] us like all the nations." But the thing displeased Samuel when they said "Give us a king to govern us." And Samuel prayed unto the Lord   (Samuel 8:4–5).

Throughout the period of the judges, Israel had been ruled by prophets and leaders raised up by God and marked by sacred and charismatic authority. The Book of Samuel tells how political rule in the form of kingship comes to Israel. It forms a bridge between the period of tribal rule and the monarchic era. This story accounts for the coming into being of legitimate, and specifically political, authority within the history of a holy people ruled by God.[1] In demanding a king, the elders do not want a particular king but the institution of kingship. Samuel's vivid description is an account of the nature of political rule inherent in kingship. The king has the right and power to draw extensively

---

1.   See Allan Silver, "Requesting a King," in Michael Walzer et al., *The Jewish Political Tradition*, Vol. I (New Haven: Yale University Press, 2000) 120–26. In the Book of Judges, it is the lone individual (like Samuel), who ultimately acknowledges God as King, and not the group. The men of Israel wished to acclaim Gideon as dynastic ruler: *Rule over us, you, your son and your grandson as well*. Gideon, however, refuses dynastic rule, *I will not rule over you myself, nor shall my son rule over you, the Lord alone shall rule over you* (Judg. 8:22–23).

on the kingdom's resources to sustain his court and retinue. He may take a tenth of grain, vintage, and flocks; fields, vineyards, and olive groves without number. The elders, their sons, daughters, and slaves will become the king's subjects. The struggles that follow between Samuel and Israel's first king, Saul, set the tone for all subsequent conflicts of prophets and kings.

Max Stern: Prophet or King (2006)
Libretto: 1 Samuel, chapter 8
Genre: Biblical episode
Medium: Baritone, two narrators (soprano and alto), chorus, instrumental ensemble and shofar
Style: Tonal / Aleatory
First Performance: Ben-Gurion University of the Negev, May 28, 2007
Duration: ca. 15 minutes

Prophet or King draws upon the attitude and mindset of mass protest. It depicts the prophet Samuel confronting a people bent on setting a man over themselves as king, in a collage of recitative, cantillation, singing, speaking and shouting. The work was commissioned for the international conference on *Spiritual Authority: Struggles over Cultural Power in Jewish Thought* and first performed at Ben-Gurion University of the Negev by a vocal and instrumental ensemble under the composer's direction on May 28, 2007.

Text and Context

This biblical episode brings up-to-date the Scriptural account of prophetic rejection by the people, reaching beyond the purely historical, to marshal power from the voice of the angry mob of all times, and place it within a contemporary context. Strikers, protesters, agitators, and grumblers of all sorts, add their voices to the ancients in demanding the needs of the moment, while ignoring the call of Eternity. Based primarily upon incidents from 1 Samuel, chapter 8, the texts for the libretto were adapted by the composer from chapter 8:4–5, 7, 9, 11:17, 19–20; chapter 11:14; chapter 12:1–3; 19–21; and Psalm 146:10.[2]

---

2.   *Prophet or King* is based on the haftorah reading to the Torah portion *Korach*, which is chanted to traditional cantillation modes (1 Samuel 11:14–12:22).

Music and Musical Exegesis

Prophet or King is an inclusive work, involving both professional musicians and university students, along with players on all levels. The ensemble includes: flutes, violins, violas, saxophones, bassoon (or cello), and percussion. Instrumentation is flexible, while vocal and instrumental demands are modest. The ancient Jewish ritual instrument *shofar* is sounded at structural points throughout the work, intended to metaphorically serve as a symbol for the spirit of prophecy: *Shall the horn be blown in a city and the people not tremble (Amos 1:4, 6)*.[3]

Analyses

Prophet or King

The melodic curves of Samuel's recitations derive from Ashkenazi-Jewish prayer modes (Dorian-Aeolian), used, also, in the cantillation of the Books of the Prophets in the synagogue: A B c d e f g a b-flat c' d'. Collective rhythmic chanting accompanies the People on their way to Gilgal. Then, one person from the crowd shouts, insultingly, at Samuel, stimulating others, likewise, to join in the barrage.

Narrators:

> Then said Samuel to the people

Samuel:

> Come and let us go to Gilgal, and renew the kingdom there.

Choir:

> And all the people went to Gilgal: and there made Saul king (11:4).
> Behold, thou art old,
> And thy sons walk not in thy ways (8:5).

Choir:

> Place a king over us; that we also may be like all the nations (8:19–20).

---

3. The *shofar* is an instrument rich in historic and ethical symbolism. It was blown on Mount Sinai at the revelation of the Divine. It is blown on the Jewish New Year (*Rosh Hashanah*) as a symbol of repentance. It will be blown in the future, heralding the Messianic Age.

Ex. 20. Max Stern: *Prophet or King*

At the onset, a Yemenite-Jewish prayer song is introduced, inconspicuously in the background, and repeated a number of times. It is used bi-functionally; here it serves as a *cantus firmus*; later, it is sung outright. The origin of the tune is significant, in that it functions in synagogue liturgy to accompany the return of the Torah scroll to the ark. The text it melodicizes: *The Lord will reign forever and ever* (Ps.146:10), introduces an enthronement motif into the liturgy, and bears a direct relationship to the theme of the entire work.[4] This association between tune and text is crucial, because, when a contrafact text is superimposed onto this tune: *Place a king over us; that we also may be like all the nations (8:19–20)*, it serves as a metaphor to imply the inverted and incongruous juxtaposition of sacred values and profane desires.

Narrators:

> And Samuel said unto all Israel (12:1):

Samuel:

> Behold, I have hearkened unto your voice and made a king over you.
> And I am old and gray headed, and
> I have walked before you from my youth unto this day (12:1–2).

Samuel, in an arioso-recitative derived from this *cantus firmus* tune, attempts to justify himself before the people. Responding passionately to his challenging query, they acknowledge and respect the Prophet's integrity, but, will accept neither his counsel nor advice.

> Here I am, witness against me — whose ox have I taken?
> Whose ass have I taken? Whom have I defrauded?
> Whom have I oppressed?
> Of whose hand have I taken a ransom (12:3)?

Choir:

> Thou hast not defrauded us, nor oppressed us,
> Nor taken of any man's hand (8:4).

The "maddening crowd" demeanor of the chorus — chanting, speaking, and shouting in rhythmic unisons and free antiphonal exchanges — is often infixed, as improvisatory sections within a wider structural

---

4. The inclusion of this verse in the present work draws upon liturgical associations with the theme of divine enthronement: *The Lord reigns, the Lord has reigned; the Lord will reign for all eternity* (*Ps. 10:6, Ps. 93:1, Exod. 15:18*).

context and frame. These verbal sections emerge out of melody in the same way that rebellious voices of the people emerge from the anonymity of the crowd. The world of thought is speech; the world of faith is song.

Narrator:

> This shall be the manner of the king that shall reign over you; he will take
> your sons, and your daughters, and fields, and vineyards, and olive yards,
> and give them to his servants, and your best young men;
> and ye shall be his servants (8:11–17).

Choir:

> Nay; but there shall be a king over us;
> That we also may be like all the nations (8:19–20)!

The voice of God is represented by treble voices. The angelic atmosphere it evokes is brighter and calmer, contrasting markedly with what has gone before. Their song is major in tonality; their soft, still, almost motionless presence silences both Samuel's sorrowful anger, and the people's anxious impatience.

Angels:

> Hearken unto the voice of the people in all that they say unto thee; for
> they have not rejected thee, but they have rejected me, that I should not
> be king over them (8:7). Now hearken unto their voice; howbeit, earnestly
> forewarn them the judgment of the king that shall rule over them (8:9).

Samuel's call for rain is echoed throughout the choir in improvised onomatopoeic mumbling, whistling, swishing, and howling. These vocal sounds integrate into the instrumental textures of the ensemble to graphically simulate a storm: *that he may send thunder and rain.*

Samuel:

> I will call unto the Lord that he may send thunder and rain;
> And ye shall know that your wickedness is great, in asking for a king (8:17).

Set for speaking voices, the phrase *Pray for thy servants* emerges in a chain reaction from the chorus, like a shiver, and denotes recognition of guilt. This supplication for forgiveness and acknowledgement of misjudgment, on the part of the sinful multitude, is spontaneous.

Choir:

> Pray for thy servants (12:19).

Samuel:

> Fear not; ye have indeed done all this evil;
> Yet turn not aside from following the Lord,
> And turn not aside after vain things.
> For the Lord will not forsake his people
> For his great name's sake (12:20–21).

Choir:

> The Lord will reign forever and ever (Ps. 146:10).

A Sephardic liturgical melody concludes the work.[5] This time, there is no irony, anger, or accusation. The original text and tune are retained. Harmonized in warm euphony, it is sung forthright, an expression of the people's sincere contrition, a gesture of reconciliation: *The Lord will reign forever and ever.*

Conclusion

Prophet or King employs traditional and unconventional techniques to convey a political theme touched upon in the Bible. The episode surrounding the coronation of the first king in the history of Israel allows Scripture to reflect on the inherently problematic nature of kingship. Spiritual leadership alone is not enough for the masses. The prophet Samuel, who retires from leadership without blemish, dramatically articulates the dangers of earthly power. The king, after coronation, will cynically and ruthlessly take advantage of the people to realize his own ambitions. Nonetheless, the people reject the prophetic voice. It was a problem then, and remains so to this day.[6]

---

5. Its metaphor both parallels and contrasts with the adaptation of a Yemenite tune, heard earlier. Yet, in synagogue liturgy, both function similarly (Psalm 146:10).

6. From the program note written by Avraham Gross, Professor of Jewish History, Ben-Gurion University of the Negev, for the premiere. See *Spiritual Authority: Struggles over Cultural Power in Jewish thought,* edited by Howard Kreisel (Beer Sheva: Ben-Gurion University of the Negev Press, 2009) 63–70.

Related Directions

Hannah's prayer or the *Song of Hannah* (1 Sam. 2:2–10) is the most important prayer uttered by a woman in the Bible. It is the paradigm for the New Testament "Canticle of the Virgin" or "Magnificat" (*Magnificat anima mea Dominum* — My soul doth magnify the Lord, Luke 1:46–55), one of the liturgical texts most frequently set, since the Renaissance. Hannah's prayer or song of thanksgiving is a paroxysm of praise, a frenzied ecstasy by a woman, joyous beyond her senses at the birth of a son, after nineteen bitter, barren, and fruitless years of sterility. As such a prayer to the Lord, filled with awe, wonder, love, and visceral confidence in her own regenerative potency, a contemporary cantata for soprano, oboe, and strings by Max Stern, interprets *Hannah's Song of Praise*. Other characters set to music include: Samuel, the High Priest Eli, and Saul.

HANNAH

Planjavsky, Peter (1947 Vienna). *Hanna und Eli*, ballad for soprano and organ.

Schutz, Heinrich (1585–1672 Dresden) *Exultavit cor meum in Domino* (1 Sam. 2:1–2), choir.

Semegen, Daria (1946 Germany/1951 USA). *Prayer of Hannah* (1 Sam. 2), soprano and piano.

Stern, Max (1947 USA/1976 Israel). *Song of Hannah* (1 Sam. 2:2–5, 9, 10), soprano, oboe and strings.

SAMUEL

Adlgasser, Anton Cajetan (1729 Germany–1777 Salzburg). *Samuel und Eli* (1 Sam. 3), oratorio.

Bartlett, Homer (1845–1920 New York). *Samuel*, oratorio.

Cassini, Giovanni Maria (1652–1719 Florence). *La nascita di Samuele* (G.M. Cassini), oratorio.

Hammerschmidt, Andreas (1612–1675 Germany). *Samuel* (J. Keimann), incidental music.

Levi-Tanai, Sara (1911–2005 Jerusalem). *The Boy Samuel*, music for Dance Theater.

Martucci, Giuseppe (1856–1909 Naples). *Samuel*, oratorio.

Mayr, Johannes (1763–1845 Germany). *Samuele*, oratorio.

ELI
The High Priest

Bonfichi, Paolo (1769–1840 Italy). *La Morte di Eli* (G.B Rasi), oratorio.
Costa, Michael (1810 Italy–1844 England). *Eli*, oratorio.

SAUL

And Saul said unto Samuel, Yea, I have obeyed the voice of the Lord...And Samuel said, Behold to obey is better than sacrifice...for rebellion is as the sin of witchcraft...Because thou hast rejected the word of the Lord, he hath rejected thee from being king (1 Samuel 15: 20–23).

Saul the son of Kish, of the tribe of Benjamin, was the first king of Israel. Although the land had been ruled by judges for many generations, the people clamored for a king, like other nations. Samuel prayed, and the Lord directed him to anoint such a king. But, although Saul defeated the Philistines in battle, and went on to defeat Moab, Ammon, Edom, the kings of Zobah, and the Amalekites, God rejected him. Why? The answer usually put forth is that Saul's disobedience consisted in not following the Lord with a whole heart. Reluctantly, Samuel concurs with the divine decree. Saul, who was commanded to destroy Amalek entirely, saved their king, Agag, and the best of their flocks.[7] After Samuel's death, the Philistines invaded Israelite territory, again. Saul had a foreboding of disaster, but, without Samuel to confer with God on the outcome of the battle, sought counsel with a witch at En Dor. The result of this séance confirmed his worst fears and divulged the bitter truth — that Saul's entire army would be routed, and he and his three sons would be killed in battle on Mount Gilboa (1 Sam. 9–31:6).

The tragedy of Saul is the story of a man 'who came in second

---

7.   Saul's ambivalent nature was the cause of his unworthiness for kingship in Israel. On the one hand, Saul reveals inability to overcome the compassionate side of his nature, to fulfill the divine command, in relation to Amalek (1 Sam. 15:9), but, on the other hand, he exhibits excessive cruelty towards the priests of Nob (1 Sam. 22:19) (Compare this with the behavior of Abraham concerning the Sacrifice of Isaac, chapter 4, or David confronting Goliath, in the next chapter).

best', the 'almost was', the 'could have been.' His, is the fate of a good, but not wholly righteous man, thrust into a position of authority and responsibility, beyond his capacity. This sympathetic attitude towards human frailty has appealed deeply to composers, making the portrayal of Saul and the disintegration of his personality, through jealousy and rage, such a moving character study.

Works List

Andreozzi, Gaetano (1763 Naples–1826 Paris). *Saulle* (F.S.Solfi), oratorio.

Arnold, Samuel (1740–1802 London). *The Curse of Saul* (1 Sam. 9–31), anthem.

Bantock, Granville (1868–1946 London). *Saul*, symphonic overture with organ.

Bazzini, Antonio (1818–1897 Italy). *Saul* (V. Alfieri), incidental music.

Berg, Carl Natanael (1879–1957 Sweden). *Saul och David* (Froeding), Baritone and orchestra.

Boyce, William (1710–1779 London). *Saul and Jonathan* (1 Sam.), cantata.

Charpentier, Marc-Antoine (1636–1704 Paris). *Mors Saulis et Jonathae* (1 Sm), oratorio.

Dello Joio, Norman (1913–2008 USA). *Lamentations on Saul*, baritone, strings, and piano.

Enescu, George (1881 Romania–1955 Paris). *La vision de Saul* (E. Adenis), cantata for soli, choir and orchestra.

Gastinel, Leon-Gustave (1823–1906 Paris). *Saul*, oratorio.

Giroust, Francois (1750–1799 France). *Les Fureurs de Saul*, oratorio.

Glanville-Hicks, Peggy (1912–1990 Australia). *Saul and the Witch of Endor*, ballet.

Gossec, Francois-Joseph (1734–1829 France). *Saul*, oratorio.

Hajdu, Andre (1932 Hungary/1965 Israel). *Saul and Michal*, choir.

Handel, George Frederick (1685 Germany–1759 London). *Saul* (N. Hamilton) (1 Sam. 16–31), oratorio.

Harbison, John (b.1938 USA). *Samuel Chapter* (1 Sam 3) (2004), collage for soprano and orchestra.

Hiller, Ferdinand (1811–1885 Germany). *Saul*, oratorio.

Hoffman, Ernst Theodor (E.T.A.) (1776–1822 Germany). *Saul, Koenig von Israel* (L. Caignez, I. von Seyfried), melodrama.

Jumentier, Bernard (1749–1829 France). *Les Fureurs de Saul*, oratorio.

Lachnith, Ludwig (1746 Prague–1820 Paris). *Saul* (Charles Morel), incidental music.

Loew, Karl (1796–1869 Germany). "Saul vor seiner letzen Schlact" (German translation of Byron: *Hebrew Melodies* by F. Theremin), song for baritone and piano.

Majo, Gian Franscesco (1740–1770 Italy). *Per la morte di Gionata e di Saule,* cantata.

Milhaud, Darius (1892–1974 France). *Saul,* incidental music.

Mondonville, Jean-Josephe (1711–1772 France). *Les Fureurs de Saul,* oratorio.

Musorgsky, Modest (1839–1881 Russia). *King Saul* (Byron), song for voice and orchestra.

Parry, Hubert (1848–1918 England). *King Saul,* oratorio.

Pearsall, Robert (1979–1856 Germany). *Saul and the Witch of Endor,* cantata.

Purcell, Henry (1659–1695 London). *In Guilty Night* (1 Sam. 28:8–20), 3 voices, and basso continuo (organ/harps).

Reutter, Hermann(1900–1985 Germany). *Saul* (A. Lernet-Holenia), opera.

Rolle, Johann Heinrich (1716–1785 Germany). *Saul oder die Gewalt der Musik* (Patzke), oratorio.

Salieri, Antonio (1750 Veneto–1825 Vienna). *Saulle,* oratorio.

Savard, Augustin (1861–1943 Paris). *La vision de Saul,* cantata.

Seyfried, Ignaz (1776–1841 Vienna). *Saul, Koenig von Israel,* oratorio.

Tal, Joseph (1910 Germany/1934 Israel–2008). *Saul at En-Dor,* opera.

Vaccai, Nicola (1790–1848 Italy). *Saul* (F. Romani), opera.

G. Dore: David and Goliath, *Bible Illustrations (1866)*

15

The biblical text is implicit rather than explicit in Johann Kuhnau's *The Battle between David and Goliath*, as extramusical ideas and images are evoked in the mind of the listener, solely by means of a keyboard instrument.

DAVID and GOLIATH

And David spoke to the men that stood by him saying: 'What shall be done to the man that killeth this Philistine, and taketh away the taunt from Israel? For who is this uncircumcised Philistine, that he should have taunted the armies of the living God (1 Samuel 17:26)?'... Thou comest to me with a sword and with a spear, and with a javelin; but I come to thee in the name of the Lord of hosts, the God of the armies of Israel (1 Samuel 17:45).

The story of David and Goliath is among the most thrilling in all of Scripture. It pits a boy, armed only with a sling shot and a few pebbles, against a giant, whose ferocity threw fear into the bravest of men. Such asymmetrical combat staggers the imagination.

Johann Kuhnau: The Battle between David and Goliath (1700)
Subtext: 1 Samuel, chapter 17
Genre: Program sonata
Medium: Keyboard music
Style: Baroque
Duration: ca. 15 minutes

Biblische Historien or *Biblical Sonatas* based on Old Testament stories[1]

---

1.   *The six Biblical Sonatas* include: I — The Battle between David and Goliath; II — Saul Cured Through Music by David; III — Jacob's Wedding; IV — The Mortally Ill and then Restored Hezekiah; V — Gideon, the Deliverer of Israel;

are among the earliest examples of program music in music history, and were the last keyboard works published by Johann Kuhnau. They are, perhaps, the most completely programmed compositions in the entire keyboard literature. Greatly admired by his contemporaries, they are, today, almost the only works of Kuhnau still regularly performed.

Biographic Context

Johann Kuhnau (1660–1722), one of the last of the Renaissance men and a major figure in late German Baroque music, combined erudition with practical musicianship. In Leipzig, he was *Director Musices* of the major churches in the city (from 1701), responsible for music at the university, as well as the city musicians. A prominent figure of his own time, Kuhnau is known today, principally as Bach's immediate predecessor as organist at the Thomaskirche, and Kantor at the Thomasschule, where he taught singing and religion.

The Kuhnau family fled from Bohemia during the Counter-Reformation because of their Protestant faith. From the age of 10, young Johann was educated as a chorister and organist by court musicians in Dresden, one of the centers of German musical culture. He studied Latin, French, and Italian at court. On his own, he learned Hebrew and Greek, as well as mathematics. He also studied law at the University of Leipzig and became a successful practicing lawyer, also publishing novels and a book (*The Musical Quack*, 1700), in which he voices his deeply moral convictions about the meaning and mission of music: *Music is something incomparable and divine. To this, even its enemies and the ignorant must acknowledge their gratitude, because they behold before them the testimony of all reasonable souls and indeed even that of the Holy Ghost... In all justice music should be granted precedence before most of the other arts, for its power on the human spirit is miraculous and indeed can frequently soften, tame, and calm not just stones and all intelligent beasts — as the poets have written of the music of Orpheus and Amphion — but also frequently the rock-hard hearts, and the bestial and untamed desires of men.*[2] During the secular and religious controversies of his tenure, when many thought that the church needed star

---

VI — Jacob's Death and Burial.

2.   Johann Kuhnau, *The Musical Charlatan*, translated by John R. Russell (Suffolk, England: Boydell & Brewer, 1997) 3.

musicians to entertain their congregants, Kuhnau, true to his convictions, remained a sober, traditional church musician and cantor, faithful to the ideals of the Reformation.[3]

Text and Context

The following fanciful account of *The Battle between David and Goliath* was written by Kuhnau and intended to be read before performing the work. It reveals an articulate and refined man, intimately familiar with, and deeply sympathetic to, the message of the Bible.

Program note by Johann Kuhnau

The portrait of the great Goliath painted in the Scriptures is rather unusual. For here we see one of nature's monsters, a giant as strong as a horse. If one were to measure him he would be longer than 6 ells. The tall brass helmet on his head makes a significant contribution to his appearance and great size. The scaly armor and the cuisses around his thighs, the great shield which he carries, and his spear, which is reinforced with iron and reminiscent of a huge beam, are enough to demonstrate that he must indeed be very strong, and that these heavy objects weighing several hundred-weight are not in the least able to inconvenience him.

If one is quite aghast at the mere description of this man, it is easy to see why the poor Israelites were terrified when they came face to face with their enemy in the flesh. For he stands before them in his brass accoutrements which as it were challenge the brightness of the sun, and makes a terrible din with the overlapping metal scales. He snorts and roars as if he wished to devour them all at once. His words resound in their ears like terrible thunder. He pours scorn on his enemies and on their weapons, and challenges a champion to come forward out of their camp. This single combat shall determine the shoulders on

---

3. The implication is that churches sought musicians, who, identifying also as entertainers, would bend to the growing secularism arising from the popularity of opera and deliver operatic church music to their congregations. See Tanya Kevorkian, *Baroque Piety: Religion, Society and Music in Leipzig, 1650–1750* (Leipzig: Ashgate Publishing, 2007) 129.

which the yoke of servitude is to weigh. He fondly imagines that in this way the scepter of the Israelites will fall into the hands of the Philistines.

But now a miracle happens. Since all the champions of Israel have lost heart, since everyone flees as soon as the giant appears, and since the monstrous warrior continues to mock his enemies in his usual manner, David appears, a young, courageous shepherd lad, and proposes to engage the fearful warrior in single combat. This, he is told, is being rather presumptuous. But David cannot be dissuaded. He adheres to his heroic proposal, and is questioned at an audience with King Saul. David tells him that only recently with God's help he had fought a bear and a lion that had stolen one of his sheep, had recovered the intended prey from the mouths of the wild beasts, and had then killed them. Thus he hopes to win the combat with the bear and lion of the Philistines. Trusting firmly in the help of God, he faces the mighty giant armed with a sling and a number of carefully selected stones.

The Philistines now think, the giant hero will sweep away his puny foe like a speck of dust, or kill him like a fly. Especially since he is enraged and has started to shower terrible curses on David, whom he considers to be a bastardly cur who is armed not with the weapons of a soldier, but with a shepherd's staff. Yet he fails to frighten David, who calls upon God and prophesies to his adversary that he will very soon fall to the ground without sword, his spear and shield, that he will lose his head, and that the rump of his body will be eaten by the birds and the wild beasts. With this David rushes towards the Philistine and slinging a sharp stone, inflicts a terrible wound upon his forehead, so that he falls to the ground. Before he can stand up again, David seizes the opportunity, throttles him with his own sword, and carries his severed head as a trophy from the battlefield.

Just as the Israelites had in the past fled from the snorting and stamping of the great Goliath, so the Philistines now flee after the victory of little David, giving the Israelites an opportunity to pursue them, and to litter the road with the bodies of the slain fugitives. It is easy to imagine how great the joy of the victorious Hebrews must have been. An idea of this is given by the fact that the women come out of the cities of the land of Israel to meet the victors with drums, violins and other musical instruments, and sing a song with many choirs. The text of this is: Saul has killed his thousands, and David his tens of thousands.[4]

Music and Musical Exegesis

In Kuhnau's preface to the original published edition, Leipzig, 1700, he writes: "So that I now may justify the more readily what I intended to show in this work, I deem it necessary to say something about the various kinds of expression attainable through music...Thus, in the first sonata, I represent the snorting and stamping of Goliath by means of the low-pitched and (on account of the dotted notes) defiant sounding theme, as well as by the rumbling sounds [of the organ or harpsichord]; the flight of the Philistines and the pursuit, by a fugue with rapid notes, because the voices follow each other quickly...And in all such cases, a sympathetic interpretation is essential..."[5]

The Battle between David and Goliath

The sonata is in eight movements; each section has an Italian caption describing the action taking place.

1

The Boasting of Goliath[6]

March-like, an ascending C major scale symbolizes the determination of the combatants. Dotted rhythms represent the steps of the giant; keyboard arpeggios (recalling trumpet-like fanfares) represent David. High and low registers contrast, and symbolically denote good and evil,

---

4. Kuhnau, *Musicalische Vorstellung Einiger Biblischer Historien*, CD notes, translated by Alfred Clayton, Gustav Leonhardt, edition, Hamburg: Teldec Classic International (1970).

5. Kuhnau's preface is reprinted in a modern edition — Kuhnau, *Biblical Sonata No. 1: The Battle between David and Goliath,* Margery Halford, editor, translated from the German by Willard A. Palmer (Port Washington, NY: Alfred Publishing, 1976).

6. These subtitles are translations of the original Italian captions supplied by Kuhnau.

as motifs are freely combined and imaginatively varied. The loosely defined form is built from four strophic-like sections.

A
(Bars 1–15, tonic-dominant harmonic motion)
A
(Bars 16–32, a cycle of fifths modulating to the subdominant)
A
(Bars 33–42, returning back to a tonic pedal)
A (coda)
(Bars 43–45, emphasizing tonic-dominant exchange)

2

*The trembling of the Israelites at the appearance
of the giant and their prayer made to God*

This movement is a chorale prelude in miniature. In slow tempo, chords, strung onto a descending chromatic bass line, change beat by beat. These underscore the 'trembling' effect (of the Israelites' fear) harmonically; while, their prayer and supplication are delineated as a sustained melodic line hovering above the chords.[7]

3

*David's courage and his desire to blunt and assail the pride of the
frightening enemy, together with his confidence placed in God's aid*

The moderate tempo, steady pace, and gentle rolling 3/4 meter of this minuet, underline David's unconquerable faith. In the face of danger, he is confident enough to sway in an *Allegretto* dance meter without being either nervous or upset. An arpeggio motif, so integrated into the melodic line as to pass almost unnoticed,[8] hearkens back to the heroic fanfare-like flourish of the opening movement and denotes the idea of

---

7. This melodic line is in fact the chorale melody to Martin Luther's hymn *Aus tiefen Noth schrei ich zu dir (1523) (From the depths of Woe I cry unto thee* (a paraphrase on Psalm 130). Kuhnau's audience would immediately have recognized the familiar tune used on Psalm Sundays in the Thomaskirche.

8. The arpeggio, placed within the phrase, is introduced and repeated three times, in bars 4, 5 and 6 (i.e. g c' g e e f), to exhibit David's courage and confidence.

assailing the giant's pride. The movement consists in three variations of a theme.

A
(Bars 1–16, tonic)
A var. 1
(Bars 17–35, dominant)
A var. 2
(Bars 36–56, tonic)

4
The battle between the one and the other and their contest

Ex. 21. Johann Kuhnau: *The Battle between David and Goliath*
© Copyright 1976 Alfred Publishing Co. Used by permission.

Each event in this recitative-like movement is depicted with marked contrasts in mood, tempo, and texture. Its three sections contain: 1) a short 10 bar episode recalling the opening movement — in content, tempo, and meter; 2) a rising circle of fifths and upward moving stepwise scale embody the will to battle; 3) and a trombone-like fanfare in the bass, sounded against sixteenth note figures in the uppermost region of the keyboard (borrowed from the third movement), manifest David's courage.

The stone, which David flings from his sling and that sinks into the forehead of Goliath, though only one bar of music, is the focal event of the sonata. Racing up the keyboard, a very rapid cadenza traces the trajectory of the stone.

Ex. 22. Johann Kuhnau: *The Battle between David and Goliath*
© Copyright 1976 Alfred Publishing Co. Used by permission.

The Philistine's demise is illustrated in a five bar segment, comprised of chromatic harmonies and repeated-note-fragments attached to a descending minor scale. Altogether, it conjures up imagery of the life-force slowly extinguished from the fallen giant's body.

Ex. 23. Johann Kuhnau: *The Battle between David and Goliath*
© Copyright 1976 Alfred Publishing Co. Used by permission.

5

*The flight of the Philistines who are hunted
and slaughtered by the Israelites*

The ensuing flight of the Philistines is displayed as a mad barrage of sixteenth notes, similar to passages found Bach's keyboard preludes and toccatas. This brief movement is only 26 bars long.

6

The joy of the Israelites in their victory

This joyful movement is a lyric siciliana dance. Framed in a moderate 3/8 meter and constructed in 8 bar periods, it flows easily, in dotted rhythms. Its eighty bars are parsed into a number of free variations.

7

The music concert given by the women in honor of David

Steadily holding its own from beginning to end, David's *music concert* is happy music. It combines previously heard trumpet fanfares with upward progressions by fifths (moving stepwise), and bears resemblance to the third movement.

8

The common rejoicing and the dancing and gaiety of the people

This final movement is a real minuet and trio. It transforms and recombines motifs from the second and seventh movements: *David's confidence in God* and *The joy of the Israelites in victory*.

Conclusion

In *The Battle between David and Goliath* and his other *Biblical Sonatas*, Kuhnau clairvoyantly demonstrates how keyboard music, without a poetic text, can capture the emotional state of an action and depict character. The sources of his inspiration are not immediately evident, and his work appears to emerge from nowhere. My hunch is that Kuhnau was influenced by the Italian madrigal and its technique of tone painting words. In these sonatas, he tries his hand at injecting something of that literary and visual imagery into instrumental music.[9] In his biography of J. S. Bach, Spitta[10] wrote, "The Biblical Sonatas... are throughout, so interesting to the musician, that they still must give pleasure to every intelligent player. Each Sonata is a collection of short,

---

9. Indeed, Northern European Renaissance and Baroque religious painting of the time, almost invariably represent biblical scenes in European landscapes and costumes. The Bible was a frame of reference.
10. See Philipp Spitta (1841–1894), *Johann Sebastian Bach*, English translation Clara Bell & J. A. Fuller-Maitland (Mineola, NY: Dover, 1979 [Reprint]).

related movements. The descriptive titles by Kuhnau give us important insights and clues into his musical symbolism."

In his attempt to tone paint the Bible, Kuhnau linked the language arts and music. The Bible played a significant, but overlooked, role in this process as a sturdy point of reference — a *cantus firmus*, if yo...u will — motivating a late Baroque master to infuse its message with life. His idea that music could tell a story or suggest a sentiment expressed in a text, applied concepts from oratory and rhetoric, familiar in his time from ancient Greek and Roman writers, such as Aristotle, Cicero, and Quintilian, whose works had emerged in the Renaissance, to musical composition. Later, such new insights became widespread, known as the doctrine of affections. Many 18th century theorists looked upon phrase structure, chord progression, rhythmic scansion, melodic construction, texture, and performance as the *rhetoric of music*. Instrumental program music was born.[11]

Related Works

The encounter between David and Goliath is dealt with in a number of significant works from the 18th to the 20th century.

Bartel, Hans-Christian (b.1932 Germany). *David and Goliath* (2000), orchestra.

Berlinski, Hermann (1910 Leipzig–2001 Washington, D.C.). *David and Goliath*, baritone and orchestra.

Bertoni, Ferdinando-Gasparo (1725 Spain–1813 Italy). *Davide triunfante di Goliat*, oratorio.

Bononocini, Giovanni (1670–1747 Vienna). *La vittoria di Davidde contra Golia* (P. Seta), oratorio.

Cuclin, Dimitrie (1885–1978 Romania). *David si Goliat*, oratorio.

Furlanetto, Bonaventura (1738–1817 Venice). *David Goliath triumphator*, oratorio; David in Sieberg, oratorio.

Detweiler, Alan (c. 1930 Canada). *David and Goliath* (1971). tenor, 2 basses, SATB, instruments, percussion, harp.

Kuhnau, Johann (1660–1722 Leipzig). *Musikalische Vorstellung einiger*

---

11. George J. Buelow, "Rhetoric and Music," *The New Grove Dictionary of Music*, Vol. 15, 793–802; Leonard G. Ratner, *Classic Music: Expression, Form, and Style* (New York: Schirmer Books, 1980) 31.

Biblischen Historien in 6 Sonaten fuer Klavier. (a) *Der Streit zwischen David und Goliath*; (b) *Der von David vermittelst der Music curirte Saul,* sonatas, klavier.

Kunzen, Adoph Carl (1720–1781 Germany). *Goliath,* oratorio.

_____. *Busse Davids,* oratorio.

Pasquini, Bernardo (1637–1710 Rome). *David trionfante contra Goliath,* oratorio.

Saint-Amans, Louis-Joseph (1740 Marseille–1820 Paris). *David et Goliath,* oratorio.

Salomon, Karel (1897 Heidelberg–1974 Jerusalem). *David and Goliath* (A. Baer), miniature opera.

Silvani, Giuseppe Antonio (1672–1727 Bologne). *Il Golia ucciso de Davidde.* 1 Samuel 17, oratorio.

Sternberg, Erich-Walter (1898 Berlin–1974 Tel Aviv). *David and Goliath* (M. Claudius), orchestra and voices.

G. Dore: Saul Attempts the Life of David

16

Le Roi David by Arthur Honegger retells the story of King David in spoken word and tone as a series of tableaus employing polytonal idioms. It was written just after the First World War and bespeaks a vernacular aesthetic devoid of Late Romantic bombast.

SAMUEL II

And Samuel said unto Jesse: 'Are these all thy children?' And he said: 'There remaineth yet the youngest, and, behold, he keepeth the sheep.' And Samuel said unto Jesse: 'Send and fetch for him; for we will not sit down till he come hither.' And he sent, and brought him in. Now he was ruddy, and withal of beautiful form, and goodly to look upon. And the Lord said: 'Arise, anoint him; for this is he'   (I Samuel 16:11–12).

A ruddy, shepherd boy and brave youth who overcomes the Philistine giant Goliath without a weapon, David became the son-in-law of Saul, Israel's first king. A musician, poet, author of Psalms, lover of many women, architect of the Temple in Jerusalem — the city he captured, built, and transformed into the capital of his monarchy — David is the most luminously gifted figure in the Bible and the archetype of ideal kingship. But, as king, himself, David, became sire to a troubled dynasty.[1] He was adored by his contemporaries and acclaimed by later generations as scion of the Messiah. Samuel I and II, originally one book, deals with events in the lives of Samuel, Saul, and David. The Talmud assigns authorship of the book to Gad the seer and Nathan the prophet (Talmud Baba Bathra 15a).

Arthur Honegger: King David (Le Roi David) (1921)
Text: Rene Morax

---

1.   Yair Zakovitch, *David: from Shepherd to Messiah* (Jerusalem: Yad Yitzhak Ben Zvi, 1995) 9.

Genre: Symphonic Psalm (Oratorio)
Medium: Soloists, mixed chorus (subdivided into men's and women's choirs), instrumental ensemble (piccolo, flute, oboe, 2 clarinets, bassoon, 2 horns, 2 trumpets, trombone, percussion, piano, harmonium)
Style: Polytonal
First performance: Theatre du Jorat, Mezieres, 1921
Duration: ca. 1 hour 10 minutes

King David (Le Roi David) retells the life of King David in a unique combination of spoken narration, songs, choruses, and instrumental portraits. Its unique designation: *Psaume symphonique*, or, a Symphonic psalm in three parts, after a drama by Rene Morax, reveals an underlying aesthetic of prayer, more so, even, than its historical revival of a biblical hero. Written for the reopening of Theatre du Jorat, a regional theatre in the Swiss village of Mezieres, it was premiered there in 1921.

Biographic Context

Composer

Arthur Honegger (1892 Le Havre, France–1955 Paris) was born and spent most of his life in France — deeply influenced by his parents' Swiss Protestant ancestry, as well as the French Catholicism of the land of his birth. He studied violin, theory, and composition at the Zurich Conservatory and Paris Conservatoire, and by the time he was discharged from the Swiss military, during the First World War (1914–1915), had already completed his studies. His style strives for a direct and popular realism, rejecting both the bombast of Late German Romanticism, as well as the refinements of French Impressionism.[2] His artistic connection to the Bible is perhaps coincidental, yet, the colorful, eclectic *King David* score he produced became a classic: lyrical, lovely, exciting, grotesque, rising even to grandeur.

---

2. These musical values were shared by many young French composers at the time. Honegger's name became affiliated with a special group of colleagues, whom history has dubbed *Les Six*. Their innovations consisted in a hybridization of the traditional French values of objectivity and clarity, with outlandish modernistic innovations.

Librettist

Rene Morax (1873–1963) was a writer of small comedies and jokes, as well as a theatre director, organizer, and promoter. He studied in Lausanne, Paris, and Berlin; and founded the *Theatre du Jorat* ("the sublime barn") as a kind of people's theatre in 1908. The tragedy of the First World War brought a pause in its activity, until 1921. In the aftermath, Morax reconsidered the role of art and his place in the artistic avantgarde. The English writer, H. G. Wells (1866–1946), who was equally shaken by the First World War, reacted by writing the popular *Outline of History*, and confesses that he did so, in an attempt to understand what had brought civilization to this brink of disaster.[3] Wells articulates the feelings of many who lived through that era: *Everywhere there were unwonted privations; everywhere there was mourning. The tale of the dead and mutilated mounted to many millions. Men felt crises in the world's affairs. They were too weary and heartsick to consider complicated possibilities. They were not sure whether they were facing a disaster to civilization or the inauguration of a new phase of human association.*[4] In consequence of the Great War and the reconstruction, Rene Morax, a jovial man of the theatre, turned to the Scriptures, reversing the 'art for arts sake' aesthetic of the pre-war period, in search of a culturally involved art that sought to inspire renewed hope amongst his contemporaries. He found what he was looking for, recounting the life of the legendary biblical king. Originally conceived as a stage work with mime and dance, Morax commissioned young Arthur Honegger to write incidental music, on the recommendation of Swiss conductor Ernest Ansermet. His *Le Roi David*, one of the most celebrated oratorios of the 20th century, consists in a series of short, picturesque tableaus, styled after French musical theatre, but with profounder purposes and objectives.[5]

---

3. During those years, many composers in our study turned to the Bible, producing works inspired from its pages (e.g. Bloch, Schoenberg, Kodaly, and Stravinsky).
4. H. G. Wells, *Outline of History*, Vol. 1 (New York, Garden City Books, 1956, [1919]) 1.
5. Honegger was swept up in this atmosphere of people bereft of all they hold near and dear, almost at the edge of sanity, turning to the Bible, and in believing, renew faith.

Text and Context

Le Roi David portrays David's story without sectarian message or didactic moralizing. Morax weaves and integrates psalms that David wrote at various stages of his career, into the events of his life. This intimate aspect of the libretto is deeply meaningful, because it affords an insight into the origins of familiar Psalms. The text draws upon I Samuel (chapters 16–31) and II Samuel (in its entirety), 1 Kings (chapters 1–2:11), 1 Chronicles (chapters 11–29), and selections from the Psalms — paraphrased into metrical verse and rhyme. The work is structured in three parts.

Synopses

Part I

From Shepherd to King

1. Instrumental Introduction and Narrator
2. Psalm 23: Song of the Shepherd David (child's voice)
3. Narrator and Psalm 18:47–49: *Praised Be the Lord* (mixed chorus)
4. Song of Victory (1 Samuel 18:6–7) (chorus)
5. Procession and Narrator
6. Psalm 11: *Fear nothing* (tenor solo) / Narrator
7. Psalm 55: *O for the wings of a dove* (soprano solo) and Narrator
8. Psalm 103:15–16: Song of the Prophets (male choir) and Narrator
9. Psalm 57: *Have mercy on me, O God* (tenor solo) and Narrator
10. Saul's Camp and Narrator
11. Psalm 27: *The Lord is my light* (chorus) and Narrator
12. Incantation: The Prophetess (recitative) and The Shade of Samuel
13. March of the Philistines and Narrator
14. Lament of Gilboa (2 Samuel 1:19–27) (female choir-mourners) and Narrator

Part II

Jerusalem

15. Narrator and Festival Song (soloists and female choir)
16. Dance before the Ark: Narrator — Chorus — Priests — Women — Warriors — Priests — Young Girls — Chorus — An Angel — Choir of Angels

Part III
Bathsheba — Absalom — Solomon — Old Age — Messiah

17. Canticle (chorus)
18. Narrator
19. Penitential Psalm 51 (chorus) and Narrator
20. Psalm 51 (chorus) and Narrator
21. Psalm 121 (tenor solo) and Narrator
22. The Song of Ephraim (soprano and female chorus) and Narrator
23. March of the Hebrews and Narrator
24. Psalm 18 (chorus) and Narrator
25. Psalm (chorus) and Narrator
26. The Crowning of Solomon and Narrator
27. The Death of David (soprano and chorus) — Narrator — Angel — Choir of Angels

Translation by Keith Anderson

Music and Musical Exegesis

Honegger, along with the other composers of *Les Six*, were informed by the French literary figure Jean Cocteau (1889–1963) and his *Appel a l'ordre* — a call to order in response to the felt catastrophic chaos of the war — rejected the indulgence of post-Romanticism for a neo-Classical musical aesthetic of discipline, order, purity, and clarity.[6] We can better understand, from this perspective, *King David's* blend of popular styles, jazz, and neo-Baroque polyphony. Each number is written in a compact and straightforward melodic idiom. Voices are heard in every combination, accompanied and *a cappella* — as soloists, in mixed choruses, and separated into choirs of women and men.[7] Two or more different keys are often sounded melodically. Harmonies are built upon primary triads enriched by added notes, and combined into polychords — which drift in planes of sonority, generating colorist effects. Parts I, II, and III conclude with extended choruses that, because they were designed to be

---

6. See Kenneth Silver, *Esprit de Corps: the Art of the Parisian Avant-Garde and the First World War, 1914–1925* (Princeton University Press and Thames and Hudson. 1989).

7. Frequently performed in a full orchestra version, this 'symphonic psalm' was originally scored for: piccolo, flute, oboe, 2 clarinets, bassoon, horn, 2 trumpets, trombone, percussion, contrabass and piano (harmonium).

performed by amateurs, employ rudimentary imitative choral textures and modest counterpoint.

Honegger's music is most of all theatrical; and strives for histrionic effects that illustrate action, define mood, and reinforce structure. For example, the trombone fanfare, accompanying the entrance of Goliath, dramatizes the text: *And there went out a champion out of the camp of the Philistines named Goliath, a giant* (17:6), by painting the battle scene. The people's accolades of victorious David — *Saul hath slain his thousands, and David his tens of thousands* (18:7) — are couched in confident brass fanfares, filled with triplets and dotted rhythms, reminiscent of French military music. Psalm 27 is sung by the mixed chorus, underlined in shining brass chords; while Psalm 57, *Have pity on me* is an air for solo tenor, accompanied by a tortured chromatic counterpoint in the English horn. In the funeral march for Jonathan and Saul at Gilboa (2 Samuel 1), incantations from a women's choir, reenact the mournful laments of wailing women (*mekonenot*).[8] In the sublime, final *Alleluia*, Honegger awakens the spirit of an ecclesiastical *jubilus*, summoning melismatic choral polyphony to accompany David's ascension into heaven.

DETAIL 1

Chantique du Berger David

Honegger sets Psalm 23 in the French vernacular, shaped and patterned after folksong. It is a paraphrased psalm translation, borrowed from French Renaissance poet, Clement Marot.[9] David sings it as if he were a young French boy. Honegger indicates musically that David is one of the people, by employing folk imagery and vernacular melody.

Yet, his style is contradictory, for, though its melody is diatonic,

---

8.   In the biblical and Talmudic period, women were actively involved in mourning rites, composing dirges, and leading responsive recitations and wailing chants.

9.   Clemet Marot (1496–1544) was one of the greatest poets of the French Renaissance. When not engaged in writing official poems at the French court, Marot spent most of his time translating Psalms. Notable for their sober and solemn musicality, his metrical biblical poetry was sung to various popular tunes, even at the Catholic court in France. They formed the basis for the *Geneva Psalter*, 1543, used by Swiss Protestant Reformer, John Calvin (1509–1564), in the psalm singing, which took place in his church.

its accompaniment is chromatic — even polytonal. Clearly, this is not pure French folk music, but rather an artistic reflection upon David's ambiguous innocence and sophistication. Through this use of polytonality, cross-relationships,[10] and augmented second intervals, Honegger evokes a kind of Orientalism, simulating the Arabic *hejaz* mode.[11] The young psalmist is accompanied, also, by wind instruments, and not, by his more traditional stringed lyre. Why? Perhaps, it is because wind instruments conjure up images of shepherds' pipes (their tones eliciting the bleating voices of the flock), so that here, we glimpse Honegger tone painting a scene, and not only setting a Psalm text.

Song of the Shepherd David (Psalm 23)

L'Eternel est mon berger / Je ne suis que son agneau.
Conduis-moi par tes sentiers /Au vallon des fraiches eaux.

L'Eternel est mon rocher / Et mon pre vert et fleuri
Il est l'ombre du figuier / Sous le soleil de midi.

L' Eternel est mon abri / Quand la foudre gronde au ciel.
L'Eternel est mon ami / Je t'aime et je te benis
Tu es L'Eternel.

—

The Lord is my shepherd
I am but his lamb.
Lead me by your paths
To the valley of fresh waters.

The Lord is my rock
And my meadow.
Green with flowers,
He is the shade of the fig-tree
Under the mid-day sun.

---

10. Cross relationships are altered and natural forms of the same pitch, within close melodic or harmonic proximity (i.e. the notes C and C-sharp used interchangeably). This effect blurs the clarity of tempered diatonic intervals, creating the aural illusion of Arabic-like quartertones.
11. An augmented second is a whole tone made larger by a half step, or a whole tone plus a semitone (e.g. C to D-sharp).

The Lord is my shelter
When thunder rumbles in the sky.
The Lord is my friend.
I love you and bless you,
For you are the Lord.

DETAIL 2

Narration (1 Samuel 16:13)

Spoken narration, drawn from the historical books of the Bible, connects episodes and numbers throughout the work. These texts perform crucial dramatic links between specific Psalms and events which defined David's character, providing emotional insight into feelings aroused within him, at the time of their composition.[12] In the musical backgrounds to these narratives, certain rhythmic patterns are associated with various moods, hypnotically prolonging them through polyrhythmic or tonal accompaniments. In a sense, these ostinati fill in time like the rhythm section of a jazz band, supplying spoken narration with an emotive underpinning.

Le Recitant

Et Samuel choisit David parmi ses freres. Et il l'oignit avec la corne d'huile. Et David etait blond et de belle figure. Et des ce jour lEspirit de Dieu resta sur lui.

Narrator

And Samuel chose David among his brothers. And he anointed him with the horn of oil. And David was fair and handsome. And from that day the Spirit of God remained with him.

DETAIL 3

Psaume 18:47–49: Choeur mixte

Loue soit le Seigneur pleine de gloire

---

12. While anyone under duress can sympathize with phobia, it was David's unique prerogative to voice his fears as prayers to God. Even more unusual, however, is the expression of gratitude and praise at the conclusion of his psalms, as if, the act of prayer were itself salvation.

Le Dieu vivant, l'auteur de ma vistoire.
Par qui je vois mes outrages venges,
Par qui sous moi les peoples sont ranges.

Quand les plus grands contre moi se soulevent
Au-dessus d'eux ses fortes mains m'elevent.
Des orgueilleux, il confond le dessein
Que pour me perdre ils couvaient dans leur sein.

Clement Marot

————

Praised be the Lord full of glory
The living God, the author of my victory.
Through whom I see my wrongs avenged
Through whom the peoples are under me.

When the greatest rise against me
His strong hands raise me over them.
He confounds the schemes of the proud
That they kept in their hearts, to destroy me.

A unison chorus, as proxy for the people, sings a lilting, through-composed melody that spins on and on in confident eighth notes, never repeating itself. This bright tune and its Gallic scansioning of text, simulates the illusion of folk music. The melody, effortlessly supported by a bass line chugging along in sixteenth notes, gravitates in the orbit of F major, dipping into the relative minor (d), and reaching its climax on a high E-flat. It is a bow to church modality, suggested by the lowered seventh tone. In transforming a major scale (F G A B-flat C D *E* F) into a mixolydian mode (F G A B-flat C D *E-flat* F), Honegger connects the vernacular to the sacred, analogous to the way a man coming in from the street, changes his behavior when he enters a church.[13]

---

13. This subtle reference to a Gregorian church mode, within the context of a vernacular French psalm, inadvertently, exposes inner tensions and dichotomies between Honegger's French-Catholic and Swiss-Protestant identity.

DETAIL 4

The Entrance of Goliath

Goliath's entrance is marked by a single, unaccompanied trombone that follows upon the Morax's narrative. His judicious adaptation of biblical verses holds close to the original.

Narrator:

> And Saul and the men of Israel were gathered together …and set the battle in array against the Philistines (17:2). And there went out a champion out of the camp of the Philistines named Goliath, a giant (17:6). And he mocked the Israelites (17:10). And David smote the Philistine in his forehead with a stone from his sling (17:49). And the Israelites shouted and pursued the Philistines unto the gate of Ekron (17:52).

Conclusion

If Morax's literary vision of David, as redeemer, is a universal affirmation of faith, Honegger catches its French dialect. The composer's musical perspective on the Bible is rooted in the land and culture of his birth. His return to naturalism and traditional national themes conjures up both the rural imagery of the French countryside and the grandeur of Louis XIV. Writing within a 20th century idiom, Honegger's vernacular setting of metrical psalms from the Geneva Psalter, reveals, too, a Swiss Protestant side to his art.[14] Both artists strive, through the story of *Le Roi David*, to project a message of hope in the aftermath of war.

This work, then, expresses the disposition of a generation who, having passed through the crises of World War I, was awakened by "the conviction that man's life is not the ease that a peace-loving generation has found it or thought to make it, but the awful conflict with evil which philosophers and saints have depicted." Morax and Honegger, having given "abundant testimony to the good and beautiful," seek in their work, also, to both give "support for faith, and distraction from a grief

---

14. Metrical psalms, in the French language, designed to be sung to secular French folksong tunes, are largely the product of the Swiss Protestant Reform (i.e. Geneva Psalter), a Calvinist preference; since French Catholics sang plainsong.

that is intolerable constantly to face, without trust in God."[15] If *Le Roi David* is a prayer, its meaning for those who created it, might best be summed up in the words of a 19th century French novelist: *To the happy and prosperous man prayer is but a meaningless jumble of words until grief comes to the unfortunate wretch to explain the sublime language which is our means of communication with God.*[16]

Despite the distance in time, and the great upheavals that his people, his kingdom, and his city have experienced, the image of David, the son of Jesse, who ruled over Israel and Judah in Jerusalem 3000 years ago, remains an imperishable figure in Western culture.[17]

Related Directions

David was the patron of the Nuremberg Meistersingers. Hans Sach's *Der klinhende Ton* (1532) tells of Jonathan saving David from Saul's assassination attempt. Settings of David's lament over Saul and Jonathan include motets by Josquin des Prés, Pierre de la Rue, and Clemens non Papa. Many prominent composers of the 17th and 18th centuries (notably A. Scarlatti, R. Keiser, A. Caldara, G. Ph. Telemann, and F. Veracini) wrote oratorios and operas on David. Prominent is an oratorio *David et Jonathans* (attributed to Carissimi); and Marc-Antoine Charpentier's stage music for Bretonneau's play. The oratorio *David's Lamentation over Saul and Jonathan* (1738) has been attributed to either John Christopher Smith or William Boyce. Johann Heinrich Rolle's oratorio *David and Jonathen*, based on Klopstock, was written in 1766.

---

15. Robert Bridges, "Preface," *The Spirit of Man: An Anthology in English and French from the Philosophers and Poets Made in 1915* (London: Longmans, Green, 1942 [1916]).
16. Alexandre Dumas, *The Count of Monte Cristo*, translation anonymous (New York: Barnes & Noble Classics, 2004) 80.
17. At the end of the oratorio, when David dies and an angel sings of future days — *a flower shall blossom from your stem, green once more (Isaiah 11:1),* we are not certain whether she is speaking of a Christian messianic redemption from sin, or a Jewish redemption of national identity under a Davidic dynasty. This verse from Isaiah, seems to embody Morax's hope that after the great powers, who nearly destroyed civilization, will be cut down, then, at last, the stock of Jesse (symbolized by the House of David or divine teaching) will spontaneously produce fresh shoots of new life to regenerate the world.

In the 19th century, the general decline of biblical oratorio and avoidance of association with politically suspect nationalistic themes, account for the relative paucity of musical works about David. Schumann's *Davidbuendelertaenze* for piano, op. 6, 1837, and the *March of the Davidbuendler against the Philistines* in *Carnival*, op. 9, 1834–1835, express his dislike of the musical philistinism[18] around him.

A certain renaissance occurred in the 20th century. Two important compositions are Arthur's Honegger's *Le Roi David* and Darius Milhaud's opera, *David*, commissioned for the 3,000th anniversary of the establishment of Jerusalem as David's capital, 1954. Descriptive compositions inspired by the figure of David include: Menachem Avidom's *David Symphony* (1947–48) and Paul Ben Haim's *Sweet Psalmist of Israel* for orchestra (1956). David the dancer is depicted by Castelnuovo-Tedesco in *Le danze del Re David* (piano solo, 1925). In folk music, an epic song with some dramatic action has been noted in the Kurdish Jewish tradition, and in a Ladino ballad, "Un pregon pregono el Rey." The Afro-American spiritual "Li'l David play on your harp," has the David theme as its first verse and refrain. Some musical works about David, whether traditional or recently composed, have become Israel folk songs. The best known of these is probably *David Melech Yisrael Hai ve-Kayyam.*

Works List

Abaelard, Petrus (1079–1142 France). *Planctus David super Saul et Jonathan* (2 Sam. 1:17), lament.

_____. *Planctus David super Abner* (2 Sam. 3:33), lament.

Achron, Josef (1886 Poland–1943 Hollywood). *David's lament* (2 Sam. 1:27), choir.

Adlgasser, Anton Cajetan (1729–1777 Salzburg). *David und Jonathan* oratorio.

Anfossi, Pasquale (1727–1797 Rome). *David contra philistaeos* (1 Sam. 17), oratorio.

Assmayer, Ignaz (1790–1862 Vienna). *Saul und David* (Chr. Kuffner), oratorio.

---

18. Philistinism implies smug conventionalism, ignorance, and indifference to artistic and cultural values.

Avidom, Menachem (1908 Poland–1995 Israel). *Symphony No. 2 — David*, orchestra.

Badia, Carlo-Agostino (1672–1738 Vienna). *La clemenza di Davidde* (S. Stampiglia), oratorio.

_____. *Il pentimento di Davidde* (S. Stampiglia), oratorio.

_____. *Il trionfo di Davidde* (S. Stampiglia), oratorio.

Barbandt, Carl (18th C. Germany). *David and Jonathan*, oratorio.

Bellermann, Konstantin (1696–1758 Germany). *Die siegende Schleuder des heldenmuethigen David*, oratorio.

Ben-Haim, Paul (1897 Germany–1981 Israel). *The Sweet Psalmist of Israel*, orchestra.

Berton, Henry Montan (1767–1844 Paris). *David dans le temple* (1 Kings), oratorio.

Binder, Abraham, W. (1895–1966 NYC). *King David*, rhapsody for piano and orchestra.

Bizet, Georges (1838–1875 Paris). *David*, chant.

Bonno, Giuseppe (1711–1788 Vienna). *La cita di Sion festeggiante nel ritorno di Davidde* (A. Bianchi), oratorio.

Bordier, Jules-Auguste (1846–1896 Paris). *David* (Milliet), lyrical scene.

Brown, Christopher (b.1943 England). *David* (Ch. Smart), cantata, mezzo-soprano, baritone, choir, orchestra.

Cafaro, Pasquale (1715–1787 Naples). *Il trionfo di Davidde*, oratorio.

Caldara, Antonio (1670 Venice–1736 Vienna). *David umilliato* (A. Zeno), oratorio.

Caproli, Carlo (17th C. Rome). *David prevaricante e poi pentito* (L. Orsini), oratorio.

Carissimi, Giacomo (1605–1674 Rome). *Historia Davidis et Jonathae*, oratorio.

Castelnuovo-Tedesco, Maria (1895 Florence–1968 California). *Le danze del re David*, Hebrew rhapsody, pianoforte.

_____. *Lament of David*, tenor and 2 choirs.

Castrisanu, Constantin (1888 Bucharest–1923 France). *Les harpes de David* (J. De Lahr), voice pianoforte.

Chorbajian, John (b.1936 USA). *When David Heard that His Son Was Slain* (1974) (2 Sam. 18), SATB.

Columbani, Quirino (18th C.). *David patientia invicta* (A. Checchio), oratorio.

Conti, Francesco Bartolomeo (1682 Florence–1732 Vienna). *Il Davidde perseguitato do Saul* (Av. Di Avanzo), oratorio.

_____. *David* (A. Zeno), oratorio.

Cortese, Luigi (1899–1976 Genoa). *David* (F. Cattaneo), oratorio.

De Leone, Francesco (1887–1948 Ohio). *David*, sacred music drama.

Desderi, Ettore (1892–1974 Florence). *Sinfonia Davidica*, soloist, choir, orchestra.

Detweiler, Alan (b.1926 Canada). *David and Goliath* (1971), soprano, 2 baritones, narrator, choir, instruments, oratorio.

Dittersdorf, Karl Ditters von (1739 Vienna–1799 Bohemia). *Davidde Penitente* (I. Pintus), oratorio.

Dresden, Sem (1881–1957 Amsterdam). *Rembrandt's Saul en David*, soprano and orchestra.

Ephros, Gershon (1890 Poland–1978 USA). *Biblical Suite: King David's Dance*, tenor, choir, pianoforte or orchestra.

Foerster, Kaspar (1616–1673 Danzig). *Dialogi Davidis cum Philisteo*, oratorio.

Foggia, Francesco (1604–1688 Rome). *David fugiens a facie Saul*, oratorio.

Franck, Johann Wolfgang (1644–1710 Germany). *Michal und David*, opera.

Fritellio, Jacobo (17th C. Italy). *Pia fraus seu Michol Davidem servans*, oratorio.

Frueh, Huldreich-Georg (1903–1945 Zurich). *Der junge David* (W.Lesch), oratorio.

Galli, Amintore (1845–1919 Italy). *David*, opera.

Gibelli, Lorenzo (1719–1812 Bologne). *Davide in Terebinto*, oratorio.

Guglielmo, Pietro Carlo (1763–1817 Naples). *Il trionfo di Davidde* (L. Caravita), oratorio.

Haim, Nicolao Francisco (17th C. Italy). *David sponsae restitus* (F. Posterla), oratorio.

Hamal, Henri-Guillaume (1685–1752 Liege, Belgium). *David*, oratorio.

Harris, Roy (1898 Oklahoma–1979 California). *Li'l boy named David*, choir, piano.

Hashagen, Klaus (1924 Java–1998 Germany). *Davids Dankgesang*, narrator, choir, band.

Hiles, Henry (1826–1904 England). *David*, oratorio.

Honegger, Arthur (1892–1955 Paris). *Le Roi David* (R. Morax), oratorio.

Horsley, William (1774–1858 London). *David*, oratorio.

Hughes, Arwel (1909–1988 Wales). *Dewisant* (A.T. Davies), oratorio.

Huybrechts, Albert (1899–1938 Brussels). *David*, symphonic poem.

Jacobson, Maurice (1896 London–1976 Brighton). *David*, ballet.

Jacoby, Hanoch (1909 Germany–1990 Israel). *King David's Lyre*, theme and variations, orchestra.

Jenkins, David (1848–1915 Wales). *David and Saul*, oratorio.

Josquin, Depres (c.1440–1521 Belgium). *Planxit autem David* (2 Sam. 1:17–27), motet, 4 voices.

Keiser, Reinhard (1674–1739 Hamburg). *Die durch Grossmuth und Glauben triumphierende Unschuld oder der siegende David*, oratorio.

Klein, Bernhard (1793–1832 Koln). *David*, oratorio.

Koenigsloew, Johann (1745 Hamburg–1833). *Saul und David im Kriege*, soloist, choir, instruments.

_____. *Davids Thronbesteigung*, oratorio.

_____. *Davids Sieg ueber die Philister*, oratorio.

Kosa, Gyorgy (1897 Budapest–1984). *David Kiraly* (M. Rabinovszky), biblical ballet with singer.

Krieger, Johann Philipp (1649–1725 Germany). *Der verfolgte David*, opera.

Leidesdorf, Maximilian Joseph (1787 Vienna–1840 Florence). *Koenig David's Lied von Schicksal* (A. Pollak), voice, pianoforte.

Lima, Bras-Francisco (1752–1813 Lisbon). *Il trionfo di Davidde*, oratorio.

MacFarren, George Alexander (1813–1887 London). *King David*, oratorio.

Malipiero, Riccardo (1914–2003 Milan). *Ciaccona di Davide*, viola, pianoforte.

Marini, Biagio (1597–1665 Venice). *Lacrime di Davide*, 2, 3, 4 voices.

Mattheson, Johann (1681–1764 Hamburg). *Der liebreiche und gedultige David*, oratorio.

Mayr, Johannes (1763–1845 Germany). *David in spelunca Engeddi* (G. Foppia), oratorio.

Mazzaferrata, Giovanni Batista (d.1691 Italy). *La caduta di David*, oratorio.

Merula, Tarquino (ca.1595–1665 Italy). *Arpa Davidica*, sacred song.

Milhaud, Darius (1892 France–1974 Geneva). *David* (A. Lunel), opera.

Naumann, Johann Gottlieb (1741–1801 Dresden). *Davide in Terebinto, figura Del Salvatore* (C. Mazzola), oratorio.

Neukomm, Sigismund (1778 Salzburg–1858 Paris). *David* (J. Webbe), oratorio.

Nielsen, Carl August (1865–1931 Copenhagen). *Saul og David* (Christiansen), opera.

Omerza, Michael (1679–1742 Slovenia). *David deprecanc pro populo*, sacred drama.

Orgad, Ben-Zion (1926 Germany–2006 Tel-Aviv). *Ha-tsevi Yisraʾel (The Beauty of Israel)* (1949/1964) (2 Sam. 1:19–27), baritone, orchestra.

Overman, Meta (1907 Rotterdam–1993 Perth). *Saul and David*, choir, baritone soloist, narrator and instruments.

Pacieri, Giuseppe (18th C. Italy). *La cetra piagenente di Davide nella morte do Gionata*, 4 voices.

Pasquali, Nicolo (1718–1757 Edinburgh). *David*, oratorio.

Piosello, Ioannes Baptisa (18th C. Italy). *David Rex* (F. Posterla), oratorio.

Pistocchi, Francesco-Antonio (1659 Palermo–1726 Bologne). *Davide*, oratorio.

Ramsey, Robert (d.1644 England). *When David Heard*, 6 voices.

Ran, Shulamit (1947 Tel Aviv/Chicago). *Ha-tsevi Yisrael* (2 Sam. 1:19), soprano, instruments.

Reutter, Georg (1708–1772 Vienna). *David*, opera.

Rieti, Vittorio (1898 Alexandria, Egypt–1994 New York). *David triomphant*, ballet.

Rispoli, Salvatore (c.1745–1812 Naples). *Il trionfo di Davide* (F. Dall'Ongaro), oratorio.

Rochberg, Georg (1918 New Jersey–2005 Pennsylvania). *David the Psalmist*, tenor, orchestra.

Rodrigo, Joaquin (1901 Valencia–1999 Madrid). *Triste está el Rey David*, choir.

Rolle, Johann Heinrich (1716–1785 Germany). *Davids Sieg in Aegypten* (Roetger), oratorio.

_____. *David und Jonathan* (F. Klopstock), oratorio.

Rorem, Ned (1923 USA). *Mourning scene* (2 Sam. 1:19–27), voice, string quartet.

Rosowsky, Solomon (1878 Riga–1962 New York). *David's crown* (P. Calderon), incidental music.

Sachs, Hans (1494–1576 Nuremberg). *Klingende Ton*, song.

Sauguet, Henri (1901 Bordeaux–1989 Paris). *David*, ballet.

Scarlatti, Alessandro (1660–1725 Naples). *Davidis pugna et victoria*, oratorio.

Sicilianos, Yorgo (b.1922 Athens). *David*, voice, orchestra, cantata.

Smith, John Christopher (1712 Ansbach–1795 London). *David's lamentation over Saul and Jonathan* (J. Lockman), oratorio.

Sternberg, Erich Walter (1891 Germany–1974 Israel) *My Brother Jonathan* (1969) (2 Sam.), mixed choir, pianoforte, strings.

Telemann, Georg Philipp (1681–1767 Hamburg). *Der koenigliche Prophet David*, oratorio.

Thompson, Randall (1899–1984 USA). *The Last Words of David* (1950) (2 Sam. 23:3–4), SATB, piano.

Tinodi, Sebestyen (c.1510–1556 Hungary). *Konig David*, voice, lute.

Trozner, Iosif (b.1904 Romania). *David singt* (R. Rilke), voices, pianoforte.

Veracini, Francesco-Maria (1690–1768 Florence). *L'incoronazione di Davidde*, oratorio.

Vitasek, Jan Nepomuk (1770–1839 Prague). *David oder die Befreyung Israels* (J. Muench-Bellinghausen), melodrama.

Wagenaar, Johann (1862 Utrecht–1941 The Hague). *Saul en David*, symphonic poem.

Ziani, Marc-Antonio (1620 Venice–1715 Vienna). *Davide liberato* (L. Verzuso Beretti), oratorio.

Zingarelli, Nicola Antonio (1752–1837 Naples). *Saulle overo il trionfo di Davide* (G. Ferreti), oratorio.

Other Directions

BATHSHEBA
(Abigail, Nabal)

The Bathsheba story occurs in several 18th century oratorios (Georg Reutter, Caldara, and Dittersdorf). Porpora's oratorio *Davide e Bersabea* (1734) was staged in London on the initiative of Handel's opponents. Mozart's cantata *Davidde Penitente* (1785) was set to a libretto probably written by Lorenzo Da Ponte and marks the start of their collaboration; the music (1782–83) is drawn largely from the Mass in C Minor (K, 427). On Abigail, the most noteworthy works are an oratorio by Francesco Durante (1736) and the oratorio *Nabal*, put together by J.C. Smith in 1764, with music taken from various Handel oratorios. An opera by

Josef Tal, *Amnon and Tamar,* with text by Recha Freier, was premiered in Jerusalem (1960).[19]

Works List

Caldara, Antonio (1670 Venice–1763 Vienna). *David umiliato* (Zeno), oratorio.

Dittersdorf, Karl Ditters von (1739 Vienna–1799). *Davidde penitente* (I.Pintus), oratorio.

Eisenmann, Willi (1902 Stuttgart–1992). *Bethsabe* (A. Gide), pantomime-oratorio.

Faccioli, Josephus (17th–18th C. Italy). *Bethsaba* (F. Lautentinus), oratorio.

Foggia, Antonio (1650–1707 Rome). *Bethsabea,* oratorio.

Grua, Carl Pietro (1700 Italy–1773 Germany). *Bethsabea,* oratorio.

Gruenenwald, Jean-Jaques (1911 France–1982). *Bethsabee,* symphonic poem for chorus and orchestra.

Lullier, Johannes (17th–18th C.). *Bet-Sabeae* (J.F. Rubini), oratorio.

Mozart, Wolfgang Amadeus (1756 Salzburg–1791 Vienna). *Davidde Penitente* (L. Da Ponte), 3 soloists, voices, choir, orchestra, cantata.

Porpora, Nicola (1686–1768 Naples). *Davide e Betsabea* (Rolli), oratorio.

Reutter, Georg (1708–1772 Vienna). *Betsabea overo il Pentimento di David,* oratorio.

ABSALOM

Absalom, the beloved third son of David (2 Samuel 13–19), was an attractive, but lawless man, who killed his half brother Amnon as revenge for the latter's rape of Tamar (Absalom's sister). Banished from the kingdom,[20] he later raised a rebellion against his father, capturing Jerusalem, but, meeting defeat in the forest of Ephraim, where he was killed by his cousin Joab, who found him caught by his long hair in an oak tree. David greatly lamented his son's death, despite Absalom's treachery, crying seven times: *O my son Absalom, my son,*

---

19. See Batia Bayer, "David," *Encyclopaedia Judaica,* Vol. 5, col. 1337–1338.
20. Amnon and Tamar are the subject of a Ladino ballad, *Un hijo tiene el Rey David*

my son Absalom! Would God I had died for thee, O Absalom, my son, my son! My son, my son! (*2 Samuel 18:33*), and prayed for Absalom's redemption from the seventh section of Hell (*Gehenna*), to which he had been consigned (Talmud Soṭah, 10b). The story of Absalom has been a popular subject for oratorios. Composers, since the Renaissance, have been particularly attracted to David's classic lament on the death of his beloved son.

Works List

Anfossi, Psaquale (1727–1797 Rome). *Assalone* (2 Sam. 13), oratorio.

Berton, Henry Montan (1767–1844 Paris). *Absalon*, oratorio.

Bertoni, Fernando-Gasparo (1725–1813 Italy). *Interius Absalom*, oratorio.

Caldara, Antonio (1670 Venice–1736 Vienna). *La Ribellione d' Assalone* (A. Zeno), oratorio.

Capocci, Gaetano (1811–1898 Rome). *Assalone*, oratorio.

Chorbajian, John (b.1936 USA). *When David Heard that His Son was Slain* (1974) (2 Sam. 18:33), SATB.

Cimarosa, Domenico (1749–1801 Venice). *Absalom*, oratorio.

Cola, Gregorius (17ᵗʰ–18ᵗʰ C.). *Absolonis Rebellio* (P. Gini), oratorio.

Colonna, Giovanni Paolo (1637–1695 Bologna). *Assalone*, oratorio.

David, Samuel (1836–1895 Paris). *Absalom*, opera.

Deering, Richard (c.1580–1630 UK). *And the King Was Moved* (1965) (2 Sam. 18:33), SSATB.

Diamond, David (1915–2005 Rochester, N.Y.). *David Weeps for Absalom* (2 Sam. 1), voice, pianoforte.

Dinerstein, Norman (1937–1982 USA). *When David Heard* (1979) (2 Sam. 18:33), SSAATTBB.

East, Michael (c.1580–1648 UK). *When David Heard that Absalom Was Slain* (2 Sam. 18:33), SSATTB.

Furlatto, Bonaventura (1738–1817 Venice). *Absolonis Rebelio*, oratorio.

Johnson, Carl (b.1935 USA). *Absalom, Absalom* (1971), tenor, SATB.

Josquin, Despres (c.1440–1521 Flanders). *Absaloni, fili mi*, 4 voices, motet.

Kunzen, Adoph Carl (1720–1781 Germany). *Absalom*, oratorio.

Lanciani, Flavio Carlo (17ᵗʰ–18ᵗʰ C. Rome). *L'Absolone ribello*, oratorio.

Moreau, Jean-Baptiste (1656–1733 Paris). *Absalon* (J. F. Duche), incidental music.

Porsile, Giuseppe (1672 Naples–1750 Vienna). *Assalone nemico Del padre amante*, oratorio.

Reindl, Constantin (1738–1799 Lucerne). *Absalom*, oratorio.

Sanders, Robert L. (1906–1974 USA). *The Death of Absalom* (1960) (2 Sam. 18:24–27, 31–33), SATB.

Schneider, Johann Cristian (1786–1853 Germany). *Absalon* (A. Brueggemann), oratorio.

Schutz, Heinrich (1585–1672 Germany). *Fili mi Absalon*, trombone quartet, basso continuo.

Soler, Antonio (1729–1783 Spain). *Absalone* (P. Calderon), incidental music.

Tomkins, Thomas (1572–1656 England). *When David Heard that Absalom Was Slain*, 4 voices madrigal.

Valentini, Giuseppi ((1680–1746 Florence). *La Superbia puita in Asalone*, oratorio.

Veracini, Francesco di Nicolo (1638–1720 Florence). *Assalone punito* (P. Canavese), oratorio.

Weelkes, Thomas (c.1575–1623 London). *When David Heard* (2 Sam. 18:33), 6 voices, organ.

Werner, Gregor Joseph (c.1695 Germany–1766 Austria). *Der so true als Heyllos wider seinen sanftmuethigen Vatter David rebellierende Sohn Absolon*, oratorio.

Ziani Pietro Andrea (1620–1684 Italy). *L' Assalone punito* (P. Lepori), oratorio.

17

This chapter focuses on the anthem *Zadok the Priest* by G. F. Handel, which transposes into music the imagery of Solomon's anointment as king. Customarily performed at British coronation ceremonies, it functions to enhance and dignify the investiture of a monarch with regal power.

I KINGS

SOLOMON

And Zadok the priest took the horn of oil out of the Tent and anointed Solomon. And they blew the ram's horn; and all the people said: 'Long live king Solomon.' And all the people came up after him, and the people piped with pipes, and rejoiced with great joy, so that the earth rent with the sound of them (1 Kings 1:39–40).

Crowned as king of Israel while still in his teens, Solomon, the second son of David and Bathsheba, ruled ancient Israel from c.970–933 B.C. His legendary adventures abound in the folklore of the Jewish people. Solomon understood the language of animals and birds, as well as men. His wisdom, wealth, and worldly fame spread far and wide during his lifetime. Great beyond himself, foreign wives turned Solomon's heart away from *following after* the God of his fathers. Sexual indulgence and over self-confidence proved tragic flaws, which, only the merit of his father, David, redeemed from immediate retributive justice by God and the people. The kingdom he ruled was divided after his death.[1]

---

1. It was a period distinguished by peace, prosperity, and lucrative foreign trade; but, also, marked by excessive taxation and oppressive forced labor, initiated in order to finance the building of the Temple, and royal palaces of unprecedented opulence.

Historical passages in the Book of Kings are not exactly chronicles of political or social events, as we know them today. More often, they are paradigms, which contemplate, examine, and evaluate moral and spiritual truths, worthiness or unworthiness: *And he did evil in the sight of the Lord and walked in the way of Jeroboam (1 Kings 15:34)*; or, *And [he] did that which was right in the eyes of the Lord, as did David his father" (1 Kings 15:11)*. So long as kings walk in the path of righteousness, all is well; but no sooner do they deviate thereof, then they becomes subject to divine retribution.[2] Originally one book, I Kings and II Kings covers Israelite history from the reign of Solomon and the period of the two kingdoms of Israel and Judah, to the destruction of Jerusalem and the Babylon captivity. Its authorship is traditionally attributed to the prophet Jeremiah.[3]

George Frederick Handel: Zadok the Priest (1727)

Text: 1 Kings 1:34, 39
Genre: Sacred Anthem
Medium: Mixed chorus (SSAATBB) and orchestra
Style: Baroque
First performance: Coronation of King George II of England, 1727
Duration: c. 5:30 minutes

Inspired from Solomon's coronation, the anthem *Zadok the Priest* was composed for the coronation of King George II of England, and has been sung at every coronation since.[4]

Anthem and Motet

The anthem is a choral setting of words from the Bible (or other religious text) that emerged during the 16th century in England, during a period that saw the establishment of the Church of England and the Commonwealth, and developed continuously into the 18th century.[5] Anthems were performed, primarily, in

---

2. I.W. Slotki, "Introduction and Commentary to the Book of Kings," *Kings* (London: Soncino Press, 1975) ix-xiii.
3. Talmud Baba Bathra 15a.
4. The words of *Zadok the Priest* have been said at every coronation since that of Edgar (944–975), crowned king of England in 973.
5. This uniquely English form is of two types: full and verse. Full anthems are

Protestant churches, where their function was similar to that of the Latin motet in the Roman Catholic service.[6] Their style was designed "for the better understanding of the layman" and tailored to the "outreach" values of the Reformation.[7] After the return of the monarchy in 1660, renamed the "Restoration Anthem," this genre took on a character of heroic grandeur, reaching its peak in the works of Handel: six Chandos anthems (1716–1718), and four Coronation anthems (1727), nearly all of which were written for special festive occasions.[8]

Both English anthem and Latin motet are single movement forms, suited to worship in churches and cathedrals. They differ in language and style, in that the anthem is less erudite and abstract than the otherworldly and contrapuntally intricate Latin motet.[9] In the anthem, English words tend to be set syllabically in short,

---

declaimed by the entire chorus, whereas, verse anthems, alternate sections for solo voices with full chorus.

6. The motet denotes any single-movement vocal composition, in continuous form, based on a sacred Latin-text. Motets were generally written for a particular holy day, and sung between the *Credo* and *Sanctus* of the Mass; performed chiefly at Vespers. Motets are often founded on the Gregorian tones of their texts, or the mass in which they appear, giving the service a sense of musical unity. See Donald Francis Tovey, "Motet," *Encyclopaedia Britannica*, Vol. 15, 849; and *Harvard Dictionary of Music*, Willi Apel, ed. (Cambridge, MA: Harvard University Press, 1972).

7. This is reflected two ways: linguistically — in the substitution of the Vernacular for Latin; constructively — in clarity of formal structure.

8. The anthem (with regard to another sacred form, the congregational hymn — which is syllabic in style, homophonic in texture, and strophic-verse in structure), has a richer, polyphonic texture, and a more dramatic and expansive character. Handel's anthem *Zadok the Priest*, conceived for state occasions, has a significantly broader scope than the usual church anthem. It is worth noting that the anthem is not a development of the hymn, but a simplification of the motet. Chandos anthems (HWV 246–251) are: Psalm 100 — *O, Be Joyful in the Lord*, Psalm 11 — *In the Lord I Put My Trust*, Psalm 51 — *Have Mercy upon Me, O God*, Psalm 96 — *O Sing unto the Lord*, Psalm 145 — *I will Magnify Thee*, Psalm 42 — *As pants the Hart*. Coronation anthems (HWV 258–261) are: *Zadok the Priest*, *The King Shall Rejoice*, *My Heart Is Indicting*, and *Let Thy Hand Be Strengthened*.

9. The late thirteenth-century theorist, Johannes de Grocheio (c. 1255–c. 1320), believed that the motet was "not intended for the vulgar [but rather] for educated people and those who look for refinement in art." See Margaret Bent, "The Late-Medieval Motet," *Companion to Medieval & Renaissance Music* (London: Oxford University Press, 1997).

easily grasped phrases, whereas the motet employs melismas. Consideration also is given to clarity of pronunciation, melodic definition, and textural transparency.

Text and Context

> Zadok the priest and Nathan the Prophet anointed Solomon King;
> And all the people rejoiced and said:
> God save the King, long live the King,
> May the King live forever!
> Amen! Allelujah!

The text is a paraphrase, based on two verses from the Book of Kings: *And let Zadok the priest and Nathan the prophet anoint him king over Israel; and blow ye the horn, and say, God save king Solomon (1:34). And Zadok the priest took an horn of oil out of the tabernacle, and anointed Solomon. And they blew the horn; and all the people said, God save King Solomon (1:39).* This regal setting has been sung at every British coronation since 1727, and, at each occasion, fills its listeners with pride of king and country.

Music and Musical Exegesis

Zadok the Priest is demarcated in three contrasting sections: introduction, acclamation, and hallelujah. The form is episodic, in that each part stands more or less complete in itself, creating a musical structure based on balance between thematic character, textures, and proportions.

Section 1

Stately Introduction (homophonic texture)

> Zadok the priest and Nathan the Prophet anointed Solomon King;
> And all the people rejoiced and said:

Zadok the Priest opens on a long and sustained crescendo, a majestic orchestral and choral introduction, regal in breadth. Its psychological impact on the onlookers conveys a sense of expectation and overwhelming suspense.

Section 2

Jubilant Acclamation (homophonic texture)

God save the King, long live the King, May the King live forever!

This introduction is followed by a jubilant choral acclamation by the people: *God save the King, long live the King, May the King live forever.*
It culminates, building through the addition of trumpets and drums, in a resplendent D major climax.

Section 3

Hallelujah Chorus (fugal and polyphonic texture)

Amen![10]

Coda

Climaxing cadence (homophonic block texture)

Allelujah!

The anthem concludes in fugal texture. Polyphony, in this context, takes on an extra-musical connotation, conveying the assent of heaven to the coronation of an earthy monarch, reinforcing the notion of imperial authority as a 'divine right of kings.' England's royalty have loved this music, for its majestic pomp and hallelujah chorus. The polyphonic sense of one singing to the other: *Allelujah! Amen!* derives from Isaiah 6:3, and climaxes in a massive block-choral cadence.

Conclusion

To an expanding British Empire, confident in its divinely favored, "sacred" right to rule other peoples, Solomon, a symbol of biblical greatness, became a model to emulate.[11] Self-assured, Imperial British

---

10. Handel's elaborate *Amen* is set as if it were a jubilant *Allelujah*.
11. This nationalistic posture of superiority is exemplified in the term — "Rule, Britannia!" a concept which first appeared in a popular song of the time: *When Britain first, at Heaven's command / Arose from out the azure main; this was the charter of the land, / And guardian angels sang this strain: "Rule, Britannia! Rule the waves: Britons never will be slaves."* See James Thomson,

theology spread Colonialism throughout the world in the person of missionaries,[12] governors, and armies. Pride justified the idea of free capitalism, class, and racial superiority. Under the guise of Solomon, however, not the values of Jerusalem, but the ambitions of Rome were reconstituted. *Zadok the King* is thus, not only the supreme paradigm of the restoration anthem; it is Handel's singular cultural contribution to 18th century Britain's theo-political ethos.

Related Works

Selections from Solomon's prayers at the dedication of the Temple were incorporated into liturgy and frequently set to music.[13] Two early musical works are the motet *Stetit autem Salomon* (1538) by Josquin Despres, and a curiosity — a canon for 96 voices by Pietro Valentini called *Nodus Salomonis* ("Solomon's Knot"), first published in 1631, and analyzed in 1650 by Athanasius Kircher in his *Musurgia Universalis;* the entire canon is nothing but a kind of "change ringing" on the G major chord. The story of the judgment of the two harlots over possession of an infant became the subject of numerous oratorios (1 Kings 3:16–28). Early oratorios include Carissimi's *Judicium Salomonis* (1669) and F.T. Richter's *L'oncoronazione di Salomone* (Vienna, 1696). The subject is taken up by northern composers: G. C. Schuermann's "spiritual opera," *Salomon* (Brunswick, 1701), R. Keiser's opera, *Salomon* (Hamburg, 1703), and M. A. Charpentier's oratorio, *Judicium Salomonis* (Paris, 1702). Ennio Porsile's *L'esaltazione di Salomone* (Barcelona, 1711) is held to be the first oratorio performed in Spain. Solomon's judgement again appears as an oratorio subject in Ignaz Holzbauer's *Guidizio di Salomone* (Mannheim,

---

The Works of James Thomson, Vol. II (published 1763) 191.

12. For an extensive elaboration of this concept, see John M. Hull, "Isaac Watts and the Origins of British Imperial Theology," *International Congregational Journal*, Vol. 4 No. 2 (February 2005) 59–79.

13. Solomon's most famous prayer was uttered on the completion of the building of the Temple: *Blessed be the Lord, that hath given rest unto his people Israel, according to all that he promised; there hath not failed one word of all his good promise, which he promised by the hand of Moses. The Lord our God is with us as he was with our fathers; let him not leave us or forsake us. That he may incline our hearts unto him, to walk in all his ways, and to keep his commandments, and his statutes, and his judgments, which he commanded our fathers* (1 Kings 8:56–58).

1766), and in a Polish work, *Sad Salomona*, a tragedy with dances and incidental music by Chopin's teacher Jozef Elsner (Warsaw, 1806). Handel's oratorio *Solomon* was first performed at Covent Garden on March 17, 1749; the "Entry of the Queen of Sheba" from this work is often performed as a concert piece (cf. Queen of Sheba).

The music for the Israeli play *Shelomo ha-Melekh ve-Shalmai ha-Sandlar* was written by Alexander Argov. *Ashmedai*, an opera based on the Talmudic legend of Satan assuming the appearance of the King, was written by Josef Tal (libretto by Israel Eliraz), and had its premiere at the Hamburg State Opera, 1971.[14]

Works List

Andriessen, Hendrik (1892–1981 Netherlands). *Salomon* (J. Vondel), incidental music.

Bantock, Granville (1868–1946 London*). King Salomon*, chorus, narrator and orchestra.

Bencini, Pietro Paolo (1680–1750 Rome). *Salomon* (F. Posterla) oratorio.

Berg, Carl (1879–1957 Stockholm). *Salomos Voga Disa*, voice and orchestra.

Broadway, Richard (18ᵗʰ C. England). *Solomon's Temple* (J. Weekes) oratorio.

Carissimi, Giacomo (1605–1674 Rome). *Judicum Salomonis*, oratorio.

Charpentier, Marc-Antoine (1636–1704 Paris). *Judicum Solomonis*, oratorio.

Colonna, Giovanni (1637–1695 Bologna). *Salomone Amante*, oratorio.

Elsner, Kasawery-Josef (1769–1854 Warsaw). *Sad Salomona* (L. Caignez) (translated A. Zablocki) oratorio.

Ford, Virgil T. (20ᵗʰ C. USA). *Give Thy Servant an Understanding Heart* (1 Kings 3:9), SATB.

Furlanetto, Bonaventura (1738–1817 Venice). *Solomon*, oratorio.

Handel, G.F. (1685 Halle–1759 London). *Solomon* (T. Morell), oratorio.

Hartmann, Johann Peter (1805–1900 Copenhagen). *Sulamith og Salomon*, Romancer og Sange, voice and piano.

Hassler, Leo (1564–1612 Germany). *Aude Domine Hymnun* (Solomon's oration in dedicating the Temple) (1 Kings 8:28–29), cantata.

---

14. See Batia Bayer, "Solomon," *Encyclopaedia Judaica*, Vol. 15, col. 110–111.

Holzbauer, Ignaz Jacob (1711 Vienna–1783). *Il Giudizio di Samone*, oratorio.

Hovaness, Alan (1911–2000 USA). *Thirtieth Ode of Solomon*, baritone, choir and orchestra.

Josquin, Despres (c. 1440–1521 Belgium). *Stetit autem Salomon II. Benedic, Domum Istam (*1 Kings 8:22–24).

Maayani, Ami (1936 Tel Aviv). *Song of Solomon*, strings.

Giovanni, Batista (1706–1784 Bologna). *L'Assunzione di Salomone al trono d'Israello* (G. Melani), oratorio.

Masini, Antonio (1639–1678 Rome). *Sposalizio di Salomone*, oratorio.

Meinardus, Ludwig (1827–1896 Germany). *Koenig Salomon*, oratorio.

Melani, Alessandro (1639–1703 Italy). *Il Giudizio Salomone*, oratorio.

Melani, Francesco (1628 Italy–1663). *Il Giudizio Salomone*, oratorio.

Naylor, Bernard (1907–1986 England). *King Solomon's Prayer*, Wisdom of Solomon, 9, soprano, choir and orchestra.

Pasquini, Bernardo (1637–1710 Rome). *L'Idolatri di Salomone* (G.B.Giardini), oratorio.

Porsile, Ennio (1810–1859 Rome). *L'esaltatione di Salomone*, oratorio.

Richter, Ferdinand (1649–1711 Vienna). *L'incorazione di Salomone*, opera.

Rispoli, Salvatore (c. 1745–1812 Naples). *I voti di Davidi per Salomone* (Ps. 71), cantata for soprano and instruments.

Schuermann, Georg Caspar (1672–1751 Germany*). Salomon* (A.U. Herzog) oratorio.

Sowerby, Leo (1895–1968 USA). Will God Indeed Dwell on the Earth? (1 Kings 8:27–30, 37–39), baritone, SATB, and organ.

Sowinski, Wojciech (1803 Poland–1880 Paris). *Sad Salomona (*Solomon's Judgment), 3 solo voices, choir and orchestra.

Thomson, Randall (1899 NYC- 1984). *Solomon and Balkis* (adapted from Kipling: "The Butterfly," opera.

Titov, Alexei (1769–1827 St. Petersburg). *Sud Zaria Solomona* (Solomon's Judgment), incidental music.

Traetta, Tommasso (1727–1779 Venice). *Rex Salomone*, oratorio.

Valentini, Pietro (1570–1654 Rome). *Canone nel nodo di Salomo* (Like Solomon's Knot), canon 96 voices.

Vellones, Pierre (1889–1939 Paris). *Le Roi Salomon*, voice and orchestra.

Veracini, Francesco-Maria (1690–1768 Florence). *La Caduta del Savio nell'idolatria di Salomone,* oratorio.

Wesley, Samuel (1810 London–1876). *O Lord My God* (Solomon's Prayer) (1 Kings 8), anthem.

Whettam, Graham (b.1927 UK). *Then Spake Solomon* (1 Kings 8:12–13, 9:3), SATB, organ.

Zannetti, Francesco (1737–1788 Italy). *Salomone*, oratorio.

Zianni, Marc-Antonio (1653 Venice–1715 Vienna). *Il Giudizio Salomone* (D.R. Cialli), oratorio.

Other Directions

QUEEN OF SHEBA

The legend of Solomon and the Queen of Sheba, the woman who ruled the ancient kingdom of Sheba (located in Southern Arabia), is one of the great love stories of all time: *[She] heard of the fame of Solomon... and came to Jerusalem with a very great train... with camels...spices... gold... and precious stones...to prove him with hard questions...she spoke with him of all...her heart... and Solomon gave to the queen... all her desire (1 Kings 10:1–13).* Ethiopian tradition, traces its royal lineage to the union of Solomon and Sheba, in a succession that spanned almost 2900 years. Their meeting became a favorite topic for operas in the 19th century, which gave prominence to the Queen of Sheba. Gounod's four-act opera, *La Reine de Saba* (text by M. Carte and J. Barbier, and Gerard de Nerval), had its premiere at the Paris Opera in 1862; but a more lasting success was gained by Karl Goldmark's *Die Koenegin von Saba* (text by S. H. Mosenthal, premiered in Vienna, 1875). Some of the melodic material is supposed to have been based on synagogue motifs. Later works on the subject are: Reynaldo Hahn's *La Reine de Scheba* (1926; text by Edmond Fleg); *Belkis, Regina di Saba,* a ballet by O. Respighi (1932); and Randall Thompson's *Solomon and Balkis,* an opera in one act, based in Kipling's *The Butterfly that Stamped* (1942).

Works List

Castelnuovo-Tedesco, Mario (1895 Italy–1968 USA). *The Queen of Sheba* (1 Kings 10:1–13), SSA, soprano, piano.

Elwart, Antoine (1808–1877 Paris). *La Reine de Saba*, opera.

Fux, Johann Joseph (1660–1741 Vienna). *La Regina Saba*, oratorio.

Goldmark, Karl (1830–1915 Vienna). *Koenigin von Saba* (S. Mosenthal), opera.

Gounod, Charles (1818 Paris–1893). *La Reine de Saba* (Jules Barbier), chorus.

Hahn, Reynaldo (1875 Caracas–1947 Paris). *La Reine de Sheba*, oratorio.

Lange-Mueller, Peter Erasmus (1850–1926 Copenhagen). *Sulamith og Salomon* (B.C. Ingerman), voice and piano.

Lavagne, Andre (1913 Paris). *Les Amours du roi Salomon et la reine de Saba*, cantata.

Milhaud, Darius (1892 France–1974 Geneva). *La Reine de Saba*, string quartet.

Schmidt, Johann Michael (1720–1792 Mainz). *Regna Saba Salomonis Hospita* (1 Kings 10), melodrama.

Spoliansky, Mischa (1898 Russia–1985 UK). *King Solomon's Mines* (1937), orchestral suite.

CHAPTER 18

Felix Mendelssohn's *Elijah*, projects the biblical prophet into a supernatural, mysterious, and fantastic German-Romantic context. Its vivid atmosphere and style combine scenes of dramatic scope with those of devotional ethos. Considered, perhaps, the greatest oratorio of the 19th century, the work has influenced a number of composers from Germany, England, and America well into the 20th century.

ELIJAH

And Ahab the son of Omri did that which was evil in the sight of the Lord...he took to wife Jezebel the daughter of Ethbaal king of the Zidonians, and went and served Baal, and worshipped him. And he reared up an altar for Baal in the house of Baal which he had built in Samaria...and Ahab did yet more to provoke the God of Israel, than all the kings of Israel that were before him... And Elijah the Tishbite, who was of the settlers of Gilead, said unto Ahab: 'As the Lord, the God of Israel liveth, before whom I stand, there shall not be dew nor rain these years, but according to my word'. (I Kings 16:30–33, 17:1).

The northern kingdom of Israel was in a state of continual unrest. In the course of its two centuries of existence (c. 876–722 B.C.) at least half of its 19 sovereigns met violent deaths at the hands of their successors.[1] Jeroboam (c. 928–907 B.C.), the first king of Israel, erected sanctuaries

---

1. The following dates of the kings of Israel is a chronological approximation, derived from the historiography of the Bible: Jeroboam (928–907 B.C.), Nadab (907–906 B.C.), Baasa (906–883 B.C.), Elah (883–882 B.C.), Zimri (882 B.C.), Omri (882–871 B.C.), Ahab (871–852 B.C.), Ahaziah (852–851 B.C.), Jehoram (851–842 B.C.), Jehu (842–814 B.C.), Jehoahaz (814–800 B.C.), Jehoash (800–784 B.C.), Jeroboam II (784–748 B.C.), Zechariah (748 B.C.), Shallum (748 B.C.), Menachem (747–737 B.C.), Pekiah (737–735 B.C.), Pekah (735–733 B.C.) and Hoshea (733–724 B.C.). Sources consulted vary considerably from the dates cited above. See the article "Jewish History: Chronological Chart of Jewish History" by Hillel Halkin and Barry Spain, *Encyclopaedia Judaica*, Vol. 8, col. 766–767.

at Dan and Bethel, introduced idolatry, set up images of bulls overlaid with gold, and deflected pilgrims from going to Jerusalem, in order to weaken the monotheistic concept of Mosaic Law. Omri (c. 887–876 B.C.), a later ruler, entered into a pact with the Phoenicians in order to develop commerce in his realm and safeguard himself from the kingdom of Damascus. He cemented this alliance by a marriage between his son Ahab, and Jezebel, daughter of the king of Tyre — who introduced alien ideas into the traditional Hebrew conception of the monarchy. Unfortunately, Ahab, an able politician and strong military ruler, was a dismal failure as king of a holy people worthy of carrying forth the blessing of God through history.

In the late ninth century (c. 860 B.C.) the prophet Elijah, a fearless advocate of the living God in the midst of Israel, emerges from obscurity to fight against the worship of Baal, introduced into the land, during the reign of Ahab by his Phoenician wife, Jezebel. He challenged the monarchy on ethical grounds,[2] denounced idolatry, and preached unconditional faithfulness to the God of Israel.[3]

Felix Mendelssohn: Elijah (1846)
Libretto: Julius Schubring, after the Lutheran Bible
Genre: Oratorio
Medium: Soprano, alto, tenor, bass, chorus, orchestra and organ
Style: Romantic
First performance: Birmingham Festival, Great Britain, 1846
Duration: ca. 1 hour 20 minutes

Mendelssohn's *Elijah* tells the story of Elijah the Prophet with soloists, chorus, and orchestra. It is an epic biblical music drama, which pivots between fiery outrage, and warm and noble contemplation. Written on commission from the Birmingham Festival in England, it was premiered there under the composer's direction in 1846.

---

2. Previous prophets were either members of prophetic schools or judges, affiliated with the royal court.
3. The last reference to the kingdom of Israel is found in 2 Kings 17:23, *so was Israel carried away out of their own land to Assyria unto this day.* Cecil Roth, *A History of the Jews* (New York: Shocken, 1970) 30–35.

Biographic Context

Felix Mendelssohn (1809 Hamburg–1847 Berlin) was the first great composer prepared for his career by well-to-do and highly-cultivated parents. Many of his youthful compositions were played at the family's private Sunday afternoon concerts, at home. Although his grandfather, Moses Mendelssohn, the famous 18th century Jewish philosopher, had played a key role in the Enlightenment, articulating the relationship of traditional Judaism to German culture; his father, Abraham, a prosperous banker, broke with family traditions, and had his children baptized in 1816. Always conscious of his Jewish origins, Mendelssohn's music is, more often than not, inspired from Lutheran sources.

Felix's affection for the music of J. S. Bach was deep, encouraged by his aunt, Sara Levy (nee Itzig), who had been a pupil of Bach's son Wilhelm Friedemann, and, who also, had supported the widow of his brother, Carl Philipp Emanuel. At 20, he conducted a performance of Bach's *St. Matthew Passion* and awakened a general revival of interest in this music. A year later, Felix conducted Handel's oratorio *Israel in Egypt*. These youthful experiences inspired his later composition of the oratorios *St. Paul* and *Elijah*.[4]

Mendelssohn was a conservative among Romantic composers. Hector Berlioz, a revolutionary colleague, recalls in his *Memoirs*, an entertaining vignette they shared together as students in Rome. It sheds more insight into the depth and seriousness of Mendelssohn's religious feelings than many a devout testimonial: *One evening we were exploring the baths of Caracalla, and debating the question of the merits or demerits of human actions and of their reward in this life. Just as I had replied by some enormity — I forget what — to his religious and orthodox enunciations, his foot slipped and he rolled down a steep ruined staircase. "Admire the divine justice," said I, as I helped him up; "I blaspheme, and it is you who fall." This impiety on my part, accompanied by an uproarious laugh, was evidently a little too much for him, and henceforth all religious discussions were tabooed.*[5] Posthumous criticism of Mendelssohn has been

---

4.   Compiled from *Mendelssohn and His World*, R. Larry Todd, editor (Princeton: Princeton University Press, 1991); Karl-Heinz Kohler, "Felix Mendelssohn," *The New Grove Dictionary of Music*, Vol. 12, 134–159; Aryeh Oron: "Felix Mendelssohn-Bartholdy" (2006). Internet resource: www.bach-cantatas. com/Lib/Mendelssohn-Felix.htm.

5.   Hector Berlioz, *Memoirs*, translated by Rachel and Eleanor Holms, annotated

harsh. His music has been criticized for lack of depth, "Victorian conformity," and "Jewish rhetoric."[6] German society, edged on by Wagner's pamphleteering, never allowed Mendelssohn to forget his origins.[7]

Text and Context

The text by Mendelssohn's friend, the Protestant minister, Julius Schubring (1806–1889) is a skillfully extracted collage of biblical citations.[8] It is, primarily, based upon 1 Kings 17–19 and 2 Kings 1–2:11, and covers the entire career of the prophet, *whose word was like a flaming torch, who shut up the heavens, brought down fire, and was taken up in a whirlwind to heaven* (paraphrase after 2 Kings 2:11). It commences with Elijah's proclamation: *As God the Lord of Israel liveth, before whom I stand: There shall not be dew nor rain these years, but according to my word (1 Kings 17:1).* This prophecy requires elucidation.

Midrash relates: Both Ahab and Elijah had met accidentally at the home of their friend Hiel, to comfort him on the losts of his two sons, who had died in the process of Hiel's seeking to rebuild the city

---

and revised by Ernest Newman (New York: Dover, 1960) 278–279.

6.   The idea that there is such a thing as a Jewish or a Christian "rhetoric" was pointed out to me, in correspondence with the Swiss theologian Edgar Kellenberger, in a letter (July 25, 2006). He writes: "I do not believe in a racial analysis of (Jewish or Christian) music. Being an exegete of biblical texts, I am interested in music as an especially precious rhetoric or Midrash. In my studies of Mendelssohn's oratorios, cantatas, and motets, I found, sometimes, Mendelssohn's exegesis [is] from a Jewish viewpoint, unlike the Christian viewpoint of Bach. It's a question of rhetoric [i.e. imagery or point of view?] not of style."

7.   During the Middle Ages the ideological pretense for assault upon Jews had been religious difference; after the Enlightenment, it was no longer a usable excuse. Nineteenth century bourgeois society invented a new weapon — Anti-Semitism — a mythology of race, blood, and national purity. See Sydney Finkelstein, *Composer and Nation* (New York: International Publishers, 1960). 134. An always important motivation (but never said) was the economic concurrence of Jews and Christians (E. Kellenberger).

8.   Schubring selects phrases from Exodus, Deuteronomy, Job, Joel, Hosea, Samuel, Psalms, Isaiah, Jeremiah, Lamentations, Malachi, Chronicles, the Gospel of Matthew, and Sirach. Originally set to words taken from Luther's German translation of the Bible, the premiere in Great Britain was translated into English.

of Jericho. While Hiel was still in mourning,[9] the following exchange between Ahab and Elijah ensued. Ahab refused to see the hand of God in what had occurred, arguing: "If the death of Hiel's sons was due to Joshua's curse,[10] then, why was the curse, uttered by Moses, the teacher of Joshua, against idol worshippers, ineffective?"[11] Ahab continued, "But now, all Israel are worshipping idols, and yet the heaven is not shut up! If the curse of the disciple [Joshua] proved effective, how much more would that of the master [Moses] have been!" Appalled by such arrogance, Elijah exclaimed, *As the Lord… liveth… there shall not be dew nor rain these years, but according to my word (1 Kings 17:1).*[12] The oratorio is structured in two parts, each containing about twenty separate numbers, divided equally between soloists and chorus.

Elijah

FIRST PART

Ahab and Jezebel have introduced the worship of pagan deities, and led the people away from the one true God. Elijah brings retribution by cursing the land with three years of drought.

Introduction (Elijah)

As the Lord of Israel liveth (1 Kings 17:11).

Overture

Famine and crisis spread across the country. The people implore God, with prayer and protest, to relieve their suffering, but to no avail. Obadiah, a loyal follower, exhorts the people to look within for salvation.

---

9. *In his days did Hiel the Bethlehemite built Jericho. With Abiram his first-born he laid the foundation thereof, and with his youngest son Segub he set up the gates thereof; according to the word of the Lord, which He spoke by the hand of Joshua the son of Nun (1 Kings 16:34).*

10. *Cursed be the man before the Lord, that riseth up and buildeth this city Jericho; he shall lay the foundation thereof with his firstborn, and in his youngest son shall he set up the gates of it (Joshua 6:26).*

11. *Moses had said: Take heed to yourselves lest…ye turn aside, and serve other gods and worship them; and the anger of the Lord be kindled against you, and He shut up the heaven so that there shall be no rain (Deut. 11:16).*

12. Talmud Sanhedrin 113a.

No. 1 Chorus and Recitative Chorus

> Help, Lord (Jer. 8:19–20)! The deeps afford no water (Lam. 4:4).

No. 2 Duet with Chorus

> Lord, bow Thine ear to our prayer (Ps. 86:1, 6)(Lam. 1:17).

No. 3 Recitative (Obadiah)

> Ye people rend your hearts (Joel 2:12–13).

No. 4 Air (Obadiah)

> If with all your hearts you truly seek me (Deut. 4:29, Jer. 29:13).

No. 5 Chorus (The People)

> Yet doth the Lord see not (Deut. 28:15, 28:22, Exod. 20:5–6).

Elijah is commanded by an angel to attend a widow in distress. In the midst of her suffering, he miraculously raises her son from the dead, and turns her heart back to God.

No. 6 Recitative (angel)

> Elijah, get thee hence (1 Kings 17:3–5).

No. 7 Double quartet (angels)

> For, he shall give His angels charge (Ps. 91:11–12).

Recitative (angel)

> Now Cherith's brook is dried up (1 Kings 17:7, 9, and 14).

No. 8 Recitative and Air (The Widow)

> What have I to do with thee (1 Kings 17:17–18, Ps. 38:7, 6:7, Job 10:15, Ps. 10:14)?

Recitative (Elijah and the Widow)

> Give me thy son (1 Kings 17:19. Ps. 86:15–16, 1 Kings 17:21, Ps. 88:11, 1 Kings 17:22–24, Ps. 116:12, Deut. 6:5, and Ps. 128:1).

No. 9 Chorus

> Blessed are the men who fear Him (Ps. 112:1, 4).

Three years having passed. Elijah resurfaces at Ahab's court, to challenge the priests of Baal. The whole kingdom gathers before the high altar to witness the encounter: Baal's followers mount an impressive spectacle, calling three times upon their gods to appear and consume the sacrifice — each time without success. Elijah steps into the silence, and calls upon the Lord, who rains down fire on the altar. The awestruck people spurred on by Elijah, set upon the idolaters and slaughter them at a brook, by the foot of the mountain.

No. 10 Recitative and Chorus (Elijah, Ahab and the People)

As God, the Lord of Sabaoth, liveth (1 Kings 18:15, 1, 17–25).

No. 11 Chorus (Priests of Baal)

Baal, we cry to thee (18:26).

No. 12 Recitative (Elijah and Priests of Baal)

Call him louder for he is a god (18:27)!

No. 13 Recitative (Elijah)

Call him louder! He heareth not (18:26, 28–29).

Chorus (Priests of Ball)

Hear and answer, Baal!

Recitative (Elijah)

Draw near, all ye people (18:30).

No. 14 Air (Elijah)

Lord God of Abraham, Isaac and Israel! (18:36–37)

No. 15 Quartet (angels)

Cast thy burden upon the Lord (Ps. 55:23, Ps. 16:8, Ps. 108:5, Ps. 25:3).

No. 16 Recitative (Elijah)

O Thou, who makest Thine angels spirits (Ps. 104:4).

Chorus (The People)

The fire descends from heaven (1 Kings 18:38–39, Deut. 6:4, 5:7).

Recitative (Elijah)

> Take all the prophets of Baal (1 Kings 18:40).

Chorus (The People)

> Take all the prophets of Baal.

No. 16 Air (Elijah)

> Is not His word like fire (Jer. 23:29, Ps. 7:12–13)?

No. 17 Air (alto)

> Woe unto them who forsake Him (Hos 7:13).

With Baal's followers in full retreat, Obadiah reminds Elijah to make good on his promise to lift the curse. Elijah calls three times on the Almighty to bring relief. A boy, sent to keep watch, finally spots storm clouds on the horizon. The heavens burst forth with rain and the people rejoice.

No. 18 and 19 Recitative and Chorus (Obadiah, Elijah, the People and the Youth)

> O man of God, help thy people (Jer. 14:22, 2 Chron. 6:27, 1 Kings 18:43, Deut. 28:23, 2 Chron. 6:26–27, 1 Kings 18:43, Deut. 28:23, 1 Kings 18:41, 2 Chron. 6:19, Ps. 28:1, 1 Kings 18:44–45).

No. 20 Chorus

> Thanks be to God (Ps. 106:1, Ps. 93:4)!

SECOND PART

No. 21 Air (Soprano)

> Hear ye Israel! Hear what the Lord speaketh (Isa. 48:1, 18, 53:1, 49:7, 41:10, 1:12, 13).

No. 22 Chorus

> Be not afraid, saith the Lord (Isa. 41:10, Ps. 91:7).

Elijah returns, to confront Ahab and his queen, reminding them, that their temporal rule depends on a legitimacy, conferred by a higher power. Jezebel seeks to reverse the tables on the prophet, portraying him as a renegade, a traitor, and a magician, who must be blamed for the suffering brought by the famine. A mob, poisoned by the queen's accusations, turns on Elijah, who barely escapes. Hidden by Obadiah, Elijah flees to the wilderness, where a band of angels watch over the prophet in his darkest hour. As Elijah rages against the injustice of his plight, the angels urge patience and endurance. He then confronts his own feelings of self-doubt.

No. 23 Recitative and Chorus (Elijah, Jezebel, and Chorus)

The Lord hath exalted thee (1 Kings 14:7, 16:30–33, 21:19, 14:15, 16, Jer. 26:11, 9, 1 Kings 21:7, 19:2. Ecclus. 48:3, 2, Jer. 26:11).

No. 24 Chorus

Woe to him; he shall perish; for he closed the heavens (Jer. 26:11)!

No. 25 Recitative (Obadiah and Elijah)

Man of God, now let my words be precious in thy sight (2 Kings 1:13, Jer. 26:11, Ps. 59:3, 57:6, Deut. 31:6, Exod. 12:12–32, Jer. 5:3, 1 Sam. 17:37, 1 Kings 19:4)!

No. 26 Air (Elijah)

It is enough, O Lord (1 Kings 19:4), Job 7:16, 1 Kings 19:10).

No. 27 Recitative (Tenor)

See, now he sleepeth beneath a juniper tree (1 Kings 19:5, Ps. 34:7).

No. 28 Trio (angels)

Lift up thine eyes to the mountains (Ps. 121:1–3).

No. 29 Chorus (angels)

He watching over Israel slumbers not (Ps. 121:4, Ps. 138:7).

No. 30 Recitative (An Angel and Elijah)

Arise, Elijah (1 Kings 19:7–8, Isa. 49:4, 64:1–2, 63:17, 1 Kings 19:4)!

No. 31 Air (An Angel)

O rest in the Lord (Ps. 37:7, 4, 5, and 1).

No. 32 Chorus (Chorale)

He that shall endure to the end, shall be saved (Matt. 24:13).

Elijah's guardian angel readies the prophet to witness the sign of hope he has been yearning for. A great commotion precedes the appearance of the Almighty — storms, tidal-waves, earthquakes, and fire, which give way to the "still small voice" of God himself. Seraphim and lesser angels command Elijah to return home, lead the faithful, and restore the kingdom of Israel to its rightful path. Bolstered by the encounter, Elijah bids farewell to the wilderness and resumes his mission.

No. 33 Recitative (Elijah and an Angel)

> Night falleth round me, O Lord (Ps. 22:19, 143:7, 6, 1 Kings 19:11, 13)!

No 34 Chorus

> Behold! God the Lord passed by (1 Kings 19:11–12)!

No. 35 Recitative (Alto)

> Above him stood the Seraphim (Isa. 6:3).

Quartet and Chorus (Angels)

> Holy, Holy, Holy is God the Lord.

No. 36 Recitative and Chorus (Elijah)

> Go, return upon thy way (1 Kings 19:15, 18)!

Recitative

> I go on my way in the strength of the Lord (Ps. 71:16, 16:2, 9).

No. 37 Air (Elijah)

> For the mountains shall depart (Isa. 54:10).

Elijah's mighty exploits and successes, as his transfiguration and ascension into heaven in a chariot of fire are chronicled. The soprano soloist declares the prophecy of Elijah's return before the Last Judgment, and the chorus foretells the promised reign of wisdom and understanding, that is to follow. A solo vocal quartet, beckons the audience to drink from the waters of the Lord's mercies, and the oratorio closes in a mood of victory and celebration.

No. 38 Chorus

Then did Elijah the prophet break forth like a fire (Ecclesiasticus 48:1, 6–7, 2 Kings 2:1, 11).

No. 39 Air (Tenor)

Then shall the righteous shine forth (Matt. 13:43, Isa. 51:11).

No. 40 Recitative (Soprano)

Behold, God hath sent Elijah the prophet (Mal. 4:5–6).

No. 41 Chorus

But the Lord, from the north has raised one (Isa. 41:25, 42:1, 11:2).

Quartet

O, Come everyone that thirsteth (Isa. 55:1, 3).

No. 42 Chorus

And then shall your light break forth (Isa. 58:8, Ps. 8:1).

Music and Musical Exegesis

Mendelssohn distributes his musical forces with consummate skill: soloists sing arioso-recitatives, arias, duets, and quartets; a large mixed chorus responds, not only accompanied by orchestra, but — sometimes also, subdivided into men's and women's *a cappella* choirs. Choral writing derives from the harmonic vocabulary of the Lutheran Chorale, the polyphonic textures of Bach's Passions, and the picturesque declamations of Handel's *Israel in Egypt*.[13]

Like Handel, Mendelssohn's melodic voice is diatonic; but his sense of orchestral line and color inhabits a Romantic countenance. Animated strings surge in arpeggio and race in sixteenth-note passages, plunging and leaping into a volatile sea of emotion that aims at all-encompassing fulfillment. Much of this turbulence and swirling

---

13. Undoubtedly, Mendelssohn absorbed these styles from his conducting experience, preparing the *St. Matthew Passion*. The steady pace of Bach's chorale harmonizations often underpins Mendelssohn's own choruses. During his career, however, Felix Mendelssohn conducted Handel's oratorio *Israel in Egypt*, more than any other work.

musical imagery derives from the urge to express and expand upon the biblical translation of Elijah to heaven in a fiery chariot,[14] which runs through the work, like an unspoken leit-motif. The organic flow of *Elijah*, it seems to me, derives as much, also, from older Latin models, such as the early Baroque master, Carissimi.[15] For example, in *Elijah*, each piece is structured with an asymmetry that permits one scene to flow effortlessly into the next. These movements complement one another, generating composite-type formal structures, quite unlike the full and rounded arias and choruses, structured as independent, self-contained units in Bach's Passions and Handel's oratorios. The following is a case in point.

Analysis

DETAIL, No. 1

Recitative with Chorus
The confrontation of Ahab and Elijah
1 Kings 17: 1, 15, 17–19, 22–25

Elijah's recitative *the Lord will then send rain* heads up the second section of Part 1. Descending pairs of tri-tones, sounded in the strings, constitute an unobtrusive, yet unmistakable motif presaging rain.

Elijah

> As God the Lord of Sabaoth liveth, before whom I stand,
> Three days this year fulfilled, I will show myself to Ahab;
> And the Lord will then send rain again upon the earth.

The racing chariot of Ahab, with wheels turning, is portrayed in this dramatic confrontation through dotted rhythms in the orchestra.

---

14. Mendelssohn traveled through Italy in 1831, and completed his *Hebrides Overture* in Rome. It is a work connected to the sea, in which he explores the same kind of surging, turbulent textures found in *Elijah*.
15. Little has been noted of Mendelssohn's connection to the Italian master, Carissimi, one of the pioneers of 17th century oratorio, whose approach to biblical subjects was, most likely, familiar to the composer from his youthful sojourn in Italy.

Ex. 24. Mendelssohn: *Elijah*, Part 1, No. 10
Reprint of Elijah from Complete Works published by Breitkof and Hartel, n.d., reissued by
Dover Publications (1995).

Ahab

> Art thou Elijah? Art thou he that troubleth Israel?

Chorus

> Thou art Elijah, he that troubleth Israel.

Underlined by these dotted rhythms, the chorus reiterates Ahab's incriminating recitative: *Thou art...he that troubleth Israel.* A background unity of rhythmic support, binding episodic elements together into a cohesive whole, links both solo accusation and choral response, thus, implying that the people are in unanimous accord with the king.

Elijah

> I never troubled Israel's peace: it is thou, Ahab, and all thy father's house.
> Ye have forsaken God's commands: and hast followed Baalim!

Elijah's response, intensified by *tremolos* in the strings, is punctuated by abrupt chords in the orchestra that resound like lightning blows from heaven.

> Now send and gather to me the whole of Israel unto Mount Carmel:
> There summon the prophets of Baal,
> And also the prophets of the groves, who are feasted at Jezebel's table.
> Then we shall see whose God is the Lord.

This time, the people are swayed by Elijah's vehemence. They echo the prophet in chorale-like declamation. It is an example of the Lutheran influence on Mendelssohn's style. Whenever Mendelssohn wishes to represent faith, he does so through the chorale.

Chorus

> And then we shall see whose God is the Lord.

Elijah's next response opens on a dry recitative and intensifies through-out. Rapidly repeated notes in the orchestra, rising to passion, confirm his fervid emotions.

Elijah

> Rise then, ye priests of Baal: select and slay a bullock,
> and put no fire under it:
> Uplift your voices, and call the god ye worship;
> And then I will call upon the Lord Jehovah:
> And the God, who by fire shall answer, let him be God.

The people are swayed by the zealousness of the Prophet. They respond by echoing his challenge.

Chorus

> Yea, and the God who by fire shall answer, let him be God.

This episode is the calm before the storm. Asymmetric in construction, it begins by proposing a trial by fire between the Lord and the priests of Baal, but closes quietly, on an unaccompanied, almost matter-of-fact recitative. It sets up a sense of expectation, which will soon be realized.

Elijah

Call first upon your god: your numbers are many: I, even I only remain, one prophet of the Lord! Invoke your forest gods and mountain deities.

DETAIL, No. 14

Recitative and Air
Elijah's prayer

Ex. 25. Mendelssohn: *Elijah*, Part 1, No. 14
© Copyright 1991 Novello. Used by permission.

Elijah's prayer *Lord God of Abraham, Isaac and Israel*, set principally in majestic E-flat major tonality, meanders expressively in and out of a number of keys. Throughout this song-filled supplication the mood is introspective, and reveals the tender, oft concealed lyric side of Elijah's nature. Its form, a truncated aria in three sections, is framed by an orchestral introduction and coda. Its position, in the overall structure of the scene, is like a parenthesis, the calm inside a storm of emotion. Like the eye of a hurricane, it affords much needed emotional relief, against the Prophet's belligerent challenges to the priests of Baal.

Air: *Prayer of Elijah*

1 Kings 18: 30, 36, 17

Introduction

9 bars (G minor modulates to E-flat major)

> Draw near all ye people: come to me!

A

6 bars (E-flat major)

> Lord God of Abraham, Isaac and Israel,
> This day let it be known that Thou art God;
> And that I am thy servant!

B

9 bars (G minor modulates to the Dominant)

> O show to all, this people
> That I have done these things according to Thy word!

C

5 bars (C minor modulates to D-flat major)

> O hear me Lord and answer me;
> O hear me Lord and answer me;

D

8 bars (D-flat major to E-flat minor-major)

> Lord God of Abraham, Isaac and Israel,
> O hear me Lord and answer me;
> And show this people that thou art Lord God;
> And let their hearts again be turned!

4 bars (C minor modulates to E-flat major)

> And show this people that thou art Lord God;
> And let their hearts again be turned!

Coda

5 bars (E-flat major)

> Lord and let their hearts again be turned!

DETAIL, No. 16

Recitative and Chorus
Slaying the priests of Baal

This section begins unassumingly, with an unaccompanied recitative by Elijah; initiating a passage, which, then, unexpectedly bursts forth into an impassioned *Allegro con fuoco* in the orchestra.

Elijah

> O thou, who makest thine angels spirits;
> Thou whose ministers are flaming fires,
> Let them now descend!
>
> (Psalm 104:4)

The violins and violas ignite, as it were, the fire from heaven, in sixteenth-note arpeggios; while the people explode into a veritable volcano of antiphonal choral declamation.

The People

> The fire descends from heaven;
> The flames consume his offering!
> Before Him upon your faces fall!

The watchword of the faith, *The Lord is God… Our God is one Lord*, is uttered as a hushed Lutheran chorale by the chorus. Then, proclaimed with full voices and organ-like orchestral support.

> The Lord is God: O Israel hear! Our God is one Lord;
> And we will have no other gods before the Lord.
>
> (1 Kings 38–39, Deuteronomy 5:7, 6:4)

Accompanied by a timpani roll, Elijah shouts his dry recitative, as if to indicate graphically, the slaying of the priests of Baal with swords. The people's unison response is immediate and unequivocal, dramatized by short, punctuated strokes from the orchestra.

Elijah

> Take all the prophets of Baal; and let not one of them escape you:
> Bring them down to Kishon's brook, and there let them be slain.

The People

> Take all the prophets of Baal; and let not one of them escape us:
> Bring all and slay them!
>
> (1 Kings 18:40)

Conclusion

The deep impression left by Elijah's ministry and his miraculous translation to heaven made Elijah a legendary figure, already, in biblical times.[16] For Mendelssohn, Elijah was not a historical being, but a living presence, a prototype for the prophet of wrath. In his music he strove for an actualization of the prophetic spirit: *such as we might again require in our own day — energetic and zealous, but also stern, wrathful and gloomy; a striking contrast to the court and popular rabble.*[17] The oratorio was so successfully received in Britain that it equaled, if not surpassed, affections for Handel's *Messiah*; and become a model to be emulated by British composers for more than half a century.[18]

---

16. Malachi, the last of the prophets, predicted that Elijah would be sent by God *before the coming of the great and terrible day of the Lord (Mal 3:23).* This prophecy became the point of departure for subsequent associations of Elijah with the Messianic Age. By the first century of the Common Era, it was taken for granted that Elijah was to be the precursor and herald of the Messiah. Jesus proclaimed John the Baptist as the reincarnated Elijah (Matthew 11:10ff, 17:10ff, Mark 9:11ff).

17. Extracted from Mendelssohn's letter to his friend and librettist, Reverend Julius Schubring (November 2, 1838); as cited in the introductory notes to Mendelssohn's vocal score, *Elijah* (London: Novello & Company, 1991).

18. Many composers drew inspiration from Mendelssohn's musical imagery. Wagner's opera *Flying Dutchman* owes much to *Hebrides* (Fingal's Cave) Overture, to say nothing of the dramatic recitatives and allusions to "fire music" in the *Ring Cycle*, traceable directly back to *Elijah*. German Reform Synagogue composer, Louis Lewandowsky (1821–1894), modeled his choral style after Mendelssohn's oratorios and psalms. Brahms' choral works and the *German Requiem* are influenced by Mendelssohn's *Psalms*, as well. Much of Late-Victorian British music derives from Mendelssohn's *Elijah* and *Saint Paul* (i.e. oratorios by Parry, Stanford, and Elgar), while, the popular and songful piano pieces, *Songs without Words*, set the standard for parlor music in 19th century America.

Related Works

An early example[19] on Elijah and the priests of Baal is Cazzati's *Il Zelante Difeso* (Bologna, 1665). Other oratorios were written for the Viennese court by composers such as Georg Reutter (1728) and Antonio Caldara (1729). A comic opera after Kotzebue by Conradin Kreutzer, *Die Schlafmuetze des Propheten Elias* (1814), was (by whim of the censor) retitled *Die Nachnuetze*. Abraham Zvi Idelsohn's opera *Elijah* has yet to be published.[20]

Other Directions

In Christianity, Elijah's ascension to heaven is equated with the ascension of Jesus. After translation to heaven, Elijah inhabits Moslem imagination as a miraculous servant, performing supernatural feats for his masters. In Jewish traditional, Elijah is both teacher and guide; protector of the innocent and accuser of the impious; comforter of the suffering, and herald of the Messiah. Elijah legends find expression in almost every genre of Jewish music from liturgy to folksong.[21] He appears in traditional liturgical chant in the blessing following the Prophetic reading,[22] in Sephardic *piyutim* for circumcision ceremonies,[23] in modern Hasidic song,[24] in Jewish-Oriental folksong,[25] and in Ashkenazi songs at the

---

19. A "History of Elijah and Ahab" occurs among Hungarian Protestant Bible songs of the 16th century. Oratorio composers from the 17th century onward made use of the subject of Elijah, when the political climate was favorable.
20. See Batia Bayer, "Elijah," *Encyclopaedia Judaica*, Vol. 6, col. 642.
21. Paraliturgical texts are devotional poems, which, though widely accepted, are not an obligatory part of synagogue liturgy.
22. *Lord our God, make us rejoice in the coming of thy servant Elijah the prophet, and in the rule of thine anointed of the house of David.* Hertz, *Prayer Book*, 497.
23. *Arrange my lips in praise of God my father, to honor the beloved of my heart, Elijah the prophet.* R. David Hasan (18th C. Morocco). "E'eroch Mahalel Nivi," *Aviah Rennanot: Shirim V'Bakashot L'Shabbatot Haggim U'Smachot* (Jerusalem: Beit Hasefarim, 1993) 195.
24. *May the All-merciful send us Elijah the prophet who shall bring us good tidings, salvation and consolation.* Hertz, *Prayerbook*, "Grace after Meals," 975.
25. *Elijah, O prophet, harness a ride in captivity for neither heart nor eyes have seen slumber.* See "Babylonian folksong," *The Sephardic Music Anthology*, edited by Velvel Pasternak (Cedarhurst, NY: Tara Publications, 2006) 97.

departing of the Sabbath:[26] *Elijah the prophet, Elijah the Tishbite, Elijah the Gilead, May he quickly come to us with Messiah, son of David (Mal. 3:23–24).*[27]

Works List

Badia, Carlo-Agostino (1672 Venice–1738 Vienna). *Il Profeta Elia* (G. Zati), oratorio.

Bonfichi, Paolo (1969–1840 Italy). *La nu volette di Elia*, oratorio.

Caldara, Antonio (1670 Venice–1736 Vienna). *Elia* (A. Zeno), oratorio.

Castelnuovo-Tedesco, Mario (1895 Florence–1968 Beverly Hills, Calif.). *Il profeti: 1. Elijah*, concerto for violin and orchestra.

Cazzati, Mauricio (1620–1677 Italy). *Il Zelante Diveso*, oratorio.

Coenen, Ludovicus (18th C. Rotterdam). *Elia on Horeb* (N. Beets), arioso, baritone and basso-continuo.

Crispi, Pietro Maria (1737–1797 Rome). *La novoletta d'Elia* (G. Pizzi), cantata.

Gabrieli, Domenico (1640 Bologne–1690). *Elia sacrificante* (1 Kings 17), oratorio.

Gray, Alan (1855 York–1935 England). *The Widow of Zarepath* (1 Kings 16), cantata.

Jacobson, Maurice (1896 London–1976). *Prophet of Fire*, broadcast music.

Kosa, Gyorgy (1897–1984 Budapest). *Elias*, oratorio.

Lavry, Marc (1903 Riga–1968 Haifa). *Meʾarat ha-Tishbi* (Sh. Hupert), voice, pianoforte.

Mendelssohn, Felix (1809 Hamburg–1847 Leipzig). *Elijah*, oratorio.

Nystedt, Knut (b.1915 Oslo). *The Burnt Sacrifice* (1 Kings 18), narrator, choir, orchestra.

Perry, George Frederick (1793 Norwich–1862 London). *Elijah and the priests of Baal*, oratorio.

Reutter, Georg (1708–1772 Vienna). *Elia* (Villati), oratorio.

---

26. *He passed through the market with his hope, and lo, the prophet Elijah came towards him.* See "Ish Hasid Hayah," attributed to Mordecai. *Zemiroth: Sabbath Songs*, translated by Nosson Scherman (Brooklyn: Mesorah Publications, 1979) 272–276.

27. *Zemirot*, 280.

Schalit, Heinrich (1886 Vienna–1951 Denver, Colo.). *Elijah the Prophet*, choir.
Veneziano, Gaetano (1656–1716 Naples). *Il sacrificio d'Elia* (G. Veneziano), oratorio.
Walliser, Christoph Thomas (1568–1648 Strasbourg). *Elias*, choir.

JEZEBEL

Wicked as Ahab was, his wife, Jezebel — daughter of Ethbaal, king of the Sidonians and mother to his sons: Ahaziah and Jehoram — was incomparably worse. According to Scripture, it was she who instigated the sins of her husband: *there was none like unto Ahab... whom his wife Jezebel stirred up (1 Kings 22:25)*. Every day, she had her husband weighed, and, the increase in gold, she sacrificed to idols (Talmud Sanhedrin 102b). She placed unchaste images in Ahab's chariot in order to stimulate his carnal desire, and, it was these, which were smeared with his blood when he was killed (1 Kings 22:38). Jezebel, herself, was trampled to death in the Jezreel Valley, by horses.[28]

Works List

Arresti, Floriano (1650–1719 Bologna). *Iezabelle*, oratorio.
Bencini, Pietro Paolo (1680–1750 Rome). *La Jezabel* (F. Posteria), oratorio.
Federici, Francesco (17th C. Rome). *Jesabel*, oratorio.
Fritello, Jacobo (17th C. Italy). *Jezabel*, oratorio.
Kapilow, Robert (b.1952 USA). *Elijah's Angel* (1998), baritone, bass, boy soprano, children's chorus, and orchestra.
Pollarolo, Carlo Francesco (1653–1722 Venice). *Jesabel*, oratorio.
Predieri, Giacomo Cesare (1671–753 Bologna). *Iezabelle* (F. Arresti), oratorio.

---

28. Louis Ginzberg, *The Legends of the Jews*, Vol. 4, 188–189.

G. Dore: Jeremiah, *Bible Illustrations (1866)*

19

In Giuseppe Verdi's opera *Nabucco*, the biblical story serves as a frame onto which are projected the national aspirations and passionate fervor of 19th century Italy.

II KINGS

And Nebuchadnezzar, king of Babylon came unto the city, while his servants were besieging it ... And he carried out thence all the treasures of the house of the Lord ... And he carried away all Jerusalem ... Jehoiachin the king of Judah ... and the king's mother ... wives ... officers, and the chief men of the land, carried he into captivity from Jerusalem to Babylon (2 Kings 24:11–15).

The concluding section of the Book of Kings deals with the fall of the kingdom of Judah and the Babylonian captivity (2 Kings 18–25). Nebuchadnezzar II (630–562 B.C.), one of the great kings of antiquity, waged many military campaigns to consolidate the Babylonian Empire. He defeated Egypt, put down revolts in Tyre, and crushed the kingdom of Judah, which had been an Egyptian tributary until Nebuchadnezzar's victory at Carchemish (605 B.C.). When Judah ceased to send tribute to Babylon, Nebuchadnezzar promptly advanced on Jerusalem to demand payment. He took Jehoiachin, Judah's 18-year-old king,[1] captive and deported him, his household, and many prominent subjects to Babylon (597 B.C.); and replaced him with his uncle, Zedekiah, a puppet king. Though at first loyal to Nebuchadnezzar, Zedekiah was later persuaded by ultra-patriotic false prophets, priests, and emissaries from Edom, Ammon, Moab, Tyre, and Sidon to join a coalition with Egypt against

---

1. The last kings of Judah are: Hezekiah (727–698 B.C.), Manasseh (698–642 B.C.), Ammon (641–640 B.C.), Josiah (639–609 B.C.), Jehoahaz (609 B.C.), Jehoiakim (608–598 B.C.), Jehoiachin (597 B.C.) and Zedekiah (595–586 B.C.).

Babylon. Hopes were raised by information received from deported exiles, predicting the speedy collapse of Babylon. It proved groundless. In 586 B.C. Nebuchadnezzar returned to defeat the coalition, once and for all. Jerusalem, the royal palace, and the Temple were sacked and burned. The population was taken in captivity to Babylon; the kingdom of Judea existed no longer.

The Bible views Nebuchadnezzar as an instrument of divine retribution, fulfilling prophecies that had hovered over Judah for generations: *Thus saith the Lord: Behold, I will bring evil upon this place and upon the inhabitants thereof, ... because they have forsaken me, and have offered unto other gods, that they might provoke me with the work of their hands; therefore my wrath shall be kindled against this place. (II Kings 22:16–17; see also Jeremiah 27).* Authorship of the book is attributed to Jeremiah.

Giuseppe Verdi: Nabucco (1840)

Libretto: Temistocle Solera
Genre: Lyric drama in four parts
Medium: Soloists, chorus and orchestra
Style: Italian Opera
First performance: La Scala, Milan, 1842
Duration: ca. 1 hour 40 minutes

The opera *Nabucco* retells the story of Nebuchadnezzar's conquest and captivity of Jerusalem, enriching the biblical narrative with a romantic subplot of love and treason in high places. Written in the late 1830s, *Nabucco* created a sensation at its premiere and established its composer as a national hero.

Biographic Context

Giuseppe Verdi (1813 Roncole–1901 Milan), the most important Italian opera composer of the 19th century, rose to fame during the struggle for Italian unification (*Risorgimento*).[2] His opera *Nabucco* is a 19th-century Italian melodrama transposed to sixth-century B.C. Jerusalem. It gave

---

2.   The *Risorgimento* describes a movement for the liberation and unification of the Italian peninsular; a period of literary and political nationalism in the 19th century that lead to a united Italy in 1870.

Italians of Verdi's generation, who identified their political fate with that of the ancient Hebrews (whose land had been occupied, and whose people oppressed, assaulted, and exiled), a voice for their pent-up feelings against the Austrian occupation of Italy and their Hapsburg rulers.

Verdi's parents were working people. His first teacher was the local church organist. At 12, Giuseppe went to the town of Busseto and started working for Antonio Barezzi.[3] There, he studied Latin with the canon at the church and music with the town band-master. At 19 he went to Milan with hopes of entering the conservatory of music, but failed to gain admission, and continued his composition studies privately. When the budding composer returned to Busseto, he was appointed conductor of the municipal band and married his protector's daughter, Margherita Barezzi. A few years later, again trying to establish himself in the big world, he resettled his little family in Milan, only to lose both wife and children to the plague. Heart broken and alone, it was at this tragic juncture in life that Verdi composed *Nabucco*. His extraordinary production of works began just at that time. Verdi is buried at the Home for Aged Musicians, which he founded in Milan.

Librettist

Librettist Temistocle Solera (1815 Ferrara–1878 Milan) commenced his career as a poet, novelist, and composer; and had written four unsuccessful operas before achieving fame as librettist in collaboration with Giuseppe Verdi. He played an active role in the *Risorgimento*, as secret courier between Cavour and Napoleon III, and as a spy on conspirators in the 1850s. Afterwards, Solera worked as an impresario and theatre director in various cities of the Iberian Peninsula, where his name appeared in recognized journals together with Spain's best writers. Solera spent his last days in poverty, trying to eek out a living as an antique dealer in Milan.

Text and Context

The libretto, which describes events in Babylon after the fall and

---

3. Antonio Barezzi was a merchant, a fanatical music enthusiast, and one of Busseto's prominent citizens. He became a second father to the young Verdi, taking him into his home, sending him to study in Milan, and in 1836, giving him his daughter Margherita in marriage.

captivity of Jerusalem, is drawn from 2 Kings 24–25, 2 Chronicles 36, and the Book of Daniel, chapters 1–4. The episode of Nebuchadnezzar's madness, repentance, and recovery, which plays such a key role in the opera, is based upon Daniel 4:30–34. The famous Slaves' chorus *Va Pensiero* is a fanciful paraphrase of Psalm 137. Both Solera and Verdi were anxious to stress their biblical sources, and supplied quotations from Jeremiah as headings for each of the four acts of the opera: Jer. 34:2 (Act 1), Jer. 30:23 (Act 2), Jer. 50:39 (Act 3), and Jer. 50:2 (Act 4). The love triangle between the principal characters (i.e. Ismaele, Abigail, and Fenena), however, is pure fantasy.[4]

Synopsis

Act 1 — Solomon's Temple in Jerusalem

Thus saith the Lord: Behold, I will give this city
Into the hand of the king of Babylon, and he shall burn it with fire.

(Jer. 34:2)

The terrified Hebrews await the arrival of Nabucco. The high priest (Zachariah) has kidnapped Nabucco's daughter (Fenena) and entrusted her to Ismaele, nephew to the king of Judah. Fenena and Ismaele fall in love, but are threatened by her jealous Amazon stepsister (Abigaille), who also desires Ismaele. The crowd returns, and Nabucco appears, ordering the destruction of the Temple.

---

4. While historical biblical events form the backdrop to this highly-charged libretto of love and jealously, intrigue and rage, revenge and remorse, Soler's direct source is a four-act French play by Auguste Anicet-Bourgeois and Francis Cornu, first performed in Paris in 1836. Various passages were apparently lifted whole sale into the libretto. The scenario of the French play was reduced and its structure simplified for the opera libretto. A secondary source is a "ballet storico" by Antonio Cortesi entitled *Nabuchodonosor,* and given at La Scala in 1838. Characters in the libretto by Solera who do not appear in the Bible are: Ismaele, Abigail, and Fenena. The high priest, Zachariah, resembles Jeremiah, who never went to Babylon. See Gabriele Dotto, "Introduction" to the vocal score of Giuseppe Verdi *Nabuchodonosor,* translated by Andrew Porter (Milan: Ricordi, 1987), in collaboration with (Chicago: University of Chicago Press, 1996) lxvii — lxxxii.

Act 2 — The palace in Babylon

Behold the whirlwind of the Lord goeth forth…
It shall fall…upon the head of the wicked.

(Jer. 30:23)

Scene 1: Abigaille discovers she is a slave's daughter, and illegitimate. The high priest of Baal circulates rumors that Nabucco has died in battle.
    Scene 2: Zachariah prays. Ismaele begs for forgiveness. Fenena converts to Judaism. Abigaille enters. Suddenly, Nabucco appears and proclaims himself a god. For this presumption, he is struck down by a thunderbolt, becoming helplessly insane.

Act 3 — At the Hanging Gardens

The wild beasts of the desert shall dwell there,
And the owls dwell therein.

(Jer. 50:39)

Scene 1: Abigaille is enthroned. Nabucco enters and realizes he is a prisoner.
Scene 2 (On the Banks of the Euphrates): The Hebrews dream of Zion.

Act 4 — At the Palace

Baal is confounded; his idols are broken in pieces.

(Jer. 50:2)

Scene 1: Nabucco repents. Supplicating the God of Israel, his reason is restored.
    Scene 2 (In front of the Statue of Baal): Zachariah, Ismaele, Fenena and Anna await execution. Abigaille takes poison, begs forgiveness from her father, and blesses her sister's union with Ismaele.

Music and Musical Exegesis

A composer of pathos, Verdi's aesthetic credo may be embodied in three words: spontaneity, naturalness, and simplicity. His style is direct and forceful. Verdi strives for immediate effect by portraying elemental human emotions, such as: jealousy, rage, contrition, love, patriotic loyalty, and betrayal. Melody is paramount in this approach. Vocal lines are drawn from a rich typology, ranging from simple declamation to speech-inflected *parlando-rubato*; short singable tunes to fully developed arias. Verdi constructs large scale dramatic scenes and acts through the juxtaposition of stock-formats, such as: *secco* and dramatic recitatives, cabalettas, cavatinas, arias, duets, ensembles, and choruses. Within the artistic framework of 19th century Italian opera, the composer slackens and heightens tensions, balancing and expanding upon them for overwhelming dramatic effects. The orchestra serves to support the voice with visceral, rhythmically dominated accompaniments; and does not often function as an independent, expressive medium.

DETAIL 1

Act II, Scene 4

Va Pensiero — Chorus of the Hebrew slaves

At the banks of the Euphrates, the Hebrew nation labors in chains. The entire ensemble (SSATTB) sings in unison *Va Pensiero*, the famous 'Slaves' Chorus'. The chorus is based on Psalm 137: *By the waters of Babylon, there we sat down, yea we wept when we remembered Zion... How shall we sing the Lord's song in a strange land?* Almost hymn-like in quality, it is a lament set to a flowing *belcanto* melody and laid out in square, four-bar phrases.[5] It is structured in clear sections, which are differentiated tonally: Tonic, Dominant, Tonic, and Subdominant — in three-part form (i.e. A B A + coda),

Formal Design

Orchestral introduction
(11 + 1 bars)

A section
Tonic (I)
Opening (16 bars)

a   +   a   +   b   +   a
(4 bars-open) + (4 bars-close) + (4 bars-break) + (4 bars-close)

Va, Pensiero, sull'ali dorate, /Va, ti posa sui clivi, sui colli (A)

---

5.   It was the *Slaves' Chorus*, almost causing a riot at its premiere, which launched Verdi's career and catapulted the unknown composer to greatness.

Ex. 26. Verdi: *Nabucodonsor*

© Copyright 1987 by The University of Chicago Press and Casa Ricordi. Used by permission.

Ove olezzano tepide e molli / L'aure dolci del suolo natal! (A)
Del Giordano le rive saluta, / Di Sïon le torri atterrate… (B)
Oh mia patria sì bella e perduta! / Oh membranza sì cara e fatal! (A)

By the waters of Babylon, Ah, we weep to recall thee, Oh Zion. (A)

May my song fly to greet thee, my homeland,
May my song fly on swift wings of gold! (A)
Greet the shores of our fair river Jordan;
Greet the shores of the fallen temple of Zion. (B)
Oh my homeland so lovely, forsaken!
Oh remembrance of fair times of old! (A)

B section
Dominant (V)
Middle (12 bars)
c   +   c   + transition
(4 bars) + (4 bars) + (4 bars)

Arpa d'ôr dei fatidici vati / Perchè muta dal salice pendi? (C)
Le memorie nel petto raccendi, / Ci favella del tempo che fu! (C)
O simìle di Solima ai fati / Traggi un suono di crudo lamento,

All our harps we have hung on the willows,
And you hang there in silence and sorrow? (C)
Let the memories of past days inspire you.
Sing a song of the days long ago! (C)

A section — Closing
Tonic (I) — Subdominant (IV)
Return (8 bars)
a   +   d
(4 bars-open) + (3 bars-close)

O t'ispiri il Signore un concento
Che ne infonda al patire virtù, (A)

Oh, lament for the fate of Jerusalem;
Raise your voices in grief and lamenting (A)

Coda
Tonic (I)
c
(3 bars)

Che ne infonda al patire virtue,
Che ne infonda al patire virtù, al patire virtù! (D)

Oh, inspire us Jehovah, with courage,
Send a new song to lighten our woe! (D coda)

Clearly not a devotional piece one might sing in church, and considerably more sophisticated than its folk-music-like frame might intimate, melodic invention in this chorus is rich and varied, supple and songlike. Its breadth and range have the character of a national anthem.

DETAIL 2

Act IV Scene 1
Dio di Giuda — Oh God of Judah

The recitative and aria *Oh God of Judah*, one of the highlights of the opera, is the supplication of a repentant sinner. In it, the deranged Nabucco pleads to the God of Israel for release from madness. Its character of sincere contrition, shares in the same ambiguities and tensions as the Psalm of supplication: It begins in anger; it continues as a plea for deliverance; and concludes in thanksgiving and praise. Nabucco hopes for salvation, but is not certain whether his prayer will be heard or answered. At the premiere, it was this aria, and not the *Slaves' Chorus*, which was encored.[6]

Analyses

Recitative and Aria of Nabucco

(Recitative)

Ah prigioniero io sono! / Dio degli Ebrei, perdono!

Ah, they have made me a prisoner!
Mighty God of Israel, hear me!

Oh God of Judah traces the various states of Nabucco's mind by way of a lyric, *basso cantante* line. This twists and turns around itself, leaps upwards, falls, climbs back upwards again, and finally, terraces downwards. Like the psalm of petition, it prays, "if you will heal me, I will do all in my power to praise and acknowledge you." This is a far cry from the presumptuous man who declared at the end of Act II, "I am

---

6. Gabriele Dotto, op. cit.

king no more, I am God!" The overall structure of the aria is a modified three-part form: (I) **A A B A** (II) **C** (III) **A A A + C (coda).**

(Aria)

Opening
A (4 bars) A (4 bars) B (4 bars) A (4 bars)

Dio di Giuda! l'ara e il tempio (A)
A te sacri, a te sacri, sorgeranno (A variation)…
Deh mi togli, mi togli a tanto affanno, (B) / deh mi togli a tanto affanno
E i miei riti, e i miei riti struggerò. (A var) / Tu m'ascolti… Già dell'empio

Oh God of Judah, altar and temple, (A)
To thy glory shall arise now. (A variation)
Ah, release me from my torment, (B) And every idol I'll destroy.
Thou dost hear me… (A variation)

The **A A** opening phrase addresses the Almighty. The **B** phrase reveals Nabucco's inner "torment," modulating into the minor mode. Then, a return to the initial **A** phrase rounds out this section and gives it a sense of closure.

Middle
C (6 bars)

Rischiarata è l'egra mente! (C)

Clouds of madness pass away and I see clearly! (C)

In this contrasting middle (**C**) section, Nabucco's sanity returns. These 6 bars function both as a break with the past, and at the same time, as a bridge back to the reprise. The dramatic weight of this section rests on the orchestra, rather than the soloist, which, unexpectedly doubles its tempo with accompanying chain-syncopations in the winds. It is an ingenious orchestral coloring, which serves as musical metaphor for Nabucco's madness evaporating away: "Clouds of madness pass away and I see clearly!"

Reprise
A (4 bars) A (2 bars) A (2 bars)

Ah, Dio verace, onnipossente, Adorarti, adorarti ognor saprò, (A var.)

Ex. 27. Verdi: *Nabucodonsor*

© Copyright 1987 by The University of Chicago Press and Casa Ricordi. Used by permission.

Adorarti ognor saprò, (A var). Adorarti ognor saprò. (A var.)

Ah, great Jehovah, Lord almighty, I'll adore Thee ever more. (A variation)
I'll adore Thee ever more. I'll adore Thee ever more. (A variation,
A variation)

This truncated reprise reinstates Nabucco's initial address of praise to the Almighty. It shifts from a mode of prayer and supplication to one of thanksgiving and adoration, tracing the emotional trajectory of the Psalm of lament. The threefold repetition of this concluding phrase signals and signifies completeness. The final adoration to Jehovah, "I'll adore thee evermore," is the most floridly ornamented passage in the entire aria, and echoes, in its way, the ecstatic pathos of the Gregorian *jubilus* — a melisma of praise.[7]

---

7.   It is notable that each section of the aria cadences with elaborate cadenzas in *bel canto* style, which serve as structural devices, to define its three-part form.

Coda
C (2 bar orchestral coda)

The reprise of (C) contributes a sense of fulfillment, finality, and closure to the aria, informing us that "clouds of madness" have passed.

Conclusion

In Verdi's hands the Bible becomes a backdrop for the expression of human pathos. His eternal truths, valid at all times and in all places, are impetuosity and ardor, love and hate, jealousy and revenge, victory and defeat.[8] It is through opposition and conflict that this biblical drama unfolds in fast-paced scenes, pressing forward towards resolution; a theater composer's histrionic sense of putting the right feeling, in the right place, at the right time — that is his goal.[9] We tend to overlook, though, that Verdi is a composer from the land of Gregorian chant and Palestrina and the 16th century Renaissance madrigal. When he needs to (as in the cloud-filled bridge passage of Nabucco's aria), Verdi knows how to take the imagery of words and paint a picture with them to evoke inner landscapes. But, at the same time, when required, he can transform a biblical psalm into a national anthem, without sacrificing either patriotic fervor or ecclesiastical purity.

In summarizing the balance between Nabucco, seen as a human drama, or, seen a biblical opera, we might conclude with the observation that the compelling and passionate humanity Verdi set to music, made him a popular opera composer, while the transference of spirit he drew from the Bible, made him a national icon.

Works List

Most musical compositions involving Nebuchadnezzar, deal largely with episodes drawn from the book of Daniel, notably the story of the Three

---

8. This point is emphasized by the non-historical subplot introduced into *Nabucco,* whose purpose is to show, how, even love, the most human of emotions, may be destroyed through mean ambition or cold-hearted malevolence.

9. This follows standard Italian opera convention, in which *bel canto* melody is framed in impassioned acts, scenes, arias, ensembles, and choruses — and music dominates the words and the actions.

Hebrews. They include an opera by Caldara (1731), Darius Milhaud's *Les Miracles de la Foi* (1951), and Benjamin Britten's *The Burning Fiery Furnace* (1966). A ballet entitled *Nabuchodonosor* was performed at La Scala, Milan, on September 6, 1838, to mark the coronation of the Austrian emperor Ferdinand I as king of Lombardy and Venice.

Albergati, Pirro (1663 Carrati–1735 Bologna). *Nabuchodonosor,* oratorio.

Ariosti, Attilio (1666 Bologna–1740). *Nabuchodonosor* (Rocco Maria Rossi) oratorio.

Dyson, George (1883–1964 UK). *Nebuchadnezzar* (1935), tenor, bass, SATB, orchestra.

Reinhard Keiser (1674–1739). *Der gestürzte und wieder erhöhte Nebukadnezar, König zu Babylon* (1704), opera.

Other Directions

HEZEKIAH

Hezekiah is among the most righteous of the kings of Judah. *He did that which was right in the eyes of the Lord...trusted...in the God of Israel; so that after him was none like him among them that were born before him (2 Kings 18:3, 5).* A number of chapters in the Bible are devoted to Hezekiah's reign (2 Kings 18–20; Isaiah 36–39, and 2 Chronicles 29–32). The prayer of Hezekiah (*Canticum Ezechia, Isa. 38*) is among the cantica of the Roman Catholic Church. His illness and recovery provide the main theme for the oratorios.

Works List

Bonocini, Giovanni (1670 Modena-747 Vienna). *Ezechia* (A. Zeno), oratorio.

Carissimi, Giacomo (1605–1674 Rome). *Ezechias,* oratorio.

Ehrlich, Abel (1915 Germany/1939 Israel–2003). *The Writing of Hezekiah,* soprano, violin, oboe, contrabass.

Gaul, Alfred (1837–1913 England). *Hezekiah,* oratorio.

Hatton, John (1809–1886 England). *Hezekiah,* sacred drama.

Krenek, Ernst (1900 Vienna–1991 USA). *Aegrotate Ezechias,* voice and piano.

Kuhnau, Johann (1660–1772 Leipzig). *The mortally ill and then restored Hezekiah*, Biblical Sonatas, keyboard.

Perry, Gorge Frederick (1793–1862 London). *Hezekiah*, oratorio.

Turpin, Edmund (1835–1907 London). *Hezekiah*, oratorio.

20

Prophecy, liturgy, and spectacle converge in Isaiah's vision-ary revelation — *Holy, holy, holy is the Lord of Hosts*. This chapter examines various settings and contexts in liturgy and art music.

ISAIAH

In the year that king Uzziah died I saw the Lord sitting upon a throne high and lifted up, and His train filled the temple. Above Him stood the seraphim; each one had six wings: with twain he covered his face, and with twain he covered his feet, and with twain he did fly. And one cried unto another, and said Holy, holy, holy, is the Lord of Hosts; the fullness of the whole earth declareth His glory   (Isaiah 6:1-3).

Isaiah was a man with a speech impediment, who could have lived comfortably and retired at ease, yet, he risked all and suffered much to bear witness to the Ineffable. Prophet and statesman, Isaiah was active in Jerusalem from 758 B.C. until 698 B.C. *in the days of Uzziah, Jotham, Ahaz, and Hezekiah, kings of Judah (Isaiah 1:1).* His father, Amoz, also a prophet, was the brother of Amaziah, king of Judah (798–769 B.C.). Uzziah, Amaziah's son, was Isaiah's first cousin, whose son, Jotham, was Isaiah's quasi-nephew. If the prophet was like a "great uncle" to Ahaz, he was revered as a kind of "great-grandfather" figure by Hezekiah. It was this close filial relationship to the ruling aristocracy which lends Isaiah's prophecies such presence and authority.[1]

---

1.   On Isaiah's speech impediment, see Louis Ginzberg, *Legends of the Jews*, Vol. 4, 261–3, and Vol. 6, note 32, 358. Jotham (758–743 B.C. regent) and Ahaz (743–733 B.C. regent, 733–727 B.C.) reigned during the lifetime of their father and grandfather Uzziah (Azariah 769–733 B.C.), who became leprous as a result of entering the Temple to offer the priestly sacrifice in 758 B.C. He was to spend the rest of his life in isolation. The period of Hezekiah's reign

Tersanctus in Synagogue and Church

It was as an 18 year-old teenager that Isaiah envisioned the angelic host of Seraphim, calling one to the other above the Temple, and proclaiming the holiness and sovereignty of God. It was his introduction to prophecy.[2] The Aramaic Targum translates this clairvoyant cry out of eternity as a manifestation of theophany — the revelation of God to man.[3]

> *And they receive word from each other and say,*
> *Holy in the highest heavens, the abode of his presence.*
> *Holy upon earth the work of His mighty power,*
> *Holy forever and to all eternity, is the Lord of hosts.*
> *The whole earth is full of His glorious splendor (Isaiah 6:3).*

The three-fold Holy[4] has had immense ethical, ritual, artistic, and musical ramifications. Each repetition is replete with meaning. Holy is a mystic idea standing for the supreme exaltedness of the Eternal. Holy, stands for the Creator's freedom from all that is imperfect, impure, and unrighteous. Holy, stands for the Almighty's fullness and complete-

---

(727–698 B.C.) overlaps the deportations in the northern kingdom of Israel. Note that these dates and others of the period are given as a frame of reference, because almost no two researchers can agree on the exact chronology of the reigns of the kings of Israel. They are compiled from: William C. Dick, *The Bible: Its Letter and Spirit* (London: J.M. Dent and Sons, Ltd., 1943) 192; Soncino Press: Books of the Bible, *Chronicles, x*; and *Encyclopedia Judaica*, Vol. 8, 766–767.

2. The years in which Isaiah began his prophetic activity were critical for both Israel and Judah. The Assyrians overwhelmed Babylon and Syria (Aram or Damascus), and set themselves to become a world power. The northern kingdom of Israel (Samaria), in response, formed a defense alliance with Syria (Aram), and sought to induce Ahaz, king of Judah to join their alliance. Upon failing to persuade him, the coalition advanced upon Jerusalem, determined to set one of their own puppets in Ahaz's place (Isa. 7:6). The southern kingdom of Judah called on Assyria for help (c. 735 B.C.). Isaiah assured Ahaz that the allied campaign would fail. Shortly afterwards his prophecy was fulfilled. Israel (Samaria) and its allies fell to Assyria. See Abraham J. Heschel, *The Prophets* (New York: Harper & Row, 1962) 64.

3. This revelation forms the prologue to a tragic prophecy of destruction and devastation which Isaiah delivered against the kingdom of Israel: *Go and tell this to the people…Until cities be waste without habitant and the Lord have removed men far away (Isaiah 6:9–12).*

4. Hebrew: *Kedusha*; Latin: *Tersanctus*; Greek: *Trisagios*.

ness — something more than good, pure, or righteous. Holy is also a regulative principle, calling for imitation of God (*imitatio deo*) through reverence for parents, consideration for the needy, honorable dealing in business, love of neighbor, refraining from tale bearing, oppression and the lie: *In all thy ways acknowledge Him (Proverbs 3:6).*[5] In an effort to bring the charismatic vision of Isaiah into social and communal consciousness, the Sages of ancient Israel introduced the Tersanctus into liturgy. As such, it forms the basis for the most important Doxology of Judaism — the *Kedusha* of the synagogue.[6] The earliest Christian congregations, which developed within the synagogue, adapted and reframed the *Kedusha* as the *Sanctus* of the Mass.[7]

Sanctus

> *Sanctus, Sanctus, Sanctus Dominus, Deus Sabaoth.*
> *Pleni sunt caeli et terra gloria tua.*
> *Hosanna in excelsis!*

> Holy, Holy, Holy, Lord of Hosts
> Heaven and earth are full of thy glory (Isa. 6:3).
> Hosanna in the highest! (Matt. 21.9)

The text *Sanctus* consists in two parts. The first part, based on Isaiah, is the *Sanctus* proper, while the second part, *Benedictus,* is adopted from Psalms via the Gospel of Matthew.[8] These two parts are often set to contrasting music. A third element, *Hosanna in excelsis,* the cry

---

5. See Joseph Hertz's commentary in *Pentateuch*, 497–498.
6. Talmud Sotah 49a. See also Eric Werner, *The Sacred Bridge: The Interdependence of Liturgy and Music in Synagogue and Church during the First Millennium* (New York: Columbia University Press, 1963) 5.
7. The first Christian reference to the *Sanctus* is that of Clement of Rome. It is the only item of the Mass Ordinary derived from an Old Testament text. See Clement of Rome, *1 Cor. 34:6,* in *The Apostolic Fathers*, Lightfoot, ed., 23, as cited in Werner, chapter 9, note 53 (1963), 308.
8. Matthew 21:9 borrowed the text from Psalm 118:26, *Blessed is thy coming in the name of the Lord*, which functioned as the greeting extended by the priests and Levites to the pilgrims upon entering the Temple precinct on the Three Festivals *(Pesach, Shabuoth, and Sukkoth).* The Latin phrase, *Benedictus qui venit in nominee Domini,* substitutes for the proof text found in the *Kedusha* that reads: *The Lord shall reign forever, thy God O Zion unto all generations (Psalm 146:10).*

which accompanied Jesus' entrance to Jerusalem, is repeated in both parts. It is a formula derived from Psalm 118:25 and signifies "highest" heavens in the Targum. *Hosanna* unifies and completes both *Sanctus* and *Benedictus,* suggesting a three-part musical treatment.[9]

> *Benedictus qui venit in nomine Domini.*
> *Hosanna in excelsis!*

> Blessed is He that cometh in the name of the Lord (Matt. 21:9) (Ps. 118:26).
> Hosanna in the highest![10]

Sanctus in Medieval Music

The oldest pan-European stratum in the development of Western art music is Gregorian plainchant. It has many roots. If the cantillation and prayer modes of the synagogue are primary sources, they are not exclusive ones; since plainchant represents a synthesis of Hebraic, Greek, Mediterranean, and North European elements.[11] In fact, much of the

---

9. Originally, the cry *Hosanna* appeared in the Psalms as a plea for help, "Please God, save now!" For Early Christianity, however, it became a kind of jubilant cry. The introduction of the *Sanctus* into the Roman Catholic Mass is ascribed to Pope Sixtus I (c. 120), while *Hosanna in excelsis* (Praise in the highest) substitutes for the phrase *Blessed be the glory of God from his place (Ezek. 3:2)* in the *Kedusha.* These changes reflect doctrinal differences between Judaism and Early Christianity. Werner, 282–290.
10. The Hebraism *Hoshana,* "Save now," originally a cry for help (Ps. 118:25) was incorporated into the liturgy of the *Sukkoth* circuits around the Temple altar as a plea for rain. In contrast, it became a cry of jubilation for Christianity (Matt. 21:9). Whether in Jewish or Christian liturgy, the exclamation *Hoshana* or *Hosanna,* provides a response that enables mortal men to participate along with the angels in affirming the supreme holiness of God; as the preface formula to *Sanctus* indicates: *Cum quibus et nostras voces, ut admitti jubeas, deprecamur, supplici confessione dicentes* (With humble confession we beg you to command that our voices be admitted together with those of the angels, saying): *Sanctus, Sanctus, Sanctus.* See Willi Apel, *Gregorian Chant* (Bloomington: Indiana University Press, 1958) 415.
11. "As for the early sources of the standard repertory [that is, of 'Gregorian' chant], it has often been noticed, though only grudgingly admitted, that none of them was written in Rome, or for that matter, in Italy. They all come from such places in Western Europe as St. Gall, Metz, Einsiedeln, Chartes, Laon, and Montpellier, in other words, from the Franco-German Empire." Apel, 79.

repertory of Gregorian song, as it has been preserved, is thought to have been formed in France during the eighth and ninth centuries.[12]

The following anonymous *Sanctus,* sung to a monodic Roman Catholic plainsong, dates from the Middle Ages (c.800). It is characterized by the rising and falling of a single line melody, undulating in a free-flowing rhythmus attuned to the inflections of the Latin text. Framed in the Aeolian mode, it exhibits a bi-partite musical form, corresponding to the literary form of the *Sanctus,* as noted above. The atmosphere produced from this disembodied melody, impacting against stone walls and echoing in the cathedral caverns of Romanesque architecture, imbues the spare unisons of plainsong with rich resonance and quasi-harmonic sonority, that fills-in the intervallic gaps and rhythmic pauses of the monophonic chant. The eternal calm and spiritual aesthetic of this music strives to recreate Isaiah's vision of Seraphic song, in tone. It is a mirror of divine adoration, phrased *in tranquil joy of spirit, with pure speech, and holy melody, responding in unison, and exclaiming with awe — Holy, Holy, Holy is the Lord of Hosts.*[13]

Anonymous: Sanctus (Gregorian chant)

Genre: Medieval liturgical music
Medium: Men's choir
Style: Monodic or Monophonic
First performance: Romanesque Cathedral, c. 800
Duration: ca. 1:30

The upward arching, threefold statement of the *Sanctus* (phrase 1) cadences on tonic (*Sanctus*), dominant (*Sanctus*), and tonic (*Sanctus*). It is contrasted by *Domini Deus Sabaoth* (phrase 2), which dips down in melodic direction and range, but incorporates motifs from the third repetition of the *Sanctus*. *Pleni sunt caeli* (phrase 3) takes its cue from the second and third repetitions of the *Sanctus*,[14] quickly climbing up

---

12. "There is a great deal of historical evidence, in support of the view, that what we call 'Gregorian Chant' represents an eighth-to-ninth century fusion of Roman and Frankish elements" (Apel, 79).
13. Isaiah was sorely affrighted by the august throne of God. Targum, Hertz, *Prayer Book,* 113.
14. The music, based on the second and third repetitions of *Sanctus*, parallels the meaning of the text: *Pleni sunt caeli* (the whole earth is full), in that each *Sanctus* refers to a different aspect of His glory: in heaven, on earth (as

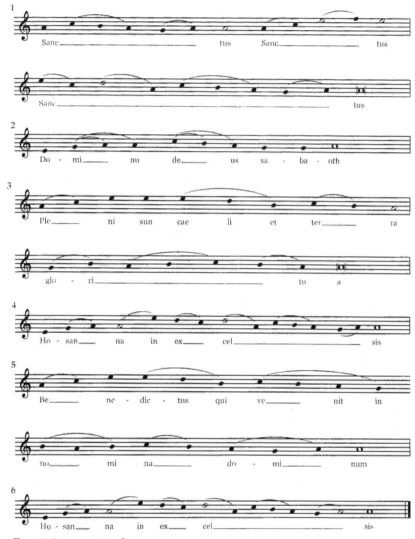

Ex. 28. Anonymous: *Sanctus*
From a recording of Our Lady of Fontgombault Abbey Choir, Rose Records, 1975. Transcribed by Max Stern

to the dominant, gently tapering down to tonic, undulating back up to

expressed in motivic paraphrase), and forever (as expressed in expansive development). These three repetitions are like concentric circles, elaborating a single meaning, and, it seems to me, represent the "wheels within wheels" of Ezekiel's vision, as well.

the mediant (C), then falling down to the tonic (A). *Hosanna* (phrase 4) sums up the first part, filling out the entire octave range of the chant, before closing with a cadence formula, derived from the third repetition of the *Sanctus*.

The second part: *Benedictus* (phrase 5) is a variation on *Pleni sunt caeli* (phrase 3), while *Hosanna* (phrase 6) repeats (phrase 4) exactly as before, rounding out the form, endowing it with a binary character. Each phrase in this plainsong either imitates or expands upon the motivic material of the Tersanctus, and, with the exception of the second *Sanctus*, cadences on the tonic. The modalities of such chants formed the theoretical basis for the church modes.[15]

One might extrapolate a theological principle, common to all sacred liturgical music, from the tonal structure of this example. Namely, that the tonal gravity of the tonic exerts such an overwhelming pull on the executants, that it quells individuality; under the sway of such piety, man can only bend in humble contrition. Art music, on the other hand, seeks a freedom of expression and individuality that oppressive conformity to ritual and liturgy does not permit. The injunction to *sing unto the Lord a new song* (Ps. 96:1) is a command for divinely directed, but free-willed creativity. It was the path that led to polyphony.

Sanctus in Renaissance Music

Giovanni Pierluigi da Palestrina: Sanctus from Missa Brevis
Genre: Liturgical
Medium: A cappella men's and boys' choirs
Style: Renaissance
First performance: St. Peters, Rome, 16th C.
Duration: ca. 5 minutes

The heavenly sound of Renaissance sacred choral music must have been created, in a conscious effort, to simulate the song of the angels in heaven, as envisioned by Isaiah. A prominent feature of this style is

---

15. Latin texts are set to plainsong melodies in three ways: syllabic (one note per syllable); neumatic (groups of two to four notes per syllable); or melismatic (a single syllable extending over a string of notes). This vocal style derives from the rhapsodic improvisations of the Eastern Mediterranean, the chant of the synagogue, and conceivably from ancient Levitical song.

its imitative counterpoint, an earthly replica of the prophetic vision *and one called to the other.* Acknowledged "Prince of Music" by the Roman Catholic Church, perhaps, no composer comes closer to this ideal than Giovanni Pierluigi da Palestrina (c.1525–1594); his creations are considered its tonal embodiment.

Ex. 29. Palestrina: *Sanctus from Missa Brevis*
© Copyright 1899 G. Schirmer.

This composer's ideal of a seamless web of euphony born of polyphony seems guided and directed by Scriptural prescription, *all take upon themselves the yoke of the kingdom of heaven one from the other, give leave one unto the other to declare the holiness of their Creator: in tranquil joy of spirit, with pure speech and holy melody.*[16] As Palestrina strives

---

16. See *Kedusha* text, Hertz, op. cit.

to duplicate, in vocal music, the adoration of the Divine Presence as revealed in a *cloud of glory (Exodus 40:34–38);* so his motifs are defined only to the extent needed to materialize textual images and ethical concepts. Whether at the level of motif, phrase, or section — rhythmic and formal outlines overlap in cloud-like formations, rather than in clear cut, neatly defined forms.

The justification for the Renaissance ideal of rich rounded euphony, against that of spare Romanesque unisons or open medieval quartal sonorities, may also be derived from these verses from Isaiah, and the exalted sounds the Prophet envisioned. In fact, all the rules of counterpoint and the handling of dissonance may be rationalized in contemplation upon the ultimate value of tertian harmony, chords of three notes built upon the interval of the third.[17] The three note chord, itself, alludes to a mystical heavenly harmony related to the eternal number "3," which symbolizes eternity and completeness. It represents a trinity of — life, substance, and intelligence; the family — father, mother, and child; the three dimensions of space — length, width, and height; and time — past, present, and future.[18] As *the whole earth is full of His glory* — so sonority, impelled forward by "earthly" dissonance, resolves into full and resonant (divinely ordained) tertian harmony.

Sanctus in Baroque Music

J.S. Bach: Sanctus from Mass in B minor
Genre: Liturgical
Medium: Mixed choir, tenor solo, orchestra
Style: Baroque
First performance: Leipzig (1724/1733)

Bach's Mass in B minor, one of the monuments of Western music, has been discussed extensively elsewhere. We focus briefly on Bach's massive treatment of the *Sanctus,* which is framed in three (or four) separate movements, each complete in itself.

Bach sets the Tersanctus as three richly textured statements by

---

17. The three basic notes of the chord are the primary harmonics in the overtone series — a phenomenon of sound, written into the acoustics of nature.
18. See Sepharial, *The Kabala of Numbers* (New York: Samuel Weiser Inc., 1970) 88–89 ff.

Ex. 30. J.S. Bach: *Sanctus from Mass in B minor*
© Copyright 1912 C.F. Peters

angelic groups of 6 voice parts. Each presentation of *Sanctus* is balanced by a descending (sometimes ascending) stepwise bass on *Sanctus,
Dominus Deus Sabaoth.* This bass line is then treated like a *cantus firmus,*
repeating nine times in counterpoint to variations and elaborations in
the upper voices, on the Tersanctus. It is similar to a *cantus firmus* in
flow, because the notes change, while the framework remains. Clearly
Bach is playing with multiples of the number 3, the numeral symbolizing perfection. This numerical relationship continues into the next
movement, *Pleni sunt coeli et terra gloria ejus,* a lively fugue in 3/8 meter,
is connected to the *Sanctus* by way of a *segue.* The closing *Osanna in
excelsis,* treated as an entirely separate movement, maintains the triple
meter. Bach conceives of it as a kind of rustic celestial dance, and sets
it for a double chorus of 8-voice parts.

Benedictus qui venit in nominee Domini is an aria for tenor and
violin (sometimes flute) obbligato that combines the rapture of the solo
voice with the descending stepwise bass line of the *Sanctus,* placed here
and there in the background. This movement evokes an Elysian mood,
placed in 3/4 meter. The blissful contemplation of the *Benedictus,* with

its ornate solo vocal and instrumental lines, is rounded out by a repeat of the previous *Osanna*. In all, Bach retains the basic structure of the text, but expands upon each section, so much so, that connections are stretched well beyond liturgical proportions.

Sanctus in Classical Music

Wolfgang Amadeus Mozart: Sanctus and Benedictus from Requiem Mass (K. 626)[19]

Genre: Sacred concert music
Medium: Soloists (SATB) and mixed choir (SATB), orchestra
Style: Classical
First performance: Vienna, 1791
Duration: ca. 1:40 and ca. 5:40

Mozart's conception of the *Sanctus* is all dignity and splendor. Overwhelmed by its glory, he represents the Holy as a royal coronation. Themes are passed between voices, in the same way that cosmic praises would have issued forth from the heavenly host on high. Poised and confident, the angels of heaven are amassed and arrayed in brilliant

---

19. Considerable controversy surrounds authorship of Mozart's *Requiem*. Austrian composer Franz Xavier Süssmayr (1766–1803), credited with its completion, was a student and cantor in a Benedictine monastery from 1779 to 1787, who, in 1791, assisted Wolfgang Amadeus Mozart as copyist with *La Clemenza di Tito* and *Die Zauberflöte*. Mozart's wife, Constanze, gave him the score to complete, only after she had already asked several other composers, who declined. Süssmayr finished the vocal score all the way to the end of the Offertory, because Mozart, before his death, had discussed several movements and the orchestration with him. Süssmayr stated that he completed the Lacrimosa and composed Sanctus, Benedictus, and Agnus Dei. Many speculate that Constanze gave Süssmayr Mozart's drafts (now lost), which contained instructions or preliminary vocal ideas, not only for Agnus Dei, but, also, Sanctus and Benedictus. Abbé Maximilian Stadler (1748–1833), a family acquaintance, writing in 1826, describes in detail Süssmayr's methods: "He made his own [copy of the] score, very like Mozart's. In this, he copied first, note for note, everything that was in Mozart's original manuscript, next, he followed the given instructions for the orchestration meticulously..., [then] composed the Sanctus, Benedictus, and Agnus Dei himself. In such fashion the work was completed." See Christoph Wolff, translated by Mary Whittall, *Mozart's Requiem: Historical and Analytical Studies, Documents, Score* (Berkeley: University of California Press, 1994).

colors, for *heaven and earth are full of His glory*. From one corner of heaven to the other, angels exalt their Creator: *Thou art holy, O thou that are enthroned amidst the praises of Israel (Psalm 22:4)*.

Ex. 31. Mozart: *Sanctus from Requiem*
Reprint of Requiem published by Breitkopf & Hartel, n.d., by Dover Publications (1987).

The *Hosanna*, an exclamation of highest praise, is set as a fugue. Seen in this context, fugal form is neither a mechanical procedure nor an academic formula, but the technical solution to mankind's finite attempts to recreate in sound — the infinite, inaudible, eternal call of praise issuing forth daily from the Seraphim and Ofanim: *We will sanctify thy Name in the world even as they sanctify it in the highest heavens*. Fugue as a collective texture is a moral experience, an exercise in both animation and patience. No one can sing a fugue alone. Performers must wait in mental readiness for their respective turns to enter. Entries need to be coordinated. Each must enter on time, neither coming-in too soon, nor too late. Such conditions establish an interrelationship of courtesy and gracefulness, involvement and enthusiasm between participants. Shared values of dignity, individuality, cooperation, and mutual respect, transform the performance of earthly singers into an act of praise approaching divinity: *they receive sanction the one from the other, and say Holy in the highest heavens, the place of his divine abode.*[20]

The *Benedictus* of the second section is set for four solo voices. Four-voice texture in this context is not a formula to be accepted automatically. It is, again, a manifestation of something divine — a representation of the four guardian archangels, who accompany the heavenly throne in intimate communion with their Creator — Michael, Raphael, Uriel, and Gabriel. Here, Mozart projects through solo voices the symbolism of angels in heaven. Such a vision frequently adorns Baroque churches of the period — endowing them with an anthropomorphic glow.[21] An abbreviated return to *Hosanna in Excelsis* concludes the *Sanctus* and transforms a 'finite' two-part form, into a rounded, and, by metaphor, 'infinite', three-part structure.

Sanctus in Romantic Music

Giuseppi Verdi: Sanctus from Requiem (1874)
Genre: Sacred concert music
Medium: Soloists (SATB) and mixed double choir (SATB/SATB), orchestra
Style: Romantic
First performance: Milan, 1874
Duration: ca. 3 minutes

Verdi's conception of *Sanctus* differs, yet, again, from that of either Palestrina or Mozart. It is earthy, dramatic, and theatrical — a military call-up, introduced with a trumpet fanfare. Assemblies of heavenly hosts, along with men of flesh and blood, are summoned to do the

---

20. Targum Isaiah 6:3 (as translated in *Kedusha*), see Hertz, *Prayer Book*, 203.
21. Not only angels, but 'angelic-like' humans have participated in this experience. The textual source of the *Benedictus* reaches back to a Midrash, deriving from a legend surrounding the death of Moses that may have been familiar to the Apostles. "God said to Moses, '*Come, I shall teach thee my great Name, that the flames of the Shekinah (Holy Presence) consume thee not.*' When the Messiah (David's son) and Aaron beheld Moses approach them, they knew that God had taught him his great Name. So they went to meet him, and saluted him with the greeting: '*Blessed is he that cometh in the name of the Lord.*' Louis Ginzberg, *The Legends of the Jews*, Vol. 3, 446, and note 905, Vol. 6, 152.

Ex. 32. Verdi: *Sanctus from Requiem*
© Copyright 1895 G. Schirmer

work of their Creator. Themes are derived from Gregorian motifs, but they are no longer ethereal in character. Energized modality has been harmonized into strong major and minor hues. No attempt is made to differentiate sections thematically, but, rather, formal contrasts are marked by change of mode modulations — from F major to D minor. When *Pleni sunt caeli* reprises, scored for women's voices only, all is lightness, air, and space. It is clear we have entered the realm of the Seraphim.

Such musical imagery, conjures up images of furtive angels, glimpsed from the sides of frescos and medieval paintings, peering into the lives of human protagonists below. Verdi's idea of Holiness is a national one — the people together — marching, shouting, and jubilant.[22] All are geared-up in readiness to obey the orders of their Almighty commander.

Kedusha in the 19ᵗʰ century Synagogue

Louis Lewandowski: Kedusha (Sanctification)
Genre: Liturgical synagogue music
Medium: Cantor, mixed choir, and organ
Style: Romantic
First performance: Berlin Reform Synagogue
Duration: ca. 6:30

The Thrice Holy is linked in Jewish liturgy, not only to Isaiah, but also to the theosophical experience of the prophet Ezekiel, *Blessed be the Glory of the Lord from His place (Ezek. 3:12).*[23] In addition to biblical

---

22. In this respect, it resembles Jesus' triumphant entry into Jerusalem: *And they went before, and they that followed, cried, saying, Hosanna; Blessed is he that cometh in the name of the Lord: Blessed be the kingdom of our father David, that comes in the name of the Lord. Hosanna in the highest. And Jesus entered into Jerusalem, and into the Temple... (Mark 11:9–11).*

23. Three types of *Kedusha* are found in synagogue liturgy (i.e. *Yotzer, week-day standing prayer, and Musaph*). The earliest version was incorporated into the opening *Yotzer* (Creator of light or seated prayer), recited before the *Shema Yisrael*. Here, the Thrice-Holy is introduced by a phrase which had a great influence on all subsequent musical settings: *Opening their mouth with jubilant song of purity and holiness, they all bless and praise the infinite sovereign holiness of God, the Ruler omnipotent, awe-inspiring and holy. Mutually accepting for themselves His heavenly rule, in unison they all give one another*

citations — introductions, interludes, and a psalm verse (Ps. 146:10) are added — to make up the week-day *Kedusha* in the synagogue.[24]

A German-Hebrew bilingual *Kedusha* was set by Louis Lewandowski (1821–1894), composer, choir master, and music director of the Jewish Community of Berlin (recognized as one of the most important com-

Ex. 33. Lewandowski: *Kedushah from Todah W'Simrah Collection*
Reprint of original edition by Hebrew Union School of Sacred Music, Sacred Music Press (1954)

---

the word to hallow their Creator in serene, pure utterance of sacred harmony, in awed chorus all reverently proclaiming: Holy, holy, holy, is the Lord of hosts, the fullness of all the earth is His glory. From the daily Morning Prayer, as cited in *Book of Prayers*, edited and translated by David De Sola Pool (New York: Union of Sephardic Congregations, 2001) 53.

24. *Kedusha* from the week day *Amidah* (standing prayer) — **Reader**: *We will sanctify thy Name in the world even as they sanctify it in the highest heavens, as it is written by the hand of thy prophet: And they called one unto the other and said,* **Congregation**: *Holy, Holy, Holy is the Lord of hosts: The whole earth is Full of His glory.* **Reader**: *Those over against them say, Blessed.* **Congregation**: *Blessed be the Glory of the Lord from His place.* **Reader**: *And in the Holy Words it is written, saying,* **Congregation**: *The Lord shall reign for ever and ever, thy God, O Zion, unto all generations. Hallelujah.* Hertz, *Prayer Book*, 135–137.

posers of synagogue music in the 19th century), and was sung at the Berlin Reform Synagogue on the evening of *Rosh Hashanah* towards the end of *Yom Kippur* and at annual confirmation services until the Holocaust.[25]

Lewandowski's liturgical *Kedusha* strives to infuse liturgical stricture with artistic stature. Solo cantorial recitatives employ traditional Western syllabic recitations, while choral passages derive from Mendelssohn's sacred choral style, in a heartfelt interplay between cantor, congregation, and organ.

KEDUSHA

Choir

> From every tongue the song is upraised to the
> Lord of Creation from the ancient of days.

Solo-Choir

> The celestial choirs do tell of His worth,
> Their voices resounding in heaven and earth:

Choir

> *Kadosh, Kadosh, Kadosh Adonai Tseva'ot,*
> *M'lo khol haarets k'vodo* (Isa. 6:3).
>
> (Holy, Holy, Holy is the Lord of Hosts!
> The whole earth is full of His glory.)

Solo-Choir

> No tongue of mere mortal can measure His worth,
> And Israel whom He sent as priests,
> Has carried His light, through peoples and lands.
> Wherever it dwelt, in every place,
> Resounded the word of joy and of praise:

Choir

> *Baruch k'vod Adonai mi-mekomo* (Ezek. 3:12).
>
> (Blessed be the glory of God from His place.)

---

25. His work is still widely used today.

Solo

> Whether the morning arises or the night descends,
> We turn upward to the Guardian, who is ever watchful,
> Who sends the power of belief to His elected people,
> The word of His holiness is eternally true.

Choir

> *Sh'ma Yisrael, Adonai Elohenu Adonai echad* (Deut. 6:4).
>
> (Hear, O Israel, the Lord our God, the Lord is one.)

Solo-Choir

> He was our Rock in darkest of days,
> He gave us strength to endure and forbear,

Solo

> He will sustain us for all our days,
> Forever and ever remains His holy praise.

Choir

> *Yimloch Adonai l'olam Elohayich Tsion l'dor va-dor.*
>
> (The Lord will reign forever, your God, O Zion unto all generations.)
> Hallelujah! (Ps. 146:10)[26]

This Great Sanctification, similar to the Additional (*Musaph*) Service for Sabbaths, New Moons, Festivals, and High Holy Days, contains a variation on the *Kedusha* core. Its text was adapted and translated for the liturgy of German Reform Judaism,[27] taking its lead from the

---

26. From the booklet accompanying a 2-CD release of pre-Holocaust recordings made between 1928 and 1930 by the Berlin Jewish Reform Community. See *The Musical Tradition of the Jewish Reform Congregation in Berlin*, with commentary by Rabbi John Levi, Melbourne, edited by Avner Bahat (Tel Aviv: Beth Hatefutsoth, 1998) 38.

27. "The German Sanctus" [*Jesaja dem Propheten geschach*] was written for Luther's German Mass, 1526. The following translation is taken from *The Hymns of Martin Luther* [Deutsche Geistliche Lieder]: set to their original melodies, with an English version edited by Leonard Woolsey Bacon (New York: Charles Scribner's Sons, 1883) 50–1. *These things the seer Isaiah did befall: In spirit he beheld the Lord of all. On a high throne, raised up in splendor*

Protestant Reformation, specifically, Martin Luther's *German Sanctus*, a poetic paraphrase of Isaiah's vision (6:1–4), that added a distinctly human element to the original. In this version, German interpolations to the *Musaph* (additional prayer), interpret the original like a modern Targum, translating the *Kedusha* into the vernacular and taking on the spirit of the Reformation — rephrasing the message of Isaiah's Revelation in the rhythm and cadence of the Lutheran chorale.[28] Its unorthodox musical innovations, borrowed also from the Reformed Church, feature a mixed choir of men and women singing together, and pipe organ.[29]

Conclusion

Isaiah is the prophet most often set to music. Perhaps, it is because, though Isaiah moved in the most privileged circles of his time, his heart reached beyond the values of wealth, intellect, and status, to a society in which God was not an idea, but a living presence. He perceived in the penetration of righteousness and justice to one's fellow man a formula for national salvation — more powerful than warlike preparations and military measures. His words of comfort and faith were later embraced by Christianity in foretelling the coming of the Messiah, and frequently are set to music in conjunction with texts from the Gospels.

---

bright, His garment's border filled the choir with light. Beside him stood two seraphim which had six wings, wherewith they both alike were clad; With twain they hid their shining, with twain they hid their feet as with a flowing train, And with the other twain they both did fly. One to the other thus aloud did cry: "Holy is God, the Lord of Sabaoth! Holy is God, the Lord of Sabaoth! Holy is God, the Lord of Sabaoth! His glory filleth all the trembling earth!" With the loud cry the posts and thresholds shook, And the whole house was filled with mist and smoke.

28. The German-Jewish reformers, by supplementing Isaiah's vision with the empirical experience of Jewish history, sought to adapt Protestant ethos to Jewish tradition. **Chor:** *Aus jeglichem Munde erschallert der Ruf / Zum Lobe des Ew'gen, der alles erschuf.* **Solo, Chor:** *Es jauchzen und jubeln die Welten in Chor, / So tont von der Erde zum Himmel empor.* **Chor:** *Heilig, Heilig, Heilig ist der Herr Zebaoth*, etc.

29. A mixed choir is forbidden in Orthodox synagogues, in the same way that monastic choirs admit only monks. The organ was considered an exclusively Christian instrument, reserved for the church, and therefore off-bounds in the synagogue.

Many composers from the 14ᵗʰ century onwards have dealt with the "Triple Sanctus" or the inspiring figure of the prophet himself, whose immortal reward for such visions of faithfulness was a glimpse into eternity and a martyr's death.[30]

Other Directions

Certain conventions in the setting of the *Sanctus* can be identified. In some works, the initial *Sanctus* is rather florid and its reiterations are expressed in progressively rising phrases. The angelic acclamation is interpreted either as an outpouring of sweet sounds (as in most 16ᵗʰ-century works), or as a mighty thundering of massed praise (as in Bach's *Mass in B Minor*). The *Sanctus* in Beethoven's *Missa Solemnis* (1823) is an exception since it begins with a whispered, stammering of awe. There are two settings by Bach of simple chorale tunes with the Latin or German (*Heilig, Heilig, Heilig*) text.

The first part of Handel's oratorio *The Messiah* contains so many passages from Isaiah that it might also almost be considered an Isaiah oratorio.[31] *Messiah* presents a Christian interpretation of Isaiah's prophecy,

---

30. When an idol was set up in the Temple by Manasseh (698 B.C.), Isaiah addressed the people predicting the destruction of the Temple and Israel's captivity under Nebuchadnezzar. Enraged, Manasseh had him seized and sawed in sunder with a wood-saw, while all the false prophets stood up and jeered. Isaiah, however, neither cried aloud nor wept, but conversed with the Holy Spirit. See Talmud Sanhedrin 103b and Louis Ginzberg, *The Legends of the Jews*, Vol. 6, note 98, 371, and note 103, 374.

31. In Christian typology these texts are considered prefiguring Christ and Christian redemption. As Christianity became a religion of Greeks and Romans, tensions grew between those raised in Gentile surroundings and those of Jewish background and culture. Paul was the first to attempt to harmonize the demands of the 'letter' of Mosaic Commandments with the 'spiritual' teachings of Jesus by means of an interpretive construct, which Christian theology terms — typology — a speculative allegorical re-reading of events of the Old Testament, construed to pre-figure events in the New Testament (see Paul: *First Letter to the Corinthians*). It is the obverse of chronological thinking, designed to create continuity between the Old Testament and the Gospels (New Testament). Christian theology, by revising and reinterpreting biblical history to conform to a new religion, appropriated the idea of a Chosen people and propagandized that God's relationship with the new Covenant of the Christian Church had replaced His original promises made to Abraham, Isaac, Jacob, Moses, and the children of Israel. Thus: the Sacrifice

viewing it as foretelling the coming of the Messiah (the Anointed one), Jesus the Christ in recitative, aria and chorus — *Comfort Ye (Isa. 40:1-3)*, *Every Valley (Isa. 40:4), And the Glory of the Lord (Isa. 40:5)*. Of the three parts of the oratorio, the first part is most often performed and heard at Advent, taking place before Christmas. It covers prophecies of the miracles surrounding the birth of Jesus: *Behold A Virgin Shall Conceive (Isa. 7:14)*; *O thou that tellest good tidings to Zion (Isa. 40:9)*; *For behold, darkness shall cover the earth (Isa. 60:2, 3)*; *The people that walked in darkness (Isa. 9:2)*; *He shall feed his flock like a shepherd (Isa. 40:11)*. The second part focuses on the Passion. It combines Isaiah citations with Psalm and New Testament texts: *He was despised (Isa. 53:3)*; *Surely He hath borne our griefs (Isa. 53:4, 5)*; *And with His stripes we are healed (Isa. 53:5b)*; *All we like sheep have gone astray (Isa. 53:6)*; *He was cut off out of the land of the living (Isa. 53:8b)*. The third part pertains to the Resurrection, Ascension, and the End of Days and consists almost entirely of New Testament texts.

Many other works for concert performance, based on extended passages from the Book of Isaiah, include Antonio Caldara's oratorio *Le profezie evangeliche d'Isaia* (1729; text by A. Zeno); Granville Bantock's *Seven Burdens of Isaiah* for men's choir (1927); Willy Burkhard's oratorio *Das Gesicht Jesaias* (1933-36); Alexandre Tansman's oratorio *Isaïe le prophete* (1951); Bernard Rogers' cantata *The Prophet Isaiah* (1954; published 1961); Robert Starer's *Ariel; Visions of Isaiah* (1959); Bohuslav Martinu's cantata *The Prophecy of Isaiah* (1963); and Ben Zion Orgad's *Isaiah's Vision;* and Jacob Weinberg's *Isaiah* (1947), an oratorio for solo voices and chorus with organ accompaniment and trumpet obbligato. Some of the most striking parts of Brahms' *Deutsches Requiem* (1857-68), also originate in this biblical book. There are also traditional tunes from various Jewish communities, Hasidic melodies, and modern Israeli folksongs such as Naomi Shemer's *Atzur Lemut Beemtza HaTammuz* (Isa. 16:9). Settings of single verses or brief passages for liturgical or concert use are numerous.

---

of Isaac foreshadows the crucifixion; the four prophets: Isaiah, Jeremiah, Ezekiel, and Daniel prefigure the four Evangelists: Matthew, Mark, Luke, and John; the twelve tribes of Israel foreshadow the Twelve Apostles, and so on.

Works List

Abravanel, Claude (1924 Montreux/1951 Jerusalem). *Shim'u amim elay* (Isa. 49:12, 65:19), soprano, tenor and pianoforte.

Adler, Samuel (b.1928 Germany/1939 USA). *God is My Salvation* (Isa. 12:1, 2, 3–6), TTBB, organ.

Alexander, Haim (1915 Berlin/1936 Jerusalem). *Le-ma'an Tsiyon lo ehesheh* (Isa. 62:1), choir.

Alman, Shmuel (1887 Ukraine–1947 London). *Va-tomar Tsiyo* (Isa. 49:14–18), 2 voices, choir.

_____. *Simchu et Jerusalem* (Isa. 61), 2 voices, choir.

Amiran, Emanuel (1909 Warsaw–1993 Israel). *Comfort Ye My People* (1940) (Isa. 40), cantata for choir and orchestra.

_____. *Ir oz lanu* (Isa. 26:1–2), voice, choir.

Amner, John (1579–1641 England). *Sing O Heavens* (Isa. 49:13–15), SSAATBB, keyboard.

Antes, John (1740–1811 Colonial America). *How Beautiful Upon the Mountains* (Isa. 52:7), SATB, orchestra.

_____. *Surely He Hath Borne Our Griefs* (Isa. 53:4–5), SATB.

_____. *I Will Mention the Lovingkindness* (Isa. 63:7), SA, keyboard.

Aufdemberge, Edgar (20th C. USA). *Behold a Branch is Growing* (Isa. 11:1–2), SAB

Babcock, Samuel (c.1760–1813 Boston). *Comfort Ye My People* (Isa. 40:1–4a, 5a), SATB.

Bach, C. P. E. (1714–1788 Germany). *Holy is God* (Isa. 6:3), SATB, organ

Bach, Johann Sebastian (1685–1750 Leipzig). Cantata 18: *Gleich wie der Regen* (Isa. 55:10–11), soprano, tenor, bass, 4 voices, choir, viola, violoncello, bassoon, basso continuo, 2 narrators.

_____. Cantata 39: *Brich dem Hungrigen dein Brot* (Isa. 58:7–8), soprano, tenor, bass, 4 voices, choir, 2 recorders, 2 oboes, strings, basso continuo.

_____. Cantata 65: *Sie warden aus Saba alle kommen* (Isa. 60:6), tenor, bass, 4 voices, choir, 2 horns, 2 recorders, 2 oboes, strings, basso-continuo.

_____. *Fuerchte dich nicht* (Isa. 41:10; 43:1), motet, 8 voices, choir.

Baeck, Sven-Erik (1919–1994 Stockholm). *Jesajas 9* (Isa. 9:2–6), chorus, orchestra.

Bantock, Glanville (1868–1946 London). *Seven Burdens of Isaiah*, mezzo soprano, choir.

Battishill, Jonathan (1738–1801 England). *O Lord, Look Down From Heaven* (Isa. 63:15), SATB, organ.

Beck, John Ness (b.1930 USA). *Every Valley* (Isa. 40:4–5), SATB, keyboard.

_____. *As he Rain* (Isa. 55:8, 10–11), SATB, keyboard.

_____. *Cry Aloud* (Isa. 58:1, 8, 60:18, 20), SATB (from Three Prophecies of Isaiah).

Beebe, Hank (20th C. USA). *Whose Minds are Stayed* (Isa. 26:3, 30:15), SATB organ.

_____. *The Lord Hath Done It* (Isa. 44:22–24), SATB, keyboard.

_____. *Isaiah's Song* (Isa. 53:3–10), 2-part, keyboard.

_____. *The Mountains Shall Depart* (Isa. 54:6–7, 10), soprano, SATB, keyboard.

_____. *Go Out With Joy* (Isa. 55:12–13), SATB or unison, keyboard.

Ben-Haim, Paul (1897 Munich–1981 Tel Aviv). *Sing, O Barren* (Roni akarah) (1957) (Isa. 54), motet choir.

_____. *Thou Shalt No More* (1957), mixed choir.

Ben-Yohanan, Asher (b.1929). *Ode to Jerusalem* (1954) (Isa., Ps.), choir.

Berger, Jean (1909 Germany–2002 USA). *And It Shall Come to Pass* (Isa. 2:2–5), choir.

_____. *Whom Shall I Send?* (Isa. 6:8).

_____. *Behold! God is My Salvation* (Isa. 12:2, 5).

_____. *All Flesh is Grass* (Isa. 40:6–8).

_____. *They That Wait Upon the Lord* (Isa. 40:31).

_____. *Quam Pulchri super Montes* (Isa. 52:7).

_____. *Arise Shine* (Isa. 60:1–2), SATB.

Bergman, Erik (1911–2006 Finland). *Jesurun* (Isa. 44:4), baritone and men's choir.

Bertouch, Georg von (1668 Germany–1743 Norway). *Du Tochter Zion freue dich* (Isa. 37), cantata for baritone, strings and basso continuo.

Bitgood, Roberta (1908–2007 USA). *They Shall Walk* (Isa. 40:28–31), SATB, keyboard.

Bliem, William (20th C. USA). *All Flesh is Grass* (Isa. 40:6–8), SATB, keyboard

Bodine, Willis (20th C. USA). *Break Forth, O Beauteous Heavenly Light* (Isa. 9:2–7), SATB, organ

Brahms, Johannes (1833 Hamburg–1897 Vienna). *Die Erloesten des*

Herrn (Isa. 35:10) (2nd movement, *German Requiem*), chorus, orchestra.

Braun, Yehezkel (b.1922 Germany/1924 Israel). *And It Shall Come to Pass* (2000), baritone, choir, orchestra.

_____. *Super montem excelsum* (1987), motet for soprano, SAB, oboe.

Bortniansky, Dimitri (1751–1825 Russia). *Comfort, All My People* (Isa. 40), SSATB.

Brandon, George (1873–1911 UK). *True Fasting* (Isa. 58:5–8) (Spiritual) 2-part, keyboard.

Brant, Henry (1913–2008 USA). *Credo for Peace* (Isa. 2:2–4), SATB, speaker, trumpet.

Bradbury, William (1816–1868 USA). *How Beautiful Upon the Mountains* (Isa. 52:7), SATB, keyboard.

Bright, Huston (1916–1970 Texas, USA). *The Vision of Isaiah*, orchestra.

Bruckner, Anton (1824–1896 Austria). *Locus iste* (Isa. 40:1), SATB.

Buck, Dudley (1839–1909 USA). *Thou Wilt Keep Him in Perfect Peace* (Isa. 26:3), SATB, keyboard.

Butler, Eugene (b.1930 USA). *How Beautiful Upon the Mountains* (Isa. 52:7), SATB, keyboard.

_____. *Seek Ye the Lord* (Isa. 55:6–7), SATB.

_____. *I Will Greatly Rejoice* (Isa. 61:10–11), SATB, keyboard.

Buxtehude, Dietrich (1637 Sweden–1707 Germany). *Fuerwahr, er trug unsere Krankheit* (Isa. 53: 4–5), choir, strings, basso continuo.

Byrd, William (1543–1623 England). *Surge Illuminare* (Isa. 60:1, 4), voice, choir.

_____. *Ecce Virgo Concipiet* (Isa. 7:14), 5 voices and choir.

_____. *Rorate Caeli Desuper* (Isa. 45:8), SAATB.

_____. *Surge Illiminare* (Isa. 60:1), SATB.

_____. *Ne Irascaris* (Isa. 64:9), SATTB, organ.

Caldara, Antonio (1670 Venice–1736 Vienna). *Le profezie d'Isaia* (A. Zeno), oratorio.

Carter, John (b.1930 USA). *How Beautiful Upon the Mountains* (Isa. 52:7), SA, keyboard.

Casella, Alfredo (1883–1947 Rome). *Ecce Deus, Salvatore meus* (Isa. 12:2–6), choir.

Clayton(Lloyd), Harold (1893–1971 UK). *They Shall Rise as Eagles* (Isa. 40:28–30), SATB.

Clokey, Joseph (1890 Indiana–1960 California). *A Canticle of Peace*, unison, keyboard.

Colaco Osorio-Schwaab, Reine (1801–1871 Amsterdam). *Jesaja 40*, narrator, pianoforte.

_____. *Jesaja 60*, narrator, pianoforte.

Davis, Katherine K. (1892–1980 USA). *Comfort Ye* (Isa. 40:1), SATB, keyboard.

Dering, Richard (c.1580–1630 England). *Duo Seraphim* (Isa. 6:2–3), SS, organ

Devidal, David (20th C. USA). *Surely He Hath Borne Our Griefs* (Isa. 53:4–6), 2-part, keyboard

Diemer, Emma Lou (b.1927 USA). *Sing, O Heavens* (Isa. 49), SATB

Distler, Hugo (1908–1942 Germany). *Lo! How a Rose E'er Blooming* (Isa. 11:1), SATB (Chorale Motet from the Christmas Story)

Dubois, Leon J. (1859–1935 Belgium). *Behold, God is My Salvation* (Isa. 12:2, 4), SATB

Effinger, Cecil (1914–1990 USA). *By the Springs of Water* (Isa. 49:10), SATB, organ.

Ehrlich, Abel (1915 Germany–2003 Israel). *The Writing of Hezekiah* (1962) for soprano, oboe, bassoon, violin.

Elgar, Edward (1857–1934 UK). *The Spirit of the Lord is upon Me* (Isa. 61:1–4, 11), SATB, keyboard.

Elvey, George J. (1816–1893 UK). *Arise, Shine for thy Light is Come* (Isa. 60:1–3), SATB, organ.

Faure, Gabriel (1845–1924 France). *Comfort All Ye My People* (Isa. 40:1, 55:1, 6–7), SATB, keyboard.

Foss, Lucas (1922 Berlin/USA). *Song of Anguish*, soloist, choir, orchestra, cantata.

Franck, Melchior (1579–1639 Germany). *Paradisus Musicus*, motets, 2–4 voices and organ.

Fritschel, James (20th C. USA). *A Great Light* (Isa. 9:2), SATB.

Galinne, Rachel (b.1949 Sweden/1975 Israel). *And We Shall Sing My Song of Praises* (1994), for 16-part mixed choir a cappella.

Gardner, John (b.1917 UK). *We Have a Strong City* (Isa. 26:1–4, 7–8), SATB.

Goudimel, Claude (1510–1572 France). *Comfort, Comfort Ye My People* (Isa. 40).

Graun, Karl H. (1704–1759 Germany). *Surely He Hath Borne Our Griefs* (Isa. 53:4), SATB.

_____. He was Despised (Isa. 55:3), SAB.

Green, Maurice (1696–1755 England). *Arise, Shine O Zion* (Isa. 60:1–3, 61:10), SATB, organ.

_____. *The Sun Shall Be No More Thy Light* (Isa. 60:19), unison, keyboard.

Guerrero, Francisco (1528–1599 Spain). *Rorate Caeli* (Isa. 45:8), SATB.

Hall, Henry (1656–1707 England). *Comfort Ye My People* (Isa. 40:1–9), alto, 2 tenors, SSATTB, organ.

Hammerschmidt, Andreas (1611–1675 Germany). *Holy is the Lord* (Isa. 6:3), SSATB, 2 violns, basso continuo.

_____. *Zion's Lament* (Isa. 49:14–16), SSATB.

Hemsi, Alberto (1898 Rhodes–1964 Paris). *Ve-hayah be-aharit ha-yamim* (Isa. 2:24), voice and pianoforte.

_____. *V'dibarti al hanevyim* (Isa. 51:16; 2:5), voice and pianoforte.

Handel, G. F. (1685 Germany–1759 England). *For unto Us a Child is Born* (Isa. 9:6).

_____. *And the Glory of the Lord* (Isa. 11:5).

_____. *O Thou That Tellest* (Isa. 40:9).

_____. *How Beautiful are the Feet of Him* (Isa. 52:7).

_____. *Surely He Hath Borne Our Griefs* (Isa. 53:4).

_____. *All We like Sheep* (Isa. 53:6), SATB, orchestra (from Messiah).

Handl, Jacob, *Duo Seraphim* (Isa. 6:3), SATB/SATB, organ.

_____. *Ecce Quomodo Moritur Justus* (Isa. 57:1–2), SATB.

_____. *Omnes de Saba Venient* (Isa. 60:6), SATTB, organ.

Hemsi, Alberto (1898 Rhodos–1964 Paris). *V'dibarti al Hanevyim* (Hos. 11:2, Amos 3:7–8; Isa. 51:16, 2:5), voice, piano.

Herbst, Johannes (1588–1666 Germany). *Der Herr ist unser Koenig* (Isa. 33:22), SATB, keyboard.

Hillert, Richard (20th C. USA). *Surely He Hath Borne Our Griefs* (Isa. 53:4–5), SATB.

Hilty, Everett Jay (1910–2006 USA). *Come Let Us Walk in the Light of the Lord* (Isa. 2:2–5), SATB.

Hopson, Hal (b.1933 USA). *For as the Rain and the Snow Come Down* (Isa. 55:10–11), SATB.

Hughes, John (b.1956 UK). *Isaiah's Vision* (Isa. 6:1–4), SATB, keyboard.

Humphrey, Pelham (1647–1674 England). *Hear, O Heavens* (Isa. 1:2, 4 11 17–18), SATB, organ.

Isaac, Heinrich (c.1450–1517 Flanders). *Ecce Virgo Concipiet* (Isa. 7:14), SATB.

Jacob, Gordon (1895–1984 UK). *O Lord I will Praise Thee* (Isa. 12), SATB, organ.

Jaeschke, Christian David (18th C. Colonial America). *The Redeemed of the Lord* (Isa. 53:10), SATB, organ.

Jennings, Arthur (20th C. USA). *Springs in the Desert* (Isa. 35:1, 4, 8, 10), tenor, SATB, and organ.

Joffe, Shlomo (1909 Warsaw–1995 Israel). *Ivru ba-she'arim* (Isa. 62:10), choir.

Joubert, John (b.1927 South Africa/UK). *Let Me Rejoice* (Isa. 61: 10–11), SATB, organ.

Knuepfer, Sebastian (1633–1676 Leipzig). *Ich will der Guete des Herrn gedenchen* (Isa. 63:7), choir.

Kohn, Karl (b.1926 USA). *Also the Sons* (Isa. 56:6–7), soprano, alto, tenor, bass, SATB, 4-hands keyboard.

Krapf, Gerhard (1924–2008 Canada). *O Lord I Will Praise Thee* (Isa. 12), unison, organ.

Krenek, Ernst (1900 Austria–1991 USA). *The Deliverance of Hezekiah* (Isa. 38:1–6), SSA, piano.

Krieger, J. P. (1651–1735 Germany). *For Unto Us a Child is Born* (Isa. 9:6–7), soprano, alto, bass, SAB, 2 violins, basso continuo.

_____. *The Righteous Shall Be Swept Away From Misfortune* (Isa. 57:1–2), SATB Strings.

Kuhnau, Johann (1660–1722 Germany). *For Unto Us a Child is Born* (Isa. 9:6), SSATB, organ.

Laderman, Ezra (b.1924 USA). *Symphony No. 5 'Isaiah'* (1982).

Lisenko, Mikola (1842–1912 Kiev). *Raduisya nivo nepolitaya* (Isa. 35) (T. Shevchenko, translator), soloist and choir, cantata.

Lasso, Orlando di (1532–1594 Flanders). *Confortamini* (Isa. 35:4), SATB

Lekberg, Sven (1899–1984 USA). *There is No God Beside Me* (Isa. 45:5–8), SATB, keyboard.

_____. *For as the Rain Cometh Down* (Isa. 55:10–13), SATB.

Leo, Leonardo (1694–1744 Naples). *Surely He Hath Borne Our Griefs* (Isa. 53:4–5), SA, keyboard.

Lewis, John Leo (1911–1971 USA). *Hast Thou Not Known?* (Isa. 40:28–31), SATB, keyboard.

Lora (John) Antonio (1899–1965 USA). *The Lord Shall Bless His People With Peace* (Isa. 52:7), SATB, piano.

Lotti, Antonio (1667–1740 Italy). *Surely He Hath Borne Our Griefs* (Isa. 53:4), SATB.

Ludlow, Ben (20th C. USA). *Cry Out and Shout!* (Isa. 12:6), speech choir, snare drum.

Lukacic, Ivan (1587–1644 Split, Croatia). *Gaudens gaudebo* (Isa. 61:10), motet, 2 voices, basso continuo.

Mancinelli, Luigi (1848–1921 Rome). *Isaias,* oratorio.

Mathews, Peter (b.1944 Canada). *Remember These Things* (Isa. 44:21–23), SATB, organ.

Mathias, William (1934–1992 UK). *Arise, Shine, For Your Light Has Come* (Isa. 60), SATB, organ.

Martin, George (20th C. UK). *Ho! Everyone That Thirsteth* (Isa. 55:1–3, 7, 12–13), bass, SATB, organ.

Martinu, Bohuslav (1890–1959 Basel). *The prophecy of Isaiah* (Isa. 24), soprano, baritone, choir, trombone, viola, timpani and pianoforte.

Mechem, Kirke (b.1925 Kansas). *A Song of Comfort* (Isa. 48:10, 66:13) (from Songs of Wisdom), SATB.

Moe, Daniel (b.1926 USA). *How Beautiful Upon the Mountains* (Isa. 52:7–8), SAB.

Morales, Cristobal (b.1500 Spain). *Ecce Virgo Concipiet* (Isa. 7:14, 9:6–7), SATB.

Moyer, J. Harold (b.1927 USA). *I Saw the Lord* (Isa. 6:1–8), SATB, organ, percussion.

Mueller, Carl F. (1892–1982 USA). *Confidence in God* (Isa. 26:1–4), SATB, organ.

Nakaseko, Kazu (1908 Kyoto–1973). *Verses from Isaiah,* soprano and cello.

Nardi, Nahum (1901 Kiev–1977 Tel-Aviv). *Ki mi-Tsiyon teze Torah* (Isa. 2:3), 2 voices and choir.

_____. *Ve-galti bi-Yerushalayim ve-sasti be-ami* (Isa. 65:19–21), 2 voices and choir.

_____. *Simhu et Yerushalayim* (Isa. 66:10), 2 voices and choir.

Natra, Sergiu (1924 Bucharest/Israel). *Dedication* (1972), two poems for mezzo soprano and orchestra.

_____. *An Ensign to the People* (1984) (Isa. 11:12), baritone, choir, orchestra, cantata.

Naylor, E. W. (1867–1934 UK). *Vox Dicentis Clama* (Isa. 40:6–11), SATB.

Neff, James (20th C. USA). *In an Acceptable Time* (Isa. 49:8–10), SATB.

Nelson, Ronald A. (1927 Illinois). *Seek Ye the Lord* (Isa. 55:6–7), SS, organ.

_____. *For Your Light Has Come* (Isa. 60:1–3), SATB, 2 trumpets and cymbal.

Newberry, Kent A. (20th C. USA). *Behold Your God Will Come* (Isa. 35:4), SATB.

_____. *Sing to the Lord a New Song* (Isa. 42:10–12), SATB.

_____. *Surely He Hath Borne Our Griefs* (Isa. 53:4–5), SATB.

_____ *For You Shall Go Out in Joy* (Isa. 55:12), SATB, piano.

Nystedt, Knut (b.1915 Norway). *Get You Up* (Isa. 10:9–11, 28–31), SATB.

_____. *Cry Out and Shout* (Isa. 12), TTBB.

_____. *Listen to Me* (Isa. 41:13, 17–20, 42:10–12), SATB.

_____. *Thus Saith the Lord* (Isa. 44:2) (from Three Motets).

_____. *Seek Ye the Lord* (Isa. 55:6–12), SSAA.

_____. *I Will Greatly Rejoice* (Isa. 61:10–11), SATB.

Oakeley, Herbert (1830 London–1903). *Who is this that cometh from Edom?* (Isa. 61:1, 63:1), anthem.

Orgad, Ben-Zion (1926 Germany–2006 Tel-Aviv). *Isaiah's Vision*, choir and orchestra.

Pelz, Walter (20th C. USA). *Day of Rejoicing* (Isa. 25: 8–9), SATB, trumpets, organ.

_____. *Arise, O God and Shine* (Isa. 60:3), SATB, organ.

Pinkham, Daniel (1923–2006 USA). *The Call of Isaiah* (Isa. 6:1–9), any voicing, organ, tape, percussion.

Pluister, Simon (1913–1995 Netherlands). *Jesaja* (Isa. 9:1–6), men's choir and wind instruments.

Pote, Allen (b.1945 USA). *Prepare Ye the Way* (Isa. 40:3–5), SATB or 2-part, piano.

Powell, Robert J. (b.1932 USA). *Prepare Ye the Way of the Lord* (Isa. 40:3), SAB.

_____. *Awake, Put On Strength* (Isa. 52:1), SAB.

_____. *All They From Saba Shall Come* (Isa. 60:1, 6b), SATB/SATB.

Proulix, Richard (b.1937 USA). *Song of Isaiah* (Isa. 12:2–6), 2-parts, 2 handbells, percussion.

Purcell, Henry (1659–1695 London). *Awake and with attention hear* (Isa. 34), bass, basso continuo.

_____. *O Lord, Thou art my God* (Isa. 25:1, 4, 7–9), choir, basso continuo.

_____. *Awake, put on thy strength* (Isa. 51:9–11), 2 voices, instruments, basso continuo.

_____. *Who hath believed our report?* (Isa. 53:1–8), choir, soloist, basso continuo.

Redman, Reinald (1892–1972 UK). *Thou Wilt Keep Him in Perfect Peace* (Isa. 26:3–4), SATB.

Roberts, J. Varley (1841–920 Oxford, England). *Seek Ye the Lord* (Isa. 55:6–7), SATB, tenor, organ.

Roff, Joseph (1911–1993 UK). *And a Little Child Shall Lead Them* (Isa. 11:5–6).

_____. *O Lord Thou Art My God* (Isa. 25:1, 4), SATB, keyboard.

_____. *Sing for Joy O Heavens* (Isa. 49:13–15), SATB, keyboard.

_____. *He Opened Not His Mouth* (Isa. 53:6–7), SATB, organ.

Sateren, Leland (1913 Norway–2007 USA). *The Abiding Presence* (Isa. 54:10), SATB.

_____. *You Shall Go Out in Joy* (Isa. 55:1–3, 11, 12, 58:11), SATB.

_____. *None Call Upon Thy Name* (Isa. 64:6–7), SATB.

Scheldt, Samuel (1587–1654 Germany). *Duo Seraphim Clamabant* (Isa. 6:2–3), SSATT/ATBB.

Schein, Johann (1586–1630 Germany). *Zion Speaks, I am by God Forsaken* (Isa. 49:4–16), SSATB.

Sweelinck, J. P. (1562–1621 Netherlands). *Ecce Virgo Concipiet* (Isa. 7:14), SSATB.

Sessions, Roger (1896–1985 USA). *Ah, Sinful Nation* (Isa. 2), SATB, piano (from Three Choruses on Biblical Texts).

Schutz, Heinrich (1585–1672 Germany). *To Us a Child is Given* (Isa. 9:6–7), SSATTB.

_____. *Trostet, Trostet mein Volk* (Isa. 40:1, 5), SSATTB, organ.

Sowerby, Leo (1895–1968). Behold, God is My Salvation (Isa. 12:2, 5–6), SA, organ.

_____. *All They From Saba Shall Come* (Isa. 60:6), tenor, SATB, organ.

Staden, Johann (1581–1634 Germany). *Die Gerechten warden Weggekrafft* (Isa. 57:1–2), SATB.

Stainer, John (1840–1901 UK). *I Saw the Lord* (Isa. 6:1–4), SATB/SATB, organ.

_____. *O Zion That Bringest Good Tidings* (Isa. 40:9), SATB, organ.

_____. *How Beautiful Upon the Mountains* (Isa. 52:7), SATB, organ.

Stern, Max (b.1947 USA/1976 Israel). *Arise Shine!* (Isa. 60:1), symphonic poem.

Stevens, Halsey (1909–1989 USA). *The Way of Jehovah* (Isa. 40:3–5), SATB, keyboard.

Tanner, J. Pater (b.1936 UK). *Sing for Joy* (Isa. 49:13), SATB, organ.

Templeton, Alec (1909 UK–1987 USA). *Hast Thou Not Known?* (Isa. 40:28–31), SATB, piano.

Thalben-Ball, George (1896–1987 UK). *Comfort Ye My People* (Isa. 40:1–3, 35:1–2, 51:3), Longfellow, bass, SATB, organ.

Thompson, Randall (1899–1984 USA). *Say Ye to the Righteous* (Isa. 3:10–11, 64:14), SATB.

_____. *Have Ye Now Known* (Isa. 50:21), SATB.

_____. *The Paper Reeds by the Brooks* (Isa. 19:7), SATB.

_____. *Ye Shall Have a Song* (Isa. 30:29), SSAATTBB (Peaceable Kingdom).

Titcomb, Everett (1885–1968 USA). *Say to Them That are of a Fearful heart* (Isa. 35:4), SATB.

_____.*Herald of Good Tidings* (Isa. 40:9–11, 28–29), SATB, 2 trumpets, organ.

Tye, Christopher (1500–1572 England). *How Glorious Sion's Court* (Isa. 26:1–3), SATB.

Van Vleck, Jacob (1751–1831 Early America). *I will Rejoice in the Lord* (Isa. 61:10), SSAA, piano.

Victoria, Tomas (1548–1611 Spain). *Vere Languores Nostros* (Isa. 53:4–5), SATB.

_____. *Sitientes, Venite Ad Aquas* (Isa. 55:1), SATB.

Vulpius, Melchoir (c.1570–1615 Germany). *Isaiah, Mighty Seer in Days of Old* (Isa. 6:1–4), SATB, organ.

_____. *Lo! How A Rose E'er Blooming* (Isa. 11:1), SATB.

Warland, Dale (b.1932 USA). *O Be Joyful O Earth* (Isa. 49:13), SATB.

Warren, Elinor Remick (1900–1991 USA). *Awake, Put On Strength* (Isa. 51: 9–11), SATB, organ.

Webber, Lloyd (1914–1982 UK). *Sing, O Heaven* (Isa. 49:13, 51:3), SAB, organ.

Wesley, Samuel S. (1766–1837 England). *The Wilderness* (Isa. 35:1–2, 4–6, 8, 10), SATB, organ.

Wetzel, Robert (b.1932 USA). *Seek Ye the Lord* (Isa. 55:6), SATB.

White, Jack Noble (20th C. USA). *The First Song of Isaiah* (Isa. 12:2–6), SATB, guitar, handbells, percussion.

Willan, Healey (1880 UK–1968 Canada). *Unto Us a Child is Born* (Isa. 9:6), SSA.

_____. *Surely He Hath Borne Our Griefs* (Isa. 53:4), SA, keyboard.

Williams, David McK (1887–1978 USA). *In the Year that King Uzziah Died* (Isa. 6:1–8), SATB, organ.

Wise, Michael (1648–1687 England). *Prepare Ye the Way of the Lord* (Isa. 40:3–9), SATB, soprano, alto, tenor, organ.

_____. *Awake, Awake, Put On Thy Strength* (Isa. 52:1–2, 7), SATB, organ.

Wynton, Alec (b.1921 UK/USA). The Vision of Isaiah (Isa. 6:1–8), SATB, brass quartet, strings.

_____. Surely it is God who Saves Me (Isa. 12:2–6), SATB organ.

Yeakle, Thomas (20th C. USA). *For a Small Moment* (Isa. 54:7–8), SATB, alto or bass, organ.

Young, Gordon (1919–1998 USA). *In the Year that King Uzziah Died* (Isa. 6:1–3), SATB, organ.

_____. *Shout Ye* (Isa. 13), SATB, organ.

_____. *Thou Wilt Keep Him in Perfect Peace* (Isa. 26), SATB.

_____. *Seek Ye the Lord* (Isa. 55:6–7), SATB.

_____. *A Canticle of Celebration* (Isa. 61:10–11), SATB, brass.

Prophetic utterance inspires Leonard Bernstein's *Jeremiah Symphony*, a symphonic essay in which the promises, denunciations, calls to repentance, and laments of Jeremiah become implicit subtexts.

JEREMIAH

And the word of the Lord came unto me saying: ...I have appointed thee a prophet unto the nations (1:4)... to root out and to pull down, and to destroy and to overthrow; to build and to plant (1:10). Woe is me... a man of strife and a man of contention to the whole earth! I have not lent, neither have men lent to me; yet every one of them doth curse me (15:10). Oh that my head were waters, and mine eyes a fountain of tears, that I might weep day and night for the slain of the daughter of my people (8:23).

Jeremiah (c.625-c.586 B.C.) is the classic prophet of rebuke and strife, sorrow and repentance. A priest from Anathoth, he prophesied in a time of political upheaval, during the reigns of the last kings of Judah.[1] Jeremiah taught that religion is an inward thing, a relation between the individual and his maker, and, that true religion does not depend upon the scrupulous observance of technicalities, not even the Temple, nor the Holy Land, but upon sincere personal seeking of God and ethical behavior (Jer. 7:5–10). For him, salvation was righteousness, and sin was *stubbornness of the heart (7:24, 9:14, and 13:10).*

The Assyrian Empire had declined, and fell to a coalition of Chaldeans and Medes (612 B.C.). Egypt, attempting to fill the void, was defeated by Babylon (605 B.C.). Judah, a former tributary of Assyria, became a vassal of Babylon. Patriots in Judah, edged on by a coalition

---

1.   These are: Josiah (640–609 B.C.), Jehoiakim (609–598 B.C.), Jehoiachin (598–597 B.C.), and Zedekiah (597–587 B.C.).

of five kingdoms in the vicinity of Jerusalem, along with diviners, sooth-sayers, false prophets, and the Temple priesthood,[2] were encouraged to support an alliance with Egypt against Babylon. Jeremiah opposed this scheme, predicting the subjection of Judah by Babylon and the destruction of Jerusalem. He advocated surrender to Babylon as God's agent in punishing idolatry: *Bend your necks under the yoke of the king of Babylon, serve him and his people, and you will live (27:11).* His prophecy infuriated the establishment of his time. All the reproaches Jeremiah suffered were the result of this political nexus.[3] The Book of Jeremiah is a collection of the Prophet's oracles as written down by his faithful disciple, Baruch Ben Neriah.

Leonard Bernstein: Jeremiah Symphony (1943)
Text: Lamentations of Jeremiah 1:1–3; 1:8, 4:14–15; 5:20–21
Genre: Symphony
Medium: Mezzo-soprano and orchestra
Style: Tonal
First performance: Pittsburgh Symphony Orchestra / Fritz Reiner, 1944
Duration: ca. 26 minutes

Although the *Jeremiah Symphony* has been called a programmatic work, it has no specific program, but rather strives to evoke the atmosphere of prophecy and the mood of the prophet. European Neo-Classicism and American Romanticism were at their peak when Bernstein wrote this symphony, while jazz was still considered a novelty in the concert music of the time (1940s). Its three-movements (slow-fast-slow) are colored in a dissonant, yet, tonal idiom.

---

2. He condemned the hypocrisy of those, who, having perverted the truth they have learned, and profaned every sacred value; still make a show of religious piety and observance. Such false prophets are the forebears of today's political advisors, media experts, and spin doctors!

3. Distressed, even by his own message of doom, Jeremiah courageously endured threats to his life and imprisonment for treason, rather than prove unfaithful to the word of God. For us today, Judah's defiance seems foolhardy. Babylon did not threaten Judah's existence. It would have been satisfied with token acknowledgement and the payment of tribute.

Biographic Context

Leonard Bernstein (1918–1990) was a multifaceted conductor, composer, writer, teacher and one of the most glamorous classical music personalities of the second half of the 20th century. His father, a Russian immigrant businessman, saw to his son's early Jewish education, and supported his musical studies with local teachers, later, at Harvard University and the Curtis Institute of Music in Philadelphia. However, he bitterly discouraged his son's professional ambitions. This conflict sowed deep seeds of resentment in the future celebrity.[4]

In addition to composing and conducting, Bernstein was fond of improvising at the piano and contributed substantially to the Broadway musical stage. His extroverted, theatrical style draws on popular music, jazz, and the Classics. These inclinations are evident in *Jeremiah,* which is inspired by synagogue melos and popular music, as well as such 20th-century masters as: Mahler, Bloch, Copeland, and Stravinsky.

Text and Context

The first two movements, *Prophecy* and *Profanation* are orchestral, while the last, *Lamentation* is sung by a female soloist. Bernstein's choice of title and selection of texts was made at a time when the truth of the Holocaust was still a rumor, and, in a sense, this symphony is his way of reaching out to identify with the plight of his people.[5] The final lines of the work are a plea for redemption.

Bernstein denied any story behind his work, and insisted that his intention was "not one of literalness, but of emotional quality."[6] Bernstein never selected specific texts to illustrate his abstract program, but clearly, the Sabbath synagogue readings from the Prophets, on the weeks preceding the 9th of Av[7] (Jer. 2:4–28; 3:4 and 4:1–2), have all the

---

4.   Humphrey Burton, *Leonard Bernstein* (New York: Doubleday, 1994) 13–18.

5.   At the time, slews of Jewish émigrés were fleeing Nazi-dominated Europe and seeking refuge in America. In some way, Bernstein senses an analogy between the ancient exile of the Jewish people from Jerusalem and their flight from war torn Germany.

6.   Bernstein's comments are cited in the liner notes for *Jeremiah (Symphony No 1),* annotated by Tim Page (New York Philharmonic / Leonard Bernstein, Sony — CD, 1999).

7.   The blackest date in the Jewish calendar is the Ninth of Av (*Tishah B'Av*),

features of such pivotal source material. Understanding these texts illuminates our perception of the emotional background surrounding the message and clout of the symphony's instrumental exegesis.

Music and Musical Exegesis

First Movement

In the first movement, the following biblical passages "parallel in feeling, the intensity of the prophet's pleas with the people," as Bernstein states: *Hear ye the word of the Lord, O house of Jacob, and all the families of the house of Israel; Thus saith the Lord: What unrighteousness have your fathers found in Me, That they are gone far from Me, And have walked after things of naught, and are become naught (2:4–5). For My people have committed two evils: They have forsaken Me, the fountain of living waters, And have hewed them out cisterns, broken cisterns, That hold no water (2:13), they, their kings, their princes and their priests and their prophets (2:26). But where are thy gods that thou hast made thee? For, according to the number of thy cities are thy gods, O Judah (2:28).*

Prophecy suggests prophetic rebuke — with its ominous hammering chords, high woodwind shrieks, and soaring string lines. Symbolic of the prophet, the horns state the principal melodic theme. It is abstractly "cantorial" in quality, mosaic in construction. Bernstein's heavily overcast urban harmonies and long stretches of American-Romantic melodic lines, recall his teachers: Aaron Copeland and Samuel Barber.

Second Movement

About the second movement, Bernstein remarks, "The scherzo, subtitled *Profanation,* gives a general sense of the destruction and chaos brought on by pagan corruption within the priesthood and the people." The following Scriptural passages suggest corresponding subtexts: *Know what thou hast done; thou art a swift young camel traversing her ways; a wild ass used to the wilderness, that snuffeth up the wind in her desire; Her lust, who can hinder it (2:23–24)? For they are all adulterers, an assembly of treacherous men. For they proceed from evil to evil, and*

which originally commemorated the destruction of the Temple in 586 B.C. Not only have many disasters befallen the Jewish people on this date, but, all subsequent calamities have been considered a consequence.

they know me not, saith the Lord (9:1–2). And they deceive every one his neighbor, and truth they speak not; they have taught their tongues to speak lies, they weary themselves to commit iniquity (9:4).

Profanation is based on the Hebrew blessing to the reading from the Prophets (*haftarah*) — a chant he learned as a boy, in preparation for his bar mitzvah in the synagogue. The liturgical ethos of the original, however, has been distorted and irregularly metered. The blessing, like a woman raped, has been subjected to visceral pulsations, trumpet ridicule, and uncouth percussive abusiveness. This jazz imagery conjures up semblances of a mocking jeer from the populace — elements reminiscent of Stravinsky's ballet, *Rite of Spring*. Bernstein is projecting us into the equivalent of a pagan celebration to *Baal*. The soaring first movement theme returns in counterpoint to this sacrilegious revelry. It appears as a prophetic judgment, a pronouncement exacting retribution, a call from on high. To no avail, the Prophet had begged the people to give up their idols and obey the spirit of the Law, which is justice, kindness, and love for others.

Third Movement

The last movement is based on "a literary conception, [it] is the cry of Jeremiah as he mourns his beloved Jerusalem, ruined, pillaged and dishonored after his desperate efforts to save it." The choice of a mezzo-soprano protagonist is not arbitrary. By employing a woman's voice, the composer is resurrecting the ancient biblical practice of hiring professional dirge singers or mourning women *(mekonenot)* to cry at funerals. Bernstein chooses her in this context to bewail a whole nation.[8] *Thus saith the Lord of hosts: Consider ye, and call for the mourning women, that they may come; and send for the wise women, that they may come; and let them make haste and take up a wailing for us, that our eyelids may run down with tears, and our eyelids gush out with waters. For a voice of wailing is heard out of Zion: 'How are we undone' (Jeremiah 9:16–18)!* Bernstein selected these citations, from the Lamentations of

---

8. In the biblical and Talmudic period, women composing dirges and leading responsive recitations were actively involved in mourning rites. To some extent, this custom continues today among Oriental Jews. Eventually, the funeral oration or eulogy took the place of the mourning women's wailing chants and instrumental playing.

Jeremiah (1:1–3; 1:8, 4:14–15; 5:20–21),[9] to lend appropriate content to her cry.

> How doth the city sit solitary that was full of people!
> How is she become a widow!
> She that was great among the nations, and princess among the provinces,
> How is she become tributary!
> She weepeth sore in the night, and her tears are on her cheeks;
> She hath none to comfort her among all her lovers;
> All her friends have dealt treacherously with her, they are become her enemies.
> Judah is gone into exile because of the affliction,
> And because of great servitude;
> She dwelleth among the nations, she findeth no rest;
> All her pursuers over took her within the narrow passes.
>
> (Lam. 1:1–3)

> Jerusalem hath grievously sinned; therefore she is become as one unclean;
> All that honored her despise her, because they have seen her nakedness;
> She herself also sigheth, and turned backward.
>
> (Lam. 1:8)

> They wander as blind men in the streets; they are polluted with blood,
> So that men cannot touch their garments.
> 'Depart ye unclean!' men cried unto them, 'Depart, depart, touch not!'
> Yea, they fled away and wandered; men among the nations;
> 'They shall no more sojourn there.'
>
> (Lam. 4:14–15)

> Wherefore dost thou forget us forever, and forsake us so long time!
> Turn thou us unto Thee, O Lord, and we shall be turned;
> Renew our days as of old.
>
> (Lam. 5:20–21)

Bernstein's lamentation evokes the aftermath to the prophet's unheeded message. It is a stylized recitation of the Book of Lamentations, with

---

9. Christian sources confirm this practice. St. Jerome adds, "This custom continues to the present day in Judea, that women with disheveled locks and bared breasts, in musical utterance invite all to weeping." As cited in *Jeremiah*, H. Freedman, ed., note 16 (London: Soncino Books of the Bible, 1968 [1949]) 71.

motifs borrowed from the traditional synagogue cantillation of the Book. Its spare orchestration, broad harmonic gestures, and tender melodic iterations by the mezzo-soprano soloist — *How doth the city sit solitary! How is she become a widow!* — are heartfelt cries. They recall similar passages of despair, that conjure up for me passages from, or references to, Bloch's *Shelomo* and Stravinsky's *Symphony of Psalms.*

Conclusion

Bitterly and powerfully Jeremiah had spoken to the people and warned that if they did not change their ways, one day the Temple would be destroyed and they would be carried off into exile. The people, unashamedly, responded with fury, not contrition. Over 2,500 years later, the spirit of the prophet touched a little boy from Lawrence, Massachusetts as he was preparing the *haftarah* reading for his bar-mitzvah. When he grew into a man, and sought, in youthful pride and ambition, to enter a prize composition competition, the most vivid impressions which fed his imagination were those words of Jeremiah, he had studied years before, in childhood. The musical language he forged draws from and parallels those literary sources and social conditions, representing a mid-20th century blend of urban-Americana and ancient-Hebraica. Through the ages, the continuity and enigma of biblical transmission, from generation to generation, is often as indirect and circumstantial as Bernstein's inspiration to *Jeremiah* — a message learned, forgotten — then remembered again in the hour of need — something passed from heart to heart and soul to soul.

Other Directions

Verses and sections from the Book of Jeremiah set for choir include Heinrich Isaac's *Oratio Hieremiae* (1538), and Samuel Scheidt's *Ist nicht Ephraim mein teurer Sohn.* The lament *Quis dabit oculis Meis* (Jer. 8:23), contained in the Good Friday liturgy, also occurs in many settings by composers of the 16th century. Oratorios on the theme include G.M. Schiassi's *Geremia in Egitto* (1727) and Ernst Hess's *Jeremiah* (1953). In Jewish musical tradition, *Ha-Ben Yakir Li Ephraim* (Jer. 31:19) has become a showpiece of the "artistic" *hazanim* of Eastern Europe; it also appears as the text of several folk songs and Hasidic *nigunim.* The original stage music for Stefan Zweig's *Jeremiah* was written by Arno Nadel.

For the Tel Aviv revival of the play in Palestine, music was composed by Yedidyah Admon. Several contemporary Israeli-popular composers have written songs based on its verses: Shmulk Kraus: *Roim Rachok* (1983) on words by Y. Rotblit after 17:8; Idan Reichel: *Mini Kolech Mibechi* (2000) on 31:15; Hami Artzi Kefir: *Ein Kavod* (2000) on 5:21. The Negro Spiritual *There is a Balm in Gilead*, based on Jeremiah 8:22, is the most conspicuous adaptation of a verse from Jeremiah into folk-lore.[10] It has been arranged in numerous choral versions by: George Brandon, Frederick Davis, William Dawson, Sam Batt Owens, Jeanne Shaffer, Irvin Cooper, C. Harry Causey, and George Kemmer.

Works List

Admon, Jedidiah (1894 Russia–1974 Israel). *Jeremias* (S. Zweig), incidental music.

_____. *Oi li al shivri* (Jer. 10:19–21), voice and pianoforte.

Alexander, Haim (1915 Berlin/1936 Jerusalem). *Ve-kibasti etkhem* (Jer. 29:14), choir.

Algazi, Isaac (1892 Izmir–1964 Montevideo). *Ha-ben yakir li Ephrayim* (Jer. 31:20), tenor, choir, organ.

Aurisicchio, Antonio (1710 Naples–1781 Rome). *Orazio Jeremiae prophetae*, 2 voices and violins.

Bach, Johann Sebastian (1685–1750 Leipzig). *Cantata 49: In deine Haende* (Jer. 31:3), bass and soprano.

_____. *Cantata 88: Siehe ich will viel Fischer aussenden* (Jer. 16:16), bass.

_____. *Cantata 102: Herr deine Augen sehen* (Jer. 5:3), choir.

Berger, Jean (1909 Germany–2002 USA). *This is the Covenant* (Jer. 31:31–34), SATB.

Bernstein, Leonard (1918 Lynn, Mass.–1990 New York). *Jeremiah Symphony*, mezzo soprano, orchestra.

Bittoni, Bernado (1756–1826 Italy). *Oratio Jeremiae Prophete*, lament.

Byrd, William (1543–1623 England). *Plorans plorabit* (Jer. 13:17–18), 5 voices, choir.

Castelnuovo-Tedesco, Mario (1895 Florence–1968 Beverly Hills, Calif.). *I Profeti: 3. (Jerusalem,* concerto for violin and orchestra.

Childs, Barney (b.1926 USA). *Heal Me, O Lord* (1964) (Jer. 17:5–10, 13–14), SATB, piano, trombone

---

10. Batia Bayer, "Jeremiah in Music," *Encyclopaedia Judaica*, Vol. 9, col. 1361.

Clark, Keith (20th C. USA). *O That My Head Were Waters* (Jer. 9:1), SATB

Clemens Non Papa, Jacobus (c.1510-c.1556 Antwerp). *Vox in Rama* (Jer. 31:15), motet.

Contino, Giovanni (c. 1513–1574 Italy). *Threni Jeremiae*, lament.

Dett, R. Nathaniel (1882–1943 USA). *Ask for the Old Paths* (Jer. 6:6, 16), tenor, SATB.

Ehrlich, Abel (1915 Germany–2003 Israel). *I Call to All Men* (1975) (an experimental graphic adventure in time) for chorus.

Hartmann, Heinrich (1582–1616 Germany). *Ist nicht Ephraim* (Jer. 31:19), 8 voices.

Hess, Ernst (1912–1968 Switzerland). *Jeremiah*, oratorio.

Hovhanes, Alan (1911–2000 USA). *Blessed is the Man* (Jer. 17:7), SATB.

Karkoff, Maurice Ingvar (1927 Stockholm). *Jeremiah 46*, cantata, choir, speakers-choir and orchestra.

Kay, Ulysses Simpson (1917 Arizona–1995 New Jersey). *Jeremiah*, cantata.

Kirschner, Emanuel (1857–1948 Berlin). *Ki hineh ha-homer* (Jer. 18:4–6), baritone and organ.

Mueller, Carl F. (1892–1982 USA). *The New Covenant* (Jer. 31:33–34), ATB, keyboard.

Nadel, Arno (1878 Vilna–1943 Auschwitz). *Jeremias* (S. Zweig), incidental music.

Naylor, John (1838–1897 England). *Jeremiah*, cantata.

Nowowiejski, Feliks (1877–1946 Poznan). *Jeremiasz* (K. Ujejski), choir a cappella.

Poser, Hans (1917–1970 Germany). *Song of Jeremiah*, chorus and orchestra.

Purcell, Henry (1659–1695 London). *Let mine eyes run down with tears* (Jer. 14:17–22), 5 voices, choir, basso continuo, organ.

Reger, Max (1873–1916 Germany). *Behold the Days Come, Saith the Lord* (Jer. 33:14–16), SATB, organ.

Sateren, Leland (1913–2007 USA). *The Word Rejected* (Jer. 8:9), SATB

Salomon, Karel (1897 Heidelberg–1974 Jerusalem). *Elegy and Dance* (Jer. 32:3), soprano/oboe solo and 2 flutes.

Saminski, Lazar (1882 Odessa–1959 New York). *Lamentation de Rachel* (Jer. 31:15–17), biblical choral poem.

Schein, Johann Hermann (1586 Grunheim–1630 Leipzig). *Ist nicht*

Ephraim mein teurer Sohn? (Jer. 31:20), motet, 5 voices and basso continuo.

Schiassi, Gaetano M. (1698 Bologne–1754 Lisbon). *Geremia in Egitto* (1 Kings), oratorio.

Schoenberg, Arnold (1874 Vienna–1951 Los Angeles). *Symphony: part 2 finale* (Jer. 7 and 17), soloist, choir and orchestra.

Schutz, Heinrich (1585–1672 Dresden). *Ist nicht Ephraim mein teuer Sohn?* (Jer. 31:20), motet, voices and choir.

Sharet, Yehuda (1901 Russia–1979 Israel). *Li-Yemey Ha-Mazor*, choir.

Shlonsky, Verdina (1913 Russia–1990 Tel-Aviv). *Jeremiah* (S. Zweig), symphonic poem.

Spicker, Max (1858 Germany–1912 USA). *Fear Not, O Israel* (Jer. 4), SATB, soprano, alto, tenor, bass, organ.

Telemann, G. P. (1681–1767 Germany). *Wave All the Flags in the Country* (Jer. 51:27–29), SATB.

Weinberg, Henry (b.1931 USA). *Vox in Rama* (Jer. 31:15), SATB.

Wenzel, Eberhard (1895–1982). *Worte des Propheten Jeremia*, choir.

Wigglesworth, Frank (1918 Boston–2003). *Jeremiah*, baritone, choir and orchestra.

Young, Carlton (20th C. USA). *We Celebrate His Love* (Jer. 33:10–11), SAB, organ, percussion, dancers.

Zelenski, Mikolaj (17th C. Poland). *Vox in Rama* (Jer. 31:15), 4 voices.

The American-Negro Spiritual *Ezekiel Saw de Wheel*, inspired from Ezekiel's vision of the Divine Chariot-Throne of Glory, illustrates one of the ways the Bible influences folk music.

EZEKIEL

And I looked, and behold, a stormy wind came out of the north, a great cloud, with a fire flashing up, so that a brightness was round about it... and out of the midst thereof came the likeness of four living creatures... And the living creatures ran and returned as the appearance of a flash of lightening. Now as I beheld... behold one wheel at the bottom hard by the creatures, at the four faces... The appearance of the wheels and their work was... as it were a wheel within a wheel (Ezekiel 1:4–5, 14–16).

Ezekiel, a priest in Jerusalem, when taken to Babylon in the first deportation of the Judeans by Nebuchadnezzar in 597 B.C., was already a decade in exile before the final Fall of Jerusalem in 586 B.C. His book foretells the destruction of Jerusalem (chapters 1–14) and predicts the restoration of Israel (chapters 25–48). It opens, however, with a fantastic vision of a Divine Chariot-Throne (*Merkavah*) drawn on "wheels" by four, four-faced living creatures: *Then the spirit lifted me up, and I heard behind me a voice of a great rushing, saying: 'Blessed be the glory of the Lord from His place. I heard also the noise of the wings of the living creatures that touched one another, and the noise of the wheels over against them, and a noise of a great rushing (Ezekiel 3:12–13).*[1]

---

1. The Doxology — *Blessed be the glory of the Lord from His place* — uttered by the celestial beings and heard by the prophet was incorporated into Hebrew liturgy as the *Kedusha*. This verse is replaced by a parallel phrase in the *Sanctus* of the Mass — *Hosanna in excelsis*.

337

The mobility of the Chariot-Throne taught Ezekiel that God may be found anywhere, not only in the Temple in Jerusalem, nor even in the Holy Land. God is eternal, but the way He is understood changes from place to place and from time to time.[2] To later ages, the vision of the chariot (*Merkavah*) became a central source of Jewish mysticism.

Anonymous: Ezekiel Saw de Wheel
Genre: Afro-American Spiritual
Medium: Voices
Style: Sacred folksong
Duration: ca. 2 minutes

Because Spirituals[3] are an improvised song form, innumerable versions of *Ezekiel Saw de Wheel* have been sung, arranged, and recorded. Each diverges from the other in its content, and number, and order of verses. Common to all versions, however, is the refrain *Way in de middle of the air*. The reference to "a wheel in a wheel" is taken from Ezekiel 1:16...*and their appearance and their work was as it were a wheel in the middle of a wheel*. The forces which keep the wheels turning are complete, uncritical and warm hearted faith and good will, *the grace of God*.

Text and Context

DETAIL

Version 1

Refrain

Ezekel saw de wheel (solo call)
Way up in the middle of the air (choral response)
Ezekel saw de wheel

---

2. Many of the innovations of the psalmists and prophets have their origin in the Torah. To cite a precedent: *In every place where I cause My name to be mentioned I will come unto thee and bless thee (Exod. 20:21).*

3. Spirituals are sacred folksongs sung by enslaved black folk in the Southern States of America, dating from the 18th century until the end of legalized slavery in the 1860s. They lend themselves easily to communal singing. See also "Biblical folksong and the Spiritual," chapter 11, Joshua.

Way in the middle of the air.
The big wheel moved by faith,
The little wheel moved by the grace of God.
A wheel in a wheel, wheel in a wheel
Way in the middle of the air.

The departure of the Divine Presence from the Temple[4] is brought on by hypocrites, people who are *brazen-faced and stiff hearted (2:4)*. The following verses give cryptic expression to these feelings, transposed as criticism of other members of the congregation.[5]

Verse 1

O, jes' let me tell you what a hypocrit'l do (solo)
Way up in the middle of the air. (chorus)
O, he'll talk about me an' he'll talk about you, (solo)
Way up in the middle of the air. (chorus) O, yes! (solo)

Refrain (all choral response)

Some verses borrow material from the New Testament, synthesizing it with citations from Ezekiel. The following references to the cross are derived from the Gospels.

Verse 2

O, mind you brother how you walk on the cross, (solo)[6]
Way up in the middle of the air. (chorus)
O, ya foot might slip and ya soul get lost, (solo)
Way in the middle of the air. (chorus) O, yes! (solo)

---

4. This vision is worked out in Ezek. 2:1–10 and 3:1–14.
5. This version is based on an early recording by the Fisk Jubilee Singers. They sang it in simple, unaccompanied block style harmony. Solo calls and choral responses were all taken at a moderate tempo. See Internet resource: "Old Time Spirituals-Black Spirituals of the Early 1900s featuring the Fisk University and Tuskegee Institute Quartets." http://www.besmark.com/spiritual.html
6. *And as they came out, they found a man of Cyrene, Simon by name: him they compelled to bear his cross (Matthew 27:32)*. See also Mark 15:21, Luke 23:26, John 19:17.

Refrain (all choral response)

DETAIL

Version 2

Another version retains the wheel imagery, but with a slight change of text.[7] The phrase *Ezekiel saw a flame-a-burnin'... a flame within a flame-a-burnin'* refers to the storm imagery of Ezekiel's vision... *a stormy wind came out of the north, a great cloud, with a fire flashing up... (1:4).*

Refrain

> Ezekiel saw a wheel a-turnin' / Way in the middle of the air
> A wheel within a wheel a-turnin' / Way in the middle of the air.
> And the little wheel turned by faith.
> And the big wheel turned by the grace of God.
> Ezekiel saw a wheel a-turnin' / Way in the middle of the air.

Verse

> Ezekiel saw a flame a-burning' / Way in the middle of the air
> A flame within a flame a-burnin' / Way in the middle of the air.
> And the little flame turned by faith.
> And the big flame burned by the grace of God.
> Ezekiel saw a wheel a-turnin' / Way in the middle of the air.

Music and Musical Exegesis

DETAIL

Version 3

This bright and lively pentatonic refrain is almost a one phrase tune. It has lots of chatty syllables and a syncopated character. It builds form through repetition: **A A A A**.[8] The text is exactly the same each time.

---

7. See Ezekiel's Wheel/ "Ezekiel saw wheel a-turning gospel Christian songs." Internet resource: http://ingeb.org/spiritual/ezekiels.html
8. The first half line of the refrain can be broken down into two motivic cells. Motif **a** tilts upwards by the interval of a third (C f f f f a), while motif **b** steps down (a a ff aa gg f). In all, it has only 4 different notes (C f a g).

The second half of the refrain creates engaging rhythmic balance, contrasting syncopated and non-syncopated figures.

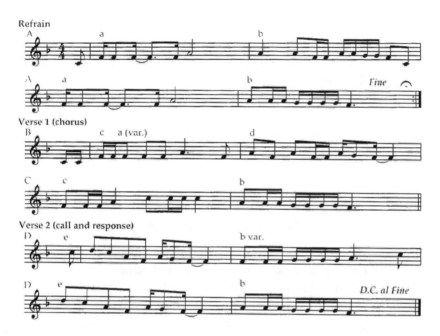

Ex. 34. Spiritual: *Ezekiel Saw de Wheel*
Transcription by the author

Refrain

A

> Ezekiel saw de wheel (a)
> Way up in de middle o' de air. (b)

A

> Ezekiel saw de wheel (a)
> Way up in de middle o' de air. (b)

A

> Ezekiel saw de wheel (a)
> Way up in de middle o' de air. (b)

A

> Ezekiel saw de wheel (a)
> Way up in de middle o' de air. (b)

Verse 1, lines **B** and **C**, contrasts syncopated with non-syncopated phrases, especially when the text speaks of the *little wheel* and the *big wheel*.[9] The final phrase, *Wheel in a wheel, wheel in a wheel,* breaks up the sing-song pattern.[10]

B

> The little wheel run by faith, (c or a)
> The big wheel run by de grace of God. (d)

C

> Wheel in a wheel, wheel in a wheel, (e)
> Way in de middle o' de air. (b)

Verses 2, lines **D D**, contrasts with both the refrain and verse 1 — in its alternating call-and-response character. Call phrases are always sung by soloists,[11] while group responses, repeat *Way up in de middle o' de air*.[12] On repetition, it is sung exactly as the refrain, resolving down by steps (a aa gggg f). Again, in contrast to syncopations elsewhere, neither the phrase *Way in de middle o' de air*, nor its variations are syncopated. Improvised slides, melismas, and a number interjections (*a whirlin', O Lord, O yes*), amplify and color this basic frame. The hand clapping, finger snapping, and foot stomping, which originally

---

9. The third motif **c** (C ff f f f a), makes use of the same pitches as the opening line, but projects a different countenance because of this non-syncopated quality, while the fourth motif **d** (a ff a ff a g f), zigzags between two notes, before stepping down.

10. It rises to a climactic high c (f ff a c cc c), which functions as a signal to return to the refrain, via repetition of the closing motif **b** *Way up in de middle o' de air.*

11. This is sung to a pentatonic motif **f** (c d c a g a g f).

12. This is the only time when motif **b** (f ff gggg a) is inverted. It occurs on the penultimate repetition of the phrase. This characteristic: of a change in pattern on the next to final statement in a melodic structure, signaling the close of a section, is found in traditional biblical cantillation, as well as in Gregorian psalmody.

accompanied these Spirituals — were later written into *a cappella* choral arrangements as vocal riffs, or simulated on piano or guitar.

Verse 2

D

> Solo: Some go to church to sing and shout (f)
> Group response: Way in de middle o' de air. (b *variation*)

D

> Solo: Before six months he's all shouted out, (f)
> Group response: Way in de middle o' de air. (b)

Conclusion

Inspiration is a quality of identification, beyond understanding; an impulse which cannot be seen, but whose effects may be manifest, unmistakably, in creative acts. What was the magic Ezekiel's vision wrought upon the minds of untutored black folk to inspire their song? Surely, it was not born of cognition, cogitation, nor logic; certainly not a theological understanding of the mysticism of the Chariot! The truth these slaves grasped was more a gut reaction: There had been a vision; God was real. This is all they knew and all they needed to know. This spirit touched the black man's soul and gave him hope, as it had given hope to Judean exiles in Babylon, so many generations before. Its message was unmistakable: Even in bondage, they were not forgotten; Salvation, however delayed, was on the way.[13]

---

13. The following Midrash on receiving the Ten Commandments at Sinai may provide an insight into the powerful effect of Ezekiel's revelation: *The people perceived the difference between the first two commandments, which they heard directly from God, and those they learned through Moses' intercession. For when they heard the words, 'I am the Eternal, thy Lord,' the understanding of the Torah became deep-rooted in their hearts, so that they never forgot what they learned. But they forgot some of the things Moses taught, for as man is flesh and blood and hence ephemeral, so are his teachings ephemeral. See Ginzberg, Legends of the Jews, Vol. 3, 109, note 243, and Vol. 6, 45.*

Related Directions

Another Afro-American spiritual "Dry Bones," often effectively arranged for vocal or instrumental ensembles, transforms the terrifying biblical scene of the rising of the dead into a syncopated, jocular description of the gradual joining together and subsequent separation of the bones. Considerable, also, are Jewish cantorial interpretations of the *Ve-ha-Ofanim* prayer from synagogue liturgy (which appears in the first blessing, *Yotzer*, before the *Shema*), and tunes adapted to many *Ofan* poems (*God, the Lord over all works...All the host render praise unto him, the Seraphim, the Ophanim, and the holy Chayoth ascribing glory and greatness*).[14] Composers of art music have generally avoided the subject of Ezekiel's vision, whereas, that of Isaiah, has established a place in the concert repertoire and Christian liturgy. The two visions were combined in the Prologue to Goethe's *Faust*, and have an ambitious setting in the prologue of Arrigo Boito's *Mefistofele* (1868, 1875). The "Valley of the Dry Bones" is described by Franz Liszt in his *Ossa arida* for choir and organ (1879). A symphonic work, *The Valley of Dry Bones*, was composed by A.W. Binder (1935). The text has also been set by several Israeli composers, generally for choir.

Works List

Bardos, Lajos (1899–1986 Budapest). *Ezekiel latomasa* (Ezekiel's vision), lament.

Ben-Haim, Paul (1897 Germany–1984 Israel). *The Visions of a Prophet* (O ye Dry Bones) (1959) (Ezek. 37), cantata for tenor, mixed choir, orchestra.

Bonno, Giuseppe (1711–1788 Vienna). *Ezechia* (A. Zeno), oratorio.

Bononcini, Giovanni (1670 Modena–1747 Vienna). *Ezechia* (A. Zeno), oratorio.

---

14. The alphabetical liturgical poem, "God, Lord over all works," reads: *He is exalted above the holy Chayoth and is adorned in glory above the celestial chariot: purity and rectitude are before his throne, lovingkindness and tender mercy before his glory.* Hertz," Eyl Adon," *Prayer Book*, 429. Some attribute a version of the text to the "Searchers in the Chariot" or Essenes. See Duncan Howett, *The Essenes and Christianity* (New York: Harper and Brothers, 1957) 202.

Brandon, George (1924–2000 USA). *Glad Tidings!* (Ezek. 47), arr. SAB, organ

Brott, Alexander (1915–2005 Montreal). *The Vision of Dry Bones* (Ezek. 37:1–14), baritone, strings, piano.

Colaco Osorio-Schwaab, Reine (1801–1871 Amsterdam). *Ezechiel 37*, recitative, instruments.

Engel, Joel (1868–1955 Paris). *Hazon Yehezkel* (Ezek. 37), voice, piano.

Ferris, William (1938–2000 USA). *I Have Seen Water* (Ezek. 47:1–2), unison, organ.

Gliere, Reinhold Morisovich (1875–1956 Kiev). *Imitation of Ezekiel*, narrator, orchestra.

Hemsi, Alberto (1898 Rhodes–1964 Paris). *Hayetah alay ruah Adonay* (Ezek. 37:1–6), voice, pianoforte.

Liszt, Franz (1811–1886 Beirut). *Ossa arida* (Ezek. 37), choir, organ.

Mays, Walter (b.1941 USA). *Voices of the Fiery Furnace*, baritone, 2 mixed choruses, and orchestra.

Milner, Moshe Michael (1886–1952 Kiev). *The Vision of the Dry Bones* (Ezek. 37), voice, piano.

Parker, Tom (20ᵗʰ C. UK). *Lead Us On, Good Shepherd* (Ezek. 34:13–16), SATB, organ.

Porrino, Ennio (1810–1859 Rome). *La visione d'Ezechiele*, orchestra.

Reichel, Bernard (1901–1992 Geneva). *La vision d'Ezechiel*, soloist, choir, orchestra.

Stainer, John (1841–1901 UK). *Ye Shall Dwell in the Land* (Ezek. 36:28, 30, 34–35), SATB, organ.

Sternberg, Erich Walter (1891 Germany–1974 Israel). *Resurrection of Israel* (1959), Cantata for baritone, choir, and orchestra.

Vaughan Willams, Ralph (1972–1958 UK). *A Vision of Aeroplane* (Ezek. 1), SATB, organ.

Weiner, Lazar (1897 Ukraine–1982 New York). *Three Biblical Songs: 3. Ezekiel*, voice, piano.

Zukerwar, Haim D. (b.1956 Uruguay/1989 Israel). *The Canticle of the Prophet* (Ezek. 37, Eccles. 1, Ezek. 40–43), Concerto for violin and strings.

G. Dore: Jonah Cast Forth from the Whale, *Bible Illustrations (1866)*

CHAPTER 23

Various works have been written on the words of the Twelve Prophets. The book of Jonah inspired the most musical creativity. This chapter surveys these books, providing brief introductory remarks about each prophet and listing compositions based upon them.

TWELVE PROPHETS

HOSEA

Hosea is the earliest of the Prophets. He lived in the Northern Kingdom of Israel during the period of its decline and fall in the 8th century B.C. He condemned the apostasy of the people, who turned away from God to serve Baal, a Canaanite god of fertility (8:4–6). He compared God's abiding love for idolatrous Israel to his own love for a wife, who proved an unfaithful whore.

Works List

Castelnuovo-Tedesco, Mario (1895 Florence–1968 California). *V'erastich li l'olam (And I will bethroth thee unto me forever)* (Hosea 2:21), voice, piano.

Harris, David (c. 1950 Boston). *Come and Let Us Return Unto the Lord (1976)* (Hosea 6:1–2), SAB, organ.

Hemsi, Alberto (1898 Rhodos–1964 Paris). *V'dibarti al Hanevyim* (Hosea 11:2, Amos 3:7–8; Isa. 51:16, 2:5), voice, piano.

Norris, Kevin (USA). *Offertory/Lent (1980)* (Hosea 6:1–2), unison, organ.

Razel, Yonatan (c. 1980 USA/Israel) *Veerastichli Leolam* (Hosea 2:11), song.

AMOS

Amos was a native Judean, and a contemporary of Isaiah, Micah, and Hosea. He prophesied in the Northern Kingdom of Israel during the reign of Jeroboam II (c.784–c.749 B.C.). He claimed to be: *Neither a prophet nor a prophet's son, but a shepherd [who] took care of sycamore trees (7:17)*. Amos prophesied the destruction of Israel (5:1–2) and declared that religion, unaccompanied by *righteousness* is anathema (5:21–24).

Works List

Bloch, Yosef Chaim (c. 1980 USA). *Hineh Yamin Baim* (Amos 8:11), song
Britten, Benjamin (1913–1976 England). *Seek the Lord* (Amos 5: 6–8), choir, organ.
Hemsi, Alberto (1898 Rhodos–1964 Paris). *V'dibarti al Hanevyim* (Hosea 11:2, Amos 3:7–8; Isa. 51:16, 2:5), voice, piano.
Jacobson, Maurice (1898–1976 England). *The Shepherd of Tekoa*, background music.
Levi, Oshik (b.1944 Israel) *Chozeh Lech Brach* (Bialik) (Amos 7:12), song.
Snyder, Wesley (1881–1965 NY). *Seek him that maketh the Seven Stars and Orion* (1964) (Amos 5:8), SATB.
Weiner, Lazar (1897 Russia–1982 New York City). *Amos*, cantata for soli and choir.

JOEL

Joel was a prophet of the kingdom of Judah. His prophecy is Messianic in nature and forecasts the 'Day of the Lord' in apocalyptic terms: *Then everyone who calls on the name of the Lord shall be saved (2:32)*. His prophesy of the outpouring of the Spirit upon all flesh was adopted by the Christian Church (Acts 2:17): *Then afterwards I will pour out my spirit on all flesh; your sons and your daughters shall prophesy, your old men shall dream dreams and your young men shall see visions (Joel 2:28).*

Works List

Bigaglia, Diogemo (1676–1745 Venice). *Giale (Joel)* (D. Giupponi), oratorio.

Carlebach, Shlomo (1925 Germany–1994 USA). *Vihuda Leolam Teshev* (Joel 4:20), song.

Demantius, Christoph (1567–1643 Germany). *Der Spruch Joel* (2:12), 5 voices.

Elgar, Edward (1857–1934 England). *Fear Not, O Land* (Joel 2:21–24), 26, SATB, organ.

Gore, Richard (d. 1994 USA). *Blow the Trumpet (1975)* (Joel 2:3), SATB, organ.

Gross (Barnard), John (b.1948 England). *Fear Not, O Land; Be Glad and Rejoice* (Joel 2:21–26), SATB, organ.

Jackson, Francis (b.1917 England). *Blow ye the Trumpet in Zion* (Joel 2:1–2, 15–17, 32), SATB, organ.

Jacobson, Joseph (20th C. USA). *Vihuda Leolam Teshev* (Joel 4:20), round.

Joffe, Shlomo (1909 Warsaw/1930 Israel–1995). *Joel, chapter 1*, alto, 9 instruments.

Laufer, Moshe (b.1958 Israel). *Veniketi Damin Lo Niketi* (Joel 4:21), song.

Morley, Thomas (1557–1602 England). *Sound Forth the Trumpet in Zion* (Joel 2:1), SAB.

Naylor, Bernard (1907–1986 England). *Motet for Whitsunday* (Joel 2:28–32) soprano, SATB.

Perti, Giacomo Antonio (1661–1756 Italy). *Inter Vestibulum et Altare* (Joel 2:17), SATB.

Purcell, Henry (1659–1695 London). *Blow up the Trumpet in Zion* (Joel 2:15–17), tenor, choir and organ.

Sumsion, Herbert (1899–1995 England). *Fear Not, O Land* (Joel 2:21–24, 26), SATB, organ.

Tallis, Thomas (1505–1585 England). *In Ieiunio et Fleta* (Joel 2:17), SAATB, optional organ.

JONAH

The story of Jonah and the whale is one of the most widely known in Scripture. A prophet in the time of Jeroboam (2 Kings 14:25), Jonah is both reluctant to obey the command of God and merciless towards the people of Nineveh, against whom he has been called to prophesy. His story demonstrates how the inviolable will of God is fulfilled against the vicissitudes of fate and human nature.

Works List

Adler, Hugo (1894 Belgium/1928 Boston–1958 USA). *Jonah*, cantata.

Anfossi, Pasqual (1727–1797 Rome). *Ninive conversa*, oratorio.

Argento, Dominick (b.1927 Pennsylvania, USA). *Jonah and the Whale* (1973), narrator, soprano, tenor, bass, SATB, 3 trombones, 3 percussions, 3 keyboards, oratorio.

Bach, J.S. (1685–1750 Leipzig). Cantata 111: *Was mein Gott will* (Jonah 1:3), aria.

Badings, Henk (1907 Java–1987 Holland). *Jonah*, oratorio for soli, chorus, orchestra, tape.

Bassani, Giovanni (1657–1716 Italy). *Jonah*, oratorio.

Berkeley, Lennox (1903–1989 England). *Jonah*, oratorio.

Bertoni, Ferdinando (1725–1813 Italy). *L'Obbedienza di Gionato*, Jona, oratorio.

Bridge, John (1844–1924 England). *The Repentance of Nineveh* (J. Bennet), oratorio.

Broadway, Richard (18th C.). *Repentance of Nineveh*, oratorio.

Caldara, Antonio (1670 Venice–1736 Vienna). *Gionata* (A. Zeno), oratorio.

Carissimi, Giacomo (1605–1674 Rome). *Jonas*, oratorio.

Castelnuovo-Tedesco, Mario (1895 Florence–1968 USA). *The Book of Jonah*, oratorio.

Hamal, Henri-Guillaume (1685–1752 Liege). *Jonas*, oratorio.

Hajdu, Andre (b.1932 Hungary/1966 Israel). *The Story of Jonah* (1987), opera for children's choir.

Franck, Melchoir (1579–1639 Germany). *Ninive, wach auf vom tiefen Schlaf der Suenden,* Jonah, 8 voices, organ.

Jacquet, de La Guerre, Elisabeth (1667–1729 Paris). *Jonas* (A.H. de la Motte), cantata for voices, instruments, basso continuo.

Kosa, Gyorgy (1897–1984 Budapest). *Jonas,* oratorio.

Lotti, Antonio (1667–1740 Venice). *Gionata,* oratorio.

Mar-Haim, Joseph (b.1940 Israel). *Jonah* (1987), Scene for mixed choir, magnetic tape.

Olivo, Simpliciano (1594–1680 Italy). *Giona,* oratorio.

Pertici, Giovanni (c.1665–1690 Italy). *Gionata,* oratorio.

Petrovics, Emil (b.1930 Hungary). *The Book of Jonah* (poem by M. Babits), oratorio.

Piccini, Nicola (1728 Italy–1800 Paris). *Gionata* (Sernicola), oratorio.

Pinkham, Daniel ((1923–2006 USA). *Jonah* (Jonah, Ps. 116, 139, Prov., Ezek.).

Stockmeier, Wolfgang (b.1930 Germany). *Da Gebet Jonas (Jonas prayer),* choir, organ.

Vieru, Anatol (b.1926 Romania). *Iona,* opera.

Vinci, Leonardo (1690–1730 Naples). *Gionata,* oratorio.

Vitali Giovanni (1632–1692 Italy). *Il Giona,* oratorio.

Vogel, Vladimir (1896 Moscow–1935 Italy). *Jona gin doch nach Ninive* (M. Buber) for baritone, narrator, speaking chorus, choir, and orchestra.

MICAH

The oracles of the Judean prophet Micah are ethical in content. He taught that the essence of religion was *only to do justly, to love mercy and to walk humbly with thy God (6:8).* He was a contemporary of Isaiah.

Works List

Adler, Samuel (b.1928 Germany/1939 USA). *God's Requirements* (Mic. 6: 6–8), unison and keyboard.

Bach, J.S. (1685–1759 Leipzig). Cantata 45 *Es ist dir gesagt, Mensch* (Mi c.6:8), chorus.

Berlinski, Herman (1910 Germany/1941 USA–2001). *It Hath Been Told Thee, O Man* (Mic. 6:8), SATB, organ.

Beversdorf, Thomas (1924 Texas–1981). *Mini Motet from Micah* (Mic. 6:1–2, 12), SATB organ or harpsichord, and optional bass.

Freed, Isadore (1900 Poland–1960 New York). *The Prophecy of Micah*, oratorio.

Gould, Morton (1913 New York–1996). *Prayer of Micah (Who is a God like unto Thee)*, choir.

Lewis, John Leo (1911–1971 USA). *Who is a God Like Thee (1977)* (Mic. 7: 18–20), SATB, organ.

Mueller, Carl F. (1892–1982 USA). *Walk Humbly with thy God* (Mic. 6:8), SATB, organ/pianoforte.

Shidlowsky, Leon (1931 Chile/1969 Israel). *Lux in tenebris* (When I sit in darkness) (Mic. 7:8), orchestra.

Stern, Max (b.1947 USA/1976 Israel). *Prophecy for the End of Days (2009)* (Ezek. 28:25–26, Mic. 4:1–2, 5), narrator, mixed choir, childern's choir, percussion, shofar, strings (organ).

NAHUM

Nahum is a prophet of the northern kingdom of Israel. He was a contemporary of Joel and Habakkuk and prophesied sometime before the fall of Nineveh in 612 B.C. His theme is the divine government of the world. So filled is he with the doom of Nineveh that he spares denunciation of his own people. It is believed that he was among the captives taken by Assyria, and died somewhere on the banks of the Tigris. I have found no musical composition based on him or his prophecy.

HABAKKUK

Habakkuk prophesied in the period before the destruction of the Jerusalem. A defender of Judah, he questions the wisdom of God (1:2), and directs his attacks against the ruling oppressors, rather than focusing on the sins of the people. Chapter 3 is a theophany, in which God appears as a warrior of infinite might, giving assurance that His will must prevail. Habakkuk reduced the essence of religion to a single phrase: *the righteous shall live by his faith (2:4).* According to rabbinic tradition, Habakkuk was the son of the Shunammite woman, whom Elisha restored to life (2 Kings 4:16) (Zohar *Beshallach*).[1]

Works List

Berlinski, Hermann (1910 Leipzig/1941 USA–2001). *Habakkuk*, cantata.
Ehrlich, Abel (1915–2003). *I Will Stand Upon My Watch* (1970), mixed choir.
Hovhaness, Alan (1911–2000 USA). *I Will Rejoice in the Lord* (Hab. 3:18–19), SATB, organ.
Gilboa, Jacob (1920–2007). *Habakkuk* (3:17–19) (1977), voice, organ.
Giroust, Francois (1750 Paris–1799). *Domine, audivi, auditionem tuam* (Hab. 3).
Hanoch, Shalom (b.1946 Israel). *Gam Ata Tsodek* (Hab. 2:4), pop song.
Karni, Yehuda (1884 Poland–1949, Israel). *Shimuni Befartzhi* (Hab. 2:11), song
Kosa, Gyorgy (1897–1984 Budapest). *Habakkuk* (chapter 3), soloist, string quartet, pianoforte.
Kosma, Jozef (1905 Hungary–1969 France). *Les Cantus* (1959)(Hab. 2:19), from oratorio.
Lutoslawski, Witold (1913–1994 Poland). *Habakkuk* (chapter 3), choir.
Roff, Joseph (1910 England–1993 USA). *The Earth Shall be Filled* (Hab. 2:14, 20), 2-part choir and organ.
Steggall, Charles (1826–1905 England). *God Came from Teman* (Hab. 3:3, 6), SATB, organ.

---

1. See "Habakkuk," *Twelve Prophets*, edited by A. Cohen, Introduction by S. M. Lehrman (London: Soncino Press, 1974 [1948]) 211.

ZEPHANIAH

Zephaniah was the great grandson of Hezekiah and an older contemporary of Jeremiah. He prophesied in Jerusalem during the days of Josiah (641–610 B.C.). Zephaniah denounced evil in Judah, predicting the *Day of the Lord (1:14)*; when, after punishment, comes a promise of salvation — the exile will end, and Zion will rejoice.

Works List

Amiran, Emanuel (1909 Warsaw/1924 Tel Aviv–1993). *Baet hahi avi etchem (At that time I will bring you back)* (Zeph. 3:20), 2-voice choir.

Bender, Jan (1909 Holland/Germany–1994 USA). *Sing, O Daughters of Zion* (Zeph. 3:14, 9:9), soprano, SAB.

Martin, George Clement (b.1844 Scotland). *The Great Day of the Lord is Near* (Zeph. 1:14, 2:3), SATB, organ.

Nardi, Nahum (1901 Kiev/1924 Tel Aviv–1977). *Rani bat Zion, Hariu Israel* (Sing, O daughter of Zion, Shout O Israel) (Zeph. 3:14), 2 voice choir.

Stout, Alan (b.1932 USA). *The Great Day of the Lord is Near* (Zeph. 1:14, 2:3), SATB, organ.

Trued, S. Clarence (c.1920 USA). *Sing Aloud!* (1980) (Zeph. 3:9–17), SATB.

Wetzler, Robert (b.1932 Pennsylvania). *Offertory/Advent* (Zeph. 3:14, 17), SATB or unison, organ.

ZECHARIA

Zechariah is a post-exilic prophet whose career began in the second year of Darius, king of Persia (c.520 B.C.). He envisions angels, as agents of Divine Providence in the working of the world, and urged the rebuilding of the Temple in Jerusalem. He looks forward to the day when the kingdom of God will be established on earth.

Works List

Alexander, Haim (1915 Berlin/1936 Jerusalem). *Jerusalem Eternal* (Zech. 2), cantata for soli, choir and orchestra.

Ankri, Etti (b.1963 Israel). *Mayim Chayim* (Zech. 14:8), song.

Antes, John (18th C. Moravia, Colonial America). *Sing and Rejoice O Daughter of Zion* (Zech. 2:10), SATB, organ.

Bartei, Girolamo (c.1565 Arezzo, Italy-c.1618). *Zachariae cantico ad Davidis Psalmo* (Venice 1607).

Charpentier, Marc-Antoine (1636–1704 Paris). *Canticum Zachariae*, chapter 5, choir.

Ehrlich, Abel (1915 Germany/1939 Tel Aviv- 2003). *Al tihyu ka'avoteichem (Be not as your fathers)* (Zech. 1:4–5), acappella choir.

Fried, Avraham (b.1959 USA). *Tanya* (Zech. 1:3), Modern Hasidic song.

Geisler, Johann Christian (18th C. Moravia, Colonial America). *Sing and Rejoice, O Zion* (Zech. 2:10), SSAB, organ.

Harnik, Meir (1927–1972 Israel). *Roni veSimchi* (Zech. 2:14), song.

Heyman, Nahum (b.1934 Israel). *Tsiyon Adom* (Leah Naor) (after Zech. 1:8), song.

Hopson, Hal H. (b.1933 Texas). *Song of Zechariah*, unison, keyboard.

Joffe, Shlomo (1909 Warsaw/1930 Israel-1995). *Ve tikare Yerushalayim ir haement* (Jerusalem shall be called a city of truth) (Zech. 8), narrator, choir, and orchestra.

Kirk, Theron (b.1951 Texas). *Sing and Rejoice* (Zech.2:10), SATB.

Krivoshey, David (b.1944 Israel). *Bechatzi Halayla* (Ettinger) (after Zech. 14:18), song.

Luzon, Eli (b.1966 Israel). *Itano Lechalot Panecho* (Zech.7:2), Mediteranean folksong.

Nardi, Nahum ((1901 Kiev/1924 Tel-Aviv-1977). *Od yeshvu zekenim uzekenot birchovot Yerushalayim* (There shall yet sit old men and old women in the broad places of Jerusalem) (Zech. 8:4), 2 voice choir.

Petzold, Johannes (1912–1985 Germany). *Rejoice Greatly* (Zech. 9:9), unison, keyboard.

Powell, Robert J. (b.1932 Mississippi). *Sing and Rejoice O Zion!* (Zech. 2:10–11), 2-part, keyboard.

_____. *Rejoice Thy King Cometh* (Zech 9:9), SAB.

Titcomb, Everett (1884–1968 Boston). *Be Joyful, O Daughters of Zion* (Zech. 9:9), SATB.

Willan, Healey (1880 London–1968 Toronto). *Rejoice Greatly* (Zech. 9:9), SATB.

MALACHI

Malachi is the last of the prophets and his theme is the love of God for Israel: *I have loved you saith the Lord (1:2).* He prophesies judgment against insincerity, and negligence in religion at the coming of the Messiah. His final message is: *Behold I will send you Elijah the prophet before the coming of the great and terrible day of the Lord (3:24).*

Works List

Byrd, William (1543 London–1623). *Ab ortu solis* (Mal.1:11), 4-voice choir.

Ouseley, Frederick Arthur (F. A.) Gore (1825–1889 England). *From the Rising of the Sun* (Mal. 1:11), SATB, organ.

Powell, Robert J. (b.1932 Mississippi). *From the Rising of the Sun* (Mal. 1:11), SATB.

Sateren, Leland (1903–2007 Minnesota). *Return unto Me* (Mal. 2:2, 3:7, 4:2), SATB.

24

The Neo-Hasidic song "Eshet Hayil" is often sung as functional music for the home, venerated by Jewish communities throughout the world. It is an exception to the rule that only music of anonymous origin may be considered 'traditional.'

PROVERBS

And Solomon's wisdom excelled the wisdom of all the children of the east, and all the wisdom of Egypt. And he spoke three thousand proverbs; and his songs were a thousand and five. And there came of all peoples to hear the Wisdom of Solomon, from all kings of the earth who had heard of his wisdom (I Kings 4:30, 32, 34).

While the prophet speaks in the name of God (*Thus saith the Lord*) and the priest instructs in religious observance, the Sages teach what they believe to be right and true. The Book of Proverbs, a section of the wisdom literature of the Bible, is a body of ethical aphorisms composed and collected by Solomon and his wise men and passed down through the generations. It was written in its present form by Hezekiah and his colleagues.[1] Taken altogether the message is clear: *The fear of the Lord is the beginning of knowledge; but the foolish despise wisdom and discipline (1:7).* Unless knowledge brings one to closer to God it is misleading and meaningless. Earnest seekers in the good life, the Sages taught in what this knowledge (or wisdom) consisted. They phrased the central truths of life into terse, memorable, poetic couplets. The final chapter of Proverbs concerns: *The words of king Lemuel;[2] the burden wherewith his mother corrected him (Proverbs 31:1).*

---

1. Talmud Baba Bathra 15a.
2. The traditional opinion holds that Lemuel is one of the names of Solomon, meaning "towards (*lemo*) God (*el*)" or one who is dedicated to Him.

Ben-Zion Shenker: "Eshet Hayil" (Woman of Valor) (1952)
Text: Proverbs 31:10–31
Genre: Sabbath song
Medium: Voice (with or without accompaniment)
Style: Eastern European Hasidic
Performance time: ca. 2:30

Considering the song *Eshet Hayil's* widespread usage, many assume its origin to be the anonymous product of a hoary past. In fact, *Eshet Hayil* was written in 1952 by Ben Zion Shenker, a Hasidic singer, cantor, and composer from Brooklyn on the occasion of his marriage.[3] Shenker set the text to music in the style of Eastern European Hasidic song and it has since become a contemporary classic, sung throughout the Jewish world. The popular tune *(nigun)* has come to symbolize the most admirable values of the virtuous wife.

Biographic Context

As a child, Ben Zion Shenker (b.1925) learned Hasidic melodies from his mother. At the age of 12 he joined a choir conducted by the eminent cantor, Joshua Weisser (1888–1952), and began studying music theory and composition in 1939. A year later, after attending a religious service led by the charismatic Polish Hasidic Rabbi Saul Taube, who had recently fled to America from Europe, and was noted for his devotional songs and wordless melodies, Ben Zion became a devotee, later becoming the Rav's musical secretary — collecting, transcribing, singing, and disseminating his *nigunim*. Following Rabbi Taube's encouragement and advice, Shenker began to write his own songs; *Eshet Hayil* is one of over 400 original melodies he composed.[4]

---

3.   Shenker's *nigunim* (wordless paraliturgical melodies), stand apart from the American-influenced neo-Hasidic songs composed by his contemporary, Shlomo Carlebach. Both Shenker and Carlebach were the most important conduits for preserving and spreading a nearly lost European musical tradition in the New World. They served as prototypes for countless performers and composers of contemporary Hasidic music.

4.   In the 1950s, Shenker produced the first commercial recordings of authentic Hasidic *nigunim*. Accompanied by a professionally arranged instrumental ensemble and male choir, singing Hebrew texts with characteristic vocals in the "Modzitzer" Hasidic tradition, Shenker's recordings were soon emulated

Hasidic Music

Hasidic music is an expression of Hasidism, a mystical Eastern-European Jewish religious movement that sets piety above learning and the expression of joy, as its chief religious duty; vocal music was seen as the best medium to achieve salvation. It originated, suddenly, in the small towns of Poland and the Ukraine in the 18th century with the appearance of the charismatic Baal Shem Tov.[5] His disciples became Hasidic rabbinical leaders, known as *zaddikim* (or righteous ones), established courts at which wordless singing and snatches of melody were raised to devotional art. The Modzitzer Hasidim, originally a Polish dynasty (sect) was founded in the 19th century by Israel of Modzitz (d.1921), regarded by some as the one who transformed the wordless melody (*nigun*) into an art form.

Israel's writings devote considerable praise to the spiritual value of music: He compared the seven tones of the scale to the seven spheres of *Kabalistic* theory; and taught that "the Temple of song is adjacent to the Temple of Repentance." His son, the second Modzitzer Rebbe, Rabbi Saul Taube (d. 1947), further popularized these melodies throughout the world.[6] The Rav composed melodies in a number of folk styles: pastoral melody (*wallach*), rhythmic dance (*rikud*), waltz, and march. From these sources Ben Zion Shenker drew inspiration.[7] His tune to *Eshet Hayil* is rounded in form, designed for strophic singing, like a ballad. It is always associated with specific times (i.e. at the Sabbath table, at the wedding canopy), or on occasions when the righteous Jewish woman is to be praised.

---

by other groups of Hasidim who had managed to settle in Brooklyn after World War II (i.e. Lubavitch, Gere, Bobov, etc.). See Sam Weiss, *Nine Luminaries of Jewish Liturgical Song.* Internet resource: www.klezmershack. com/articles_s/luminaries/-56K

5. Rabbi Yisroel ben Eliezer (1698–1760), also known as the Baal Shem Tov or Besht was a mystical Jewish rabbi, considered the founder of Hasidic Judaism. Born in a small village, now part of the Ukraine, his parents were poor, upright, and pious. At school, he distinguished himself by frequent disappearances, being found in the lonely woods, rapturously enjoying the beauties of nature. Many of his disciples believed that he was descended from the royal house of King David.

6. Neil Levin, *Zemirot Anthology* (Cedarhurst, NY: Tara Publications, 1981) note 7, 132.

7. Velvel Pasternak, *Beyond Hava Nagila* (Owings Mills, Maryland: Tara Publications 1999) 81.

Text and Context

A proverb is not simply an abstract moralizing homily; behind each is a story or fable from which its lesson is derived. Aggadah relates that King Solomon married Pharaoh's daughter on the day of the Temple's dedication. She kept him awake the whole night with music, so that he slept late into the morning; and, since he kept the keys to the Temple's gates under his pillow, the morning sacrifice was delayed. Thereon, his mother, Bathsheba, exhorted him to avoid debauchery and rule justly: *Give not thy strength unto women nor thy ways to that which destroyeth kings (31:1–9).* The verses which follow (31:10–31) are her advice — they describe the character of the ideal wife, and remain, to this day, a paradigm of the virtuous woman. The tune Shenker composed is intended to be sung to the original and unaltered Hebrew text, arranged alphabetically, verse by verse.[8]

Eshet Hayil mi yimtsa, verachot mipeninim michra.
Batachba lev baalah, veshlalal loyechsar.
Gamalt hu tov, velo rah, kol yemey chayeha.
Darsha tsemer ufishtim, vataas bechefetz kapeyha (31:10–13).

Patach piha bechoch ma, vetorat chesd al leshonah.
Sofiya chalichot beytah, velechem atslut lo tochal.
Kamu baneyha veyashruha, baalah vayehallelah.
Rabot banot asu chayil, veat alit al kulanah (31:26–29).

A woman of valor who can find?
For her price is above all rubies.
The heart of her husband doth safely trust in her,
And he hath no lack of gain.
She doeth him good and not evil,
All the days of her life.
She seeketh wool and flax,
And worketh willingly with her hands (31:10–13).

---

8. As the Psalms, so also the couplets of Proverbs are structured on the principle of parallelism. This implies, that at times, the second clause is synonymous with the first (repeating the same idea in other words); at other times, it is antithetical (contrasting and contradicting the first phrase); while at still other times, the second phrase continues the initial idea, building and synthesizing it into a more complex unit of thought.

She openeth her mouth with wisdom;
And the law of kindness is on her tongue.
She looketh well to the ways of her household,
And eateth not the bread of idleness.
Her children rise up, and call her blessed;
Her husband also, and he praiseth her:
'Many daughters have done valiantly,
But thou excellest them all' (31: 26–29).

Music and Musical Exegesis

The music neither paints the imagery of the words, nor attempts to express the text dramatically; rather, it creates a general mood, onto which — like every good ballad tune — words are strung. There is a significant difference in content and construction, however, between this Jewish "ballad" and the popular form prevalent in medieval Christendom. Firstly, *Eshet Hayil* consists in words of praise only; it tells no story of love or death, nor sings of victory in war. Secondly, the text is free flowing, not structured in poetic meter and rhymed stanzas. It is the melody, alone, that generates, from this prose text, a strophic ballad-form.

Each musical phrase completes a verse from Proverbs, and the

Ex. 35. Ben-Zion Shenker: *Eshet Hayil*
Transcription by the author

entire tune fills out eight verses. Shenker's two-period[9] structure contains four 4-bar phrases: **A A B B**. Its tonal underpinning derives from a synagogue prayer mode *(Ahavoh Rabboh)*: (F) G A-flat B C D E-flat (F). A more in depth view of the song's formal design reveals that **A** phrases subdivide into two bar units: **A** = 2 + 2 or a + a; while **B** phrases are constructed of multiple 1-bar patterns. These sequence stepwise, downwards on the notes of the mode: **B** = 1 + 1 + 1 + 1 or b + b + b + c, or more precisely, b + b var. + b var.2 + d. The contrasting motivic patterning between the two lines of the tune, lend it an attractive and engaging symmetry.

Conclusion

Ben Zion Shenker is a composer whose work appeals as a realignment of traditional elements; in this case, a Hasidic Jewish ethos. His song is an example of a composition that neither strives for, nor needs to be original in an artistic sense; it is enough if the tune has merit in the eyes of a congregation who sing and cherish it as their own. It is a written melody that has entered the realm of oral tradition. At the heart of all oral traditions, and this includes the Scriptural text before it became canonized, lays a similar process of individual creativity, and collective approval and preservation. This unassuming Sabbath table song permits us occasion to encounter the music of the Bible, in our own time, as the expression of a community of faith.

In a larger sense, we glimpse into the workshops of pious and devoted, but anonymous craftsmen of earlier ages though the visor of this contemporary Hasid's creativity; those who sought not the accolades of men, but created for the glory of God. The Russian writer, Alexander Solzhenitsyn, upon winning the Noble Prize for literature, in 1970, gave voice to this ethos in his acceptance speech: *One kind of artist imagines himself the creator of an independent spiritual world and shoulders the act of creating ... When failure overwhelms him, he blames it on the age-old discord of the world, on the complexity of the fragmented and torn modern soul, or on the public's lack of understanding. Another*

---

9. A period, generally, contains eight measures of music, consisting of two phrases (question and answer), which end on a cadence. These form a complete musical sentence or statement.

artist acknowledges a higher power above him and joyfully works as a common apprentice under God's heaven.[10]

Other Directions

Proverbs in Art Music

An entirely different direction in setting Proverbs is to be found in the madrigal *Freue dich des Weibes deiner Jungen* ("Rejoice in the wife of thy youth"), from *Israelis Brunlein (The Fountain of Israel)* (1623) — a collection of 21 sacred compositions for 5 and 6 voices and continuo by German Baroque composer Johann Hermann Schein (1586–1630).[11]

Text
Proverbs 5:18–19
Freue dich des Weibes deiner Jungen

Rejoice with the wife of thy youth.
Let her be as the loving hind and pleasant roe;
Let her breasts satisfy thee at all times;
And be thou ravished always with her love.

This four-minute work cuts across the boundary between sacred and secular music, with rhythms that are lively, often dance-like. Characteristic Italian madrigal motifs mold the text into expressive melodic shapes that both: imitate and interweave in polyphonic textures, and alternate in homophonic chordal blocks.

Insofar as Schein's primary aim is that the spiritual message of the text be transmitted with the greatest degree of conviction, he does not hesitate to incorporate into his work the latest Italian secular styles of his day. We observe the curious interface between the prevalent culture of another age and personal religious beliefs, at once serious and religious — though not necessarily liturgical. It is a paradigm repeated again and

---

10. Alexander Solzhenitsyn, *Nobel Lecture*, translated by F.D. Reeve (New York: Farrar, Straus and Giroux 1972) 4.
11. Schein, an early predecessor of J.S. Bach's at St. Thomas Church, studied both law, as well as music. His work at St. Thomas, from 1616, required him to teach ten hours of Latin and four hours of singing each week. Although sacred music was his love, secular music was not foreign to his world.

again throughout history — drawing techniques of the secular into the sphere of the sacred.

Works List

Alexander, Haim (b.1915 Berlin/1936 Jerusalem). *Oved admato* (Prov. 28:19), choir.

Alman, Shmuel (1887 Ukraine–1947 London). *Etz hayyim* (Prov. 3:18, 17), choir.

Asgeirsson, Jon (b.1928 Iceland). *From the Proverbs*, motet, choir.

Ben-Haim, Paul (1897 Munich–1981 Tel Aviv). *Ashrey adam* (Prov. 3), voice, pianoforte.

_____. *Divrey Agur* (Prov. 30), soprano, mezzo-soprano, pianoforte/ orchestra.

Berger, Jean (1909 Germany–2002 USA) *For The Lord Giveth Wisdom* (Prov. 2:6–8), SATB.

_____. *Happy is the Man* (Prov. 3:13–16), SATB.

_____. *Go to the Ant, Thou Sluggard* (from Of Wisdom and Folly) (Prov. 6:8–9), SATB

Blank, Allan (b.1925 New York). *Lines from Proverbs*, choir.

Brahms, Johannes (1833 Hamburg–1897 Vienna). *Denn es gehet den Menschen* (Prov. 3:19–22), choir.

_____. *Ich wandte mich und sahe.* (Prov. 4:1–3), choir.

Brandon, George (1924–2000 USA). *Trust in the Lord* (Prov. 3:5, 6), SATB, keyboard.

Braun, Yehezkel (b.1922). *Proverbs* (1992), Cantata for children's choir (SMA), flute, harp.

_____. *King Solomon's Proverbs* (1993). 28 canons for 2–3-part equal voices.

Castelnuovo-Tedesco, Mario (1895 Italy–1968 USA). *Proverbs of Solomon*, 2 tenors, 2 basses.

Clark, Keith (20th C. USA). *Happy is the Man Who Finds Wisdom* (Prov. 3), SATB.

Cram, James (d. 1973 USA). *Favor and Good Understanding* (Prov. 3:1–4), SATB, keyboard.

Da-Oz, Ram (1929 Berlin/1934 Haifa). *Yesh mit'asher ve-eyn kol* (Prov. 13:7), SA.

_____. *Al tithalel be-yom mahar* (Prov. 27:1), SA.

_____. *Pagosh dov shakul be-ish* (Prov. 17:12), SA.

Dagan, Yisrael (b.1961 Israel). *Oz Vehadar* (after Prov. 31:25).

Davis, Katherine (1892–1980 USA). *Trust in the Lord* (Prov. 3:5–6), SATB or SSA, keyboard.

Effinger, Cecil (1914–1990 USA). *Forget Not My Law* (Prov. 3:1–6), TTBB, organ.

Ehrlich, Abel (1915 Germany/1939 Israel–2003). *I Call to All Men* (1975), for 2-part choir (SS).

Ford, Virgil T. (1912–1980 USA). *Be Not Wise in Your Own Eyes* (Prov. 3:5, 7, 13–14, 19), SATB, keyboard

Freed, Isadore (1900 Poland–1960 USA). *A Woman of Valor* (Prov. 31), SATB

Gesius, Bartholomaeus (c. 1560–1613 Frankfurt). *Proverbiorum Salomonus*, 8vv.

Gideon, Miriam (1906 Greeley, Colorado–1996 New York). *The Habitable Earth*, cantata for soloist, choir, oboe, and pianoforte.

Goehr, Alexander (b.1932 Germany/UK). *Little Cantata of Proverbs*, SATB.

Hajdu, Andre (b.1932 Hungary/1966 Israel). *Three Songs from the Book of Proverbs* (1990) for 2-part women's or children's choir (SA), 2 percussions, pianoforte.

Hutson, Wihla (1901–2002 USA). *In All Thy Ways Acknowledge Him* (Prov. 3:6), SATB, organ.

Intzik, Smuel (b.1938 Israel). *Eshet Hayil* (Prov. 31:10), song.

Janequin, Clement (c. 1525–1555 France). *Proverbes de Salomon*, 4 voices.

Krejci, Miroslav (1891–1964 Prague). *Kniha prislovi*, voice, pianoforte.

Krenek, Ernst (1900 Austria–1991 USA). *There Be Three Things* (Prov. 30:18–19), SATB.

_____. *There Be Four Things* (Prov. 30: 24–28), SATB.

Kriti, Oded (b.1983 Israel), Gideon Levi (b.1976 Israel). *Bani* (after Prov. 10:15), song.

Lasso, Orlando di (1532–1594 Flanders). *Beatus Homo* (Prov. 3:13–14), 2-part.

_____. *Expectatio Justorum* (Prov. 10:28–29), 2-part.

Lavry, Marc (1903 Riga–1968 Haifa). *Oved admato* (Prov. 1:8, 12:11).

Levy, Ernst (1895–1981 Switzerland). *Hear Ye Children* (Prov. 4:1, 7–8), SSA/SSA.

Linn, Robert (1925–1999 USA). *Anthem of Wisdom* (Prov. 3: 16–17, 8:1–5, 9:1–6), SATB, pianoforte.

McCormick, Clifford (20th C. USA). *Trust in the Lord* (Prov. 3:5–7), SATB, keyboard.

Mechem, Kirke (b.1925 USA). *Songs of Wisdom* (1970), soprano, alto, tenor, bass, SATB.

Mellnas, Arne (1933–2002 Sweden). *Ten Proverbs* (1981), soprano, alto, tenor, bass, SATB.

Milhaud, Darius (1892 France–1974). *Cantata from Proverbs*, women's choir, harp, oboe, violoncello.

Moe, Daniel (b.1926 USA). *Exhortation from Proverbs* (Prov. 3:1–2, 13–16), SATB, 2 trumpets, 2 trombones, horn, tuba.

Nystedt, Knut (b.1915 Norway). *If You Receive My Words* (1973) (Prov. 2:1–15, 3:1–4), SATBB.

_____. *The Path of the Just* (Prov. 4:18–23), SATB.

_____. *All the Ways of a Man* (Prov. 16:2–9, 16–20), SATB.

Parker, Alice (b.1925 USA). *A Merry Heart* (Prov. 17:22), 7-part.

_____. *Bow down Thine Ear* (Prov. 22:17), 5-part (from Sunday Rounds).

Powell, Robert J. (b.1932 USA). *Trust in the Lord* (Prov. 3:5–7), SATB, organ.

_____. *Honor the Lord with thy Substance* (Prov. 3:9–10), SAB.

Rorem, Ned (b.1923 Indiana). *Two Psalms and a Proverb* (Prov. 23:29–35), choir, string quartet.

Salomon, Karel (1897 Heidelberg–1974 Jerusalem). *Ha-lo hokhmah tikra* (Prov. 8), alto, organ, string quartet.

Schein, Johann Hermann (1586–1630 Leipzig). *Freue dich desWeibes deiner Jugend* (Prov. 5:18–19), 5 voices, basso continuo.

_____. *Wem ein tugendsam Weib bescheret ist* (Prov. 31:10–13), 5 voices, basso continuo madrigal.

_____. *Lieblich und schoene sein ist nichts* (Prov. 31:30–31), 5 voices, basso continuo, madrigal.

Sowerby, Leo (1895–1968 USA). *My Son, If Thou Wilt Receive* (Prov. 2:1–6, 8), SATB, organ.

Spies, Claudio (b.1925 Chile/USA). *Proverbs on Wisdom* (Prov. 1:20–23, 33, 3:7, 19–20), TTBB, organ, piano.

Starer, Robert (1924 Vienna–2001 N.Y.). *Five proverbs on love*, choir.

Stocker, Richard (b.1938 England). *Proverbs* (1971), SATB, organ (or 2 oboes, clarinet, 2 bassoons, 2 trumpets, 3 trombones).

Wagner, Naphtali (b.1949 Israel). *For Out of It* (1991), children's choir (SSAA), oboe.

Weckerlin, Jean Baptiste (1821–1910 France). *Four proverbs*, voice and pianoforte.

Weissensee, Friedrich (1560–1622 Germany). *Hochzeitslied aus den Sprichwoertern Salomonis* (Prov. 31), 6 voices.

Wiesenberg, Menachem (b.1950 Israel). *Go to the Ant you Sluggard* (1991), Motet for 3-part choir (SSA).

Wilkinson, Scott (20th C. USA). *Happy the Man* (Prov. 3:13), SATB.

Wood, Ralph Walter (b.1902 London). *Happy is the man that findeth wisdom*, choir, pianoforte.

William Blake: The Lord Answering Job out of the Whirlwind, *Illustrations of the Book of Job* (1826)

Ralph Vaughan Williams' ballet suite, *Job: a Masque for Dancing*, places ultimate purpose on stage. By contrasting euphony with dissonance, and the regular flow of Renaissance dance with disjunctive 20th-century rhythm, it finds musical analogy to philosophical dialectic — in pondering the moral question: "Why do the righteous suffer?"

JOB

And the Lord said unto Satan: 'Hast thou considered my servant Job, that there is none like him in the earth, a whole-hearted and an upright man, one who feareth God, and shunneth evil? Then Satan answered the Lord and said: 'Doth Job fear God for nought? Hast Thou not made a hedge about him, and about his house, and about all that he hath, on every side? Thou hast blessed the work of his hands, and his possessions are increased in the land. But put forth Thy hand now and touch all that he hath, surely he will blaspheme Thee to Thy face.' And the Lord said unto Satan: 'Behold, all that he hath is in thy power; only upon himself put not forth thy hand.' So Satan went forth from the presence of the Lord   (Job 1:8–13).

Job denied the resurrection of the dead and judged the prosperity of the wicked and the woes of the pious only by their earthly fortunes.[1] Yet, his faith in God is unshakeable. He serves God, neither for reward in the present, nor the hereafter, but, solely and unconditionally for love. Most of this philosophical book struggles to reconcile faith with reason over the question: In a world governed by a just and omnipotent God, why do the righteous suffer? Is affliction simply a punishment for sin or has it dimensions beyond human comprehension?[2] The book's conclusion

---

1.   *He that goeth down to Sheol shall come up no more (Job 7:13).* "This shows that Job denied the resurrection of the dead" (Talmud Baba Bathra 16a).
2.   The book speaks powerfully and comfortingly to people who, in their search for meaning, have found orthodox faith difficult, and cannot be reconciled to

is that man cannot comprehend divine wisdom.[3] One of the wisdom books of the Bible, Job tells the story of the most pious Gentile that ever lived. Its authorship has been attributed to Moses.[4] The Book of Job is considered among the great works of world literature.

Ralph Vaughan Williams: Job — A Masque for Dancing (1930)

Scenario: Geoffrey Keynes and Gwendolyn Raverat
Genre: Ballet
Medium: Symphony orchestra
Style: Modal
First performance: Cambridge, England, 1931

Job is a ballet-pantomime inspired from illustrations by English engraver and mystic, William Blake. It tells Job's story of suffering in a lush and piquant score, which breathes the air of rural England. The *Masque* owes its direct existence to Geoffrey Keynes, a Blake scholar and ballet fan who devised the scenario in 1928, during the centenary year of the artist's death. Keynes' assistant was his sister-in-law, scenic designer Gwendolyn Taverat, who also happened to be a cousin of Ralph Vaughan Williams.[5] She suggested Vaughan Williams for the project, who completed the score in 1930.

Biographic Context

Ralph Vaughan Williams (1872–1958) is perhaps the most important English composer of the 20th century. His father, a clergyman, died

---

the clichés and formulas of conventional religion (which frequently equates poverty and suffering with punishment for sin; health and prosperity with reward for righteousness).

3. It is beyond human ken. Next to all the great good that God does, individual suffering is insignificant. Temporary setbacks may occur to the righteous, but ultimately great reward is given.

4. Talmud Baba Bathra 15a argues that Job was a contemporary of Moses and cites, through inference from similarity of phrases, the verse: *Would that they were inscribed in a book (Job 19:23)*, implying that it is Moses (who is called inscriber), as it is written, *And he choose the first part for himself, for there was the lawgiver's* [literally translated from the Hebrew as inscriber's] *portion reserved (Deut. 33:21)*.

5. The work was offered to the Russian impresario Sergei Diaghilev (1872–1929), who turned it down.

when the future composer was still a boy. An aunt taught him piano and theory at home. At primary school Ralph learned the violin. Studies at Trinity College and the Royal College of Music under Parry, Stanford, and Wood were later supplemented under Max Bruch in Berlin (1897), and with Maurice Ravel in Paris (1908). English folk song and church music, along with the sophisticated English madrigal of the Tudor period (16th and 17th centuries), shaped and influenced his musical style. Much of Vaughan Williams' connection to the Bible derives from his editorship of *The English Hymnal*, a collection of 800 country tunes and sacred vocal works from the 16th to the early 20th century, which he gathered together and published in 1906.[6]

Text, Context, and Subtext

According to Midrash, Job was a wealthy landowner, merchant, and the king of Edom. His book portrays him as a charitable, upright, and God fearing man — whose life was struck by tragedy. His oxen and asses were stolen. A fire burned his sheep. Bandits fell on his camels. His servants were killed. A tornado smashed the house where his children were eating and drinking, and killed them. His body was stricken with disease (1:13–19). Yet, for all this, Job refuses to acknowledge personal guilt for his suffering nor curse his maker. *And he said: Naked came I out of my mother's womb, and naked I shall return thither; The Lord gave and the Lord hath taken away; Blessed be the name of the Lord (1:21).*

Four relatives come to comfort Job during the week of his mourning (*Shiva*);[7] each, in turn, attempts to rationalize Job's tragic misfortune. His uncle, Eliphaz the Temanite, said: *Shall mortal man be just before God (4:17)?* Job replies: *Is there injustice on my tongue (6:30)?* A distant cousin, Bildad the Shuhite, remarked: *Doth God pervert judgment (8:3)?*

---

6. Besides composing and lecturing in Europe and the United States, Vaughan Williams served as professor of composition at the Royal College of Music (1919–1939), and for nearly half a century, he was conductor of the Leigh Hill Festival (1905–1953).

7. The *Shiva* is an ancient seven day mourning period in the house of a mourner. According to tradition, Job was the great-grandson of Esau. His four friends (Eliphaz, Bildad, Zophar and Elihu) are all relatives. Their fathers Shuah, Namat, and Barachel were brothers, sons of Buz, and grandsons of Abraham's brother Nahor. Job's first wife died during the seven-year period of his tribulation. His second marriage was to Jacob's daughter, Dinah.

Job retorted: *I am innocent (9:21)*. Then, Zophar the Naamathite added, accusingly: *If iniquity be in thy hand, put it far away (11:14)*. Job again, protested: *Though He slay me, yet will I trust in Him (13:15)*. And finally, a younger cousin, Elihu, the son of Barachel the Buzite, perked up: *God will not do wickedly; the Almighty will not pervert justice (34:12)*. It was enough; rationality had reached its limits. It was time for God to intervene. *The Lord answered Job out of the whirlwind (37:1)*. In Job's defense, God appeared to Eliphaz: *'My wrath is kindled against thee and against thy two friends; for ye have not spoken of Me the thing that is right, as My servant Job hath' (42:7)*. This revelation is puzzling; for, while suffering is no sure proof of sin — ultimate purpose and meaning are beyond human comprehension. The consolation of the righteous is to be found, then, only in the knowledge that they are never completely cut off from the fellowship of God. *So the Lord blessed the latter end of Job more than his beginning (42:12)*.[8]

Literary and Visual Sources

The ballet *Job — a Masque for Dancing* owes its existence to a single literary and visual source: William Blake's *Illustrations of the Book of Job* (1826).[9] Blake's interest in the Book of Job dates from early in his career. He illustrated it according to his own religious lights, drawing upon Judeo-Christian tradition and a uniquely personal spiritual understanding. These illustrations consist in 21 lithograph plates, with accompanying commentary, taken mostly from the Book of Job, but explained and amplified in verses drawn from the Old and New Testaments, including the Apocrypha.[10] Blake's images do not entirely

---

8.   Ginzberg, *Legends of the Bible* (1956) 266 ff.
9.   William Blake (1757–1827) was a pre-20th-century engraver and mystic multimedia artist who developed a technique for engraving metal plates with both text and illustrations, which he then lithographed and colored by hand. He envisioned a parallel between the man of his time, whom he saw as a cog in an increasingly materialistic industrial revolution, and the biblical Job, caught in a web of laws and rationality. In Blake's vision, imagination and forgiveness were religious virtues — Man and Job could become free through belief in the spiritual and artistic nature of salvation. Although Blake's eccentric work was little understood by his contemporaries, he is recognized today as one of the giants of the Romantic Movement, both as artist and poet, and seems to embody all that we now think of as poor but misunderstood genius.
10. These are: Genesis, Deuteronomy, 1 Samuel, Psalms, Isaiah, and Daniel; as

follow the sequence of events as narrated in the Bible, and scenes are added, which do not always tally with the text. The scenario of the ballet, *Job,* on the other hand, follows the sequence of the story as it appears in the Bible. The essential action is divided into nine scenes, which summarize six chapters of Job: 1, 2, 3, 32, 38, and 42. Most of the teleological arguments of the book have been excluded from the ballet.

The Masque

In the late Middle Ages, the Masque was a form of festive and courtly entertainment — involving music, dancing, singing, acting, and elaborate stage design. English court masques were often performed at wedding feasts in the 16th century. For subject matter, a masque might combine mythology and fable with timely political, social, and ethical allegory. Ralph Vaughan Williams' *Job* is closer to a ballet than an authentic court masque, since the designation 'masque' serves to indicate that its dance movements derive, from Renaissance dances, rather than from abstract modern dance.

Music and Musical Exegesis

Ralph Vaughan Williams' score, while written in a sophisticated 20th-century musical idiom, draws upon English folk music and the madrigal of the Elizabethan period for its substance. Embracing the idyllic spirit of rural England, he evokes the gentle, everyday feelings of the common people by means of this countryside music, and, largely ignores the proud, pompous confidence of the ruling gentry — the music of 18th-century England, personified in the works of Handel. It is Vaughan Williams' metaphor for righteousness.

SCENARIO
Job, a Masque for Dancing

SCENE I
Job and His Family. Thus Did Job Continually (Blake: PLATE 1)

Introduction, part 1: The blessed Job — *There was a man in the land of*

---

well as Matthew, Luke, Corinthians 1 & 2, John, and Revelation.

Uz, whose name was Job; and the man was whole hearted and upright, and one that feared God and shunned evil. And there were born unto him seven sons and three daughters (1:1–2).

DETAIL

Scene I
Introduction. Pastoral Dance. Satan's appeal to God.
Saraband of the Sons of God.

Scene 1 is like the exposition of a symphony. A gently flowing string theme represents Job, seated with his wife; while his daughters dance to a solo flute. A woodwind figure sounds the bleeps of far-off flocks. The blessings of Job and the choir of angels are presented in rich modal polyphony. Satan's entrance is marked by truncated thrusts and sinister minor chord gestures in the brass. God is revealed in majestic euphony. A stately Saraband (in three-quarter time) symbolizes the adoration of the sons of God.

Satan before the Throne of God (Blake: PLATE 2)

Part 2: The Dialogue: Satan enters. The heavens open. God in His majesty — *Hast thou considered my servant Job, that there is none like him in the earth, a whole hearted and upright man that feareth God, and shunneth evil (1:3)?* Satan — *But put forth Thy hand now and touch his bone and his flesh, surely he will blaspheme Thee to Thy face (2:5). And the Lord said unto Satan: 'Behold he is in thy hand; only spare his life'* (2:6).

Vaughan Williams approaches the dialogue between Satan and God, as a musical duel for the soul of Job. Vaughan Williams tells the story of suffering and anguish, forces of love at war with forces of hate, through the transformation of tender, human folk themes. He depicts this duality melodically, harmonically, and rhythmically. Consonance opposes dissonance, diatonicism challenges chromaticism, symmetry versus asymmetry, flowing meter confronts spastic gesture. Lyricism, major chords, and rich polyphony serve as tonal metaphors for Job, God, and the Angels, while the Devil is portrayed in harsh sonorities and angular rhythms. Within this basic dichotomy, themes interact and metamorphose. It is, as if to say: 'the devil is not inhuman, only a distortion of human feelings'. This technique, while primarily illustrative and narrative, takes on symphonic dimensions through motivic juxtapositions and contrasts, repetition, variation, and development.

SCENE II

Satan Going Forth from the Presence of the Lord (Blake: PLATE 5)

Satan's Dance of Triumph — *So Satan went forth from the presence of the Lord (1:12).*

DETAIL

Scene II

God's throne is empty. Satan in wild triumph seats himself upon it.

Satan's satanic glee and triumph are depicted in a wild distortion of Scene 1. Vaughan Williams introduces a grotesque variation of the *Saraband of the Sons of God* in the guise of a scherzo.[11] It symbolizes mock adoration of the Almighty by Satan; a distortion of the plainsong *Gloria in excelsis* is sounded in the brass. Eventually, Satan assembles the host of hell and seats himself on the divine throne. It is a perverse variation on God's majestic theme and purpose.

SCENE III
Job's Sons and Daughters Overwhelmed by Satan (Blake: PLATE 3)

Minuet of the sons of Job and their wives: tranquility is visited by disaster. Satan converts the scene from contentment to lament: *Then came a great wind, and smote the four corners of the house and it fell upon the young men, and they are dead (1:18).*

SCENE IV
Job's Evil Dreams (Blake: PLATE 11)

Job's Dream — *Then thou scarest me with dreams, and terrifiest me through visions; so that my soul chooseth strangling, and death (7:14–15).*

SCENE V
The Messengers Tell Job of His Misfortunes (Blake: PLATE 4)

Dance of the Three Messengers — *And there came a Messenger unto Job and said: 'The oxen were plowing and the Sabeans came down and they have slain the young men with the sword' (1:14–15). While he was yet speaking, there came another and said: 'The fire of God is fallen from heaven, and hath burned up the flocks, and the young men, and consumed them and I only am escaped alone to tell thee' (1:16).*

---

11. It is based on Beethoven's String Quartet, Op. 135. Vaughan Williams notes in his chapter, "A Musical Autobiography," *I cribbed Satan's dance from Job deliberately from the Scherzo of Beethoven's last quartet.* See Ralph Vaughan Williams, *National Music and Other Essays* (London: Oxford University Press, 1963) 190.

Satan Smiting Job with Boils (Blake: PLATE 6)

Naked I came out of my mother's womb, and naked I return thither; The Lord gave, and the Lord hath taken away; blessed be the name of the Lord (1:20).

SCENE VI
Job's Comforters (Blake: PLATE 7)

Dance of Job's Comforters — *What, 'Shall we receive good at the hand of God and shall we not also receive evil'(2:10)? And when they lifted up their eyes afar off, and knew him not, they lifted up their voice and wept; and they rent every man his mantle, and sprinkled dust upon their heads towards heaven (2:12).*

Man that is born of a woman is of few days, and full of trouble. He cometh forth like a flower, and withereth; he fleeth also as a shadow, and continueth not. And dost Thou open Thine eyes upon such a one, and bringest me into judgment with Thee (14:1–3)?

DETAIL

Scene VI
Dance of Job's comforters. Job's curse. A vision of Satan.

Job's dialogue with his friends is caricatured by an alto saxophone solo. Initially it feigns faint concern, then rises to anger and reproach in an accusing staccato. Pushed beyond endurance, a parody of Heaven's noble theme bursts forth suddenly in the orchestra. Job cowers in fearsome terror. Satan stands triumphant.

Job's Despair (Blake: PLATE 8)

Job's Curse — *Let the day perish wherein I was born, and the night wherein it was said: 'A man-child is brought forth' (3:3).* Satan's Celebration.

SCENE VII
The Wrath of Elihu (Blake: PLATE 12)

Part 1 — Elihu's Dance of Youth and Beauty — *I am young, and ye are very old; wherefore I was afraid, and durst not declare you mine opinion. Lo, all these doth God work, twice, yea thrice, with a man, to bring back his soul from the pit, that he may be enlightened with the light of the living (32:6; 33:29–30).*

DETAIL

Scene VII (There is no break between VI and VII)
Elihu's dance of youth and beauty. Pavane of the Heavenly Host.

Elihu's rebuke is depicted by a solo violin; it is a pentatonic theme
embellished with chromatic alterations. Thus, Vaughan Williams

portrays ambivalence; human nature, partaking both of (a diatonic) Heaven and (a chromatic) Hell.

The Lord Answering Job out of a Whirlwind (Blake: PLATE 13)

Part 2 — Pavane of the Sons of the Morning — *Then the Lord answered Job out of the whirlwind, and said: Who is this that darkeneth counsel by words without knowledge (Job 38:1–2)? Who maketh the clouds his chariot and walketh on the wings of the wind (Psalm 104:3)?*

In contrast, resplendent triads symbolize the Lord's answer to Job. The *Pavane of the Sons of God* opens up into an outpouring of divine grace, majesty and grandeur. It is cosmic emanation played-out within the frame of a Renaissance dance.

SCENE VIII
The Fall of Satan (Blake: PLATE 16)

Part 1 — Satan enters and is dismissed — *Hell is naked before Him, and destruction hast no covering (26:6).*

When the Morning Stars Sang Together (Blake: PLATE 14)

Part 2 — Galliard of the Sons of the Morning — *Where wast thou when I laid the foundations of the earth; when the morning stars sang together, and all the sons of God shouted for joy? Canst thou bind the chains of Pleiades, or loose the bands of Orion (38:4, 7, 31)?*

Job's Sacrifice (Blake: PLATE 18)

Part 3 — Altar Dance — *Now therefore, take unto you seven bullocks and seven rams, and go to My servant Job, and offer up yourselves a burnt-offering; and my servant Job shall pray for you (42:8).*

SCENE IX
Job and His Family Restored to Prosperity (Blake: PLATE 21)

Epilogue — *So the Lord blessed the latter end of Job more than his beginning; so Job died, being old and full of days (42:12, 17).*

Conclusion

Vaughan Williams was a gruff, down-to-earth man who loathed pretentiousness, and shared much in common with Blake's iconoclastic brand of Protestantism. Throughout his career, Vaughan Williams pursued the democratic, egalitarian ideals he believed in. Born into the privileged intellectual middle class, he rejected an officer's commission and enlisted as a common British soldier in the First World War. Later in life, he refused knighthood. His personal beliefs were humanistic and agnostic. When he set sacred texts, it was to express a sense of communion with people, rather than affirm religious faith. Vaughan Williams' composition is a metaphor, asserting the healthiness of folk music and the deeply human values of rural England.

Stylistically, these attitudes translate into a rejection of many 20th-century musical axioms: Popular music — because of its vulgarity and commercialism; Impressionism — because of its sophisticated 'art for art's sake' aloofness; and Dodecaphony — because of its convoluted and abstract intellectualism. Vaughan Williams' artistic voice is his personal way of standing up for something fundamental and true, negating, in tonal terms, as did Job in his protests, the smug notion that God rewards the righteous while punishing the wicked.

Related Directions

Among the saintly patrons of music, Saint Job appeared suddenly, during the 14th–18th centuries in France, Germany, England, and especially in Holland and Belgium. This tradition is thought to derive from an interpretation of Job's complaint: *Therefore is my harp (kinnor) turned to mourning, and my pipe (uggav) into the voice of them that weep (Job 30:31).* Another possible source lies in the Job mystery plays, which were based largely on the apocryphal *Testament of Job*. All these traditions are reflected in the many paintings and illustrations which show Job being consoled (and, sometimes, also mocked — cf. Job 30:1, 7, 9, 14) by musicians (mostly wind-instrument players).

Motet collections of the first half of the 16th century include a number of settings from the Book of Job (by Claudin de Sermisy, Pierre de La Rue, L. Senfl, L. Morales, T. Crecquillon, and J. Clemens non Papa), mainly of the sadder verses (a symptom of the early Baroque period's emphasis on demonstrative repentance scenes). These treatments culminate in Orlando di Lasso's two extended settings for four voices: *Sacrae lections novem ex propheta Hiob* (1565) and *Lectiones sacrae ex libris Hiob excerptae musics numeris* (1582). The first setting is extremely pathetic, the second, more restrained. Further settings of the period were those by Jacobus (Handl) Gallus and Joachim á Burck (1610).

From about the turn of the seventeenth century, Protestant composers increasingly favored the half-verse: *I know that my Redeemer liveth (Job 19:25)*, of which there are two settings by Heinrich Schutz. The rise of the oratorio form had, meanwhile, produced several works on the subject by G. Carissimi, P. d'Albergatti, and Bach's Cantata no. 160, *Ich weiss dass mein Erloeser lebt*. The most famous setting of this text is the contralto aria from G. F. Handel's *Messiah* (1742), *I know that my Redeemer liveth,* engraved on the scroll held by Roubillac's statue of Handel on the composer's grave in Westminster Abbey.

There are few oratorios on the theme in the 19th century. Frederick Shepherd Converse's *Job* (performed in Hamburg, 1908), was one of the first works by an American composer to be represented in Europe. Besides Vaughn Williams' *Job* suite for orchestra, he also wrote *The Voice out of the Whirlwind*, for choir and organ. Jacques Maritain adapted the biblical text for Nicolas Nabokov's oratorio *Job* (1932). Other modern works include György Kósa's *Hiob* (cantata, 1933); Hugo Chaim Adler's *Hiob* (oratorio, 1933); Lehman Engel's *Four Excerpts from Job* (for voice and piano, 1932); and Luigi Dallapiccola's *Giobbe* (oratorio, 1949).

Petr Eben's *Job for organ and narrator* (1987) (58') is an eight-movement meditation on destiny, faith, and the mystery of creation. An episodic, densely textured work, its often obtuse and massive exterior is made comprehensible through Scriptural citations narrated between sections. A completely different approach is found in Max Stern's *Song of the Morning Stars* (1979) (8'). This orchestral prelude depicts the stars glistening at the dawn of creation, in mixed meters and bright tonalities. Its binary structure parallels the verse: *When the morning stars sang together, and all the sons of God shouted for joy (Job 38:7).*

Works List

Adler, Hugo Chaim (1894–1955). *Hiob*, cantata.

Albergati, Pirro (1663–1735 Bologne). *Giobbe*, oratorio.

Andriessen, Hendrik F. (1892–1981 Netherlands). *Job* (Job 37:1–3), bass, choir and organ, cantata.

Anfossi, Pasquale (1727–1797 Rome). *Giobbe* (N. Angeletti), oratorio.

Bach, Johann Christian (1735 Leipzig–1782 London). *Parce mihi, Domine* (Job 7:16), soprano and orchestra.

_____. *Taedet animam meam* (Job 10:1), soprano and orchestra.

_____. *Manus tuae* (Job 10:8), soprano and orchestra.

Bach, Johann Michael (1648–1694 Germany). *Ich weiss dass mein Erloser lebt* (Job 19:25–27), SATBB.

Baird, Tadeusz (1928–1981 Poland). *Egzorta*, narrator, choir and orchestra.

Barber, Samuel (1910–1981 USA). *Motetto on Words from the Book of Job* (1930), double chorus.

Barker, Ken (20th C. USA). *Where Were You?* (1981) (Job 38:4–7), SATB, piano.

Bartulis, Vidmantas (b.1954 Lithuania). *Job the Loser* (2003), oratorio for 5 soloists, mixed choir and orchestra.

Ben-Haim, Paul (1897 Munich–1981 Tel-Aviv). *Wenn man doch meinen Kummer* (Job 6, 2), soprano, alto, tenor, 2 basses.

_____. *Der Mensch vom Weibe geboren* (Job 14:19), soprano, alto, 2 tenors, 2 basses.

Berger, Jean (1909 Germany–2002 USA). *Man Born of Woman* (Job 14: 1–2), SATB.

Bergsma, William (1921–1994 USA). *Confrontation from the Book of Job* (1963), SATB, 2 flutes, clarinet, bass clarinet, saxophone, 2 horns, 2 trumpets, 2 trombones, tuba, timpani, 4 percussions, pianoforte, violoncello, double bass.

Bitgood, Roberta (1908, Connecticut–2007). *Job*, cantata for choir,

Boyce, William (1710–1779 England). *O Where Shall Wisdom Be Found?* (Job 28:12–13, 15, 23–28), SATB, organ.

Brahms, Johannes (1833–1897 Vienna). *Warum ist das Licht* (Job 3:20–23), choir and instruments.

Byrd, William (1543–1623 England). *Cunctis diebus* (Job 10:20–22), 6 voices and choir.

Carissimi, Giacomo (1605–1674 Rome). *Job*, oratorio.

Converse, Frederick Shepherd (1871–1940 Newton, Mass.). *Job*, oratorio.

Dallapiccola, Luigi (1904–1975 Florence). *Job*, oratorio.

Desderi, Ettore (1892 Italy–1974). *Job*, cantata.

Dittersdorf, Karl Ditters von (1739 Vienna–1799 Bohemia). *Giobbe* (I. Pintus), oratorio.

Eben, Petr (1929–2007 Czech Republic). *Job* for organ and narrator.

Ehrlich, Abel (1915–2003 Israel). *Job's Last Answer* (1976) for mixed choir.

384

_____. *Job* (1990), oratorio for tenor, baritone, mixed choir, children's choir, and orchestra.

Eisenmann, Will (1906 Stuttgart–1992). *Die Klage Hiobs*, symphonic cantata for bass, choir and orchestra.

Engel, A. Lehman (1910 Jackson, Mississippi–1982 New York). *Job,* voice and pianoforte.

Epstein, David (1930–2002 USA) *The Lament of Job* (1980), 3 sopranos, 3 altos, tenor, SATB, 3 speakers, 2 percussions, pianoforte, 2 violoncellos.

Guerrini, Guido (c.1890–1965 Rome). *Il lamento di Job*, bass, pianoforte, gong and strings.

Guy, Noa (b.1949 Israel). *And Everyone an Earring of Gold* (1984), for women's or children's choir (SSA).

Haas, Joseph (1879–1960 Munich). *Die Hochzeit des Jobs* (L. Andersen), opera.

Haines, Edmund (20th C. UK). *Dialogues from the Book of Job* (1965) (Job 21:22–23, 25–26, 28–29), soprano, alto, SSAA, piano.

Haller, Hermann (1914 Switzerland–2002). *Erbarmt euch mein*, alto, choir and organ, cantata.

Handel, G. F. (1685–1759 London). *The ways of Zion do mourn* (Job 29:11–12, 14), funeral anthem.

Hensel, Fanny Cecilia (1805 Hamburg–1847 Berlin). *Hiob*, alto, choir and orchestra, cantata.

Herder, Ronald (20th C. USA). *The Job Elegies* (1966) (Job 3:3, 13, 18–21a), alto, SATB.

Huber, Klaus (b.1924 Bern). *Hiob* (P. de Chardin), baritone, organ and tape.

Jacobi, Frederick (1891–1952 New York). *Hagiographa: Job*, string quartet and pianoforte.

Jergenson, Dale (20th C. USA). *The Lament of Job* (1975), SATB.

Josquin, Depres (c.1440–1521 Belgium). *Responde mihi* (Job 13:22–28), 4 voices, motet.

Kapp, Artur Josepowitsh (1878–1952 Estonia). *Iow* (J. Kalijuvee), oratorio.

Kelterborn, Louis (1891–1933 Switzerland). *Hiob*, oratorio.

Klein, Bernhard (1793–1832 Koln). *Job*, oratorio.

Klenau, Paul (1883–1946 Copenhagen). *Hiob*, choir.

Kosa, Gyorgy (1897–1984 Budapest). *Hiob*, cantata, baritone and instruments.

Kunc, Bozidar (1903 Zaghreb–1964 USA). *Two chapters from the Book of Job*, cantata.

Lasso, Orlando di (1532–1594 Munich). *Sacrae lectiones ex Propheta Job*, 4 voices, motet.

Le Flem, Paul (1881–1984 France). *Job* (L. Bertus), radiophonic oratorio.

Leeuw, Ton de (1926 Rotterdam–1996 Paris). *Job* (L. Bertus), radiophonic oratorio.

Loewe, Karl (1796–1869 Germany). *Hiob*, cantata.

Manneke, Daan (1939- Netherlands). *Job*, men's choir and instruments.

Mechem, Kirche (b.1925 USA). *The Protest of Job* (1970) (Job 3:3, 23–26; 14:7, 9, 11–12), SATB.

Milhaud, Darius (1892–1974 France). *Job* (Job 37:1–13), cantata, bass, choir and organ.

Morley, Thomas (c.1557–1602 England). *I Know That My Redeemer Liveth* (Job 19:25–27), SATB.

Nabokov, Nikolai (1903 Belarus–1978 New York). *Job* (J. Maritain), oratorio.

Newbury, Kent (20ᵗʰ C. USA). *Wisdom and Understanding* (Job 28:20–21, 23–28), SATB.

Oertzen, Rudolf von (1910–1990 Belgium). *Hiob*, choral symphony.

Otto, Julius (1804–1877 Dresden). *Hiob* (J. Mosen), oratorio.

Parry, Hubert (1848–1918 England). *Job*, oratorio, soloist, voices, choir and orchestra.

Perroni, Giovanni (1688 Italy–1748 Vienna). *Giobbe*, oratorio.

Peters, Flor (1903–1986 Belgium) *I Know That My Redeemer Liveth* (Job 19:25), SATB, organ.

Prohaska, Karl (1869–1927 Vienna). *Aus dem Buch Hiob*, 8 voices and organ.

Purcell, Henry (1659–1695 London). *Let the night perish* (Job 3), solo song, basso continuo.

_____. *Man that is born of woman* (Job 14:1–2), choir and basso continuo.

Queralt, Francisco (1740–1825 Barcelona). *El santo Job*, cantata.

Rabaud, Henri (1873–1949 Paris). *Job* (Ch. Raffalli & H. de Grosse), oratorio.

_____. *Deuxieme poeme lyrique sur le livre de Job* (tr. E. Renan), baritone, orchestra.

Reger, Max (1873–1916 Leipzig). *Mein Odem ist schwach* (Job 17), 5 voices, choir and organ, motet.

Russell, William (1777–1813 London). *Job*, oratorio.

Schreck, Gustav Ernst (1849–1918 Leipzig). *Woher kommt denn die Weisheit* (Job 28:20–28), choir.

Schutz, Heinrich (1585–1672 Germany). *I Know That My Redeemer Liveth* (Job:25–27), SSAATBB.

Schulz, Svend Simon (1913 Denmark). *Job*, oratorio.

Schwab, Felician (1611–1661 Germany). *Cithara patientis Jobi*, motet.

Senfl, Ludwig (1486 Basel–1555 Munich). *Cum aegrotasset Job*, 5 voices.

Stern, Max (1947 USA/Israel). *Song of the Morning Stars* (1979) (Job 38:7), prelude for orchestra.

Studer, Hans (1911 Bern–1984). *Die Leiden Hiobs*, oratorio.

Vaughan Williams, Ralph (1872–1958 London). *Job* (K. Keynes), A Masque for Dancing, ballet-orchestral suite.

_____. *The Voice of the Whirlwind* (Job 38:1–11, 16–17, 40:7–10, 14), SATB, organ

Vellones, Pierre (1889–1939 Paris). *Job*, oratorio.

Veretti, Antonio (1900 Verona–1978 Rome). *Job*, oratorio.

Wesley, Samuel S. (1766–1837 England). *Man That is Born of a Woman* (Job 14:1–2).

Wilbye, John (1575–1638 England). *Homo natus de muliere* (Job 14:1–2, SSAATB

Ziani, Marc-Antonio (1653 Venice–1715 Vienna). *Il mistico Giobbe*, oratorio.

26

This chapter discusses a contemporary Israeli motet, Yehezkel Braun's *Cantici Canticorum*, in its relation to historic interpretations of Song *of Songs*. It treats the text as a national religious allegory and strives for a style touched by the arid landscape of the Holy Land.

SONG OF SONGS (CANTICLES)[1]

The Song of Songs, which is Solomon's. Let him kiss me with the kisses of his mouth, for thy love is better than wine (1:1–2)... The king hath brought me into his chambers (1:4)... By night on my bed I sought him whom my soul loveth; I sought him, but I found him not (3:1)... Go forth, O ye daughters of Zion, and gaze upon king Solomon, even upon the crown wherewith his mother crowned him... In the day of the gladness of his heart (3: 11).

Song of Songs is a series of erotic love poems. One of the most popular books of the Bible, tradition assigns authorship of the text to Solomon,[2] divinely anointed king of Israel, noting that it was written by him in his youth.[3] All the same, it remains a puzzlement how such a manifestly sensual poem could enter into Holy Writ. Perhaps, authenticity validates tradition: Just because of the scroll's truly exalted origin and

---

1. This collection, one of the shortest in Scripture, containing only 117 verses, is known by many names. In the Hebrew Bible it is called *Shir Hashirim*, in the Latin Bible its title is *Canticorum*. These terms are often translated as *Song of Songs* and *Canticles*. In the King James Version, it is named *Song of Solomon*.
2. Meaning that it was either written or commissioned by him. See Max Stern, "Three Faces of King Solomon: Musical Interpretations of Songs of Songs, Proverbs, and Ecclesiastes," *Wisdom of Life & Life Poetry*, ed. by L. Makovetsky, N. Davidovitch, O. Bartana (Ariel University Center, Israel 2008) xx–xxvii.
3. "For it is the way of the world that when a man is young he composes songs of love" (Midrash Song of Songs Rabbah 1.10).

the allegory attached to it — interpreting Song of Songs as an allegory of steadfastness and love between God and Israel — Song of Songs was admitted into the canon, despite rabbinic misgivings centuries later.[4] The early Christian church embraced this exegesis, identifying Solomon himself as the bridegroom, and the daughter of Pharaoh as the bride; but transposed the allegory of the sanctified union between man and woman to Christ and his church — the love of Jesus for the individual soul, or the love of the soul for God, the most intimate of relationships.[5]

Yehezkel Braun: Cantici Canticorum Caput III (1973)
Text: Song of Songs, chapter 3
Genre: Motet
Medium: Solo and choir (SATB)
Style: Modal
First performance: Eighth Zimriya Festival, Israel, July 1973
Duration: ca. 11 minutes

Biographic Context

Yehezkel Braun (b.1922, Breslau, Germany/1924, Palestine) belongs to the first generation of Israeli composers, educated in Palestine, who sought a renewal of the ancient homeland[6] through the creation of ethically oriented works, outside the forms and formats of traditional liturgy. Lyrically conceived, his modal choral music represents the "acceptable" Israeli choral style, and is frequently performed by school

---

4. See Gerson D. Cohen, "The Song of Songs and the Jewish Religious Mentality," *The Canon and Mesorah of the Hebrew Bible*, ed. by Sid Z. Leiman (Ktav, New York 1974) 262–282. This is also the view of Eliezar Schweid, Professor Emeritus of Jewish philosophy at Hebrew University of Jerusalem, in conversation with the author on May 13, 2008.
5. See Saint Bernard of Clairvaux (1090–1153), "Sermons on the Songs," available in full on Internet resource: http://www.pathsoflove.com/bernard/songof-songs/contents.html
6. Modern Zionism is a political movement for the ingathering of the Jewish people and reestablishment of a Jewish national state in the ancient homeland. It is an offshoot of the prophetic concept of Zion, a hill in Jerusalem, the heavenly city, the site of the Temple, the royal residence of David and his successors, and the place of God's habitation on earth: *For out of Zion shall go forth the law, and the word of the Lord from Jerusalem (Isa. 2:3).*

choirs and those of the kibbutz movement. In these works Braun brings Renaissance polyphonic technique and knowledge of Gregorian chant to bear upon the folk music of Israel's ingathered Oriental communities, which he fuses into a style at once thoughtful and accessible. His *a cappella* choral motet *Cantici Canticorum Caput III* was commissioned for the 25th anniversary of The State of Israel and premiered at the Eighth International Zimriya Choral Festival, 1973.

Growing up in the settlement of Rishon LeZion, as a child Yehezkel was exposed to the rich ethnic traditions of Yemenite, Persian, Babylonian, and Sephardic Jewish communities. In his 20s, Braun joined Kibbutz Mishmar Hanegev (1940–1951),[7] and there absorbed the Zionistic concept of music as a social coordinate.[8] Both experiences left their mark on his style. He later studied composition with pioneer Israeli composer and critic, Alexander Uriah Boskovich (1907–1964), at the Tel-Aviv Academy of Music (1947–1953), returning there to teach until his retirement. In the 1970s, Braun pursued other directions: studies in Classics at Tel-Aviv University (MA, 1972), and Gregorian chant at the Benedictine monastery of Solesmes (1975). *Cantici Canticorum* is a product of this period. Yehezkel Braun received the prestigious Israel Prize for lifetime achievement in 2001.

Text and Context

Braun seeks to establish (through its Latin title, *Cantici Canticorum*), a connection between contemporary Israeli choral music and the Latin motet of the Middle Ages. He sets each verse (or couplet) of chapter 3 as a separate movement, following Catholic practice: I — verses 1–2; II — verses 3–4; III — verse 5; IV — verse 6–7; V — verse 9–10; VI — verse 11.

---

7. He served four of those years in the Jewish Brigade during WWII.
8. Throughout the 19th century choral singing and music festivals were associated with nationalism. Zionism was a late comer to the movements that stirred up national consciousness among the peoples of Western and Eastern Europe. The first Jewish choral group, called Hazomir Choral Society, 1899 was organized in Lodz, Poland; others followed. Early choral singing in Palestine began in the kibbutz, a collective settlement in Palestine for the resettlement of the land. The kibbutz repertoire consisted in group singing of arrangements of Eastern European and Yiddish folk songs, along with Hasidic *nigunim* — to Hebrew texts.

Song of Songs, Chapter 3

I

By night on my bed I sought him whom my soul loveth;
I sought him, but I found him not.
I will rise now, and go about the city in the streets,
And in the broad places I will seek him whom my soul loveth:
I sought him, but I found him not (3:1–2).

II

The watchmen that go about the city found me: to whom I said,
Saw ye him whom my soul loveth?
It was but a little that I passed from them, but I found him whom
my soul loveth:
I held him, and would not let him go, until I brought him into my
mother's house,
And into the chamber of her that conceived me (3:3–4).

III

I charge you, O ye daughters of Jerusalem, by the roes, and by the hinds
of the field, that ye stir not up, nor awake my love, till he please (3:5).

IV

Who is this that cometh out of the wilderness like pillars of smoke,
Perfumed with myrrh and frankincense, with all powders of the merchant?
Behold his bed which is Solomon's;
Threescore valiant men are about it, of the valiant of Israel.
They all hold swords, being expert in war;
Every man hath his sword upon his thigh because of fear in the night
(3:6–8).

Each movement combines studied simplicity with sophisticated innocence — often characteristics of popular love songs. It is an approach
that harmonizes with traditional interpretations of the book — viewing
Song of Songs, not, as deeply personal erotic love poetry between man
and woman, but as a national religious allegory between God and his
people.[9]

---

9. Shlomo Kaplan, program note from the score.

DETAIL

V

Solo:

> King Solomon made himself a palanquin of the wood of Lebanon.
> He made the pillars thereof of silver, the top thereof of gold,
> The seat of it purple, the inside thereof being inlaid with love,
> From the daughters of Jerusalem (3: 9–10).

On the surface, these verses would appear to portray Solomon in his majestic palanquin.[10] Allegorically, the *palanquin* represents the Tabernacle.[11] The *silver* signifies the hooks of the Tabernacle's pillars. The *gold* refers to the covering of the Ark. The *seat of it purple* symbolizes the partition between the Holy and the Holy of Holies (with its ark, cover, Cherubim, and Tablets). *The inside thereof,* the inner sanctum of the Holy of Holies, stands for the passionate conjugal *love* that exists between God and Israel. The God-fearing ones, the *daughters of Jerusalem* are those beings, spiritually whole before the Holy One, blessed be He.[12]

Music and Musical Exegesis

Braun sets movement V as an extended soprano solo, evocatively sung by one of the daughters of Jerusalem. Its descriptive quality recalls the Oriental introductory improvisation *(taqsim)*. Its function is the same — to introduce the rhythmic and dance-like movement which follows.

It starts with an upward leap of a minor seventh (A [c] — g), then gravitates downwards, stepwise, in a stylized tumbling strain (g f e d e). It is a characteristic of many improvised introductory sections *(petichot)* to liturgical poetry *(piyutim)* in Near Eastern synagogue *(bakashot)* traditions. Plaintively, the singer recounts the *pillars,* the *seat,* the top of

---

10. A palanquin is a covered carriage, usually for one person, carried by poles on the shoulders of two or more men, or placed on the back of a camel or elephant.

11. These interpretations are based on Rashi (1040–1105), leading commentator on the Bible and Talmud, from *Shir Hashirim*: Song of Songs / An allegorical translation by Nosson Scherman (New York: Mesorah Publications, 1977).

12. Ibid., 123–4.

Ex. 36. Yehezkel Braun: *Cantici Cantorum Caput III*
© Copyright 1973 by Hamercaz Letarbut Ulechinuch. Used by permission.

gold, and the inside of the *palanquin inlaid with love*. Then, this quasi-archaic cantilena winds its way along, in an East–West mix, resolving downwards by the skip of a perfect fourth, like an Ashkenazi cantorial recitation.[13] Three elements define this wistful solo: its initial leap, its slow cascading descent, and its final plagal cadence.[14]

DETAIL

VI

The last movement contrasts imagery of the *daughters of Zion* and *crown*. The biblical commentator Rashi interprets *daughters of Zion* as

---

13. It is a plagal cadence, descending from d to A.
14. It calls to mind also the relationship between Gregorian antiphon and hymn, and prompts us to conjecture: Is this Oriental pattern of free improvisation and rhythmic, dance-like song, the source for the Western liturgical sequence of antiphon and hymn?

those distinguished to behold God — by virtue of circumcision, phylacteries *(tefillin)*, and fringes on garments *(tzitzis)*. The *crown* represents natural phenomena and human deeds — vehicles, through which God manifests himself in the world.

Chorus:

> Go forth, O ye daughters of Zion, and gaze upon king Solomon,
> Even the crown, wherewith his mother hath crowned him in the day of his
> espousals, And in the day of the gladness of his heart (3:11).

Ex. 37. Yehezkel Braun: *Cantici Cantorum Caput III*

© Copyright 1973 by Hamercaz Letarbut Ulechinuch. Used by permission.

This lively, syncopated movement juxtaposes block format with many-voiced imitative polyphony. The phrase, *Go forth, O ye daughters of Zion,* is presented with march-like determination, while the following phrase, *Even the crown wherein his mother crowned him*, is defined by imitative texture. Such differences contrast the candid, innocent call to the daughters of Zion to *Go forth*, with the complex inner world of Solomon's regal *gladness of heart* — symbolic of the complex calculations involved in the building of the Temple. Modality is pure "white note" throughout — Dorian, Aeolian, and Phrygian modes (with cadences on D, A, F, G).[15] It is Braun's way of indicating — by way of tonality — unadulterated innocence and freedom from sin. The summation of the entire motet, on a triumphant A-major triad, stands for Solomon's wedding day, allegorically, the day on which Israel received the Torah on Sinai.

Conclusion

Yehezkel Braun's choral works strive to realize of the Zionist "melting pot" ideology of his generation, and often integrate biblical texts with Eastern Mediterranean and Ashkenazi Jewish folk song. Braun's themes are informed with textual implications. His approach is to smooth and homogenize the "kinks" out of ethnic sources, distilling them into something new and original. The purity and clarity of the vocal cantilena is molded equally after Sephardic synagogue cantillation and Yiddish folk song. The "Israeli" quality of the harmony derives from its free interweaving of tertian triads with quartal sonorities. In the manner of a Renaissance madrigal, he contrasts and blends homophonic and polyphonic writing: textures varying from solo monologue to full ensemble, often expanding elastically from block harmony into imitative counterpoint. Each of the six movements of *Cantici Canticorum* builds to a climax.

Rabbi Akiva (ca. 50–135 AD) declared that if the other books of the Bible are holy, Song of Songs is "the holy of holies."[16] As if this were not praise enough, this greatest of Jewish sages added that "the whole world attained its supreme value only on the day when the Song of Songs was given to Israel."[17] One of the ways Braun translates Akiva's

---

15. The role of white notes (i.e. on the piano) consciously reverts back to the simplicity of Gregorian modes, and, consequently, ecclesiastical attitudes about music.
16. Talmud Megillah 7a.
17. Mishnah Yadaim iii.5.

biblical vision into music is by side-stepping visceral rhythms and the tactile quality of instruments, and alluding to the free flowing natural-ness and purity of folk song and dance. Braun associates the worlds of biblical cantillation, Oriental melisma, Yiddish folk song, Gregorian modality, and Palestrina-like polyphony — with a world of virtue. This sense of repressing the physical is revealed, also, in his rejection of the color saturation and sensual innuendos of Late Romanticism. Braun's strict avoidance of chromatic harmony is a conscious musical choice, suggesting the subjugation of flesh to spirit. All these technical devices reinforce the rabbinic interpretation of the text and serve the aim of Social Zionism: that of creating music for a society touched by the spirit of tradition and the arid purity of the Holy Land *(Eretz Yisrael).*

Related Works

Ralph Vaughan Williams: Flos Campi Suite (1925)
Subtext: Song of Songs
Medium: Viola, chorus, small orchestra
Style: English modal
First performance: Royal College of Music, London, 1925

Ralph Vaughan Williams' *Flos campi (Flower of the Field)* (1925), a suite for viola solo, wordless chorus, and small orchestra, is an unusual 20th-century work. Latin texts from Song of Songs are printed in the score, intended to be understood by the listener, but neither spoken nor sung. It alternates wistful speech-like viola calls with yearning choral responses, in a free rhapsodic form. Vaughan Williams once described this lush sensual work as one "concerned with the spirit's liberation and the incarnation of spirit in flesh."[18]

DETAIL

Flos Campi

1. *Sicut Lilium inter spinas (2:2, 5)*

As the lily among the thorns, so is my love among the daughters...

---

18.   As cited in Cecil Bloom, "The Hebrew Bible in Music," *Midstream* (New York: Theodore Herzl Foundation, January/February 2007) 43.

Stay me with flagons; comfort me with apples; for I am sick of love.

2. *Jam enim hiems transit (2:10–11)*

> For, lo, the winter is past, the rain is over and gone,
> The flowers appear on the earth;
> The time of the singing of birds is come,
> And the voice of the turtle is heard in our land.

3. *Quaesivi quem diligit anima mea (3:1; 5:8; 6:1)*

> I sought him whom my soul loveth, but I found him not…
> 'I charge you O daughters of Jerusalem, if ye find my beloved, that ye tell
> him that I am sick of love'…'Whither is my beloved gone, O thou fairest
> among women? Whither is thy beloved turned aside?
> That we may seek him with thee'.

4. *En lectum Salomonis (3:7–8)*

> Behold his bed [palanquin] which is Solomon's;
> Three score valiant men are about it…
> They all hold swords, being expert in war.

5. *Revertere, revertere Sulamitis! (7:1–2)*

> Return, return, O Shulamite! Return, return, that we may look upon thee…
> How beautiful are thy feet with shoes, O Prince's daughter!

6. *'Pone me ut signaculum super cor tuum' (8:6)*

> 'Set me as a seal upon thine heart'.

Other Directions

In the music of the 15th and more frequently the 16th century, settings of Canticles in the Vulgate were generally composed for liturgical purposes since its verses and sections formed part of Marian celebrations.[19]

---

19. Marian celebrations commemorate events in the life of Mary, mother of Jesus, which take place throughout the year in the Catholic Church. They honor the Blessed Virgin Mary, asking for her intercession before the throne of God. Four of the most famous antiphons attached to them are: "Alma Redemtoris Mater," "Ave Regina Caelorum," "Regina Coeli," and "Salve Regina." See *Dictionary of Mary* (New York: Catholic Book Publishing Co., 1985) 387–392.

Early examples are settings of *Quam pulchra es* by John Dunstable and King Henry VIII of England. Sixteenth-century composers of motets and motet-cycles include most of the great "Netherlanders" and their Italian successors. On the other hand, in the 17th century the functions and forms of settings became diversified. Although Monteverdi's choral *Nigra sum* and *Pulchra es* were used as Marian praises, his *Ego flos campi (I am a flower of the field and lily of the valleys)* and *Ego dormio* were composed as songs for alto voice and continuo.

German Protestant settings were mostly intended as wedding songs. With the rise of Pietism, they once more assumed a religio-allegorical function. Among Schutz's many settings in both Latin and German, *Ich beschwoere euch* (1641) is a *dialog* approaching dramatic form. *Meine Freundin du bist schoen* by Johann Christoph Bach, another wedding piece, practically concludes a period in the musical history of Song of Songs. The 18th century did not favor the text, although one rare exception was William Boyce's *Solomon, a Sereneta ... taken from the Canticles* (1743), with dialogues between "He" and "She" and choirs.

In the 19th and 20th centuries, the dramatic, or at least dialogic, potential of the text again appealed to composers. The 19th-century works include: *Total pulchra es* by Bruckner; Charbrier's cantata, *La Sulamite;* Leopold Damrosch's oratorio, *Sulamith;* and oratorios entitled *Canticum cantorucum* by Enrico Bossi and Italo Montemezzi. 20th-century composers include: Virgil Thompson (*Five phrases from the Song of Solomon,* for soprano and percussion); Jacobo Ficher (*Sulamita,* symphonic poem); Rudolf Wagner-Regeny (*Shir Hashirim,* for choir; German text by Manfred Sturmann); Lukas Foss (*Song of Songs,* for soprano and orchestra); Jean Martinon (*Le Lis de Saron,* oratorio); Stanislaw Skrowaczewski (*Cantique des cantiques,* for soprano and 23 instruments); Arthur Honegger (*Le Cantique des Cantiques,* ballet); Carl Berg (*Das Hohelied,* for choir); and Mario Castelnuovo-Tedesco (*The Song of Songs,* scenic oratorio); also settings of "Set me as a seal upon thine heart," for Reform Jewish wedding ceremonies.

Among settings by Israeli composers, the best known are the oratorio *Shir ha-Shirim* by Marc Lavry, and the solo song *Hinach Yafah* by Alexander Uriah Boscovich (based on the traditional Ashkenazi intonation of the text). Several choral settings have also been composed for the introductory parts of the Kibbutz Seder ceremonies, which traditionally open with the celebration of Spring. Folk-style settings of single verses and combinations of verses are especially numerous (i.e. Nissimov: *Ana*

Halakh Dodekh, Kol Dodi). Their role was particularly important in the formative years of Israeli folk dance, during the late 1940s. The need for lyric couple-dances — as against prevailing communal dances (i.e. Hora, Debka, and Polka-like couple-dances) — led to an ideological conflict, which was resolved by basing the new, more tender dances on the so-called "historical" spiritualized precedent of Song of Songs. It is noteworthy that Song of Songs scarcely appears in traditional Jewish music outside its liturgical function — no doubt because of rabbinic prohibition against singing it "like a folksong" (Talmud Sanhedrin 101a). Contemporary Israeli popular, folk, and even, rock songs on texts from Songs of Songs, abound:

- Aloni, Yair: *Ani Yesna Velibi Er* (5:2).
- Ariel, Meir: *Shir Ganuv* (after 7:1–11)
- Eilat, Dafnah: *Ki Hineh Hastav Avar* (2:11).
- Galili, Rivka: *Ani Yesna Velibi Er* (5:2–6).
- Hatzlil Ha Oud: *Hanhilah Hitbalbeleh* (2:4), Mediteraneanized folksong.
- Heyman, Nahum: *Nitzanim Nirim Baaretz* (2:11–13); *Megadim* (7:14); *Im Lo Tedilach* (1:15–17, 2:1–2).
- Nissim, Meir: *Shechora Ani Venavah* (1:5, 2:1).
- Reichel, Idan: *Hinach Yafah* (4:1–3).
- Sharabi, Boaz: *Shir Hashirim* (1:1–3).
- Shuki, Shuki: *Gan Naul Achoti* (4:12).
- Tabib, Michael: *Achot Lanu Ketanah* (8:8).
- Teplo, Naomi: *Ki Hineh Hastav Avar* (2:1).

Works List

Ahle, Johann Rudolf (1625–1673 Germany). *Komm meine Braut vom Libanon*, 4 voices and 4 instruments.

Amiran, Emanuel (1909 Warsaw–1993 Tel Aviv). *Shehorah ve-na'avah* (Sg 1:5–6), voice and pianoforte; *Shuvi, shuvi, ha-Shulamite* (Sg 7:1), 2 voices, and choir.

Avni, Tzvi (b.1927 Germany/1933 Tel Aviv). *Three Songs from Song of Songs* (1957) for soprano or tenor, and piano.

Bantock, Granville (1868–1946 London). *The Song of Songs*, soloist, voices, choir and orchestra.

Bardi, Benno (b.1890 Germany/1933 London). *Hymn to Love*, oratorio.

Bardos, Lajos (1899–1986 Budapest). *Enek a dalrol*, mixed voices.

Baudoin, Noel (1480–1529 Antwerp). *Quam pulchra es* (Sg 4), choir.

Ben-Haim, Paul (1897 Munich–1981 Tel Aviv). *Ani havatselet ha-Sharon* (Sg 2:1), soprano and pianoforte.

_____. *Gan na'ul*. (Sg 4:12–13, 15–16), soprano, mezzo soprano, pianoforte/orchestra.

Berg, Carl Natanel (1879–1957 Stockholm). *Solomos voga disa*, voice and orchestra.

Berneker, Konstanz (1844–1906 Germany). *Das hohe Lied*, choir.

Billings, William (1746–1800 Boston). *The Rose of Sharon* (Sg 2:1–11), 4 women's voices, anthem.

Blackford, Richard (b.1954 UK). *From Song of Songs*, soprano, pianoforte.

Boisdeffre, Rene Le Mouton de (1834–1906 France). *Le cantique des cantiques*, Opus 80 (E. Cabrol), soprano, tenor and pianoforte.

Boskovich, Alexander (1907 Transylvania–1964 Tel Aviv). *Hinakh yafah ra'ayati*, voice and pianoforte.

_____. *Behold Thou Art Fair* (1947), alto, orchestra (or string quartet).

_____. *Daughter of Israel*, tenor, choir and orchestra.

Bossi, Enrico (1861–1925 Rome). *Canticum Canticorum*, cantata, bass, soprano, choir, orchestra, organ.

Bouzignac, Guilaume (d.1641 France). *Tota pulchra es*, choir.

Braun, Yehezkel (b.1922 Germany/1924 Israel). *Shir ha-shirim* (Sg 3:1–11), choir.

_____. *Nigra sum* (1995), alto, violin

Britten, Benjamin (1913–1976 England). *My beloved is mine*, canticle.

Bruckner, Anton (1824–1896 Vienna). *Tota pulchra es*, choir and organ.

Burian, Amil-Frantisek (1904–1954 Prague). *Pisen* (M. Brod), voice, band, instr.

Buxtehude, Dietrich (c.1637–1707 Lubeck). *Ich bin eine Blume zu Sharon* (Sg 2:1–3), alto, strings, basso continuo.

Carissimi, Giacomo (1605–1674 Rome). *Nigra es sed Formosa*, 2 sopranos, basso continuo, motet.

_____. *Quam pulchra es*, soprano and basso-continuo.

Castelnuovo-Tedesco, Mario (1895 Florence–1968 Beverly Hills, Calif.). *Songs of the Shulamite*, soprano, flute, harp and string quartet.

_____. *The Song of Songs*, a rustic wedding idyll, soprano, tenor, baritone, choir, dancers and orchestra.

Chausson, Ernst (1855 Paris–1899). *Tota pulchra es* (Sg 4:7), choir.

Clemens Non Papa, Jacobus (c.1510-c.1556 Antwerp). *Adjuro vos filiae Jerusalem*, 3 voices.

_____. *Ego flos campi*, 3 voices.

_____.*Tota pulchra es*, 3 voices.

_____.*Veni in ortum meum*, 3 voices.

Crueger, Johannes (1589–1663 Berlin). *Achtstimmig Hochzeitsgesang* (Sg 4), 8 voices, choir.

Damrosch, Leopold (1882 Posen–1885 New York). *Sulamith*, soloist, choir, orchestra.

Danielis, Daniel (1635 Belgium–1696 France). *Adjuro vos filiae Sion*, voice, 2 violins, basso continuo.

David, Karl Heinrich (1884–1951 Italy). *Das hohe Lied Salmonis*, soprano, tenor, women's choir, orchestra.

Dessau, Paul (1894 Hamburg–1979 Berlin). *Song of songs*, 4 women's choirs a cappella.

Dunstable, John (1370–1453 London). *Quam pulchra es* (Sg 7), 3 voices.

Edel, Yitzchak (1896 Warsaw–1973 Tel Aviv). *Shir ha-Shirim*, 3 songs, soprano, pianoforte.

Elwart, Antoine (1808–1877 Paris). *Tota pulchra es* (Sg 4:7), 2 sopranos, organ.

Ephros, Gershon (1890 Poland–1978 USA). *Biblical suite*, tenor, choir, pianoforte/orchestra.

Erbse, Heimo (1924 Germany–2005 Austria). *Das Hohelied Salomo's*, soprano, baritone and orchestra.

Fabritius, Albinus (16th C. Italy). *Quam pulchra es*, 6 voices and choir.

Foss, Lucas (1922 Berlin/1937 USA). *Song of Songs*, soprano, orchestra/pianoforte.

Fossa, Johannes (c.1540–1603 Munich). *Adjuro vos filiae Jerusalem*, 4 voices and viola da gamba.

Franck, Melchior (1579–1639 Germany). *Geistliche Gesaenge aus dem Hehenlied Salomonis*, 5/6/8/ voices.

Friedmann, Aron (1855–1936 Berlin). *Salomo's hohe Lied* (M. Mendelssohn), voice and pianoforte.

Gabrieli, Andrea (1510–1586 Venice). *Filiae Jerusalem*, choir.

Geist, Christian (1640–1711 Copenhagen). *Adiuro vos o filiae Jerusalem*, 4 voices, 2 violins and basso-continuo.

Gnessin, Michael (1883–1957 Moscow). *Song of Songs* (M. Gnessin), voice and pianoforte.

_____. *Ahot lanu ketanah*, voice and pianoforte.

Gombert, Nicolas (c.1505-c.1556 Europe). *Quam pulchra es*, 6 voices.

Gorczycki, Grzegorz Gerwazy (1664–1734 Cracow). *Tota pulchra es*, choir.

Grainger, Percy Aldridge (1882 Australia–1961White Plains, NY). *Love verses from the Song of Solomon*, choir and orchestra.

Grimm, Carl Hugo (1890–1978 Ohio). *Song of Songs*, choral work.

Hawes, Patrick (b.1958 UK). *Song of Songs*, soprano, SATB, violin.

Hemsi, Alberto (1898 Rhodes–1964 Paris). *Shir ha-Shirim* (Sg 1:4), soprano, pianoforte.

_____. *Hinakh yafah ra'ayati* (Sg 1:14–16), voice, pianoforte.

Honegger, Arthur (1892–1955 Paris). *Le Cantique des cantiques*, oratorio.

Horst, Anton van der (1899 Amsterdam–1965). *Two fragments from Song of songs*, choir and orchestra.

Hovland, Egil (b.1924 Norway). *The Song of Songs*, soprano, violin, percussion instruments and pianoforte.

_____. *Lilja-Ord um kjoerleik*, narrator and orchestra.

Jacobson, Maurice (1896 London–1976 Brighton). *Song of Songs*, voice and pianoforte.

Johannes de Limburgia (15th C. France). *Pulchra es anima mea*, 3 voices.

_____. *Descendi in ortum meum*, 3 voices.

_____. *Tota pulchra es*, 4 voices.

_____. *Surg propera amica mea*, 4 voices.

Johansson, Bengt (1914–1989 Helsinki). *I sat down under his shadow*, choir.

_____. *Set me as seal*, choir.

Josquin, Depres (c.1440–1521 Belgium). *Ecce tu pulchra es* (Sg 1:14–16, 2:1–5), 4 voices, motet.

_____. *Descendi in ortum meum* (Sg 6:10–12), 4 voices, motet.

Keller, Wilhelm (b.1920 Austria). *Lied der Freundlin*, soprano, flute and harp.

Krein, Alexander (1883–1951 Moscow). *Ani havatselet ha-Sharon*, soprano and pianoforte.

Laderman, Ezra (b.1924 USA). *Song of Songs* (1977), soprano, flute, viola, violoncello.

Ladmirault, Paul (1877 France–1944 Italy). *Tota pulchra es* (Sg 4:7), soprano, violin, organ, string quartet.

Lasso, Orlando di (1532–1594 Munich). *Quam pulchra es*, 5 voices.

_____. *Veni in hortum*, 5 voices.

Lavry, Marc (1903 Riga–1967 Haifa). *Song of Songs* (Max Brod) (1940) for soprano, tenor, bass, bass, mixed choir, orchestra, oratorio.

Lechner, Leonhard (1553–1606 Stuttgart). *Das Hohelied Salomonis*, 4 voices.

Lederer, Joseph (1733–1796 Germany). *Das hohe Lied Salomonis*, musical; *Cantica Salomonis* (A. Weyermann), voice and harpsichord.

Leeuw, Ton de (1926 Rotterdam–1996 Paris). *Car nos vignes sont en fleur*, choir.

Leichtentritt, Hugo (1874 Germany–1951 Cambridge, Mass.). *Song of Solomon*, alto and orchestra, cantata.

Leoni, Leone (c.1560–1627 Italy). *Adjuro vos filiase*, 2 voices.

_____. *Ego dormio*, 8 voices.

_____. *Nigra sum sed formosa*, 8 voices.

Levi-Tanai, Sara (1911–2005 Jerusalem). *Kol dodi*, voice and pianoforte.

Levy, Yehuda (b.1939). *For Lo, The Winter is Past* (1990) for 2-part women's or children's choir (SA).

Lier, Bertus van (1906–1972 Netherlands). *Het Hooglied*, soloist, choir, orchestra.

Loewe, Karl (1796–1869 Germany). *Das hohe Lied Salomonis* (Byron) (translated by F. Theremin), voice and pianoforte.

Lorenzini, Raimondo (c.1730–1806 Rome). *Nigra sum sed formosa*, choir and basso continuo.

Lukacic, Ivan (1587–1644 Croatia). *Osculetur me* (Sg 1:2–3), voice, basso continuo.

_____. *Trahe me post Te* (Sg 1:4–5), voice, basso continuo.

_____. *In lectulo meo* (Sg 3:1–4), 2 voices, basso continuo.

_____. *Quam pulchra es* (Sg 4:1–7), 4 voices, basso continuo.

Lupi, Johannes (1506–1539 France). *Nigra sum sed formosa*, 4 voices.

Mackenzie, Alexander (1847 Edinburgh–1935 London). *The rose of Sharon* (J. Bennet), oratorio.

Martinon, Jean (1910–1976 Paris). *Le lis de Saron*, oratorio.

Melartin, Erkki (1875–1937 Finland). *Morning song*, cantata.

Mezzogori, Giovanni Nicolo (17th C. Italy). *Song of Songs* — 13 motets, 2–4 voices and basso-continuo.

Monteverdi, Claudio (1567–1643 Venice). *Quam pulchra es*, 1–8 voices.

_____. *Nigra sum sed formosa filiae Jerusalem*, 1–8 voices.

Mussorgsky, Modest (1839–1881 Russia). *Hebrew song* (L. Mey), voice and pianoforte.

Nakaseko, Kazu (1908 Kyoto–1973). *Two songs of Solomon,* soprano and pianoforte.

Nardi, Nahum (1901 Kiev–1977 Tel Aviv). *Samuni notera et ha-keramim* (Sg 1:6), soloist, 2 voices and choir.

_____. *Ha-yafah ba-nashim* (Sg 1:8), soloist, 2 voices, choir.

Nissimov, Nissim (1909 Bulgaria–1951 Israel). *Ki hiney hastav avar* (Sg. 2:11–13), choir.

_____. *Ana Halakh Dodekh* (Sg 6:1–4), choir.

Nivers, Guillaume Gabriel (1632–1714 Paris). *Quam pulchra es,* 2 voices and basso continuo.

Novak, Jan (1921–1984 Czech Republic). *Carmina Sulamitis,* mezzo-soprano and orchestra.

Orgad, Ben-Zion (1926 Germany–2006 Israel) *The Good Dream* (1995) for alto and violin.

Palestrina, Giovanni Pierluigi (1525–1594 Rome). *Song of Songs,* 4–5 voices, 31 motets.

Partos, Oedoen (1907–1977). *By Night on My Bed* (1991), SSAA.

Patachich, Ivan (1922–1993 Budapest). *Music of the Bible,* voices and pianoforte.

Pedrell, Felippe (1841–1922 Barcelona). *Filia Jerusalem,* soprano, choir, string quartet, and harmonium.

Penderecki, Krzysztof (b.1933 Cracow). *Canticum Canticorum Salomonis,* 16 voices, choir and orchestra.

Petrushka, Shabtai (1903 Berlin–1997 Jerusalem). *Song of Songs,* chamber suite, flute, violin, violoncello and percussion.

Pisador, Diego (c.1509-c.1560 Spain). *Tota pulchra es* (Josquin), voice and vihuela.

Pizzetti, Ildebrando (1880–1968 Italy). *Adjuro vos filiae Jerusalem,* cantata.

Pololanik, Zdenek (b.1935 Czech Republic). *Shir ha-Shirim,* oratorio.

Purcell, Henry (1659–1695 London). *My beloved spake,* voices, choir, instruments, basso continuo.

Rasiuk, Moshe (b.1954 Israel). *By Night on My Bed* (1991) for girls' choir (SSAA).

Reutter, Hermann (1900 Stuttgart–1985). *Aus dem Hohelied Salomonis,* alto, baritone, clarinet and orchestra.

Rimski-Korsakov, Nikolai (1844–1908 Russia). *Hebrew song,* voice and pianoforte; Song of songs, duet and orchestra.

Ritter, Christian (c.1648–1717 Germany). *Ich beschwoere euch ihr*

Toechter Jerusalem, contralto, tenor, bass, 2 violins, viola and basso-continuo.

Rochberg, George (1918 Paterson, New Jersey–2005 Bryn Mawr, Pennsylvania). *Song of Solomon*, voice and pianoforte.

Rodriguez, Robert Xavier (b.1946 Texas, USA). *The Song of Songs* (1992), soprano, narrator, instrumental ensemble.

Roseingrave, Daniel (1650 London–1727 Dublin). *The voice of my beloved*, motet.

Rosowsky, Solomon (1878 Riga–1962 New York). *Shir ha-Shirim*, choir and pianoforte.

Rubinstein, Anton (1829 Moldova–1894 Russia). *Shulamith*, oratorio.

Sadai, Yizhak (1935 Sofia/1949 Israel). *Divertimento*, alto and 3 instruments.

Saminski, Lazar (1882 Odessa–1959 New York). *Shir ha-Shirim*, soprano, pianoforte.

Schenck, Johan (1656–1712 Germany). *Hooglied van Salomon*, voice, basso continuo.

Schutz, Heinrich (1585–1672 Dresden). *Song of Songs*, 7 songs (tr. C. Becker), choir and basso-continuo.

Scontrino, Antonio (1850–1922 Florence). *Tota pulchra*, vocal quartet.

Shenderovas, Anatoly (b.1945 Lithuania). *Simeni Kahotam al Libeha (Set Me as a Seal)* (1992), soprano, bass, percussion solo, orchestra.

Seter, Mordechai (1916 Russia–1994 Tel Aviv). *Cantata L'Shabbat* (Sg 1:1–4), choir and instruments.

_____. *I Call Upon Thee* (1975), choir (SMA), Song of Songs.

Shapleigh, Bertram (1871 Boston–1940 Washington, D.C.). *Song of Solomon*, cantata.

Shatal, Miriam (b.1903 Netherlands–2006 Israel). *I Call Upon Thee* (1975) for 3-part women's choir.

Skrowaczewski, Stanislaw (b.1923 Lvov). *Cantique des cantiques*, soprano and 23 instruments.

Snizkova-Skrhova, Jitka (1924 Prague–1989). *Pisen Salomonova* (J. Seifert), alto, narrator, and chamber orchestra with harp.

Snunit, Zevi (1933–1957 Tel Aviv). *Hinakh Yafah* (Sg 4:1), 2 voices, choir.

_____. *Ma Yafah Dodayikh* (Sg 4:10), 2 voices and choir.

_____. *Mi zot ha-nishkafa* (Sg 6:10), 2 voices and choir.

Sowinski, Wojciech (1803–1880 Paris). *Tota pulchra es*, choir and orchestra.

Sternberg, Erich-Walter (1898 Berlin–1974 Tel Aviv). *Kol dodi* (Sg 2:8), 2 voices and choir.

Stravinsky, Igor (1882 Russia–1971 New York). *Canticum sacrum* (Sg 4:16), tenor, bass, choir and orchestra.

Tanaka, Karen (b.1961 Japan). *The Song of Songs* (1996), violoncello, electronics.

Tavaris, Manuel de (1585 Portugal–1638 Spain). *Veni in hortum meum*, 8 voices.

Thomson, Virgil (1896 Kansas City, Mo.–1989 Manhattan). *Five phrases from the Song of Solomon*, soprano and percussion.

Todeschi, Simplicio (c.1600-c.1637 Italy). *Adjuro vos*, motet, 3 voices and organ.

_____. *Nigra sum*, motet, 3 voices and organ.

Vackar, Dalibor (1906–1984 Czech Republic). Canticum Canticorum, choir madrigal.

Vaughn-Williams, Ralph (1872–1958 London). *Flos campi*, suite, viola, small choir and small orchestra.

Vellones, Pierre (1889–1939 Paris). *Cantique des cantiques*, 8 songs, soprano, tenor, bass, flute and bassoon.

Victoria, Tomas Luis de (1548–1611 Madrid). *Nigra sum sed formosa*, sacred motet, 2 sopranos, alto, 2 tenors and a bass.

Wagner-Regeny, Rudolf (1903 Hungary–1969). *Shir ha-Shirim*, cantata, alto, baritone, women's choir and small orchestra.

Walton, William (1902 England–1982 Italy). *Set me as a seal upon thine heart*, voice and pianoforte.

Weissensteiner, Raimund (1905–1997 Vienna). *Das hohe Lied*, soloist, choir and orchestra.

Werder, Felix (b.1922 Berlin/1940 Melbourne). *Shir ha-Shirim*, mezzo-soprano and strings.

Wolf-Ferrari, Ermano (1876–1948 Venice). *La Sulamita*, biblical chant, soloist, choir, orchestra and organ.

Wolpe, Stephan (1902 Germany–1972 New York). *Semolo tahat roshi*, alto and pianoforte.

Zagwijn, Henri (1878–1957 Netherlands). *Het Hooglied van Salomo*, recitative, flute, viola and harp.

Zarlino, Giuseppe (1517–1590 Venice). *Nigra sum sed Formosa* (Sg 1:4), 5 voices.

_____. *Ecce tu pulchra es* (Sg 1:14), canon fugue, 3 voices.

G. Dore: Boaz and Ruth, *Bible Illustrations (1866)*

27

Jewish tradition drew upon the Bible as a musical as well as a textual source, because cantillation accompanies most of its books. In this extract from the Broadway epic, *The Eternal Road*, Kurt Weill's score demonstrates a convergence of age old traditions with vernacular Western culture.

RUTH

And she said: 'Behold, thy sister-in-law is gone back unto her people and unto her god; return thou after thy sister-in-law. And Ruth said: 'Entreat me not to leave thee, and to return from following after thee; for whither thou goest, I will go; and where thou lodgest, I will lodge; thy people shall be my people, and thy God my God; where thou diest, I will die, and there I will be buried; the Lord do so to me, and more also, if aught but death part thee and me. And when she saw that she was steadfastly minded to go with her, she left off speaking unto her. So they two went until they came to Bethlehem   (Ruth 1: 15–18).

The decisive victories of the judges secured lengthy periods of peace and tranquility in which social and domestic life flourished. According to its superscription, the Book of Ruth takes place during such a period and complements the more turbulent Book of Judges.[1] Unshaken by the difficulties of Mosaic commandments, and the hardship of being a Moabite stranger in the Holy Land, Ruth affirms her readiness to follow Jewish customs and law.[2] "And when Naomi said: *We have one Torah, one law, one command; the Eternal our God is one, there is none beside him.* Ruth answered: *Thy people shall be my people, thy God my God.*"

---

1.   For this reason, while the Hebrew Bible places the Book of Ruth in the category of Writings, the Greek translation (Septuagint) places this scroll immediately after the Book of Judges.

2.   Midrash fragment published by Hartmann, *Ruth in der Midrasch-litteratur,* as cited in Ginzberg, *The Legends of the Jews,* Vol. 6, 190.

As a reward for her devotion, Ruth wed Boaz, a prince of Israel, and became great-grandmother to David, ancestor of the Messiah. Boaz, of whom it is said, fathered and buried sixty children during his lifetime, died on the day after the wedding.[3] Its authorship is attributed to the prophet Samuel.

Kurt Weill: The Eternal Road (1935)

Libretto in German: Franz Werfel
English translation: Ludwig Lewisohn
Genre: Biblical Pageant
Medium: 245 actors, actresses and singers, and symphony orchestra
Style: Broadway Musical
First performance: Manhattan Opera House, New York City, 1937
Duration: ca. 5–7 hours (excerpt 10 minutes)

The Eternal Road is a biblical morality play recounting the saga of the Jewish people as set forth in the Old Testament.[4] Conceived and created in the mid-1930s, it is told as a flashback in a synagogue during a midnight vigil, where a group of modern Jews have gathered to escape persecution. It was first performed in New York City in 1937. The original Broadway production was set on five stages a full acre in size, involving a cast of nearly 250 and a 100-piece orchestra; envisioned as a production of heroic proportions, which would encompass the narrative of the Hebrew Bible in a single evening. The play implicitly suggests Zionism's

---

3. See Midrash Ruth Rabbah 5.15. Boaz is identified with Ibzan of Bethlehem (Judges 12:8). Ruth was 40 years old and Boaz was 80 years old when they married (Ruth Rabbah 6.2). See also Talmud Baba Bathra 91a and Midrash Ruth Zuta 4.13. Commentary on the Book of Ruth inevitably remarks on its idyllic pastoral charm, simple faith, and lovely depiction of womanhood. In accord with the Midrash, one can scarcely imagine the tragedy she faced the day after the book closes — as a twice widowed woman who now bears Boaz's child. Boaz's death the day after the wedding is considered questionable, since the Bible makes no mention of it.

4. *The Eternal Road* was the idea of Zionist leader Meyer W. Weisgal (1894–1977), as a response to events in Europe at the time of Nazi persecution in Germany. For creative suggestions, Weisgal turned to Austrian theatrical director and impresario Max Reinhardt (1873–1943) — famous for his vast and spectacular productions — who had recently fled Germany. Reinhardt proposed two fellow expatriates to author the libretto and set it to music: poet and playwright, Franz Werfel, and composer, Kurt Weill.

answer to the age-old historical wandering, persecution, and suffering of the Jewish people — a vision of national rebirth — specifically, a return to the "Promised Land" as a solution to exile.

Biographic Contexts

Librettist

Franz Werfel (1890–1945), Austro-German novelist, poet, playwright, and one of the most popular German-language writers of his time, wrote the libretto to *The Eternal Road* (i.e. *Der Weg der Verheissung* or *The Path of Promise*) while still in Vienna.[5] Werfel had been born into a prosperous and assimilated Jewish family in Prague. There, he befriended such Expressionist writers as Franz Kafka and Max Brod in the cafés of Prague, where he hung out as a youthful idealist. Though attracted to the universal religious values of faith and the brotherhood of man, which later became central themes in his writings, Franz's own Jewish identity was ambiguous.[6] His marriage to Alma Mahler, a rabid anti-Semite and widow of the composer, Gustav Mahler, paved his way into Viennese intellectual society, but did so at the price of renouncing his Jewishness, without formally converting. Following the Nazi takeover of Austria (*Anschluss*) in 1938, Franz fled with Alma to France, then, after the German invasion and occupation of Paris, he fled again, this time to the United States.[7] Late in life, the now famous author learned Hebrew and studied the Bible and Talmud.

Composer

Composer Kurt Weill (1900–1950) was born in Germany. He imbibed traditional Jewish values from his father, the cantor of the Neue Dessau Synagogue, where he sang as a child in the choir. In his teens, however,

---

5. John Simon, "Love and Torments of a Man-Child," The New York Times Book review, April 29, 1990, Peter Stephan Jungk, *Franz Werfel: A Life in Prague, Vienna, and Hollywood,* translated by Anselm Hollo (New York: Weidenfeld, 1990).

6. In childhood, a nurse would take him to her own Roman Catholic Church as well as the synagogue. Many of Werfel's essays attempt to reconcile the two religions, among them, the book *Paul Among the Jews* (1926).

7. There he wrote "The Song of Bernadette" about the saint from Lourdes, 1941, where he had stopped on his journey westward, op. cit.

while neither denying nor disavowing his Jewish roots, Weill set aside the ritual observance of Judaism. As a young man, Kurt studied with Engelbert Humperdinck (1854–1921), composer of the opera *Hansel and Gretel*, and Wagner's last assistant at Bayreuth.[8] Dissatisfied with merely imitating Late Romantic tradition, Weill enrolled in the Berlin composition class of modernist, Ferrucio Busoni (1866–1924), and produced a number of avant-garde concert works.

His reputation, however, rests on the theater music he wrote in collaboration with socialist poet, playwright, and theater director, Bertolt Brecht (1898–1956) — *The Three Penny Opera* (1928) and *The Rise and Fall of the City of Mahagonny* (1930). The gritty cabaret style of these works, coined during the Weimar Republic, blended classical music elements with Latin rhythms and jazz. Shortly thereafter, Weill experienced the chill of the Hitler regime that gripped Germany. Despite theatrical success, the works he produced with Bertolt Brecht were discredited and sabotaged. In perturbation, he abandoned Germany for Paris, where he composed the music to *The Eternal Road* (1935–1937). Through the efforts of impresario Max Reinhardt, Weill was able to resettle in New York, where he supervised the original production, and went on to be acknowledged as one of the most influential theatre composers of the 20th century.

Text and Context

The Eternal Road consists in a series of flashbacks told in a synagogue, during an all-night vigil, in which a Jewish community has taken refuge from a pogrom raging outside. The dramatic structure of the action moves back and forth between biblical reenactments to musings on modern events in the 1930s — in a timeless debate on the perpetual recurrence of persecution in Jewish history. During the night, in an attempt to sustain the people's courage, the Rabbi recalls incidents from the Bible, reminding them of their heritage and God's eternal covenant.[9]

The story of Ruth comprises a 10-minute fragment from this pageant. Franz Werfel draws upon the entire Book of Ruth in creating the

---

8. This influence lingers on in Wagnerian-like leit-motif techniques he employs in the score for *The Eternal Road*.

9. From Neil Levin's program notes to the Milkin Archive of American Jewish Music CD, *Kurt Weil: The Eternal Road (highlights)* (Canada: Naxos, 2003).

libretto, a luminously poetic translation and paraphrase, imbuing it with warm personal insights and humanistic perspectives. The excerpt from Act III, scene 24 is based upon Scripture and skillfully compresses the book into four compact episodes. In addition to Werfel's text, italicized verses below (cited from the Book of Ruth) afford the reader comparison between the original and this libretto.

LIBRETTO

Chapter one: Naomi and Ruth's dialogue
Chapter two: Reaping in the field
Chapter three: The love scene between Ruth and Boaz
Chapter four: The Wedding

Part I — Naomi and Ruth
Ruth accompanies Naomi to Bethlehem (chapter 1)

Rabbi:

And Naomi cautioned Ruth and said to her:

Naomi:

Thou hast gone with me, Ruth,
All the way from Moab.
Now to thy land and god return again.
No more remember the God we two have worshiped.
Find with thy people contentment again.

(1:8) And Naomi said unto her two daughters-in-law: 'Go, return each of you to her mother's house; the Lord deal kindly with you, as ye have dealt with the dead, and with me.'

Ruth:

Nay, where thou goest will I go also.
And I shall dwell wherever thou abidest,
For thy God is my God
And thy folk are my folk.
And shoudst thou die,
Then I would die with thee,
For so thy soul and mine are knit together.
Until the grave then let the bond endure.

> Thy God is my God,
> And thy faith, my faith.
> May God reward me happiness or sorrow,
> As death alone can tear us asunder.
> And where thou goest, will I go also,
> And I shall dwell wherever thou art.

(1:16–17) And Ruth said: 'Entreat me not to leave thee, and to return after following thee; for whither thou goest, I will go; and whither thou lodgest, I will lodge; thy people shall be my people, and thy God my God; where thou diest, will I die, and there will I be buried; the Lord do so to me, and more also, if aught but death part thee and me,'

Naomi:

> Blessed be thy faith my daughter,
> And the love which brings thee to the shelter of the Lord.

Ruth:

> To know and love the Lord is all of life,
> To leave Him is bereavement.

(2:12) 'The Lord recompense thy work, and be thy reward complete from the Lord, the God of Israel, under whose wings thou art come to take refuge.'

Part II — a harvest field
Ruth gleans in the field of Boaz (chapter 2)

Naomi:

> Yes, Boaz brings the harvest in.

(2:1–2) And Naomi had a kinsman of her husband's, a mighty man of valour, of the family of Elmelech, and his name was Boaz. And Ruth the Moabitess said unto Naomi: Let me now go the field, and glean among the ears of corn after him in whose sight I shall find favor. And she said unto her: 'Go, my daughter.'

Boaz: (addressing a reaper)

> God be with you.
> Who is the stranger there?

(2:4–5) And, behold, Boaz came from Bethlehem, and said unto the reapers: 'The Lord be with you.' And they answered him: 'The Lord bless thee.' Then said Boaz unto his servant that was set over the reapers: 'Whose damsel is this?'

A Reaper:

> She came recently from Moab.

(2:6) And the servant that was set over the reapers answered and said: 'It is a Moabitish damsel that came back with Naomi out of the field of Moab.'

Boaz:

> Then it is Ruth, the faith fullest of women.
> But woe to any man who dare distress
> The gentle lady in the humble dress,
> And when she wearies from the sun and heat,
> Prepare her food that she may rest and eat.
> And when the day of harvest work is fled,
> Bring also vinegar to cool her head.

(2:8–9) Then Boaz said unto Ruth: 'Hearest thou not, my daughter? Go not to glean in another field, neither pass from hence, but abide here fast by my maidens. Let thine eyes be on the fields that they do reap, and go thou after them; have I not charged the young men that they shall not touch thee? And when thou art athirst, go unto the vessels, and drink of that which the young men have drawn.' (2:14) And Boaz said unto her at meal time: 'Come hither, and eat of the bread and dip thy morsel in the vinegar.'

Rabbi:

> Boaz feasted that evening and was merry,
> And rejoiced for the harvest.
> He went to the threshing floor;
> Nearby the grain, he lay and slept.
> And then Ruth came softly
> And lay down near him in the darkness.

(3:7) And when Boaz had eaten and drunk, and his heart was merry, he went to lie down at the end of the heap of corn; and she came softly, and uncovered his feet, and laid her down.

Part III — Boaz and Ruth
Ruth seeks betrothal with Boaz (chapter 3)

Rabbi:

But suddenly, Boaz awoke in the night. And lo, a woman was there.

(3:8–12) And it came to pass at midnight, that the man was startled, and turned himself; and behold, a woman lay at his feet.

Boaz:

Who art thou?

(3:9) And he said: 'Who art thou?'

Ruth:

I am Ruth.

Boaz:

Yes, thou art Ruth.

Ruth:

To thy near kinsmen was I wed in youth.

(3:9) And she answered: 'I am Ruth thy handmaid; spread therefore thy skirt over they handmaid; for thou art a near kinsman.'

Boaz:

And utterly to the Eternal given.

Ruth:

From mine own life and mine own people driven,
I wander widowed in a world forlorn.

Boaz:

And gleanest ears amidst the alien corn.
How camest thou that lovely faith to cherish?

Ruth:

God wills that not one branch of Jacob perish.
Thus speak thy lips; thine eyes, oh let me see.

Boaz:

> Oh, any youth, however deep his dreaming,
> Could love thee for the beauty from thee streaming.
> Why seekest thou an aging man like me?

(3:10) And he said: 'Blessed be thou of the lord, my daughter; thou hast shown more kindness in the end than at the beginning, inasmuch as thou didst not follow the young men, whether poor or rich.'

Ruth:

> Not I, but God hath placed me here before thee.

Boaz:

> Nay child, on bended knee I should adore thee,
> That bringest me the highest good so late.

(3:11–12) And now my daughter, fear not; I will do to thee all that thou sayest; for all the men in the gate of my people do know that thou art a virtuous woman. And now it is true that I am a near kinsman; howbeit there is a kinsman nearer than I.

Ruth:

> Shall I now go?

Boaz:

> Ruth, till the morning wait. Make here thy fragrant bed,
> And with security sleep through the night, untroubled for thy purity.
> But rise before the early morning-tide,
> That none may see, nor words be said, to shame thee.
> When day burns high, I shall appear to claim thee,
> Redeeming thee, and making thee my bride.

(3:13) Tarry this night, and it shall be in the morning, that if he will perform unto thee the part of a kinsman, well; let him do the kinsman's part; but if he be not willing to do the part of as kinsman to thee, then I will do the part of a kinsman to thee, as the Lord liveth; lie down until the morning.'

Part IV — The Wedding
Boaz marries Ruth (chapter 4)

Chorus of men:

> To thy word Boaz, all shall witness be,
> No branch or leaf shall die on Jacob's tree.

(4: 11) And all the people that were in the gate, and the elders, said: 'We are witnesses. The Lord make the woman that is come into thy house like Rachel and like Leah, which two did build the house of Israel.

MORAL
Men and Women:

> Free was thy choice, thy faith sought no reward.[10]
> Therefore be thou exalted, be thou exalted of the Lord.

Music and Musical Exegesis

Weill's score for *The Eternal Road* is an eclectic blend of theatrical set pieces, choral numbers, solo arias and ensembles, fanfares, synagogue recitatives, and triumphant marches modeled after French Grand opera. At times, it paraphrases Mozart's *Requiem* and *Don Giovanni*, along with Wagnerian "twilight" music from the *Ring Cycle*, and jazz elements from the 1920s. Running throughout, and binding this mosaic into a coherent whole, are leit-motifs derived from biblical cantillation and Jewish liturgy.

Scene 24 is an "endless" arioso, a flowing recitative that adapts Werfel's poetic and prose texts to warm, flowing orchestral melody. It is a thought process, involving recurring musical themes, with deep roots in Weill's German-Jewish heritage. Leit-motif is presumed to be a technique Weill inherited from Wagner, via his teacher, Humperdinck. Nonetheless, leit-motive is not the exclusive property of Wagner. The same technique follows German-Jewish musical practice among Ashkenazim, since the Middle Ages.[11] The adaptation of 19th-century

---

10. The phrase *thy faith sought no reward* captures the essence of all prophecy. It is the same conclusion reached by Schoenberg in the opera *Moses and Aaron*.

11. The idea of leit-motif or a recurring musical theme, associated with a particular person, place, or idea, was familiar to Weill from the synagogue. These are the M*issinai* tunes — ancient Ashkenazi melodies associated with specific

"Wagnerian" leit-motif technique by Weill, then, was not something foreign to his musical thinking; but, in fact, an integral component of Weill's compositional vernacular. Another device Weill employs is *contrafact*,[12] that is, the fitting of new words to a pre-existing melody.

Conclusion

Ruth — a woman of mixed heritage — is both a stranger from a strange land and grandmother of the messianic King David. Considered a prototype of the ideal proselyte, she leaves family, friends, and homeland to follow in the footsteps of the God of Israel. *The Eternal Road* places her in a slightly different context — one imbued with a humanist perspective. Weill's score exhibits a corresponding cross-fertilization in melodic style and musical technique. One example is leit-motif, another is *contrafact* — procedures for thinking about music, which he, too, inherited, not only from his environment and teachers, but from his home and medieval German-Jewish forebears. This operatic excerpt from her life presents the Bible in a similar mix, demonstrating that culture is a diverse heritage, blended from many currents. It is not so pure as liturgy, nor so dry and sanctimonious as theology, but a dynamic, living presence. *The Eternal Road*, as Broadway musical, bears witness to this symbiosis in its vernacular transformation of the Bible.[13] "Religion," writes Werfel "is the everlasting dialogue between humanity and God. Art is its soliloquy."[14]

Jewish prayers, especially on the Festivals and Holy Days of the year.

12. *Contrafact* has many connotations. It may imply a new musical composition built out of an already existing one; or a new melody overlaid onto a familiar harmonic structure; or the creation of a new text sung to a pre-existing melody. In practice, almost any text can be fitted to a given melody if it is distorted, compressed, drawn out, repeated, or spiced with humming sections. This procedure was familiar to Weill from the Sabbath Zemirot he sang at home as a child. Among Ashkenazi Jews, even psalm texts were adapted to medieval German popular and folksongs.

13. This idea of the continuity of the generations, through character traits and ideals, is one of the themes of the Book of Ruth. Ruth bestowed on her great-grandson the biblical heritage of faith and love: *There is a son born to Naomi; and they called his name Obed; he is the father of Jesse, the father of David (Ruth 4:17)*. It is a Scriptural principle: the deeds of the fathers are repeated in the sons (*maaseh avot siman lebanim*).

14. Cited from Franz Werfel's posthumous novel *Zwischen Oben und Unter*

Another Instance of the Bible on Broadway

George and Ira Gershwin: Porgy and Bess (1935)

As the Bible found its way onto Broadway and into the opera house through *The Eternal Road*, so, in many unsuspecting ways, biblical ethos entered, integrated, and vitalized America's popular culture. The folk opera *Porgy and Bess* by George and Ira Gershwin, for example, contains a number of biblical references, particularly in the song, "It Ain't Necessarily So," which places familiar biblical characters — David, Goliath, Jonah, Moses, and Methuselah — into a humorous theatrical context, replete with Southern-black dialect and traditional African call-response form.

It Ain't Necessarily So

It ain't necessarily so. It ain't necessarily so.
De t'ings dat yo li'ble to read in de Bible, It ain't necessarily so.

Li'l David was small, but oh my! Li'l David was small, but oh my!
He fought Big Goliath who lay down and dieth. Li'l David was small, but oh my!

Wadoo! Wadoo! Zim bam boddle-oo, Zim bam boddle-oo.
Hoodle ah da waah da! Hoodle ah da waah da! Scatty way! Scatty way!

Oh Jonah, he lived in a whale. Oh Jonah, he lived in a whale.
Fo' he made his home in dat fish's abdomen. Oh Jonah, he lived in a whale.

L'il Moses was found in a stream. L'il Moses was found in a stream.
He floated on water 'till Ole Pharaoh's daughter
She fished him, she says from dat stream.

Wadoo! Wadoo! Zim bam boddle-oo, Zim bam boddle-oo.
Hoodle ah da waah da! Hoodle ah da waah da! Scatty way! Scatty way!

It ain't necessarily so. It ain't necessarily so.
Dey tell all you chillum De Debble's a villun. But 'tain't necessarily so.

To get into Hebben don't snap fo' a sebben — live clean! Don' have no fault!

(Unknown Binding), 1946, as cited in Sol Liptzin's article "Franz Werfel," *Encyclopaedia Judaica*, Vol. 16, col. 451.

Oh, I takes dat gospel whenever it's pos'ple — but wi a grain of salt!

Methu'lah lived nine hundred years. Methu'lah lived nine hundred years. But who call dat livin' when no gal'll give in to no man what's nine hundred years.

I'm preachin' dis sermon to show,
it ain't nessa, ain't nessa, ain't nessa, ain't nessa, It ain't necessarily so!

Works List

The story of Ruth has been dramatized and set to music dozens of times from the 18th to the 20th centuries in many genres: oratorio, cantata, song, instrumental and incidental music. It continues to arouse interest and inspire creativity. *Ruth Hamoaviyah* (1988) is a contemporary paraphrase of the story by Batia Karmi, set to music by Israeli popular song composer Nurit Hirsh. For an extensive musicological discussion of the book see Helen Leneman, *The Story of Ruth in Opera and Oratorio (The Bible in the Modern World 11)* (Sheffield, England: Sheffield Phoenix Press, 2007).

Avison, Charles (1709–1770 England). *Ruth*, oratorio.

Ayres, Paul (c.1980 UK). *Ruth*, SSATB.

Berkeley, Lennox (1903 Oxford–1989). *Ruth* (Crozier), opera.

Berlinski, Herman (1910 Germany–2001 USA). *Entreat Me Not* (1963) (Ruth 1:16), baritone, SATB, keyboard.

Braun, Yehezkel (b.1922 Wroclaw/1924 Israel). *Illuminations to the Book of Ruth*, orchestra.

Castelnuovo-Tedesco, Mario (1895 Florence–1968 Beverly Hills, California). *Naomi and Ruth*, cantata, soprano, choir and pianoforte.

Costa, Michael (1810 Naples–1844 Brighton). *Naomi and Ruth*, oratorio.

Cowen, Frederic Hymen (1852 Jamaica–1935 London). *Ruth* (J. Bennet), oratorio.

De Leone, Francesco (1887–1948 Ohio). *Ruth*, sacred music drama.

Ebert, Hans (1889–1952 Berlin). *Biblische Balladen: a. Ruth b. Boaz* (E. Lasker-Schueler), voice and pianoforte.

Eckert, Karl (1820–1879 Berlin). *Ruth* (F. Foester), oratorio.

Elwart, Antoine (1808–1877 Paris). *Turh et Boaz*, oratorio.

Erbse, Heimo (1924 Germany–2005 Austria). *Ruth* (G. Hoffman), ballet.

Farinelli, Giuseppe (1769–1836 Trieste). *La nozze de Ruth*, oratorio.

Feo, Francesco (1691–1761 Naples). *Ruth,* oratorio.

Franck, Cesar (1822 Belgium–1890 Paris). *Ruth*, biblical eclogue for soloist, choir and orchestra.

Gal, Hans (1890 Austria–1987 Edinburgh). *Ruth* (Levertov), incidental music.

Gaul, Alfred (1837–1913 England). *Ruth*, sacred cantata.

Giardini, Felice (1716 Turin–1796 Moscow). *Ruth*, oratorio.

Goldman, Maurice (1910–1984 USA). *Entreat Me Not to Leave Thee* (1970) (Ruth 1:16), soprano, SATB, keyboard.

Goldschmidt, Otto (1829 Hamburg–1907 London). *Ruth*, cantata for soloist, choir, orchestra.

Gounod, Charles Francois (1818 Paris–1893). *Ruth*, oratorio.

Hart, Fritz (1874 London–1949 Honolulu). *Ruth and Naomi* (F. Hart), opera.

Howe, Mary (1882–1964 USA). *Song of Ruth* (1940) (Ruth 1:16–17), soprano, SATB, organ.

Ippolitov-Ivanov, Mikhail (1859–1935 Moscow). *Ruf* (A. Tolstoy), opera.

Jacobi, Frederick (1891 San Francisco–1952 New York). *Hagiographa: Ruth*, string quartet, and pianoforte.

Joffe, Shlomo (1909 Warsaw–1995 Bet Alpha, Israel). *Ruth*, symphonic suite.

Kosakoff, Reuven (1898–1987 USA). *Ruth and Naomi* (1965), soprano, alto, bass, and pianoforte.

Le Sueur, Jean-Francois (1760–1837 Paris). *Ruth et Noemi*, oratorio.

Litolff, Henry (1818 London–1891 Paris). *Ruth et Boaz*, oratorio.

Ludlow, Joseph (20th C. USA). *The Words of Ruth* (1967) (Ruth 1:16), SATB, keyboard.

Meller, Wilfred (1914–2008 UK). *The Song of Ruth*, cantata, soprano, mezzo-soprano, bass, orchestra.

Naumbourg, Samuel (1815 Bavaria–1880 Paris). *Ruth et Noemi* (tr. Plouvier), voice and pianoforte, elegie.

Nowowiejski, Feliks (1877–1946 Poland). *Klosy Ruth* (P. Calderon), incidental music.

Peters, Flor (1903–2986 Belgium). *Wedding Song* (1962) (Ruth 1:16–17), soprano, SATB, and organ.

Sacchini, Antonio (1730 Florence–1786 Paris). *Nuptiae Ruth* (Acenzione), oratorio.

Schletterer, Hans Michael (1824–1893 Germany). *Ruth*, soprano, alto, cantata for choir and pianoforte.

Schumann, Georg Alfred (1866–1952 Berlin). *Ruth*, oratorio.

Slater (Edson), Jean (20th C. USA). *Entreat Me Not to Leave Thee* (1944) (Ruth 1:16), SATB.

Spies, Claudio (b.1925 Chile/USA). *Verses from the Book of Ruth* (1961), SSA, narrator, and pianoforte.

Stampiglia, Silvio (1664–1725 Naples). *Il matrimonio di Rut* (G. Perroni), oratorio.

Tadolini, Giovanni (1793–1872 Bologna). *Boaz*, cantata for 2 tenors, baritone, and orchestra.

Weiner, Lazar (1897 Russia–1982 New York). *Three biblical songs*, 1. Ruth, voice and pianoforte.

Wesley, Samuel (1766–1837 London). *Ruth*, oratorio.

G. Dore: The People Mourning Over the Ruins of Jerusalem, *Bible Illustrations* *(1866)*

28

Born of the cataclysm of war, Ernst Krenek's *Lamentations of the Prophet Jeremiah* brings religious imagination to bear upon events in the 20th century, in an *a cappella* choral work that grieves of human suffering; hybridizing angelic imagery and plainsong with serial techniques.

LAMENTATIONS

How doth the city sit solitary that was full of people! How is she become as a widow! She that was great among the nations, and princess among the provinces, how is she become tributary. Jerusalem remembereth in the days of her affliction and of her anguish all her treasures that she had from days of old; now that her people fall by the hand of the adversary, and none doth help her, the adversaries have seen her, they have mocked at her desolations (Lamentations 1:1, 7).

A national elegy — the Book of Lamentations contains five dirges of grief, astonishment, and desolation, bewailing the destruction of the Temple, the fall of Jerusalem, and exile of the Jewish People in 586 B.C. The scroll not only acknowledges the role of suffering and exile, as punishments for sin, but, prescribes its antidote through remorse and repentance. Thus, individuals and the nation may attain forgiveness, reconciliation, and restoration. Lamentations is acrostic in structure. Initial verses as well as internal lines are arranged according to the 22 letters of the Hebrew alphabet. Tradition attributes the scroll to the prophet Jeremiah, who wrote it in this form to indicate that God's full fury was unleashed against the people of Israel because they *transgressed the Torah which was given to them with twenty-two letters*.[1]

In Christian theology, Lamentations foreshadows the sorrow over the sins of the people and their rejection of God — expressed by Jesus

---

1.   Talmud Sanhedrin 104a.

as he approached Jerusalem and looked ahead to her destruction at the hands of the Romans (Luke 19:41–44).

Ernst Krenek: Lamentatio Jeremiae Prophetae (1941–42)
Latin Text: Lamentations
Genre: Choral music
Medium: A cappella chorus (SATB)
Style: Atonal
First performance: Kassel, Germany, 1958
Duration: ca. 1 hour

Lamentatio Jeremiae Prophetae (Lamentations of the Prophet Jeremiah) is a major 20th-century choral work inspired by Catholic liturgy. It was written after the outbreak of World War II by Ernst Krenek, as a despairing response to the destruction of European civilization, as he knew it. Scholastic in conception, it blends the austerity of plainsong with techniques of medieval polyphony and serial atonality.[2]

Biographic Context

Ernst Krenek (1900–1991) was a serious intellectual, whose lofty idealism often expressed itself in a heavy, ponderous style.[3] Incongruously,

---

2.   The recitation of Lamentations in the Roman Catholic Church includes not only the text itself, but also the opening sentence *Incipit lamentatio Jeremiae prophetae.* The Hebrew letters *aleph, beth* etc., mark the beginning of each verse or stanza in chapters 1 to 4. Each chapter concludes with the sentence: *Jerusalem, convertere as Dominum Deum tuum.* The Hebrew letter names are set to melisma, a procedure imitated in various art music settings of Lamentations (*Eikhah*). Until well into the 17th century these settings were always based on traditional Gregorian melodies, which formed a "skeleton" for their construction. Many other Gregorian patterns evoke association with various Jewish recitations of Lamentations, as well. The resemblance of Gregorian chant to Yemenite Jewish melodies was pointed out by A.Z. Idelsohn nearly a century ago. See Idelsohn, *Jewish Music,* 51, 55–56.
3.   The following convoluted quotation, from remarks the composer delivered at a lecture about *Lamentatio Jeremiae Prophetae* in 1960, provides insight into Krenek's deeply thought out, but hardly spontaneous approach to art: *Only he who has fully absorbed the history of the Occident and sees himself as a link in a chain of events (which reaches from the darkest past to a still darker future), will have to recognize that the significance of his own contributions depends*

he believed firmly in the "superiority of feeling over thought."[4] This conflicted outlook expressed itself in the many different phases Krenek embraced throughout his career, which encompass most of the major stylistic trends of the 20ᵗʰ century.

Krenek grew up in Vienna as the son of pious Czech Catholics, profoundly touched by Roman Catholicism. His early works, however, were secular, styled in a Late Romantic idiom influenced by Ernst's teacher, Austrian composer, Franz Schreker (1878–1934). Then, following a visit to Paris in the early 1920s, he adopted Neo-Classicism. In Germany, the most successful work of this Weimar period was the opera *Johnny spielt auf* (Johnny Strikes Up, 1926), which concerns a promiscuous black jazz band leader. In this work, Krenek adopted stylistic elements from jazz, Negro Spirituals, and various cabaret idioms. The composer continued to occupy himself with theater music — despite Nazi anathema to jazz opera — until the Second World War. An atonal opera, *Karl V*, written in 1934, endeared him even less to the Nazis, since it was outright pro-Austrian Catholicism. Here, Krenek extolled the universalism of the Holy Roman Empire in a work that symbolized his view of Hitler's National Socialism destroying Europe, in the same way that nationalism destroyed Karl V.[5] True to his creative vision, in life as well as in art, *Karl V* marked the composer's return to Roman Catholicism.[6] Fleeing to the

---

upon the originality of his testimony. Because, it will be evident to him how in history, the new (that which is still unspoken in its present form, the unheard which deviates courageously from tradition), again and again is regarded as essential and decisive for an era (not only by later generations, but is seen already by even his own contemporaries), as a valuable, although often also uncomfortable, frightening, even threatening acquisition. See program notes by Leo Samama to the disc *Ernst Krenek: Lamentatio Jeremiae Prophetae* recorded by the Netherlands Chamber Choir, conducted by Uwe Gronostay (Globe Records, The Netherlands, 1992).

4. See John L. Stewart, *Ernst Krenek: The Man and His Music* (Berkeley: University of California Press, 1991).

5. Karl or Charles V (1500–1558) was ruler of the Holy Roman Empire from 1519. As the heir of four of Europe's leading dynasties — he ruled over extensive domains in Central, Western, and Southern Europe — as well as the various Castilian (Spanish) colonies in the Americas. Aside from this, Charles is best known for his role in the convocation of the Council of Trent.

6. See Oliver Daniel, "Ernst Krenek," *The New Grove Dictionary of Music*, Vol. 10, 254.

United States, in 1938, Krenek reinvented himself again, and became an academic.

Among the many faculty posts he assumed in America, it was while serving as professor of music at Vassar College (until 1942) that he wrote *Lamentatio Jeremiae Prophetae* — a work of deep mourning.[7] Formerly, labeled a "cultural Bolshevist" by the Nazis, it was not the bright lights of the theatre, the *bon vivant* sophistication of Krenek's youthful Parisian escapades, nor the political activism of his German years that sustained the composer from 1940 onwards — rather, it was the ardent Roman Catholicism of his childhood. Krenek wrote *Lamentations* as a testament of faith.

Text and Context

The custom of publicly reading the Book of Lamentations dates from biblical times. The institution of prayers — recited in commemoration of Jerusalem and the restoration of the Land of Israel — developed out of the rabbinic conception of God's mourning the destruction of the Temple.[8] The hour of midnight was chosen, because David arose at this hour to study and pray.[9] The psalmists also prayed frequently,[10] and the Apostles adopted their practices.[11] Based on such precedents, Early Christianity instituted the canonical hours of prayer — transferring the reading of the Book of Lamentations to the night vigils, and singling out the middle of the night as the hour par excellence for prayer.[12] From

---

7. Perhaps it expresses Krenek's personal grief, the termination of his European life, and his activities as a theatre composer.
8. *Should I weep in the fifth month* [the 9th day of the month of Av, commemorating the destruction of the First Temple in 586 B.C.], *separating myself as I have done these so many years* (Zechariah 7:3). And also: *Woe to the children, on account of whose sins, I destroyed My house and burnt My temple, and exiled them among the nations* (Talmud Berachoth 3a).
9. *At midnight I will rise to give thanks unto Thee* (Ps. 119:62 as cited in Talmud Berachoth 3b-4a).
10. *Seven times a day I have given praise to thee* (Ps. 119:64).
11. *And at midnight, Paul and Silas, praying, praised God* (Acts 16:25).
12. These were read at services commemorating the Last Supper, the Crucifixion, and the Vigil for the Resurrection. Byzantine or Eastern Orthodox rite refers to these services as "Lamentation upon the Grave" (*Epitaphios Threnios*), recited at ceremonies marking the death and resurrection of Christ, on the last two days of Holy Week.

the older Jewish liturgy of national lament, the Roman Catholic service adopted the practice of reading sections or lessons from Lamentations. Krenek sets excerpts from the Book of Lamentations, as they are recited in the liturgy of the Roman Catholic *Tenebrae* lessons on the three sacred days of Holy Week (*Triduum sacrum*) — Maundy Thursday, Good Friday, and Holy Saturday before Easter Sunday.[13] Each lesson is rounded off with the call: *Jerusalem converte ad Dominum Deum tuum* (Jerusalem, return unto the Lord thy God) (Hosea 14:1).

The Lessons

Maundy Thursday (Commemorating the Last Supper)
Part One — Lesson I, chapter 1: 1–5; Lesson II, chapter 1: 6–9; Lesson III, chapter 1: 10–14.

Good Friday (Commemorating the Crucifixion)
Part Two — Lesson I, chapter 2:8–11; Lesson II, chapter 2:12–15; Lesson III, chapter 3: 1–9.

Holy Saturday (Commemorating the Vigil for the Resurrection)
Part Three — Lesson I, chapter 3:22–30; Lesson II, chapter 4:1–6; Lesson III, chapter 5:1–11.

Krenek's choice of texts emulates Latin versions, which have been set to music by composers, since the Council of Trent, 1545.[14] It is significant that translators of the Vulgate retained the original Hebrew letters at

---

13. The term "vigils" originally derived from the Latin *vigiliae* or nocturnal watches of the Roman guards, which lasted twelve hours — from six o' clock in the evening until six o' clock in the morning — divided into three: from 6:00–10:00 P.M., 10:00 P.M. to 2:00 A.M., and 2:00–6:00 A.M. These "watches" were sometimes, also divided into four "vigils" of three hours each. Later, the "vigils" or "night offices" were reduced to three: "Nocturnes" or "Matins Offices" (approximately from 9:00 till midnight, from midnight till 3:00 A.M., and from 3:00 A.M. till dawn). In the Roman Catholic service, Lamentations replace of the three regular lessons during the first Nocturne of Matins: on Thursday, Friday, and Saturday nights of Holy Week. See "Canonical Hours," *Catholic Encyclopaedia*.

14. The same text was set by French Baroque composer Marc Antoine Charpentier in his *Lecons de Tenebres*, and many others.

the beginning of each verse, which, in Gregorian recitation, became occasion for extended melismas — a practice Krenek also retains.[15]

LECTIO PRIMA

Incipit lamentation Jeremiae Prophetae

ALEPH. Quomodo sedet sola civitas plena populo: facta est quasi vidua domina gentium: princeps provinciarum facta est subtribito.

BETH. Plorans ploravit in nocte, et lacrimae ejus in maxillis ejus: non est qui consoletur eam ex omnis caris ejus; omnes amici ejus speverunt eam, et facti sunt ei inimici.

GHIMEL. Migravit Judas propter afflictionem, et multitudinem servitutis: habitavit inter Gentes, nec invenit requiem: omnes persecutores ejus apprehenderunt eam inter angustias.

DALETH. Viae Sion lugent eo quod non sint qui veniant ad solemnitatem: omnes portae ejus destructae: scaerdotes ejus gementes: virgines ejus squalidas, et ipsa oppressa est amaritudine.

HE. Facati sunt hostes ejus in capite, inimici ejus locupletati sunt: quia Dominus locutus est super eam propter mutitudinem iniquitatum ejus: parvuli ejus ducti sunt in captivitatem, ante faciem tribulantis.

Jerusalem converte ad Dominum Deum tuum.

FIRST LESSON

Here begins the lamentation of the Prophet Jeremiah.

ALEPH. How lonely sits the city that was full of people. How like a widow has she become. She that was a princess among the cities, has become a vassal.

BETH. She weeps bitterly in the night, tears on her cheeks; among

---

15. The practice of reading the letters publically is an early one, perhaps, derived from ancient Hebrew custom (retained in Catholic ritual), but discontinued by later generations when the scroll of Lamentations was chanted, on the 9th day of the month of Av, in the synagogue. Besides its Latin translation, Catholic renditions of Lamentations differ from Hebrew in two ways: The initial phrase *Incipit lamentation Jeremiae Prophetae* (translated from the Septuagint), does not appear in the Hebrew. Nor does the Latin phrase *Jerusalem converte ad Dominum Deum tuum*, a moral refrain closing each lesson.

all her lovers she has none to comfort her; all her friends have dealt treacherously with her, they have become her enemies.

GHIMEL. Judah has gone into exile because of affliction, and hard servitude; she dwells now among the nations, but finds no resting place; her pursuers have all overtaken her in the midst of her distress.

DALETH. The roads to Zion mourn, for none come to the appointed feasts; all her gates are desolate, her priests groan; her maidens have been dragged away, and she suffers bitterly.

HE. Her foes have become the head and her enemies prosper, because the Lord has made her suffer for the multitude of her transgressions; her children have gone away captives before the foe.

Jerusalem, convert to your God.

Music and Musical Exegesis

Krenek's *Lamentatio Jeremiae Prophetae* blends medieval formalism with contemporary atonality, in a mosaic of epigrammatic musical statements. The movements setting Hebrew letters, only, vary from between 11 to 30 seconds in duration. While, more elaborate, individual verses, span between 2 to 3 minutes. If the step-wise quality of melodic line is Gregorian — smooth, flowing, and devoid of pointillist angularity — its pitch content is atonal. The initial four tones of the six-note row (**F G A B-flat** D-flat E-flat),[16] derive from a Gregorian intonation: **F G A B-flat** A G A/ A G F G F. In an effort to simulate angelic singing, transposition and serial procedures such as: retrograde, inversion, and retrograde inversion — shape this abstract row into sustained melodic gestures. This hybridization of ancient and modern creates the illusion of other worldly voices, heard seemingly from outer space.[17] To sustain these ethereal effects, Krenek employs a veritable encyclopedia of contrapuntal techniques: imitation, strict canons, augmentation,

---

16. The series is transposed and adjusted at the tri-tone to generate 12-tone symmetry: B C D E F-sharp G-sharp, but corresponding half and whole tone intervals are not retained.

17. *Transposition* refers to moving notes up or down in pitch by a constant interval. In *Retrograde* the order of notes is reversed. *Inversion* refers to turning the order of notes upside-down. For instance, if the original melody has a rising third, the inverted melody has a falling third. The inversion played backwards is called *retrograde inversion*.

contrary motion, perpetual canons, and cancrizans.[18] Krenek's setting of the letter Aleph (*Lectio Prima*) demonstrates this technique in brief.

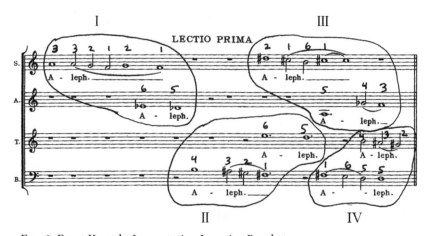

Ex. 38. Ernst Krenek: *Lamentation Jeremiae Prophetae*
© Copyright 1957 by Berenreiter-Verlag-Kassel-Basel-London-New York-Praha. Reproduced by permission of Berenreiter-Verlag.

Analysis

Lectio Prima
Aleph

This movement utilizes three transpositions of the six-note row. In its original form (I) F G A B-flat D-flat E-flat, represented as, 1 2 3 4 5 6; transposed a semi-tone higher (II) F-sharp G-sharp A-sharp B D E; transposed a minor sixth up (or diminished fourth down) (III & IV) C-sharp D-sharp F G-flat A B. He sets the letter *Aleph* in four clause-like

---

18. *Imitation* describes a musical motif repeated in other voices, retaining (more or less) its original rhythmic and intervallic structure. *Strict canon* is a contrapuntal device in which an initial melody is exactly repeated in another voice part (not necessarily at the same pitch level). *Contrary motion* refers to the movement of two melodic lines in opposite directions. In *Perpetual canon*, each part repeats continually (*ad infinitum*). *Augmentation* designates lengthening rhythms or widening of melodic intervals. *Cancrizans* is the technique of mirror imaging. The palindrome: A MAN A PLAN A CANAL PANAMA, for example, reads identically backwards and forwards. See Leonard Bernstein, *The Infinite Variety of Music* (New York: Simon and Shuster, 1966) 141.

gestures, articulated by paired-voices. These, in turn, clump together into two longer phrase units: soprano-alto (I version of the row)/bass-tenor (II version of the row) and soprano-alto (III version of the row)/ bass-tenor (II version of the row). Krenek disguises the seeming symmetry of this parallelism by the shape of each gesture and number of notes used (I) 6 notes-2 notes/(II) 4 notes-2 notes; and (III) 4 notes-3 notes/(IV) 4 notes-3 notes. He applies the same technique to durations (I) 9 beats-4 beats/(II) 7 beats-6 beats; and (III) 8 beats-6 beats/ (IV) 6 beats-3 beats. He further distorts symmetry by foreshortened and overlapping entries. We get the impression of imitation, but nothing quite imitates; we get the impression of repetition, but nothing quite repeats. In the end, we have a logical structure that is consciously blurred, constantly and continuously changing, as mobile as a drifting cloud.

Conclusion

For all its complexity and cogitation, *Lamentatio Jeremiae Prophetae*, in its address to Eternity, manages to capture the essence of liturgical music. Throughout, Krenek seems to be praying a mournful monologue. Yet, amidst loss, tears, and pain — there is hope. Jewish legend recalls: *On the day the temple was destroyed the Messiah was born.* Perhaps, what this means is, curiously, that when there is nothing left to lose, just then, and only then, hope, miraculously emerges of itself from the ashes of desolation, to console and to comfort. It is this message of hope, imbedded in the most remote regions of nature, the soul, and the cosmos, that is Krenek's musical hermeneutic.[19]

Related Directions

The first polyphonic settings of Lamentations made their appearance in the 15th century in the works of the Netherlands composers. In 1454,

---

19. Commenting on the verse: *Because the comforter is far from me (Lam. 1:16)*, Midrash Lamentations Rabbah 1.51 allegorizes: *On the day the temple was destroyed the Messiah was born* (Jerusalem Talmud, chapter 2, section 4). When questioned about the whereabouts of her son, the mother of the Messiah replied, *Did I not tell you that a hard fate is in store for him? Misfortune has dogged him... strong winds and a whirlwind came and carried him off.* The man who questioned her replied, *Did I not tell you at his coming [birth] [the Temple] was destroyed, and at his coming [return] it will be rebuilt.*

Guillaume Dufay wrote a four-voice motet on the fall of Constantinople, *O tres piteux*, for the "Banquet of the Pheasant," held in Lille by Philip the Good of Burgundy, intended to open a new Crusade. The liturgical melody of Lamentations is sung in Latin by the tenor, while the other voices sing the French poem. Two collections of polyphonic Lamentations by various composers were among the first products of music printing (Petrucci, Venice, 1506); and by the end of the 16th century, more than a dozen similar collections had appeared in Italy, France, and Germany. Cristobal Morales' *Lamentations* (1564) represents the first unified composition of the entire text by a single composer, which later became common practice. The list of composers of *Lamentations* is practically identical with that of the major composers of the 16th century. Until 1587, the Papal Chapel sang the settings by Eleazer Genet (Carpentras); these were replaced by those of Palestrina, which were superseded by those of Allegri. Other notable settings were those of William Byrd, Lodovico Viadana, and Johann Rosenmueller. The most frequently performed settings today are those by Palestrina, Gregorio Allegri, Orlando de Lasso, Thomas Tallis, and Marc-Antoine Charpentier.

From the 17th century, a new genre of solo — basso continuo settings of *Lamentations* became numerous (i.e. Carissimi, Frescobaldi). The liturgical melody was abandoned in favor of free composition, although other principles were retained, namely: the *Incipit lamentatio*, the melisma on the Hebrew letter names, and the call *Jerusalem, Jerusalem* — which was frequently set during the Baroque period, as a series of calls, preferably with echo effects. Extended compositions of the text became particularly prominent in French music, usually, under the name of *Leçon de Tenebres*. The *Leçons* of Marc-Antoine Charpentier, Michel-Richard de Lalande, and Francois Couperin are particularly well known. Johann Sebastian Bach's Cantata No. 46, *Schauet doch und sehet* (Leipzig, 1723–27) is based mainly on *Lamentations* 1:12–13. Other interesting 18th-century settings are by Antonio Soler and the motet for solo voice and basso continuo on the Latin text of *Lamentations*, Chapter 1, by Jean-Jacques Rousseau (1772).

Though the Book of Lamentations was virtually ignored by composers of the 19th century, there has been a significant revival of interest during the 20th century. The most notable modern works are Ernst Krenek's *Lamentatio Jeremiae Prophetae*; Manuel Rosenthal's *Deux priers pour les temps malheureux* (1942); Leonard Bernstein's *Jeremiah Symphony* (which contains a movement on the Hebrew text of *Lamentations* chapter 1, sung by a mezzo-soprano); Alberto Ginastera's *Hieremiae prophetae Lamentationes*, three motets for *a cappella* mixed choir (1946); Edmund Rubbra's *Tenebrae: 9 Lamentations* for orchestra (1951); and Igor Stravinsky's *Threni, id est Lamentationes Jeremiae Prophetae* (to the Greek translation) for soloists, choir, and orchestra (1958).[20]

Works List

Agricola, Alexander (c.1445–1506 Europe). *Lamentationes Jeremiae*, 3 and 4 voices.

Alcarotti, Francesco (1535–1596 Italy). *Lamentazioni di Geremia*, 5 voices.

Allegri, Gregorio (1584–1652 Rome). *Lamentationes Jeremiae*, choir.

Andriessen, Jurriaan (1925–1996 Netherlands). *Vier Revinsliederen*, voice, orchestra.

Asola, Giovanni Matteo (1524–1609 Venice). *Lamentationes Ieremiae Prophetae*, 6vv.

Averitt, William (20th C. USA). *O Vos Omnes* (Lam. 1:12), SATB.

Bar-Am, Benjamin (b.1923). *The Lamentations of Jeremiah* (1997), alto, baritone, mixed choir, motet.

Bardos, Lajos (1899–c.1987 Budapest). *Jeremias siralma*, choir.

Barlow, David (1927–1975 UK). *Behold and See* (Lam. 1:12), SATB.

Berchem, Jachet (c.1505–1567 Belgium). *O Vos Omnes* (Lam. 1:12), SATB.

Bernier, Nicolas (1664-c.1735 Paris). *Lecons de tenebres: laments, motets*, choir, basso continuo.

Bernstein, Leonard (1918 Lawrence, Massachusettes–1990 New York city). *Jeremiah Symphony: 3. Lamentation*, mezzo soprano and orchestra.

Bittoni, Bernado (1756–1826 Italy). *Oratio Jeremiae Prophetae*, lamentations.

Bona, Valerio (1560–1620 Italy). *Lamentationi con l'orazione di Jeremia*, 4 voices.

Boucher, Boris (17th C.). *Lamentationes Jeremiae*, choir, organ and orchestra.

---

20. See Batia Bayer, "The Book of Lamentations," *Encyclopaedia Judaica*, Vol. 10, col. 1375–1376.

Bouzignac, Guilaume (d.1641 France). *Prima lamentatione Jeremiae prophetae*, 5 voices.

Brummel, Antoine (1460–1525 Europe). *Lamentations*, 2 voices.

Brunetti, Gaetano (c.1744–1798 Madrid). *Lamentazione Jeremiae.*

Byrd, William (1543–1623 England). *De lamentatione* (Lam.2:8–10), 5 voices, choir.

_____. *Vide, Domine quoniam tribulor*, Lam. 1:20, 5 voices and choir.

Calvisius, Sethus (1556–1615 Leipzig). *Zion spricht: der Herr Hat Mich verlassen.*

Casals, Pablo (1876 Spain–1973). *O Vos Omnes* (Lam. 1:12), SSAATTBB.

Cavalieri, Emilio de (ca.1550–1602 Rome). *Lamentationes Hieremiae Prophetae*, 1–5 voices.

Chappell, Herbert (b.1934 UK). *Lamentations of Jeremiah*, SATB.

Compere, Loyset (c.1445–1518 Flanders). *O Vos Omnes* (Lam. 1:12), SATB.

Cooper, Paul (b.1926 USA). *Symphony No. 3 'Lamentations,'* strings.

Correa, Carlos (1680–1747 Portugal). *O Vos Omnes* (Lam. 1:12), SATB.

Couperin, Francois (1668–1733 Paris). *Lecons de tenebres* (Lam. 1:1, 14).

Croce, Giovanni (1557–1609 Italy). *O Vos Omnes* (Lam. 1:12), SATB.

Dentice, Fabrizio (1560–1635 Naples). *Lamentationi*, 5 voices.

Dufay, Guillaume (c.1397–1474 Europe). *O tres piteux.*

Duron, Sebastian (1660–1716 Spain). *O Vos Omnes* (Lam. 1:12), SATB, organ.

Ehrlich, Abel (1915–2003). *How is the Gold become Dim*, SATB/SATB, orchestra.

Elvey, George (1816–1893 England). *The ways of Zion do mourn*, anthem.

Esquivel de Barahona, Juan (c.1560-c.1625 Spain) *O Vos Omnes* (Lam. 1:12), SATB.

Falconio, Placido (16th C. Italy). *Threni Hieremiae Prophetae una cum Psalm*, 4 voices.

Ferrabosco I, Alphonso (1543–1588 Italy/England). *Vocem meam audisti, Lam.* 3:56, 58, ATTBB.

Fetler, Paul (1920 USA). *Lamentations* (1973) Lam, Ezek, Isa, Jer, Ps, SATB, Narrator, amplified flute, 4 percussions, organ.

Fevin, Antoine (c.1470-c.1512 France). *Lamentationae Jeremiae*, 3–4 voices.

Frescobaldi, Girolamo (1583–1643 Rome). *Lamentationes Jeremiae.*

Garcia Fajer, Francisco Javier (1730–1809 Spain). *Lamentationae*, 8 voices, orchestra.

Genet, Eleazar (Carpentras) (1475–1548 France). *Liber lamentationum Hieremiae*, 2–5 voices.

Gesualdo, Carlo (1566–1613 Italy). *O Vos Omnes* (Lam. 1:12), SSATB

Ginastera, Alberto (1916 Buenos Aires–1983 Geneva). *Hieremiae Prophetae Lamentationes* (1946) 3 motets, SATB.

Golijov, Osvaldo (b.1960 Argentina). *Tenebrae* (2002), Opera.

Handel, George Frederic (1685–1759 London). *The Ways of Zion Do Mourn*. Lamentations 1:4, 11 and 2:10, funeral anthem.

Haudimont, Joseph, Abbe (1751–1792 Paris). *Lecons de Jeremiae*, 2 voices, choir and basso-continuo.

Haydn, Michael (1737–1806 Austria). *O Vos Omnes* (Lam. 1:12), SATB

Heinichen, Johann David (1683–1729 Germany). *Lamentationes Jeremiae*, voice and orchestra.

Hilton, John (1599–1657 England). *The Lamentations of Jeremiah*, SAB, keyboard.

Hollaender, Christian (1515–1569 Europe). *Lamentationes Hieremiae Prophetae*, 6 voices.

Isaac, Henricus (1450–1517 Florence). *Oratio Hieremiae*, 4 voices.

Isnardi, Paolo (1525-ca.1600 Italy). *Lamentationes*, 5 voices.

Jachet da Mantova (1495 France–1559 Mantua, Italy). *Lamentationes primo, secundo ed tertio*, 4 voices; *Oratio Hieremiae Profetae*, 5 voices.

Joffe, Shlomo (1909 Warsaw–1995 Bet Alpha, Israel). *Kinah*. Lamentations 3, 7, voices and a cappella choir.

Jommelli, Nicolo (1714–1774 Italy). *O Vos Omnes* (Lam. 1:12), SATB, organ

Jochsberger, Tzipora (b.1920 Germany/USA/Israel). *Kinnah and Kaddish* (1981), SATB.

Kohn, Karl (b.1926 USA) *Sensus Spei* (Lam. 3:22–23), SSAATTBB, piano.

Kornizer, Leon (1888–1947 Hamburg). *Eli Tsiyon*, voice and pianoforte.

Krenek, Ernst (1900 Vienna–1991 Palm Springs, Calif.). *Lamentatio Jeremiae Prophetae*, a cappella choir.

La Hele, Georg (1547 Antwerp–1587 Madrid). *Lamentatio Jeremiae*, 5 voices; Lamentatio Jeremiae, 8 voices.

La Lande, Michel-Richard (1657 Paris–1726 Versailles). *Lamentationes Jeremiae Prophetae*, soprano/tenor and basso-continuo.

Lapicida, Erasmus (c.1450–1547 Vienna). *Lamentatio Jeremiae*, 3 voices.

Laquai, Reinhold (1894–1957 Switzerland). *Aus den Klageliedern Jeremias*, 6 voices and a cappella choir.

Laurens, Jean-Bonaventure (1801–1890 France). *Lamentations de Jeremie*, 2 tenors and a bass.

Le Boucher, Maurice Georges Eugene (1882–1964 Paris). *De lamentatione Jeremiae prophetae*, choir, organ and orchestra.

Leo, Leonardo (1694–1744 Naples). *Lezioni lamentationen*, soprano and alto.

Lidon, Jose (1748–1827 Madrid). *Lamentatione Jeremiae*.

Locke, Matthew (1630–1677 London). *How doth the city sit solitary*, 5 voice and basso-continuo.

Lotti, Antonio (1667–1740 Italy). *O Vos Omnes* (Lam. 1:12), SATB

Lupi II (17ᵗʰ C. France). *Lamentationes des Jeremiae*.

Marcello, Benedetto (1686–1739 Italy). *I treni de Geremia*.

Martini, Giovanni (1706–1784 Italy). *Behold and See* (Lam. 1:12), SATB.

Mazzaferrata, Giovanni Batista (17ᵗʰ C. Italy). *Lezioni e lamentationi*, voices and instruments.

Monnikendam, Marius (1896–1977 Netherlands). *De Klagsangen von Jeremias*, alto, choir and organ.

Morales, Christobal de (1512 Seville–1553 Malaga). *Lamentazionae Jeremiae*, 4–6 voices.

Nakseko, Kazu (1908 Kyoto–1973). *Lamentations of Jeremiah*, soprano, violin and pianoforte.

Nanino, Giovanni Maria (1545–1607 Rome). *Lamentationae Jeremiae*, voices.

Nasco, Jean (d. 1611 Italy). *Lamentationi*, 4 voices.

Nebra, Jose de (1688–1768 Madrid). *Lamentationes Jeremiae*, voices.

Nivers, Guillaume Gabriel (1632–1714 Paris). *Lamentationes Jeremiae Prophetae*.

Nowakowski, David (1848 Kiev–1921 Odessa). *Hashivenu Adonay eilekha* (Lam. 5:21), choir.

Obrecht, Jacob (c.1430 Utrecht, Netherlands–1505 Ferrara, Italy). *O vos omnes* (Lam. 1:12), motet, 3 voices.

Orto, Mabrianus de (16ᵗʰ C. Belgium). *Lamentationum Hieremiae Prophetae*.

Ouseley, Frederich A. Gore (1825–1998 UK). *Is It Nothing To You?* (Lam. 1:12), SATB.

Palestrina, Giovanni Pierluigi (1525–1594 Rome). *Lamentationum Hieremiae Prophetae*, motet, men's choir.

Phinot, Dominique (d. 1557/60 France/Italy). *Lamentationes Jeremiae*, Lam. 5:1–8, SATB/SATB

Pinkham, Daniel (1923–2006 Massachusetts). *Lamentations of Jeremiah*, choir.

Powell, Robert J. (b.1932 USA). *It is of the Lord's Mercies* (Lam. 3:22–26), SATB

Praetorius, Hieronymous (1560–1629 Germany). *O Vos Omnes* (Lam. 1:12), SATTB.

Preindl, Joseph (1756–1823 Vienna). *Lamentatio Jeremiae Prophetae*, choir.

Pujol, Juan (1573–1626 Barcelona). *Lamentazionae Jeremiae*, motet, 4–8 voices.

Ramsey, Robert (d.1644 England). *How doth the Cittie remayne desolate*, 6 voices; Woe is me that I am constrayned, 6 voices.

Raphael, Günter (1903 Berlin–1960). *Aus den Klagelieden Jeremiae*, choir.

Raval, Sebastino (c.1550–1604 Italy). *Lamentationes Hieremiae Prophetae*, 5 voices.

Rebello, Joao Leurenco (1610–1661 Portugal). *Lamentationes Hieremiae Prophetae.*

Rimonte, Pedro (c.1570–1618 Spain). *Lamentationae Hieremiae Prophetae*, 6 voices.

Robledo, Melchior (c.1520–1587 Spain). *Lamentations*, 4 voices.

Rodriguez de Ledesma, Marian (1779–1848 Madrid). *Lamentationes de samana sancta.*

Rosenthal, Manuel (1904–2003 Paris). *Deux prieres pour les temps malheureux*, voice and orchestra.

Rousseau, Jean-Jacques (1712 Geneva–1778). *Quomodo sedet sola civitas*, 2 voices and basso-continuo.

Roze, Abbe Nicholas (1745–1819 France). *Lecons de Jeremie.*

Sateren, Leland (1913–2007 USA). *His Compassions Fail Not* (Lam. 3:22–26), SATB.

Schalk, Carl (b.1929 USA). *Four Choruses from Lamentations* (Lam. 1:13, 18, 4:13–15, 5:1, 7, 15–16), SATB.

Schidlowsky, Leon (b.1931) *Lament* (1966), a cappella choir.

Sermisy, Claude de Claudin (c.1490–1562 Paris). *Lamentatio*, 4 voices.

Speranza, Alessandro (1728–1797 Naples). *Lamentazione Jeremiae.*

Stravinsky, Igor (1882 Russia–1971 USA). *Threni id est Lamentationes Jeremiae Prophetae*, soloist, choir and orchestra.

Szamotulczyk, Waclaw (1526–1560 Poland). *Lamentationes Hieremiae Prophetae*, men's choir.

Tal, Josef (1910 Germany–2008 Israel). *Lamentations* (1982) Cantata for alto and orchestra (Lamentations, Jeremiah).

Tallis, Thomas (1505–1585 England). *Incipit lamentatio*, 5 voices a cappella; *De Lamentatione*, 5 voices.

Tinctoris, Johannes (1435–1511 Belgium). *Lamentationes Jeremiae Prophetae*, 4 voices.

Torres, Jose de (1655–1738 Madrid). *Lamentatione*, 4 voices.

Tromboncino, Bartolomeo (1470–1535 Italy). *Lamentazionae Jeremiae*, voice and choir; *Lamentationum liberum secundus*.

Vallotti, Francesco Antonio (1697–1780 Italy) *O Vos Omnes* (Lam. 1:12), SATB.

Vargas, Urban de (d. 1656 Valencia). *Incipit lamentatio*, 14 voices and basso-continuo.

Varotto, Michele (c.1525–1599 Italy). *Lamentatione Hieremiae Prophetae*, 5–8 voices and instruments.

Vaughan Williams, Ralph (1872–1958 UK). *O Vos Omnes* (Lam. 1:12), SSAATTBB, alto-solo.

Vecchi, Orazio (1550–1605 Italy). *Lamentazione Hieremiae*, 4 voices.

Verheyen, Pierre Emmanuel (1750–1819 Ghent, Belgium). *Lamentationen*.

Viadana, Lodovico (1560–1645 Italy). *Lamentationes Hieremiae*, 4 voices.

Victoria, Tomas Luis de (1548–1611 Madrid). *Lamentationes Jeremiae*, 4–5 voices.

Vinci, Pietro (c.1535 Nicosia–1584 Italy). *Il primo lib. Delle Lamentationi*, 4 voices.

Weckmann, Matthias (1621–1674 Hamburg). *Die Klagelieder Jeremias*, 3 viola da gambas.

Werbecke, Gaspar van (1440 Belgium–c.1520). *Incipit lamentatio Jeremiae Prophetae*.

Werner, Gregor Joseph (c.1695–1766 Austria). *Die betruebte Tochter Zion*, oratorio.

Wise, Michael (1648–1687 England). *The Ways of Sion Do Mourn*, soprano, bass, SATB and organ, anthem.

Zelenka, Jan Dismas (1679 Bohemia–1745 Dresden, Germany). *Lamentationes Jeremiae Prophetae*, voices, instruments and basso-continuo.

Zumaya, Manuel (1680 Mexico City–1740). *Lamentationae*, choir.

Zur, Menachem (b.1942 Israel). *Lamentations* (1982), alto and orchestra, cantata.

29

Ernest Bloch's *Schelomo*, for cello and orchestra, is one of the few original musical compositions of Jewish conscious-ness to have entered the international concert repertory. Its motto replicates the opening words of the book, *Vanity of vanities; all is Vanity (Ecclesiastes 1:2)*.

ECCLESIASTES

The words of Koheleth, the son of David, king in Jerusalem. Vanity of vanities, saith Koheleth; vanity of vanities, all is vanity. What profit hath man of all his labor wherein he labor-eth under the sun? One generation passeth and another genera-tion cometh; and the earth abideth for ever. That which hath been is that which shall be, and that which hath been done is that which shall be done; and there is nothing new under the sun   (Ecclesiastes 1:1–4, 9).

The Book of Ecclesiastes is a work of deep pessimism, which, in the end, rises to a *reverence for God and obedience to his commandments, for this is the whole man (12:13)*. Fatalistic and stoic in character, the Sages wished to exclude the scroll from the Bible "because its words are self-contradictory." Yet, they did not "because its beginning and end are religious teaching."[1] According to tradition, Solomon wrote Ecclesiastes in his old age.[2] It contains the meditations of a world-weary man, overcome by a sense of the futility of all things.

Ernest Bloch: Schelomo: Hebrew Rhapsody (1915)
Subtext: Ecclesiastes
Genre: Program music
Medium: Cello and orchestra

---

1.   "Fore when a man becomes old, he speaks of the vanity of things" (Talmud Sabbath 30a).
2.   Midrash Ecclesiastes Rabbah 1.10.

Style: Post-Romantic-Impressionism
Duration: ca. 20 minutes

Biographic Context

Ernest Bloch (1880 Geneva–1959 Portland, Oregon) is the foremost creator of Jewish music in the 20th century.[3] His style merges influences from Wagner and Strauss, Mussorgsky and Debussy — with Hebraic cantillation and Orientalism.

Following musical studies — on violin with Eugene Ysaye in Brussels, composition with Jaques Dalcroze in Geneva, and Iwan Knorr in Frankfurt — Bloch returned to work in his father's shop of Swiss tourist goods, while continuing to compose, teach, and conduct. Bloch's father, Maurice (Meyer) Bloch, an introvert and pessimist in temperament, appears to have had an Orthodox background. In his youth, "Old Bloch" planned to study for the rabbinate, but upon reaching maturity became a merchant and turned agnostic. He imparted his understanding of Jewish customs and ceremonies to his children through songs and stories. Like his father, Bloch was an agnostic and did not practice Jewish customs or ceremonies; he had little faith in institutional religion. "From what father told me, I don't think [Hebrew] lessons had much of an impact;[4] though he absorbed the essence or atmosphere of whatever he was exposed to — and when he composed the Jewish Cycle (1912–1916) — this is what came out," wrote Bloch's daughter Suzanne, many years later. Bloch maintained a conviction that Judaism, at its prophetic best, possessed cosmic scope far beyond the limiting formulas of pride and knowledge, custom and ceremony.[5]

The outbreak of World War I, in 1914, confirmed Bloch's despair over the future of mankind, and brought to the surface a deep vein of pessimism latent in the composer's soul. His feelings soon found their outlet in what is his most famous work, the Hebrew Rhapsody for cello

---

3. Central to Bloch's music is his Jewish consciousness, and he is the first composer of world stature to think in such terms.
4. Ernest and his sister did not take their Hebrew lessons seriously; they would tease their old teacher who came to the house to teach them.
5. Suzanne Bloch (1907–2002), a Renaissance music specialist, showed me Bloch's sketchbooks at her apartment in New York City in the early 1970s, and enthusiastically informed me that her father had a large crucifix hanging on the wall of their living room.

and symphony orchestra, *Schelomo*. It had already been written by the time he came to the USA in 1916, as conductor for the dance company of Maud Allan (1873–1956).[6] Bloch went on to become a seminal figure in American music as mentor to some the most eminent composers and composition teachers of the next generation: Roger Sessions, Bernard Rogers, George Antheil, Frederick Jacobi, and Quincy Porter.

Text and Context

The career of Solomon and his court (described in 2 Chronicles 1–9) frames the subtext to this programmatic work. The following extracts from Bloch's program notes for the concert he conducted at the Royal Academy of Saint Cecelia in Rome, January 22, 1933, illumine the psychic imagery that informed his musical creativity.

> *If one likes, one may imagine that the voice of the solo cello is the voice of King Solomon. The complex voice of the orchestra is the voice of his age, his world, his experience. There are times when the orchestra seems to reflect his thoughts, as the solo cello reflects his words. The Introduction, which contains the germs of several essential motifs, is the plaint, the lamentation — 'nothing is worth the pain it causes; Vanity of Vanities — all is Vanity' — an emotional, nearly physiological reaction. The cello cadenza then puts this pessimistic philosophy into words — this beginning is a soliloquy. A new and important motif — violas! This mood changes, but the atmosphere of pessimism almost despairs — there comes his life, his world. Is it Solomon himself who tells us his dark reflections? There are the rhythms of languorous dance — a symbol of passion? The rhapsodist says: 'I have tasted all of this, and this too is Vanity!' The orchestra enlarges on the main theme; it becomes rich as though his wives and concubines could displace these thoughts. He enters into their seductive dance. The theme returns in the orchestra and here it becomes the royal pomp — the concubines, the slaves, the*

---

6. Maud Allen (1873 Toronto–1956 Los Angeles) trained in Europe and made her debut there. She danced to critical acclaim in London, and between 1910 and 1918 toured the world. Although she is almost forgotten now, at the height of her success she was as well known as Isadora Duncan. Her style of interpretive dancing helped expand the definitions of modern dance.

treasure, all that man might desire. Here, the exotic panoply of an Oriental world. 'I am the King. This is my world!' And then the revulsion: 'To what end? Vanity!'

The rhapsodist comments — gentler, more desolate, it is the broken idealism of Solomon. The languorous dance returns, but Schelomo spurns it. The grand tutti — tumult, barbaric splendor, power — and then Schelomo. And all of this — nothing, nothing. I cannot describe the next episode. It is a motif my father sang in Hebrew. Is it the call of a Muezzin; this strange motif of the bassoon, which permeates the orchestra? Is it the Priests? At first Schelomo seems to withstand it. Soon he joins in. Is it the crowd; their prayers? Again one hears the lament, their growing fevered anguish. Again tutti — is it Schelomo or the crowd — the maddening crowd hurling blasphemies against the universe? 'Vanity, vanity all is vanity.' The tumult is appeased. Schelomo alone mediates, a shudder of sadness — 'I have seen it all — wasted effort — the triumph of evil — I too knew hope; it is become barren, sterile, a gesture of despair. All is Vanity.'

The orchestra leaves this world to enter into a vision, where peace, justice, loving kindness live again. Schelomo drifts into the dreams, but not for long. The splendors of power and the throne topple like tarnished fanes into ruins. Here Schelomo thinks through the orchestra as his voice, and the solo cello cries imprecations. The orchestra magnifies these thoughts. This time the cadenza is a downfall, then alone in silence, 'Schelomo: Vanity of Vanities, all is Vanity!'

Music and Musical Exegesis

Bloch's music speaks almost like a Hasidic lament, an impassioned outcry of the heart, in which the voice of the solo cello is echoed, reiterated, elaborated, and commented upon by the orchestra. Rhapsodic in development, it gives the impression of being free, almost improvised in form. Yet, it is clearly structured in three sections — each climaxing in a resplendent, polychromatic orchestral surge. *Schelomo* recounts the regal pomp, power, and worldly splendor of Solomon's court with all the Impressionistic resources of the Late-Romantic orchestra. The real focus, however, is not its suggestive portrayal of nature, but rather, the spirit of the Bible, which Bloch is intent upon tone painting. In evoking the pathos of nature, clothed in quasi-oriental orchestral coloring, he is seeking, primarily, a musical metaphor to describe the opening nine verses of the book, a vision encased in swirling instrumental imagery: *the wind returneth again to its circuits...all rivers run into the sea...all things toil to weariness (1:1–9).*

Analysis

Schelomo opens with a lengthy cello cadenza. It represents the pessimistic voice of Solomon, in the Jewish *Ahavoh Rabbah* mode (A G F-sharp E-flat D C B-flat A), at first musing, later rising to a feverish pitch of despair. The middle section, dominated by a tune used in the study of the Talmud (*gemora nigun*), is characterized by reiterated recitation tones — as if the various instruments were mumbling a liturgical text. This section ends, as the first, in a bewildered cry against the universe. It is a world Solomon turns from in disgust. The third section, cast in the major mode, portrays Bloch's utopian vision of an ideal world. Notwithstanding, he is unable to maintain the ideal, and after citing several previous themes, *Schelomo* abandons this vision of eternal bliss to plunge once again into an anguished whirlpool of emotion. It is a cry that builds to a final, culminating convulsion, before closing on a chromatic descent into despair — the voice of the solo cello, mirroring *the words of the Preacher, the son of David, king in Jerusalem (1:1).*

Conclusion

Bloch's musical credo may be summed up in an oft cited autobiographical quotation: *It is the Jewish soul that interests me, the complex, glowing, agitated soul that I feel vibrating throughout the Bible; the freshness and naïveté of the Patriarchs; the violence of the Prophetic Books; the savage Jewish love of justice; the despair of Ecclesiastes; the sorrow and the immense greatness of the Book of Job; the sensuality of the Song of Songs. All this is in us, all this is in me, and it is the better part of me. It is all this that I endeavor to hear in myself and to transcribe in my music: the venerable emotion of the race that slumbers way down in our souls.*[7]

---

7.   Henry Taylor Parker, "Unique Music by Ernest Bloch Receives Notable Expositions" (San Franscisco: Mary Margearet Morgan Co., 1925), quoting from *Musical America* (May 12, 1917) 17, as cited in Robert Strassburg, *Ernest*

Through the Bible, Ernest Bloch's music unearths a philosophy of life. Triggered by events of the First World War, Bloch seeks mooring for his existential distress, beyond time and place. He finds symbolic resonance for turbulent inner emotions by way of identification with the aged figure of Solomon, king of Israel, despairing of his world. It is eternity speaking to him.

Related Directions

Johannes Brahms: Four Serious Songs *(Vier ernste Gesange)*, Op. 121 (1896)

Texts: Ecclesiastes 3:19–22, 4:1–3, Sirach (Ecclesiasticus) 41:1–21, 1 Corinthians 13:1–3, 12–13
Genre: Art Song
Medium: Voice and piano
Style: Late Romantic

Four serious songs for alto voice and piano, one of Johannes Brahms' last works, reveals the reflective, rather than dramatic side of Scripture. In this song cycle, Brahms seeks to relate to the tragic pessimism of *Ecclesiastes,* without reference to Solomon at all. It is a completely different direction of exegesis than Bloch's. In this textually composite work, verses are also included from the Apocrypha and New Testament. He sets them all as intimate meditations, posing the central questions of human existence.

Song 1: If man dies as beasts do, what about man's spirit? What distinguishes man from beasts? What outlasts death? *Who knoweth the spirit of man that goeth upward...? For who shall bring him to see what shall be after him? (Ecclesiastes 3:19–22).*

Song 2: What about evil and all the injustice which befalls man because of oppression by others (Ecclesiastes 4:1–3)?

Song 3: Death is bitter for men who live comfortably, but, for those who are tortured and in pain, death is deliverance (Sirach 41:1–2).

Song 4: And though I am gifted with skill, brilliance, wisdom, and even give to the poor, if I have not charity (a sense of loving-kindness towards others) *it profiteth me nothing...But now abideth faith, hope,*

Bloch, 41. See also Peter Gradenwitz, *The Music of Israel* (Portland, Oregon: Amadeus Press, 1996) 285–290.

and charity... but the greatest of these is charity (1 Corinthians 13:1–3, 12–13).

Works List

Adler, Samuel (b.1928 Germany/1939 USA). *Seasons of Time* (Eccles. 3, 11, 12), unison choir, piano, and percussion.

Bacon, Ernst (1898–1990 USA). *Ecclesiastes* (1936), soprano, baritone, SATB, and orchestra

Bantock, Granville (1868–1946 London). *Vanity of vanities,* choral symphony.

Ben-Haim, Paul (1897 Munich–1981 Tel Aviv). *U-zekhor et bor'eha* (Eccles. 12:1–7), 2 tenors, 1 baritone, and 2 basses.

Buxtehude, Dietrich (1637–1707 Germany). *Ich sprach in meinem Herzen,* soprano, strings, basso continuo.

Carissimi, Giacomo (1605–1674 Rome). *Vanitas vanitatum I and II,* soprano, tenor, choir, basso continuo.

Dello Joio, Norman (1913 New York–2008). *Meditations on Ecclesiastes* (Eccles. 11:1–8), strings.

Dessau, Paul (1894–1979 Berlin). *Havel havalim,* choir and orchestra.

Ehrlich, Abel (1915 Germany/1939 Israel–2003). *For the Memory of Them is Forgotten* (1975) for small mixed choir, flute, bassoon, horn, viola, violoncello.

_____. *Thou Knowest Not* (1986) for 4-part children's choir SSMA and violin.

Even-Or, Mary (1939–1989 Israel). *Time* (1985), voice and piano.

Fissinger, Edwin (1948–1990 USA). *To Everything There is a Season* (Eccles. 3:1), SATB and narrator.

Goemanne, Noel (b.1926 Belg./USA). *A Time for Everything* (Eccles. 3:1–8), unis, organ.

Glarum, L. Stanley (1908–1976 USA). *Remember Now Thy Creator* (Eccles. 12:1–2, 6–7), SATB.

Hajdu, Andre (b.1932 Hungary/Israel). *Vanity of Vanities* (1982), soprano, choir, pianoforte.

Harlap, Aharon (b.1941 Canada/Israel). *Kohelet or the Preacher* (2000) for mezzo soprano, violin, violoncello, pianoforte, song cycle.

_____. *Vanity of Vanities* (1982), for soprano, mixed choir and piano.

Holmboe, Vagn (1909–1996 Copenhagen). *Vanitas vanitatum,* 8 part, choir, motet.

Hovhaness, Alan (1911–2000 USA). *Wisdom* (Eccles. 8:1, 9:17–18), SATB (from *Three Motets*).

Korte, Karl (b.1928 USA). *Of Time and Season* (1975) (Ecclesiastes and other), SATB, marimba and piano.

Krenek, Ernst (1900 Austria–1991 USA). *The Earth Abideth* (Eccles. 1:4–5, 7), SSA.

_____. *Go Thy Way* (Eccles. 9:7, 9, 10), SATB (Three Motets).

Lang, David (b.1957 USA). *Again* (after *Ecclesiastes*) (2005), SSAATB.

Lewis, John Leo (1911–1971 USA). *Rejoice* (Eccles. 11:9).

_____. *Remember Now* (Eccles. 12:1), SATB.

London, Edwin (b.1929 USA). *Better Is* (Eccles. 4:6), SSA (9 soloists).

Mailman, Martin (1932–2000 USA). *To Everything There is a Season* (Eccles. 1–2, 4, 8, 10), SATB.

Mechem, Kirke (b.1925 Wichita, Kansas). *Songs of Wisdom* (Eccles. 1:18, 4:13, 7:9, 16, 9:11, 11:9), cantata.

Mueller, Carl F. (1892–1982 USA). *A Time for Everything* (Eccles. 3:1–8), SATB

Nowak, Lionel (1911–1995 USA). *Wisdom Exalteth Her Children* (Eccles. 4:11–12), SSA/SSA.

Orff, Carl (1895–1982 Germany). *Omnia Tempus Habent* (Eccles. 3:1–8), TTTBBBB

Patterson, Paul (b.1947 UK). *To Everything There is a Season* (Eccles. 3:1–2, 4, 8), SATB (from Requiem).

Pinkham, Daniel (1923–2006 Mass.). *Three songs from Ecclesiastes*, high voice and strings.

Pizzetti, Ildebrando (1880–1968 Italy). *Vanitas vanitatum* (Eccles. 1), cantata, men's choir and orchestra.

Playman, Gordon (20th C. USA). *Remember Now Thy Creator* (Eccles. 12:1–7), SATB, organ.

Red, Buryl (20th C. USA). *Ecclesiastes 4:11*, SA(T)B, keyboard.

Roza, Miklos (1907 Hungary/1939 USA–1995). *To Everything There is a Season* (Hienieden Alles has seine Stunde), op. 21 (1946) (Eccles. 3), SATB.

_____. *Vanities of Life* (Die Eitelken des Lebens), op. 30 (1967) (Eccles. 1:1–18), SATB (pianoforte or organ, ad lib.).

Sadai, Yitzchak (b.1935 Bulgaria/Israel). *Koheleth*, cantata for alto, baritone, and instruments.

Schein, Johann Hermann (1586–640 Leipzig). *Siehe an die Werk Gottes* (Eccles. 7:13–14), motet.

Schutz, Heinrich (1585–1672 Dresden). *Iss dein Brot mit Freuden* (Eccles. 9:7), motet.

Scott, Cyril (1879–1970 Liverpool). *Let us now praise famous men*, choir and orchestra.

Seeger, Pete (b.1919 New York City). *Turn! Turn! Turn!: To everything there is a season* (Eccles. 3:1–8), folk song.

Shaw, Christopher (1924–1995 UK). *A Lesson from Ecclesiastes* (Eccles. 5:1–7), SATB, organ.

Sleeth, Natalie (1930–1992 USA). *It's All in the Hands of God* (Eccles. 3:1–10), 2 pt, keyboard.

Starer, Robert (1924 Vienna–2001 Kingston, NY). *Kohelet: To everything there is a Season* (Eccles. 3:1–8), SATB (from *On the Nature of Things*), cantata.

Steggall, Charles (1826–1905 UK). *Remember Now Thy Creator* (Eccles. 12:4, 7–8), SATB, organ.

Sweelinck, Jan Pieterzoon (1562–1621 Amsterdam). *Vanitas vanitatum*, 4 voices, canon and unison.

Toch, Ernst (1887 Vienna–1964 St. Monica, California). *Vanity of vanities*, 2 voices and 5 instruments, cantata.

Tryhall, Gilbert (20th C. USA). *A Time to Every Purpose* (Eccles. 1:3–7, 3:1–8), SATB, Tape.

Wagemans, Peter-Jan (b.1952 Hague). *Ecclesiastes* (Eccles. 4:1–3), 4 sopranos, 4 altos, 4 tenors, 4 basses, 2 clarinets and 2 basses.

Weinberger, Jaromir (1896 Prague–1969 St. Petersburg, Fla.). *Ecclesiastes*, soprano, baritone, choir and organ.

Wiesenberg, Menachem (b.1950 Israel). *To Every Thing There is a Season* (1988) for women's or children's choir (SSA).

Werder, Felix (1922 Berlin-Melbourne). *Shir Kohelet*, solo violin.

Wolpe, Michael (b.1960 Israel). *To Every Thing* (1991), 3-part children's choir (SSA), pianoforte.

Yeakle, Thomas (20th C. USA). *Go Thy Way* (Eccles. 9:7–8), SATB.

Zorman, Moshe (b.1952 Israel). *To Every Thing* (1991), 3-part children's choir (SSA), pianoforte.

G. Dore: Esther Acsusing Haman, *Bible Illustrations (1866)*

30

The adaptation of the Book of Esther, in plays with music for school and community, and, in concert oratorios, indicates its breadth of appeal. This chapter focuses on biblical stories as a source of music for children, via two Purim songs.

ESTHER

So the king and Haman came to the banquet with Esther the queen. And the king said again unto Esther ... 'whatever thy petition queen Esther, it shall be granted thee... Even to the half of the kingdom' ... Then Esther the queen answered and said: 'If I have found favor in thy sight, O king, ... let my life be given me at my petition, and my people at my request; for we are sold, I and my people to be destroyed, to be slain, and to perish' ... Then spoke the king Ahasuerus and said ... 'Who is he, and where is he, that he durst presume in his heart to do so?' And Esther said: 'An adversary and an enemy, even this wicked Haman' (Esther 7:1–6).

The Book of Esther (*Megillah Esther*) takes place during the Persian Period (c.538–c.323 B.C.) and tells of the deliverance of the Jewish nation, brought about by God through Esther.[1] It reveals how Haman's

---

1.   A complicated and much disputed chronology surrounds the end of the Babylonian exile and the subsequent period of Persian rule, in which events in the Book of Esther occur. Scripture deals with these as follows: About a century before Ahasuerus, a Mede, became king (c.444 B.C.), Cyrus, a Persian (c.538 B.C.) had given the order to rebuild Jerusalem: *Thus saith Cyrus king of Persia, the Lord God of heaven hath given me all the kingdoms of the earth; and he hath charged me to build him an house at Jerusalem, which is in Judah. Who is among you of all his people... let him go up to Jerusalem... and build the house of the Lord (Ezra 4:2–3).* However, during the reign of Ahasuerus, referred to in Scripture as Artaxerxes (Ezra 4:6–7), word condemning the Jews, caused him to nullify the earlier decree of Cyrus: *Be it known now unto the king, that*

plot to destroy the Jews was foiled by Esther and Mordecai and transformed into the Feast of Purim. The sequence of events recorded in
Megillah Esther, occurs over a period of nine years — from the third
year of King Ahasuerus' reign (Esther 1:3) until the twelfth year (Esther
3:7). Ahasuerus' banquet, which opens the book, takes place after
Belshazzar's Feast (Daniel 5). Its purpose, like Belshazzar's, was to celebrate the unfulfilled prophecy of Jeremiah.[2] Ahasuerus, like Belshazzar
before him, had miscalculated the years of the Exile, and profaned the
Temple implements — using them as secular drinking goblets. The
Hebrew title *Megillah Esther* signifies the hidden hand of the Eternal
concealed behind apparent chance and coincidence. It is an encoded
secret, revealed through the agency of history.[3] The Feast of Purim is a
celebration of divine mercy, miraculously transforming fear and despair

---

*if this city be builded... [The Jews] will not pay toll, tribute, and custom, and...
endamage the revenue of the kings (Ezra 4:13).* King Artaxerxes (Ahasuerus)
responded, *it is found that this city of old time hath made insurrection against
kings, and that rebellion and sedition have been made therein (Ezra 4:19).* The
justification for Artaxerxes ('Ahasuerus') halt to the rebuilding the Temple,
in response to this account of resistance, becomes clear, and so....*they went
up in haste to Jerusalem unto the Jews, and made them to cease by force and
power (Ezra 4:23).* Haman's plot proposed a permanent solution to an existing
situation, and thus, he succeeded in persuading the king to do away with the
Jews entirely (Esther 3:6–15). To complete the story, we must jump ahead to
Darius (Darius II, the son of Esther and Ahasuerus) in the next generation
(c. 419 B.C.), who reinstated the decree of Cyrus: *Let the work of this house of
God alone (Dan. 6:7),* and sanctioned the rebuilding of Jerusalem: *In the first
year of Darius the son of Ahasuerus, of the seed of the Medes, was made king
over the realm of the Chaldeans (Dan. 9:1).* Thus was the prophecy of Jeremiah
fulfilled: *I will gather you from all the nations and places where I have banished
you and will bring you back to the place from where I carried you into exile (Jer.
25:11).*

2. *For many nations [Medes and Persians] and great kings shall make slaves of
    them; and I will recompense them according to their deeds, and according to
    the work of their hands (Jer. 25:14). For thus saith the Lord, that after seventy
    years be accomplished I will visit you, and perform my good word toward you,
    in causing you to return to this place (Jer. 29:10).*

3. All is contained in the names *Esther* and *Megillah.* Megillah means "to
    uncover" (Hebrew, *legalot*) or "reveal." Commentators derive the name
    Esther from the root meaning "to hide" *(hastir)* from the verse: *I will hide
    my face from them, I will see what their end shall be (Deut. 32:20).* The title
    Megillah Esther, can thus be interpreted as "the revelation of that which is
    hidden."

into joy and happiness. The *Megillah* was composed by the Men of the Great Assembly,[4] and is considered the last book of Scriptural writings.[5]

PURIM SONGS
Music for School and Community

Although music was banned in Jewish life, as a sign of national mourning, following the destruction of the Temple, at Purim celebrations music was permitted and even encouraged.[6] The two selections discussed in this chapter are drawn from a large repertoire of Purim songs popularly sung in homes, schools, communities, and synagogues throughout the Jewish world. Many Purim songs originated within dramatizations of the Purim story, known as *Purim-Spiele* (Purim plays).[7] These folk dramas, which date at least from the ninth and tenth centuries in Germany, were continued later in Eastern Europe. They appear to parallel the development of Medieval liturgical drama in the Christian world. In various contexts, Purim plays are performed to the present day.

Text and Context

Music is not foreign to the Book of Esther, which is sung to a special cantillation. Four verses of redemption (2:5, 8:15, 8:16, and 10:3) are recited in the synagogue, but in an unusual and uncharacteristic way. The congregation, rather than the reader, first reads the verse; then, this verse is repeated by the reader — a reversal of the conventional solo-congregation responsorial pattern of liturgy. The text to the song "U-Mordecai Yatsa" is based on two of the above verses: *And Mordecai went forth from the presence of the king in royal apparel of blue and white,*

---

4. These are the prophets, scribes, sages, and teachers who continued the spiritual regeneration of Israel, begun by Ezra. Tradition states that they laid the foundations of liturgy, edited several books of Scripture, and, all but fixed the biblical canon.

5. Talmud Baba Bathra 15a.

6. The jovial character of the feast is illustrated in a Talmudic maxim, later codified into Jewish law: One should drink on Purim until he can no longer distinguish between *cursed be Haman* and *blessed be Mordecai* (Talmud Megillah 7b).

7. *Spiele* is a Yiddish word meaning play or skit.

and with a great crown of gold, and with a robe of fine linen and purple; and the city of Shushan shouted and was glad. The Jews had light and gladness and joy and honor (8:15–16).

Music

DETAIL No. 1

U Mordecai Yatsa (*And Mordecai Went Forth*)
Text: Esther 8:15–16
Genre: Purim song
Medium: Voices
Style: Yiddish-Hasidic song
Duration: ca. 1 minute

The lively music to "U Mordecai yatsa" is sung syllabically. Its tonality is based on a natural-minor prayer mode, while the tune resembles a Yiddish folksong in structure: two symmetrical 8-bar periods. The first 4-bars (**A**) are open and cadence on the dominant; the next 4-bars (**A**) are closed and cadence on the tonic. This pattern of open and closed phrases is duplicated in the **B** period. Altogether, it generates a standard folksong form: **A A B B**.

U Mordecai yatsa milifney hamelech

Ex. 39. Purim Song: *U Mordecai Yatsa*
Transcribed by the author

Belevosh malchut vaateret zahav (8:15 paraphrase).
Layehudim hayta ora vesimcha.
Ora vesimcha ve sason v' yikak (8:16).

And Mordecai went forth from the presence of the king
In royal apparel and a great crown of gold (8:15 paraphrase).
The Jews had light and gladness.
Light and gladness and joy and honor (8:16).

DETAIL No.2

A Wicked, Wicked Man
Text and Music: Anonymous (English)
Arranged by S.E. Goldfarb
Genre: School song
Medium: Voices
Style: Strophic song (March)
Duration: ca. 1 minute

The school song "A Wicked, Wicked Man" summarizes, in a spoofing manner, the main characters of the story in short, pithy phrases. Each stanza of its freely invented English text, while it does not, directly, cite Scripture, has a scriptural origin; revealing its anonymous author's familiarity with the narrative: Verse 1 (3:5–6), verse 2 (7:2, 6), verse 3 (4:7), verse 4 (7:3–5), verse 5 (8:7) and verse 6 (9:20–22).

The tune to leaps about in triadic formations, like a trumpet reveille or a German folksong. The two-line 8-bar tune (**A B**) is constructed in verse-refrain. Each 8-bar line sub-divides into two 4-bar phrases (A = a + a) and (B = b + b). The verse is symmetrically constructed (2 + 2) and always cadences on the tonic. The refrain is balanced asymmetrically (3 + 1). The origin of tune is unknown; perhaps, it is an original melody, or perhaps, it is an American adaptation of an earlier folksong.[8]

---

8. The song "A Wicked, Wicked Man" appears in a collection, entitled, "The Jewish Songster" (1925), compiled by Rabbi Israel Goldfarb and his brother Samuel Eliezer Goldfarb, head of the music department at the Bureau of Jewish Education, who is credited with being the song's arranger. It has been sung in Jewish-American religious schools ever since.

Ex. 40. Purim Song: *A Wicked, Wicked Man*
Transcribed by the author

Verse 1.

Oh! Once there was a wicked, wicked man, And Haman was his name, Sir.
He would have murdered all the Jews; through they were not to blame, Sir.

Refrain:

Oh, today we'll merry, merry be,
Oh, today we'll merry, merry be,
Oh, today we'll merry, merry be,
And *Nash* some *Homen tashen.*

Verse 2.

And Esther was the lovely queen of king Ahasuerus.
When Haman said he'd kill us all, Oh my, how he did scare us.

Refrain

Verse 3.

But Mordecai her cousin bold, Said,"What a dreadful *chutzpah,*
If guns were but invented now, This Haman I would shoot, Sir.

Refrain

Verse 4.

When Esther speaking to the king, Of Haman's plot made mention,
"Ha, ha" said he, "Oh, no he won't! I'll spoil his bad intention."

Refrain

Verse 5.

> The guest of honor he shall be, this clever Mr. Smarty.
> And high above us he shall swing, at a little hanging party.

Refrain

Verse 6.

> Of all his cruel and unkind ways, this little joke did cure him.
> And don't we owe him thanks, for this jolly feast of Purim.

Refrain

Conclusion

Comparing the two songs, we note that "And Mordecai Went Forth" is primarily a congregational song, sung in homes, schools, synagogues, and community settings, whereas, "A Wicked, Wicked Man," is a school song — written for, and exclusively sung by children. This sociological distinction is significant. The congregation is an all-inclusive body and represents the traditional Jewish world-view: *We will go with our young and with our old, with our sons and with our daughters (Exod. 10:9)*. The idea of a separate repertoire of children's music is unknown to Jewish Tradition before the Enlightenment (*Haskalah*). It represents a segregation based on age-grouping, and is a unique contribution of the modern world to biblical study. Its introduction to 20th-century American-Jewish education, and its parallel in elementary education in Palestine at the same period, duplicates something akin to the development of children's literature in the West, two centuries earlier.[9] From the above examples, we observe, one of the ways in which the Bible

---

9.   In Western literature, there are no written records of children's songs until the 17th century. Before that time, children learned chants and songs by rote. This development, though, has had an inverse effect upon the adult population, tending to infantilize the deep ethical and historic vistas of religion, and characterize Bible stories by such condescending remarks as: "they are just stories for children." Curiously, this tendency to minimalize Scriptural narrative enters culture through the door of jest, satire, and parody. It is characteristic of the Purim play: *and the scorners delight in their scorning (Proverbs 1:22)*.

penetrated the world of little children. It was through such songs that the Book of Esther left the liturgical milieu and entered into the brightly colored world of the kindergarten.

Related Directions — Concert Works

An early musical treatment of the subject is a 14th-century motet for three voices, *Quoniam Novi probatur*, in which Haman voices his complaint. Palestrina wrote a five-voiced motet, *Quid habes Hester?* (1575), a dialogue between Esther and Ahasuerus, on a text taken from apocryphal additions to Esther 15:9–14. From the late 17th century and early 18th century, the Esther story attracted the attention of many serious composers. Some works include: A. Stradella's oratorio *Ester, liberatrice dell' popolo ebreo* (c. 1670), Marc Antoine Charpentier's quasi-oratorio *Historia Esther* (date unknown), G. Legrenzi's oratorio *Gli sponsali d'Esther* (1676), J.B. Moreau's choruses for Racine's *Esther* (1712), and A. Caldara's oratorio *Ester* (1723). One of the few works on the subject in the second half of the 18th century was K. Ditters von Dittersdorf's oratorio *La liberatrice del popolo giudaico nella Persia a sia l'Esther* (1773). Handel's masque *Haman and Mordecai (1718)*, with text by John Arbuthnot and (probably) Alexander Pope, and based on Racine's drama, was Handel's first work in the direction of oratorio, first performed in 1720, and later worked it into a full English oratorio, *Esther (1732)*. The libretto was translated into Hebrew by the Venetian rabbi, Jacob Raphael Saravaal (1707–1782); two copies of it survive in the *Etz Haim* Library, Amsterdam.

The 19th and 20th centuries saw a few operatic variants of the story, such as Guidi's *Ester d'Engaddi*, set by A. Peri (1843) and G. Pacini (1847); while Eugene d'Albert wrote an overture to Grillparzer's *Esther* (1888). For performances of Racine's play at the Comedie Française, choruses were composed by several undistinguished musicians; later contributions include those by Reynaldo Hahn (1905) and Marcel Samuel-Rousseau (1912). *Esther*, an opera by Jan Meyerowitz with text by Langston Hughes, was written in 1956. Meyerowitz also wrote a choral work, *Midrash Esther* (1957). The most notable modern work on the subject is Darius Milhaud's opera *Esther de Carpentras* (1938), which dramatized an old Provençal Purim play, with the threat posed by a conversionist bishop of Carpentras.

Purim Plays *(Purim-Spiel)*

The music of Jewish Purim plays has not survived in notation except for a few songs collected by 20th-century folklorists. Isaac Offenbach's play *Koenegin Esther* (1833) includes some couplets, in which the court jester seems a more important figure than the biblical personages. Hermann Cohn's five-act parody *Der Barbier von Schuschan* (1984) was an imitation of P. Cornelius's *Barbier von Baghdad; Abraham Goldfaden's Kenig Akhashverosh* (c. 1885), produced no memorable tune, and M. Gelbart wrote *Akhashverosh*, a Purim play in New York (1916). The Purim-Spiele, with their wealth of songs and choruses, also influenced the creation of Yiddish Theater, and, in turn, the American Musical Theater. In Palestine, for the production of K.J. Silman's *Megillat Esther*, music was written by Yedidya Admon. The music for the production of Itzik Manger's *Di Megille* was written by Dov Seltzer in a revival style, reminiscent of East European Jewish folksong and Yiddish theatre in particular. Nahum Nardi's songs to Levin Kipnis' kindergarten Purim play *Mishak Purim*, written in the early 1930s, have become popular Israeli folksongs. A large repertoire of 20th-century children's songs (with non-liturgical texts) is sung on and around the Purim holiday in Jewish homes, schools, and synagogues throughout the world. Some of these include: *Once There Was a Wicked, Wicked Man, Ani Purim, Chag Purim, Mishe Nichnas Adar, Shoshanas Yaakov, Al HaNisim, VeNahafoch Hu, LaYehudim Hayesa Orah, Kacha Yay'aseh, Chayav Inish,* and *Utzu Eitzah*.[10]

Works List

Adlgasser, Anton (1729 Inzel–1777 Salzburg). *Esther*, oratorio.
Albergati, Pirro (1663–1735 Bologne). *Esther* (F. Grillparzer), overture.
Anfossi, Pasquale (1727–1797 Rome). *Ester* (N. Angeletti), oratorio.
Arrigoni, Carlo (1697–1744 Florence). *Ester*, oratorio.
Aurisicchio, Antonio (1710 Naples–1781 Rome). *Ester*, componimento dramatico.
Bellinzani, Paolo Benedetto (1690 Mantua–1757 Recanati). *Esther* (G.M. Ercolani), oratorio.

---

10. See Batia Bayer's summary from the article "Book of Esther," *Encyclopaedia Judaica*, Vol. 6, col. 912.

Bellman, Carl Michael (1740–1795 Stockholm). *Ester* (A.M. Ercolani), oratorio.

Bonfichi, Paolo (1769–1840 Italy). *Ester, ossia la morte di Ammano* (F.S. Salfi), oratorio.

Borghi, Giovanni Battista (1738–1796 Italy). *Il trionfo di Mardocheo*, oratorio.

Brod, Max (1884 Prague–1968 Tel Aviv). *Esther* (M. Brod), incidental music.

Brunetti, Gualberto (1706–1787 Italy). *Ester*, oratorio.

Caldara, Antonio (1670 Venice–1736 Vienna). *Esther* (R. Fozio), oratorio.

Castelnuovo-Tedesco, Mario (1895 Italy–1968 USA). *The Book of Esther*, oratorio.

Cerne, Titus (1859–1910 Romania). *Esther*, cantata, voice and orchestra.

Charpentier, Marc-Antoine (1636–1704 Paris). *Historia Esther*, oratorio.

Clari, Giovanni Carlo (1677–1754 Pisa). *Esther* (Pistoia-Gatti), oratorio.

Cola, Gregorius (18th C.). *Esther*, oratorio.

Comella, Luciano Francisco (1757–1812 Madrid). *Esther*, oratorio.

Coquard, Arthur (1846 Paris–1910). *Esther* (J. Racine), opera.

Dittersdorf, Karl Ditters von (1739 Vienna–1799 Bohemia). *La liberatrice del popolo guidaico nella Persia o sia l'Esther* (I. Pintus), oratorio.

Edelmann, Johann Friedrich (1749 Strasbourg–1794 Paris). *Esther*, oratorio.

Ettinger, Max (1874 Lwow–1951 Basel). *Koenigin Esther*, soloist, choir and orchestra.

Fatioli, Mercurio (18th C. Rome) *Humilium et superborum exitus* (Ph. Capistrellus), oratorio.

Ferrari Trecate, Luigi (1884 Alexandria–1964 Rome) *Regina Ester* (A. Montanari), opera.

Fritellio, Jacobo (17th C. Rome). *Aman depressus*, choir, organ and instruments.

Gabrielli, Conte Nicolo (1814 Naples–1891 Paris). *Ester*, opera.

Gasparini, Francesco (1668–1727 Rome). *Esther*, oratorio.

Gideon, Miriam (1906 Colorado–1996 New York). *Three Biblical Masks: Haman, Esther, Mordecai*, violin and pianoforte.

Gordigiani, Luigi (1806–1860 Florence). *Esther*, oratorio.

Hahn, Reynaldo (1875 Caracas–1947 Paris). *Esther* (J.B. Racine), incidental music.

Handel, George Frederic (1685 Halle–1759 London). *Esther* (A. Pope), oratorio.

Hart, Fritz (1874 London–1949 Honolulu). *Esther* (F. Hart), opera.

Jacquet (de La Guerre), Elisabeth (1667–1729 Paris). *Esther* (A.H. de la Motte), voice and basso continuo, cantata.

Kaufmann, Walter (1907 Karlovary, Cz.–1984 USA). *Esther* (H. Politzer), opera.

Konigsloew, Johann (1745–1833 Germany). *Esther*, oratorio.

Kozlowski, Jozef (1757 Warsaw–1831). *Esther* (J. Racine), incidental music.

Lavry, Marc (1903 Riga–1968 Haifa). *Queen Esther* (M. Lavry), opera.

Lefebvre, Charles Edouard (1843 Paris–1917*). Esther* (J. Racine), incidental music.

Legrenzi, Giovanni (1626–1690 Venice). *Gli sponsali d'Ester*, oratorio.

Leichtentritt, Hugo (1874 Posen–1951 Cambridge, Mass.). *Esther*, music drama.

Leidesdorf, Maximilian Joseph (1787 Vienna–1840 Florence). *Esther*, oratorio.

Lotti, Antonio (1667–1740 Venice). *L'umilta coronata in Esther*, oratorio.

Majo, Gian Francesco (1740 Naples–1770 Rome). *Esther*, oratorio.

Manna, Christoforo (18th C. Naples). *Esther*, oratorio.

Mariotte, Antoine (1875–1944 Paris). *Esther, princesse d'Israel* (A. Dumas and Ch. Leconte), opera.

Mathieu, Julien (1734 Versailles–1811 Paris). *La reine Vashti*, oratorio.

Mees, Joseph Henri (1777 Brussels–1856 Paris). *Esther*, oratorio.

Mereaux, Nicolas-Jean Lefroid de (1745–1797 Paris). *Esther*, oratorio.

Messner, Joseph (1893–1969 Salzburg). *Hadassa*, biblical opera.

Meyerowitz, Jan (1913 Germany–1998 France). *Esther*, opera.

Milhaud, Darius (1892 France–1974 Geneva). *Esther de carpentras* (A. Lunel), opera.

_____. *Le candelabre a sept branches*: e) Purim, pianoforte.

Moreau, Jean Baptiste (1656–1733 Paris). *Esther* (J. Racine), incidental music.

Moreira, Antonio Leal (1758–1819 Lisbon). *Ester*, oratorio.

Naumbourg, Samuel (1815 Ansbach–1880 Paris). *U'Mordechai yatza lifne hamelech*, men's choir.

_____. *La Jehudim hajeta ora vesimchah*, choir.

Orlandini, Giuseppe Maria (1688 Bologne–1750 Florence). *Esther* (G. Melani), oratorio.

Paisiello, Giovanni (1740–1816 Naples). *Ester*, oratorio.

Palestrina, Giovanni Pierluigi (1525–1594 Rome). *Quid habes Hester* (Esther 15:9–14), motet.

Pasquini, Bernardo (1637–1710 Rome). *Assuero* (Nencini), oratorio.

Plantade, Charles-Henri (1764–1839 Paris). *Esther* (J. Racine), choirs.

Rose, Alfred (1855–1919). *La-Yehudim*, choir and organ.

Rousseau, Alexandre-Samuel (1853–1904 Paris). *Esther, princesse d'Israel* (J. Racine), incidental music.

Sacchini, Antonio Maria (1730 Florence–1786 Paris). *Esther*, oratorio.

Sarri, Domenica Natale (1678–1744 Naples). *Ester riparatrice*, oratorio.

Schuster, Joseph (1748–1812 Dresden). *Ester*, oratorio.

Springer, Max (1877–1954 Vienna). *Esther*, opera.

Stradella, Alessandro (1645 Naples–1682 Genoa). *Ester, liberatrice del popolo hebreo*, oratorio.

Strung, Nicolaus Adam (1640–1700 Dresden). *Esther* (J. Koeler), singspiel.

Szulc, Jozef Zygmunt (1875 Warsaw–1956 Paris). *Esther*, symphonic overture.

Tarchi, Angelo (1759 Naples–1814 Paris). *Esther* (I. Pergola), oratorio.

Valle, Pietro della (1586–1652 Rome). *Esther*, oratorio.

Volkert, Franz (1776–1846 Vienna). *La-Yehudim hayetah orah* (Esther 8:10), choir.

Werner, Gregor Joseph (c.1695–1766 Eisenstadt). *Die glueckh-seeligst vermaehlte u. bis zum hoechsten Gipfel der ehren erhobene Durchlaeuchtige Braut Esther*, oratorio.

CHAPTER 31

The colorful *Belshazzar's Feast* by William Walton is one of the first major oratorios of the 20th century to be influenced by jazz. Declamatory and rhythmic in character, it telescopes the Babylonian exile and redemption into three concise scenes.

DANIEL

Then they brought the golden vessels that were taken out of the temple of the house of God, which was at Jerusalem; and the king, and his princes, his wives, and his concubines, drunk in them. They drank wine, and praised the Gods of gold, and of silver, of brass, of iron, of wood, and of stone. In the same night came forth finger's of a man's hand, and wrote over against the candlestick upon the plaster of the wall of the king's palace: and the king saw the part of the hand that wrote. Then the king's countenance was changed, and his thoughts troubled him…. Now let Daniel be called and he will show the interpretation (Daniel 5:3–6, 12).

Daniel, one of the captives taken when Jerusalem fell into the hands of Nebuchadnezzar, was brought to Babylon as a child, in the first deportations from Judea in 597 B.C.[1] Extraordinarily pious, and clairvoyant in spirit, Daniel was the most distinguished member of the Babylonian Diaspora, and rose to become advisor to Nebuchadnezzar, Belshazzar, Darius, and Cyrus. The Book of Daniel focuses on his experiences, interpretations of dreams, and visions. The twelve chapters of the book fall into two groups. The first six chapters relate incidents in the life of Daniel and his friends; the remainder are visions. The book is placed in the Writings of the Hebrew Bible and among the Prophets in the

---

1.   Louis Ginzberg, *Legends of the Bible*, 633.

Christian Bible. Tradition attributes its authorship to the Men of the Great Assembly.[2]

Christian theology regards the Book as one of the most important in Scripture — connecting the Old and New Testaments, citing it as the foundation for the book of Revelation. It regards Daniel as saint and prophet — foretelling the Messiah, the destruction of Jerusalem, and the Temple in 70 (Dan. 9:24–27). Jesus brings attention to Daniel as prophet (Matt. 24:15), attributing phrases from Daniel's visions — such as 'son of man' (Dan. 7:13) — to himself.

William Walton: Belshazzar's Feast (1930)
Libretto: Osbert Sitwell
Genre: 20th C. Oratorio
Medium: Baritone soloist, chorus, brass ensemble and orchestra
Style: Pantonal and Polytonal
First Performance: Leeds Festival, October 8, 1931
Duration: ca. 35 minutes

Biographic Context

William Walton (1902–1983) is the major British composer to emerge in the period between the two World Wars. His style juxtaposes modernity with Neo-Romantic idioms. Walton was born in the industrial town of Oldham, where his father was a choirmaster and singing teacher. When the boy was 10 years old, hoping to advance his son's education, the father arranged an audition for him as chorister at Christ Church Cathedral, Oxford University. The dean of the church took an interest in young William, and subsequently, at the early age of 16, arranged for him to attend Oxford. Then followed a period when Walton was the "adopted brother" of the brilliant and wealthy Sitwell family, which included poet Sacheverell (who had befriended William as an Oxford undergraduate), and his siblings, Osbert and Edith. For more than ten years, Walton lived and traveled with the Sitwell family, continuing to compose and broaden his horizons, while freed from financial worries. For a year, he played piano with a jazz band, and this experience

---

2. The Men of the Great Assembly were prophets, scribes, sages, and teachers who continued the spiritual regeneration of Israel that was begun by Ezra (Talmud Baba Bathra 15a).

influenced the music he wrote to accompany the poetry of Edith Sitwell — *Façade* an 'entertainment' for speaking voice and six instruments. In 1929, Walton was invited by the British Broadcasting Corporation (BBC) to compose a small choral work for broadcast; it blossomed into *Belshazzar's Feast*.

Text and Context

The libretto to *Belshazzar's Feast* by Osbert Sitwell is based on the Book of Daniel (5:1–30). Its three sections are: Part 1 — *Isaiah's ominous prophecy against Babylon*, Part 2 — *Belshazzar's feast*, and Part 3 — *the Exiles redeemed*. They flow together without pause.

I

Prophecy of the Destruction of Babylon

The libretto supplements the account from the Book of Daniel with prophetic citations[3] foretelling the destruction of Babylon: *Howl ye for the day of the Lord is at hand; as destruction from the Almighty shall it come (Isaiah 13:6)*. Psalm 137 is alluded to as well, adding historic vividness to the scene by invoking the suffering of the exiled Judeans at *the waters of Babylon*.[4]

II

Belshazzar's Feast

Belshazzar's pride is an illusion, founded on a miscalculation of the duration of the exile. The king had arrogantly thought that the Almighty had reneged on his promise of deliverance for the Judeans, and Jeremiah's prophecy had not been fulfilled: *And it shall come to pass, when seventy years are accomplished, that I will punish the king of*

---

3. Isaiah 39 describes Hezekiah revealing his treasures to representatives of the king of Babylon. *Thus spake Isaiah: Thy sons that thou shalt beget, they shall take away and be eunuchs in the palace of the king of Babylon (Isa. 39:5, 7)*.

4. *By the waters of Babylon there we sat down; yea we wept and hanged our harps upon the willows. For they that wasted us required of us a song. Sing us one of the songs of Zion. How shall we sing the Lord's song in a strange land? If I forget thee, O Jerusalem, let my right hand forget her cunning. If I do not remember thee, let my tongue cleave to the roof of my mouth. Yea, if I prefer not Jerusalem above my chief joy (Psalm 137)*.

Babylon, and that nation, saith the Lord, for their iniquity, and the land of the Chaldeans; and I will make it perpetual desolation (Jer. 25:12). For thus saith the Lord: After seventy years are accomplished for Babylon, I will remember you, and perform My good word toward you, in causing you to return to this place (Jer. 29:10).

III

The Redemption of the Exiles and the Fall of Babylon

Supplementary descriptions from the New Testament, replete with references to the wealth of Babylon,[5] serve to intensify the eventual fall of the Chaldean city, when it does arrive. The cries of the redeemed exiles are voiced in Psalm texts,[6] drawing the oratorio to its exultant conclusion.

Music and Musical Exegesis

Belshazzar's Feast is dramatic in character but narrative in form. Its demonstrative expression flows with the action; there are no arias, choruses, or extended recitatives as in Handel. It employs large performing forces and makes extensive use of percussion instruments. Choral passages are frequently rhythmic, assertive, animated, almost jazzy, and sparked by pungent dissonances. Practically every syllable is set to a different tone cluster.[7] Sonorities are mostly tertian, but at other times, also, quartal.[8] The choral proclamations are provided with

---

5. *Babylon was a great city, her merchandise was of gold and silver, of precious stones, of pearls, of fine linen, of purple silk and scarlet, all manner vessels of ivory, all manner vessels of most precious wood, of brass, iron and marble, cinnamon, odors and ointments, of frankincense, wine and oil, fine flour, wheat and beasts, sheep, horses, chariots, slaves and the souls of men (Revelation 18:10–13).*

6. *Then sing aloud to God our strength, make a joyful noise to the God of Jacob. Take a psalm, bring hither the timbrel, blow up the trumpet in the New Moon. Blow the trumpet in Zion, for Babylon the great is fallen. Alleluia (Psalm 81:1–3)!*

7. Each four note cluster is comprised of a triad plus an added tone — a sixth, a seventh, or a ninth — often in inverted position. That is, a change or reversal in the natural order of the notes of a triad (i.e. instead of root position 1–3–5–6, it might be 3–5–6–1 or 5–6–1–3).

8. Quartal sonorities are made up of intervals of fourths or fifths, piled one on

tonal support from the orchestra. Once its difficult vocal demands are surmounted, the score makes a brilliant effect. The following excerpt from Part II, interplaying block and contrapuntal textures, contains some of Walton's most imaginative choral writing.

DETAIL

Excerpt from Part II

A short, unison orchestral introduction opens this segment, foreboding events about to transpire. The following texts, which set the scene, are voiced in four-note block-choral texture.

Chorus

> Thus in Babylon, the mighty city,

Chorus

> Belshazzar the King made a great feast,
> Made a feast to a thousand of his lords.
> And drank wine before the thousand.

Chorus

> Belshazzar, whiles he tasted the wine

Walton portrays Belshazzar's guests becoming inebriated with consummate musical skill. A feast is in the offing, and as the guests, metaphorically, taste the wine and get drunk, short melismas sprout forth in each voice, and strict homophonic texture opens up into a tipsy polyphonic web. A short orchestral interlude follows.

Then, in the following *tutti* choral passage, the text, *command us to bring*, is recited as rhythmicized chant. An asymmetric continuity of phrases stirs up anticipation and excitement for *the gold and silver vessels*. Besides providing tonal underpinning, the orchestra, in-between choral declamations, adds its own polymetric interludes. Clarion brass timbres emerge, with orchestration taking its cue from the text's metallic imagery — *the gold and silver vessels*.

---

top of the other, for example: d-g-c'-f' or g-d-a'-e'.

Ex. 41. William Walton: *Belshazzar's Feast*

Belshazzar's Feast by William Walton. Words selected from biblical sources by Osbert Sitwell. Music by William Walton. © Copyright Oxford University Press 1931. Reproduced by permission. All rights reserved.

Chorus

> Commanded us to bring the gold and silver vessels
> That his Princes, his wives and his concubines
> Might rejoice and drink therein.

The vocal textures froth, and phrases continue to expand into longer and longer free polyphonic melismas, as all *rejoice and drink*. Antiphonal exchanges between the two choruses graphically illustrate the differences between Belshazzar's wives and his concubines. The wives' phrases are short and to the point; the concubines' are longer and sensually drawn out. Another short orchestra interlude follows.

Chorus

> After they had praised their strange gods,
> The idols and the devils,

Chorus

> False gods who can neither see nor hear,

Walton, then, introduces free chromaticism into block sonorities as allusions to strange gods, idols, and devils. Another short orchestral passage transitions into imagery of alien, sacrilegious, false gods. Because false gods are many, Walton, insightfully, subdivides the choral parts and introduces imitation and increasing complexity. Many voice-parts illustrate, metaphorically, the concept of idolatrous moral blindness by way of musical texture, since 'false gods are many.'[9] In stark contrast, however, unisons invoke the inviolable monotheistic word of the one true God. An orchestral interlude seats us in the hall, alongside the guests' calls for timbrel and harp. This *a cappella* passage, begun in complex imitative choral polyphony, gradually coalesces into a radiant unison on the word — *king*.[10] A pounding orchestral interlude ushers in another *a cappella* declamation.

---

9. A verbal commentary, on the other hand, might have noted, 'the people do not think for themselves; they merely imitate alien gods who can neither prosper nor help.'

10. This touch by Walton is filled with symbolism. The king is the model for the people. It is He to whom all flows, and from whom, all emanates. We find this interpretation of the Hebrew word for king (*Melech*) in Hirsch's commentaries to *Psalms* (10:16, 21:2, and 24:7–9).

Chorus

> Called they for the timbrel and the pleasant harp
> To extol the glory of the King.

Chorus

> Then they pledged the King before the people, crying,
> Thou, O King, art King of Kings: O King, live for ever...

Such clamoring choral statements alternate with orchestral responses, and build to a climactic pronouncement. Engaging antiphonal choral dispositions resemble Anglican psalmody,[11] showing us how a traditional liturgical format may become integrated into a complex modern work. Then, once again, the mixed choral sonority coalesces into a vibrant unison, sustained against a pounding orchestra.

Narrator

> And in that same hour, as they feasted came forth fingers of a man's hand
> And the King saw the part of the hand that wrote.

This spare, solo baritone recitative, beginning in "medio" range, stretches up, then, fractures down, to introduce the writing on the wall sequence. It produces an ominous effect, after so much tutti singing.

Narrator

> And this was the writing that was written:
> 'MENE, MENE, TEKEL, and UPHARSIN'[12]

Chorus

> 'THOU ART FOUND WEIGHED IN THE BALANCE AND FOUND WANTING.'

The text 'MENE, MENE, TEKEL, and UPHARSIN' is declaimed parlando, with long pauses between phrases, against spine tingling

---

11. These choral techniques are used naturally by Walton, schooled in antiphonal Anglican Church psalmody from childhood.

12. These mysterious words are a play on their meaning in Aramaic: *Mene*: God has *measured* your sovereignty and put an end to it; *Tekel*: you have been *weighed* in the balance and found wanting; *Parsin*: your kingdom has been *divided* and given to the Medes and the Persians. *The Jerusalem Bible*, Alexander Jones, ed., note f (Garden City, NY: Doubleday & Company, 1966) 1435.

sonorities in the orchestra. The soloist begins on a frightening low B-flat, then, bounds up a major seventh, to interpret the mysterious writing on the wall. Men's choral voices utter the frightening Divine Pronouncement, protracted for greater dramatic effect, on an F-sharp minor/major seventh chord.

Ex. 42. William Walton: *Belshazzar's Feast*

© Copyright Oxford University Press 1931. Reproduced by permission. All rights reserved.

Narrator

> In that night was Belshazzar the King slain.
> And his Kingdom divided.

The narrator, completely unaccompanied, erupts into a cry on the name "Belshazzar." Cadenza-like, it descends from middle to low register, then ascends all the way up into the highest head tones.

It makes a striking impression, conjuring up a dramatic flashback, telescoping the king's entire career into a single breath. The choir reiterates the narrator's pronouncement, shouting aloud the fatal word — *slain!* The effect is electric, like a knife jabbing into the king's gut.

Ex. 43. William Walton: *Belshazzar's Feast*

© Copyright Oxford University Press 1931. Reproduced by permission. All rights reserved.

Conclusion

If not generally categorized as a national composer, William Walton, in drawing upon his experience as a boy chorister in the Anglican Church, gives this 20th-century biblical oratorio a voice that is thoroughly British. In his scansion of text, Walton's masterful *Belshazzar's Feast* presents an incisive and insightful modern exegesis, integrating tradition with innovation. Avoiding excessive introspection, he portrays the story almost cinematically; bearing testimony to the Book of Daniel's guiding light: The Eternal will frustrate the schemes of proud and mighty kings, but defend and keep his faithful servants from all harm. Fate is not blind, history is the unfolding of a divine plan, and destiny is determined by the will of God. At the end of days, righteousness will triumph and the Kingdom of God will be established on earth.

Play of Daniel and Other Works

The *Play of Daniel* mentioned in the following paragraph gives us occasion to note the role of the church in the development of the concert hall, theater, and opera house, since in the Middle Ages it functioned as all three. This ecclesiastical drama is but one example drawn from a larger repertoire, which synthesized dramatic action, speech, antiphonal singing, and music derived from ecclesiastical rites — antiphons, responsorials, sequences, and hymns into a coherent whole.

Mediaeval liturgical drama generally used little in the way of elaborate costumes and scenery, forbade the use of instruments, and contained large quotations of unmeasured plainsong. The *Play of Daniel*[13] is exceptional. It is a medieval opera, closely following the biblical story at the court of Belshazzar, with large portions of the text being poetic rather than strictly liturgical. Its music combines composed songs and traditional church melodies, many borrowed from earlier works. Significantly, the monophonic manuscript indicates pitch only, but not rhythm, compelling performers to do their own scansion based on the natural accentuation of the Latin text.

Handel's powerful oratorio *Belshazzar* (1745, text by Charles Jennens) did not deter later composers from attempting versions of their own. Other treatments of the theme include Sibelius' *Belsazars gastabud* (1906), written as incidental music to a drama by the Finish-Swedish poet Hjalmar Procope and reworked into an orchestral suite in 1907; and a setting of Heine's *Belsazar* by Bernard van Dieren (1884–1936). Joseph Achron composed incidental music to a play on the theme in 1928, later reworked as two tableaux for large orchestra.

The dramatic episodes of the Daniel cycle,[14] including and often combining the canonical and apocryphal parts, have always been

---

13. The *Play of Daniel (Ludus Danielis)* refers to two liturgical dramas of the 12th and 13th centuries. The first, one of the plays in the Fleury Play-book, a 13th-century manuscript, contains ten liturgical dramas by the Latin poet Hilarius or Hilary the Englishman (fl. 1125), without musical accompaniment. The second is a 13th-century drama with monophonic music written by clerical students at the Beauvais Cathedral (ca. 1230), the highest chancel in Europe, at the time.

14. The "Daniel cycle" refers to six legends, from chapters 1–6, about righteous people, who, through unswerving trust in God were able to survive against overwhelming odds. These, also, include apocalyptic texts from the Septuagint (e.g. Three Children in the Fiery Furnace, Prayer of Azariah, Song of the Holy Lads, Prayer of Nabonidus, Daniel in the Lion's Den, and sometimes, the stories of Susanna, as well as, Bel and the Dragon). Wayne Sibley Towner, *Daniel Interpretation: A Biblical Commentary for Teaching and Preaching* (Louisville, KY: John Knox Press, 1984) 7–8.

favored by composers. Notable 18th-century settings of the Daniel cycle are Caldara's opera and Hasse's oratorio (both presented at the Viennese court in 1731). 20th-century settings include: Darius Milhaud's *Les Miracles de la foi* (1951), a cantata for tenor, chorus, and orchestra based on passages from the Book of Daniel; and Benjamin Britten's modern "parable for church performance," *The Burning Fiery Furnace* (1966), with text by William Plomer. Vachel Lindsay's *The Daniel Jazz* was set to music in the jazz idiom by Louis Gruenberg for tenor and eight instruments (1923); and by Herbert Chappel (1963) for unison voices and piano.

The Song of the Three Children (*Canticum trium Purorum*, Vulgate Dan. 3:52–90)[15] is a prayer of praise to God which does not appear in the Masoretic Version or the Protestant Bible, but is included in the Catholic liturgy. It resembles Psalm 148, and has inspired many fine musical settings: notably by Josquin des Prés (15th century), polychoral settings by Heinrich Schutz and Michael Praetorius (17th century) and Karlheinz Stockhausen's *Gesang der drei Juenglinge* (1956), which dissolves and reconstitutes the human utterances by electronic manipulation.[16]

Notable is the Negro spiritual "Daniel, Daniel Servant of the Lord," arranged by Undine S. Moore (1904–1989). On the popular level, the spiritual *Shadrack, Meshack, Abednego*, made famous by the jazz trumpeter and singer Louis Armstrong, and thought to be authentic, was composed by Robert MacGinney. A contemporary Israeli folk-rock song by Meir Ariel (1942–1999) (*Chayat Habarzel*) draws upon imagery from the vision of the four great beasts that came up from the sea (Dan. 7).

Works List

Achron, Josef (1886–1943 Hollywood). *Belshazzar* (J. Roche), incidental music.

---

15. *Then these three, as with one mouth, praised and glorified and blessed God, in the furnace, saying: Blessed art thou, O Lord, the God of our fathers; and worthy to be praised…in all ages.* R.H. Charles, *The Apochrpha*,Vol. 1 (Oxford: Clarendon Press 1963 [1913]) 625–637; also Jerusalem Bible.
16. See Batia Bayer, "Daniel in Music," *Encyclopaedia Judaica*, Vol. 5, col. 1277 and "Belshazzar in the Arts," Vol. 4, col. 449.

Adamis, Michael (b.1929 Pireus). *The Fiery Furnace* (Dan. 3), liturgical drama.

Albergati, Pirro (1663–1735 Bologne). *Il convito di Baldassare,* oratorio.

Anfossi, Pasquale (1727–1797 Rome). *Il convitto di Baldassare* (Dan. 5), oratorio.

Ariosti, Attilio (1666 Bologne-c.1740). *Dario,* oratorio.

Bertoni, Fernando-Gasparo (1725–1813). *Balthasar,* oratorio.

Bigaglia, Diogemo (1676–1745 Venice). *Il profeta Daniele* (D. Giupponi), oratorio.

Bonfichi, Paolo (1769 Milan–1840). *La morte di Baldassare,* oratorio.

Bosmans, Henriette (1895–1952 Amsterdam). *Belsazer* (H. Heine), alto, orchestra.

Bridge, Joseph (1853 Rochester–1929 St. Albans). *Daniel,* oratorio.

Bristow, George Frederick (1825–1898 New York). *Daniel* (W.A. Hardenbrook), oratorio.

Britten, Benjamin (1913–1976 England). *The Burning Fiery Furnace* (Miracle play / P. Plomer), canticle.

Brossard, Sebastian de (1655–1730). *Baltassar* (Dan. 5), cantata.

_____. *Les trois enfants de la fournaise de Babylone* (Dan. 3), cantata.

Butler, Eugene (20ᵗʰ C. USA). *Song of Daniel* (Dan. 2:20–23), SATB, keyboard, percussion.

Caldara, Antonio (1670 Venice–1736 Vienna). *Daniello,* oratorio.

Carissimi, Giacomo (1605–1674 Rome). *Oratorio di Daniele Profeta,* oratorio.

_____. *Baltasar,* oratorio.

Castelnuevo-Tedesco, Mario (1895 Italy–1968 USA). *The Fiery Furnace,* baritone, children's choir, pianoforte and percussion.

Clasing, Johann Heinrich (1779–1829 Hamburg). *Belsazar* (B. Wolf), choir and orchestra.

Dieren, Bernard van (1884 Rotterdam–1936 London). *Balsazar* (H. Heine), choir and orchestra.

Felici, Alessandro (1742–1772 Florence). *Il Daniello,* oratorio.

Furlanetto, Bonaventura (1738–1817 Venice). *Baltassar,* oratorio.

Galuppi, Baldassare (1706–1785 Venice). *Daniel in lacu leonum* (P. Chiari), oratorio.

_____. *Tres pueri hebraei in captivitate Babylonis* (P. Chiari), oratorio.

Georges, Alexandre (1850–1938 Paris). *Balthasar ou La fin de Babylone* (Ch. Grandmougin), opera.

Gilboa, Jacob (1920 Slovakia–2007 Tel Aviv). *Katros upsanterin* (Dan. 3), harp, harpsichord, pianoforte & orchestra.

Gollmick, Adolf (1825 Frankfurt am Main–1883 London). *Balthasar*, opera.

Gray, Alan (1855–1935 Cambridge). *The Vision of Belshazzar*, cantata.

Greenberg, Noah (1919–1966 New York). *The Play of Daniel*, liturgical drama.

Griesbach, John Henry (1798 Windsor–1875 London). *Belshazzar's feast*, opera (revised as an oratorio *Daniel*).

Hadley, Henry Kimball (1871–1937 Massachusetts). *Belshazzar*, cantata.

Handel, George Frederic (1685–1959 London). *Belshazzar* (Ch. Jennens) (Dan. 5), oratorio.

Harris, Charles (1862 London–1929 Ottawa). *Daniel before the king*, cantata.

Hasse, Johann-Adolf (1699 Bergedorf–1783 Venice). *Daniello* (A. Zeno), oratorio.

_____. *Il cantico de tre fanciulli* (S. Pallavicino), oratorio.

Josquin, Depres (ca.1440–1521). *Benedicite omnia opera Domini* (Dan. 3:57–74), 4 voices, motet.

Koreschtschenko, Arsenij Nikolayevich (1870–1922 Moscow). *Pir Baltassara*, opera.

Lang-Zaimont, Judith (b.1945 Queens, N.Y.). *Sweet Daniel*, pianoforte.

Lasso, Orlando di (1532–1594 Munich). *Daniels knaben drey ist Gott gestanden bey*, choir.

_____. *Daniel gworffen war zur grossen Loewenschar*, choir.

Lukacic, Ivan (1587–1644 Split). *Sacredotes Dei* (Dan. 3:81–87), 2 voices, motet.

Mabellini, Teodulo (1817–1897 Florence). *Il convito di Baldassare* (Dan. 5), opera.

Mattheson, Johann (1681–1764 Hamburg). *Der aus dem Loewen-Graben befreyte himmlische Daniel*, oratorio.

Messi, Franciscus de (17th C.). *Balthasarius epulum et inheritus* (B. Vacondo), oratorio.

Milhaud, Darius (1892–1974 Geneva). *Miracles of Faith: (a) Daniel and Nebuchadnezzar (b) Daniel and Belshazzar (c) Daniel and Darius*, for tenor, narrator, choir, and orchestra.

Naylor, Bernard (1907 UK–1986 Canada). *Ascension Day* (Dan. 7:13–14), SSATB

Nicolini, Giuseppe (1762–1842). *Daniel nel lago dei leoni* (C. Capelli), oratorio.

Opienski, Henryk (1870 Crakow–1942 Lausanne). *Daniel*, oratorio.

Perry, George Frederick (1793 Norwich–1862 London). *Belshazzar's Feast*, cantata.

Pinkham, Daniel (1923–2006 USA) *Daniel in the Lion's Den* (1973) (Dan. 6, Apocrypha, Ps. 116, J. Newton), SATB, tenor, bariton, narrator, timpani, 4 percussions, electronic tape, 2 pianofortes.

Pollarolo, Carlo Francesco (1653–1722 Venice). *Convito di Baldassar* (P.A. Ginori), oratorio.

Predieri, Giovanni Battista (1678–1760 Italy). *Daniele liberato dal lago de'lioni*, oratorio.

Purcell, Henry (1659–1695 London). *Bendicite omnia opera* (The Song of the Three Children). Daniel 3, choir, voices and basso continuo.

Reinecke, Karl (1824–1910 Leipzig). *Belsazar* (F. Roeber), oratorio.

Samson, Joseph (1888–1957 France). *Cantique des trois enfants*, choir a capella.

Schuermann, Georg Caspar (1672–1751 Germany). *Daniel* (A.U. Herzog), oratorio.

Schumann, Robert (1810–1856 Germany). *Belsatzar* (H. Heine), voice and pianoforte.

Sibelius, Jean (1865–1957 Finland). *Belshazzar's Feast* (H.J. Procope), strings, incidental music-suite.

Souweine, C.J. (19th C. Netherlands). *Daniel* (Meyer Roelandts), opera.

Stanford, Charles Villiers (1852 Dublin–1924 London). *The Three Holy Children*, oratorio.

Statkowski, Roman (1859–1925 Warsaw). *Uczta Baltazara* (Belshazzar's feast), cantata.

Stockhausen, Karlheinz (1928–2007 Germany). *Gesang der Juenglinge im Feuerofen*, electronic sound with 5 loudspeakers.

Vancorbeil, Auguste-Emanuel (1821–1884 Paris). *Cantique des trios enfants*, 3 voices.

Walton, William (1902 England–1982 Italy). *Belshazzar's Feast*, oratorio.

Weigl, Joseph (1766–1820 Vienna). *Baals Sturz oder Daniel in der Loewengrube*, opera.

Wenzel, Eberhard (1896–1982 Germany). *Belzazarlied* (Dan. 4–6), voices, choir.

Werner, Gregor Joseph (c. 1695–1766 Eisenstadt). *Daniel*, oratorio.

G. Dore: Ezra Ready the Law in the Hearing of the People, *Bible Illustrations* (1866)

While many works have been written about the destruction of Jerusalem and the subsequent exile of the Jewish People, comparatively few compositions have been inspired by their return from captivity.

EZRA and NEHEMIAH[1]

Ezra came up from Babylon; he was a ready scribe versed in the Law of Moses, which the Lord, the God of Israel, had given; and the king granted him all his request, according to the hand of the Lord his God upon him   (Ezra 7:6).

The Books of Ezra and Nehemiah are devoted to events occurring in the land of Israel at the end of the Babylonian Exile, a period of approximately one century (beginning in 538 B.C.). Ezra details the return of the Judeans from captivity, and their efforts to rebuild the Temple up to the decree of Artaxerxes — events covered at the beginning of the Book of Nehemiah. Chapters 1-6 deal with the First Return under Zerubbabel and the building of the Second Temple. Chapters 7-10 focus on the career of Ezra. Over one-half century elapsed between chapters 6 and 7. The characters in the first part of the book had died by the time Ezra began his ministry in Jerusalem. Tradition attributes authorship of the Book to Ezra.[2]

---

1. Considerable controversy and uncertainty surrounds chronology in the Books of Ezra and Nehemiah, which were originally one book, and may, also, have formed the conclusion to the Book of Chronicles. Haggai was the main prophet in the days of Ezra, while Zechariah was the principal prophet in the days of Nehemiah.
2. Modern critical scholarship reverses the order of events in Ezra and Nehemiah, as presented in the Bible, claiming that Nehemiah preceded Ezra. Oesterley and Robinson, *An Introduction to the Books of the Old Testament* (London: Society for Promoting Christian Knowledge, 1949 [1934]) 109-30.

Works List

Jackson, William (1815–1866 England). *The Deliverance from Babylon,* oratorio.

Jacquet de La Guerre, Elizabeth (1667–1729 Paris). *Le Temple Rebasti* (A.H. de La Motte after Ezra), cantata for voice and basso continuo.

NEHEMIAH[3]

So the wall was completed on the twenty-fifth of Elul, in fifty-two days. When all our enemies heard about this, all the surrounding nations were afraid and lost their self-confidence, because they realized that this work had been done with the help of our God   (Nehemiah 6:15–16).

The Book of Nehemiah continues the story of Israel's return from Babylonian captivity and the rebuilding of the Temple in Jerusalem. A high official at the court of Artaxerxes, Nehemiah, though born in Babylon, was living in Persia when word reached him of the rebuilding of the Temple. Knowing that there was no wall to protect the city, he prayed to God to utilize him to save the city. Nehemiah's prayer was answered, when the Persian king gave him permission to return to Jerusalem as governor, in charge of reorganizing the Judean province and rebuilding the walls of the city. Despite opposition, the wall was rebuilt in only 52 days. This united effort was short-lived, however, and Jerusalem fell back into apostasy when Nehemiah left. After 12 years, he returned to find the walls strong, but, the people weak, and set about the task of reestablishing true worship.

---

3.   Nehemiah is identified as Zerubbabel in Talmud Sanhedrin 38a.

Works List

Britten, Benjamin (1913–1976 England). *Stand up and Bless the Lord* (Neh. 9:5–6), chorus, organ.

Jacobi, Frederick (1891–1952 USA). *From the Prophet Nehemiah*, 3 excerpts, voice and 2 pianos.

Nardi, Nahum (1901 Kiev/1924 Tel Aviv–1977). *Lchu vnivne et Chomat Yerushalaim* (Neh. 2:17, 4:16).

Natra, Sergiu (1924 Romania/1961 Israel). *Igereth Nehemia* (Nehemiah Builds the Second Temple), baritone, chorus, orchestra.

Stevens, Halsey (1908 New York–1989 California). *Blessed be Thy Glorious Name* (Neh. 9:5–9, 11–12), SATB.

Wolff, S. (Stanley) Drummond (1916 England/1946 Canada–2004 San Diego). *Praise to the Lord* (Neh. 9:6), SATB, organ (optional brass).

G. Dore: Cyrus Restoring the Vessels of the Temple, *Bible Illustrations (1866)*

CHAPTER 33

Compositions in bibliographic lists are cited in this chapter without comment. All are based on texts from Chronicles.

CHRONICLES I & II

Adam, Sheth, Enosh, Kenan, Malaleleel, Lamech, Noah, Shem, Ham and Japheth... Thus saith Cyrus king of Persia. All kingdoms of the earth hath the Lord God given me; and he hath charged me to build him an house in Jerusalem, which is in Judah. Who is there among you of all his people? The Lord his God be with him, and let him go up (1 Chronicles 1:1–4; 2 Chronicles 36:23).

Chronicles is a composite history of the Jewish People from the Creation of the World until the destruction of the First Temple and Babylonian Captivity — a period of about three and one-half millennia. The book consists in genealogical lists (1 Chron. 1–9), accounts of the reigns of David and Solomon (1 Chron. 10–28 and 2 Chron. 1–9), and the story of the kingdom of Judah until the exile in 586 B.C. (2 Chron. 10–36). The final verses are a decree from Cyrus calling for the return to Jerusalem and the rebuilding of the Temple.[1]

Chronicles 1 & 2 was originally one book (similar to Samuel 1 & 2, Kings 1 & 2, and Ezra and Nehemiah). The Hebrew title *Divrey*

---

1. Before the dispersion, the Prophets were privy to the Eternal's Will and were able to interpret cosmic intentions behind natural events. After the dissolution of national life, the blessing of God became hidden and unfathomable (i.e. *Megillah Esther*). Henceforth, there could be no prophetic testimony, only shadowy inference by scholarly deduction, or conformity to the wisdom of the past. See Eli Cashdan, "Introduction and Commentary to Malachi," *The Twelve Prophets* (London: Soncino Press, 1974 [1948]) 335–6.

Hayamim means "words of the days." The Greek (Septuagint) designation *Paralipomena*, signifies "things left out" or events unrecorded in earlier biblical history. Chronicles was designated by Saint Jerome in the 4th century as a "chronicle of divine history" or *Liber Chronicorum*.[2] Jerome perceptively understood that Chronicles traces something more than archival records of family inheritance and tribal heritage. The genealogical lists which open the book trace the destiny of the 'Blessing' which God bestowed to mankind at the dawn of Creation. Chronicles records the dispersion of this 'Blessing' among the fathers, the sons, and their descendents, from generation to generation.[3] Authorship is traditionally attributed to Ezra (c. 400 B.C.).

Works List

Of particular artistic interest are descriptions of David bringing the Ark to Jerusalem and the Temple music (1 Chron. 16); David's charge to his son Solomon to build the Temple (1 Chron. 28–29); and celebrations following completion of the Temple by Solomon (2 Chron. 5).

Byrd, William (1543–1623 England). *Laetentur Coeli* (Be Glad, Ye Heavens) (1 Chron. 16:31), SATBB.

Campbell, Sidney (1909–1974 England). *Be Strong and of Good Courage* (1 Chron. 28:20), SATB, organ.

Ferguson, Edwin Earle (b.1910 USA). *I Have Built an House* (2 Chron. 6:2, 18–20, 41), SATB, organ.

Foss, Lukas (1922 Germany /1939 USA–2009). *Behold! I Build a House* (1949) (2 Chron. 6), SATB, piano or organ.

Harper, Marjorie (b.1937 Minnesota). *Deliver us* (1 Chron. 16:35), SATB, organ or piano.

---

2. See I. W. Slotki, "Introduction," *Chronicles* (London: Soncino Press, 1974) xi-xiv.

3. This intangible blessing is the most sought after possession in the world, for it carries with it the fullest realization of heavenly favor; in a sense, biblical narrative is the story of its transference from soul to soul, heart to heart, and generation to generation. But, it also presupposes responsibility: Who is worthy of this blessing? By what means may it be attained? By what means is it forfeited? In a sense, the blessing is unconditional; on the other hand, it demands faithfulness. Biblical history is a tug-of-war between these two principles, a saga of divine tutelage, wherewith mankind learns to be human.

Krause, Ken (20th C. USA). *His Love is Eternal* (1 Chron. 16), SATB, keyboard.

Matthews, Thomas (1915–1999 Oklahoma). *The Trumpeters and Singers Were as One* (2 Chron. 5:13), SATB, organ.

Mead (Johnson), Edward (fl.1572–1601 England). *Sing unto the Lord All the Earth* (1 Chron. 1:16, 23–25, 29–31), SATB piano or organ.

Poston, Elizabeth (1905–1987 England). *Laudate Dominum* (2 Chron. 5:13–14), SATB, organ.

Powell, Robert (b.1933 Mississippi). *The Trumpeters and Singers Were as One* (2 Chron. 5:13), SATB, organ, 2 trumpets, 2 trombones, timpani.

Price, Milburn (b.1938 Alabama). *O Give Thanks Unto the Lord* (1 Chron. 16: 8–12, 14, 23–25), SATB, 3 trumpets, 2 trombones, tuba.

Roesch, Robert (20th C. USA). *Give Thanks to Him* (2 Chron. 20:21), SATB, keyboard.

Schalk, Carl (b.1930 USA). *Offertory* (1 Chron. 16: 28–29, 34), unison, organ.

Yancey, Thomas Leland (c.1934 Missouri). *The Song of David* (1 Chr. 29:10–13), SATB, organ.

Urbaites, Mindaugas (b.1952 Lithuania). *The Book of the Jerusalem of the North* (1 Chron., Tobit)(2001), tenor, violin solo, male choir, percussion, pianoforte, celeste.

Zarai, Yonatan (b.1929 Hungary/Israel). *Viven Uziyahu Migdal Biyerushalayin* (2 Chr. 26:9), song.

G. Dore: The Rebuilding of the Temple, *Bible Illustrations (1866)*

Conclusion

How music touches on the Bible, and how the Bible touches on music, has been the subject of this book. Whether in letter or spirit, the biblical "Word" interpreted and reinterpreted through the ages, contains within it a voice, a tone, a dimension that awakens our care and concern. It is the influence this impulse makes on its meandering course through the musical consciousness of Western Civilization — whether shallow or deep, high brow or low brow, sacred or secular that this book has sought to follow. It is the golden thread of an ancient faith tracing itself through the clay substance of human flesh, transforming material reality with a divine resonance that manifests itself in works of folk, popular, and fine art.

Reflecting on many levels about works in all genres of music, it has examined the creative response of individuals and peoples, who, in stretching towards the Divine, have tried to define that experience in time and tone, through word, voice, and instruments. This book has sought, as well, to understand the "why" of those moved to identify, within the context of the Bible, and express this creatively, through the medium of music.

For these reasons, we have treated such disparate artistic creations as: a plainchant, an anthem setting of a single Bible-verse, a Negro Spiritual, a grand opera, and a popular musical loosely based on a biblical episode — on an equal footing — meriting serious discussion and consideration. This hodgepodge has not been an exercise in Post-modernism. It does not advocate blurring the distinctions between high and low culture, nor, try to demonstrate that absolute truth is unobtainable. Nor, ought avoidance of chronological contextualization be construed as delighting in the arbitrariness of incongruous juxtapositions, alone. *Behold, God is mighty, and despiseth not any, he is mighty in strength and wisdom (Job 36:5).*

Rather, our biblical organization, selecting a diverse cross-section of genres from various historical periods has been an attempt to challenge traditional norms in looking at music, the Bible, and their interface. This approach presupposes two different ways of rationalizing culture and religion — not contradictory, but complementary. Like Jacob's ladder, they differ in direction of thought, more than in content.

The culture of man is an ascent from the earth. By metaphor, it means climbing up the ladder of time, step by step, through trial and error, colored by experiences, feelings, ideas, and images. Only much later, does humanity try to make sense of this blind struggle; imposing the logic of cause and effect upon arbitrary accumulations of facts, individual perceptions and achievements, collective traditions and historical experiences. This is man's way of building civilization.

The Bible — for all its variety and multiplicity of authorship — is the opposite. It is one. It marks the descent on the ladder from heaven to earth. It reveals a unified divine light, made manifest upon earth in words, deeds, thoughts, and chance happen-stance. Albeit, expressed differently at different times, in different places, by different people, in different circumstances — the enduring perception of the Bible suggests a single vision of perfection, a cognizance shared throughout the generations: *One generation shall praise thy works to another, and shall declare thy mighty acts (Psalm 145:4).*

Styles, like ideas, come and go. Ways of looking at things change and transform. This book has tried to relate to some of the ways those moved to trace into musical form, something of that encounter, have done so. Such creations rise from the place where they stand to meet the Divine. But, they descend from heaven too, partaking of, and joining something of their fleeting and finite dust to that soft, warm, gentle, and Infinite light, which shines, if only for a moment, on each of us.

Music may rise to prophecy or remain descriptive. It may function as a sacrificial offering in tone or suffice as a functional tool, filling in a liturgical lacuna or serving as a thread on which to bead a text. In each and every instance, however, that music forms a specific relationship with the biblical Word and Voice. Such selections have enriched the mosaic of civilization greatly. They may be found in every style, form, historic period, category, and performing genre. The numbers of works which have attempted this synthesis are vast, and much remains untouched, awaiting further exploration and elucidation.

APPENDIX 1
Index of Biblical References to Music

This index cites verses relating to various aspects of music in the Bible. These include: production and characteristics of sound (i.e. vocal or instrumental, clapping, shouting, etc.), types and forms (i.e. hymn, song, lamentation, acrostic, etc.), function (i.e. times of gladness, signals of warning, Temple ritual, blowing the horn, etc.), performers (i.e. Asaph, Zechariah, Jehiel, Levites, etc.), power of music (i.e. to effect prophecy, sooth the soul, etc.), the imagery of music in nature (i.e. trees shout, floods clapping hands, etc.), heavenly host (i.e. angels of praise, morning stars, etc.), dance, and Voice of God. When taken together these verses present a picture of music in speech and song, cry and exaltation — a living expression of biblical emotion sympathetically reverberating with the cosmos.

Genesis: 3:8, 3:10, 4:21, 4:23, 27:22, 31:27

Exodus: 4:11, 15:1–2, 15:20–21, 19:13, 19:16, 19:19, 20:18, 28:33–35, 32:17–19, 39:25–26

Leviticus: 9:24, 23:24, 25:9

Numbers: 1:47, 1:49–50, 2:33, 3:15, 3:39, 7:89, 8:6, 8:9, 8:10, 8:24–26, 10:2–10, 21:17, 29:1, 31:6

Deuteronomy: 4:12, 4:33, 4:36, 5:22–26, 5:28, 10:8, 18:16, 27:14, 21:19, 31:21–22, 31:30, 32:1, 32:43–44

Joshua: 6:4–8, 6:9, 6:10, 6:13, 6:16, 6:20

Judges: 3:27, 5:1, 5:3, 5:11, 5:12, 6:34, 7:8, 7:16, 7:18, 7:19, 7:20, 7:21, 7:22–23, 11:34, 11:40

1 Samuel: 1:10, 1:13, 4:5, 4:6, 6:12, 7:10, 10:5, 13:3, 16:16–18, 16:23, 18:6–7, 18:10, 19:9, 21:11, 29:5

2 Samuel: 1:17, 2:28, 3:32–33, 6:5, 6:14–16, 15:10, 18:16, 19:35, 20:1, 20:22, 22:1, 22:7, 22:14, 22:50, 23:1

1 Kings: 1:34, 1:39, 1:40, 1:41, 1:45, 4:32, 8:28, 8:55, 10:12, 13:30, 19:11–13

2 Kings: 3:15, 4:31, 9:13, 11:14, 12:13

Isaiah: 5:1, 5:12, 5:26, 6:3–4, 7:18, 10:14, 10:30, 12:2, 12:4–6, 13:2, 13:4, 13:6, 14:7, 14:11, 14:31, 15:2–5, 15:8, 16:10–11, 18:3, 18:15, 23:15, 23:16, 24:8, 24:9, 24:14, 24:16, 25:5, 26:1, 26:19, 27:2, 27:13, 28:23, 29:4, 29:6, 30:29, 30:30–32, 33:3, 35:2, 35:5–6, 35:10, 38:20, 40:3, 40:9, 42:2, 42:10, 42:11, 43:14, 44:23, 48:20, 49:13, 51:3, 51:11, 52:8–9, 54:1, 55:12, 58:1, 58:4, 61:7, 65:14, 65:19, 66:6

Jeremiah: 3:21, 4:5, 4:8, 4:19, 4:21, 4:31, 6:1, 6:17, 6:23, 6:26, 7:16, 7:29, 7:34, 8:19, 9:10, 9:17, 9:18, 9:19, 9:20, 11:14, 14:12, 16:5, 16:9, 20:13, 20:16, 22:10, 22:18, 22:20, 25:9, 25:10, 25:30–31, 25:34, 25:36, 29:18, 30:5, 30:19, 31:4, 31:7, 31:12, 31:13, 31:15–16, 33:10–11, 34:5, 42:14, 46:22, 48:20, 48:31, 48:33, 48:36, 49:2, 49:3, 49:17, 50:13, 50:15, 50:42, 50:46, 51:8, 51:14, 51:27, 51:37, 51:54–55

Ezekiel, 1:24–25, 2:10, 3:12, 3:13, 7:14, 7:16, 8:14, 8:18, 9:1, 10:5, 19:1, 19:14, 21:22, 23:42, 24:16–17, 24:23, 26:10, 26:13, 26:15, 26:17, 27:2, 27:28, 27:30, 27:31, 27:32, 27:36, 28:12–13, 30:2, 32:2, 32:16, 33:3–6, 33:32, 37:7, 43:2

Hosea: 5:8, 7:14, 8:1

Joel: 1:5, 1:13, 2:1, 2:5, 2:11, 2:12, 2:15, 3:16

Amos: 1:2, 1:14, 2:2, 3:6, 5:1, 5:16, 5:17, 5:23, 6:5, 8:3, 8:10

Jonah: 2:9

Micah: 1:8, 1:11, 2:4, 4:9, 6:16

Nahum: 2:7, 3:2

Habakkuk: 3:1, 3:9, 3:13, 3:16, 3:19

Zephaniah: 1:10, 1:11, 1:14, 1:16, 2:14–15, 3:14

Zechariah: 2:10, 7:5, 9:9, 9:14, 10:8, 11:2, 11:3, 12:10–12

Malachi: 2:13

Psalms: 3:1, 3:2, 3:4, 3:8, 4:1, 4:2, 4:4, 5:1–2, 5:11, 6:1, 7:1, 7:5, 7:17, 8:1, 9:1, 9:2, 9:11, 9:16, 9:20, 11:1, 12:1, 13:1, 13:5–6, 14:1, 15:1, 16:1, 17:1, 18:1, 18:6, 18:13, 18:49, 19:1, 20:1, 20:3, 20:5, 21:1–2, 21:13, 22:1, 23:1, 24:1, 24:6, 24:10, 25:1, 26:1, 26:7, 27:1, 27:6, 27:7, 28:1, 28:2, 28:6, 28:7, 29:1, 29:3, 29:4–5, 29:7–9, 30:1, 30:4, 30:5, 30:11, 30:12, 31:1, 31:22, 32:1, 32:5, 32:7, 32:11, 33:1–3, 34:1, 35:1, 35:18, 35:27, 36:1, 37:1, 38:1, 39:1, 39:5, 39:11, 40:1, 40:3, 41:1, 41:11, 42:1, 42:4, 42:8, 43:4, 44:1, 44:8, 45:1, 46:1, 45:11, 47:1, 47:4–7,

Index of Musical Instruments in the Bible[1]

The creation of music and dance may originate in the mystery of the soul, but it derives its content from the rhythmic impulse of the body, the dexterity of the hand, the ethos of the voice, and the constructive power of the imagination. Music existed in prehistoric times. String instruments began with a one-stringed hunter's bow; wind instruments, perhaps, from either a bamboo cane or a blade of grass. Yuval, the father of music in the Bible, and the great-great-great-grandson of Cain, must have been a genius of the first order. He taught men the power that lay hidden in the simplest of sound makers:[2] *Yuval, the father of all such as handle the harp (kinnor) and organ (uggav) (Gen. 4:21).*

Bells (*paamonim*)

Bells were attached to the hem of the High Priest and made humming sounds as he went about his ministrations.[3]

---

1. There seems to be disagreement on almost every aspect of identification and classification of instruments in the Bible. We have tried to define terminology as clearly as we understand it. For an extensive discussion on musical instruments in the Bible and their various interpretations in biblical commentaries see Alfred Sendrey, *Music in Ancient Israel* (New York: Philosophical Library, 1969), Section VI — *The Musical Instruments*, 262–420. For a more up-to-date survey see Joachim Braun, *Music in Ancient Israel/Palestine: archaeological, written, and comparative sources* (Grand Rapids, MI: Wm. B. Eerdmans Publishing Co., 2002).

2. Plucking on strings and tooting on pipes are limitations of sound sources, not of talent. In primitive culture, men of music made their instruments from the earth. *Kinnor* is a category designating string instruments, while *uggav,* signifies, perhaps, all the winds.

3. Ethno-musicology has thrown light onto the meaning of biblical instruments, examining and comparing them to present-day instruments from high cultures of the Orient and primitive society. See Curt Sachs, *The History of*

Exod. 28:34–35, Exod. 39:25–26

Cymbals (*mitzeltayim* or a pair of cymbals)

Bronze cymbals are the only percussion instruments admitted unreservedly into the sacred service. It would appear that loud sounding cymbals (*zilzeleh teruah*) were signaling instruments, while high sounding cymbals (*zilzeleh shamah*) may have been used to mark off phrases, either, following the literal sense of the Psalm verses, or, functioning musically in an abstract, independent cyclical pattern, similar to the medieval concept of isorhythm.[4]

2 Sam. 6:5, Ps. 150:5 (*zilzeleh shamah* or loud sounding cymbals), Ps. 150:5 (*zilzeleh teruah* or high sounding cymbals), Neh. 12:27, 1 Chron. 13:8, 1 Chron. 15:16, 1 Chron. 15:19, 1 Chron. 15:28, 1 Chron. 16:5, 1 Chron. 16:42, 1 Chron. 25:1, 1 Chron. 25:6, 2 Chron. 5:12–13, 2 Chron. 20, 25

Flute (*halil*, cane pipe, metal tube, double flute, double oboe or transverse flute)

Flutes were made of reed or wood sometimes covered with gold or silver, and rarely with metal. They had connotations of joy as well as mourning, and came to be associated with the Festival of Tabernacles.

1 Sam. 10:5, 1 Kings 1:40, Isa. 1:12, Isa. 30:29, Jer. 48:36

Gittit (zither)

The 'gittit' could have been a zither-like instrument with strings strung parallel to the frame, either square or harp shaped, like a grand piano. Zithers were played both plucked by the fingers (like the modern Iraqi instrument, *kannun*), or with mallets (like the modern Persian instrument, *santur*).

Musical Instruments (New York: W.W. Norton, 1968) 105–127, for an extensive discussion on musical instruments during the Nomadic Epoch and the time of the Kings (with reference to Mishnaic and Talmudic sources).

4. There is no clear evidence about which instrument was used for *zilzeleh shamah*. It is my hunch that these may indicate small hand cymbals, similar to those found today in South East Asia (India and Thailand). In Oriental orchestras of the Far East, finger cymbals are used to mark off the beginning of each phrase-rhythmic cycle (*tala*). Thus, it is plausible that these smaller cymbals might have found a place in the music of the Temple, as well.

Ps. 8:1, Ps. 81:1, Ps. 84:1

Hand Clapping

Hand clapping is used to this day to provide rhythmic support for melody and dance. Clapping, body slapping, stamping, snapping of fingers — always imply metered melody, with clearly defined phrases, as opposed to free vocal chant.

Isa. 55:12, Ps. 47:1, Ps. 98:8

Lyre (*kinnor*, harp, or hand held harp/ lyre)

The lyre, sometimes translated as harp or *kinnor*, is the instrument of King David. It is held in the hands with strings strung parallel to the sounding board.

Gen. 4:21, Gen. 31:27, 1 Sam. 10:5, 1 Sam. 16:16, 1 Sam. 16:23, 2 Sam. 6:5, 2 Sam. 10:12, Isa. 5:12, Isa. 16:11, Isa. 23:16, Isa. 24: 8, Isa. 30:32, Ezek. 26:13, Ps. 33:2, Ps. 43:4, Ps. 49:4, Ps. 57:8, Ps. 71:22, Ps. 81:2, Ps. 92:3, Ps. 98:5, Ps. 108:2, Ps. 137:2, Ps. 147:7, Ps. 149:3, Ps. 150:3, Job 21:12, Job 30:31, Neh. 12:27, 1 Chron. 13:8, 1 Chron. 15:6, 1 Chron. 15:21, 1 Chron. 15:28, 1 Chron. 16:5, 1 Chron. 25:1, 1 Chron. 25:3, 1 Chron. 25:6, 2 Chron. 5:12, 2 Chron. 9:11, 2 Chron. 20:28, 2 Chron. 29: 20, 25

Nehilot

This term is an unusual one, and appears to be a designation for performance by wind instruments, as distinguished from the usual accompaniment by string instruments.[5]

Ps. 5:1

Psaltery (harp or *nevel*)

The psaltery, a translation of the Hebrew term *nevel,* is a plucked string instrument often referred to along with the lyre or *kinnor* (sometimes translated as harp). It is a larger and heavier instrument than the lyre, played resting on the knee or on the floor, with strings strung

---

5.   Commentators derive this interpretation from the similarity between the words *hali*l (flute) and *nehil*ot. Also, it is considered a derivative of the word for dance — *mahol* (see Sendrey, 318–320).

perpendicular to the sound board. The different kinds of *'nevels'* are categorized according to the number of strings. Generally speaking, harps were used in connection with the singing voice and not as purely instrumental music. It is important, also, to keep in mind that during the biblical period there were neither standard numbers of strings nor standard tunings. The harp of 8-strings was referred to as *Sheminith* (Ps. 6:1, Ps. 12:1, 1 Chron. 15:21); while the harp of 10-strings, was termed *Asor* (Ps. 33:2, Ps, 92:3, Ps. 144:9). These designations appear as titles to Psalms.[6]

1 Sam. 10:5, 1 Sam. 6:5, 1 Kings. 10:12, Isa. 5:12, Isa. 14:11, Amos 5:23, Amos 6:5, Ps. 33:2, Ps. 57:8, Ps. 71:22 (see note[7]), Ps. 81:2, Ps. 90:3, Ps. 108:1, Ps. 144:9, Ps. 150:3, Neh. 12:27, 1 Chron. 13:8, 1 Chron. 15:16, 1 Chron. 15:28, 1 Chron. 16:5, 1 Chron. 25:1, 1 Chron. 25:6, 2 Chron. 5:12, 2 Chron. 9:11, 2 Chron. 20:28, 2 Chron. 29:25

Rattles (*na'aneim* or sistrum)

Rattles and sound makers of all kinds provide an endless variety of timbres and rhythmic accompaniments. The *groger* sounded on Purim during the reading of the Megillah is such an example.

2 Sam. 6:5, Judg. 7:18–20, Judg. 7:22, 1 Sam. 13:3, 2 Sam. 2:28, 2 Sam. 6:15, 2 Sam. 15:10, 2 Sam. 18:16, 2 Sam. 20:1, 2 Sam. 20:22, 1 Kings 1:34, 1 Kings 1:39, 1 Kings 1:41, 2 Kings 9:13, Isa. 18:3

Shofar (ram's horn)

In the ancient world sound was known to influence matter.[8] The

---

6. These instruments had symbolic significance: *Those hymns of the Temple praising the presence of God on earth and the union with God of all things earthly are played on a harp of 7-strings. The song of the days of the Messiah, when final redemption will come to all, sounds forth on the harp of 8-strings. The harp of 10-strings, however, is reserved for the song which shall arise on that day when the world that is to be, will be united in one harmonious whole.* See commentary by Samson Raphael Hirsch, *The Psalms*, 35.

7. This verse sums up the function of the harp, and the essence of all biblical music: a demonstration of gratitude to God — repaying, in some measure, one's debt for the gift of life, through singing and playing an instrument: *I will also praise thee with the psaltery (nevel), even thy truth, O my God: unto thee will I sing with the harp (kinnor), O thou Holy One of Israel (Ps. 71:22).*

8. David Tame, *The Secret Power of Music* (NY: Destiny Books, 1984) 13 ff.

shofar or ram's horn, for example, has always been considered a magical instrument, associated with the revelation of God's voice at Mount Sinai: *There were thunders and lightening, and a thick cloud on the mount and the voice of a horn exceedingly loud (Exod. 19:16).* Joshua brought down the walls of Jericho with shofar blasts.

Exod. 19:16, Exod. 19:19, Exod. 20:18, Lev. 25:9, Jos. 6:4–6, Jos. 6:8–9, Jos. 6:13, Jos. 6:16, Jos. 6:20, Judg. 3:27, Judg. 6:34, Judg. 7:8, Judg. 7:16, Isa. 27:13, Isa. 58:1, Jer. 4:5, Jer. 4:19, Jer. 4:21, Jer. 6:1, Jer. 6: 17, Jer. 42:14, Jer. 51:27, Ez. 33:3–6, Hos. 5:8, Hos. 8:1, Joel 2:1, Joel 2:15, Amos 2:3, Amos 3:6, Zeph. 1:16, Zech. 9:14, Ps. 47:5, Ps. 81:3, Ps. 98:6, Ps. 150:3, Job 39: 24–25, Neh. 4:18, Neh. 4:20, 1 Chron. 15:14

Tof (timbal or tabret)

Tof is a generic name for hand drums of all sizes. Mostly, frame drums, which were played almost exclusively by women. Perhaps the term also includes goblet form pottery drums, similar to the modern darabukka.

Gen. 31:27, Exod. 15:20, Judg. 11:34, 1 Sam, 18:6, 2 Sam. 6:5, Jer. 13:4, Isa. 5:12, 24:8, 30:32, Ezek. 28:13, Ps. 68:26, Ps. 1:3, Ps. 149:3, Ps. 150:4, 1 Chron. 13:8.

Trumpets (*hazotsrot*)

Trumpets were made of silver and used as signaling instruments: *calling the assembly, journeying of the camps... one trumpet to gather the princes... if ye go to war (Num. 2–9);* and, as ritual instruments in the sacrificial service: *in day of gladness... solemn days... beginning of months,... burnt offerings... sacrifices....peace offerings as a memorial before God.* They were blown exclusively by priests: *the priests shall blow with the trumpets (Num. 10:10).*

Num. 10:2, Num. 8–10, Num. 21:6, 2 Kings 11:14, 2 Kings 12:13, Hos. 5:8, Ps. 98:6, Ezra 3:10, Neh. 12:35, Neh. 12:35, Neh. 12:41, 1 Chron. 13:8, 1 Chron. 15:24, 1 Chron. 15:28, 1 Chron. 16:6, 1 Chron. 16:42, 2 Chron. 5:12–13, 2 Chron. 7:6, 2 Chron. 13:12, 2 Chron. 13:14, 2 Chron. 20:28, 2 Chron. 29:27–28

Uggav (a vertical flute or *nay*)

Uggav is a wind instrument, considered variously as a syrinx or pan-pipes, whistle-head recorder, double pipe oboe, or bagpipe. The noted authority on musical instruments, Curt Sachs, conceived of it as a Middle Eastern (Persian) *nay*, producing a deep-toned flute-like tone.[9]

Gen. 4:21, Ps. 150:5, Job 21:12, Job 30:31, 1 Sam. 10:5, 1 Kings 1:40, Isa. 5:12, Isa. 30:29, Jer. 48:36, Ezek. 28:13

---

9. Curt Sachs, *History of Musical Instruments*, 106.

APPENDIX III
Table of Contents
in Historical Context

Ancient and Medieval Periods (until 1400)
Anonymous: *Sanctus (6th–10th C.)*

Renaissance Period (1400–1600)
Giovanni Pierluigi da Palestrina (c.1524–1595): *Sanctus* from *Missa Brevis (1570)*

Baroque Period (1600–1750)
Johann Hermann Schein (1586–1630): *Israeli Brunlein (1623)*
Giacomo Carissimi (1605–1674): *Jephte (1649)*
Johann Kuhnau (1660–1722): *David and Goliath (1700)*
George Frederic Handel (1685–1759): *Israel in Egypt (1739)*
Zadok the Priest (1727)

Classical Period (1750–1800)
Joseph Haydn (1732–1809): *The Creation (1798)*
Wolfgang Amadeus Mozart (1756–1791): *Sanctus* from *Requiem (1791)*

Romantic Period (1800–1900)
Spiritual: *Ezekiel Saw de Wheel (18th–19th C.)*
Spiritual: *Go Down Moses (18th–19th C.)*
Spiritual: *Joshua Fit de Battle of Jericho (18th–19th C.)*
Gioachino Rossini (1792–1868): *Moses in Egypt (1818)*
Felix Mendelssohn (1809–1847): *Elijah (1846)*
Giuseppe Verdi (1813–1901): *Sanctus* from *Requiem (1874)*
Nabucco (1840)
Louis Lewandowski (1821–1894): *Kedusha (c. 1860)*
Johannes Brahms (1833–1897): *Four Serious Songs (1896)*
Camille Saint Saens (1835–1921): *Samson and Delilah (1877)*

20th-Century Music(1900–1980)

Ralph Vaughan Williams (1872–1958): *Job, Masque for Dancing (1930)*
Flos Campi (1925)

Arnold Schoenberg (1874–1951): *Jacob's Ladder (1917–1922)*
Moses and Aaron (1932)

Ernest Bloch (1880–1959): *Sacred Service (1933)*
Schelomo (1915)

Igor Stravinsky (1882–1971): *Abraham and Isaac (1963)*
Symphony of Psalms (1930)

Arthur Honegger (1892–1955): *King David (1921)*

Darius Milhaud (1892–1974): *Cain and Abel (1945)*

Hebrew Community song: *U' Mordecai Yatza (19th–20th C.)*

Children's song: *A Wicked, Wicked Man (19th–20th C.)*

Kurt Weill (1900–1950): *The Eternal Road (Ruth excerpt) (1935)*

Ernst Krenek (1900–1991): *Lamentations Jeremiae Prophetae (1942)*

William Walton (1902–1983): *Belshazzar's Feast (1930)*

Benjamin Britten (1913–1976): *Noyes Fludde (1957)*

Leonard Bernstein (1918–1990): *Jeremiah Symphony (1943)*

Yehezkel Braun (b.1922): *Shir Hashirim Chapter 3 (1973)*

Shlomo Carlebach (1925–1994): *Eso Eynai (1961)*

Ben Zion Shenker (b.1925): *Esheth Hayil (1952)*

Contemporary Music (1980–2010)

Max Stern (b.1947): *Balaam and the Ass (1990)*
Ha'azinu (Song of Moses) (1989)
Prophet or King (2006)

Andrew Lloyd Webber (b.1948): *Joseph and the Amazing Technicolor Dreamcoat (1976)*

Discography of
Musical Examples

Haydn, Franz Joseph: Die Schopfung (The Creation) / Janowitz, Ludwig,Wunderlich, Fischer-Discau,Berry, Weiner Singverein, Berliner Philharmoniker / Herbert Von Karajan, DGG 449 761–2, ADD, 1969. CD1-Bands 2 (2:58) & 3 (4:01)

Britten, Benjamin: Noye's Fludde, Finchley Children's Music Group/ Nicolas Wilks, SommCD 212, DDD, 1997. Bands 9 (4:18) & 10 (4:54)

Strawinsky, Igor: Abraham and Isaac / Fischer-Dieskau, Radio-Symphonieorchester Stuttgart / Bertini, Orfeo C015821, DDD, 1982. Band 7 (12:09)

Schoenberg, Arnold: Die Jakobsleiter / BBC Singers, BBC Symphony Orchestra / Pierre Boulez, Sony SMK48 462, ADD, 1978/82. Band 2 (4:46)

Handel, George Frideric: Israel in Egypt / Choir of Christ Church Cathedral, Oxford, English Chamber Orchestra / Simon Preston, Decca 443 470–2, ADD, 1975. CD1-Bands 20 (0:51), 21 ((1:31), 22 (1:05), CD2-Bands 15 (2:04)

Bloch, Ernest: Sacred Service / Aron Marko Rothmuller, London Philharmonic Choir and Orchestra / Ernest Bloch, Jewish Music Heritage Recordings CD 015, AAD, 1949. Band 7 (7:40)

Stern, Max: Balaam and the Ass / Stuart Taylor, trombone, Gene Cipriani, percussion Institute for Social Integration in the Schools, Bar Ilan, AAD, 1991. Bands 1 (1:41), 2 (1:42), 3 (0:32), 4 (0:44)

Stern, Max: Haazinu / Gary Karr, contrabass, Jerusalem Symphony Orchestra / Arthur Post ACUM-IBA MS 1, AAD, 1993. Band 1 excerpt (10:41)

Spirituals / Joshua Fit de Battle of Jericho / Paul Robeson, bass-baritone, Lawrence Brown, piano-vocals, Columbia Odyssey LP, 1945. (1:49)

Carissimi, Giacomo: Jephte / Ensemble Jacques Moderne/ Joel Suhubiette, Ligia Digital, Lidi 0202129–03, DDD, 2003. Bands 5 (4:57), 6 (4:43)

Saint-Saens: Camille / Gorr, Vickers, Chours and Orchestra du Theatre National de l'Opera de Paris / Georges Pretre, EMI, ADD, 1963/2001. Act 2 (excerpt) Bands 11 (3:07), 12 (5:15)

Honegger, Arthur: Le Roi David / Martin, narrator, Chœur Regional Vitorria d'Ile de France, Orchestre de la Cite/Michel Piquemal, Naxos 8.553649, DDD, 1997. Bands 2 (1:18), 3 (2:02), 4 (0:39)

Kuhnau, Johann: Biblical Sonatas (David and Goliath) / Gustav Leonhardt, Teldec 3984–21763, ADD, 1970/1998. Bands 5 (0:30), 6 (0:33), 7 (0:58)

Mendelssohn, Felix: Elijah / Rundfunkchor Leipzig, Gewandhausorchester Leipzig / Wolfgang Swallish, Philips 438 368–2, ADD, 1993. CD1 Bands 14 (3:17), 16 (3:01)

Verdi, Giuseppe: Nabucco / Chor und Orchester der Deutschen Oper Berlin / Sinopoli, DGG 457 196–2 (Voices from Heaven compilation), 1983/1997. CD 1 Band 2 (4:57); Tito Gobbi/ Vienna Opera Orchestra/ Gardelli, Helicon Compilation 476038–2 (Opera's Golden Voices), 1965/2003. CD 4 Band 10 (2:45)

Gregorian Chant (Sanctus) / The Monks Choir of Our Lady of Fontgombault Abbey/Duchene, Rose Records, 1975. Band 7 (1:23)

Palestrina, Giovanni: Missa Brevis (Sanctus) / The Madrigal Choir, Marin Constantin, Electrecord EDC 178, ADD, 1995. Band 1 (5:04)

Mozart, Wolfgang Amadeus: Requiem (Sanctus) / Zylis, Dominguez, Schreier, Crass, South German Madrigal Choir, Consortium Musicum/Wolfgang Gonnenwein, Seraphim 7243 5 69734, 1966/1997. Bands 11 (1:40), 12 (5:40)

Verdi, Giuseppe: Requiem (Sanctus) / Freni, Ludwig, Cossutta, Ghiaurov, Wiener Singverein, Berliner Philharmoniker/von Karajan, DGG 453 091–2, 1972. CD 2 Band 2 (3:09)

Lewandowski, Louis: Sanctification / The Musical Tradition of the Jewish Reform Congregation in Berlin, Joseph Schmidt, tenor, Choir and Organ / Herman Schildberger, Beth Hatefutsoth, 1928/1997. CD 1 Band 1 (6:18)

Bernstein, Leonard: Symphony No. 1 "Jeremiah"/ New York Philharmonic, Bernstein, Sony SMK 60697, ADD, 1962/1999. Bands 1 excerpt (2:40) 2 excerpt (1:46)

Spiritual: Ezekiel Saw De Wheel / Tuskegee Institute Choir, Dawson, MCA MSD-35340, 1955/1992. Band 1 (2:15)

Moditzer Melody:Eshet Hayil (The Soul of the Sabbath) / The Zamir Chorale Boston, Joshua Jacobson, HZ-915 2001. Band 5 (2:20)

Schein, Johann Hermann. Israelis Brunnein. Ensembel Vocal Europeen/ Philippe Herreweghe. France: Harmonia Mundi, HMA 1951574, 1996. Band 2.

Vaughn Williams, Ralph: Job, A Masque for Dancing (Galliard) / Munich Symphony Orchestra / Douglas Bostock, Olufsen ClassCD 244, 1999. Band 10 (2:13)

Braun, Yehezkel: Cantici Canticorum Caput III (The Songs Live On) / Zamir Chorale, Jacobson, HZ-914, 1999. Bands 6 (1:06) 7 (2:39)

Weill, Kurt: The Eternal Road (scene 24) / soloists, Rundfunk-Sinfonieorchester Berlin / Schwartz, Milken Archive-Naxos 8.559402, DDD, 2003. Band 10 (4:51)

Krenek, Ernst: Lamentio Jeremiae Prophetae / Netherlands Chamber Choir/Gronostay, Globe.Glo 5085, DDD, 1992. Band 1 excerpt (1:55)

Bloch, Ernst:Schelomo / Nelsova, London Philharmonic/Bloch, JMHR CD 015, ADD, 1950/1997. Band 1 excerpt (5:49)

Walton, William: Belshazzar's Feast /Atlanta Symphony Orchestra and Chorus/Robert Shaw, Telarc CD-80181, DDD, 1989. Band 1 excerpt (5:41)

Bibliography

Biblical Texts and Rabbinical Literature

Charles, Robert Henry, ed. *Apocrypha and Pseudepigrapha of the Old Testament in English.* 2 vols. Oxford: Clarendon Press, 1963 (1913).

Cohen, Abraham, ed. *The Soncino Books of the Bible.* Hebrew and English Translations with introductions and commentary. London, Jerusalem, and New York: Soncino Press, 1974.

De Sola Pool, David, ed. *Book of Prayers: According to the Custom of the Spanish and Portuguese Jews.* New York: Union of Sephardic Congregations, 1997.

Epstein, Isidore, trans. and ed. *Babylonian Talmud.* 18 vols. London: Soncino Press, 1961.

Freedman, H., and Simon, Maurice, eds. *The Midrash Rabbah.* 5 vols. London: Soncino Press, 1977.

Friedlander, M. ed. *Holy Scriptures.* Hebrew and English Text from London Edition 1881. Tel-Aviv: Sinai Publishing, 1971.

Gruber, Mayer, ed. and trans. *Rashi's Commentary on Psalms.* Leiden, Brill, 2004.

Gryson, Roger, ed. *Biblia Sacra Vulgata:Iuxta Vulgatam Versionem.* Stuttgart: Deutsche Bibelgesellschaft, 1994.

Hahasid, Judah ben Samuel. *Sefer Hasidim* 2 vols., ed. Shimon Goodman. Jerusalem: Institute of Responsa Literature, 2006 [Hebrew].

Hertz, Joseph Herman, ed. *Authorized Daily Prayer Book.* London: Soncino Press, 1976.

_____. *The Pentateuch and Haftorahs.* English translation and commentary. London: Soncino Press, 1960 [Hebrew].

Hirsch, Samson Raphael, trans. and commentary. *The Psalms.* New York: Feldheim Publishers, 1977.

Jones, Alexander, ed. *The Jerusalem Bible.* Garden City, NY: Doubleday, 1966.

Maimonides, Moses. *Guide to the Perplexed,* translated by M. Friedlander. New York: Dover Publications, 1956 [1904].

Scherman, Nosson, trans. *Shir haShirim*. ArtScroll Tanach Series. New York: Mesorah Publications, 1977.

_____. *Zemiroth: Sabbath Songs*. Brooklyn: Art Scroll Mesorah Series, 1979.

Sperling, Harry, and Simon, Maurice, trans. *The Zohar*. 5 volumes. London: Soncino Press, 1934.

Music History, Literature, and Cultural Studies

Abrams, Joshua, "The Eternal Road," Performance review Brooklyn Academy of Music, March 4, 2000. *Theatre Journal* 53.1 (2001): 148–151.

Apel, Willi. *Gregorian Chant*. Bloomington: Indiana University Press, 1958.

Baron, Salo Wittmayer. *A Social and Religious History of the Jews*. 3 vols. New York: Columbia University Press, 1937.

Berger, Melvin. *Chamber Music: A Listener's Guide*. New York: Doubleday, 1990.

Bernstein, Leonard. *The Infinite Variety of Music*. New York: Simon and Schuster, 1966.

Bridges, Robert, ed. *The Spirit of Man*. London: Longmans, Green and Co., 1916.

Chase, Gilbert. *America's music: From the Pilgrims to the Present*. New York: McGraw-Hill, 1955.

Conlon, Joan Catoni. *Performing Monteverdi: A Conductor's Guide*. Chapel Hill, NC: Hinshaw Music, 2001.

Copeland, Robert M. "The Christian Message of Igor Stravinsky," *Musical Quarterly* 68.4 (1982): 563–579.

Cormack, Malcolm. *William Blake: Illustrations of the Book of Job*. Richmond, VA: Virginia Museum of Fine Arts, 1997.

Dante. *The Inferno, The Purgatorio, The Paradiso*, comments and translation by John Ciardi. New York: New American Library, 1964.

Du Bois, W. E. Burghardt. *The World and Africa: An inquiry into the part which Africa has played in world history*. New York: Viking Press, 1947.

Farmer, Henry George. "The Music of Ancient Mesopotamia," in *Ancient and Oriental Music*. vol. 1. Edited by Egon Wellesz. London: Oxford University Press, 1957.

Finkelstein, Sidney. *Composer and Nation*. New York: International Publishers, 1960.

Fletcher, Harris F. *Milton's Rabbinical Readings*. Urbana: University of Illinois Press, 1930.

Ginzberg, Louis. *Legends of the Bible*. Philadelphia: Jewish Publication Society, 1956.

_____. *The Legends of the Jews*. 7 vols. Baltimore: Johns Hopkins Press, 1998 (originally published Philadelphia: The Jewish Publication Society of America, 1938).

Gorali, Moshe. *The Old Testament in Music,* Jerusalem: Maron Publishers, 1993.

Gradenwitz, Peter. *The Music of Israel: From the Biblical Era to Modern Times*. Portland, OR: Amadeus Press, 1996.

Grout, Donald Jay. *A History of Western Music*. New York: Norton, 1960.

Guthrie, Harvey H. *Israel's Sacred Songs: A Study of Dominant Themes*. New York: Seabury Press, 1966.

Hamilton, Edith. *Mythology*. New York: New American Library, 1957.

Henrikson, Alf. *Through the Ages: An Illustrated Chronicle of Events from 2000 BC to the Present*. New York: Crescent Books, 1983.

Heschel, Abraham J. *The Prophets*. 2 vols. New York: Harper & Row, 1969.

Howett, Duncan. *The Essenes and Christianity*. New York: Harper & Brothers, 1957.

Idelsohn, A.Z. *Jewish Music In Its Historical Development*. New York: Schocken Books, 1975 [1929].

_____ *Jewish Liturgy and Its Development* (New |York: Schocken Books, 1972 [1932].

Keller, James M. Program notes for Joseph Haydn, *Die Schopfung (The Creation), Hob XXI:2*, New York Philharmonic, February 2004.

Kingman, Daniel. *American Music: A Panorama*. New York: Schirmer Books, 1979.

Kodaly, Zoltan. *Folk Music of Hungary*. Translated by Ronald Tempest and Cynthia Jolly. New York: Praeger Publishers, 1971.

Levy, Calmann. "The Prophets of Israel: Their Part in the Political Life of the Jewish Race," Book Review (James Darmester: *Les Prophetes D'Israel*). New York, The New York Times, August 28, 1892. http://query.nytimes.com/gst/abstract.html?res=9805E2DB1E39E033A2575BC2A96E9C94639ED7CF

Levin, Neil, ed. *Z'mirot Anthology: Traditional Sabbath Songs for the Home*. Cedarhurst, NY: Tara Publications, 1981.

Machlis, Joseph. *The Enjoyment of Music*. New York: W. W. Norton, 1984.

Margolis, Max L., and Alexander Marx. *A History of the Jewish People*. New York: Atheneum, 1974.

McKinnon, James. "On the Question of Psalmody in the Ancient Synagogue." In *The Temple, the Church Fathers and Early Western Chant*. Brookfield, VT: Ashgate Publishing, 1998.

Neville, Don. "Opera or oratorio?: Metastasio's sacred *opera seria*," *Early Music*, 26.4 (1998): 596.

Pasternak, Velvel. *Beyond Hava Nagila*. Cedarhurst, NY: Tara Publications, 1999.

Plassman, Thomas/Joseph Vann. *Lives of Saints*. New York: John Crawley, 1954.

Quintilian, Lacus Curtius. *Institutio Oratoria*, Book XI, Chapter 3. Translated by Harold Edgeworth Butler. New York: Loeb Classical Library, vol. 4, 1920–22.

Ratner, Leonard G. *Classic Music: Expression, Form, and Style* (New York: Schirmer Books, 1980).

Raynor, Henry. *A Social History of Music: From the Middle Ages to Beethoven. (New York: Schocken Books, 1972)*.

Reese, Gustave. *Music in the Middle Ages*. New York: Norton, 1940.

_____. *Music in the Renaissance*, New York: W. W. Norton, 1959.

Sachs, Curt. *Our Musical Heritage: A Short History of Music*. Englewood Cliffs, NJ: Prentice-Hall, 1955.

_____. *Rise of Music in the Ancient World*. New York: W. W. Norton, 1943.

_____. *World History of Dance*. New York: W. W. Norton, 1965.

Sackett, Theodore Alan. Book Review: *Donna K. Heizer: Jewish-German Identity in the Orientalist Literature of Elsie Lasker-Schuler, Friedrich Wolf, and Franz Werfel* (Columbia, SC: Camden House, 1996). *South Atlantic Review*, 1997.

Sendrey, Alfred. *Music in Ancient Israel*. New York: Philosophical Library, 1969.

_____. *The Music of the Jews in the Diaspora*. New York & London: Thomas Yoseloff, 1970.

Solzhenitsyn, Aleksandr. *Nobel Lecture*. Translated by F. D. Reeve. New York: Farrar, Straus, and Giroux, 1972.

Steinsaltz, Adin. *Biblical Images*. Translated by Yehuda Hanegbi, Yehidut Keshet, and Michael Swirsky. New York: Basic Books, 1994.

Stern, Max. "Elijah in Music: An Aesthetic Interpretation." In *Elijah and Elisha: And God Said, "You Are Fired,"* edited by Mishael Caspi and John T. Greene, 251–260. North Richland Hills, TX: Bible Press, 2007.

_____"Organizing Procedures Involving Indeterminacy and Improvisation," *Interface*, edited by Marc Leman, Herman Saabe, Jos Kunst, and Frits Weiland, Vol. 17, The Netherlands: Swets & Zeitlinger, 1988) 103–114.

_____ "The Influence of Minnesang on the Musical Voice of Megillas Vintz," Judentum und Umwelt, Johann Maier, ed. Heft 34 (Frankfurt am Main: Peter Lang, 2007/8) 165–172.

Strunk, Oliver, ed. *Source Readings in Music History*. New York: W. W. Norton, 1950.

Tame, David. *The Secret Power of Music*. New York: Destiny Books, 1984.

Truron, Walterus. "The Rhythm of Metrical Psalms Tunes," *Music & Letters* 9.1 (1928): 29–33.

Tumasonienė, Violeta. *The Holy Scripture motives in new music of Lithuanian composers*. Latvia: Daugavpils University Musicological Journal "Saule," 2008) 57–70.

_____. *The Aspects of Verbum — Toni Against the Background of Biblical Tradition*. Daugavpils University Musicological Journal "Saule," (2009) 35–48.

Wagner, Peter. *Introduction to the Gregorian Melodies*. Translated by Agnes Orme and Edward Gerald Penfold Wyatt. London: Plainsong and Mediaeval Music Society, 1901.

Weber, Max. *The Rational and Social Foundations of Music*. Translated and Edited by Don Martindale, Johannes Riedel, and Gertrude Neuwirth. Carbondale: Southern Illinois University Press, 1958.

_____. *The Sociology of Religion*. Translated by Ephraim Fischoff. Introduction by Talcott Parsons. Boston: Beacon Press, 1964.

Wells, Herbert George. *The Outline of History*. 2 vols. New York, Garden City Books, 1956.

Werner, Eric. The Sacred Bridge: The Interdependence of Liturgy and Music in Synagogue and Church during the First Millennium. New York: Columbia University Press, 1963.

Wolff, Christoph, translated by Mary Whittall; Mozart's Requiem:

Historical and Analytical Studies; Documents; Score. University of California Press, Berkeley, 1994.

Zakovitch, Yair. *David: From Shepherd to Messiah.* Jerusalem: Yad Yitzhak Ben Zvi, 1995 [Hebrew].

Dictionaries, Encyclopedias, Commentaries, and Bibliographies

Aharoni, Yochanan, ed. *Carta's Atlas of the Bible.* Jerusalem: Carta, 1974 [Hebrew].

Apel, Willi, ed. *Harvard Dictionary of Music.* Cambridge, MA: Harvard University Press, 1972.

Bloesch, Richard J., and Weyburn Wasson. *Twentieth Century Choral Music: An Annotated Bibliography of Music Appropriate for College and University Choirs.* Lawton, OK: American Choral Directors Association, 1997.

Dick, William C. *The Bible: Its Letter and Spirit.* London: J.M. Dent and Sons, Ltd., 1943.

Freedman, David Noel, ed. *Eerdmans Dictionary of the Bible.* Grand Rapids, MI: William. B. Eerdmans Publishing Company, 2000.

Gorali, Moshe, Betty Hirshowitz, and Tali Turel. *The Old Testament in the Works of Johann Sebastian Bach* (Haifa, Israel: Haifa Music Museum, 1979).

Hindley, Geoffrey, ed. *The Larousse Encyclopedia of Music.* English edition of original French edition. London: Hamlyn Publishing, 1979.

Hofman, Shlomo. *Miqra'ey Music: A Collection of Biblical References to Music.* Tel-Aviv: Israel Music Institute, 1974.

Howley, George Cecil Douglas, Frederick Fyvie Bruce, and Henry Leopold Ellison, eds. *The New Layman's Bible Commentary in One Volume.* Grand Rapids, MI: Zondervan Publishing House, 1979.

Kuiper, Kathleen, ed. *Merriam Webster's Encyclopedia of Literature.* Springfield, MA: Merriam-Webster, 1995.

Laster, James. *Catalogue of Choral Music Arranged in Biblical Order.* Metuchen, NJ: Scarecrow Press, 1983.

Nulman, Macy, ed. *The Concise Encyclopedia of Jewish Music.* New York: McGraw-Hill, 1975.

Oesterley, W. O. E., and Theodore H. Robinson. *An Introduction to the Books of the Old Testament.* London: Society for Promoting Christian Knowledge, 1934.

Roth, Cecil, ed. *Encyclopedia Judaica.* 17 vols. Jerusalem: Keter Publishing House, 1978.

Sadie, Stanley, ed. *The New Grove Dictionary of Music and Musicians.* 20 vols. London: MacMillan, 1980.

Salzman, Eric. *Twentieth-Century Music: An Introduction.* Englewood Cliffs, NJ: Prentice-Hall, 1967.

Strimple, Nick. *Choral Music in the Twentieth Century.* Portland, OR: Amadeus Press, 2002.

Timor, Matatiyahu, ed. *Encyclopedia of History.* Tel-Aviv: Academia, 1954 [Hebrew].

Wetterau, Bruce, tr. *Macmillan Concise Dictionary of World History.* New York: Macmillan Publishing Company, 1983.

Yust, Walter, ed. *Encyclopedia Britannica.* 24 vol. London: William Benton, 1960.

Composers

Berger, Arthur. "Problems of Pitch Organization in Stravinsky," *Perspectives of New Music 2*, 1 (1963): 11–42. As cited in Benjamin Boretz and Edward T. Cone, eds. *Perspectives on Schoenberg and Stravinsky,* 2nd edition, 123–154. New York: W. W. Norton, 1972.

Berlioz, Hector. *Memoirs of Hector Berlioz.* Translated by Rachel and Eleanor Holms. Annotated and Revised by Ernest Newman. New York: Dover, 1960.

Burton, Humphrey. *Leonard Bernstein.* New York: Doubleday, 1994.

Frisch, Walter, ed. *Schoenberg and his World.* Princeton, NJ: Princeton University Press, 1999.

Geiringer, Karl. *Brahms: His Life and Works.* 3rd ed. New York: Da Capo, 1981.

Jacobson, Joshua R. "The Choral Music of Salamone Rossi," *American Choral Review* XXX.4 (1988).

Harran, Don. *Salamone Rossi: Jewish Musician in Late Renaissance Mantua,* NY: Oxford University Press, 1999.

Kellenberger, Edgar, D. Letter to author about Mendelssohn, July 25, 2006.

Mahler, Alma. *Gustav Mahler: Erinnerungen Und Briefe.* Amsterdam: Allert de Lange, 1940, as cited in Alfred Mathis-Rosenzweig,

Gustav Mahler: New Insights into His Life, Times and Work. Translated and annotated by Jeremy Barham. Surrey, UK: Ashgate Publishing, 2007.

Moser, Hans Joachim. *Heinrich Schutz: His Life and Work*, 2nd revised ed. Translated by Carl F. Pfatteicher. St. Louis: Concordia, 1959.

Mudde, Willem. "Heinrich Schutz: Composer of the Bible," in *The Musical Heritage of the Lutheran Church*, vol. 5, edited by Theodore Hoeltz Nickel. St. Louis: Concordia, 1959, p. 86.

Schoenberg, Arnold. *Letters.* Edited by Erwin Stein. Translated by Eithe Wilkins and Ernst Kaiser. Berkeley: University of California Press: 1987.

Schrade, Leo. "Henrich Schutz and Johann Sebastian Bach in the Protestant Liturgy." Vol. 4 of *The Musical Heritage of the Lutheran Church.* Edited by Theodore Hoeltz Nickel. St. Louis: Concordia, 1954.

Stewart, John L. *Ernst Krenek: The Man and His Music.* Berkeley: University of California Press, 1991.

Strassburg, Robert. *Ernest Bloch: Voice in the Wilderness.* Los Angeles: California State University, 1977.

Stern, Max. "Three Settings of Psalm 150 by Heinrich Schutz." PhD diss., University of Colorado, 1985.

Todd, R. Larry, ed. *Mendelssohn and his World.* Princeton, NJ: Princeton University Press, 1991.

Tymoczko, Dimitri. "Stravinsky and the Octotonic: A Reconsideration," *Music Theory Spectrum* 24.1 (2002): 68–102.

Wellez, Egon, ed. *The New Oxford History of Music: Ancient and Oriental Music*, vol. 1. London: Oxford University Press, 1957.

White, Eric Walter. *Stravinsky: The Composer and his Work.* London: Faber & Faber, 1966.

Williams, Ralph Vaughan. *National Music and Other Essays.* London: Oxford University Press, [1934] 1963.

Scores

Bloch, Ernest. *Sacred Service (Avodath Hakodesh)*, a Sabbath Morning Service according to the Union Prayer Book for Baritone (Cantor) Mixed Chorus and Organ or Full Orchestra. New York: Broude Brothers, 1965.

_____. *Schelomo*, Hebrew Rhapsody for Cello and Orchestra. New York: Dover Publications, 1996.

Braun, Yehezkel. *Cantici Canticorum Caput III* (The Song of Songs, Chapter 3). Tel-Aviv: Education and Culture Centre of the General Federation of Labour-Histadrut, 1973.

Britten, Benjamin. *Noye's Fludd*, The Chester Miracle Play, Op. 59 (1958). London: Boosey & Hawkes, 2000.

Carissimi, Giacomo. *Jephte*, Oratorio a 6 voice basso continuo. Critical Edition by Adelchi Amisano. Milan: Casa Ricordi, 1977.

Dvorak, Antonin. *Biblical Songs, Op. 99*. New York: G. Schirmer, 1895.

Goldfarb, Israel, and Samuel E. Goldfarb, eds. "A Wicked, Wicked Man," in *The Jewish Songster: 120 Festival Songs in Hebrew, English, and Yiddish arranged for Voice and Piano*. New York: Congregation Beth Israel Anshe Emes, 1925.

Handel, Georg Fredrick, Felix Mendelssohn-Bartholdy, and Horace Wadham Nicholl. *Israel in Egypt*, a sacred oratorio for 2 sopranos, alto, tenor & 2 bass soli, SATB & orchestra. Edited by Felix Mendelssohn-Bartholdy. London: Novello Publishing, 1990. Reprint of the 19th century octavo edition.

Harlap, Aharon. *The Sacrifice of Isaac*, for mixed Choir (1979). Tel-Aviv: Israel Music Institute, 2007.

Haydn, Joseph. *The Creation*. New York: Dover Publications, 1990.

Honegger, Arthur, and René Morax. *Le Roi David*, Psaume symphonique en trois parties d'apres le drama de Rene Morax (original version). English version by Edward Agate (Foetisch Frères SA, 1925). Lausanne: Foetisch (Hug Musique), 1952.

Kodaly, Zoltan. *Psalmus Hungaricus, Op. 13*. The 55th Psalm in a Hungarian paraphrase by Michael Veg, for tenor solo, chorus, and orchestra. Vienna: Universal Edition, 1955.

Krenek, Ernst. *Lamentatio Jeremiae Prophetae*, fur Chor a cappella. Kassel: Barenreiter, 1957.

Kuhnau, Johann. *Biblical Sonata No. 1 "The Battle between David and Goliath."* Margery Halford, editor. Introduction translated from the German by William A. Palmer. Port Washington, NY: Alfred Publishing, 1976.

Lewandowski, Louis. *Todah W'Simrah*, Vierstimmige Chore und Soli fur den Israelitischen Gottesdienst, reprint. Introduction by Hugo Chaim Adler. New York: Sacred Music Press, 1954.

Mendelssohn, Felix. *Elijah*, An Oratorio for soprano, alto, tenor, and bass soli, SATB, orchestra, and organ, Op. 70. Text derived from the Lutheran Bible by Julius Schubring. English version by William Bartholomew. London: Novello & Company, 1991.

Mozart, Wolfgang Amadeus. *Requiem, K. 626*. New York: Dover Publications, 1987.

Palestrina, Giovanni Pierluigi da. *Missa Brevis*. Edited by Frank Damrosch. New York: G. Schirmer, 1927.

Pasternak, Velvel, ed. *The Sephardic Music Anthology*. Cedarhurst, NY: Tara Publications, 2006.

Rossi, Salamone. *Hashirim Asher Lish'lomo* (The Songs of Solomon). 2 vols, Edited by Fritz Kikko. New York: The Jewish Theological Seminary, 1967–69,

Saint-Saens, Camille. *Samson and Delilah*, Opera in Three Acts. Libretto by Ferdinand Lemaire. New York: G. Schirmer, 1964.

Schoenberg, Arnold. *Die Jakobsleiter*, Oratorium (fragment) (1917–1922) scored for performance following the composer's instructions by Winfried Zillig. Vienna: Universal Edition (Belmont Music Publishers), 1980.

_____. *Moses und Aaron, Opera in Three Acts*. Mainz: Schott, 1957.

Stern, Max. *Balaam and the Ass*, for trombone and percussion. Ramat Gan, Israel: Institute for the Advancement of Social Integration in the Schools, Bar Ilan University, 1994.

_____. *Ha'azinu (Song of Moses)*, for Contrabass and Orchestra. Beer-Sheva: manuscript, 1988.

Stravinsky, Igor. *Abraham and Isaac: A Sacred Ballad for Baritone and Chamber Orchestra*. London: Boosey & Hawkes, 1965.

Vaughan Williams, R. *Flos Campi: Suite for Solo Viola, Small Orchestra and Small chorus*. London: Oxford University Press, 1927.

_____. *Job: A Masque for Dancing*. London: Oxford University Press, 1934

Verdi, Giuseppe. *Nabucodonosor*. Libretto: Dramma lirico in four parts by Temistocle Solera. Milan: The University of Chicago Press and Casa Ricordi, 1987.

_____. *Requiem to the Memory of Alessandro Manzoni*. New York: G. Schirmer, 1895.

Vivaldi, Antonio. *Laudate Pueri, RV 601, Salmo 112 per Soprano e orchestra*. Milano: Ricordi, 1998.

Walton, William. *Belshazzar's Feast*, for mixed choir, baritone solo, and orchestra. Text arranged from biblical sources by Osbert Sitwell. Oxford: Oxford University Press, 1959.

Recordings, Programs, and Liner Notes

Bahat, Avner. *The Musical Tradition of the Jewish Reform Congregation in Berlin (1928–1930)*. Historic Recordings-Beth Hatefutsoth Records, 1999.

Blyth, Alan. *Brahms: Ein Deutsches Requiem*. Berlin PO/Kempe. EMI. 1993.

Bortnyansky, Dimitri. *Concertos for Choir (Nos. 34, 2, 14, 13, 17, 31, 22, 26, 6)*. The USSR Ministry of Culture Chamber Choir/Valeri Polyansky. Melodiya, 1990.

Bossuyt, Ignace. Translated by Derek Yeld. *Schein:Israelis Brunnlein*. Ensemble Vocal Europeen/Phillippe Herreweghe. Harmonia Mundi, 2005.

British Symphonic Collection, vol. 2. *Job: A Masque for Dancing*. Municher Symphoniker/Douglas Bostock. Olufsen Records, 1999.

Burrows, Donald. *Handel: Israel in Egypt*. English CO/Preston. Decca-CD, 1994.

Buslau, Oliver. Translation: Mary Whittall. "Gregorian Chant: The Beauty of Austerity." *Panorama: Gregorian Chant.* Germany, Deutsche Grammophone-CD, 2000.

Constantino, Cedric. Translation: Geoffrey Marshall. *Giacomo Carissimi: Historia di Jephte*. Ensemble Jacques Moderne/Joel Suhubiette. Harmonia Mundi, 2003.

Dawson, William. *Interpretation of the Religious Folk-Songs of the American Negro*. Spirituals/Tuskegee Institute Choir/ Dawson. MCA Records, 1992.

Eppstein, Ury, editor: Voices of Jerusalem, Eastern Church Music, Collection, Largo 5151, CD, 2006.

Ferey, Mathieu. Translation: Keith Anderson. *Honegger: Le Roi David (Original version)*. Orchestre de la Cite/Michel Piquemal. Naxos-CD, 1997.

Fess, Eike. Translation by Alan Seaton. *Arnold Schoenberg: Moses Und Aaron*. Vienna State Opera/Daniele Gatti. DVD Vienna: ORF, ArtHaus Musik, 2006.

Furber, Martin. *Gregorian Chant: Mass for the Dedication of a Church*.

The Monk's Choir of Our Lady of Fontgombault/Duchene. Rose Records, 1995.

Gottwald, Clytus. Translation: Stewart Spencer. *Schoenberg: Die Jakobsleiter.* BBC Singers and SO/ Boulez. Sony-CD, 1993.

Haylock, Julian. *Mature Work of a Youthful Prodigy, Mendelssohn's "Elijah."* Rundfunkchor und Gewandlausorchestra Leipzig/W. Sawallisch. Philips, 1993.

Herzog, Myrna. Program Notes, "The Play of Daniel," Israel, 2008.

Hirshberg, Jehoash. Program Notes, "Elijah." 1992.

Huglo, Michel. *Chant Gregorien: Processions Pascales.* Deller Consort. France: Harmonia Mundi, 1974.

Jacobson, Joshua. *The Songs Live On (Braun: Song of Songs).* The Zamir Chorale of Boston/Jacobson, 1999.

_____. *The Soul of the Sabbath (Ben-Zion Shenker: Eshet Hayil).* The Zamir Chorale of Boston/Jacobson. 2001.

Jones, Nick. *Walton: Belshazzar's Feast/Bernstein: Chichester Psalms.* Atlanta Symphony Orchestra & Choir/Robert Shaw. Telarc-CD, 1989.

Knapp, Alexander. *Bloch Performs Bloch.* Jewish Music Heritage Recordings, London, 1997.

Lichtenberger, Eva. *Cori Spezzati: Venetian Polychoral Music.* Chamber Choir of Europe/Matt. The Netherlands: Brilliant Classics, 2002.

Levin, Neil W. *Genesis Suite (1945)* Berlin Radio SO/Schwartz. Milken Archive of American Jewish Music. Naxos-CD, 2004.

_____. *Kurt Weil: The Eternal Road (highlights)*(2003). Berlin Radio SO/Schwartz.

Lindlar, Heinrich. Translation: Richard Sterling. *Igor Strawinsky: Abraham and Isaac.* Stuttgart Symphony Orchestra/Fischer-Dieskau/ Gary Bertini. Orfeo-CD, 1982.

Marlow, Richard. *Heinrich Schutz: Psalmen Davids.* Choir of Trinity College, Cambridge/Marlow. Conifer-CD 1991.

Milken Archive of American Jewish Music. Naxos-CD, 2003.

Mozart, Wolfgang Amadeus. *Requiem.* Consortium Musicum/Wolfgang Gonnenwein. Seraphim, 1997.

Osborne, Richard. *Joseph Haydn: Die Schopfung (The Creation).* Berlin Philharmonic Orchestra/Von Karajan. Deutsche Grammophon-2 CDs, 1969

_____. *Saint-Saens: Samson et Dalila.* Theatre National de l' Opera de Paris/Georges Pretre. EMI Classics, 2001.

Page, Tim. *Jeremiah (Symphony No 1)*. New York Philharmonic/Leonard Bernstein. Sony-CD, 1999.

Place, Adelaide de. *Brahms/Mendelssohn*. Ensemble de Lausanne/ Corboz. UK: Virgin Classics, 2004.

Roseberry, Eric. *Britten: Noye's Fludde*. Finchley Children's Music Group. Somm-CD, 1997.

Samana, Leo. Netherlands Chamber Choir/Uwe Gronostay. Globe-CD, 1992.

Stenzl, Jurg. Translated by Susan Marie Praeder. *Nicola Porpora: Il Gedeone*. Wiener Aklademie/Martin Haselbock. CPO, Germany, 1999.

Stern, Max. *Biblical Compositions (Haazinu, Balaam, and the Ass)*. Jerusalem Symphony Orchestra/Karr/Fagen and Taylor/Cipriani. ACUM/MS 1 /Israel, 1993.

Verdi, Giuseppe. *Nabucco*. Teatro Alla Scala Production, Milan/ Riccardo Muti. NVC Arts-DVD, 1987.

Victrola Internet resource: Old Time Spirituals — Black Spirituals of the Early 1900s featuring the Fisk University and Tuskegee Institute Quartets. *www.besmark.com/sprititual.html*

von Karajan, Herbert. Deutsche Grammophon-CD, 1997.

von Pufendor, Lutz. Translation: Stewart Spencer. *Zoltan Kodaly: Psalmus Hungaricus*. RIAS SO Berlin/Ferenc Fricsay. Deutche Grammophon, 1999.

Warrack, Jack. *Dvorak: Requiem-Biblical Songs*. Czech PO/Ancerl & Dietrich Fischer-Diskau/Jorg Demus, piano. Deutche Grammophon GmbH, 1997.

Internet Resources

Bible Stories In Opera and Oratorio (Originally published Early 1900's) (2008). *www.oldandsold.com/articles30/biblical-operas-4.shtml*

Buster, David. Program notes, *Chichester Psalms*, North Country Chorus (2009) *www.northcountrychorus.org/programnotes.html*

The Canonical Hours. *www.fisheaters.com/hours.html*

Covendale, Miles. Translation: Psalm 100. *www.greatsite.com/timeline-english-bible-history/index.html*

Dorman, Marianne. Gregory The Great (2007). *http://mariannedorman.homestead.com/Gregory.html*

Ernst, Carl W. *Interpreting the Song of Songs: The Paradox of Spiritual and Sensual Love* (2007) *www.unc.edu/~cernst/articles/sosintro. htm*

Ezekiel Saw The (De) Wheel (various versions of texts): *http://www. my.homewithgod.com/heavenlymidis2/ezekiel.   http://www. negrospirituals.com/news-song/zekiel_ezekiel_saw_the_wheel. htm.   http://www.spitualy.cz/component/option,com_mjoosic/ page,song/task. http://www.ingeb.org/spiritua/ezekiels.html*

Fisk Jubilee Singers. *Our History* (2006). *www.fiskjubileesingers.org/ our_history.html*

Foster, Marshall. "The History and Impact of the Geneva Bible," *Vision Forum Ministries*, 2006. *http://www.visionforumministries.org/ issues/news_and_reports/the_history_and_impact_of_the.aspx*

Freed, Richard. Program notes: *Leonard Bernstein: Symphony No. 1, "Jeremiah."* The John F. Kennedy Center, 2005. *www.kennedy_ center.org/calendar/index.cfm?fuseaction*

Goldfarb, Samuel E. *www-dev.lib.washington.edu/specialcoll/findaids/ docs/ papersrecords/GoldfarbSamuelE2784.xml*

Gosta, Predrag. "Monteverdi: Vespers (1610): Historical Context, Performing Practice, Analysis of Work and Recordings." PhD diss., Georgia State University, 2007. *www.monteverdivespers. com/home.htm*

Hadfield, Duncan. *Nabucco* (2001). *www.ellenkent.com/synopsis/ nabucco*

Higginson, Thomas Wentworth. "Negro Spirituals" from the *Atlantic Monthly*, June 1867. *http://xroads.virginia.edu/~HYPER/TWH/ Higg.html*

Hirsch, Emil G. *Song of Song, The* (reprint of 1906) (2007). *www.jew-ishencyclopedia.com/view.jsp?artid=968&letter=S*

Hong Kong Bach Choir — The French Concert, program notes (2006). *www.bachchoir.org.hk/concerts/2006/TheFrenchConcert.html*

Hull, John M. "Isaac Watts and the Origins of British Imperial Theology." *International Congregational Journal* 4.2 (2005): 59–79. *www. johnhull.biz/Articles2/IsaacWatts2.html.*

Jacobson, Joshua. Salamone Rossi Hebreo. *Jewish Musician in the Italian Renaissance* (2003). *www.zamir.org/composers/rossi/rossi2.html*

Jeffcoat, John L III. *English Bible History* (2002). *www.greatsite.com/ timeline-english-bible-history/index.html*

Leonard, Richard C. Singing the Psalms: A Brief History of Psalmody (1997). *www.laudemont.org/a-stp.htm*

Keller, Theodore. "Psalter Schemas" (2006). *www.kellerbool.com.*

Killian, Greg. *Megillat Esther* (2008). *www.betemunah.org/esther.html*

Knight, Kevin. *The Catholic Encyclopedia.* New York: Robert Appleton Company, 1912 (2007). *www.newadvent.org/cathen/1327a.htm*

Lewis, Randolph. "Nathaniel of Southhampton or Balaam's Ass," *ChickenBones: A Journal for Literary & Artistic African-American Themes* (2007). *www.nathanielturned.com/balaamsass.htm*

Liu, James C. S. "Notes on the Carissimi Oratorio, Jephte." *Choral Music Notes* (2003). Notes on the Carissimi Oratorio. *http://members. macconnect.com/users/j/jimbob/classical/Carissimi_Jephte.html*

Mahan, Asa: "Solomon's Song," *The Oberlin Quarterly Review.* February, 1848. article lxiv. *http://truthinheart.com/EarlyOberlinCD/CD/ Mahan/SolomonsSong.htm*

Malick, David. *The Book of Ruth* (2007).*www.bible.org/page. php?page_id=888*

Marxsen, Eduard.*www.kunstbus.nl/muziek/eduard+marksen.html*

Morrison, Chris. Program notes, *Chichester Psalms,* All Media Guide, Dayton Philharmonic (2007–2008). *www.daytonphilharmonic. com/content.jsp?articleld*

Moses, Oral. *The Spiritual: A Source for Modern Gospel* (2010). *www. thenegrospiritualworkshop.com/article_the_spiritual_a_source_ for_gospel.htm*

Oron, Aryeh. "Felix Mendelssohn-Bartholdy" (2006). *www.bach-cantatas.com/Lib/Mendelssohn-Felix.htm*

Predrag Gosta. *Monteverdi: Vespers (1610). www.predraggosta.com/ PREDRAG-GOSTA-CONDUCTING-RESUME-03–2009.*

Saint Philip Neri, Confessor-1515–1595, from *"Lives of Saints,"* New York: John J. Crawley & Co. (2006). *www.ewtn.com/library/MARY/ PHILIP.htm*

Saint-Saens, Camille. Essays (2007). *www.oldandsold.com/articles18/ music-19.shtml*

Schwartz, Steve. *Le Roi David by Arthur Honegger* (1995). *www.classical. net/music/comp.1st/works/honegger/roidavid.html*

Schweissinger, Marc J. "Franz Werfel." *The Literary Encyclopedia (2005)* (2008). *www.litencyc.com/php/speople.php?rec=true&UID=5468*

Smith Creek "Music.Literary Aspects of a Hymn" (2008). *www. smithcreekmusic.com/Hymnology/Hymn.mechanics/Hymn. mechanics.html*

Stahl, Samuel M. *Felix Mendelssohn: Musical Genius and Jewish Casualty* (1998). *www.beth-elsa.org/be_s0220.htm*

Sternhold and Hopkins: The Whole Book of Psalms Collected into English Metre (2007). *www.cgmusic.com/workshop/oldver/psalm_100.htm*

Verdi, Giuseppe. il sito officiale. *Temistocle Solera* (2003). *www.giuseppe-verdi.it/Inglese/page.asp?IDCategoria*

Weiss, Sam. "Nine Luminaries of Jewish Liturgical Song" (2006). *www.klezmershack.com/articles_s/luminaries/-56K*

Westminster School Bulletin. *www.westminster.org.uk/academiclife/index.asm*

Wikipedia, the free encyclopedia. *http://en.wikipedia.org/wiki*

Index of Scriptural References

Index of Composers

General Index

DATE DUE

APR 0 9 2014			
APR 1 4 2016			
MAY 0 7 2019			
MAY 1 6 2019			
NOV 07 2019 NOV 2 7 2019			